The Essential Mayberry

8.00
8.00
5.00
8.00

47.00
27.00
────
20.00

29.00
39.00
8.00
────
47.00

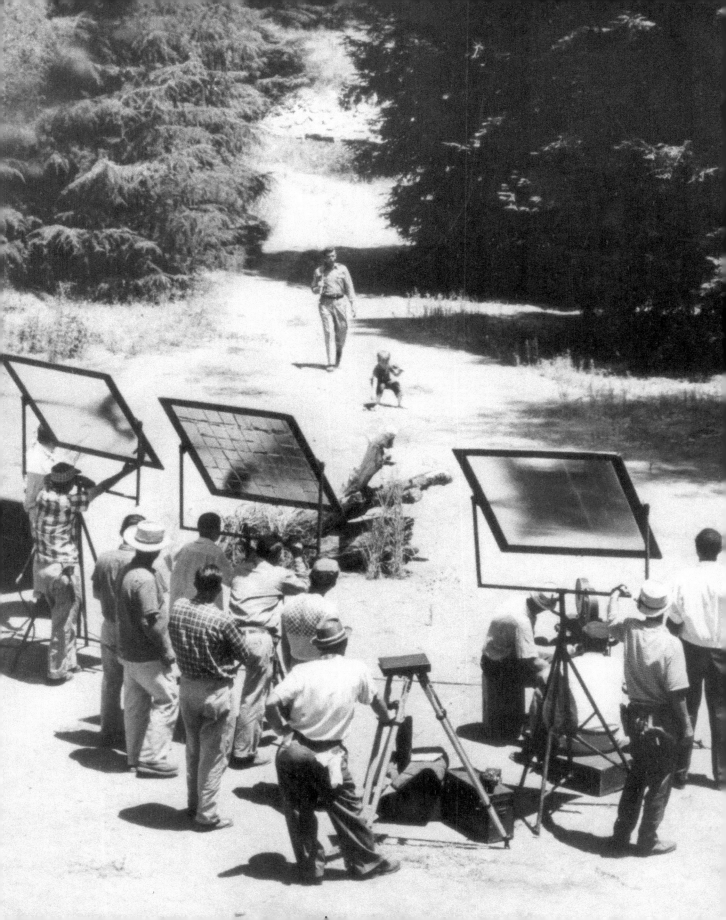

THE ESSENTIAL MAYBERRY

BEHIND THE SCENES OF
The Andy Griffith Show

Neal Brower

BLAIR | 2023

Blair is an imprint of Carolina Wren Press.

The mission of Blair/Carolina Wren Press is to seek out, nurture, and promote literary work by new and underrepresented writers.

We gratefully acknowledge the ongoing support of general operations by the Durham Arts Council's United Arts Fund and the North Carolina Arts Council.

All photographs courtesy of *The Andy Griffith Show* Rerun Watchers Club.

ISBN 9781958888124

Library of Congress Control Number: 2023937740

In memory of the Mayberry wordsmiths:
Jack, Charles, Everett, Jim, Harvey, Ray, Sam, and Bill . . .
and Andy Griffith, the guiding star

Contents

1962–1963

1963–1964

Foreword

Born in North Carolina in 1960, the same year that *The Andy Griffith Show* premiered, I can't remember a time when I wasn't completely captivated by this much-beloved TV show. I enjoy watching stories about Mayberry folks so much that, in 1979, I joined three college buddies in founding *The Andy Griffith Show Rerun Watchers Club (TAGSRWC)*.

As TAGSRWC has grown over the past four decades to have nearly 1,500 chapters founded and tens of thousands of members, I'm often asked, "Why do you think *The Andy Griffith Show* has endured? Why is such an old TV show still so popular after all these years?"

These questions asking "Why?" are frequently paired with a companion question: "Is the continuing popularity simply because the show is so wholesome and nostalgic?"

My usual answer throughout all these years (including in my foreword for *Mayberry 101*, Neal Brower's 1998 prologue to this expanded study of *The Andy Griffith Show*) has been that, yes, the show is wholesome and nostalgic. Those qualities are part of its appeal, but if the show were merely wholesome or just nostalgic, generations of viewers wouldn't still be tuning in to watch the same episodes over and over.

I then typically go on to observe that the core of the show's enduring appeal is that viewers continue to be entertained by *The Andy Griffith Show*'s outstanding stories, which were created by a group of people—writers, actors, directors, musicians, and other crew and staff—who were unsurpassed both in their talents and in their dedication to the shared goal of producing the best TV show that they could.

No one was more devoted to that mission than Andy Griffith himself. He often said that the show is mainly about one thing: *what it is, is love*. And indeed no one loved the show and cared for it more than Andy Griffith. As an ardent participant in the show's production once said, "They call it *The Andy Griffith Show* for a reason."

So, okay, at this point, there's no real debate about whether *The Andy Griffith Show* was created by some immensely talented people telling compelling, timeless stories. Once we accept that admittedly very general assessment, then an even more interesting question naturally follows: *How did they do it?*

That's where Neal Brower and *The Essential Mayberry: Behind the Scenes of The Andy Griffith Show* come in. Neal, who's the same age as Ron Howard, has been teaching courses, presenting lectures, and writing about *The Andy Griffith Show* for more than three decades. His particular focus has been on the mechanics of the show's production.

Echoing actor Tom Jacobs (Danny Thomas's brother) asking Andy Taylor, "How'd they do it, Sheriff?" after seeing Gilly Walker's car parked inside the Mayberry Courthouse in "Goober Takes a Car Apart," Neal has continually wondered, "How'd they do it?" about the making of *The Andy Griffith Show*. In this volume, Neal has looked under the hood of scores of favorite *Griffith* episodes in order to provide all of us Goobers with high-test answers.

And how'd Neal do it? Well, he corresponded with and talked to many of the show's key writers, who, collectively, wrote nearly half the episodes of the entire series—and, more crucially, who wrote the majority of everybody's favorite episodes.

Neal has shrewdly chosen to focus on *The Andy Griffith Show*'s writing, and the writers themselves—the people who first put Mayberry's wonderful characters and stories on paper. With this approach, along with a close examination of original scripts and their revisions, Neal has been able to assemble the origin story of each *Griffith* episode. He does so with every bit as much skill as Goober demonstrates when taking Gilly's car apart and putting it back together in the Mayberry Courthouse.

While Neal also probes the Who, What, When, Where, and Why of each episode, it's his resolute pursuit of the How that reveals the most interesting information about the creation of Mayberry. Episode by episode, Neal meticulously unveils the essence of the processes that ultimately produce so many highly satisfying moments in Mayberry.

And while he also includes information and perspectives from some of the show's actors and others, Neal stays centered on how the stories themselves were shaped during writing and rewriting. As often as not, he asks the questions and then largely lets the writers tell us how they did it.

At the same time, Neal also has an eagle eye for the choices and techniques used in directing episodes, and he likewise has a keen ear for the musical scoring. He artfully weaves insights about those elements into the overall storytelling for each episode.

The result is an impressive and absorbing collection of essays that offer a rare look behind the scenes. Together, they provide a fascinating, thoughtful study of a legendary TV show that so many of us love. By reading this truly essential Mayberry book, any fan of *The Andy Griffith Show* is sure to find an even deeper appreciation and enjoyment of the show.

Happy reading and continued watching!

Jim Clark

P.S. After you've read *The Essential Mayberry*, just remember, to paraphrase Andy Taylor: *Mayberry knowledge is a fine thing, but don't flaunt it.*

Introduction

Mayberry is my passion. I love *The Andy Griffith Show*. I have watched *The Andy Griffith Show* throughout my life . . . and I was not alone. Throughout its production, *The Andy Griffith Show* (*TAGS*) remained among the top-ten programs in the A. C. Nielson Ratings. Reruns of the series continued their high ratings for decades after production had ended. Today, *The Andy Griffith Show* continues to attract new fans through current streaming and network broadcasts.

I think the evergreen appeal of *TAGS* is a result of its great writing, talented cast, and the on-screen creation of a community of citizens who treat one another with love and respect.

In 1985, the Mayberry bug bit me. I read a book, *The Andy Griffith Show* by Richard Kelly (still in print, by the way). In the back of the book, Kelly listed all 249 episodes. I was now a person with a mission: I would tape all 249 episodes. (Yes, remember when we *taped* shows?)

I eventually accomplished my mission. While doing so, I got caught up in the lives of Mayberry's residents and the loving spirit in their town. I also joined the fan club, *The Andy Griffith Show* Rerun Watchers Club, and I began to accumulate a wealth of material about the show.

I compiled my Mayberry materials into a teaching format and developed a college course about the show. To date, I have taught this course more than twenty-five times at eight different community colleges. Also, I began to write a column for *The Bullet*, the fan club's newsletter, and eventually, that work led me to the writers. I wanted to know how they got ideas for their scripts, where they found their details, how they did such a great job at depicting small-town life.

I got to meet, interview, and correspond with many of these writers, and the result was the first edition of this book, titled *Mayberry 101*. I wrote that manuscript with the help of three outstanding *TAGS* writers: Sam Brobrick, Everett Greenbaum, and Harvey Bullock. I also drew upon the insights of producer Aaron Ruben and several of *The Andy Griffith Show* cast members.

This book has been a big seller with my publisher, Blair, for many years.

You'd think I'd be done. But no . . .

Soon after the publication of *Mayberry 101*, I contacted writer Jack Elinson. Jack wrote or cowrote thirty-four *TAGS* episodes. Jack agreed to answer my questions about his scripts. We corresponded by mail beginning in January 2000. We completed the project nine months later.

In 2020, I retired after thirty-nine years as a United Methodist minister. It now seemed the time to write a follow-up to *Mayberry 101*. In the meantime, Andy Griffith had donated all 249 of his *TAGS* scripts to the University of North Carolina at Chapel Hill library. In the fall, I drove to Chapel Hill and began researching Andy Griffith's *TAGS* scripts.

I clearly remember the first day of working with Andy's scripts. It was hard to believe that Andy Griffith's actual working scripts were in my hands. I felt Andy had donated them with me and other fans in mind. I had never had the opportunity to interview Andy Griffith in person, but he, through his scripts, was going to speak to me now!

The scripts gave Andy a voice from the time when they were produced. Notes, in his own hand, were evidence of how well he understood what was "right" for a small southern town. The scripts revealed what was originally written by the scriptwriters and the rewrites of producer and story consultant Aaron Ruben.

It was now time to return to Jack Elinson's answers. (His letters had been in storage for twenty-three years!)

I discovered through Jack's letters that the primary focus of his writing was the creation of a believable small-town atmosphere. Jack never hesitated to acknowledge the great talent of the *TAGS* cast and crew. He was always confident that the contributions of Andy Griffith and Aaron Ruben would make his scripts better.

There was not a day during the writing of this book's draft that I did not feel the spirit of Jack Elinson. The pages of Jack's correspondence, written in his own hand, became, for me, a conversation with him. It was a joyous and wonderful experience.

In this revised and retitled edition of what was *Mayberry 101*, the episodes of Jack Elinson and Charles Stewart take their place alongside the classic *TAGS* episodes written by Jim Fritzell and Everett Greenbaum, Harvey Bullock and Ray Saffian Allen, and Sam Bobrick and Bill Idelson.

Jack and Charles's place among this group is well deserved. Their "The New Housekeeper" and "Manhunt" scripts introduced the viewing audience to the Taylor family and the comic genius of Don Knotts, performing the role of Barney Fife. The two writers introduced the leadership role of women in the community through their Ellie Walker episodes (something seldom seen on 1960s television). Jack and Charles also wrote such *TAGS* classics as "Barney and the Choir," "Aunt Bee the Warden," and "Andy on Trial."

The Essential Mayberry places Jack's episodes with the episodes that appear in *Mayberry 101*. Most of Jack's scripts were written for the first two seasons, so they will be among the first chapters. All the episodes included in this book will appear in chronological order.

My aim is to give the Mayberry lover insights into the creative process of each of these episodes of *The Andy Griffith Show*. My hope is that you will enjoy this book and that while you are reading it, you will feel the very spirit of Mayberry and the people who created it.

1960–1961

"The New Housekeeper"

Episode 1

First Broadcast on
October 3, 1960

Written by
**Jack Elinson and
Charles Stewart**

Directed by
Sheldon Leonard

"Charles and I had a nice feel for *The Griffith Show,* even though we were both northerners. Charles came from Seattle, and I was from New York City."
—JACK ELINSON

"I became a comedy writer the old-fashioned way—nepotism," says writer Jack Elinson, principal writer on many of the first episodes of *The Andy Griffith Show* (*TAGS*). "Back in the thirties, when I was a teenager, my brother, Izzy, was already a very successful radio comedy writer. He wrote for *The Eddie Cantor Show* and *The Abbot and Costello Show,* among others.

"I was excited by his work, listening to the laughs his jokes were getting, and I got the bug. I wanted to be like him. Over the years, he helped to open doors for me until I established my own career. Izzy, by the way, wrote a few Griffith scripts with his partner, Fred Fox.

"I met my writing partner, Charles Stewart, in the fifties. We both had the same agent, and he suggested that we become a team. We did, and happily we clicked and had many wonderful years together.

"When *The Griffith Show* was sold to a sponsor, Charles and I were already writing *The Danny Thomas Show.* Producer Sheldon Leonard then asked us to write some scripts for Griffith."

Jack and Charles began writing scripts for *TAGS* in the early spring of 1960. Six scripts were completed and turned in to Aaron Ruben, who had been hired as the producer and story consultant for the new series.

"There wasn't any particular one of the six scripts that was designated to be the first one on the air," recalls Jack. "We wrote the scripts and then planned to decide later which one should be the series opener."

"There was actually a disagreement about this when the time came to make a decision. Sheldon and Aaron wanted to do one of the scripts titled 'Manhunt' first, but CBS chose 'The New Housekeeper,' and being the network, CBS won."

Aaron, Sheldon, and series star Andy Griffith felt that the "Manhunt" script, which featured Deputy Barney Fife, was comedically stronger than "The New

Housekeeper." Andy personally felt "Housekeeper" was "soft" and that the series opener should feature Don Knotts, who Andy, Aaron, and Sheldon agreed should be the series' comic lead, while Andy played the role of a straight man.

On Thursday, July 21, 1960, director Sheldon Leonard, producer Aaron Ruben, and "The New Housekeeper" cast gathered in a conference room on the Desilou Studios production lot. The group began the day by reading through the "Manhunt" script, which would begin production the following Thursday.

The "Manhunt" script was then put aside, and the remainder of the day was spent reading through "The New Housekeeper." All participants in the read-through were encouraged to make suggestions if they had any ideas they thought would improve the script.

On Friday, July 22, 1960, the cast spent the day rehearsing the script. All interior and exterior scenes were rehearsed inside Stages 1 and 2 on the Desilou lot. Saturday and Sunday, July 23 and 24, were weekend time off. The cast spent this time memorizing their lines. Monday through Wednesday, July 25, 26, and 27, were filming days. The exterior scenes were filmed on Monday, weather permitting.

During inclement weather, the interior scenes were filmed first, and the exteriors were rescheduled for later in the week.

"The New Housekeeper" script began with the script directions:

Andy's Living Room—Day

Where ANDY is officiating at a wedding ceremony. BARNEY FIFE is best man. The bride is ROSE MOSS, Andy's ex-housekeeper. The groom, a nervous one, is WILBUR PINE. An unhappy witness is little OPIE, Andy's son.

Jack and Charles's script directions set the scene and give insight into the characters' mindsets and their roles in the scene. The opening script directions set the scene in Andy's living room. In the filmed episode, this was changed to the interior of the courthouse. Barney Fife is cast in the role of best man, which is not obvious in the film. Andy's ex-housekeeper's last name is Moss, though this is never mentioned in the episode. Wilbur Pine is described as a nervous groom, and little Opie is not happy with the proceedings.

"The New Housekeeper" begins with an exterior shot of the Mayberry Courthouse that quickly cuts to the signs on its front doors. The signs read "Sheriff" and "Justice of the Peace." This shot dissolves into a close-up of Andy Taylor conducting the wedding ceremony of Wilbur and Rose.

Charles and Jack originally set the opening of the episode in the interior of Andy's living room. The decision to change this setting to the courthouse and a close-up of its signs gives the viewing audience a clearer introduction to Andy in his roles of sheriff and justice of the peace.

"The opening shots of the episode were the work of Sheldon Leonard, the director," says Jack.

The unhappy Opie interrupts the ceremony. He speaks now so he "won't have to forever hold his peace." Rose immediately kneels beside Opie and explains that he is not losing her forever. She plans to visit often.

While Rose is kneeling beside Opie, he places his hand on a pile of newspapers on the edge of Andy's desk. In the preceding medium shots of the desk, the newspapers are not in this position. The newspapers move in and out of this position throughout the remainder of the scene.

This continuity error is the result of filming *TAGS* with one camera. With this filming setup, each scene was performed and filmed numerous times. The master shot was a medium shot. All close-ups were filmed during another performance of the scene with the camera filming only the actor seen in the close-up. The close-ups and master shots were put in proper order during the editing process after the filming of the episode was completed.

The moving newspapers are the result of filming the master shot of the opening scene several times, moving the newspapers for one performance and removing them for another. The editor then selected master shots from different run-throughs for the finished episode and was either unaware of the error or thought the viewing audience would never notice the difference.

Near the end of the ceremony, Andy tells Barney to "get ready." Barney responds by getting his "mouth organ" out of his pocket and playing a few notes.

Charles and Jack's script direction have Barney playing "The Wedding March" as the couple exits the courthouse. The performance was dropped from the scene.

"We couldn't have Barney just standing there during the wedding ceremony, so we gave him a harmonica to play," says Jack.

In the next scene, a short time after the wedding, Opie asks if Rose has called. Andy answers that Rose hasn't called and isn't likely to because she is on her honeymoon. "Besides that, Aunt Bee will be coming pretty soon and that'll be just like having Rose here."

Andy then tells Opie that Aunt Bee had raised him and "done a pretty good job." He attempts to reassure Opie. "She'll raise you just fine and love you like she loved me."

Opie replies that he "ain't gonna love no one besides Rose."

This scene is set outdoors and was filmed on Monday, July 25, when all exterior photography for the episode was scheduled.

"Having the exteriors of the town was so great," says Jack. "The Danny Thomas Show was done in front of a live audience, so they were confined to interiors. It was so interesting to see both shows back-to-back on Monday nights. The Thomas Show looked like a play, and The Griffith Show looked like a movie."

Charles and Jack's script directions end the father-son discussion:

Opie rushes off tearfully. Andy would go after him, but Barney enters officiously. He salutes Andy.

Barney salutes and states that he is "reporting with an important message."

Andy reminds Barney that he doesn't have to salute: "It's just me and you."

Barney explains he wants to do things right. He would like "the folks of this town to realize" that Andy picked him to be his deputy because he "was the best suited for the job." Barney concludes the explanation, "And I want to thank you, Cousin Andy."

"Making Barney Andy's cousin was obviously done to explain why Andy would hire a misfit like Barney," says Jack. "Sheldon, Aaron, and Andy felt it would become a one-joke thing, so we voted to drop it."

Barney's important message is that "Aunt Bee called to say she's comin' in tomorrow."

The next day begins with Opie ambitiously preparing breakfast alone. The scene's script directions were: *Opie has eggs boiling on the stove, the table is set and as the scene opens, he is pouring juice into one of the glasses. He pours a little too much and it spills over slightly. He bends over to slurp the surplus.*

The filmed scene replaced the spilled juice with Opie dropping a grapefruit half on the floor, brushing it with a cleaning brush, and then scratching his head with the brush.

Andy enters the kitchen. Opie explains that he has prepared breakfast to "show that we don't need Aunt Bee. We can get along without her."

A knock on the door announces Aunt Bee's arrival. The script describes her as *a pleasant, round-faced woman.*

"Soon after the pilot was sold, the cast was set," says Jack. "The Aunt Bee character and the actress, Frances Bavier, who would play her was a done deal. Charles and I take no credit for Aunt Bee's look. That came from our wardrobe lady, and I'm sure that Sheldon, Aaron, and maybe Andy had a few things to add. My only contribution was naming Aunt Bee. My wife had an Aunt Bee, who was a nurse. The name had a nice sound to it."

Aunt Bee is excited to meet Opie. Raising Opie will "be just like raising Andy all over again."

Aunt Bee requests that Opie "give her a little sugar." Andy repeats the request, "Go on now, give her a little sugar. Give her some good."

"The 'come give me a little sugar' and 'give her some good' lines obviously came from Andy Griffith himself," says Jack. "People from Seattle and New York don't talk that way."

That evening Aunt Bee prepares fried chicken especially for Opie. Opie, however, isn't hungry, because Aunt Bee makes it different from Rose.

Aunt Bee is a bit hurt by the comment but hides it as best she can. She goes into the kitchen to "get us some coffee."

After her departure, Andy says to Opie, "And to think I was glad when you learned to talk."

"Charles had two young sons and I had three, so we knew a little about kids who get bratty," says Jack. "Andy's response to Opie came from me. I said that to my kids when they said something they shouldn't have."

Andy gets up to help Aunt Bee in the kitchen. He sends Opie up to his room. Before leaving the table, Opie fills his plate with two additional pieces of chicken.

The script directions for the next scene:

INT. OPIE'S BEDROOM

Opie is wolfing down the last of the dinner, obviously with a great deal of relish. He is just finishing a chicken leg when he alerts to a sound in the hall outside. But, before he can hide the plate, the door opens and Andy enters. Opie tries to stand in front of the plate.

Andy has come to look for Opie's plate, which has disappeared from the table. He sees the plate and wonders "how it got all the way up here to Opie's room and licked clean, to boot."

In reply, Opie explains he brought it up for his bird, Dickie. Dickie loves fried chicken, biscuits, and honey.

"When Andy enters Opie's room, he knows, of course, Opie has devoured the food," says Jack. "Andy plays along with the 'Dickie the bird' story. Amused, Andy knows it's just a matter of time before Opie starts warming up to Aunt Bee."

The episode's first act ends with Opie kneeling by his bedside, saying his prayers. In the script, the prayer begins, "God bless my Paw . . . and my dog, _____, and my bird, Dickie . . . and my frog, Jumpie."

Jack and Charles do not name the dog in the prayer. The actor, Ronny Howard, had a dog named Gulliver, and that name was given to Opie's pet. Jumpie the frog is omitted from the filmed prayer.

The door to the bedroom is left ajar. Aunt Bee walking in the hall past the door stops and listens to Opie. Opie ends the prayer and then thinks of something else. "Oh, I forgot somebody important!" Aunt Bee, still standing in the doorway, beams in anticipation. Opie ends his prayer, "God bless Rose, even though she ran off and got married!"

The episode's second act begins with Barney escorting a prisoner into the courthouse. The prisoner is Emma Watson, *a fragile little old lady who walks with the help of a cane.* Barney has arrested Emma for jaywalking. Andy enters as Barney starts to fingerprint the prisoner and reminds Barney, "We don't never stop Emma. We figure if she can save a step or two here and there, she'll just be with us that much longer." Much to Barney's irritation, Andy releases Emma to "go ahead on home."

"It's obvious that Barney is very light in this script," says Jack, "so we came up with this scene just to keep him alive and remind the audience he's a bumbling character."

Later that day, Andy enters Opie's bedroom. Opie asks Andy if he can run away from home. Andy explains that if that's what's on your mind you "ain't supposed to ask your Paw. First you write a note sayin' that you are running away and then you do it."

Andy and Opie's dialogue creates humor by presenting Opie's viewpoint. Opie understands the concept of running away, but his viewpoint reveals the perspective of a child. He believes he should get his father's permission before "going any-place far." After learning that a note is required, Opie admits he "doesn't know how to write." Andy then graciously agrees to write the note for him.

"The father-son relationship between Andy and Opie couldn't have been better," says Jack. "It was one of the strengths of this show. Ronny was six years old at that time, and that's exactly what would happen. We didn't have to exaggerate. It was real."

Opie eventually realizes that he doesn't want to "leave you, Paw." Andy asks Opie if his reason for wanting to run away is Aunt Bee. Opie explains that Aunt Bee "can't fish, or hunt frogs, or play baseball with me like Rose did."

Later in the day, Andy decides to show Aunt Bee a "little bit about baseball." Andy hands Aunt Bee a bat. She asks, "What's that?" and then attempts to hold the big end and hit with the little end.

"Someone like Aunt Bee would have been totally ignorant of all sports, hence the wrong end of the bat," says Jack. "If she saw a football, she'd wonder why it wasn't round like other balls."

The fishing scene that follows was shortened from what appeared in the original script. The original has Aunt Bee catching two fish rather than one. The first is a "limp" fish taken out of a sack that Andy attaches to Aunt Bee's hook after pulling her line out of the water with his toes. This may explain why Andy is barefooted in the scene.

The filmed episode has Aunt Bee pulling her only catch out of the water, screaming at the squirming fish on the line, dropping the pole, and running away. Opie asks, "What did she do that for?"

In the original script the fishing trip is followed by a scene that was deleted from the filmed version. In the scene: *Andy is at the wheel of a vehicle. Next to him Opie sleeps with his head on Aunt Bee's shoulder. She has her arm around him. Andy and Aunt Bee exchange looks. Aunt Bee is apparently in seventh heaven with the boy in her embrace. But after a moment Opie stirs, awakes, recognizes where he is, and indignantly sits erect. Aunt Bee feels the rebuff.*

Arriving home, Andy carries a sleeping Opie to bed. Opie awakes and quickly realizes Dickie is gone. Aunt Bee confesses that she "cleaned out the cage this morning, and maybe I didn't shut the cage door tight enough." Aunt Bee, completely defeated, leaves the room.

"The thought of having a bird and Aunt Bee accidentally leaving Dickie's cage open was in the original storyline before the script was written," says Jack. "We needed something like that to make Opie angry at her and want her out of the house."

Charles and Jack's script directions provide a wonderful narrative to what happens next.

Morning—Opie is in bed.

He looks up at the sound of voices. He feigns sleep. The door opens and Aunt Bee enters. She is dressed for travel. Behind her stands Andy with her packed suitcase in his hand. She bends over and brushes Opie's cheek with her lips. She exits.

Opie ~~tries to feel the elation~~ he thinks he should feel at successfully rid-
~~ding himself of Aunt~~ Bee. But he cannot. He goes to crouch next to the open
window.

In the yard, Aunt Bee tells Andy she would love to stay and "do the things Opie likes to do, but he's a very smart little boy. I ~~couldn't fool him~~. You know, he's going through a very hard time."

Charles and Jack write, "Suddenly Opie ~~makes his decision~~ and ~~climbs out the window calling~~ 'Paw! Aunt Bee! ~~Wait!~~'"

It's interesting that the writers visualize Opie's bedroom being on the ground floor and have him climb out the window into the yard. In the filmed episode, Opie's bedroom is upstairs and will remain so throughout the series.

Opie tells Aunt Bee he wants her to stay. He asks, "If she goes, what will happen to her? She doesn't know how to do anything." So, he must teach Aunt Bee how to play ball and catch fish: "She needs me!"

"Turning Opie around was, of course, the happy ending we needed," says Jack. "Opie's lines were perfect and touching, yet funny with the 'you need me' line. I don't think we could have done better."

The episode concludes with Andy and Aunt Bee sitting on the front porch. Andy is playing guitar and singing. Aunt Bee sits in a rocking chair, smiling and ~~tapping~~ her foot. Opie rushes out of the house and joyfully announces that "~~Dickie~~ has come back!" The family celebrates the bird's return. Andy resumes playing and singing "The ~~Crawdad Song~~," Opie joins in, repeating the last word of each line, and Aunt Bee hums along.

"Andy playing and singing on the porch was our idea," says Jack. "It was Andy Griffith who selected 'The ~~Crawdad Song~~.' We left it up to Andy to pick out the songs throughout the series, because he was an expert when it came to music."

"The ending with everyone ~~joining~~ in was not scripted. It just happened when they filmed it. ~~My bet~~ is that it was ~~Andy's idea~~."

"We were all pleased about the way 'Housekeeper' turned out," says Jack. "Since this was the first show on the air, we had to hold our breaths waiting to see how the viewers reacted to it. ~~Happily~~, the reaction was very positive, and we could breathe again.

"Some of the critics, however, didn't care for it. To these critics, *The ~~Griffith Show~~* was 'country.' Now here we are, years later. The show is still on the air and loved by so many people. I think we can now safely say that those few critics don't bother us at all."

"I have no other special memories of 'Housekeeper,'" admits Jack. "It was just one of several scripts we wrote before we started filming. We had no idea how any of them would turn out. Thank the good Lord, they all turned out great!"

January 2000

Neal,
In case you're won-
dering why I'm writ-
ing in longhand, I just
got a new computer,
which I don't know
how to use yet and
my typewriter needs
servicing. I kinda
like writing longhand
instead of charging
into all that high-
tech stuff out there.
Writing in longhand
is sort of Mayberry,
don't you think?
—Jack

In the Beginning

"When *The Andy Griffith Show* was being put together by Danny Thomas and Sheldon Leonard in Los Angeles, Andy and I were in New York City," says *The Andy Griffith Show* associate producer Richard O. Linke. "The four of us would go back and forth by phone, and Sheldon flew in a couple of times. When it came time to hire the line producer, who is usually the head writer and the day-to-day guy in charge of what happens, we thought Sheldon was going to hire a man by the name of Fred DeCordova. DeCordova was a big, big movie and television director in Hollywood. I said, 'Man, that's great.' But it turned out that DeCordova wasn't available.

"So Sheldon sent us a list of names of other possible candidates. It's funny because all the persons that were recommended were both New York-bred and Jewish. At first, I said to myself, 'This sounds a bit funny. How would they know about an Andy Griffith and the South?'

"The list was narrowed down to Aaron Ruben and Marvin Marks, who was the head writer for *The Jackie Gleason Show*. I had heard about Aaron Ruben, but I didn't know too much about his work. Andy and I talked to both candidates and were sort of confused about who to hire.

"I remember my office was a two-room suite at the Park Sheraton Hotel, and Andy used to come over there for meetings. He was doing *Destry Rides Again* on Broadway at the time. So Andy said, 'What do you think?' And I said, 'Jeez, I don't know.' It was almost a flip of the coin at that stage. Finally we said, and I don't remember if Andy said it to me or I said it to Andy, 'Let's go with Aaron Ruben.'

"Our decision was not based on any big knowledge or document. But it was probably the luckiest and the best decision we ever made because Aaron turned out to be a really top, top writer-producer and a very brilliant guy in his own field. And that was it. We called Sheldon with our decision, and the William Morris Agency, who put the *The Andy Griffith Show* package together, did the actual hiring."

"As the producer of the series, my main responsibility was to be sure we had a good, workable script on that first day of shooting," says Aaron Ruben. "If necessary, I would do a rewrite and make certain all of us—Andy, the director, the executive producer, and I—were agreed we were ready for the camera. The other responsibilities I had to attend to were casting, conferring with the editor, the composer, the wardrobe people, and the writers."

"Manhunt"

Episode 2

First Broadcast on
October 10, 1960

Written by
**Charles Stewart
and Jack Elinson**

Directed by
Don Weis

"Charles and I rented an apartment which we used as an office. We had equal strengths both on stories and comedy. Charles did the typing while I paced. As for our writing credits, we always alternated which name would come first. That was our agreement."—JACK ELINSON

"As I mentioned earlier, our first script on the air came down to either 'The New Housekeeper' or 'Manhunt,'" says Jack. "Some of us voted for 'Manhunt' because Barney was so strong in it. Others voted for 'The New Housekeeper' because Opie was so strong in that one. CBS, who had the final say, wanted 'Housekeeper' because it was such a pure 'family' show. It was homey.

"As for Don Knotts's character, it was apparent that Barney was hilarious. We struck gold! 'Manhunt' was just the beginning of his character's development. All the scripts that came afterward honed the character more and more.

"Don Knotts himself contributed so much through his acting ability. He came up with so many funny things on the set that embellished the scripts. What was funny on paper became hysterical on film. It didn't take long before Andy and the rest of us realized that Don should be the funny one and Andy should be the straight man."

"Manhunt" opens with Andy and Opie in a rowboat fishing. Opie asks, "Paw, what kind of bait are you puttin' on my line?" Andy replies, "It's a piece of ham from our lunch." Andy throws Opie's line into the water and explains that a piece of ham might "perk up" the fish.

Opie immediately gets a bite and says of the fish, "You were right, Paw, he sure went for the ham." Andy agrees, "He sure did. Looky there, he's still smacking his lips."

"As for Andy using ham as bait, Charles did a lot of fishing and he told me that he used ham now and then and had luck with it," says Jack. "Andy's line about the fish 'smackin' his lips' was the result of Charles and I writing southern. Any writer worth his weight is able to capture the characters they're writing about.

It's ~~important to have an ear~~ for the ~~way~~ people ta~~lk~~. In ad~~dition~~ to writing ~~scripts~~ for *The ~~Griffith Show~~*, Charles and I als~~o wrote scripts~~ for *The ~~Real McCoys~~*. ~~That~~ show was ab~~out~~ southern~~ers~~ who ~~moved~~ to California. Havi~~ng done~~ that ~~show, I~~ became ver~~y familiar~~ with ~~the way~~ southerners ~~talk~~."

In response to ~~his ham-baited catch~~, Op~~ie~~ admiringly sa~~ys~~, "G~~olly, Paw~~, you know ~~just~~ about ev~~erything~~. You~~'re the sheriff~~, the ju~~stice~~ of the pe~~ace~~, I bet ~~you're~~ the m~~ost important man-in~~ the w~~hole world~~."

Andy looks down and notices the boat "has sprung a leak." He rows the boat to shore, where he and Opie hide it "out of sight under the bushes" to prevent anyone from taking the leaking boat out on the water.

The script directions for the ending of the scene are very detailed. Andy and Opie *are soaked from the knees down*. In the filmed episode, Andy's pantlegs are rolled up and not wet, but Opie's pantlegs are wet from the knees down, as the script suggested.

Barney drives up in the squad car and excitedly announces, "You'll never guess what's happened! Somethin' big! Biggest thing ever happened in Mayberry! Real big! Big! Big!" He reports that a dangerous criminal has escaped from state prison and is believed to be headed toward Mayberry.

"We didn't think of making Barney's 'Something big' line a running joke at first," says Jack, "but we found occasion to use it a second time and then we realized it would make a funny 'runner.' The repetition worked great."

Andy, Barney, and Opie quickly return to the courthouse. Before entering the building, Andy sends the six-year-old Opie home to clean the fish.

"When Andy tells Opie to clean the fish, it was of course a way to get Opie out of the scene," says Jack. "I don't think it was far-fetched since Opie and Andy go fishing together all the time. You could assume that Andy has taught Opie how to clean fish."

Andy enters the courthouse. Otis Campbell, a jailed prisoner, asks if he "can go now." Otis's twenty-four hours "are about up," so he reaches through the cell bars, gets the keys hanging on the wall, unlocks the cell, and lets himself out.

"We created Otis as an example of how a small-town jail is run," says Jack. "Otis had nothing to do with the plot, but in between the story points, we didn't want to forget the flavor of the Mayberry jail."

"Otis, the drunk, was the first of the many Mayberry characters that came along over the years. Charles and I saw Otis as someone who only got drunk on Saturday nights. After he had one too many, he walked over to Andy's office and let himself into a cell. The next morning, after a good night's sleep, he let himself out, waving goodbye to Andy. Since it was Sunday morning, he then walked directly to church to ask the Lord's forgiveness for drinking so much."

Otis's release upsets Barney. He is concerned about what the state police will think when they find "we got an empty jail." Andy reassures him that the jail will be filling up as soon as "we catch that criminal." Barney brightens at the news and remembers, "I better check my arms." He begins patting his various pockets and, frowning, says, "I can't find my bullet!"

"Charles and I came up with the one-bullet idea," admits Jack. "From the moment it was read by everyone, it was agreed unanimously that Barney would only have one bullet always. It wasn't hard to think of the idea. Barney was such a bumbler there was no way Andy would trust him with more than one bullet."

Sirens are heard in the distance. Outside, a "whole regiment" roars up to stop in front of the courthouse. The regiment consists of two motorcycles and three patrol cars. A group of nine troopers and their leader, Captain Barker, dismount.

"The whole point of 'Manhunt' was to show that a huge number of troopers with all the very newest technology and weapons aren't a match for a shrewd country sheriff," explains Jack. "The vehicles and large cast cost some extra money, but the show never went over budget and didn't have a lot of extra sets other than Andy's office and home. *TAGS* wasn't an expensive show."

Captain Barker marches past two men sitting on a bench and briskly enters the courthouse. The script directions describe the two as *old men playing chess*. In Andy Griffith's working copy of the script, the word *chess* is marked through in pencil and replaced with *checkers*.

Once inside the courthouse, Barker immediately picks up the telephone. He sternly instructs the operator to keep the line open to the state capitol.

Andy grabs the telephone as Captain Barker is about to slam down the receiver. He gently tells the operator, Sarah, Barker's instruction is "alright," and she should call his home phone if any sheriff business comes up.

"We felt that even in the early sixties, there were still the good old telephone operators," says Jack. "Mayberry, of all places, would be a reality for someone like Sarah. Naturally, Sarah would be picking up the phone and getting the folks through to whomever they wanted to talk to."

Captain Barker ignores Andy's offer of help. He orders a map set beside Andy's desk and places a magnetized marker upon it. Andy is impressed. He still uses pins, which are in short supply since the Woman's Club used the pins to hem up costumes for their Halloween play.

"About Andy's fascination with the magnetic pins on Barker's map—Andy was just having a little fun with Barker," Jack explains. "Andy pretended to be awed by Barker's 'latest tool in crimefighting.' Hence Andy's line about the Women's Club."

Pictures of the escaped criminal are passed out. The photograph of "a mean, criminal type" is briefly shown in the filmed episode. Barney looks at the picture and in the original script says, "Darned if he doesn't look just like the mayor's wife." Barney's line was eventually changed to "That's a nice snapshot of him."

"Barney's remark about the criminal's mug shot is sincere," says Jack. "Andy could have done the same line, but out of his mouth it would have been tongue in cheek."

Aunt Bee and Opie arrive. Opie tells Barker, "You don't have to worry, sir. My paw will catch the criminal for sure."

Barker and his men depart, leaving Andy and Barney to "stay and handle your local affairs."

Opie doesn't understand why an important person like Andy has been excluded. Andy explains that Barker is probably saving him and Barney for a special assignment.

Jack and Charles's script directions for what follows are *Opie brightens, but not nearly so much as Barney who fairly bubbles.*

Barney pulls the gun from his holster with a quick draw. The gun catches and

Barney accidentally fires, almost shooting off his own toe. The others leap back in alarm. Andy just holds out his hand without a word. Miserably, Barney hands over the gun. Andy breaks it, empties out the bullets, closes the gun, and hands it back to Barney, who puts it in his holster, a very unhappy deputy. END OF ACT ONE.

The second act begins with Opie and a small "knot" of Mayberry citizens gathered outside the courthouse. Andy is asked, "How come you're not to be out on the roadblock?" Opie quickly speaks up: "You don't have to tell my paw anything! He knows what he's doing!"

"Opie's adoration of Andy was so powerful," says Jack. "His belief in his dad was a very important part of 'Manhunt.' No father wants to let down his son. He wants his son to be proud of him. No way would Andy disappoint Opie."

Andy decides, "He's got to do something." He takes a box of bullets from his desk drawer and tells Barney to load his gun. The two are going on patrol!

Andy lets Barney out on an old road down by the lake. He instructs Barney to keep his eyes on the road and "don't let anything pass without you checking it."

Barney replies, "You can trust me, Sheriff. You're talking to Reliable Barney Fife, you know."

"'Reliable Barney Fife' was just a happenstance in the 'The New Housekeeper,'" says Jack. "We never intended it to be a runner throughout the series. But like so many other things, what we thought was a one-shot line turned out to be too good not to repeat it in a lot of the shows. It was the way that Don Knotts did the line that made it so funny."

After Andy drives away, Barney spots a vehicle approaching. He stops it, recognizes the driver, and warmly greets his friend Cal Jones. Barney orders Cal to get out of his truck. Barney must frisk him to be sure he is not the criminal disguised as Cal.

Later, another man is frisked. Barney completes the task and says to the man, "Be sure and say hello to the little woman, Mayor!"

Still later, Barney is frisking an older woman. Barney says, "I'm sorry about this, but us lawmen can't take chances." The woman turns and replies, "But Barney. I'm your mother!"

"I think the roadblock scene was the only time we did exaggerated over-the-top sketch comedy on *The Griffith Show*," admits Jack. "We especially stretched it when Barney gives his own mother such a hard time. It was just too funny not to do. Obviously, Andy, Don, and producer Aaron Ruben felt the same."

Barney takes a break from his roadblock duties. While Barney is relaxing, the criminal, Dirkson, sneaks up behind him and takes his gun. In the original script, Dirkson points the gun at Barney, and he faints *dead away*. Barney eventually *comes out of his faint* and is found by Andy. Barney begins explaining what happened, but *the word picture is too much. He faints again.* The scene was revised, and in the filmed episode Barney is left gagged and bound.

Andy finds Barney, releases him, and reports to Captain Barker that they "made contact" with the criminal. Andy has an idea but is cut off by Barker before he can share it.

Andy tells his idea to Barney: "If I was a criminal headed through the woods, I'd stop at Molly Brand's house." Molly bakes pies daily and sets them out on the window to cool. The pies' aroma would simply be too much for a starving criminal to resist.

Andy and Barney stop by Emma Brand's house. Andy warns Emma about "the escaped convict on the loose." Andy then asks about Emma's sciatica. Emma replies, "It's fine" and quickly closes the door. Andy realizes something "curious" is going on. Emma's sciatica is never "fine." Andy believes Dirkson is inside the house. He knocks on the door and tells Emma in case she was to see the criminal, "Don't say a word about my boat being laid down by the lake under a clump of bushes. The criminal could use the boat to "get away."

"I have no memory of why the name Molly was changed to Emma," says Jack. "I likewise know nothing about the character having a sciatica problem."

The character's name change and sciatica problem were likely a revision made after the script read-through on Thursday, July 28, 1960.

Andy radios Captain Barker and tells him that he has made "the necessary arrangements to wind this whole thing up." Andy suggests that Barker go by his house and pick up Opie, who can show him the way to the lake where the criminal can be found.

"The filmed episode ran twenty-four minutes," says Jack. "With the time restraints you have to move your story along pretty fast. We didn't feel that any of the moves that Andy made were unrealistic. Andy is a very clever guy, so the smell of Molly's pies and mentioning the boat so the criminal will overhear is not out of line. One of the general rules on *The Griffith Show* was to always be real."

Andy and Barney drive to the lake and see Dirkson pulling the hidden boat into the water. The State Patrol arrive soon afterward, with Opie in tow, as Dirkson is rowing away from shore. Captain Barker reprimands Andy for "letting the criminal get away." Opie then has a realization. Andy purposely allowed the criminal to take the boat.

"Opie doesn't say that the boat is sinking," explains Jack. "What he says is, 'Paw, that's our boat isn't it? And you let him take it on purpose, didn't you?' What Charles and I did was build this moment to its climax. We just wanted to keep the suspense going."

The boat quickly sinks. Dirkson dives out and swims toward his capture.

The original script ends act 2 at this point. The revised script adds additional dialogue. Andy looks at Opie and says, "You know this morning when we were fishing, I sure didn't enjoy having a hole in that boat. I'll tell you the truth, right now, I wouldn't take a dollar and a quarter for it."

"As for the 'I wouldn't take a dollar and a quarter' line," says Jack, "I think that came from Andy."

The episode ends outside the courthouse. Dirkson sits in the back of a patrol car waiting to be taken away. Charles and Jack's script directions are *Barney steps to the window of the car to glare defiantly at the prisoner. Dirkson lunges at Barney with a snarl. Barney, his courage suddenly drained away, steps back, his eyes roll up, and he faints dead away.*

The scene is revised with a much better ending. Barney tells Dirkson, you "won't get the drop on me again." He then pulls his gun from the holster, starts a fancy gun twirl, and snags his finger.

The "Manhunt" script earned Charles and Jack a Writer's Guild of America award for best writing in a comedy or variety series.

"Naturally, we were thrilled to get the Writer's Guild award," says Jack. "The way this award works is that any writer who feels that his or her script is worthy of an award can submit it for consideration. It has to be a script that was produced and shown on the air. The interesting thing about this award is that it's judged by the script only, not by the film that is broadcast.

"Since I worked on so many scripts over my career it's hard to pick a favorite, but if I had to pick one, it would have to be 'Manhunt.' First, it was the show that kicked off the Barney character. It was almost like writing a pilot just for a Barney show. So much was learned from that episode. The one-bullet stuff, the bumbling, the trying so hard to be the absolute best police officer in the business. Stewart and I took such pride in that episode.

"A second reason the episode is a favorite is we won the Writers Guild Award that year for 'Manhunt.' How sweet it was!"

"The Guitar Player"

"Next Christmas, when I send Andy Griffith a holiday card, I'm gonna come out and ask him what a spavined horse is."—JACK ELINSON

Spavined—Arthritis of the smaller hock joint. Often seen in older horses.

Jack Elinson and Charles Stewart were hired to write six *Griffith Show* scripts in the early spring of 1960. The scripts were scheduled to be put into production in July of that year and would be among the earliest episodes of *The Andy Griffith Show*.

Each script began with a consultation with *TAGS* producer and story consultant Aaron Ruben. Charles, Jack, and Aaron would discuss possible story ideas. Six of these ideas were approved for further development.

The next step in the process was the creation of a story outline.

"Before a script is written, the story outline is of utmost importance," says Jack. "Everything is laid out scene by scene. It's vital to know how it'll flow from beginnings and endings. To make sure everyone is in agreement, the outline is discussed thoroughly, during which changes are made. When everyone is satisfied, we start writing the script."

Jack and Charles would then submit the first draft of the script for feedback.

"Every script was done with the input of all the key people," says Jack. "It was always a collaboration of executive producer Sheldon Leonard, Aaron Ruben, Andy Griffith, and us."

After a collaborative meeting, Charles and Jack were given the "go-ahead" to write the script's final draft.

"Very often, during the writing, if we came up with new ideas that might make it better, we checked it out with the others to get their opinions," says Jack. Charles and Jack turned in their second draft of "The Guitar Player" on July 14, 1960. Their work on the episode was finished. The script was now in the hands of story consultant Aaron Ruben.

"Aaron Ruben's work was monumental," says Jack. "His contribution to the

Episode 3

First Broadcast on
October 17, 1960

Written by
Jack Elinson and
Charles Stewart

Directed by
Don Weis

James Best
Guest Stars as
Jim Lindsey

series was one of the reasons it became a giant hit. He wasn't just a script consultant; he was the producer who kept things humming. Every script that was written was always rewritten by Aaron. His touch was what kept *The Griffith Show* consistent and great."

"The Guitar Player" script was first read by the cast on the morning of Thursday, July 28, 1960. The script was then set aside. The remainder of the day was spent on a final read-through of the "Manhunt" script.

Aaron Ruben submitted the first revisions to "The Guitar Player" on Tuesday, August 2, for typing, copying, and insertion into Charles and Jack's script. An in-depth cast read-through of the script was done on the afternoon of Thursday, August 4, during which additional revisions were made. A revised script was assembled later that evening and ready for rehearsals on Friday morning, August 5. Filming of "The Guitar Player" was scheduled for Monday through Wednesday, August 8–10.

The episode begins with a group of townsfolk gathered in front of Monroe's Mortuary. Jim Lindsey, "a youngish, indolent fellow," is playing a guitar. Proprietor Orville Monroe is angry that the performance is in front of his business.

"Since we knew that music was one of Andy Griffith's many interests, it was no surprise that Andy would like to feature some music in the series," says Jack. "This script was the first of quite a few shows where Andy and others did their musical stuff."

"James Best did a fine job in the role of Jim Lindsey, the guitar player," says Jack. "James was a top actor at that time. That was why we grabbed him. The character he played was inspired by Elvis Presley and all the other rock 'n' rollers like him."

Mortician Orville Monroe complains to Andy. He wants Jim arrested for disturbing the peace.

"Strangely, there can be a lot of humor in death," says Jack. "Years ago, on radio, there was a show called *The Life of Riley*. One of the regular characters was a mortuary director whose exit line every week was, 'It's time to be shoveling off.' I wonder why Orville Monroe wasn't used in the series as much as Floyd Lawson, the barber. Done tastefully, a funeral director is a great character."

Andy cordially arrests Jim. Afterward in the sheriff's office, Andy joins Jim in playing and singing "New River Train."

"When it came to music, all we usually did in a script was write *Andy sings (blank)*," says Jack. "Andy Griffith picked the music. For the length of the musical performance, they just played as long as they wanted to. If the show ran too long, the performance was shortened in the editing room."

Actor Jim Lindsey was not a musician and did not play the guitar. A professional guitarist was hired to record Jim's parts and instruct James Best on the proper finger placements for the close-ups of his hands.

Andy asks Jim, "Why don't you do something about yourself?" Andy enters the cell and, without asking, pours Jim a cup of coffee. He then sits and says, "You got real talent. Wouldn't you like to earn yourself some real money?" Jim, however, feels that "he's not ready."

"Andy entering the cell and serving Lindsey coffee, then sitting in a rocking chair was not in our script," says Jack. "Sometimes these small moves were suggested by Andy and then worked out on the set by the director. The people working on the show were always looking for whatever made the show real and comfortable."

"We approached the Griffith scripts in a general comic manner and then adapted the humor to the setting," says Jack. "First and foremost, we wanted to be funny. But we also wanted to capture the feel of a small town in the South. That's what made *The Griffith Show* a hit. People living in small towns all over America could relate to it. The highly sophisticated looked down their noses at us, but as we found out, we didn't need them. We captured America. The show was a smash!"

Later, Barney is putting new wanted posters on the bulletin board. He is carefully watched by Mayberry postmaster Talbot Martin. When Barney turns his back, Talbot reaches for a wanted poster placed on a nearby chair. He is caught in the act.

Talbot's action is motivated by the fact that he has not received any federal wanted posters "lately." He wants a state poster to put on his "half-empty" post office bulletin board.

Barney and Talbot get into a heated argument. Andy decides to interrupt their disagreement and mollify the postmaster.

He tells Talbot, "You may not have many posters, but you got quality. Master criminals rather than petty thieves."

Andy advises Talbot and Barney to "look at their bulletin boards with pride and count your blessings."

"By this point, Andy Griffith had decided that his character would be the 'Solomon' of Mayberry, and Barney and all the other town folks would be the funny characters," says Jack. "Andy was the wise man who settled all arguments and kept all things in order. The argument between Barney and Talbot was a demonstration of the silly little things people argue about."

As Talbot exits, Andy and Barney see a band bus parking across the street. The bus has "Bobby Fleet and His Band with a Beat" painted on its side.

"Many of the names we came up with had no significance," says Jack. "Bobby Fleet is an example. The last name, Fleet, only had to rhyme with beat to give the band's name a corny effect."

After parking, the band members enter a diner. Bobby Fleet immediately begins loudly joking about the slow service and the small-town life of Mayberry.

Andy and Barney enter the diner. Andy becomes the new target of Fleet's joking. Andy attempts to tell Fleet about Jim Lindsey's talent but is interrupted.

Andy and Barney step outside. Barney angrily tells Andy, "You were awful nice to that smart-alecky fellow. It's a good thing he didn't start in on me. I'm a mean man when I get riled."

"When the guys in the band hurl their insults at Andy, Barney the clown becomes Barney the defender," says Jack. "Barney's no fool at that moment. It was stuff like that which allows the character to show some depth."

Andy dislikes Fleet but would like to get him to hear Jim play. Andy is confident Jim could "make it if he had a chance."

Andy suddenly has an idea. Fleet's bus is parked in a one-hour zone. The bus takes up two parking spaces and is thus "only entitled to a half a hour." In a "little bit" the musicians will be violating the law.

Bobby Fleet and his band are brought in for sentencing. The parking penalty is twenty dollars or twenty-four hours in jail. Fleet protests. He insults the "dignity" of Andy's robes and offers a bribe to avoid the sentence. Andy continues to raise the fine, and Fleet decides he will not pay it. He and the band will serve their sentence in jail.

Andy sends Barney out to "arrest Jim Lindsey and his guitar with him."

Barney eventually brings Jim in for questioning. Fleet figures out the situation and says, "I'm not going to listen to this kid!" Jim, angered, replies that he has no intention of playing.

Andy takes Jim's guitar and attempts to tune it. He pretends to have trouble and asks Jim to tune the guitar for him. Jim reluctantly complies. Bobby Fleet laughs at Jim's tuning strum. More laughs and insults accompany Jim's tuning efforts.

Charles and Jack's script directions describe what happens next: *Jim gets himself set, and with a look of angry defiance, he plunges into the number. As the number progresses it becomes obvious this boy is good.*

"When Lindsey gets angry at Fleet's insults, the close-up of Lindsey's furious face was the work of director, Don Weis," says Jack. "We never put camera-shot directions in our scripts."

Jim's angry playing turns into a joyous performance. Bobby Fleet nods his head in rhythm. The jailed musicians take out their instruments and play along. Andy grins with satisfaction. Barney conducts the band and breaks into a spontaneous dance.

"Barney dancing as he conducts the band is something that happened as they were staging the scene," says Jack. "That was not in the script. In many cases, as they rehearse a scene, ideas pop up. Ideas can come from either the director or Andy or Don or Aaron Ruben, or who knows, perhaps the script girl."

"All the music was prerecorded," says Jack. "It was done in a recording studio and then during filming, the performers react to the soundtrack. This was standard procedure."

Afterward, Andy asks Fleet, "If Jim was available, would you hire him?" Fleet answers that he "digs" Jim and "could always use a good guitarist." Andy then "talks money" with Fleet.

Jim eventually speaks up for himself, "You two been talkin' over me like I was a spavined horse on an auction block." Jim will take the job. His salary can be negotiated later.

"I know for sure 'the spavined horse' dialogue was not in our script," says Jack. "I don't even know what that means! That had to have been one of Andy Griffith's contributions."

The second act ends with Andy's farewell words to Jim: "One thing about this fellow Fleet. He digs you, so you be nice and dig him back."

"When we did this script, we hadn't started shooting yet and had no idea that 'The Guitar Player' would be show number three," says Jack. "Everybody liked the way it came out and didn't mind that we featured a guest star so soon. In the beginning of a new series, you should concentrate on the main characters and develop them fully. But, then again, nothing in the Declaration of Independence says you can't go another way. That's show biz."

"Ellie Comes to Town"

Episode 6

First Broadcast on
October 24, 1960

Written by
**Charles Stewart
and Jack Elinson**

Directed by
Don Weis

"All of us know an Emma Brand. We're even guilty ourselves. Every other week, a bunch of us old writers meet for lunch, including *TAGS* producer Aaron Ruben. The first discussion when we sit down is about our aches and pains. There isn't one of us who hasn't got a medical report to give."
—JACK ELINSON

Charles and Jack began "Ellie Comes to Town" with the following detailed script directions: *Exterior street in front of Walker's Drug Store. It is early morning. The sheriff's car pulls up to the curb. Barney is at the wheel. Aunt Bee is in the middle, Andy on the passenger side. Andy and Aunt Bee climb out of the car.*

Andy and Aunt Bee walk to the drugstore and discover the front door is locked. Fred Walker, the pharmacist, must be "having another spell of sickness." Andy reaches above the door, finds a key, and lets Aunt Bee and himself inside.

Andy, feeling at home in a familiar place, steps behind the counter and waits on Aunt Bee, who requests a bottle of toilet water.

Aunt Bee's request in the original script included two additional items: a bottle of oil of wintergreen for her arm and "something for Opie's sniffles." Andy suggests nose drops because "that boy always uses the spray for a water pistol."

Outside, Ellie Walker arrives and finds the front door of the drugstore unlocked. She panics, sees Barney sitting in the parked squad car, and yells, "Burglars!"

In the original script, Barney *tries to jump out of the squad car without opening the door.* This was revised during the script cast read-through on Thursday, August 25. The revision is more visually comedic. Barney has parked the car beside a mailbox that blocks the opening of the driver's door. Barney, responding to Ellie's cries for help, can barely squeeze out of the car.

Barney, followed by Ellie, rushes into the drugstore. He identifies the intruders and introduces them. Ellie replies that she is "Fred's niece" and has "come to help out." Andy refers to Ellie "as the new lady druggist."

"Ellie's character came out of a discussion with executive producer Sheldon

Leonard," recalls Jack. "Sheldon thought it might be a good idea if we created a possible romance for Andy. If it worked, then she would become a series regular. If it didn't work, then we could write her out. Luckily, it worked out nicely. Elinor Donahue did a fine job. She was very appealing.

"We decided to make Ellie a pharmacist to show she was not only pretty, but she was also smart. Actually, we were ahead of our time. Remember this was 1960 and the feminist movement hadn't really begun yet.

"Andy, addressing Ellie as 'lady druggist' goes right along with the fact that in 1960, not too many women had jobs like that. This led to Andy's confusion as to what he should call Ellie. She was the first 'lady druggist' he ever saw."

Ellie would like an explanation of why Andy is in the store "before it is opened." Andy explains he always helps himself even when Ellie's uncle Fred "is here." He totals up Aunt Bee's order while giving the explanation, then opens the cash register to pay his bill. Ellie steps in and finishes the transaction.

Barney and Aunt Bee leave the drugstore. Andy stays behind. He thinks maybe he could help Ellie "find out where things are." Ellie slowly warms up to Andy. Andy eventually decides to "go on." He walks toward the door as a customer, Emma Brand, enters.

"Charles and I liked the Emma Brand character, and it only made sense to use her," says Jack. "The actress, Cheerio Meredith, was perfect for the part. She was just hilarious!"

Andy greets Emma. She complains, "I ran out of my pills last night and couldn't sleep a wink." Even watching the late movie couldn't put her to sleep.

In the revised script, Andy replies, "Yes, I saw that movie. Unfortunately, it was good. Sure does keep a body awake when they slip in a good one on that late show."

Andy Griffith changes the dialogue in his script. In pencil, he crosses out "unfortunately" and inserts "pretty" before "good." The ending of the third sentence, "on that late show," is crossed out and replaced with "like that."

The dialogue, after these changes, reads, "Yes, I saw that movie. It was pretty good. Sure does keep a body awake when they slip in a good one like that."

The dialogue was changed further prior to the filming of the episode. Andy's first sentence becomes, "I know it. I saw it." The phrase "wasn't it" is inserted after "it was pretty good."

These small changes make a difference. The dialogue sounds more natural and appropriate to the small southern town setting.

Emma describes her pain to Andy in detail. Ellie emerges from the back room. Emma holds out a dime and asks for her pills. She has no prescription, however, and Ellie refuses to give her the pills. Emma, angered, storms out of the store.

Later, Emma visits the courthouse to report a murder. She explains the situation to Andy. Emma feels if she doesn't get her pills it's "just a matter of time" before she will be dead. Andy explains to Emma that the law doesn't allow him to force Ellie to hand over the pills.

Jack and Charles set the next scene at the front door of the drugstore. Their detailed script directions are, *Ellie is cleaning the front window. She has applied window cleaner which has formed into a powder. She now starts to wipe the powder away with a circular motion. As she wipes the first circle, she is startled to discover the little face of Opie. Opie pulls his mouth wide at the corners with his fingers and sticks out his tongue. He is surprised when Ellie makes a face right back at him! This is something new in adult behavior.*

"The 'funny faces' between Opie and Ellie were all in the script," says Jack. "If I do say so myself, it was a wonderful 'hunk.'" ("Hunk" is Jack's shorthand for "a piece of writing.")

Opie enters the drugstore, introduces himself, and tells Ellie he came by to see the new "lady druggist." Ellie asks if Opie would like an ice-cream cone. Opie would, but he "ain't got no money." Ellie agrees to give Opie an ice cream free of charge if he doesn't say "ain't" anymore.

"The 'ice-cream' and 'ain't' stuff was a good way to show what a nice person Ellie was, especially with a child," says Jack. "Since this was her first time on the show, it was important to flesh out her character as quickly as possible."

Andy enters the drugstore. After Opie's departure, he turns the subject to a matter "that was brought to his attention." Ellie is distracted by something she sees. A hunched-over person is sneaking behind a counter. The person's cover is blown by a feather in her hat that bobs above the countertop. It is Emma attempting to get her pills.

Andy defends Emma. Ellie stands her ground. Andy responds, "You don't care about seeing a human being suffer. Someday you might get sick and aching and see who helps you." He angrily leaves the store.

"As in all romance stories, the formula that still works is boy meets girl, boy loses girl, boy wins girl," says Jack. "In keeping with this tradition, we had to create a quarrel between Andy and Ellie. It wasn't difficult. As nice as Ellie was, she was a druggist and knew all the rules. She cannot dispense a prescription without a doctor writing one. Ellie was absolutely right. Andy, on the other hand, was being Andy with his argument that Emma had been taking these pills forever. So both had a legitimate point. It was a perfect stand-off and place for Andy and Ellie to be so soon after they've first met."

Later in the day, Andy enters the courthouse and finds Barney studying an open book. The book is a sheriff's manual. Barney has been memorizing the "sheriff's rules." He asks Andy to "check" him on it.

"Don Knotts came up with Barney's memory of the sheriff's manual himself," says Jack. "Don may have done a routine similar to it on *The Steve Allen Show*. He was a regular on that show and frequently played a nervous man."

Don's idea was discussed with story consultant Aaron Ruben. Dialogue was written along with the script direction, *All action is up to actor.*

In the filmed scene, Andy Griffith and Don loosely follow the scripted dialogue. The two perform the scene with a natural spontaneity. Words and phrasing are changed. The actors are guided by the script but allowed the freedom to create in the moment.

Aunt Bee arrives carrying a pot of soup. She tells Andy that Emma has taken to her sickbed and requests that the soup be delivered. Andy picks up a book as he and Barney depart the courthouse. He hopes to use it to find some "technicalities" that will allow Emma to receive her pills.

Barney searches the book on the way to Emma's. The closest thing he can find is *Wilson v. Thorpe's Pharmacy* in Mount Corey, 1952. The case dealt with the selling of arsenic. Thorpe claimed arsenic would be dangerous and refused the sell.

Wilson protested, proved himself responsible, won the case, and purchased his arsenic. He was buried three days later.

"The *Wilson v. Thorpe's Pharmacy* case was our invention," admits Jack. "It was purely fictional."

Andy and Barney deliver the soup and find Emma propped up on a couch surrounded by food. She is eating a turkey drumstick.

A knock is heard. Andy opens the front door and finds Ellie carrying a container of soup along with a bottle of pills. Emma quickly takes a pill and "feels better already."

Ellie departs followed by Andy. Ellie explains to him that she talked with her uncle Fred, learned that the pills were only sugar with no medicinal qualities, and decided "What's the harm?" She further explains that she previously insisted upon a prescription because there are rules that a pharmacist is sworn to follow.

Andy says that rules aren't everything. "You've got to think about people too." That's the human equation.

Andy then notices a car parked next to a fire hydrant. He takes out his citation book and begins writing a ticket. Ellie reminds Andy of the human equation and suggests that perhaps the driver had an emergency. Andy, feeling generous, decides to overlook the violation. Upon seeing this, Ellie smiles, gets into the car, and drives away.

"Ellie outsmarting Andy was in our story outline," says Jack. "We knew that was our finish before one word of the script was written. Andy and Ellie play a cat-and-mouse game. Andy is a shrewd one, but so is Ellie. Each one holds their own in a likable way. By the episode's end, Andy has met his match and the stage is set for his and Ellie's relationship in the series. I think viewers looked forward to their relationship from this show on."

"Ellie for Council"

"Yes, we did enjoy writing the 'weak-kneed, chicken-livered, yellow-streaked turncoat' line. In fact, I think if we threw in three more of those, it would have been even funnier."—JACK ELINSON

Episode 12

First Broadcast on December 12, 1960

Written by
Jack Elinson and Charles Stewart

Directed by
Bob Sweeney

"Ellie for Council" was directed by Bob Sweeney, the first of eighty *TAGS* episodes he would direct. Bob, producer Aaron Ruben, and the cast spend the afternoon of Thursday, October 6, 1960, reading the script. The cast members were returning from their first weeklong "layoff" since beginning production of the series in mid-July.

Jack and Charles set the opening of the episode at a "picnic spot near a lake." The camera closes in on Opie, who is "wolfing" down his fourth hot dog. Andy, Ellie, Barney, his girl Hilda Mae, and Aunt Bee are seated behind him. Andy is strumming his guitar. He becomes aware of the others staring at Opie and stops playing. Andy warns Opie to stop eating or he will swell up and his "freckles will fall off."

"I believe Andy playing the guitar was Andy Griffith's idea," says Jack. "Andy was the star of the show, so who were we to say no?"

"I admit we may have gone overboard with Opie's voracious appetite. Sometimes when you're doing comedy, you exaggerate. When you're looking for laughs, you go across the line of reality."

Barney suggests to Hilda Mae that they take a "little walk down by the lake." Barney, standing, reaches down to help Hilda Mae to her feet. Her weight causes him to stumble, and it is Hilda Mae who steadies Barney.

"Since Andy and Ellie are together at the picnic, we felt Barney should have a girlfriend too," says Jack. "We knew from the beginning that Barney would be hilarious in the presence of women. What could be funnier than Barney trying to be Clark Gable?"

Opie asks Aunt Bee to take a walk with him and "look for gophers." The two depart, leaving Andy and Ellie alone.

"As for Opie and Aunt Bee walking off to 'look for gophers,' I think we wrote 'look for squirrels' and somebody changed it," says Jack. "Being a city guy, I never would have come up with gophers. Writing *The Griffith Show* was actually bilingual—English as we always knew it and southern talk as we eventually learned it."

Andy lies on his back to relax and covers his face with a newspaper. Ellie glances at the paper and notices an article about candidates for the city council. Ellie looks closer and discovers that all the candidates are men. She feels this is "awful" and questions why there aren't any women running.

Andy feels Ellie's idea about women running for council is "plain silly." Ellie, angered by the comment, rushes off.

"We felt it would be nice to open the episode on a picnic, showing everyone relaxing outdoors," says Jack. "We wanted a peaceful setting before the story began with Ellie spotting the news about the city council. The scene opened with Andy and Ellie having a good time. It ended with Ellie storming off in anger. The scene went full circle from peaceful to stormy."

Later in the sheriff's office, Andy types out an apology to Ellie. In the note, Andy asks forgiveness for the comments he made about women.

Otis Campbell, "a prisoner behind bars," listens as Andy reads his apology aloud. Otis advises Andy to "fight it out" with Ellie.

"Otis was designed to be an ongoing character throughout the series," says Jack. "In some episodes, he was just in for a short bit, but in this episode, he had a big part and was strongly involved in the story. He is sober in this episode, but right from the start, he'd get drunk every Saturday night."

Barney rushes into the office with exciting news. Ellie has signed up to run for council! A petition to get her name on the ballot is being passed around. Barney accidentally admits that he signed it. His girlfriend, Hilda Mae, persuaded him.

"Since we already made Ellie a pharmacist, we thought we'd go another step forward and have her run for council," says Jack. "It was a continuation of the feminist angle. We have to pat ourselves on the back for doing that in 1960, especially in the South."

Andy feels the situation calls for a "talk" with Ellie. During their conversation, he suggests that Ellie let the "men worry about government business." Ellie, however, stands her ground and refuses to withdraw her candidacy.

Back at the sheriff's office, Aunt Bee brings lunch and shares the news that Ellie got the one hundred names she needed for the petition. She will be running for council!

Andy, Barney, and Otis are joined by hardware merchant Sam Lindsay and grain dealer Lyle Nugent. (The two men's occupations and last names are included in the script directions but not given in the filmed episode.) The men are upset and turn on Barney for signing Ellie's petition. Sam calls him "a weak-kneed, chicken-livered, yellow-streaked turncoat."

"One of the formulas that's been around as long as comedy has is the 'comparing lines,'" says Jack. "The 'weak-kneed, chicken-livered, yellow-streaked turncoat' line is an example. Small-town comparisons are especially rich."

Andy reminds the men that they control the "purse strings" and suggests that they stop their wives' charge accounts if they get too "cute" about the election.

Jack and Charles write detailed script directions to illustrate Andy's suggestion put into action. Charge accounts are refused in a millinery store, a shoe shop, and a dress shop. In the dress shop, the stunned wife walks outs clothed only in her slip. The dialogue in these scenes is pantomimed.

"The charge account refusal sequence had a lot of ground to cover to establish what's happening," says Jack. "We chose pantomime instead of hearing the dialogue in order to move along quickly."

"Having the lady leave the dress store wearing only a slip was over the line, but we just couldn't pass up the chance to get a big laugh," Jack admits. "The only defense we could use is the lady was so flustered by her charge refusal and in such a huff, she forgot to put on her dress."

The angry wives meet in the drugstore to discuss their husbands' actions. Ellie reminds them that they have some "pretty potent weapons" to fight back with.

Jack and Charles use pantomime again to show the women's weapons in action. Lyle Nugent must prepare his own breakfast, Sam Lindsay mends holes in his socks, and Otis irons his shirt.

The montage ends in Andy's kitchen. He is frying eggs. He scraps the burned eggs onto Opie's plate. Aunt Bee offers Opie some of the homemade stew she has cooked, but he refuses and says, "No, I'm sticking with the men."

Ellie knocks on the back door and enters. She announces that she is withdrawing her name as a candidate. She doesn't want to start a civil war in Mayberry between the men and the women.

Opie, after hearing this, celebrates, and says, "We beat them females. We kept them in their place." Andy is embarrassed by Opie's comments,

"Since Andy was no better about his attitude toward women than all the men in Mayberry, it wasn't difficult to make him see the light," says Jack. "Using Opie to be the conduit to make it happen was the perfect way. Teaching Opie the wrong message is the last thing Andy would ever do."

Ellie, followed by Andy, departs. The two arrive at a political rally organized by the women. The women, seeing Ellie, begin chanting, "We want Ellie." Andy speaks up. He would like to say something. Andy confesses his behavior has wrongly influenced Opie and ends up admitting that "if Ellie wants to run for council, she has a right to."

Ellie, hearing this, smiles, steps forward, and kisses Andy on the cheek. The two are instantly reconciled.

In the filmed epilogue, Andy, Ellie, Aunt Bee, and Opie are sitting on the Taylor front porch. They are joined by Barney. Andy notices a "little red smug" on Barney's jaw and discovers it is some of Hilda Mae's lipstick. Andy jokes with Barney about this in song. He finishes the "ditty" with a verse about Ellie running for council.

Jack and Charles's original ending was very different. Ellie, Hilda Mae, Andy, and Barney are double dating. The boys are serenading, Andy strumming guitar and singing, Barney playing harmonica. Ellie looks at her wristwatch and suddenly realizes she is late for a special committee meeting. Hilda Mae, who has become Councilwoman Walker's aid, is also running late.

After the two depart, Andy says of his guitar, playing, "Doggone if I wasn't going real good with Ellie sitting there to inspire me." He then picks up a small vine covered with leaves and drapes it over Barney's head to give the appearance of a girl's hair. Andy says to Barney, "Alright now, smile as pretty as you can. Come on smile! You ain't much, but you're the best I got!" Andy goes back to strumming his number and the scene fades out.

"The Horse Trader"

Episode 14

First Broadcast on January 9, 1960

Written by
Jack Elinson and Charles Stewart

Directed by
Bob Sweeney

"One of my favorite old jokes is about this cannon in the square that fired a shot every day at noon to indicate the time. This was done as far back as anyone could remember. One day the cannon didn't fire. Stone silence at noon. All the townsfolks stared at each other and asked, 'What was that?'"
—JACK ELINSON

"The Horse Trader" opens in the sheriff's office. Andy is in one of the cells sprucing up in front of a mirror. He is preparing himself for a council meeting. Barney, a council member, tells Andy he can't understand why the council is thinking about getting rid of the town's cannon. The cannon is a Mayberry landmark.

"I've always been intrigued by cannons," says Jack. "Cannons seem to be in so many small towns in the town square. It's so American."

Barney has decided to vote to keep the cannon. He likes things "to stay the way they are." Barney gives Andy an example of a change that bothers him. He is "frosted" by the stamp machine in the post office. He doesn't think it's right for the U.S. government to "be transacting business through a slot machine."

"There are still people who yearn for the past and wish all the high-tech miracles would go away," says Jack. "We arbitrarily chose Barney to demonstrate this. We did this back in 1960, long before high technology took hold. I personally despise ATM machines. I still like to go into a bank and talk to an actual person. Barney reflects this sentiment."

Andy and Barney are about to exit the office when Opie enters carrying a small bag. The bag contains seeds to grow licorice sticks. Opie traded his new cap pistol for the seeds. (In Jack and Charles's unrevised script, Opie trades away his whittling knife.) Opie is on his way to trade another friend the licorice seeds for a pair of roller skates.

Andy reminds Opie of the Golden Rule and instructs his son "to be honest and square-dealing with other folks."

In the filmed scene, Andy Griffith changes words and adds small phrases to the scripted dialogue. Ronny Howard, on the other hand, delivers Opie's lines exactly as Jack and Charles wrote them.

After Andy and Barney exit, Opie remains behind and asks himself, "If honesty is such a good policy, how come I'm out a cap pistol?"

"A character talking to oneself is hardly a new technique when writing a TV show," says Jack. "When it comes to children, they do a lot of talking to themselves. When my kids were Opie's age, I would pass their rooms, and if they were by themselves, I'd often hear talking. Perhaps they were play-acting cowboys and Indians. So, Opie talking when alone was realistic childhood behavior."

The episode's next scene is set in the mayor's office. Mayor Pike is presiding at the council meeting. "Andy, Barney, Ellie, and others" are present.

"We put Ellie in the council meeting since she had won a seat in a previous episode," says Jack. "Her presence also kept the character alive in the series."

The council meeting in Aaron Ruben's revised script is much shorter than what Jack and Charles originally wrote. Andy addresses the council. He reports that the cannon was never in good shape and after the last Fourth of July, it didn't get any better. The muzzle was cracked during the celebration.

In Jack and Charles's script, Andy gives newcomer Ellie Walker a detailed account of what happened: "We had this parade recreating the Revolutionary War and one float had a bunch of fellers dressed up like British soldiers. Well, Buzz Fluehart, he had a still back of Bear Creek, come into town having consumed just a little too much of his own product. Well, when he saw them redcoats, he just knew they'd started the war all over again! Quick as sin, he run down to the town square and shoved a pound of gunpowder and a lawn bowling ball into the cannon and tried to fire it! Cracked that muzzle like it was a ripe watermelon."

As the meeting progresses the council members learn that a public-spirited former citizen, Milford Phillips, has donated a plaque to be placed in Mayberry's town square.

In the unrevised script, Ellie shares a sketch of the plaque that includes the state motto, "To be rather than to seem!"

The motto is the actual state motto of North Carolina. The on-screen revealing of North Carolina as Mayberry's home state would not occur, however, until much later in the series. Prior to the revelation, Mayberry was located somewhere in the South.

A motion to get rid of the cannon is voted upon and unanimously approved. Suggestions are made to donate the cannon to the state museum or to sell it. The mayor appoints Andy and Barney to a "Get Rid of the Cannon" committee, and the meeting is adjourned.

Jack and Charles's unrevised script has the mayor quickly adjourning the meeting because he "has a golf date." In response to being given the task of getting rid of the cannon, Andy says, "When it comes to leaving things to others, the mayor is in a class by himself."

The writers use Andy's comment for an additional joke. Andy explains that the mayor didn't even write his own acceptance speech when he won his office. "He passed the buck to Winston Churchill and read the 'blood, sweat, and tears' stuff. Made no sense at all!"

The filmed episode shows Andy and Barney attaching the cannon to the back of the squad car. Their attempts to get rid of the cannon are shown in pantomime. The two take the cannon door-to-door, to an antique dealer; finding no buyer, they take it back to the town square.

"Just as in 'Ellie for Council,' the montage device with no audible dialogue is a good way to show Andy and Barney getting turned down wherever they go," says Jack. "Our script was revised by Aaron Ruben and changed from Barney going out by himself to Andy and Barney going together. The marching music heard on the soundtrack was put in by Earle Hagen, the musical director."

The montage was filmed on Monday, October 31 (Halloween Day). Filming exteriors on Mondays was a standard practice that allowed flexibility. If the weather was inclement, interior filming was substituted and the exterior filming was rescheduled for either Tuesday or Wednesday.

After returning the cannon to the town square, Andy attempts to sell the cannon to Barney. A close viewing of the filmed episode shows condensation occasionally coming from the actors' mouths as they say their lines. Culver City, California, where the exteriors were shot, was having a cool Halloween Day.

In Jack and Charles's unrevised script, Andy visits the drugstore while Barney is out trying to sell the cannon. Orville Monroe, the undertaker, is seated at the fountain drinking a soda. Andy attempts to sell the cannon to Orville, telling him the cannon could be used to "lay to rest dignitaries with a twenty-one-gun salute." Orville refuses and explains that he tries to keep his business "in a mood of quiet serenity."

Opie enters the drugstore and climbs on the stool beside Andy. He asks if he can have some of Andy's "cool drink." Ellie places a second straw in the soda and asks, "How was school today?" Opie's reply is muffled. He refuses to release the straw from his lips.

"Opie's muffled reply is a good example of capturing childhood behavior," says Jack. "Charles and I drew from memories of our own children when they were Opie's age. Kids are kids and for the most part, they're all the same. In addition, I consider Ronny Howard the best child actor that ever was. He was just himself and deserves all the credit for making it real."

Barney enters and reports that he received an offer from the junk dealer to take the cannon if the dealer is paid fifteen dollars. His conversation with Andy is interrupted when Ralph Mason, an out-of-towner, enters the drugstore.

Mason notices an old-fashioned copper washtub sitting on a counter. The tub is used as a bin for displaying a "load" of soap topped by a sale sign reading "Bar Soap 6 for 39 cents." (The wording on the sign was given in the script.) Mason, an antique dealer, expresses an interest in buying the washtub.

In Jack and Charles's unrevised script, the washtub is the second item Mason purchases. Upon entering the drugstore, Mason browses through a display of postcards.

Andy notices this, approaches, extracts a postcard from the display, and hands it to Mason. The postcard is a photograph of Rutledge's Stump. Andy then shares the stump's story.

"Rutledge's Stump is a big sycamore stump on the old Rutledge place. Old Henry Rutledge was quite a whittler and decided that stump would be a real good spot for whittling out the faces of some famous presidents. The only trouble was the faces didn't come out looking like any presidents you'd recognize. That didn't faze Henry. He just put down that they were vice presidents. Nobody ever remembers what they look like, so who could call him on it? Anyway, it's a mighty artistic piece of work. Henry has gotten every detail of the faces in there . . . right down to the little eyeballs."

Andy, realizing that Mason is in a shopping mood, asks if he would be interested in purchasing a cannon. Andy and Barney take Mason to the town square to look at the "historical treasure." Opie joins them.

Andy tells Mason the cannon fired the first shot at Fort Sumter and, later, was dragged up San Juan Hill by Teddy Roosevelt. Barney, upset by Andy's deception, departs.

Opie, listening, interrupts. He is stopped mid-sentence by Andy and told to "go find a barrel ring and tell Barney to put it away."

"In my script, Andy says to Opie, 'You go back to the office and get the frauvis and tell Barney to put it away,'" says Jack. "What 'frauvis' means, I have no idea. Charles and I came up with that phony word and gave it to Andy to use in the spur of the moment."

Later in the drugstore, Barney and Ellie are discussing Andy's dealings with Mr. Mason. Andy rushes in with exciting news. He has sold the cannon to Mason for $175! Barney and Ellie stare coldly at Andy. Andy, angered that his "horse trading" is not appreciated, leaves.

As Andy comes out of the drugstore, Opie roller-skates toward the door. Andy stops him and asks where Opie got the roller skates. Opie answers that he got the skates and enough money for an ice-cream cone from his friend in exchange for one of Andy's broken cuff links. Opie explains that he was able to make the trade because his friend believed the broken cuff link was a button off the uniform of General George Washington.

Without a word, Andy reaches out, grabs Opie by the arm, and rolls him home. Opie doesn't understand "what's the matter." He dealt with his friend the same way that he had seen Andy deal with Mr. Mason. Andy explains that he was only doing a "little innocent horse trading." Opie feels he was doing the same and tells Andy, "I think we both broke the Golden Rule." Andy looks at Opie for a moment and understands that his son has taught him a lesson.

Andy's anger disappears. He affectionately pats Opie on the stomach. The two agree that Opie will return the roller skates and Andy will "mend some fences of his own."

"The main reason for this story was to show a switch," says Jack. "During the series, Opie was always getting words of wisdom from his paw. We thought it would be interesting if Andy, the Solomon of the town and always Honest Abe, suddenly did some lying himself. It was a very simple and clean story. We set it up in the first part of the episode with Opie wanting to make the licorice-seed trade. What we intended, in the end, was Andy, in his zest to get rid of the cannon, goes about it deceitfully. After talking with Opie, he realizes he's done what he's told Opie never to do. This time, Andy learned something from his son."

Inside the drugstore, Barney is seated at the soda fountain, drowning his sorrows over Andy's deceitful dealings. He finishes a root-beer float and grimly slides the glass back to Ellie for a refill. Ellie is reluctant to comply and reminds Barney he has already consumed four floats inside of fifteen minutes.

"We thought it was funny for Barney to drown his sorrows with ice-cream sodas, but playing it like it was booze," says Jack. "Don Knotts played it like a real drunk, insisting on another drink and threatening to go elsewhere if Ellie didn't serve him. It was a wonderful bit."

Mr. Mason enters with a check to purchase the cannon. Andy arrives soon afterward and refuses Mason's check because their deal was based upon lies. Mason, however, still wants to honor the deal. Andy, in an effort not to cheat Mason, negotiates the price down to twenty dollars. Barney and Ellie watch the transaction and are proud of Andy for doing "the right thing."

In the epilogue, Ellie delivers a "wire" from former Mayberry citizen Milford Phillips. Mr. Phillips is sending something better than a plaque. The town will be receiving a "genuine civil war cannon with a crack down the muzzle from actual combat at San Juan Hill."

"We knew, going in, that the cannon should land back in Mayberry," says Jack. "It was a funny, ironic finish after all the fuss about it. Personally, I'm glad the cannon came back. I got another story out of it down the line."

"Those Gossipin' Men"

Episode 15

First Broadcast on
January 16, 1961

Written by
**Charles Stewart
and Jack Elinson**

Directed by
Bob Sweeney

Manhattan Shoe Company slogan:
"When you take a Manhattan Shoe out, it's a shoo-in."

"Those Gossipin' Men" opens inside the drugstore. Aunt Bee, Clara Lindsay, and Emma Watson are busy gossiping. A bored Opie stands close by.

The women are discussing Millie Parson's hair. Millie has dyed the tips blonde in hopes of attracting the attention of the new postman.

"It was fun writing 'women talk,'" says Jack. "It was our way for us to kid women in general. The women normally make us men look like fools. This is a fact that goes back to Eve having the last word over Adam."

Pharmacist Fred Walker walks behind the counter to ring up an order for Emma. Among the purchased items is a bottle of peroxide. Emma quickly explains that the peroxide is for gargling, not hair coloring. She says she is in her forties and never tries to hide her age.

"In our script, Ellie has the role given to her uncle Fred in the film," says Jack. "Ellie was not only in the show but was the key character who would come up with the idea of turning the tables on the men. I frankly don't know why she was left out. Perhaps the actress Elinor Donahue was unavailable due to illness."

Opie is surprised by Emma's age and is about to reveal how old Aunt Bee is when she sends him to get a candy bar.

"Opie leaving to get a candy bar is his last appearance in the script," says Jack. "Since this was a grown-up's story, there wasn't much for Opie to do, but we still wanted him in every show, no matter how small the part."

After Opie's departure, Aunt Bee immediately directs the conversation toward a new target, Rose Blake. She tells the others that Rose recently traveled to Raleigh to buy a new set of teeth.

Rose Blake is a character that was seen but not named in "The Guitar Player." According to the episode's script directions, Rose is the proprietor of the diner where Bobby Fleet and His Band with a Beat eat lunch. She serves water to the musicians.

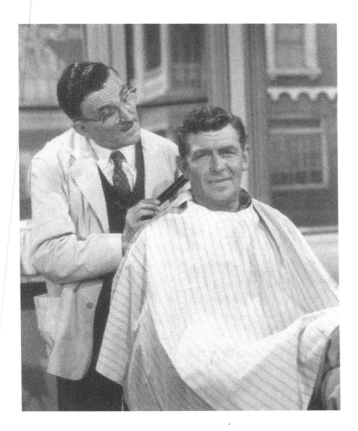

Andy enters the drugstore and requests some sulfa powder. He explains that Barney was taking his gun apart and cut his finger. The sulfa powder will prevent any infection.

The women believe the explanation is an unlikely story and suspect there "is more to this than meets the eye." Their gossip quickly spreads. The story begins with Barney scratching his finger and, after numerous retellings, escalates to Barney shooting himself in the chest.

Later in the sheriff's office, Andy examines Barney's finger. The scratch is so small that Barney must direct Andy's eye to it. The telephone rings. Barney answers and is told that he "is dead!" Barney shares this with Andy and the two have a good laugh. Andy kids Barney about his demise. Barney, however, grows uncomfortable with his line of kidding.

"We thought it was perfectly normal for Barney to be amused at first," says Jack. "When Andy picks at him so relentlessly, Barney doesn't appreciate being called 'dead.' This shows how 'square' the character is."

Barney eventually says to Andy, "You're a scream. You ought to get a job on one of those excursion boats."

"I believe Barney's 'you ought to' line was the first time it was used," says Jack. "It was a great comeback and the phrase with a different ending was reused numerous times in the series."

Aunt Bee rushes in. She has heard that Barney is "gone." Barney comes out of the back room and denies this. Andy tells Aunt Bee that the women's gossip is responsible for the misinformation and that gossiping comes natural to women.

Jim and Charles comically express Andy's belief in a line deleted from their script. Andy says, "Women can no more keep a secret than a hen can keep an egg."

Aunt Bee storms out as mortician Orville Monroe steps in. Orville consoles Andy over the loss of Barney. Barney, emerging from the back room, startles Orville, who realizes Barney is "still with us." Orville leaves to move the hearse that is backed up to the door.

"This part of the story was so much fun to write," says Jack. "It was not difficult once we got the idea of Barney's false death. Having the mortician show up was the perfect punch line to end the segment."

Later Aunt Bee and Emma Watson are seated at the drugstore's fountain discussing Andy's biased comments about their gossiping. They are angered by Andy's "smugness." The conversation ends when Wilbur Finch enters.

"The only description we had of Wilbur Finch in the script was 'a rather unprepossessing man, a traveling shoe salesman,'" says Jack. "Our character descriptions in the scripts were usually short and to the point."

Mr. Finch orders a root beer, sits down next to Aunt Bee, and identifies himself as a shoe salesman. He asks if the ladies would like to buy a pair of shoes, quickly finishes his drink, and departs.

Andy and Barney enter the drugstore. Andy asks about the "stranger that was just in here." Aunt Bee answers that the man is a shoe salesman from New York City. Hoping to make Andy curious, she adds, "At least that's what he says he is." Aunt Bee concludes by pointing out that it seems strange that a person would travel all the way from New York to sell shoes in Mayberry.

Andy and Barney, curious about the shoe salesman, decide to drop by the hotel in hopes of learning more about Wilbur Finch. Andy checks the hotel's register and examines a business card Finch left with Jason, the hotel "keeper."

Andy and Barney are on their way toward the door as Finch enters the hotel lobby from upstairs. Barney almost backs into him. He prevents the collision by spinning around Finch and walking into a wall.

"Barney walking into the wall wasn't in the script," says Jack. "That happened during the staging of the scene. We didn't have any set rules about using physical comedy in *The Griffith Show*. When it was natural, it was written or worked into the scene during rehearsal. We never forced it in just to get a sight laugh."

Wilbur Finch asks Jason for a television in his room and is told the hotel doesn't provide that service. Disappointed, he says, "Television is mighty important to me."

Jason rushes to the barbershop. He tells Floyd, the barber, and Orville Monroe, who is getting a haircut, about Finch's request. The three step outside when they see Finch approaching from across the street. Finch tells them he tried to rent a television but couldn't get one.

"Writing for Floyd the barber was a blast," says Jack. "This was the first time we wrote for him, and only his second appearance on the show. Casting Howard McNear for the role was a brilliant choice. He added so much. His performance went way beyond the words in the script."

Floyd, Orville, and Jason begin spreading the news. Their gossip turns Finch into an important talent scout for the *Manhattan Show Time* television program.

"Wilbur Finch being mistaken for a talent scout was in the script outline," says Jack. "The out-of-control gossiping was necessary to cause the men to think Finch was a big-time show biz guy. This idea made the whole last half of the script work."

The men are excited and would like for their children or themselves to audition for Finch. Andy suggests that they "play along" with Finch's shoe salesman facade.

Later, a defeated Wilbur Finch returns to his room. He has had an unsuccessful sales day and decides to check out early. There is a knock at the door. Floyd and his son Randolph, carrying a saxophone, enter. Floyd has "come to buy shoes," and cleverly asks Randolph to provide some background music.

The hallway outside Finch's room is crowded with auditioners. Floyd and son are followed by Barney playing his harmonica, Orville Monroe's daughter Annabelle playing her accordion, and many others. By the evening's end, Finch has sold sixty-seven pairs of shoes, a new company record for one day's sales.

The next morning, a group of men accompany Wilbur Finch to his car. He is leaving. Before driving away, he confesses that he was about washed up as a shoe salesman, but the previous night's sales gave him new confidence. After hearing this, the men realize Wilbur Finch is only a shoe salesman.

Aunt Bee and Emma are watching from across the street. Jack and Charles's script directions are the ladies smile at Andy who has narrowed a look at them that says, "So that's where it all began!"

"As in 'Ellie for Council,' this too is a look at the ever-present battle of the sexes, which is always good for a laugh," says Jack. "The strange thing, though, is just like in the episode, the women always win."

"Alcohol and Old Lace"

Episode 17

First Broadcast on
January 30, 1961

Written by
**Charles Stewart
and Jack Elinson**

Directed by
Gene Reynolds

**Gladys Hurlbut
and Charity Grace**
Guest Star as
Clarabelle and
Jennifer Morrison

"I hope I never bump into the playwright who wrote *Arsenic and Old Lace*. He wouldn't appreciate me stealing his story, but I'm glad I did."
—JACK ELINSON

"We're trying to develop a flower that smells like witch hazel."
—JENNIFER MORRISON

"I have to confess that 'Alcohol and Old Lace' was a direct steal from *Arsenic and Old Lace*," says Jack. "I saw the play when I was a teenager. It was a big hit on Broadway, and I remember that Boris Karloff was in it. The play was later adapted into a movie starring Cary Grant.

"Charles and I wrote several scripts before Aaron Ruben came aboard. After Aaron became producer, we cleared storylines with Aaron and executive producer Sheldon Leonard. Our deal was to write fifteen scripts during the first and second seasons. During that time, we were also writing scripts for *The Danny Thomas Show*."

"Alcohol and Old Lace" may have been one of the earliest Stewart/Elinson scripts. Will Hoople is listed in the episode's character list. Will was the town drunk in the pilot episode for *The Griffith Show*. The pilot was an episode of *The Danny Thomas Show*.

Otis Campbell appears in the second *TAGS* episode, "Manhunt." Jack and Charles named the character. It is likely that "Alcohol and Old Lace" was written prior to "Manhunt" but was held back until filming was done on November 21, 22, and 23, 1960 (Thanksgiving week). By that time Otis Campbell was established as the town drunk and his name replaced Will Hoople's in the script.

"Alcohol and Old Lace" opens inside the barbershop. Floyd, the barber, is putting the finishing touches on Andy's hair. Andy checks himself in the mirror and says, "My sideburns, they're both even!"

Charles and Jack's script directions are a wonderful narrative of the scene:
Floyd places himself before Andy squinting his eye and holding his thumb out as

though it were a level, measuring the sideburns. Apparently, the phenomenon has occurred. They are even! Floyd is delighted.

Floyd measures the sideburns with his comb and afterward makes a notch in the comb with his thumb. This is Andy's notch and will be used in the future to cut his sideburns evenly. Floyd concludes the haircut with a witch-hazel rub.

"The opening scene was the way we pictured a small-town barbershop would be," says Jack. "Floyd's customers were all men he knew intimately. Floyd always aimed to please. When Andy tells him his sideburns are perfectly matched, he's kidding a little bit, but Floyd takes it dead serious. That's why he measures them carefully in that crazy way with his comb. Floyd takes great pride in his haircuts. Andy, being the sweet guy that he is, realizes this and wants to show his respect for Floyd's profession. He immediately puts his kidding aside. Andy would do the same for a termite inspector."

Jennifer and Clarabelle Morrison, *spinsters whose garb provides more than a hint at a bygone era*, approach the barbershop.

Jennifer, seeing Andy inside, starts to enter the barbershop. She has some news she would like to report. She is also attracted by the odor of witch hazel. Jennifer is stopped by Clarabelle.

"In a small town like Mayberry, two very proper ladies like the Morrison sisters would never enter a male barbershop," says Jack. "That is the reason Clarabelle stops Jennifer, who has apparently lost her head. God forbid they might walk in right in the middle of a dirty joke."

Andy Griffith had a great ear for authentic southern dialect. He continually tweaked the scripted dialogue to make it more authentic. Word changes, written in pencil, were frequently made. When Andy greets the Morrison sisters outside the barbershop, he was to say, "What is it?" Andy Griffith changes this to "Good morning," which communicates southern hospitality.

Clarabelle tells Andy that she knows the whereabouts of a moonshine still. The sisters saw the still with their own eyes. It is owned by Ben Sewell and located on Council Flats. Andy decides to act on the tip.

Clarabelle leads Jennifer away, but not before Jennifer, *like a moth drawn to the flame*, takes one last sniff of Andy's witch hazel.

"We thought it'd be funny to have an old biddy like Jennifer Morrison still have romance in her old bones," says Jack. "Sniffing the witch hazel is as close as she'll ever get to romance. This was funny, but also sad."

The Morrison sisters' tip leads Andy and Barney to a still operated by Ben Sewell. Andy calls out to the moonshiner and is answered with a gunshot. Andy identifies himself. Ben is happy to see Andy and Barney. He welcomes the two and invites them to have a taste of his wares. Ben apologizes for shooting and explains he did so because he "thought they were the law."

"When Andy and Barney get shot at by Ben Sewell, the funny idea was Ben not considering Andy as the law," says Jack. "Andy is just a nice fella who'd never make trouble."

Andy and Barney later visit the Morrison sisters, who are standing in front of a hothouse working in flowers. Andy has come to officially thank them for their help in the apprehension of Ben Sewell. Afterward, the sisters give Andy another tip. During one of their walks, they saw Rube Sloan running a still at Furnace Creek.

"When the sisters tip off Andy about the location of another still, it points out how clever they are, given their ages," says Jack. "It's always nice to have elderly people, who should be in their rocking chairs, be this sharp and active."

After the lawmen leave, the sisters "get back to their work." They enter the hothouse and begin filling jars with moonshine. The sisters are running a still!

"It was fun doing a moonshine story, since it's been so prevalent in this country," says Jack. "Charles and I had never actually seen a real still. We handed it off to a propman to do the research and build it for the show."

The episode's second act begins with Barney bringing in Rube Sloan. Rube sees Ben Sewell locked in a cell. The two moonshiners accuse the other of turning them in. Rube thinks carefully and realizes the Morrison sisters were by his place recently and turned both him and Ben in.

Otis Campbell visits the Morrison sisters. Ben and Rube, his regular suppliers, are in jail. Otis asks why the sisters haven't been caught. He is told that the sisters do not sell moonshine for drinking purposes. They sell elixirs for celebrations and special occasions. Otis purchases some elixir to celebrate "Sir Walter Raleigh Landing in Virginia Day."

"In 'Arsenic and Old Lace,' the two sweet old ladies murdered men and tucked them in the basement," says Jack. "I'm sure, in their minds, they were doing it for a very good reason. The two Morrison loonies were the same. They believed a body has a right to nip now and then when there's an occasion."

Andy releases Ben and Rube on probation. Barney informs Ben, who lingers behind, that he has smashed his still to smithereens. He took a great big axe and "pow, pow, pow!"

Ben is distressed by this and says, "I made that still with my own hands. She was my masterpiece."

"It was our idea to have Barney repeat the 'pow, pow, pow' whenever possible," says Jack. "It was such fun to have this skinny, harmless deputy doing Clint Eastwood."

"Ben's description of his still as a 'masterpiece' was a bit of satire," says Jack. "Ben was talking about the still as though he was talking about Michelangelo painting the Sistine Chapel. To Ben, his still was the Sistine Chapel."

Andy and Barney celebrate the end of moonshining in Mayberry. The celebration is interrupted by Otis. He drunkenly staggers in and locks himself in a cell.

The Morrison sisters continue to sell their elixir. Their latest customer makes a purchase to celebrate Mohammed's birthday.

"We knew that celebrating Mohammed's birthday was out of character for the South," says Jack. "That's why we chose such a crazy, far-out celebration. It's something that's totally foreign to the folks in Mayberry. It might be something they've heard about happening in a far-off land somewhere, but they've never actually seen a Muslim in their lives. For local drinkers, that's good enough."

Opie arrives and tells the sisters that he has gotten into trouble at school and would like some of their flowers to give to his teacher. He hopes the flowers will make her "unmad."

The Morrison sisters tell Opie to help himself and go about their business. Opie, unobserved, steps into the hothouse where the "special" flowers are grown.

At the sheriff's office, Barney is interrogating Otis. Otis, following a town-drunk code, refuses to reveal the still's location. The scene's script directions are:

Barney taps a ruler in the palm of his hand. He smashes the ruler down on the edge of the desk. The ruler breaks in half, putting a feeble end to this Gestapo tactic.

"Barney's third-degree questioning of Otis was a satire of police inflicting pain with the ruler until the suspect confesses his horrible crime," says Jack. "Barney has seen all this in movies and is simply imitating those tough detectives. Otis's defense of not ratting on other stills is again satire, like in a war, if you're captured, give only your name and serial number, torture be damned."

Opie runs into the sheriff's office with his arms full of flowers. He places the mason jar holding the flowers on Andy's desk, removes the flowers, and goes into the back room to get a vase.

Andy and Barney are looking at a map laid out on the desk. They are planning their strategy for locating the operating still. An unusual odor disturbs their concentration.

Opie returns with the flowers and tells Andy he got them from the Morrison sisters' flower-making machine. He describes the machine in detail. Andy realizes that Opie has seen a still. Andy sniffs the mason jar and is convinced. The Morrisons are making moonshine!

"As in any script, we had to know how the problem would be resolved," says Jack. "I'm sure we had several ways to wrap it up. We eventually decided to have Opie go into the sisters' hothouse to get some flowers for his teacher and thereby coming across this strange thing with tubes and a jar with funny-tasting stuff."

Andy and Barney, carrying his axe, confront the Morrison sisters about their criminal activities. The sisters claim their elixir is only for celebrating special occasions. Andy, curious, asks for clarification.

The sisters define what they consider to be special occasions. These are national holidays, like Christmas and the Fourth of July, as well as occasions not as well known. Among these are National Potato Week, Panama Canal Day, and Bastille Day. Two other occasions, St. Swithins Day and the annual Homecoming at Mayberry College (which Andy points out does not exist), were deleted from the filmed episode.

"It was fun digging up all the celebrations that called for a nip or two," says Jack. "Panama Canal Day was a direct reference to *Arsenic and Old Lace*."

Andy escorts the sisters aside and tells Barney to "do your duty." Barney grabs his axe and "pow, pow, pow!" Moonshine spurts from the wreckage, covering Andy's face. Andy licks his lips and justifies the action as a celebration of National Still-Smashing Day.

"Andy's line, 'After all it is National Still Smashing Day,' is a great 'button' for the ending," says Jack. "How did we come up with such good lines? My only answer is that's what we were paid for."

In the epilogue, the Morrison sisters have begun making preserves instead of moonshine. They deliver a sample to Andy and Barney. Andy is given his jar outside the sheriff's office. Inside, Barney has already received his jar and is busy tasting it. Andy enters to find Barney in a state of intoxicated enjoyment and realizes the rehabilitation of the Morrison sisters is not complete.

"After Barney gets his first taste of the ladies' preserves, he loves the unusual glow it causes and he digs in for more and more," says Jack. "It's always funny to see someone getting tipsy without knowing why. The silly grin on Barney's face tells you how much he's enjoying the experience."

"The Beauty Contest"

Episode 20

First Broadcast on
January 23, 1961

Written by
**Jack Elinson and
Charles Stewart**

Directed by
Bob Sweeney

Lillian Bronson
Guest Stars as
Irma Bishop
(spinster)

"We've sure seen us a pack of feminine pulchritude today!"
—ANDY TAYLOR (dialogue deleted from script)

"The Beauty Contest" begins inside Floyd's Barbershop. Mayor Stoner is seated in the chair ready for a shave. Floyd is stropping the razor and says, "If you ask me what's wrong with people today, Mayor, I say it's selfishness. It's me first and devil take the hindmost."

Floyd continues talking as he goes about shaving the mayor. The mayor is stopped from joining the conversation by Floyd pulling his lower lip taut or putting a hand under his chin.

The filmed episode deletes this opening, which was written by Charles and Jack to set up the storyline.

Floyd covers the mayor's face with a wet towel as Andy enters. Andy is soliciting ads for the Founders' Day program. Andy suggests Floyd place his usual ad, "Compliments of Floyd's Tonsorial Parlor." Floyd adds a slogan, "Best Clip Joint in Town."

"'Tonsorial Parlor' goes way back in time," says Jack. "We remembered it along with those striped poles that were outside every barbershop."

"Frankly, I was surprised Barney was left out of this script," says Jack. "Perhaps Don Knotts was given the week off. Doing a script without Barney was like writing it with one hand tied behind our backs. Obviously, Barney could have added a lot of laughs in a story like this. Thank goodness we had Howard McNear to fill the void. He was heavily used in this show and very funny."

Andy tells Floyd the Founders' Day celebration will include the usual activities. Among these are a street dance, game booths, a white elephant sale, a pie-eating contest, and free watermelon.

"Charles and I participated in or knew all the activities that went on at county fairs and Fourth of July celebrations," says Jack. "We made a list of these and used them for Mayberry's Founders' Day celebration. My favorite was always the pie-eating contests, which defied cholesterol."

Andy expresses a wish for a "new grand finale." He feels that "folks are sick and tired of the mayor's wife riding out on that horse singing that opera stuff." Hearing this, the mayor removes the towel covering his face and agrees.

"Since we haven't seen the mayor's wife yet at this point, we wanted to paint a picture of her," says Jack. "That's what led to 'riding out on a horse and singing all that opera stuff.' The image conjured up is of a large woman wearing a breastplate and carrying a spear. She is singing something very German. As for the mayor overhearing Andy's comments, the towel covering worked beautifully."

The Founders' Day grand finale is discussed at a council meeting later in the day. Floyd suggests a beauty contest be added to the traditional founding of Mayberry pageant. Everyone agrees. The council turns to selecting a judge for the beauty contest. Ellie nominates Andy, and the council unanimously approves.

"I don't think there's anything more American than beauty contests," says Jack. "Big towns and small towns have girls in them that dream of becoming Miss America, Miss Universe, Miss Anything. We felt it was a fitting subject for Mayberry."

Afterward, Andy thanks Ellie for the nomination and assures her that he will pick her as the winner. Ellie is angered that Andy would believe that her nomination was made for this reason. Seething, she confesses that she has no intention of entering the contest.

At home, Andy tells Aunt Bee of Ellie's reaction. Aunt Bee feels Andy needs to get Ellie "into the contest or he will have a time finding a likely Miss Mayberry." Aunt Bee recalls that she never passed up participating in beauty contests when she was younger.

In Jack and Charles's script, Aunt Bee shares details of being crowned "Miss Jasper Junction of 1933." She recalls that a winner's sash was draped around her. She still has the sash but doesn't think it would "go around me anymore." This information is deleted from the filmed episode.

There is a knock on the door. Darlene Swanson, a prospective Miss Mayberry, enters. She has come to borrow a cup of sugar. On the way to the kitchen, she charmingly displays herself to Andy.

Barbara Sue Lindsay, another prospective Miss Mayberry, enters as Darlene is leaving. Barbara Sue is dressed as a southern belle with a parasol on one shoulder and a bag of peat moss over the other. She is making a delivery from her father's store. Barbara Sue enters and parades before Andy.

"I have to admit that the Miss Mayberry 'audition' stuff was on the sketchy side," says Jack. "You have to remember that we had a lot of ground to cover as quickly as possible. We had to show the avalanche of young women strutting their 'talent' and we wanted it all to be funny, not straight."

Opie suggests Andy choose his classmate, Mary Wigginbottom, as Miss Mayberry. Mary is the prettiest girl in the first grade and has "genuine gold braces."

(Her last name was changed to Wiggins and the gold braces dropped in the filmed episode.)

Aunt Bee again tells Andy to get Ellie to enter the beauty contest. Her participation will "solve a lot of problems."

The following morning, Andy receives thirteen calls from parents asking him to pick their daughter to be Miss Mayberry. The mayor drops by and encourages Andy to not let people push him around. The mayor then tells Andy he doesn't mind which one of his three daughters wins the contest.

Andy, frustrated, telephones Ellie. He apologizes for accusing her unjustly and asks her to enter the beauty contest. Ellie hangs up.

Irma Bishop, a town spinster, enters the sheriff's office. She volunteers to help put on the Founders' Day pageant. Andy appreciates the generous offer.

Floyd enters soon afterward and proudly announces that he is writing a song to be sung to the triumphant Miss Mayberry.

Later, at the community hall, Miss Bishop is directing a rehearsal of the Founders' Day pageant. The script directions for the scene are *From behind the curtain comes Floyd in a partially completed Pilgrim's costume. He is followed by two men and two women also in half-completed costumes and carrying sacks. They walk with an exaggerated trudge.*

Floyd, playing the title role of John Mayberry, fumbles his lines. The other actors give half-hearted performances.

"The rehearsing scene was great," says Jack. "There's nothing like amateurs trying to be 'show biz.' Howard McNear was dynamite and a joy to write for."

Andy, watching, applauds enthusiastically. Floyd proudly accepts Andy's praise, announces that he has finished his song, and eagerly performs it.

"There's nothing that's more fun than writing real bad song lyrics," says Jack. "'Hail to Thee, Miss Mayberry' will rank right along with 'Three Little Fishes in the Itty-bitty Pool.'"

Floyd requests that he be the one who sings "Hail to Thee, Miss Mayberry" when the winner is announced. Andy responds, "If I catch anyone else trying to sing it, I'll hit them right in the mouth."

"Andy saying, 'I'll hit them right in the mouth' was added to our script after we'd turned it in," says Jack. "The line is so uncharacteristic coming from such a gentleman. Any kind of violence would be Andy's last resort. That's what made it so startling and unexpected."

Floyd tells Andy there is something he would like to talk to him about. Andy agrees to listen and says, "Floyd, you and Miss Bishop have been rays of sunshine in the sea of selfishness."

"Andy calling Floyd and Miss Bishop 'rays of sunshine in a sea of selfishness' was a flowery tribute to their goodness," says Jack. "It actually sounds like something out of a fortune cookie. Maybe that's where Andy found it."

Floyd requests that Andy pick his niece, Virginia Lee, as Miss Mayberry. Andy refuses.

The Founders' Day celebration arrives. The mayor introduces the beauty contestants. Ellie is sitting in the audience and is stunned when the mayor calls her name. (Aunt Bee has entered Ellie in the contest.)

Ellie reluctantly walks to the stage and whispers to Andy that she will never speak to him again if he picks her.

Andy stalls, delaying the announcement of the winner. He asks for the robe that will be placed upon the winner's shoulders. Miss Bishop brings it.

Charles and Jack's script direction are *Andy looks at Miss Bishop, realizes that she has been working right up to the last minute, knocking herself out with no reward, and content to stay in the background. An idea forms.*

Andy explains to the audience that real beauty is "inside beauty." He asks Miss Bishop to bring the robe to him. He places the robe around Miss Bishop and pronounces her "Royal Highness Miss Mayberry."

"Andy asking for the robe was the perfect way to get Miss Bishop on stage," says Jack. "This was a Cinderella story. The plain Jane capturing the prize. Andy's decision left all the pushy mothers and fathers and their 'beauties' enraged."

"Andy's acknowledgment of inner beauty was a way of ending our story with a moral," says Jack. "We often ended our stories this way. We always tried not to get too preachy. The morals were taught with warmth and humor."

"Cyrano Andy"

Episode 22

First Broadcast on
March 6, 1961

Written by
**Jack Elinson and
Charles Stewart**

Directed by
Bob Sweeney

"Thelma Lou, you're the cats!"—BARNEY FIFE

The Andy Griffith Show cast sat down on Thursday, January 5, 1961, to read through the "Cyrano Andy" script. The cast was returning from a Christmas layoff (the second since production began in late July 1960.) The layoff was from December 23, 1960, through January 4, 1961.

The episode's opening scene is set in Ellie Walker's home. Andy is playing guitar. Ellie serves coffee. Barney sits stiffly on a sofa beside his date, Thelma Lou. All four are singing with enthusiasm.

"The whole opening was scripted," says Jack. "We called for a song that was 'old and familiar' and they came up with 'Seeing Nellie Home.' I'm sure Andy Griffith suggested it. He oversaw the song department."

"I don't remember anything about Barney's former girlfriend," says Jack. "Maybe the actress who played Hilda Mae wasn't what they were looking for and Betty Lynn was a better choice. We had no special image of Thelma Lou. Producer Aaron Ruben made all the casting decisions."

At the song's end, Andy causally drapes an arm around Ellie. Jack and Charles write a wonderful description of what happens next:

Barney tries to emulate Andy. His arm crawls toward Thelma Lou's shoulder like a stalking animal. He is almost there when Thelma Lou sees the arm and is quite ready to have it put around her shoulders, even scrunches a little to make it easier . . . but Barney hastily starts scratching his head as though that was all he ever intended.

The lights suddenly go out due to a power failure. The room is dark. When the power is restored, Barney is revealed sitting beside Andy!

"It wasn't difficult to write Barney's shyness," says Jack. "With Don Knotts doing it, it flowed easily. Who could have performed it better than Don?"

Later, Barney walks Thelma Lou home. He concludes with an explanation of the fundamentals of fingerprinting as the two reach Thelma Lou's front porch. Thelma Lou longs for something more. Barney starts to leave, turns back, and promises to tell her about the "assembling and oiling of the .38 caliber revolver" the next time they are together. Thelma Lou, fighting back tears, watches as Barney walks away.

In Jack and Charles's script, Thelma Lou invites Barney in for coffee so he can warm his feet and hands before walking home. Barney refuses the offer. He plans to keep his circulation going by clapping his hands and jogging home.

Barney jogs along, then suddenly stops near a telephone pole under a light. He looks back toward Thelma Lou's house. Half resolutely, he takes a step as if to return, but then he pauses as he pictures in his mind and half-pantomimes the actions he envisions as taking place if he should return. He holds out his arms as if around a girl and begins to tilt the imaginary Thelma Lou back for a kiss. Abruptly he realizes he can only go through with it in his imagination and that in reality he'd flub again just as he did before. Barney looks back and sees Thelma Lou's porch light go off. Angry at himself and his inadequacy, he balls his right fist, punches the telephone pole, and then strides away.

It was not hard to imagine that this scene, given life through the talents of Don Knotts, would have been very special. It is a disappointment that it was cut from the script.

The next day, Andy and Opie are playing checkers in the sheriff's office. Andy does some deep thinking and moves his checker. Opie makes the jump that has opened up. Andy starts to make a move, but Opie stops him and continues jumping five more checkers.

Andy tousles Opie's hair and says, "I got plans to stop playing with you! You're a riverboat sharpie, that's what you are!"

"Even though I've never been on a Mississippi River boat, I remember seeing movies showing the 'riverboat sharpie' at work," says Jack. "It was funny to compare Opie to that breed."

Barney enters and is asked by Andy if he did all right with Thelma Lou last night. Barney, uncomfortable with Opie's presence, doesn't answer. Andy suggests that Opie run along and play. Opie, understanding the reason for the request, replies, "Gee whiz, you'd think I never heard about kissing before."

"It was also funny to have Opie, do the 'kissing' line," says Jack. "Children always listen to what grown-ups say and understand a lot about what they do."

After Opie's departure, Andy warns Barney that he may be in danger of losing Thelma Lou if he doesn't soon let her know how he feels about her. In the original script, Andy explains, "A girl expects a little kissy and a little squeezy. You know, a little lifey." These lines were crossed out by Andy Griffith on his copy of the script and deleted from the filmed episode.

Barney admits there are plenty of things he can think of to say to Thelma Lou when he is alone.

Andy encourages Barney to share with him some of the things he would say.

He makes the request in a smiling, lighthearted manner, but as Barney shares his feelings, Andy understands that what he is hearing is a sincere, heartfelt declaration of love. This is not a time for hilarity. Andy deeply respects Barney and the feelings he is comfortable sharing. Andy affirms Barney by telling him that what he has shared is "beautiful!"

"We liked writing how Barney feels about Thelma Lou," says Jack. "It was very touching and enhanced in the finished episode by Earl Hagen's music. Hagen was great! We loved the way the whole scene was done. 'You're the cats' didn't come from me. I never heard the phrase. Charles Stewart came up with it."

"The scene also expressed the feelings about Andy and Barney's relationship to one another," says Jack. "These are two guys who do love and respect one another. You see that in so many of the episodes. Their relationship made the series what it is."

Afterward, Andy realizes that Barney needs someone to tell Thelma Lou how he feels about her. Andy decides to visit Thelma Lou and speak on Barney's behalf.

"We definitely thought of Cyrano de Bergerac from the start," says Jack. "That was the nugget that got us going on the story."

Andy visits Thelma Lou and speaks for Barney. Thelma Lou is pleased by what she hears but would like to hear it from Barney's "own thin lips."

After Andy departs, Thelma Lou gets an idea. She telephones Barney and reports that Andy "just came calling on me."

Charles and Jack's script directions are a narrative of how Barney reacts to the report. *Barney opens the door of the sheriff's office and stalks in grim-faced. Andy watches curiously as Barney stalks to the desk, removes his gun belt and lays it on the desk, places his hat on top and, finally removes his star and places it on top of the gun belt and hat."* (Barney does not remove his badge in the filmed episode.) *Then he turns to face Andy, puts his fists in a John L. Sullivan pose, and challenges Andy.*

"The nice scene of Andy respectfully listening to Barney express his feeling for Thelma Lou was a setup for the angry scene," says Jack. "A misunderstanding between two friends is always grist for the mill. In our script, Barney challenges Andy to boxing, a little judo, or to arm wrestle. Barney calls Andy a Judas and a love thief."

Barney asks Andy how he would feel if he tried to steal Ellie away from him. Andy laughs at the idea. Barney, angered, calls Floyd's Barbershop and schedules the "works." If it "smells," Barney wants it.

"Ellie Walker was specifically written into the series to give Andy a romantic interest," says Jack. "By the time we did 'Cyrano Andy,' the romance between them was growing. We cracked up when we wrote the 'If it smells, I want it' line. We cracked up even more when we saw Don Knotts perform it."

Later, Barney enters the drugstore. It is obvious Floyd has given him the "works." He removes his hat, revealing a spit curl over his forehead. Barney tells Ellie that she is "his kind of woman." Ellie laughs at Barney and tells him that she doesn't have time for "this nonsense."

"Barney's spit curl was scripted," says Jack. "Talk about cracking up! We immediately knew the curl was a great visual. As for his sweet talk, we just did Barney trying to be Frank Sinatra. The dialogue came easily."

Later, Ellie tells Andy of Barney's romantic advances. Barney enters the sheriff's office. He believes Andy has stolen Thelma Lou from him and decides, under the circumstances, to resign as deputy.

Andy and Ellie must do something. Andy believes that if Ellie would call Barney's bluff, he would run back to Thelma Lou "like a scared rabbit." Ellie suggests that Andy do the same with Thelma Lou.

Andy and Ellie put their plan into action. Andy encounters Thelma Lou on her front porch. Ellie woos Barney in the back room of the drugstore. Declarations of love and kisses on the check are given. The filmed narrative cuts back and forth between Andy revealing his true feelings to Thelma Lou and Ellie making advances on Barney.

"Charles and I had to work out 'the scared rabbit' scenes very carefully," says Jack. "There was a lot going on. Andy and Ellie were role-playing. Barney and Thelma Lou were reacting. Misunderstandings had to be corrected, and we had to do it all in the episode's run time of twenty-four minutes. The cuts back and forth between Andy and Thelma Lou, and Barney and Ellie were all carefully scripted."

Afterward, a visibly shaken Barney tells Andy what happened at the drugstore. He believes he is the one that Ellie wants and confesses his conquest is a "hollow victory."

Outside the sheriff's office, Thelma Lou approaches Barney and confesses that she made up the whole thing with Andy to make Barney jealous. She declares that Barney is the one she wants. Barney answers that Thelma Lou is the only girl for him.

"After all the goings-on, we had to get back to reality," says Jack. "Barney and Thelma Lou's reconciliation was played straight with very little comedy. We ended the scene with Barney leading his lady fair down the street."

The original epilogue was set in Ellie's living room. Barney tells Thelma Lou it is time they started walking home. Ellie accompanies Thelma Lou to a back room to get her coat. Andy tells Barney he would like to walk with the couple and get some fresh air. The girls return. Barney offers Thelma Lou his arm in a suave fashion and says to Andy, "You wouldn't want to walk with us. We're taking the long way." Barney gives Andy a large wink and exits.

The epilogue that appears in the filmed episode was written by producer and story consultant Aaron Ruben. In his version, Andy helps Ellie in the kitchen.

Barney, alone with Thelma Lou, wants a kiss. Andy repeatedly interrupts Barney's intentions with questions about pie and coffee. A frustrated Barney eventually leaves Thelma Lou and storms off to the kitchen to get the pie and coffee himself.

"Aaron's epilogue was better than ours," says Jack. "Andy was having fun teasing Barney. It was a much funnier finish."

"Of all the scripts we wrote, 'Cyrano Andy' was the sketchiest," says Jack. "The comedy was broad, almost on the verge of farce. This was not the typical soft, gentle show which characterized the series."

"The New Doctor"

Episode 24

First Broadcast on
March 27, 1961

Written by
**Charles Stewart
and Jack Ellison**

Directed by
Bob Sweeney

George Nadar
Guest Stars as
Dr. Robert Benson

"If a chicken hawk is hangin' around, a wise rooster don't bury his head."
—BARNEY FIFE

"Aw, come on, Paw, get married. Be a good scout."—OPIE TAYLOR

Charles and Jack begin "The New Doctor" in the Taylor kitchen. Aunt Bee is checking a chocolate layer cake she is baking for the Saturday night "social." She opens the oven door and looks in.

"Aunt Bee's way of checking on the cake was changed in the filmed episode," says Jack. "Aunt Bee sticks a broom straw in the cake to see if it's done. I never saw my mother do that, nor my wife. The broom straw was a nice touch for the small-town southern setting. I imagine it was the idea of Andy Griffith."

Aunt Bee asks if Andy has invited Ellie Walker to the social. Andy hasn't. He explains that he and Ellie have an understanding and take it for granted that they will go together. Aunt Bee advises that a "girl likes the courtesy of being asked."

Opie enters. He asks, based upon the conversation he has overheard, when Andy is going to ask Ellie to marry him. Opie would like to have a "maw that owns a drugstore with a soda fountain."

"We loved writing for Opie, especially knowing that Ronny Howard was doing the part," says Jack. "Ronny was the best child actor ever on TV. As for writing from a child's viewpoint, Charles and I were both fathers and knew about kids."

Barney picks up Andy and drives the short distance to the sheriff's office with the siren blasting.

"In our script, Andy says to Barney, 'Let's not break everyone's eardrums letting them know we're open for business,'" says Jack. "Story consultant Aaron Ruben tweaked the dialogue and added a great closing line, 'You keep playing with the siren like that and I'm going to take it off the car.'"

Before going into the sheriff's office, Andy decides to walk over to the drugstore. He explains to Barney that he has something he would like to ask Ellie.

Inside, Ellie introduces Andy and Barney to a *youngish well dressed* man, Dr. Robert Benson. Benson is the new doctor in town.

"We indicated in the script directions that Dr. Benson be handsome in order to make him a threat to Andy," says Jack. "Aaron Ruben chose actor George Nadar for the role."

Andy asks about Dr. Benson's family and learns that Benson is not married. Barney has never heard of a doctor that wasn't married.

"Both Charles and I had this feeling that doctors are all married," says Jack. "Doctors have to go to medical school, then intern, then start their practice. All this adds up to a lot of years. By then, they're all in their thirties, so of course they're married. We had Barney share our belief."

Ellie takes Dr. Benson into the back room to show him the prescription department. Andy steps behind the fountain counter and gets Barney and himself a soda.

Barney, while drinking his soda, reflects upon Dr. Benson's young age and appearance. He says to Andy, "If you aren't worried, why should I be?"

Andy asks for an explanation. Barney answers, "Two plus two makes four." Ellie and the doctor are unmarried, young, and good-looking. Barney, hearing laughter coming from the prescription department, adds, "Two young people lost in a world of pills."

"When Barney warns what could happen between Benson and Ellie, it really is an example of his mixed-up logic," says Jack. "What he should have said is 'one plus one makes two.'" Poor Barney got a little confused, which is what Charles and I intended."

"Andy tells Barney he believes that he has been blowing the siren so much that it's loosened his brains," says Jack. "This was our second time referring to the siren in the squad car. Repetitions are often used in comedy. We call them 'runners.' It's a formula that seems always to work."

Charles and Jack included script directions throughout the drugstore scene that guide Andy from no suspension to a state of worry about a possible romantic relationship between Ellie and Dr. Benson. The directions were *Andy speaks with some asperity. Andy reacts with a trace of a little concern. There is a threat in Andy's tone.*

Andy Griffith was very aware of the dynamics and subtle changes in his character's emotions. At the beginning of the scene, he writes on the margin of his script, "How to play."

Back at the sheriff's office, Andy reflects on the situation as Barney rattles on about Ellie and Dr. Benson. Aunt Bee enters and excitedly announces there is a new doctor in town. She too feels he is young and good-looking. Barney adds "unmarried" to the doctor's desirable qualities.

Aunt Bee also feels that Andy may have a reason to be concerned. Andy, hearing this, has heard enough. He decides to leave to tend to some sheriff business.

After Andy's departure, Barney says, "Darn guy! Somehow or another he just brings out the big brother in me. I guess I'll just try to help the kid."

"The Barney character is growing one script after another," says Jack. "Don Knotts kept coming up with new stuff, with the help of Andy Griffith and Aaron Ruben. That was what kept us finding new stuff in our scripts. Barney playing the big brother was an example. The character continued to evolve and by the end of the second season, Barney was full-blown."

Barney keeps a close eye on Dr. Benson. He stands outside the drugstore and spies on the doctor from behind a raised newspaper. Barney flattens himself against a wall and works himself into position to watch inside activities through the drugstore's front door.

"I loved the scene where Barney decides to do a little spying," says Jack. "We drew inspiration from the old Inspector Clouseau movies. The inspector was a totally inept detective who did everything wrong, but it never fazed him. That was Barney!"

Barney telephones Aunt Bee with a spy report. He has seen Dr. Benson enter the drugstore fourteen times in the last two days. Barney feels it is time for him to "take the bull by the horns," and he knows just what to do.

"The scene that followed blew my mind," says Jack. "Barney in the doctor's office was pure gold. Remembering the scene for the first time in forty years brought back memories. I remembered it before I even got to reading it. The scene was probably the funniest thing we ever wrote. When I got to Barney's last line, 'Forget about them. Will I pull through?,' I absolutely fell on the floor laughing."

Barney's examination scene begins with Barney lying on a table, stripped to the waist with only a T-shirt on. Dr. Benson checks Barney's lungs, blood pressure, and pulse. All the while, Barney asks questions about the doctor's numerous visits to the drugstore. He tells Benson that Ellie is Andy's girl and Andy is insanely jealous.

The doctor, busy with the examination, barely listens and is concerned that Barney's blood pressure is low. Aware that the doctor has found something, Barney's interest has a new concern, himself.

The doctor writes Barney a prescription. In the script, Jack and Charles creatively write Barney's response: *Barney grabs for the prescription, clutching the life-giving words of Latin to his frightened little bosom.*

That evening, Andy, Aunt Bee, and Opie are relaxing on the front porch. Andy is strumming his guitar. Aunt Bee asks if he has invited Ellie to the social. Andy hasn't. Aunt Bee disapproves of his hesitance. She warns that one day he will go to call on Ellie and her husband and two children will greet him.

Opie, playing with his wooden blocks but carefully listening to the adults, says, "Come on, Paw. Get married. Be a good scout."

"The porch scene was originally set in the Taylor living room," says Jack. "Aaron Ruben decided to shift it to the front porch. We had Andy reading a magazine. The rewrite has Andy strumming his guitar. I admit the porch was a better setting. It helped set the personal mood of the scene."

Andy, alone on the porch, reflects upon Aunt Bee's warning. He rushes to Ellie's home and formally asks her to the social. There is a knock on the door. It is Dr. Benson. Ellie asks if Benson is planning on attending the social. He is not, so Ellie invites the doctor to join Andy and herself. Andy is not pleased with the invitation.

The next day, Andy and Barney see Dr. Benson entering the drugstore. Andy sends Barney to see what Ellie and the doctor are doing.

Prior to Barney's arrival, the doctor is showing Ellie photographs of his fiancée.

Barney enters and positions himself to overhear the conversation. The doctor, referring to his fiancée, tells Ellie he would like to get married. Ellie suggests that Andy, as justice of the peace, perform the ceremony.

The scene's script directions are *Barney is dying. Ellie and Benson stabbing his beloved Andy this way! Barney dashes madly back to Andy.*

Barney reports that Ellie and the doctor are talking marriage. Andy rushes to the drugstore to fight for what is his. Barney, in a panic, believes there is going to be bloodshed.

In the original script, Barney picks up the telephone and asks Sarah, the operator, to get the police. Realizing he is the police, he hangs up. Barney pulls out his gun, attempts to open a locked drawer to get a bullet, returns his gun to its holster, sits down, and starts biting his nails.

In the filmed scene, Barney, realizing he isn't wearing his gun, runs into a jail cell to retrieve the gun from the bunk. Barney swings the door open. While reaching for the gun, the door swings back, locking Barney inside.

"The gun on the bed was another Aaron Ruben rewrite," says Jack. "Given the small-town informality of the sheriff's office, Aaron didn't feel it was necessary to explain why Barney's gun was in the cell. Remember, Barney's in a tizzy about the whole situation, so he's capable of doing nutty things."

In Aaron Ruben's rewrite, Barney's participation in what he believes may be a dangerous confrontation is prevented by a locked door. The original scene has Barney panicking in the face of danger. He is defeated and sits biting his nails. In contrast, the rewrite doesn't belittle Barney's courage. It is a locked cell door rather than fear that stops Barney from taking further action. The rewrite allows Barney to be more than a fearful caricature.

Andy rushes into the drugstore and makes an implied proposal of marriage. In response, Dr. Benson suggests that Andy and Ellie join him and his fiancée in a double wedding ceremony.

Andy slowly realizes the situation is different from what he thought. Andy, however, intends to honor his proposal. He tells Ellie to set a date. Ellie points out that she never gave his proposal an answer. She does not want to rush into marriage and answers "no" to the proposal.

Jack and Charles close the second act with *In his ecstasy, Andy kisses Ellie quickly on the cheek. He turns to the doctor and in his enthusiasm, almost starts to kiss him too. He catches himself and runs out.*

In the epilogue, Andy and Barney enter the drugstore. The two hear voices coming from the back room. Ellie says, "'Darling, sweetheart,' and the phrase, 'I love you.'"

Andy and Barney rush to "catch Ellie with a new lover." Instead, they find Ellie and Dr. Benson putting a bandage on Opie's skinned elbow.

"The tag was funny," says Jack. "Our only concern was that the audience might guess who Ellie was talking to. We hoped that they would be surprised when Opie was revealed."

The script ends with the following: *Opie holds up his elbow to show bandage. Andy looks at Barney and both would now like to crawl into one of the two-ounce medicine bottles. FADE OUT.*

"The Inspector"

Episode 26

First Broadcast on
April 10, 1961

Written by
**Jack Elinson and
Charles Stewart**

Directed by
Bob Sweeney

Tod Andrews
Guest Stars as
Inspector Ralph
Case

"This jail doesn't even seem like a jail."—INSPECTOR RALPH CASE

"The Inspector" begins in the sheriff's office. Barney is alone, playing a game of checkers. He carefully studies the board, makes a move, then walks to the other side of the board and makes a move. Andy enters carrying the mail and a small package. He is curious when he sees Barney's one-person game.

"Barney playing checkers against himself isn't that crazy," says Jack. "People who are bored and have nobody to talk to have been known to play against themselves. Especially if they've played solitaire a hundred times and they're sick of it. We chose to open the show that way."

Andy sees the package is from the Hubacher brothers, who are currently serving time at State Prison. Barney feels the three brothers are the nicest fellows he and Andy ever "sent up." The package contains a wallet for Andy and a leather bookmark for Barney. The brothers are learning leathercraft as a trade, and the gifts are a sample of their work. Barney suggests that he and Andy drive up to State Prison some Sunday for a visit.

"I'm sure the idea of a letter from the Hubacher brothers was suggested by Aaron Ruben," says Jack. "Aaron asked us to include a letter from them as we were forming the story. Showing Andy and Barney's fondness of the three guys they put in jail helped set the unusual friendliness of Mayberry's small-town sheriff's office."

Barney looks through the mail and finds a postcard from the state inspector's office. He reads it and learns that a man is coming to inspect the jail. Andy assures Barney that the inspection is routine procedure.

Andy looks at the card and discovers the inspection is scheduled for later that day. Hearing this, Barney becomes frantic. Andy advises Barney not to "get his skinny little veins popping." The inspector, Sam Allen, is one of his buddies.

"In comedy, if someone is fat, you do fat jokes," says Jack. "Barney is skinny, so we wrote skinny jokes. Giving Andy the 'thin veins' line was impossible to resist."

Barney realizes that the jail cells are empty. He feels a prisoner is needed to "dress up the place," and departs to find one.

Jack and Charles give the departure a colorful description: *And, with his nose twitching and his hand on his holster, Barney strides out into the jungle.*

Later, Barney returns with Otis Campbell, the town drunk. Otis has his arm affectionately around Barney's shoulder. Otis announces that it is his birthday and is pleased to celebrate it with his good friends, Andy and Barney. Andy has an idea. He will ask Sam Allen, who knows Otis, to celebrate Otis's birthday when he arrives.

"We loved writing for Otis," says Jack. "Along with fat jokes and skinny jokes, drunk jokes are hard to resist. Making it Otis's birthday was the perfect device to enrage the new inspector. We had no trouble coming up with it."

While Andy is out getting a birthday cake, Otis dozes in his chair. The door opens and Ralph Case, a new inspector, arrives. Case has replaced Sam Allen. Inspector Case sees Otis asleep at Andy's desk and wants to know why the prisoner is not in a cell.

"Our only description of Ralph Case was 'wears civilian clothes, but has an obviously official air,'" says Jack. "Ruth Birch was an outstanding casting director. She worked on *The Griffith Show*, *The Danny Thomas Show*, and several others. She was, at that time, one of the top casting people in the business. Ruth selected the actors and submitted their names to Aaron Ruben for final approval."

Andy enters carrying a birthday cake. Barney identifies Case as the new inspector. Andy introduces him to Otis and asks if he would like to do some fishing while in Mayberry. Case is not interested in celebrating Otis's birthday or in fishing. He walks into a cell, inspects the doilies placed on the chairs, and says, "This jail doesn't even seem like a jail."

"The inspector's line, 'This jail doesn't even seem like a jail,' is the perfect description of life in Mayberry," says Jack. "That's what this story, and the series, is all about."

The inspector asks Andy if he has ever read any sort of police manual. Andy answers that he used to subscribe to the *Police Gazette* but had to cut it out when Deputy Fife joined the force. Andy explains that the *Gazette* had a lot of girlie pictures in it and Barney has never been married.

"We loved doing the *Police Gazette* stuff," says Jack. "It showed Andy digging a hole for himself, making it deeper and deeper. Even though the girls' pictures in the *Police Gazette* were nothing like *Playboy* magazine, it was fun writing something slightly naughty."

Case asks for Barney's sidearm. He inspects the gun and discovers there are no bullets in the cylinder. Andy explains that Barney keeps his bullet in his pocket. Case orders Barney to load his weapon. Barney eagerly places his bullet in the cylinder, flips the cylinder shut, and fires a shot into the floor.

"From the very first time Barney accidentally fired a shot, we knew it would be a running joke throughout the series," says Jack. "We likewise knew that Andy would only trust Barney with one bullet."

Case has seen enough. He plans to call his boss and have him come and see for himself the worst case of a jail he has ever seen. Case also threatens the impeachment of Andy and Barney from their duties.

Case departs, and Andy comments, "That fellow sure does have a lot of nasty in him."

"I have a sneaking feeling that the 'nasty' line came from Andy Griffith," says Jack. "That wasn't the way Charles and I talked. If you want to do southern speech, who better to suggest it than a southerner?"

The script's second act opens with Andy sweeping the sheriff's office. Opie enters carrying a paper bag. He tells Andy that Barney was at their house and told Aunt Bee that an inspector was making trouble.

Opie imitates Barney's nervous pace and arm waving, saying, "Oh, this is awful, awful. Oh, we're never gonna get outa this one."

Opie's imitation is wisely deleted from the script. His scripted behavior is not appropriate for the character. Barney is loved and respected by the Taylor family. Opie may at times overhear Andy describe Barney as high-spirited, but he never thinks of Barney as someone to make fun of.

Another deletion from the script is a joke based upon a child's misunderstanding of adult conversation. Opie says to Andy, "Barney said the inspector was going to give you a peach and throw you out of office." Andy explains the word is "impeach."

The script concludes the scene as it appears in the filmed episode. Opie tells Andy that Barney said he might have a chance if he wore a hat and tie. Opie opens the paper bag and brings out a polka-dotted tie and a fedora fishing hat.

Barney enters as Andy comes out of the back room wearing his new accessories. Barney reports that Inspector Case has called his boss. Andy walks into one of the cells and places fresh linens on the bed. He is followed by Barney, who swings the cell door open. Momentum swings the door back, locking the two inside.

"Just like Barney accidentally shooting his gun, locking himself in the cell would become a 'runner' in the series," says Jack. "When you find comic gold, you don't waste it. The details of how Barney would accidentally lock the door were all in our stage directions."

Inspector Case enters. He is not happy with what he sees. Case believes the locked cell, the polka-dot tie, and fishing hat, along with his earlier observations, will result in a "housecleaning" of the sheriff's office.

"In a story like this one, the whole trick is to make Andy look worse and worse," says Jack. "The inspector reacts with disbelief and wonders, 'What kind of looney) bin is this?' It wasn't difficult to come up with Mayberry-type things, like Aunt Bee's doilies, that the inspector would completely misunderstand."

Inspector Case's "housecleaning" comment panics Barney. A line of dialogue deleted from the filmed episode communicates Andy's acknowledgment of this. Andy says, "I ought to call you Barney P. Fife . . . 'P' for panic."

Andy says to Case, "You can make threats against me all you like, but you're scaring my deputy and I'd like for you to stop."

Andy is calm and confident. He doesn't know what the end results of the inspection will be, but he believes in the way he conducts himself as sheriff.

Mayberryian Sam Truett enters and reports that Luke Reimer is operating his still and, fearful of being turned in, is shooting at anyone who comes near his place.

Inspector Cases suggests the state police be called. Andy ignores this and exits.

The squad car, with Andy, Barney, and Case, arrives at the Reimer place. Luke begins shooting. Andy, Barney, and Case take cover behind the car.

Case asks for a portable loudspeaker. He wants to let Luke know they "mean business."

Barney opens the trunk. Jack and Charles write a detailed description of its content: *The trunk is littered with fishing tackle, creel, 2 fishing poles, old inner tube, large thermos (1 gal), picnic basket, hip boots, bat and glove, football, swim fins, sleeping bag rolls. Among the mass is a portable loudspeaker.*

(The asked-for items, except for the inner tube, baseball glove, and swim fins, were all assembled by propman Frank Myers.)

"Opening the trunk to find Andy's fishing equipment and a whole lot of other nonessential things was still another nail for Case to pound into Andy's coffin," says Jack.

Case uses the loudspeaker to order Luke to come out with his hands up. Luke answers with gunfire. Case's hat is shot off his head.

"Luke Reimer shooting off Case's hat was called for in the script," says Jack. "Since we had no idea how that could be executed, it was easy for us to say, 'Do it,' and let someone else take care of it. The propman, Frank Myers, was the one who made it all happen on screen. He figured out how to have the hat fly off and how to do the gunshots kicking up dirt. In those days, that was considered a nifty special effect. Now it would be considered kindergarten."

Case suggests smoking Luke out and asks if there are any tear gas bombs in the trunk. Andy doesn't take the idea seriously.

The script has Barney digging out a box of tear-gas bombs from the trunk. Case poises a bomb to throw but stops after seeing a label on the box. He bends closer and reads, "Not to be used after March 1953." He tosses the bomb aside. It explodes in a harmless little puff. The exploding tear-gas bomb is deleted from the filmed episode.

Andy wants to give Luke some time to simmer down and stops Case from radioing the state police.

Andy eventually decides the time is right and bravely walks toward Luke. Luke continues to fire his gun.

"Luke Reimer's still has been shut down many times by Andy," says Jack. "Luke, however, is still fond of Andy and would do nothing to harm him. Andy understood this. In that context, having Andy walk unarmed into Luke's gunfire is quite believable."

Case's boss, Mr. Brady, arrives and watches as Andy peacefully disarms Luke. Brady compliments Andy on the arrest. He then turns his attention to Case and asks about his complaints. Case reports the birthday cake, a gun accidentally fired, doilies on chairs, a polka-dot tie, and then, considering the bravery Andy has just demonstrated, is speechless. Case, defeated, walks away.

After the departure, Andy confidentially says to Brady, "That boy's been working too hard. He's right curious acting."

"The 'right curious acting' line was not ours," says Jack. "As a writer, I hate to give so much credit to someone else, but once again I must conclude the line came from Andy Griffith. Thank God he never asked for a writer credit!"

"~~Quiet Sam~~"

Episode 29

First Broadcast on
May 1, 1961

Written by
**Jim Fritzell and
Everett Greenbaum**

Directed by
Bob Sweeney

William Schallert
Guest Stars as
Sam Becker

"I had no idea when we wrote 'Quiet Sam' that it was the beginning of a lifetime association with Mayberry."—EVERETT GREENBAUM

"I guess Jim Fritzell and I wound up with *TAGS* [*The Andy Griffith Show*] as a result of our knack for writing Americana," says writer Everett Greenbaum. "Aaron Ruben and *TAGS* executive producer Sheldon Leonard were familiar with our writing from *Mr. Peepers* and *The Real McCoys*.

"But there was another thing. Bob Sweeney (who directed most of the shows in the early years) went to high school in San Francisco with Jim Fritzell. A year ahead of Jim in high school, Bob was Jim's idol, because he had been head of debate and was later a success in show business. Bob helped Jim get started in Hollywood and may have encouraged Aaron to give us a try.

"At the time, Jim and I didn't have any trouble finding writing assignments, and I wasn't overly thrilled about being hired to write a *TAGS* script because what I really wanted to do was write movies. I had only watched the show a couple of times. But I had loved Andy in *No Time for Sergeants* as well as his record, 'What It Was, Was Football.'"

Everett and Jim's finished script opens with Barney and Floyd standing in front of the barbershop. Barney sees a truck parked close to a fire hydrant and suspects a violation of "Code 8, Section B." The truck belongs to Sam Becker, "a strange duck" who "doesn't say word one."

"We kind of borrowed the code dialogue from Jack Webb's *Dragnet* show, which was number one in the ratings in those days," says Everett.

Barney tries to get Sam to talk but is unsuccessful. After Sam drives away, Andy walks up, and Barney tells him that Sam has all the characteristics of a criminal. Barney asks, "Doesn't it bother you the way he won't look you in the eye? The way he's always in a hurry. The busiest man in the world has five minutes to pass the time of day."

"Sam Becker had to have a quality of shyness and mystery in the beginning, and William Schallert, who was cast in the role, fit my image of the character

72

very well," says Everett. "When writing a script, I used names I knew rather than stopping to make one up. The Becker family lived across the street from us in Buffalo."

Another example of Everett's method for selecting names was the naming of Nate Pike, Opie's wise four-year-old acquaintance. Opie mentions Nate as a thunderstorm begins. Opie asks Andy if he thinks lightning will hit the backyard and requests a penny. Andy questions Opie about the request and is told Nate Pike said "a penny hit by lightning is worth six cents."

"Nate Pike was a great big bully who used to beat me up in school," recalls Everett. "Nate's theory about a penny hit by lightning grew out of a childhood memory. As kids, we thought a penny run over by a train was lucky, so we extended it to lightning strikes."

Barney stops by the Taylors' to report on the "Becker case." Barney has checked the sales records at the drugstore and found that Sam has purchased large amounts of absorbent cotton, antiseptics, vitamins, tranquilizers, and swab sticks. Barney thinks Sam is harboring someone with a bullet in him and convinces Andy that they should go look around.

Andy and Barney park at a distance when they arrive at Sam's house. They watch as Sam plows his field in the middle of the night. Barney suggests that Sam's strange behavior may be due to the fact that Sam is growing marijuana.

This is somewhat surprising dialogue for 1961, especially in a small southern town. "I think we wrote the script about the same time marijuana was in the news because Robert Mitchum had been arrested for possession," explains Everett. "Barney's comment was inspired by the extensive news coverage of the incident."

Soon after Andy and Barney return to Mayberry, Andy receives a call that there is trouble at the Becker place. Andy leaves word for Barney, who is out checking doorknobs, that he is returning to the Becker place.

As Andy arrives at Sam's home, a thunderstorm occurs. The on-screen lightning storm visually communicates the feeling of mystery initially created by the suspicious behavior of Sam Becker. The *TAGS* production crew realistically created the storm through the use of wind machines, sound effects, variations in lighting, simulation of pouring rain, and the addition during the editing process of actual footage of lightning flashing across the sky.

Soon after arriving at Sam's house, Andy learns the real reason for Sam's suspicious behavior—he and his wife are expecting a baby.

Meanwhile, Barney gets the message about Andy's whereabouts and jumps to the conclusion that Andy is in serious trouble. Barney telephones Floyd and instructs him to round up anyone he can find to help rescue Andy.

The careful attention given to detail on *TAGS* is evident in the brief telephone-conversation scene between Floyd and Barney. Pouring rain can be seen through the window behind Floyd. Such detail enabled Mayberry to come alive as a real and believable place.

When Barney arrives at the Becker place, he learns that the birth is going to happen at any time. Barney becomes nervous when he learns that the inexperienced Andy is going to perform the delivery. Barney reminds Andy that he flunked "Miss Webster's biology class in the spring of 1938."

"Biology class dissection jokes have always been grist for the comedy mill, so we had Barney remind Andy about flunking Miss Webster's biology class—while dissecting a grasshopper, he froze," says Everett.

Andy tells Barney and Sam that they need to get their minds on something other than babies. Andy diverts the conversation by bringing up Barney's army service. Barney shares his memories about his experience "across the big pond" in Staten Island's three-thousand-book PX library. Sam tells of his service in Korea. As the two talk, Andy quietly leaves to deliver the baby.

After "army story number seventeen" has been told, Andy returns with Sam's baby boy. Sam takes his son but soon calls upon the sheriff to help the baby "Andy" stop crying.

Everett comments, "Jim and I liked the humor of Barney's army experience so well that several years later we used it a second time in the Don Knotts movie *The Reluctant Astronaut*. Becker naming the baby 'Andy' ended the second act on a sentimental note and was a surefire crowd-pleaser, like waving a flag in vaudeville."

"Quiet Sam" concludes with a group of Mayberry residents celebrating Andy's birth. The celebration includes a forty-second performance of "She'll Be Comin' 'Round the Mountain."

"There was no musical performance in our script," says Everett. "I imagine the filmed script was too short and the music was added to fill in the remaining time."

"The Guitar Player Returns"

Episode 31

First Broadcast on
May 15, 1961

Written by
**Charles Stewart
and Jack Elinson**

Directed by
Bob Sweeney

James Best
Guest Stars as
Jim Lindsay
(Lindsay was spelled
Lindsey in Episode 3,
"The Guitar Player")

(Indicating jacket) "Custom made. You know what the guys in the band call this? A set of threads."—JIM LINDSAY

"Everyone was pleased with 'The Guitar Player' episode," says Jack. "The work of actor James Best especially stood out. Because of this, we decided to write another 'guitar player' script. It wasn't difficult to come up with another story for the character."

Charles and Jack open the script with Andy rushing into the drugstore with exciting news. Andy tells Barney and Ellie that Jim Lindsay is coming to Mayberry! Ellie has never heard of Jim. Barney is surprised. He tells Ellie that Jim is the guitar player with Bobby Fleet and His Band with a Beat. Barney can't believe Ellie hasn't heard his classic hit, "Rock 'n' Roll Rosie from Raleigh."

"It was our intention to have Barney tell Ellie all about Jim Lindsay," says Jack. "It was a smooth way to do a recap and remind the audience who Jim was. I believe the title, 'Rock 'n' Roll Rosie From Raleigh,' came from us. We were really good at coming up with bad song titles."

Andy and Barney hurry to the barbershop to share the exciting news with Floyd and the mayor, who is getting a haircut.

The four plan a welcoming reception for Jim. The plans include a "Welcome Home" banner, the participation of the Mayberry Drum and Bugle Corps, and an official police escort into town.

Later at the sheriff's office, Barney is working out the details of the escort. He is concerned about the banner. Barney fears that Charlie, one of the banner holders, will let his end drop. Andy advises Barney to calm down or he is "going to bust his little corpuscles."

"We would never skip an opportunity for Andy to refer to Barney's little corpuscles," says Jack. "In 'The Inspector' script we had Andy concerned that Barney was going to pop his little veins. Andy loved teasing Barney with lines like these. Barney's worry about Charlie 'letting his end of the banner drop' showed his excitement and nervousness to make sure Lindsay's reception would be perfect."

Barney can't find his whistle. He believes the whistle is an escort essential. Andy suggests an alternative, "You might try blowing across an empty pop bottle—sound like a boat coming in."

"Andy's line about using an empty pop bottle was another way of teasing Barney," says Jack. "Barney's excitement about Jim Lindsay's arrival kicked us into his misplacing his whistle, which in turned kicked us into Andy's pop bottle line."

Barney goes to the back room in search of his whistle. Andy talks to Barney with his back to the front door. Outside Jim has arrived unannounced.

The episode's script directions give Jim a detailed introduction: *A flashy, foreign sports car has just pulled up to the courthouse. Out steps JIM LINDSAY, the picture of show biz success. Jim is wearing a handsome sport shirt with open collar, and a bright hound's tooth sport jacket.*

Jim opens the courthouse front door and sneaks in. He is holding a guitar. He brings his arm up and comes down with a loud opening chord. Jim launches into a "bright" number. Andy turns, sees Jim, grabs his own guitar, and joins in.

"As in the first 'Guitar Player' show, we had to watch the timing," says Jack. "Whenever you do a show with musical numbers, you must shorten the scripts. So, the time is carefully watched from the first read-through to each scene filmed." (Jim and Andy's performance lasts fifty-two seconds.) "That way, we don't get surprised when the show is completed. As careful as we were, we'd often have to make a few more cuts."

Andy and Barney are overjoyed to see Jim. Barney, remembering the big welcoming plans, is concerned that Jim's early arrival may disrupt things. He insists the police escort not be canceled and leads Jim, with siren blasting, the short distance to the hotel.

The mayor and a group of citizens, including Aunt Bee and Opie, are waiting for Jim on the front porch of the hotel. After an official welcome, Jim enters the hotel. Before doing so, Aunt Bee invites him to supper that evening at the Taylors'.

In Jim's absence, Opie is left holding a handful of confetti he had planned to throw. Andy suggests Opie throw it at him. Opie does so and shouts, "Welcome home, Paw!"

"Andy and Opie's father-son relationship was one of the backbones of the show," says Jack. "The relationship started out with Andy and Opie walking toward the lake with their fishing gear in the opening titles. That opening shot, with Earle Hagen's great theme music, told you everything you needed to know about Andy and Opie. There have been a lot of father-son relationships on TV, but nothing to compare to this one. Charles and I were both parents who knew about fathers and sons. As dads, it was a pleasure to write scripts for this show."

That evening after supper, Jim and Andy play "The Midnight Special." Andy sings and adds custom lyrics about "Deputy Fife."

"We had nothing to do with selecting 'The Midnight Special,'" says Jack. "All we had in the script was 'Andy and Jim are in the midst of a duet.' Andy Griffith took it from there."

Barney compliments Jim on the "slick-looking duds," he is wearing. Jim says the guys in the band call his clothing a "set of threads." Afterward, Barney explains to Aunt Bee and Ellie that a set of threads is a suit.

"It's always funny when a square like Barney tries to be hip and 'with it,'" says Jack. "Don Knotts always played the big shot beautifully."

Aunt Bee asks, "Jimmy, what brought you here?"

"Aunt Bee calling Jim 'Jimmy' wasn't in the script," says Jack. "Frances Bavier came up with it during filming."

Jim explains that he has returned to Mayberry to rest. He also shares the news that he has left Bobby Fleet's band to "go out on his own."

Aunt Bee answers a knock on the door. A stranger asks to speak to Jim. Jim steps out onto the porch. The stranger identifies himself as a representative of a finance company and reminds Jim that he is behind on his car payments. The representative has come for Jim's car.

Jim hands over the keys and comes back inside. He says nothing about what has happened. Instead, he picks up his guitar and expresses his feelings through his fingers. He mournfully begins playing the blues.

"The script direction was *Jim starts picking a plaintive blues tune*," says Jack. "I imagine musical director Earle Hagen or the guitarist who you hear playing on the soundtrack took it from there."

The second act opens in Walker's Drug Store. Ellie is bagging the items Jim has picked out to purchase. The items, *shaving cream, a toothbrush, a magazine, and a carton of cigarettes* are carefully listed in the script.

Jim reaches for his wallet and discovers he has left it at the hotel. He tells Ellie to put the purchase on his tab. Ellie reluctantly does so and later shares with Andy her concern that Jim never pays for anything he buys.

"This episode was Elinor Donahue's last show," says Jack. "I don't recall any problems with Elinor. I thought she and her character fit into the show just fine. I never had a clue as to what factored into her departure."

Andy, growing suspicious, visits the barbershop. Floyd and Jason, the hotel clerk, tell him that Jim has been running up quite a bill at the barbershop and hotel. Jason also mentions that Jim hasn't received any work offers through the mail.

Barney enters. He has recently loaned Jim ten dollars. After hearing this, Andy decides it's time to talk with bandleader Bobby Fleet.

Andy learns from Bobby Fleet that Jim got cocky and wanted to become his partner. Fleet turned him down and Jim left in anger. Fleet confides that he would, however, be willing to take Jim back.

Andy goes to the hotel and confronts Jim with the truth. Jim refuses to meet with Fleet, who is waiting at the sheriff's office. Andy decides to take matters in hand. He arrests Jim for vagrancy and not paying his bills.

At the sheriff's office, Bobby Fleet agrees to pay Jim's outstanding bills and offers him a salary raise. Jim gladly shakes on the deal.

Andy advises Jim to "act like he's got some smarts now" and reminds him that he has "a set of threads, a little red car, and three guitars to feed."

Andy's words of wisdom were a rewrite by producer and story consultant Aaron Ruben. In the original script, Andy advises Jim to stop wearing custom-made shirts. He explains that the shirts fit so snug around the collar that "they been choking off all the common sense."

The episode concludes with Andy and Jim playing their guitars. Barney enjoys the music and suggests playing his harmonica during the next number.

As Barney speaks, Andy takes away his harmonica. Jim and Andy flank Barney, lift him straight off his feet, carry him into a cell, and lock the cell door.

Andy and Jim, with Barney securely separated from his harmonica, return to their instruments and happily resume the music.

"We enjoyed writing the epilogues," says Jack. "Since the story was finished at the end of the second act, it was always an enjoyable challenge to squeeze out one more joke."

"Bringing Up Opie"

Episode 32

First Broadcast on
May 22, 1961

Written by
**Jack Elinson and
Charles Stewart**

Directed by
Bob Sweeney

**"You can go out and plant two whole rows of spinach!
It'll be very educational."—AUNT BEE**

The opening of "Bringing Up Opie" is set in the sheriff's office. Andy is booking Otis Campbell, the town drunk. Otis, intoxicated and unsteady on his feet, stands before Andy.

Andy asks Otis to stop weaving long enough for him to read the violation, intoxication in a public place. Otis answers, "I'm not weaving . . . the room's moving."

"At this point in the series, Otis showing up drunk was a running thing," says Jack. "It was always fun writing these scenes and they were easy to do, because they were so outrageous."

"Our opening 'the room's moving' joke was cut out by producer Aaron Ruben," says Jack. "Perhaps it was cut out to shorten the scene, or Aaron may have felt it was more important to get right into the action that followed."

The "action" is described in the scene's script directions. After being sentenced, *Otis heads for the cell. He takes down the key ring to unlock the cell door and let himself in.*

Opie enters carrying his schoolbooks. He greets his "paw" and, upon seeing Otis, asks if he's "got a snootful again." Andy doesn't like to hear Opie use such words.

The details of Opie's physical movements are written in the script: *Opie swings his books onto the desk. Andy helps Opie up onto the desk. Opie sits with his legs crossed.*

Ronny Howard delivers his dialogue word for word as it is written in the script. Andy Griffith occasionally makes minor changes to give his dialogue a more natural conversational feel. He changes, "All right, we'll let it go at that" to "Well, I guess we'll have to let it go at that."

After Opie is seated, Andy tells the story of "The Beauty and the Beast." The "telling" lasts one minute and twenty seconds.

"I'm sure 'The Beauty and the Beast' story was a bit from one of Andy Griffith's comedy routines when he was doing stand-up," says Jack. "I know we didn't write it."

In his story, Andy describes the beast looking at Beauty with his "small, little, ugly eyes" and smiling a "small, sad, ugly smile."

Opie imitates what he is hearing. He squints his eyes as he imagines the beast would and smiles a "sad, ugly" smile.

"Opie squinting and smiling was not asked for in the script," says Jack. "The facial expressions and the close-up of them was the director, Bob Sweeney, at work."

As Andy is finishing the story, he notices that Opie's shoe is untied. He places Opie's foot on his knee and ties the lace as he promises the telling of "King Arthur and the Knights of the Round Table" tomorrow.

"Andy's tying Opie's shoelace was not in the script," says Jack. "It was either the director's idea or maybe it came from Andy Griffith. Perhaps Ronny Howard actually had a loose shoelace that Andy Griffith noticed and, staying in character, tied as the scene was being shot."

Aunt Bee enters and, seeing Opie, says he should be working on his homework instead of hanging around the sheriff's office. Opie explains that the students in his class asked the teacher questions until time for the bell to ring and the teacher didn't have time to give any homework assignments. The students "beat the rap."

"'Beat the rap' was a phrase we all learned from gangster movies starring the biggest gangster of all, Edward G. Robinson," says Jack. "The slang meaning of 'rap' is escaping punishment. That is what Opie thought he and his classmates had done."

Barney enters and, seeing that Opie is wearing his toy gun, challenges Opie to a fast draw. Barney then gives Opie some helpful suggestions on how to draw his gun faster.

Aunt Bee is not happy with this behavior or Opie's language. She tells Andy she received a call from the school principal earlier in the day. During lunch, Opie handcuffed one of his classmates to the flagpole.

Andy is shocked and, after questioning Opie, learns that Barney had given him an old, rusty pair of handcuffs.

"This is a story about how Andy's job as sheriff affects Opie," says Jack. "The boy is obviously thrilled that his dad is a lawman. What other kid in Mayberry can make that statement? So, Opie emulates Andy and Barney, who shows the kid how to draw a gun properly. If Opie didn't have to go to school, he'd spend all day in the sheriff's office, learning the business, getting ready to step into Andy's shoes when he grows up."

Later at home, Aunt Bee tells Andy that Opie is spending too much time at the jail. The jail is a bad influence that is affecting Opie's language and behavior negatively. Andy reluctantly agrees and goes to have a talk with Opie.

The script directions set the scene: *Opie is in bed, leafing through a comic book. As the door opens and Andy enters, he brightens.* Andy explains that he has come up to have *a little talk* with Opie. *Opie slides over and makes room for Andy to sit on the edge of the bed. Andy fidgets.*

Andy explains that the jail is no place for a little boy. Opie is not to come there anymore. Andy assures Opie that he is not trying to get rid of him. His desire is for Opie to be a normal, happy child.

Andy asks Opie to trust him and believe that what he is asking is for the best. Andy looks at Opie with eyes full of love, kisses his cheek, gently pats his head, and leaves with a sad smile on his face.

"The Andy and Opie bedroom scene was lovely, indeed," says Jack. "A father-son relationship can't get any better than that."

The next day, Andy and Barney are sitting in the sheriff's office. Otis is in his cell. All three are brooding. Barney looks at his wristwatch and sees it is almost time for Opie to be getting out of school. (Musical director Earl Hagen cleverly opens the scene with the ringing of three bells before the accompanying background music begins. The dismissal bell at Opie's school rings at three o'clock.)

The trio agrees they are a bad influence on the boy. Andy decides he will go on patrol. While he is out, he plans to drive by the house and see how things are going.

After Andy's departure, Barney asks Otis if he would like to learn the fast draw. Otis is not enthusiastic but takes the gun Barney hands him. Otis points the gun at Barney and demands to be let out of his cell. Barney grabs the gun out of Otis's hand.

Otis then explains the reason for his earlier lack of enthusiasm over learning the fast draw: "Even if I wanted to break out, you wouldn't let me."

"The Barney-Otis scene was a beauty," says Jack. "First, the situation was funny, Barney looking for someone to teach his gun moves. Second, the two actors playing the scene were dynamite! As a writer, you can't ask for better 'firepower.'"

At the Taylor home, Opie is in the kitchen with Aunt Bee, "dawdling" over his milk and cookies. Opie feels there is nothing to do. Aunt Bee takes a packet of Northrup King Company spinach seeds out of a drawer and suggests Opie go outside and plant "two whole rows." She believes the project would be educational.

Opie is not convinced. The thought of planting spinach is not exciting.

Opie is watering the newly planted seeds when he sees the patrol car drive up. He runs to the car. Andy grimaces when he learns Opie is planting spinach but agrees that it is educational. Before Andy drives away, Opie asks, "Paw, when you drive off, will you give her a blast on the siren?"

"Personally, I love spinach, but polls taken say people hate it," says Jack. "Popeye did a lot to recommend spinach for the building of muscles, but that doesn't impress Opie. We ended the scene with Opie asking Andy to blast the siren as he drives away, which was a great way to show how much he misses the sheriff's business."

Later in the sheriff's office, Andy and Barney see Opie outside waving at them through the window. Barney, forgetting the restriction, invites Opie in. Before he enters, Aunt Bee appears, picks Opie up, and carries him away.

Andy goes to the window and watches until Aunt Bee and Opie have disappeared. He reminds himself that he had planned to tell Opie the story of "King Arthur and the Knights of the Round Table."

"In this story, Aunt Bee's concern for Opie's welfare results in Andy and Opie's separation," says Jack. "Aunt Bee is the problem causer, but it would be difficult to ever believe that she was the villain. She is the sweetest lady who ever appeared on TV. She only wants the best for Opie. She's the mother in his life. We never intended for the audience to harbor any negative thoughts about America's Aunt Bee."

Later, Opie is outside. He sees a watering can but decides he can't take any more spinach tending. An overflowing garbage can is nearby. Opie sees a can on the ground, aimlessly kicks it, follows it into the street, and decides this could be a way to pass the afternoon.

Opie's can-kicking leads him to an abandoned mine shaft. Opie attempts to pry away one of the boards blocking the mine's entrance. His efforts cause a minor mine-shaft collapse.

"The mine caving in was a special effect we requested," says Jack. "It was more elaborate than what we usually asked for. I don't recall any cost concerns from producer Aaron Ruben."

Opie continues kicking the can. He eventually comes upon a boy eating apples. The boy, seeing the can, draws his leg back to give it a kick. Opie stops him, and the two make a deal—five apples in exchange for the can.

Opie eats the apples, lies down in the bed of a nearby Elm City delivery truck, and falls asleep. Later as night approaches, the truck's driver, unaware of Opie's presence, gets in and drives away.

Opie's can-kicking adventure, done entirely in pantomime, is detailed in the script's directions. The description of the action takes one and a half pages and lasts three minutes and forty seconds on screen. Musical director Earle Hagan's accompanying soundtrack features a variation of the opening theme song and is a perfect audio companion to the on-screen action.

"Pantomime is always a useful tool when you're showing a character alone and nobody to talk to," says Jack. "It's the only tool, outside of a voice-over, which was never done in the Griffith series."

"When I was a kid, kicking the can was considered a major sport," says Jack. "I don't think any boy in the country didn't kick a can. It was part of being a boy and the perfect way to start Opie on an odyssey."

Aunt Bee calls Andy in a panic. It is almost suppertime and Opie is missing. Andy and Barney go in search of Opie. Hours later, they arrive at the Taylor home without Opie. Soon afterward, the telephone rings. It is Sheriff Fred Jordon of Elm City calling with the news that Opie is with him.

Andy returns with Opie and asks him to tell Aunt Bee and Barney about his adventures. Andy tells Opie his "wandering off" is bad and that he will have to be punished.

Aunt Bee defends Opie. She feels Opie has gotten into trouble because he hasn't been seeing enough of his father. She would like Opie to resume visiting Andy at the jail and suggests that Andy and Barney correct the behavior that had previously been a negative influence.

Andy warns Opie that there will be consequences if he uses "a bad choice of words" like "snootful" when describing Otis. Andy says to Opie, "Do you understand, or do you want to spend the rest of your days planting spinach? And one other thing. If a certain little boy ever handcuffs another little boy to a flagpole, he'll not only be planting spinach, he'll be doing it standing up!"

"A father bawling out a child in a funny way is always rich stuff," says Jack. "Andy is angry, but not overly threatening."

Aunt Bee tells Opie she will fix him supper before he goes to bed. She promises to serve a special dessert with the meal—his favorite, apple pie.

The already apple-filled Opie grimaces at the thought.

The episode ends with Andy telling Opie, who has received a star for good behavior at school, the story of "King Arthur and the Knights of the Round Table." Barney listens to the story and disagrees with Andy about which of the knights was the bravest. The disagreement escalates until Opie heads toward the door. Before leaving, he tells Andy and Barney, "I'm going home. This place is a bad influence!"

"There's a discrepancy here," says Jack. "In my script, the 'Knights of the Round Table' piece came long before the end of the show. Andy tells the story to Barney after Opie has appeared at the doorway of the sheriff's office and isn't allowed inside. After Opie leaves, Barney asks Andy to tell him the story, which Andy does just to practice his storytelling. Nowhere in my script is Opie saying, 'I got another star for being good' and exiting saying, 'This place is a bad influence.' My script ends with Aunt Bee offering Opie a piece of apple pie and Opie looking sick."

"As for Andy and Barney's argument over which knight was the bravest, Sir Lancelot or Sir Gawain, I'm in the dark also," says Jack. "I'll bet on Andy and go with Sir Lancelot."

"Bringing Up Opie" Shooting Schedule

1st Day Monday, March 27, 1961

Locations: 40 Acres, Culver City and Stage 2, Desilu/Cahuenga

1—Andy's Yard (Residential Street)
   Andy out on patrol—stops by to see how Opie is doing
2—Andy's House Ext. Garden
   Opie ditches watering can—leaves
3—Sheriff Office interior—looking out front door (Coaltown Street—40 Acres)
   Opie wants to come in—not allowed
4—Roadway Ext.
   Opie starts kicking can

5—Ext. Farmhouse (Mudd House)
   Opie meets boy—gets apples—falls asleep in truck
6—Ext. Mine Entrance
   Cave collapses
   Move to Stage 2 Desilu/Cahuenga
7—Int. Sheriff Office
   Booking Otis—telling "Beauty and Beast" story to Opie—Aunt Bee says jail bad influence
8—Int. Sheriff Office
   All miss Opie—Barney does gun bit with Otis
End of Day 1

2nd Day Tuesday, March 28, 1961

Location: Stage 2, Desilu/Cahuenga

1—Int. Sheriff Office
   See Opie pass by—Andy tells Barney "King Arthur" story (deleted from the finished episode)
2—Int. Sheriff Office
   Epilogue—Andy tells story
3—Int. Sheriff Office
   Post Toasties commercial (Broadcast at end of "Bringing Up Opie")

4—Int. Sheriff Office
   Sanka Coffee commercial
5—Int. Sheriff Office
   Andy gets a call from Aunt Bee
6—Int. Sheriff Office
   Opie wants to come in—not allowed
End of Day 2

3rd Day Wednesday, March 29, 1961

Location: Stage 2, Desilu/Cahuenga

1—Int. Kitchen
   Get call from Elm City
2—Int. Kitchen
   Post Raisin Bran commercial
3—Int. Kitchen
   Aunt Bee sends Opie outside to plant spinach
4—Int. Kitchen
   Opie bored—Aunt Bee sends Opie outside to water garden

5—Int. Kitchen
   Aunt Bee calls Andy
6—Int. Opie Room
   Andy tells Opie to stay away from office
7—Int. Living Room
   Opie tells what he did that afternoon—Aunt Bee suggests Opie visit the sheriff's office
8—Int. Dining Room
   Aunt Bee telling Andy that the sheriff's office is a bad influence
End of Day 3

Season 1 Wrap-Up

"Bringing Up Opie" was the last first-season episode produced and broadcast. Its production concluded on the evening of Wednesday, March 29.

The season began with the cast read-through of "The New Housekeeper" script on Thursday, July 21, 1960. The next nine episodes were produced on a weekly basis before the first company layoff, which ran from September 28 through October 4.

Production resumed on October 5. Eleven episodes were produced before a Christmas/New Year layoff that began on December 22 and ran through January 4, 1961. Six additional episodes were produced before a February 16 through February 22 layoff. The final five episodes, including "Bringing Up Opie," were produced following the February layoff.

The summer layoff was scheduled for "March 30 THRU ?." (Production of the second-season episode "Barney's Replacement" began on Thursday, July 13, 1961, with the cast read-through of the script.)

The May 22, 1961, broadcast of "Bringing Up Opie" was followed by five weeks of reruns. The rerun order and dates of broadcast were "Andy the Matchmaker" on May 29, "Andy and the Gentleman Crook" on June 5, "The Horse Trader" on June 12, "Manhunt" on June 19, and "Cyrano Andy" on June 26. The five weeks of reruns were followed by network summer replacement programming.

The Andy Griffith Show's first season was broadcast by the CBS network on Monday nights at 9:30 p.m. The series ended its first season ranked fourth in national television ratings with an estimated weekly audience of 13.12 million viewers.

The Andy Griffith Show's second season began with the broadcast of "Opie and the Bully" on October 2, 1961. (The episode followed "Barney's Replacement" in production order. Episodes were not broadcast in order of production.)

1961–1962

"Barney's Replacement"

"You better gird your loins, Buster! You've got a fight on your hands!"
—BARNEY FIFE warning temporary deputy Bob Rogers

Loins—The part of the body on each side of the spinal cord between the hip bone and the false ribs.

Note in a letter postmarked June 19, 2000: "Sorry to report that Charles Stewart passed away a few days ago after a long illness. He was 85."—JACK

Episode 33

First Broadcast on October 9, 1961

Written by
Jack Elinson and Charles Stewart

Directed by
Bob Sweeney

Mark Miller
Guest Stars as Bob Rogers

"This script came out of a meeting we had between seasons with producer Aaron Ruben and executive producer Sheldon Leonard," says Jack. "When the meeting finished, we came away with twelve stories, which was always our goal. Sheldon also used this system on the other series he produced. It was an effective plan and always got Charles and I off to a good start."

"Barney's Replacement" begins with Andy at his desk going through the mail. He extracts a wanted poster and reads aloud, "Wanted for armed robbery." He then comments on the criminal pictured on the poster, "They get younger every year."

"Since this was forty years ago, it's surprising that we came up with 'They get younger every year,'" says Jack, "given the horror of school shootings going on these days. We sadly were way ahead of our time."

Andy goes to the bulletin board to post the notice. Barney, who oversees the board, stops Andy.

Andy notices the poster of a criminal that has been captured. News of the capture was on television and in the newspaper.

Barney, however, refuses to remove the poster until he receives official notification in the mail. Barney mutters about taking the poster down and eventually accuses Andy of "blowing his top." Barney angrily removes the poster, picks up a broom, and heads out the door.

"This opening scene was a good way to get the story started," says Jack. "This story centered upon Andy finding fault with Barney and Barney's fear of

being replaced. The out-of-date poster was the first thing to put Barney on the defensive."

Opie enters. He saw Barney "sweeping clear down the street," and asks Andy what's wrong. Andy explains that Barney is a "little excited," and believes the sweeping may be a good thing. "If Barney sweeps as far as Walker's Drug Store, then maybe he'll go in and get himself a soda and cool off."

Andy Griffith marked out the name "Walker" from his script. This may be in response to Elinor Donahue and her character Ellie Walker's departure from the series. Andy also changes "soda" to "bottle of pop."

"In New York, we called a soft drink a 'bottle of soda,'" says Jack. "I always assumed the rest of the country did the same. I was surprised that the phrase was changed to 'bottle of pop.'"

A "bottle of pop" may sound strange to many southerners. In central North Carolina, soft drinks were most often referred to by their brand names. Barney would get a Coke or Pepsi at the drugstore. *The Griffith Show*, however, could not use actual soft-drink names because of advertising restrictions.

Andy affectionately tickles Opie on the stomach and sends him off to school with the instructions to "Do a good day's work and act like somebody."

"The 'act like somebody' line is interesting," says Jack. "When I saw my children off to school, I used to say, 'Be smarter today than you were yesterday.' 'Act like somebody' wasn't in our script. [The line likewise does not appear in Andy Griffith's working copy of the script.] I imagine it may have been a spontaneous comment that fit the scene and could have been added during rehearsal or when the scene was being filmed."

Later in the day, Andy and Barney are on patrol. Andy notices a stop sign hanging loose and asks Barney why he hasn't fixed it. Barney doesn't want to make the repair until he receives the work order from the county.

Andy and Barney arrive at the sheriff's office. A visitor's car is parked by the front door. Barney, driving, eases the squad car to a stop and lightly touches the bumper of the parked car.

Barney becomes defensive when Andy comments on his driving. He feels Andy has been picking on him lately and he can't do anything right.

Andy and Barney enter the sheriff's office. Bob Rogers is waiting inside. Rogers is *a youngish, alert-looking fellow in a neat business suit.*

Rogers introduces himself and explains that he has been sent by the State Attorney's Office. Ralph Baker, an old friend of Andy's, would like Rogers, a lawyer, to observe Andy and Barney's daily activities. While in Mayberry, Rogers will serve as a temporary deputy.

"I wasn't aware of and am amazed we named Andy's friend Ralph Baker," says Jack. "Ralph Baker was the name we gave to the boy Opie handcuffed to the flagpole in 'Bringing Up Opie.' This was a goof that nobody spotted."

Barney later visits Thelma Lou. He is upset and tells Thelma Lou that Andy has gotten a replacement for him. Barney knows Mayberry is not a two-deputy town and realizes he is "on his way out."

Barney thinks the situation through and tells Thelma Lou he will not help train Rogers. He will "hold back" and let Rogers "swim alone."

"In the filmed episode, Thelma Lou has her hair covered, is wearing an apron, and holding a cleaning cloth," says Jack. "In our script, we didn't indicate that she was house cleaning during Barney's visit. I'm sure this realistic touch was the director Bob Sweeney's idea."

"We gave Barney an out-of-date phrase in this scene," says Jack. "Barney, referring to himself training Rogers, says, 'Not on your tintype.' A tintype was the 1850s equivalent of a 1960s Polaroid instant photograph. The phrase is like the oath, 'Not on my life.' The 'tintype' line is proof that a writer never knows what obscure phrase will come to mind when writing dialogue."

The next morning, Rogers is carefully studying the bulletin board. Barney enters, notices Rogers, and says he is too busy to explain the proper procedure for posting wanted posters.

Rogers, undeterred, has found a "keeping-the-bulletin-board-up-to-date system" in the Law Officer's Manual. He reads the system's guidelines aloud as Andy enters. Andy feels Rogers has discovered a "pretty good system."

Barney, irritated by the praise, says, "I haven't got time to discuss trivial trivialities," and storms out.

"I can't remember if we referred to an actual Law Officer's manual for the bulletin board guidelines or just made them up," says Jack. "'Trivial trivialities' is a silly combination of words spoken by Barney, who is flustered by the situation. It's certainly not great English, which is what makes it funny."

Later in the day, Barney sees Rogers inside the squad car checking out the equipment. Barney slides into the car and begins a technical explanation of the two-way radio operation. Barney picks up the microphone and says, "You talk in here." He points to the speaker in the car's dash and says, "You listen in here."

Rogers points to a switch above the microphone. Barney slaps his hand away. The switch operates the siren. With an exaggerated motion, Barney uses his index finger to flip the switch on. The siren starts up. Barney flips the switch off. The siren continues blasting!

Jack and Charles's script directions describe what follows: *Barney looks at Rogers in exasperation. Climbs out of the car, slamming the door, and opens the hood. Rogers gets out to observe and, by now, several onlookers have gathered, along with Andy.*

Barney suggests cutting the wire to the siren. Rogers reaches for a pencil from Barney's pocket, reaches under the hood, and taps the condenser box. The siren immediately turns off.

"Barney's siren-operation instructions were very funny," says Jack. "We either researched how to stop a stuck police siren, or somebody who was knowledgeable about cars told us how it works."

Later inside the sheriff's office, Rogers shows off a statistical chart he has made. The chart should predict the pattern of law violations for the year. Rogers, reading from his chart, predicts the type and number of future violations. Among the violations is a wife-beating case, a violation that seldom occurs in Mayberry.

"We made up the business about the chart that Rogers shows Andy," says Jack. "Rogers was kind of a square guy, so we figured someone like that would come up with a statistical chart."

Andy and Barney are skeptical about the chart's accuracy. The telephone rings. The caller reports that "Ad Simpkins just gave his wife what for."

Barney is eager to get on the case, but Andy stops him. Andy feels "Bob" should investigate the reported violation since he predicted it. Barney reluctantly hands over the keys to the squad car.

Insight into a character's emotions and motivation was often given through script directions. Barney, battling insecurities, is eager to respond to the reported violation in an attempt *to salvage some slight importance.*

The script's directions are sometimes very interesting. In the script, Barney is to *walk over to Rogers and, like General Lee surrendering to General Grant, hand over the keys.*

That night at Thelma Lou's, ~~Barney~~ discusses his ~~work situation~~. ~~Throughout the conversation,~~ Barney's ~~wrists~~ are ~~wrapped in yarn~~, whi~~ch Thelma Lou rolls into a ball~~.

~~Barney admits~~ that ~~Rogers~~ is an excell~~ent deputy~~, and ~~he feels like a "fifth wheel"~~ on the way out. As he and ~~Thelma Lou talks,~~ Barney comes ~~to the realization that Andy~~ is ~~too good of~~ a friend to ~~fire him~~ and ma~~kes the decisi~~on to help And~~y out~~. He ~~will "bow out."~~

"~~The whole~~ wrapping ~~yarn stuff was in the script~~," says Jack. "It gave us a bit of humor while the discussion was going on. Ba~~rney was nervously twist~~ing his ~~hand~~s as he talked and ~~eventual~~ly beco~~mes~~ hopelessly c~~uffed by the~~ yarn. The foul~~ed up yar~~n, rath~~er~~ than what Barney says, is Thelma Lou's primary concern. Thelma Lou, however, eventually becomes aw~~are of the serious~~ness of the conversation. The twi~~sted yar~~n and Thelma Lou's ~~redirecte~~d conc~~ern~~ are ~~deleted from the film~~ed scene."

The n~~ext day, Barney places his c~~ap, ~~tie~~, ba~~dge~~, ~~gun~~, and ho~~lster~~ on A~~ndy's desk~~. He admits that he is resigning because of the "new man." Barney explains that he has been thinking about stepping away for some time but hasn't because he didn't want to leave Andy short-handed.

"~~Barney deciding to quit~~ to save Andy ~~from firing~~ him is a real ~~gesture~~ to a good friend," s~~ays Jack~~. "~~Barney gives reasons~~ for the resi~~gnation~~, but ~~down deep he's hurt~~ about the whol~~e thing.~~"

~~Barney gives another~~ reas~~on for~~ his resignatio~~n~~. He tells Andy tha~~t he and Thelma Lou will~~ "be hi~~tching up one of these day~~s," and aft~~erward~~, he ~~doesn't want Thelma Lou worrying~~ about the da~~nger~~s he m~~ay face while~~ "~~doing lawman's work.~~"

"For whatever reason, there was never any set policy on whether Barney would ever get married," says Jack. "This flexibility, which applied to Andy also, allowed us to have Barney mention the possibility of a future marriage. Having Barney or Andy married would have given us new material for future scripts."

Andy is speechless in response to Barney's resignation. The two sadly confess that they will miss one another, and Barney bravely departs.

"Andy's response to Barney quitting was not in our script," says Jack. "It was a nice addition, likely written by story consultant Aaron Ruben. The two men acknowledging that they will miss the other is evidence of their deep friendship."

Barney soon takes his place in "big business." Wearing a salt-and-pepper business suit and carrying a vacuum cleaner, Barney knocks on Clara Rush's front door. (The character played by Hope Summers is later given the last name Edwards.)

"Barney's civilian clothes weren't scripted by us," says Jack. "The salt-and-pepper suit, bow tie, and white hat Barney wears were a combination of Don Knotts's, Aaron Ruben's, and the wardrobe person's thoughts."

Clara thinks Barney is pretending to be a vacuum-cleaner salesman and playing a joke on her. She is busy, however, and quickly dismisses Barney.

Barney's next prospective customer is Emma Watson. Emma listens to Barney's vacuum-cleaner spiel, but she is more interested in why Barney is not wearing his uniform.

Emma, still thinking of Barney as a deputy, asks if the vacuum cleaner Barney carries is a new type of gun. To her it looks like a bazooka. Emma is familiar with the weapon. She once received a photograph of a bazooka from her nephew while he was in the war. (This interesting dialogue was deleted from the filmed episode.)

Emma eventually understands that Barney is not a deputy and becomes angry when she remembers that he once arrested her for jaywalking.

"We gave Emma a confused understanding of Barney's work identity," says Jack. "She finally accepts that Barney is a salesman. This causes her to wonder if he was ever a real deputy. She remembers that he once arrested her for jaywalking. The jaywalking she had in mind resulted in her arrest in the very first episode, 'The New Housekeeper.'"

Later, Barney, a defeated salesman, walks slowly along the street. He sees Andy and quickly straightens his posture and quickens his pace to look successful.

Andy asks Barney to rejoin the Mayberry Police Force. Barney refuses and says he doesn't want to give up the income from his vacuum-cleaner sales.

Andy reaches for Barney's order book, thumbs through it, and finds only blank pages. Barney explains that Andy is looking at his second order book. His first book is full of orders. Andy is puzzled and watches Barney slowly walk away.

"It wasn't difficult for Andy to know that Barney was striking out," says Jack. "It wasn't just the evidence of the empty order that convinced him. Andy also believed that Barney's failure as a salesman was inevitable."

Andy visits Thelma Lou to confirm his suspicions. Thelma Lou admits that Barney never wanted to be a salesman. Andy responds, "That boy weighs about a hundred pounds, and fifty of it is proud." Andy shakes his head and repeats the word "proud" six more times.

In the script, Andy uses the word "stubborn" to describe Barney and repeats the word twice.

The word "stubborn" is crossed out in Andy Griffith's working copy of the script. "Proud" is written in the margin in handwriting that is noticeably different from Andy's. The writing is most likely that of script continuity person Hazel Hall.

"I didn't realize that 'stubborn' had been replaced with 'proud,' says Jack. "What makes the line to Thelma Lou so good is the punctuation that Andy Griffith used in his delivery."

Andy knows he must get Barney back on the force. The way to accomplish this presents itself when Rogers approaches Andy on the street and asks if Barney applied for a license to sell door-to-door. Rogers informs Andy that Barney, selling without a license, is in violation of the Green River Ordinance.

Andy, believing that Barney will be outraged if arrested, sends Rogers to bring him in.

"The 'Green River Ordinance' was fictitious," says Jack. "We figured there must be a required license to sell door-to-door, but we didn't want to take the time to look it up, so we made up the name."

Rogers returns with Barney and locks him in a cell. Rogers tells Andy he is not surprised by Barney's violation. It was predicted in his charts.

Barney is angered that Rogers sees him as a figure on a chart rather than as a human being. Andy heads toward the back room as Barney tells Rogers that his concern with statistics has made him ignorant of people. Barney finishes his tirade and declares that he will fight to get his job back.

Andy returns with Barney's uniform. Barney, seeing the uniform, smiles, thanks Andy, and, with a sense of duty, goes to the back room to put the uniform on.

"When Andy hands Barney back his uniform, the script reads, *Barney gathers it awkwardly in his arms*," says Jack. "The pride Barney showed in the filmed episode was the wonderful Don Knotts at work."

The episode ends with Rogers saying goodbye. Barney is writing Rogers a ticket as he and Andy step outside the sheriff's office. The ticket is for illegal parking. Rogers, now dressed as a civilian, has parked his car in a spot reserved for police parking only.

Barney eventually tears the ticket up and reminds Rogers not to get too technical whenever he works with people.

Rogers drives away. Andy looks at Barney with admiration. Barney too has learned an important lesson.

The filmed episode concludes with a low-angle shot. The camera looks up at Barney as he confidently struts across the street, content in his role of bringing law and order to Mayberry.

Barney will keep the lesson he has learned in his heart, but in his head, he is still a by-the-book deputy whose behavior is often determined by his emotions and insecurities.

"Andy and the Woman Speeder"

Episode 35

First Broadcast on
October 16, 1961

Written by
**Charles Stewart
and Jack Elinson**

Directed by
Bob Sweeney

Jean Hagen
Guest Stars as
Elizabeth Crowley

"I'm real disappointed in my deputy. He's a law officer and ought to know better."—ANDY TAYLOR

"Charles and I were very aware this script was similar to *The Andy Griffith Show* pilot. (The pilot, 'Danny Meets Andy Griffith,' was written by Arthur Stander and broadcast February 15, 1960, as an episode of *The Danny Thomas Show*.) We thought it was a good idea to do this version of the story using a good-looking woman instead of a not-so-good-looking Danny Thomas. The change gave the show a whole different slant."

"Andy and the Woman Speeder" begins with Andy, Opie, and Floyd walking to the squad car. The car, with the trunk open, is parked on the roadside near a woodsy area. The three are carrying fishing equipment.

The scene's script directions have Andy *opening the turtleback*.

A turtleback is a turtle-shaped back cover of a vehicle and is an unusual way to refer to the truck of the squad car. (In the third-season episode "Convicts at Large," Barney and Floyd will use Floyd's turtlebacked car on a fishing trip.)

Andy evaluates the day's catch and feels there are enough fish for a "mighty fine fish fry." Opie responds, "Don't forget what Uncle Barney will be bringing in." "Uncle" appears in the script but was deleted from the filmed dialogue.

Barney eventually arrives from his secret fishing place. He is wonderfully dressed as a fisherman and carries a fish creel. The script directions instruct Andy to open Barney's creel and take out a frog.

The filmed discovery of the frog is very different! Andy takes the creel from a protesting Barney. Barney takes the creel back. Andy grabs the creel away from Barney. Barney retrieves the creel, and Floyd quickly snatches it away. Barney slaps Floyd's hand and recaptures the creel. Andy takes the creel from Barney; Barney takes it back; Floyd takes the creel from Barney; and Andy, after taking the creel from Floyd, opens it and takes out a frog. Andy, in response to what he has pulled from the creel, calls Barney "old frog man."

The creel exchange takes fifteen seconds on-screen. The exchange is an un-

scripted "bit" of physical comedy that was carefully choreographed prior to filming. Andy calling Barney "old frog man" was not in the script.

"The opening gave us immediate laughs right at the beginning," says Jack. "Barney, even keeping the frog, is funny."

Suddenly, a Ford Thunderbird convertible drives by doing seventy in a forty-five-mile-per-hour zone. The four fishermen jump into the squad car and give chase. The driver of the speeding car eventually stops. The driver is *an attractive girl, Liz Crowley.* Andy asks to see her driver's license and discovers Miss Crowley is from Washington, DC. Andy feels that someone from the capital of the United States should set a better example.

"We indicated that Liz Crowley is driving a red sports car in the script," says Jack. "Andy's reference to Washington was interesting. He assumes that everyone who lives in the capital is always a law-abiding citizen. This is funny by itself, given the fact that laws are broken in that town every day."

Miss Cowley apologizes for speeding, explains that she is in a hurry to get back to Washington, and starts to drive away. Andy stops her. He gives Miss Crowley a speeding ticket and informs her that she will have to appear in court.

Miss Crowley's demeanor immediately changes. She accuses Andy of setting speed traps for out-of-state vehicles and demands to see Mayberry's Justice of the Peace.

The scene quickly cuts to Andy sitting at his desk. He turns around a desk sign that reads "Sheriff" to read "Justice of the Peace" and raps a gavel.

Miss Crowley is shocked to discover Andy is the Justice of the Peace. Andy fines Miss Crowley ten dollars for speeding. She is surprised that the fine is so low and accuses Andy of having a foolproof system.

Andy fines Miss Crowley another ten dollars for the insinuation. Miss Crowley believes Andy has no intention of letting her go until he has drained her dry. Hearing this, Andy fines her another ten dollars for contempt.

Miss Crowley compares Andy to Western outlaw Jesse James. Andy charges her with insulting the dignity of his robes. The fine for robe insulting is thirty dollars. The fees total sixty dollars, but Andy agrees to settle for twenty-five.

"By this time in the series, Charles and I had fallen into the funny way Andy expressed himself," says Jack. "'There you went and contempted again' and 'fined another ten dollars for robe insulting' were examples of our new-learned grasp of southern jargon. Having Andy playing games with the English language was always on our minds."

Miss Crowley refuses to pay the fine. She decides to plea "not guilty" and stand trial before "an honest-to-goodness judge." Miss Crowley will appear in Mayor's Court and is told by Andy that she is entitled to legal counsel.

Andy and Barney discuss the availability of Mayberry's two lawyers, Rafe Peterson and Clarence Polk. (The script's cast list includes another lawyer, Charles Carey, who was to appear on-screen. This character was later dropped.) Peterson is currently selling aluminum siding but Polk, who has not yet started umpiring ball games for the summer, may be available. Miss Crowley decides to pass on these "brilliant barristers" and act as her own counsel.

"I really don't know if there are Mayor's Courts in small towns," says Jack. "We just made it up because the actor who portrayed the mayor was part of our cast and very available. The conversation about available lawyers is perfect small-town stuff. It's very Mayberry."

Miss Crowley's decision to appear in Mayor's Court causes a problem. The mayor doesn't hold court until the next day. Miss Crowley will have to be kept in jail overnight. Andy is not prepared for "lady customers." He suggests Miss Crowley pay the fee and save everybody a "heap of trouble."

Miss Crowley stubbornly refuses. Andy decides he can be just as stubborn. He orders Barney to lock up Miss Crowley and buy some pink towels.

Later, Andy and Barney arrive at the sheriff's office and find the front door locked. Andy bangs on the door and calls for Aunt Bee, who is serving as Miss

Crowley's matron. Inside, Andy and Barney find *the prisoner seated before a temporary vanity, combing her hair, a very attractive sight. A less attractive sight is a temporary clothesline hung with stockings and other feminine unmentionables.*

Aunt Bee and Miss Crowley have become friends and are on a first-name basis. The two women have made a list of needed items, nail polish, and cologne. Barney reluctantly takes the list, and he and Aunt Bee depart.

Andy approaches the cell and points out that Miss Crowley has Aunt Bee "eating out of her hands." Miss Crowley denies this and thanks Andy for sending Aunt Bee to serve as her matron. This word of thanks opens the door to more cordial conversation. Miss Crowley and Andy eventually agree that they wish the "whole thing" hadn't happened.

Andy lets Miss Crowley out of the cell and the two attempt to start over. Miss Crowley happily agrees to pay the original ten-dollar fine. Andy reminds her the fine is now twenty-five dollars. Miss Crowley becomes furious, redeclares she will take the matter to court, returns to the cell, and locks herself inside.

Later, Barney returns with the items he has purchased. Miss Crowley thanks him and sees an opportunity to charm Barney.

She begins by calling Barney "Sheriff." The script directions for this error are *It is eight to one this is no honest mistake.*

Miss Crowley next asks Barney to break the twine that binds the package containing the purchased items. Barney complies and Miss Crowley acknowledges his strength. In response, Barney *hunches and rolls his shoulders like a fighter.*

Miss Crowley leads Barney into a discussion of his love life. She assures him that there are plenty of women who would like to be his girl.

Miss Crowley ends her charm-weaving by telling Barney he has "an amazing resemblance to Frank Sinatra." Hearing this, Barney *tilts his hat forward, swaggers à la Sinatra,* and begins singing, "It's a quarter to three . . ."

"I loved Sinatra's singing, but I didn't care for him as a person," says Jack. "Barney doing Sinatra worked great for us and for Don Knotts. Don's imitation was so funny!"

Later, Aunt Bee has turned the cell *into a beauty parlor.* She is combing out Miss Crowley's hair as Floyd Lawson enters. Floyd has dropped by to see how the case is going.

Floyd drifts over to the cell to watch the combing with *professional interest.* Miss Crowley sees this as an opportunity *to turn the witness to her side.* She asks Floyd to comb out her hair. She looks at Floyd's *artistic hands* and is sure he has the *touch.*

The script directions describe the response to the compliment: *Floyd practically swoons with the thrill of the opportunity. He is excited, and a thoroughly hooked sucker. He combs away with joyous zest.*

"Speaking of funny, Floyd was right behind Barney," says Jack. "The hair stuff played like a charm. Charles and I had such fun writing Crowley vamping these two guys."

Later, the mayor's court is called to order. Floyd Lawson is the first witness. Miss Crowley starts the questioning. Floyd reports that he has been having trouble with his glasses and is not sure he saw Miss Crowley speeding. Upon hearing this, Andy has no other questions.

Barney is the next witness. Andy requests to question the witness first. Barney becomes uncomfortable on the stand and states that it is hard to tell how fast a car is going when the observer is standing still. Barney feels Andy is "making too much out of this."

Opie is the final witness. He holds a baseball signed by the New York Yankees while he sits in the witness chair. The ball was given to him by Miss Crowley.

Andy, seeing the ball, realizes he is defeated. He has no further questions. The mayor dismisses the case.

"The fun continued in the trial scene with all the turncoats really turning against Andy," says Jack. "The trial was a switch from *The Danny Thomas Show* spin-off. Story consultant Aaron Ruben liked the difference and never felt the similarity in storylines was a bad idea."

"Even though I had once lived in the Bronx, which is where Yankee Stadium is, I wasn't a Yankees fan," says Jack. "I rooted for the Giants, who played in Manhattan. My loyalty to the Bronx was nonexistent. It pained me to give Opie a Yankees-signed baseball, but the Giants left New York for California in 1958 and it seemed more likely that Miss Crowley, living in Washington, would have easier access to an East Coast team."

After the dismissal, Andy tells Miss Crowley that she has outsmarted justice and turned three people against him whom he believed would never leave his side. Miss Crowley suddenly is not so happy over her victory.

Later, Barney assists Miss Crowley with her luggage. She is leaving Mayberry. Prior to driving away, she apologizes for the "rift" she has caused between Andy and Barney.

The script directions narrate what happens next. Andy exits the sheriff's office. *He just looks at Miss Crowley and, turning away, walks toward the patrol car. Miss Crowley suddenly gets an idea. She shoves the car into gear and tromps on the accelerator. Andy and Barney jump into the squad car and roar off after the speeder.*

Andy catches up to Miss Crowley, and both pull to a stop. Andy imposes the usual fine of ten dollars. Miss Crowley pays the fine and twenty-five dollars more from the previous case. She admits she won that case by "highly questionable methods."

Andy gladly accepts the money and says he feels better about her former conduct. Miss Crowley feels the same.

"This was about the only way we could wrap up the story," says Jack. "It was important to have Crowley show her good side."

Before driving away, Miss Crowley reminds Barney that he bears an amazing resemblance to Frank Sinatra.

The remark stays in Barney's mind. Later, in the sheriff's office, he tilts his hat forward, loosens his shoulders, begins snapping his fingers, and breaks into a rendition of "One for My Baby." Sadly for Barney, Andy doesn't recognize the singer or the song.

"No way would we have missed the opportunity to milk the Sinatra bit just one more time," says Jack. "It was the perfect way to end the script."

"Barney on the Rebound"

Episode 36

First Broadcast on
December 30, 1961

Written by
**Charles Stewart
and Jack Elinson**

Directed by
Bob Sweeney

Jackie Coogan
Guest Stars as
George Stevens

Beverly Tyler
Guest Stars as
Melissa (Gladys)
Stevens

"Why would a girl like Melissa want to get involved with a squirt?"
—ANDY TAYLOR

The "Barney on the Rebound" script begins with Barney and Thelma Lou arriving at the sheriff's office. Barney parks the squad car, gets out, walks around the car, and opens the passenger door for Thelma Lou.

In the filmed episode, Barney and Thelma Lou open their own doors. The changed action plays into the storyline. Barney will soon be eagerly opening the car door for another woman.

Thelma Lou thanks Barney for the ride with a kiss on the cheek. A man passing by notices the kiss. Barney is embarrassed and tells Thelma Lou a deputy should not be kissed in public.

The man who notices the kiss is Thomas Yaqoob. Yaqoob used the stage name Tom Jacobs and appeared as an extra in more than sixty *The Andy Griffith Show* episodes. Yaqoob/Jacobs was a brother of Danny Thomas.

Barney sees a car parking directly behind the squad car. The car stops in a restricted area marked "Sheriff's Parking Only." Thelma Lou departs to do her grocery shopping, leaving Barney to handle the violation.

The driver of the illegally parked car is new Mayberry resident Melissa Stevens.

"Melissa is described in the script as *a rather striking looking blonde, and just a bit too flashy for Mayberry*," says Jack. "The 'head-to-toe' once-over Barney gives Melissa wasn't written in the script. Don Knotts did it as a natural reaction at the sight of a beautiful girl."

Thelma Lou exits from the grocery store in time to see Barney enraptured with Melissa. Her grocery shopping is completed too quickly to be realistic. Thelma Lou has picked out her groceries and had them bagged, totaled, and paid for in forty-two seconds!

Melissa is looking for the post office. Barney eagerly assists her. He opens her car door and gives an elaborate "follow me" signal. Barney gets into the squad car and, with the squad car siren blasting, makes a U-turn. Melissa follows. The

~~procession~~ comes to a stop ~~in front of the post~~ office located directly ~~across the~~ ~~street. Barney~~ jumps out, ~~opens Melissa's door~~ for her, and ~~taking her arm, es-~~ ~~corts~~ her into the ~~post office.~~

"Rereading the script, I ~~cracked up at the U-turn~~ to the ~~post~~ office across the ~~street," says Jack~~. "I ~~had completely~~ forgotten that ~~bit~~. It certainly was ~~fun to~~ ~~write.~~"

Later, an ~~unhappy~~ Thelma ~~Lou~~ tells Andy ~~what happened~~. She ~~feels Barney~~ was acting ~~as if he was leading~~ Melissa "dow~~n the Oregon Trail~~."

"~~Thelma Lou's reference~~ to the ~~Oregon Trail~~ is the result of us looking for a place as ~~far away from Mayberry as possible~~," says ~~Jack~~. "It could have been India or ~~China~~. The effort ~~Barney~~ ~~put into directing Melissa~~ was appropriate for a ~~much longer trip~~."

~~Barney~~ enters the ~~sheriff's office still aglow~~ from his time spent with ~~Melissa~~. When ~~Thelma Lou~~ asks about the ~~girl, Barney~~ gives a very ~~detailed description~~ of ~~Melissa~~ and her father, ~~George. Barney~~ also says he spent time pointing out all the post office's ~~highlights to Melissa~~.

"It's ~~funny~~ to see a ~~guy~~ talking himself into trouble and not realize it," says Jack. "The ~~huge~~ amount of detail Barney knows ~~about Melissa~~ had me on the floor. ~~Barney~~ ~~compares~~ the Mayberry post office to one in a big city. His idea of '~~big~~' is ~~hilarious~~. Andy tries to shut Barney up, but it's too late, Barney has fallen ~~down the well~~."

~~Barney~~ and Thelma Lou begin arguing. Andy advises Barney to "drop the subject." The argument escalates. Barney accuses Thelma Lou of being jealous. ~~Thelma Lou~~ tells him that she and he are both as "free as birds" and storms out.

~~Later~~ in the day, ~~Barney~~ returns to the sheriff's office. Things are no better between him and ~~Thelma Lou~~. Andy listens and advises that Thelma Lou will eventually simmer down and then Barney can enjoy the kissing and hugging of making up. Andy feels that the couple's current argument serves as good practice for married life.

"We always felt that Andy should have his own way of saying things," says Jack. "Andy telling Barney that 'Thelma Lou got a mad on at you' is an example. Andy has always thrown curves at the English language, grammar be damned. Andy equating Barney's fighting with Thelma Lou as good practice for married life is funny because Andy thinks he's said something positive about their argument."

A frustrated Barney vows that he is through with women. The telephone rings. Barney answers. He is all business until he recognizes Melissa's voice. She invites him to supper and Barney cordially accepts. Andy warns Barney that this will only make Thelma Lou madder.

That evening after supper, Barney draws upon his talents to entertain Melissa and her father. He tells a "two five-hundred-pound canaries" joke. Melissa and her father laugh with gusto. Barney, *still pounding the joke*, repeats the punchline.

Next Barney causally takes out his harmonica, and after announcing selections from his repertory, he performs.

"The titles in Barney's repertory were all real songs," says Jack. "One of the songs, 'Kitten on the Keys,' was normally played on piano and prized by piano players for showing off their fingerwork. Its inclusion in Barney's repertory was funny because he was going to perform it on harmonica. As for the 'two five-hundred-pound canaries' joke, we tried to make up the worst joke we could think of for Barney to tell. I think we succeeded."

The next morning, Barney enters the sheriff's office still pleased with his previous night's success. He reports that he didn't "hit the sack until almost ten-thirty." Andy advises Barney to forget Melissa and make up with Thelma Lou. Barney ignores the advice. He already has another date with Melissa.

"If I had it to write over, I'd make Barney's bedtime nine-thirty," says Jack. (This is an interesting comment since Barney's original scripted bedtime, which was changed in the filmed episode, was eleven-thirty.) "For some reason, going to bed late is a lot more sophisticated than going to bed early. Moving the bedtime up to nine-thirty would have been more proof that Barney is not a sophisticated man of the world."

That evening, Barney is again the center of attention. He is playing the big man as George and Melissa listen raptly. After supper, George retires upstairs, leaving Barney and Melissa alone. Melissa sits beside Barney on the couch. She reaches behind him and turns off a table lamp. Barney is uncomfortable with the situation. Melissa moves closer and embraces him. She asks if he "would like to stay like this forever." Barney hesitantly answers yes.

Hearing this, Melissa jumps to her feet, turns on the lamp, and calls to her father. When George enters, Melissa reports that Barney has proposed marriage. Barney is as surprised to learn this as George is.

"I wish I could say that the scene of a very aggressive woman making advances toward a very bashful and frightened man is an original idea, but it's not," says Jack. "This type of scene has been done in many forms and is considered a staple. It's also been done many times in reverse with an aggressive male wooing a nervous female. Don Knotts's performance is what made this staple scene shine."

The next morning, the Taylors are finishing breakfast. Aunt Bee is reading the newspaper. She suddenly gasps and reads aloud from the "Mayberry Merry-Go-Round" column. The column reports that Barney and Melissa are ready to set a wedding date.

"No matter how small the town, I bet there's a 'Mayberry Merry-Go-Round' column in every newspaper," says Jack. "The presence of the column proves that everyone loves gossip—the juicier, the better."

Barney bursts into the kitchen through the back door. He has seen the column and is very upset. He asks Andy to help him get out of the mess he is in.

In the script, Barney *flops into a chair, head hanging between his arms.* The reality of what has happened hits him full force and he pleads with Andy to help him get Thelma Lou back.

Andy, frustrated with Barney, asks, "Why don't you keep playing the field, staying in circulation, having fun?" Barney replies, "Andy!!! Where do you get these modernistic ideas? Why, sometimes you shock me!" (Barney's realization of the seriousness of the situation and the dialogue are deleted from the finished episode.)

Andy agrees to help Barney get Thelma Lou back. He and Barney drive to Thelma Lou's house. Andy instructs Barney to remain in the squad car until he has talked with Thelma Lou alone.

Andy tells Thelma Lou he is taking a survey and has dropped by to get her thoughts on the upcoming Founders' Day celebration. Andy brings up the celebration's parade and mentions the participation of the Drum and Fife Corps. Andy, after opening the subject of Fife, begins talking about Barney.

Thelma Lou doesn't want to talk about Barney. She walks to the door and opens it to indicate that Andy should leave, and Barney, listening outside the door, falls inside.

Andy immediately comes to Barney's defense and explains that all Barney wants is Thelma Lou's forgiveness. Barney was a victim of circumstance, a "pawn in the hands of a wily woman." Barney agrees and promises to cut things off with Melissa.

Thelma Lou eventually softens and grants her forgiveness. In response, Andy instructs Thelma Lou to give Barney a "little sugar on the jaw."

"Charles and I were much better at writing 'southern' by this point, but 'give him a little sugar' was still beyond us," says Jack. "I don't remember ever hearing that phrase. I believe it was a southern expression Andy Griffith put into the script."

Later, Barney returns to the sheriff's office. He enters with a jaunt in his step and is once again "a man of the world." He has successfully ended things with Melissa.

The telephone rings. It is George Stevens!

The telephone conversation was scripted to visually cut back and forth between Andy and Stevens. Stevens calls Barney a "weaselly deputy" and reports that Barney ended the relationship without a face-to-face meeting with Melissa. Stevens intends to start a breach-of-promise suit against Barney for alienation of affection. (George Stevens's on-screen appearance and dialogue are deleted from the filmed episode.)

"This is the kind of story where we figured out the end first and then went backward to the beginning," says Jack. "We brought the scam couple into Mayberry looking for their prey. What prey could be funnier than Barney. We then tied that into the Barney/Thelma Lou relationship, and the writing fell into place."

Andy suggests that Mr. Stevens and Melissa come to the sheriff's office the next day and an attempt will be made to settle the matter.

The next morning, Stevens and Melissa are in the sheriff's office. Melissa is in tears. Stevens demands satisfaction but may be willing to settle the breach-of-promise suit out of court for a cash settlement.

Barney enters. Andy instructs him to stand beside Melissa. Andy takes a book out of his desk drawer, stands, and begins reading aloud the marriage ceremony.

Barney, George, and Melissa are stunned! George interrupts Andy. Melissa announces that she has no intention of marrying a "squirt" like Barney.

Andy's suspicions are confirmed. George and Melissa, whose name is really Gladys, are married to one another. Andy threatens to jail the couple for the scam they were attempting to pull but instead demands that they leave Mayberry.

The Stevenses depart. Barney is "flabbergasted" by what has just happened. He questions Andy about starting the marriage service. How could Andy have been sure that Melissa wouldn't go along with the ceremony?

Andy explains that Mr. Stevens was too anxious to make a cash settlement and Melissa was crying fake tears, but what really gave him the confidence to begin the marriage ceremony was the realization that a flashy, pretty, big-city girl like Melissa would never agree to marry a squirt.

Barney is insulted. His lines prior to the conclusion of the episode's second act are, "Squirt! Now just a minute, I don't care what a gal like that wants. Thelma Lou thinks I'm pretty good." (These lines were deleted from the filmed episode.)

"It was always a pleasure writing Barney stuff," says Jack. "In the episode's epilogue, Andy visits Barney and Thelma Lou after a passionate making-up session. Barney is shown with his hair messed up and smeared lipstick on his face. The way Don Knotts performed this was a beautiful thing to watch. He was funny without saying anything. I think all the writers who did The Griffith Show loved writing Barney scenes."

"The Perfect Female"

"My goodness that girl can do everything!"
—AUNT BEE, referring to Karen Moore

Episode 37

First Broadcast on
November 27, 1961

Written by
**Jack Elinson and
Charles Stewart**

Directed by
Bob Sweeney

Gail Davis
Guest Stars as
Karen Moore

"The Perfect Female" was inspired by the great Broadway musical *Annie Get Your Gun* starring Ethel Merman," says Jack. "Remember that terrific song, 'Anything You Can Do'? That's what our story is. It's also the equality theme that was beginning to take shape in the 1960s. We didn't write the script with any special actress in mind. It went the usual way—write the script, then cast it. We didn't think of making the Karen Moore character a series regular. We took it one step at a time. There was always the thought that Andy should eventually have a girlfriend, and doing stories like this was a good way to try out actresses now and then. If one hit big, she'd be the one. Simply put, it was like auditioning."

The episode begins with Barney parking the squad car in Thelma Lou's driveway. Thelma Lou comes outside for a private discussion. The two would like to get Andy and Thelma Lou's cousin, Karen Moore, together.

"I checked back to 'Cyrano Andy,' and nowhere in our script did we give Thelma Lou a last name," says Jack. "She was just Thelma Lou. Apparently, nobody else bothered to give her a last name either. Maybe it was for the best. Thelma Lou is such a nice name, why ruin it with a last name like 'Stottlemeyer'?"

The cousin, Karen Moore, is in Mayberry on vacation and has no desire to participate in matchmaking. Neither does Andy. Barney has set Andy up on blind dates in the past and been "burned." One date was a talker with fat knees, and another looked like Benjamin Franklin.

"Blind date disasters are part of life," says Jack. "The girl who looked like Benjamin Franklin was funny when you think of old Ben with the long hair. He could have been an ugly woman."

Thelma Lou and Barney decide to have Andy and Karen meet at three o'clock in the coffee shop. Barney is confident he can get Andy there and shares his plan with Thelma Lou.

Later at the sheriff's office, it is almost three o'clock. Barney subtly suggests that he and Andy go out for a cup of coffee. Andy, busy with paperwork, would prefer to drink coffee in the office. Barney looks up at the ticking wall clock and begins to panic. At the stroke of three, he blurts out his intention of getting Andy to the coffee shop to meet Thelma Lou's cousin. Andy agrees, but Barney, still pleading his case, doesn't hear.

"One of the elements in Barney's character is his confidence that he has everything in perfect control," says Jack. "He is totally on top of every situation. Then when it counts, he falls apart. He is just like *The Pink Panther*'s Inspector Clouseau, who felt he was number one in his business but, in reality, was the biggest screwup of all time."

Andy gets up from his desk and walks toward the door. Barney asks where Andy is going and is relieved with the answer. Barney replies, "You knew you were gonna go but you had to do a little picking first." Barney then repeats "pick" five times and ends with "you beat everything." (Barney's lines are shortened and modified in the filmed episode.)

Andy and Barney arrive at the coffee shop before the girls and sit on stools at the counter. Thelma Lou and Karen arrive. Barney and Thelma Lou act surprised to see one another. Thelma Lou suggests the foursome take seats in a booth.

On the way to the booth, Andy whispers to Barney, "She's kind of cute." Barney responds, "Cute! You think she's cute, huh? I knew you would." (In the filmed episode, this conversation is changed to Andy whispering to Barney with a smile on his face.)

Barney directs the group into a booth, making sure Andy sits beside Karen. Barney takes a seat beside Thelma Lou and immediately announces that Andy and Karen have a lot to talk about. He gets to his feet and ushers Thelma Lou out the door.

Andy and Karen make the most of an uncomfortable situation. They both agree to talk further and begin joking about getting married.

"For me, the best part of the coffee scene was after Barney and Thelma Lou leave," says Jack. "Andy and Karen showing their amusement at such obvious matchmaking was a joy to write."

Later, Barney is eager to find out how things went with Karen. Andy, picking at Barney, reports that he and Karen had coffee and then got married. Andy invites Barney to drop by that evening for a visit. He suggests Barney come early so he "can see the children before they go to bed." (The "children" line is deleted from the filmed episode.)

Barney doesn't appreciate the joke. He says to Andy, "Oh, you're funny. You are! You ought to go on radio and be an all-night disc jockey!"

"'You ought to . . .' is a handy formula whenever someone tries to be funny and it's not appreciated by the listener," says Jack. "We used it repeatedly during the series. In this case, Barney is seriously trying to match Andy with Karen and has no interest in jokes."

Andy assures Barney that he and Karen hit it off just fine. The two even have a date to go out to Finnegan Flats and shoot crows. (In the script the couple plan a *little chicken hawk hunting*.)

Barney is stunned by the news. Shooting crows is a poor dating activity! Andy questions Barney about his first date with Thelma Lou and learns that on that occasion, Barney sat with her on the front porch and demonstrated how to take his gun apart in the moonlight. (This romantic remembrance is deleted from the filmed episode.)

Andy leaves to purchase some shotgun shells. After his departure, Barney says aloud to himself, "Looks like I'm going to have to guide the kid all the way."

"Barney was always funny when he took the role of a 'Man of the World,'" says Jack. "Barney sees himself as a man who's seen it all and knows it all. In this scene, he was Andy's 'big brother' guiding the 'kid.'"

Karen tells Thelma Lou that she likes Andy and the two already have a date for the following day. Thelma Lou, like Barney, is surprised to learn that the couple will be shooting crows. She asks Karen if she told Andy she is a skeet shooting champion. Karen didn't.

Casting director Ruth Burch selected Gail Davis to portray Karen Moore. The actress, approved by producer Aaron Ruben, was a perfect match for the shooting champion character. Gail Davis had previously starred on television as the title character in the *Annie Oakley* series.

The next day the couple arrives at Finnegan Flats. Andy removes a *picnic basket, blanket, two camp stools and his gun* from the back seat of the squad car. The basket contains chicken, potato salad, lots of goodies, and a leaky thermos. (All of these details are given in the script directions and the items asked for were supplied by Prop Master Reggie Smith.)

Andy makes a fuss over Karen. He sets up a stool for her so she will be comfortable and instructs her to cover her ears whenever he shoots his gun. He compliments her beauty and treats her like a lady.

Later, Karen tells Thelma Lou that she enjoyed the date. She never mentioned to Andy that she was an expert with a gun. The fact didn't seem important. Andy was a gentleman, and she was a lady. That was more than enough. Nothing more needed to be said.

"The reason we didn't have Karen show her stuff on the first date was pure theatrical license," says Jack. "If she showed her shooting skills that soon, the show would be over right there and, as story writers, we'd have nowhere to go. It was more dramatic to show her skill later in the story."

Barney anxiously awaits news of how Andy's date with Karen turned out. Andy reports that the date was "very nice." Barney begins whistling "Here Comes the Bride." Andy stops him, and in a man-talk discussion, he says he needs to talk with Karen some more and "see how she measures up." Andy plans to do so later that evening when Karen comes over for supper.

That evening after supper, Andy sends Opie up to his room to get ready for bed. Opie, though enjoying Karen's visit, doesn't protest. (Growing up, whenever I protested having to go to bed, my parents would ask why I couldn't be more like Opie.)

"We weren't trying to make Opie a role model when he leaves quietly as he's told," says Jack. "This was a simple way to exit Opie so Andy and Aunt Bee can do their grown-up talk. When I was a kid and my parents wanted to say something, they didn't want me to hear, they didn't ask me to leave the room—they simply started talking in Russian!"

After Opie's departure, Andy and Aunt Bee begin interrogating Karen. They ask if she likes little boys, if she can bake gooseberry pie, what type of books she reads, and if she likes music.

After the questioning, Aunt Bee asks Andy to show off his musical talents. She suggests he perform something lively like "Sourwood Mountain."

In the script, Aunt Bee asks Andy to "sing the one about the Turtle Doves." The script directions instruct Karen to join Andy in wordless obbligato, a vocal part that is integral to a piece of music.

"Andy, who was always a gentleman, behaves very nicely in this scene," says Jack. "Despite Aunt Bee's unsubtle questions, Andy manages to make Karen feel very much at home. As for gooseberry pie, I have no idea what that is. Somebody else came up with that."

"We didn't indicate what song Andy should sing in the script," says Jack. "I guess 'Sourwood Mountain' would have been Andy Griffith's choice. The song wasn't put in to add length to the script. It was there to add warmth, especially with Karen joining in. At this point, you think these two are going to get romantically serious."

The next day Barney visits Thelma Lou. He has some exciting news! Andy is very pleased with Karen.

Karen enters adjusting the sleeves of her sweater. (The script directions have Karen adjusting her belt as she enters: *Putting the finishing touches on her dressing.* The writers thus provide a visual explanation for why Karen is not in the living room when Barney arrives.)

Barney tells Karen she has hooked "a mighty big fish." (This is changed from a mighty "tough" fish in the script.) According to Barney, Karen has passed the muster.

"By this point in the story, it's obvious we're dealing with two very eligible people," says Jack. "It's clear neither one is in a rush to get married. It's Barney, of course, who messes things up by telling Karen how lucky she is to get a catch like Andy. That was the main point of the story we were heading to, creating the conflict."

"When Barney tells Karen how lucky she is to get Andy, it's obvious she'd get furious," says Jack. "That wasn't difficult for us to write. Karen's a very strong lady, and her response was right in character."

The telephone rings. It is Andy calling to invite Karen to an upcoming skeet shooting contest he will be participating in. At first, Karen wants to turn the date down, but seeing a way to teach Andy an important lesson, she agrees to the outing.

At the contest, Karen, dressed in a shooting vest, steps forward to participate in the contest. She will be shooting against Andy!

Andy hits twenty-three targets. Karen hits twenty-five, a perfect score, and is the winner of the contest.

Barney regrets Andy's loss and mournfully says, "Losing to a woman; it's the end of an era."

"Barney's disappointment at Karen beating Andy was representative of attitudes expressed during the feminist movement," says Jack. "Negativity was definitely a unfortunate part of the movement that started in the 1960s."

A humbled Andy congratulates Karen on her victory. Karen confidently begins questioning Andy to see if he too passes the muster. (In the script, Karen asks Andy if he likes Russian composer Sergei Prokofiev and what he thinks of French writer Guy de Maupassant. Both artists' names are deleted from the filmed episode, and the questions asked are less specific.) Karen then walks away.

Andy acknowledges that he has learned a behavior-changing lesson. Realizing this has made him a better person, he goes after Karen hoping to make amends.

"Charles and I definitely wanted to make the statement that women weren't going to be second-class citizens anymore," says Jack. "Forty years later, women have come a long way, and they're going to get stronger in the future."

In the epilogue, Andy, Karen, Barney, and Thelma Lou have gathered for a little target practice. In the script, Thelma Lou is not part of the group. Andy Griffith wrote "Thelma Lou" at the top of his script page as a reminder that she should be included.

Andy hands Karen his pistol, and *with the skill of a marksman, she steps up, takes aim and fires three rapid shots. All five bottles are shattered.* (The script directions are incorrect in the number of shots and bottles. The filmed episode has Karen firing six shots and shattering six bottles.)

Barney reluctantly compliments Karen's shooting and qualifies the merits of her shooting ability. It isn't too difficult to shoot when someone takes careful aim. It's another matter when the shooter performs the quick draw. Andy, Karen, and Thelma Lou persuade Barney to demonstrate his quick draw.

Charles and Jack carefully detail every movement of the quick draw and its *aftermath. Barney goes through all the mannerisms of getting himself set. He makes a slight tug at each sleeve, looks down at the holster, flexes his fingers, spreads his feet just so many inches apart, goes into a cat-like pose . . . then suddenly he reaches to draw out his gun and BANG! It goes off in his holster!*

Barney is ready to explode. He turns and angrily walks out to the boards upon which the bottles are placed, gives them a good kick, knocking over the bottles. (In the filmed episode, Barney knocks the bottles over with his hand. This change is more visually pleasing.) *He stands glaring at Andy and Karen who are still smothering their laughter.*

"Barney shooting his gun in its holster was too good to pass up," says Jack. "I think if we ended every show that way, the public would never have tired of it."

"Mayberry Goes Bankrupt"

Episode 39

First Broadcast on
October 23, 1961

Written by
**Jack Elinson and
Charles Stewart**

Directed by
Bob Sweeney

Andy Clyde
Guest Stars as
Frank Myers

"This is the second of our scripts that Barney wasn't in. (The first script
without Barney was 'The Beauty Contest.') I can only guess Don Knotts was
not available for whatever reason."—JACK ELINSON

"Mayberry Goes Bankrupt" begins in the mayor's office. The town council is
meeting to discuss what to do about Frank Myers. Frank is delinquent on paying
his taxes. This has gone on for eight quarters. (In the script Frank is fifteen quarters behind.)

"Charles and I made up most of the names we gave our characters," says Jack.
"Occasionally, if we wanted an unusual-sounding name, we would flip through
the telephone book until something caught our eye. For this script, we apparently just decided to use the name of our production manager, Frank Myers, for
the fun of it."

"The veteran actor Andy Clyde was cast in the role," says Jack. "We never wrote
a role with a specific actor in mind. We may have suggested people now and then,
but the final pick was by producer Aaron Ruben."

The town council agrees that Frank must be evicted from his home. Andy, however, is sympathetic and asks if perhaps council member Harlon Fergus could
extend Frank a loan from his bank. The bank president refuses Andy's request.

The town council feels eviction is the best action to take. Frank's house is an
eyesore and a tourist deterrent. Out-of-towners, seeing Frank's house, want to
leave Mayberry as fast as they can. The mayor tells Andy he is "just wasting his
sympathy."

"We wrote the 'wasting your sympathy' line because we wanted to point out
the irony of the mayor telling nice guy Andy not to be nice," says Jack.

In the script, the mayor says to Andy, "Frank had the same chance as the rest of
us had. I started the same as he did . . . with two bare hands, two legs, a brain . . ."
Andy finishes the sentence, "and a rich uncle."

The mayor suggests that the town "ought to build some good-looking landmark on Frank's property. Maybe something Mayberry would become famous
for like Paris with its Eiffel Tower or Italy's Leaning Tower of Pisa."

Andy responds, "Well, if that's what you want, you won't find anything that leans more than Frank's house." (The comical exchange was deleted from the filmed episode.)

"The first scene was a long one and played pretty straight all the way," says Jack. "Evicting Frank from his home was serious stuff, and it was difficult to find laughs along the way. If Barney was there, I'm sure we could have found some comedy through him. Without Don Knotts, we were like a baseball team with one of its star players out with an injury."

Don Knotts was signed for twenty-eight episodes in the 1961–62 season at his request. The role of Barney Fife was very demanding, and the actor needed time off to rest. (Knotts was under contract for seventeen appearances in the first season of the series. Due to the key comedic role Knotts played, his contract was renegotiated, and he appeared in twenty-eight first-season episodes.)

Later, Andy reluctantly arrives at Frank's house to serve the eviction notice. The house is in disrepair. Discarded furniture and junk litter the yard. A goat and a flock of chickens loiter around the back gate.

"We wrote an extensive description of Frank's house, both outside and inside," says Jack. "We included details like the back gate falling off. We described the inside as having a 'Ma and Pa Kettle' interior worse than the outside. In the movies, Ma and Pa Kettle were poorer than Frank."

Frank meets Andy at the back door and invites him inside. A chick roosts on the couch. Frank shoos the bird away and offers Andy the seat. Andy, after removing a feather from the couch, prefers to stand. (The chicken is named Hazel. Perhaps a nod to script continuity person Hazel Hall.)

"Besides the hen, we almost indicated a goat and a pig be inside the house, but we decided that was a little much," says Frank. "The hen did just fine all by herself. Today that hen is still a member of the Screen Actors Guild."

Frank discusses his financial status with Andy. He explains that business has been bad lately. Andy agrees that making berries for women's hats isn't a "hot business right now." Frank shows Andy his backlog of berries and predicts that he will be sitting pretty when the styles change.

"I don't remember how we came up with making berries for women's hats for a vocation, but for a guy like Frank, it had to be the silliest occupation possible," says Jack.

That evening, the Taylors relax on the front porch. Andy mournfully strums his guitar, Aunt Bee quietly sews, and Opie plays with a set of cowboy figures. Aunt Bee acknowledges that Andy evicting Frank was an unpleasant task. Opie is listening to the adult conversation and asks about the meaning of eviction. Andy explains that Frank had to move from his house because he had not paid his taxes. Opie is curious about where Frank will move to and suggests that

Frank move in with the Taylors. Andy and Aunt Bee consider the suggestion and after finding no reason not to, invite Frank to stay with them.

"We set this scene on the front porch because it was a place where the Taylors often sat after supper," says Jack. "The porch was a place for reflection. We had Andy softly pick at his guitar. This helped set the mood."

"We thought it'd be good if Opie, with his simple innocence, would come up with the idea to bring Frank into their home," says Jack. "From the mouths of babes comes true wisdom. Inviting Frank to stay was an example of neighborly love. Love was a very big part of Mayberry and explains why the show is still alive and well after so many years."

"After Andy and Aunt Bee agree to invite Frank, Andy was greatly relieved," says Jack. "We wrote that *Andy begins playing a lively tune on guitar.* The music was an audible way to express Andy's joy."

Frank arrives at the Taylor home with his suitcase and a strongbox containing his "valuables." Andy suggests that Frank should perhaps sell some of the items to raise funds to pay his taxes. Frank takes the items out one by one and explains their sentimental value. After going through the items, Frank realizes they are worthless. Andy calls the valuables "fine items" and advises Frank to hold on to them for their sentimental value.

"Anybody who's ever traveled during their lifetime winds up with 'treasures' and then wonder why they're still holding on to the silly things," says Jack. "We all have drawers full of useless stuff to remember all the trips we've taken. After we turned in the script, we realized we had the wrong date for one of the 'valuables,' the St. Louis World's Fair medallion. The fair was held in 1906 not 1904, as Frank says. I wasn't even born when the fair was held, so how would I know?"

"Here again, we see what a sensitive guy Andy was when he brings up the 'sentimental value of Frank's belongings' as a reason not to sell them," says Jack. "Somebody else might say, 'Get rid of this junk,' but not Andy."

Opie discovers a "funny" looking paper in the strongbox. The paper is a bond issued to Frank's great-great-granddaddy by the town of Mayberry back in 1861. Andy examines the bond and discovers it is redeemable at $100 at 8½ percent interest compounded annually over the last hundred years. Andy calls the bank president to confer.

Afterward, Andy and Frank meet with the town council. Andy, with great satisfaction, announces that the town owes Frank $349,119.27! Franks tells the council he will take the money in cash.

"I would think we did the mathematics of the total worth of the $100 bond," says Jack. "The closing line of act one, 'I'll take it in cash,' was one of the greatest lines in the series, if I say so myself."

"Turning the tables always makes for good stories," says Jack, "especially when a poor guy like Frank is being pushed around by the town council. Then suddenly the shoe is on the other foot. The audience enjoys seeing the heavies sweating bullets and Andy enjoying every minute of it."

"If, by the wild chance, the audience didn't know what Andy's character is like, they knew with this script," says Jack. "He was pained about having to evict Frank, then so happy when the tables turned, putting the bad guys into a corner. Enough said."

The second act begins with a content Frank Myers puffing a cigar. The town council is paying Frank a personal visit. They plead with Frank to be reasonable. However, Frank is determined to cash his bond.

"This scene was easy to write," says Jack. "The ball is now in Frank's court, and he's milking it to the hilt. Our script direction describing Frank at this point was *The little pigeon has suddenly become a hawk.* Puffing a cigar is a perfect symbol to show who's on top at the moment."

Later, Andy meets with the mayor and bank president Fergus. The scripted opening of the scene has the mayor on the telephone. He hangs up and says, "Roanoke won't lend us a cent! It's the same all over—Elm City, Vicksburg, Kerryville. You'd think in time of need, one troubled town would help another! What happened to togetherness? Where is that 'Great Big Heart of America'? Gone, gone."

Andy responds, "Mayor, maybe you're trying the wrong towns. Seems to me, when you're begging you ought to think big, like Philadelphia or Baltimore or about Washington. Them fellas are known for giving out money." (This dialogue was deleted from the filmed episode.)

The mayor asks Andy, the only one Frank likes, to make a deal with Frank on the town's behalf. Andy hesitantly agrees.

Andy visits Frank and finds him looking through a mail-order catalogue. Frank is picking out items for his house. The scene directions are *Frank rips out a page of a mail-order catalogue and stuffs it in a manila envelope when he comes upon an item he wants.* Frank encourages Andy to order something for himself, Aunt Bee, and Opie. (The filing and invitation to order something was deleted from the filmed episode.)

Andy sadly tells Frank the town will not be able to cash the bond. The town does not have the money. Frank is disappointed and confesses to Andy that "it sure isn't fun being known as the fella with the worst house in town."

Andy suddenly has an idea. Maybe something can be done about Frank's house.

Andy's idea is revealed in the next scene. The members of the town council are busy working, making needed improvements to Frank's house and yard.

"Andy's idea to have the town council fix up Frank's house is still another way of showing Andy's concern for a friend," says Jack. "In this episode, Andy is like a fairy godmother who makes happy things happen."

While the workers are cleaning up, Frank asks the mayor for some paint to touch up the frame of a portrait of his great-great-granddaddy shaking hands with General Robert E. Lee. Banker Fergus, hearing this, realizes that Frank's bond was bought with Confederate money and can only be paid back in the same currency. The bond is thus worthless!

The town council wants Frank evicted. Andy points out that the council has done something nice for a fellow townsman and should let it go at that. Frank's house, thanks to their hard work, is now a showplace that will encourage out-of-towners who see it to spend some time in Mayberry.

"It wasn't difficult to reveal that the bond was worthless since Mayberry was in the South," says Jack. "The Confederate money angle was the easy way to go. The solution to the story wasn't tough. With Andy calling the shots, pointing out that Frank's house is a thing of beauty now, it all made sense."

An out-of-town couple drives up and stops in front of Frank's house. Andy welcomes the couple to Mayberry. The couple thought they were in Elm City and quickly drive away.

"After doing a show about a big crisis in Mayberry, it was a nice change of pace to have out-of-towners drive in looking for Elm City," says Jack.

In the epilogue, Andy and Frank visit the mayor to show him a letter Frank has from the president. The president is answering an invitation to visit Mayberry. The mayor examines the letter and discovers it is signed by Jefferson Davis, president of the Confederate States of America. (It's interesting that a portrait of President George Washington has been placed on the wall behind the mayor.)

"Frankly, I wasn't too wild about the epilogue," says Jack. "I felt it was one too many Confederate jokes. But, hey what do I know? I'm from the North."

"After thinking about the episode, I have an afterthought," says Jack. "Despite the absence of Don Knotts in this episode, you can see that Andy Griffith was in firm control all the way. He was the backbone of the series."

"Opie's Hobo Friend"

Episode 40

First Broadcast on
November 13, 1961

Written by
Harvey Bullock

Directed by
Bob Sweeney

Buddy Ebsen
Guest Stars as
David Browne,
the Hobo

"In my brief career, I had never written alone before, or for any of the Hollywood studios or producers. I knew nobody in town. I had no contacts. The only familiar thing in sight was my battered, old, Royal manual typewriter."—HARVEY BULLOCK

"There was always a special joy in doing an 'Opie' story," says producer Aaron Ruben. "We always tried to open the new season with an 'Opie' script because they had such enormous appeal, and we felt it was a smart way to hook an audience for the start of the new season. 'Opie's Hobo Friend' was a wonderful story, and just the kind that Harvey Bullock was so capable of writing—lots of heart, warmth, a solid moral lesson, and always the meaningful relationship between Andy and Opie."

"'Opie's Hobo Friend' has a very special meaning for me," says Harvey Bullock. "It was the first one I wrote for the series. I was new in town, having left my wife and three infant daughters back in New York while I sought employment in the booming sitcom business in Hollywood.

"I was living in a run-down motel and driving a rent-a-wreck when my agent managed to get me a meeting with Aaron Ruben. This was my big chance. *The Griffith Show* was the absolute Tiffany of all comedies. A writing assignment on that highly respected show would almost guarantee assignments on any other show in town.

"The thought of the meeting made me very nervous. But being from a small town, I felt comfortable with the Mayberry style. I also recognized the obvious—their stories were emotional and character driven, not physical farce.

"I have always delighted in older, colorful characters who were not the stuff of convention. The bare bones of the story I had in mind featured an irresponsible vagrant who seemed to live in glorious freedom and would thus be appealing to a youngster who didn't recognize the pitfalls. But it was important the vagrant be somewhat glib, educated, articulate, even likable—all of which made him an even more effectively tempting role model.

"I went in to meet Aaron with all fingers, toes, arms, legs, and, certainly, stomach crossed. To my immense relief, he turned out to be the most friendly, understanding, and helpful producer I have ever met. I think he sensed I was nervous and went out of his way to relax me. He prodded, added, spent time, and gradually the 'Hobo' evolved. 'Go home and get started on it,' I remember Aaron saying. 'It'll be a good one.' After the meeting, I drove my old rented wreck of a car out the studio gate—and the wheels never touched the ground."

Harvey's finished script came alive through the wonderful acting abilities of *TAGS* cast and guest star Buddy Ebsen. "Buddy Ebsen was cast as the hobo because he is a fine actor, and he had that easygoing, happy-go-lucky look one might associate with a guy who has dropped out of the competitive world and embarked on an aimless, wandering existence," says Aaron Ruben. "The process of hiring guest stars begins with hiring a good casting director. Having been told by the producer what the part calls for, he or she will then go through their file on the actors they are familiar with and decide which would be most suitable for the role. They will submit a short list of possibilities to the producer and, thus, spare him the lengthy process of having to audition an endless parade of candidates."

Harvey drew upon his past during the writing of the episode. "I actually had a friend whose name was Dave Browne," says Harvey. "It came up accidently that he had an *e* [on the end of his last name] and we teased him mercilessly. It [the name Browne] seemed to fit the hobo character, who used that little touch as a subtle claim to class."

Harvey introduces Dave Browne in the episode's opening scene. Andy and Opie meet Mr. Browne as they arrive at a lake for a morning of fishing. After Andy and Opie are out of sight, Mr. Browne helps himself to a sandwich from the lunch bag in the back seat of the squad car.

Later that afternoon, Barney brings Mr. Browne in on a vagrancy charge. After Andy and Opie return from fishing, Barney tells Andy that Mr. Browne doesn't have a cent on him. When Mr. Browne asks for a coin, he explains that money disappears whenever he has it, and when he needs more it reappears. Mr. Browne illustrates this by making the coin magically disappear and reappear from Opie's ear. Andy dismisses the vagrancy charge, and Mr. Browne leaves.

Barney objects to Andy's release of Mr. Browne. Not wanting Opie to hear Barney's objections, Andy gives Opie a penny for the gumball machine down the street. Barney feels Browne "is no ordinary hobo" and vows to keep "his baby blues" on him.

When Opie encounters Mr. Browne at the gumball machine, Mr. Browne tells Opie he doesn't need money as long as he has "the magic touch and knows the magic word." Mr. Browne demonstrates by saying "Tuscarora," as he taps the top of the gumball machine. Although he retrieves a gumball using his magic touch, he is actually reaching behind the machine and jimmying the machine with a pick.

"I grew up in Binghamton, New York, a town about halfway between New York City and Buffalo, near the Pennsylvania border. My parents would sometimes take my sister and me on car trips in our vintage Plymouth. Often we would return to Binghamton on Route 17, and near Deposit, New York, the road went near the top of Tuscarora Mountain and then descended in a very long stretch of highway. My father would say the magic word, 'Tuscarora,' and to our squeals of delight, he would turn off the motor, and we coasted down in the quiet for miles.

"I had completely forgotten about it. Then thirty years after, as an ink-stained wretch laboring over my typewriter in the small hours, doing a story about a roguish hobo, the word jumped out of my subconscious, slid through my finger-tips and onto the paper. And it somehow seemed exactly right."

One of the strengths of *TAGS* was its realism. An excellent example of detailed realism is present in the Tuscarora scene. Mr. Dave and Opie are standing in front of a store window. A pedestrian walking on the sidewalk on the other side of the street can be seen in the window's reflection.

"The assistant director on 'Opie's Hobo Friend' was Bruce Bilson," says Harvey, "and one of his duties as AD was to set up background happenings, extras cross-ing the street, etcetera, so the director could concentrate on the main action with the principal players. I could always tell when Bruce was the AD. He would have layers of happenings to give flavor to the film. Most importantly, they were always muted enough so they did not distract. I used to kid him about his great eye and inventiveness for detail, how he would have a man mowing his lawn in the background three blocks away!"

Later in the episode, Barney arrests Mr. Browne for loitering. Not wanting to imprison Mr. Browne, Andy gives him a job trimming hedges. Before he begins the job, Mr. Browne discusses the job with Opie and reaches the conclusion that he will cut the hedges tomorrow—"the perfect day to start any job."

Mr. Browne's philosophy makes an impression on Opie. The next morning Opie decides to "wait until tomorrow" to pick up his room. After breakfast, Opie leaves for school and encounters Mr. Browne. Mr. Browne tells Opie he can hear the fish jumping at the lake and shows him a homemade fishing lure he calls the "Gollywobbler Super Fish Catcher."

"The name of Mr. Dave's homemade fishing lure just jumped out. *Gollywob-bler* was a word used for a stomach disorder. It always intrigued me, so I bent it around to embellish a homemade fishhook," says Harvey.

Influenced by Mr. Browne again, Opie decides to play hooky from school and go fishing. Barney catches Opie and takes him home.

Andy decides it is time to pay Mr. Browne a visit. He explains to Browne that Opie is having trouble being able to tell the difference between right and wrong. Andy decides that Mr. Browne is not a good role model and invites him to leave town. Andy explains to Mr. Browne that he has a lot of "unscrambling to do" to straighten Opie out.

Shortly after this exchange, Barney brings Mr. Browne in a third time. This time he is arrested for purse snatching. The purse found on Mr. Browne has Aunt Bee's name inside it. Opie enters the courthouse and overhears the charge. He questions Mr. Browne about the theft. Mr. Browne offers no explanation. Opie turns to leave but stops. He takes the gollywobbler from his pocket, hangs it on a bar of Mr. Browne's cell, and departs.

After Barney and Opie leave, Andy walks over to the cell and tells Mr. Browne that he knows the pocketbook is one Aunt Bee had thrown in the trash. A train whistle is heard blowing in the distance. Andy opens the cell and says, "Mr. Dave, I'd say you got a train to catch."

"Several weeks after completing 'Hobo' I was on my way out of the studio when Sheldon Leonard, the king himself, intercepted me," Harvey recalls. "He had gone out of his way to find me and tell me how much he enjoyed the script of 'Hobo.' His final words were, 'I find your writing very literate.' I rushed home to read the script again. What part was he referring to? I never did know exactly, but I reveled in having pleased that man and was thrilled at having the chance to contribute to such a class show. Happily, the episode worked well. That opened the door for me, and I went on to do some thirty-odd more. But the 'Hobo' will always be the most meaningful."

"The Pickle Story"

Episode 43

First Broadcast on
December 18, 1961

Written by
Harvey Bullock

Directed by
Bob Sweeney

"I have fond memories of almost every aspect of working for Sheldon, Aaron, and Andy during those halcyon days."—HARVEY BULLOCK

"The storyline for 'The Pickle Story' evolved from one of the legendary writers' seminars conducted by *TAGS* executive producer Sheldon Leonard," says writer Harvey Bullock. "Sheldon and producer Aaron Ruben would invite a half-dozen writers to a 'spitball session' wherein everyone would toss ideas in the air. It was a wide-open, invigorating exercise with all those active minds spinning at once.

"At the time, I had just come to Hollywood and had written only one *TAGS* episode, 'Opie's Hobo Friend,' which turned out extremely well. I was very flattered to be invited to the seminar based on one credit and was totally in awe of the veteran writers I was privileged to mingle with.

"In the seminar, the bare bones of 'The Pickle Story' emerged. Among the writers attending that day was the team of Fred Fox and Izzy Elinson. Fred, one of the most affable, popular, and talented guys in the business, had an extreme stammer which he (and we) all joked about.

"At the end of the seminar, Sheldon doled out each story to whichever writer he thought might be best suited for it. Evidently, Fred coveted 'The Pickle Story' because when Sheldon came to that one, Freddy raised his hand but was so excited his stammering overcame him. He struggled to get the words out, unnoticed by Sheldon. In desperation, Fred tugged at his partner's arm. But Izzy was busy making notes about a previous story allotted to them.

"Poor Freddy was apoplectic but, sadly, also still speechless. Hardly looking up from his notes, Sheldon finally decreed: 'Okay Harve, you take that one.' At that point, but too late, Freddy finally found his voice and bemoaned loudly, 'F-F-F-F-F-For P-P-P-P-P-Pete's sake, Izzy, you just b-b-b-b-b-blew "The Pickle Story."' Nobody else requested it, and to be honest, I didn't have strong feelings about it myself. I was just wildly anxious to get an assignment—any story at all would do. By the way, Freddy later got another story he liked equally as well."

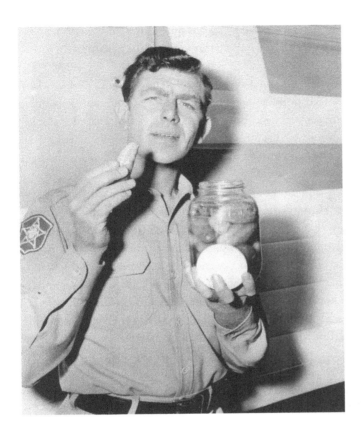

Harvey developed the assigned story into a wonderful comedic script that begins with Clara Johnson and Aunt Bee in the kitchen. Clara has brought over a jar of her homemade pickles. Aunt Bee has recently made pickles as well, and the two comment on the pickle contest they have entered for the past eleven years. Clara and Aunt Bee sample the pickles. Clara's pickles are "simply delicious." According to Clara, Aunt Bee's pickles are "very nice" and need only a few changes.

This opening scene has some inconsistencies with previous *TAGS* episodes. Although Aunt Bee has entered and lost the pickle contest for eleven years, at this point in the series she had only been in Mayberry one or two years. Aunt Bee is also known as an excellent cook, yet she cannot make good pickles.

"The time inconsistency never seemed to bother any of us," says Harvey. "It never came up in the comprehensive review each script underwent. I think we never equated the two years the series was on the air as necessarily two years passing in Mayberry—the stories didn't purport to happen a week apart. It was not a contemporary show, so time was malleable. Furthermore, when a character became a series regular, they seemed to be granted an endless past.

"Aunt Bee's inability to prepare edible pickles posed absolutely no problem to me. It's believable (and even endearing) that a master of anything can have a drastic weak point or two."

The first courthouse scene begins with Andy and Barney singing "Tell My Darling Mother I'll Be There." "My copy of the script has the courthouse scene opening with Barney whispering to a passed-out Otis in his cell," says Harvey. "Barney is trying to probe Otis's subconscious mind into revealing where his whiskey still is operating. The replacement of this with the singing could have been the decision of Andy or Aaron Ruben."

Harvey's idea, however, was too good to discard. It was renamed "The Barney Fife Subconscious Prober Primer" and used one week later in the episode, "Sheriff Barney" (Episode 44), written by Leo Solomon and Ben Gershman.

At this point in the episode, Aunt Bee brings lunch, including a jar of her homemade pickles, to the courthouse. Andy and Barney are hesitant to try the pickles but do so to satisfy Aunt Bee. After she departs, they decide to dispose of the whole batch of homemade pickles and replace them with good "store" pickles.

After the switch is made, Aunt Bee notices that Andy, Barney, and Opie really seem to like her pickles. Encouraged by this, she decides to enter the pickles in the contest again.

Andy and Barney are faced with a dilemma. Aunt Bee might win the contest with the store pickles. Andy realizes the severity of the situation after Clara Johnson brings a jar of her pickles and a scrapbook containing her blue ribbons to the courthouse. The contest means a lot to Clara, and Andy wouldn't be able to forgive himself if she "got nosed out by a store pickle."

Andy tells Barney they have to eat up all the store pickles so Aunt Bee will make more to enter in the contest. Barney can't believe that Andy wants Aunt Bee to make another batch of "those kerosene cucumbers."

"Annabelle Folker, my late mother-in-law, was a feisty, outspoken delight," recalls Harvey. "She had a wondrous vocabulary and sure called 'em as she saw them. One time my wife Betty made some new salad dressing. Belle took one taste and immediately pronounced it 'kerosene.' I thought it was uproariously funny and stuck it in my mind for future use."

TAGS musical director Earle Hagen's talents are highlighted in the fifty-second scene showing Andy, Barney, and Opie eating up the store pickles. Earl reinforces the on-screen action with variations of the *TAGS* theme song that fit the scene perfectly. For example, he slows the music's tempo to audibly communicate the characters' feelings of being stuffed.

Andy, Barney, and Opie eventually consume the store pickles and encourage Aunt Bee to make another batch. Aunt Bee "has to hurry some," but the pickles are prepared and entered in the contest.

The pickle-judging scene that concludes the second act includes an interesting and beautifully photographed fifteen-second segment in which the camera is positioned behind the seated Clara Johnson. The camera fluidly pans right, around the end of the aisle where Clara is seated, and stops directly in front of her.

The scene likewise uses silence to heighten its dramatic impact. The carousel music playing in the background stops as the judges taste Aunt Bee's pickles. The music resumes after the judges react negatively to the kerosene cucumbers.

Once again, Clara's pickles win the blue ribbon. After the winner is announced, Opie is seen standing on a chair behind Aunt Bee. He affectionately reaches out and places his hand on her shoulder. This small gesture is a wonderful expression of love.

Andy comforts Aunt Bee by telling her she may win next year. Aunt Bee replies that as long as her family likes her pickles "that's blue ribbon enough for me." She then announces that the boys are still going to be winners because she's made a new batch of pickles for them. She noticed that they liked them so much, she's made sixteen jars this time.

The epilogue ends the episode on a comic high note. Barney drops by during breakfast. Andy asks him to have some toast and jelly. The two become aware of an unidentifiable odor. Barney discovers the odor's source when he opens the lid on the jelly container. Aunt Bee has been making marmalade!

"The idea for the bad marmalade came out of the blue," says Harvey. "I usually did not write an epilogue until after the script was complete. By then I had a better sense of which story elements had worked best, what loose ends there were, and a general feeling of the story's momentum.

"The popularity of 'The Pickle Story' [it ranked second in 1994 when *The Andy Griffith Show* Rerun Watchers Club (TAGSRWC), the show's fan club, published a poll of club members' favorite episodes] has a certain sweet irony to me. Years after the series, someone told me when the 'pickle' script was first read by the actors there was a deadly silence. Consensus seemed to be that the script just somehow did not work. They all wondered if my previous success with the 'Hobo Friend' story had been a fluke. But they had no time to replace it, so they proceeded to give it their best shot."

"I don't recall a deadly silence at the first reading of the 'pickle' script," says producer Aaron Ruben. "If there was no enthusiastic response, it was because the story was a rather light one and did not have the weightier subject matter that episodes like 'Opie's Hobo Friend' had. In the end, it was fun doing it and a most enjoyable show."

"The Farmer Takes a Wife"

Episode 45

First Broadcast on
January 1, 1962

Written by
**Charles Stewart
and Jack Elinson**

Directed by
Bob Sweeney

Alan Hale Jr.
Guest Stars as
Jeff Pruitt

"Doggone it, Thelma Lou, you're mine and, you know it! And you better let him [Jeff Pruitt] know it!"—BARNEY FIFE

"Bringing in strong characters from the outside, such as Jeff Pruitt, served the series well."—JACK ELINSON

"The Farmer Takes a Wife" begins on the streets of Mayberry. The opening script directions paint a word picture of the action. *A pickup truck, dusty from travel, pulls up. A giant-sized fellow, Jeff Pruitt, leaps out, cups his hands to his mouth, and bellows: "Hey, Andy! Barney! I'm here!"*

"We created Jeff Pruitt as a larger-than-life, unrestrained character," says Jack. "Getting Alan Hale Jr. for the part was perfect casting. The inspiration for this story was the great musical 'Seven Brides for Seven Brothers.' Since we were a half-hour show with a low budget, we made it one guy, but the way Alan played it, he made it feel like seven guys."

The script places Andy and Barney inside the sheriff's office when Jeff arrives in town. The two are busy going over some reports. The filmed episode is different. Andy is in front of the bookshelf placed by the doorway to the back room. Barney stands outside one of the cells and is cleaning a spittoon.

"Barney cleaning out a spittoon was never in our script," says Jack. "Who decided on that piece of business is a mystery to me."

Jeff enters the sheriff's office and is overjoyed to see Andy and Barney. Jeff warmly shakes Andy's hand. He calls Barney "Little Buddy!" (In the script, Jeff's greeting is "Little Barney!")

Jeff, in his excitement, picks Barney up off his feet. The script directions for this action give an insight into how Barney feels about the elevated embrace. *Jeff scoops Barney off the floor, in one arm, completely destroying the he-man deputy image.*

"We had Jeff pick up Barney to show what a friendly big guy he was," says Jack.

"Jeff gave everybody in sight a bear hug. He was a very outgoing guy. Jeff picking Barney up became a 'runner' we repeated several times in the episode."

Jeff tells Andy and Barney he has come to Mayberry to look for a bride. Andy asks why Jeff doesn't marry Bertha who lives on the farm next to his.

Jeff explains that Bertha is neighborly, fun to be with, and good competition for milking cows, calling hogs, and picking tobacco. Jeff, however, wants to marry a female type—a woman who is soft and squishy. Bertha does not fit the bill.

"All the competitive things between Jeff and Bertha were in the script," says Jack. "Milking cows and calling hogs sounded like routine farm work. The 'picking tobacco' reference wasn't ours. I'm sure that was a contribution from Andy Griffith. Andy, a North Carolinian, would have known that tobacco was grown there."

Barney asks Jeff if he would like some help finding a bride. Andy, playing along, suggests that "the next time we go out on a manhunt we'll make it a woman-hunt too." Jeff roars with laughter at Andy's suggestion.

"Andy does the 'manhunt' and 'woman-hunt' line as his little joke," says Jack. "Jeff roars with laughter like Andy was the funniest stand-up comic around. Johnny Carson would love to have Jeff in his audience every night."

Later, Opie stops by the sheriff's office. He tells Andy he just saw Jeff Pruitt "standing on the corner picking up girls." Andy, surprised by the comment, asks Opie to explain. Opie answers that he saw Jeff pick up a girl and say, "Pardon me, ma'am. Just checking your weight."

Andy sends Opie home and goes out to look for Jeff. He finds Jeff doing exactly as Opie said. Andy stops him and explains, "Main Street isn't a marketplace for brides." Andy, wanting to get Jeff off the streets, invites him over to the house to "have a mouthful to eat."

At the Taylor home, Andy, Aunt Bee, Opie, and Jeff finish lunch. The four move to the living room. Aunt Bee apologizes to Jeff for serving only one leg of lamb. Jeff reassures her that he normally eats a light lunch and then makes it up at supper. Jeff's typical supper would be beef, chicken, pork, and duck or a different combination of main courses.

Jeff asks Aunt Bee if she knows of any possible brides he can look over. Aunt Bee explains that Jeff is using the wrong approach to find a wife. People generally like to take the time to get to know one another before getting married.

Jeff defends his technique. He always conducts himself in a gentlemanly manner. He walks up to a girl, tips his hat, and says, "How do you do? Let's get hitched, please."

Opie, who has been listening, agrees that Jeff's approach seems polite. Andy, having forgotten that Opie was present, sends him out to play. The scene ends with Opie acknowledging that he understands what Andy is doing. Opie says, "Whenever grown-ups want to talk about something interesting, they say, 'Go out and play.'"

The scene was rewritten for the filmed episode. In the rewrite, Opie is never present for lunch. Andy, Aunt Bee, and Jeff remain in the kitchen instead of moving to the living room. The dialogue about Jeff's supper menu and his gentlemanly manner of picking up a wife is deleted. The filmed scene also includes the addition of a small but realistic mannerism, Jeff sipping coffee from a saucer.

"The lunch scene was rewritten by story consultant Aaron Ruben," says Jack. "The leg of lamb Aunt Bee serves for lunch was scripted. I since have learned that lamb is rarely served in North Carolina. It's interesting that this was not changed in the rewrite."

"Jeff sipping coffee from a saucer was not in the script, although my parents used to do the same thing with hot tea," says Jack. "Saucer-sipping sounds like something Andy Griffith would have suggested or perhaps Alan Hale contributed to that."

Barney enters the kitchen brimming with excitement. He has the solution for Jeff's wife search. Thelma Lou is hosting a "hen party" at her house that evening. (The script describes the gathering as a meeting of the sewing circle.) Andy, Barney, and Jeff will casually drop by, and Jeff can look the women over to see if any have bride potential. Barney tells Jeff that he is going to have himself a "regular smorgasbord of Mayberry pulchritude!" (Barney's "buffet of beauty" phrase is deleted from the filmed episode.)

That evening, the three men quietly arrive at Thelma Lou's. Barney walks around to the back of the house to converse with Thelma Lou before the men make an entrance. He sees her inside the house, taps on the widow, and asks if everything is ready for Jeff.

Barney calls Thelma Lou "honey," tells her she is "sweet to help out" and kisses her on the cheek.

"The intimacy between Barney and Thelma Lou was there to remind the audience about their relationship," says Jack. "A lot of regular viewers knew the couple cared about one another, but we were nervous comedy writers who wanted to cue in any new viewers. The affection also sets up Barney's jealous reaction to what happens later in the story."

The three men enter the house and act surprised to find a room full of girls. Jeff immediately gets busy looking over the "crop." (Jeff's scripted term for a group of women was deleted from the filmed episode.)

Thelma Lou enters from the kitchen and catches Jeff's attention. Jeff steps over to Andy and Barney to tell them he has found a "winner." Jeff points across the room to Thelma Lou who is temporarily blocked from view by a plump woman.

Barney, intending to introduce the two, accompanies Jeff toward the plump woman. Jeff, however, heads straight toward Thelma Lou. Jeff's misdirection puzzles Barney. Puzzlement quickly turns to panic as Barney understands what has happened.

"When Barney realizes Jeff has chosen Thelma Lou, his reaction resulted in some of the funniest stuff he ever did on the series," says Jack. "Don Knotts's performance was hysterical."

The next day, Barney and Andy are in the sheriff's office discussing the events of the previous evening. Barney expresses his disappointment in Andy for not stopping him from helping Jeff find a bride.

"Barney lashing out at Andy, accusing him of being the one who screwed things up, is also hysterical," says Jack. "Poor Andy knows he will have a hard time convincing Barney he is blameless. Instead, he suggests that Barney talk with Jeff."

While Andy and Barney are talking, Jeff is paying a visit to Thelma Lou. Jeff drives up in his truck, screeches to a top, gets out, and hollers, "Thelma Lou, Honey, I'm here."

Jeff calls Thelma Lou "my little blossom in the garden of love." He hands Thelma Lou a bouquet of flowers and tells her they won't need watering. The flowers will live "just by drinking in her beauty."

Jeff places Thelma Lou's hand on his chest and declares that "underneath that muscle is my heart . . . thumping for you."

Jeff confesses that whenever he looks at Thelma Lou he feels like poetry "has just got to come pouring out." He looks at Thelma Lou soulfully and begins reciting, "The boy stood on the burning deck."

Jeff's extended courtship was wisely deleted from the filmed episode. The scripted dialogue and actions present Jeff as a ridiculous Romeo rather than a joyous, overeager, confident suitor.

The visit ends as it was originally scripted. Thelma Lou tells Jeff there is something they "should clear up" before things go further. Jeff, thinking about what should be clarified, suddenly realizes that proposing marriage on a first date is not respectable. He decides to leave and return later. A marriage proposal on a second date would be respectable.

In celebration, Jeff lifts Thelma Lou off her feet and spins her around. Barney, wanting to talk with Jeff, arrives in time to see the jubilant expression of affection. He is not amused!

Barney tells Jeff he can't have Thelma Lou because she is his girl. Jeff inquires if Barney has asked Thelma Lou to marry him. Barney answers, "Not yet." Jeff, in contrast, is ready to propose and believes this makes Thelma Lou more his girl than Barney's.

After Jeff's departure, Barney orders Thelma Lou to stop seeing Jeff. "Nip it! Nip it in the bud!"

"'Nip it, nip it' was something we wrote real early in season one," says Jack. "The phrase was a 'runner' for the rest of the series and became even funnier as Don Knotts added another 'nip it' or two as he went along."

Barney's jealousy pleases Thelma Lou. She playfully tells Barney that she has no evidence to prove that she is his girl. Thelma Lou inspects her finger and states, "I don't see a ring and they still call me 'Miss.'" Barney sarcastically laughs off the comment. (Thelma Lou's dialogue and Barney's reaction are deleted from the filmed episode.)

Later, Barney recounts his recent experience to Andy. Barney says he had to adopt a get-tough policy with Thelma Lou. Andy looks out the window as he listens to Barney and sees Jeff walking with Thelma Lou.

Barney sees Jeff with his arm around Thelma Lou and madly dashes for the door. He is going to fight for what is his.

Andy warns Barney that Jeff could kill him in a fight. Barney responds, "Yeah, I know he'll probably beat me to a pulp. I won't stand a chance but doggone it, Andy, what do you expect me to do? Just roll over and play dead? There's such a thing as self-respect. A feller can lose a lot of things, but he can't lose that."

Barney acknowledging that he is facing a winless physical confrontation makes his character more believable. Barney's uncontrolled emotional response to seeing Jeff and Thelma Lou together doesn't blind him to the reality of the situation, Jeff is a giant of a man, and Barney is a "little buddy." Barney's motivation to participate in the physical battle is not uncontrolled emotion but a human need for self-respect.

Andy forbids Barney, a deputy, to brawl with a civilian. The scene's script directions are *Barney's resolve is shaken. Deep down he wouldn't mind being talked out of this suicidal mission if he could escape with honor. Barney likes the beautiful "out," but still plays the reluctant tiger. Barney slumps, crosses the room, and sits down with his head between his knees.*

Barney's prediction about the fight's outcome and the necessity of holding on to his self-respect are deleted from the filmed episode. The scene concludes instead with Barney shaking in frustration over not being allowed to fight and pounding his fist into his hand.

In an effort to help Barney, Andy pays a visit to Thelma Lou. He tells her that Barney figures he has lost her to Jeff.

Thelma Lou admits that at first she was amused by Jeff's advances. She also thought if she encouraged Jeff, it would perhaps motivate Barney to become more serious about his relationship with her. Andy calls this tactic "getting Barney off the dime."

Thelma Lou is fearful that Jeff's intentions may have gotten out of hand. She picks up a box from a table, opens it, and shows Andy the contents, a wedding ring.

Thelma Lou tells Andy that Jeff refuses to take "no" for an answer and has ordered her to pack her things for a move to his farm.

Thelma Lou, reflecting on the situation, admits she could never live on a farm. Andy knows that Jeff could never live in the city. If forced to do so, he would "kick like a bronco." Andy gets an idea! It's time he and Thelma Lou did a little "bronco-busting."

Andy's visit with Thelma Lou is shortened in the filmed episode. Thelma Lou's confession of wanting to make Barney jealous and showing Andy the wedding ring are deleted.

Later, Andy begins the "bronco-busting." He tells Jeff there is a chance Thelma Lou might not want to marry him. To prevent rejection, Jeff must become Thelma Lou's idea of a "dream prince."

Andy gives Jeff some pointers. He must cut out the rough stuff. He can no longer pick Thelma Lou up and shake her. Instead, when greeting Thelma Lou, he should bow at the waist and give Thelma Lou's fingertips a "little kissy."

Andy tells Jeff there is one thing Thelma Lou "lives and breathes . . . dancing." Andy recruits Aunt Bee, who Andy says is "one of the finest dance instructors in the whole state," to teach Jeff. Andy puts on a record. A waltz begins playing and, urged on by Aunt Bee, Jeff with Aunt Bee as a partner stumbles around the room. (The dance lesson is deleted from the filmed episode.)

The next pointer is the result of Thelma Lou's desire for a man with etiquette and social grace. Andy and Aunt Bee have Jeff balance a teacup on one knee and a cookie plate on the other. Jeff, practicing a social grace, attempts to pick up the teacup. The cookie plate falls on the floor, and Jeff juggles the teacup until eventually catching it in his hand.

The final pointer is appearance. Jeff must wear a suit when courting Thelma Lou.

Andy accompanies Jeff to a men's clothing store to purchase a new suit. A man exits the store as Andy and Jeff are about to enter. The man is Carl Griffith, the father of Andy Griffith.

Andy Griffith moved his parents, Carl and Geneva, from North Carolina to California shortly after the series was renewed for a second season. The couple lived in a guesthouse adjacent to Andy's residence in the town of Toluca Lake. The parents eventually relocated to a permanent residence at a retirement village in Newhall, California.

"Andy tutoring Jeff was influenced by 'My Fair Lady,'" says Jack. "Instead of Julie Andrews, who played Eliza Dolittle on Broadway, it was Alan Hale playing Jeff Pruitt. I think that Jeff had a lot more trouble becoming a gentleman than Eliza had becoming a lady."

"I was never aware that the customer leaving the clothing store was Andy Griffith's dad," says Jack. "I hope Andy paid him for his 'work.'"

Jeff is now ready for a date with Thelma Lou. He arrives tightly bound in his new suit. Thelma Lou invites Jeff to have something to eat. She removes a cloth covering a plate and reveals finger sandwiches.

Jeff tries a sandwich and admits it whets his appetite for supper. (The meal is called "dinner" in the script.) Thelma Lou informs Jeff that the finger sandwiches are supper. The tiny sandwiches are the result of her desire to stay trim. Jeff responds that there isn't enough food on the plate "to get skinny on."

"'There ain't enough meal there to get skinny on' was simply a line we wrote to show what Jeff expects a meal to be," says Jack.

Andy rushes in and interrupts the meal. He has news about a job opening for a shoe salesman. Thelma Lou, without conferring with Jeff, decides the job would be perfect.

Jeff has had enough! He will not practice social graces or live in town!

Jeff announces he is going home to Bertha. He asks for the return of the wedding ring and declares "the deal is off." (The "ring return" line is deleted from the filmed episode.)

Barney enters. He is ready to do "what a man's got to do." He demands Jeff fight him or get out of "here."

Jeff leaves. Barry responds with dazed disbelief.

The script direction for what follows is *Suddenly feeling very virile, Barney turns to Thelma Lou. He is now the heavy lover and says, "To the winner belongs the spoils." Barney reaches for Thelma Lou's hand and pulls her to him like an Apache dancer.*

In the script, Barney is almost knocked over by the impact of pulling Thelma Lou into his arms. The filmed episode eliminates the lovers' collision and concludes with Barney celebrating his victory with a satisfying kiss.

"Barney was never funnier than when he thought he solved a problem all by himself," says Jack. "Barney is totally unaware he had nothing to do with Jeff leaving. He thinks only about how great he is."

In the epilogue, Andy and Barney are standing in front of the sheriff's office. Barney is philosophizing. He tells Andy he has learned that you don't have to use physical force if you just show the other fellow you mean business.

A car pulls up and parks in a zone marked "Sheriff Parking Only." The driver, a big man, gets out.

Barney approaches the driver with an "I mean business" attitude and demands the car be moved. The driver moves threateningly toward Barney.

Andy, standing behind Barney, gestures with real authority for the driver to move the car. The driver complies.

Barney smiles smugly. He says to Andy, "That's the way I like to handle it. Be firm and send them on their way. I hate fighting. It's ugly."

"Again, Barney doesn't know what's going on and he takes full credit for shooing away the man who's illegally parked," says Jack. "Barney, unaware of Andy's role in what happened, has only one thought . . . how lucky Andy is to have him for a deputy."

"Keeper of the Flame"

First Broadcast
January 8, 1962

Written by
Jack Elinson and
Charles Stewart

Directed by
Bob Sweeney

Everett Sloane
Guest Stars as
Jubal Foster

"Jubal, Jubal, Jubal, Jubal, Juuuuubal!"—An intoxicated BARNEY FIFE

The "Keeper of the Flame" script begins with a detailed script direction. *Int. Barn—Day. OPEN CLOSE on Opie who is kneeling with his right hand raised. Opie's face is revealed by the flickering light of a candle. He wears an expression of awe.*

The camera pulls back to reveal a ring of four other boys. The oldest is ten or so. The others are around nine. Opie is the youngest of the group.

The boys are members of a secret club, the Wildcats. Opie is repeating the vows for membership.

Opie promises not to reveal any of the secrets of the Wildcats and to not tell anyone there is "such a club as the Wildcats." If Opie breaks the vows he will be struck down by the Curse of the Claw. The club members certify Opie's membership with the sign of the Wildcats, three claw swiping gestures of the hand, accompanied by a growl.

"If I remember correctly, my partner Charles Stewart came up with this story idea," says Jack. "One of his sons was in a secret club. Once we came up with the 'Wildcat' name, the 'claw action' and the 'growl' followed."

Everybody in the Wildcats is given an important job. Opie's job will be Keeper of the Flame. It's his responsibility to take care of the sacred candle and bring it to every meeting.

The script directions describe how seriously Opie takes his job. *The candle is put in a small box and handed to Opie. Opie clutches the box as though to guard it with his life. He nods manfully that he'll be faithful to this trust.*

Opie, reflecting upon his new responsibility, asks what happens "when the scared candle gets all used up?" The members have never thought of this and are confused about the proper procedure. The leader of the Wildcats, Tom, rises to the occasion and says that another sacred candle will be purchased at the dime store.

"'The Keeper of the Flame' seemed like a position necessary for a secret club,"

says Jack. "Tom's suggestion that they get another sacred candle at the store shows why he's the head guy in the club. This kid is going to go far."

The meeting is quickly ended when Old Man Foster is seen outside the barn. Foster warns the boys to stay off his property and chases them away.

"There was no description of Jubal Foster in the script," says Jack. "It was obvious by his demeanor and harsh voice that he was a grouch. I don't remember how we came up with his name."

Later, Opie enters the sheriff's office. He is aglow with secret club excitement. He asks Andy and Barney to guess where he's been. Andy thinks for a second, gives up, and asks "where." Opie replies, "I can't tell you." Opie admits that he has joined a secret club but the club's name, meeting location, and his club job can't be told. He likewise can't tell why he can't tell because if he did, something bad would happen to him. He can't tell this either. Opie then explains he just dropped by to tell Andy and Barney about the club.

Opie asks Andy if there are any chores he can do to earn money to pay his club dues. Andy suggests emptying the wastebasket. Opie picks up the basket and goes out the back door.

After his departure, Andy asks Barney if he ever belonged to a secret club. Without missing a beat, Barney answers, "I can't tell you."

"Once we got Opie's 'I can't tell you' response, we wrote the dialogue in a matter of minutes," says Jack. "The questions and answers seemed to flow and build to a comical conclusion."

Jubal Foster storms into the sheriff's office. He has come to make a complaint about the boys who have been trespassing on his property.

Opie returns from emptying the wastebasket, Foster sees him and identifies him as one of the trespassers. Foster moves angrily toward Opie.

Andy faces Foster and tells him to stop scaring Opie. Andy orders Foster to leave. Barney backs Andy up and, likewise, orders Foster "out."

After Foster's departure, Barney says if Foster would have said one more word, he would have been forced to get physical with him.

Andy, speaking to Opie, confirms that Barney would have too.

"Whenever he could, Andy would say something nice to Barney to bolster the macho in Barney's skinny little body," says Jack. "In this situation, Barney would have defended Opie without any fear of Foster."

The Wildcats reconvene to discuss moving to a new meeting location. The members, after a short discussion, realize it is hard to find a secret meeting place and decide to continue meeting in the Foster barn. The meeting is adjourned. As the boys leave the barn, they see Foster approaching and make a run for it.

Opie picks up the sacred candle, blows out the flame, and carries it with him.

After the boy's departure, Foster enters the barn. He mutters threats against the boys as he lights a kerosene lamp, unlocks a padlocked door, and steps into a room containing a moonshine still.

Foster places the lighted lamp on a shelf, samples his moonshine, reaches for an empty jug, and accidentally knocks over the lamp. The lamp falls to the ground. Flames ignite the straw littering the ground, and a fire quickly spreads.

Foster picks up parts of his still, carries them away from the fire, and stores them in an adjacent building. The barn burns to the ground.

"Everything you see on the screen was in the stage directions in the script," says Jack. "Every single detail of the fire was written out. The filmed results were very impressive."

Musical director Earle Hagen's dramatic background music strengthens the impact of the scene. After the musical score was written, Earle conducted the small orchestra that performed the composition. The music was performed and recorded at Danny Thomas's Marterto production studio in Culver City.

Andy and Barney drive out to the scene of the fire. Foster accuses the boys he saw running away from his barn of starting the fire. Andy decides the situation calls for an investigation.

Barney, reflecting on the investigation, feels the situation calls for a lineup. Boys would be brought in, and Foster would look them over and identify the ones who were in the barn.

"The idea of every kid being hauled in for a lineup was vintage Barney," says Jack. "Barney wants to be Clint Eastwood so bad."

At the Taylor home, Aunt Bee is cleaning Opie's room. As she works, she listens to her favorite radio soap opera, *The Secret Life of Celia Gordon*, and learns that John, Celia's lover, has secretly married Beverly.

Aunt Bee is shocked by the revelation and becomes frustrated with "men" in general. She angrily picks up a pillow from the bed and fluffs it. The pillow's removal reveals the hiding place of the Wildcats' sacred candle box.

"When we wrote the shows in the sixties, it was the sixties in our mind," says Jack. "That's why it's so fantastic that it's still being seen years later. It's interesting that whenever you see the show, it's the present time . . . in other words . . . timeless."

"Radio soap operas, more appropriate for decades prior to the sixties, have been the butt of ridicule for ages," says Jack. "The people listening to them, however, loved them. Frances Bavier was wonderful in the bedroom scene. Her reactions to the soap opera prove what a fine actress she was."

Aunt Bee hears Andy announce his arrival for lunch. She hurries downstairs with the candle box in hand.

Aunt Bee, arriving in the kitchen, places the box on the table. Andy, seated at the table, teases Aunt Bee about her devotion to the soap opera character Celia. He idly picks the box up, opens it, and looks at its contents. A frown comes upon Andy's face. His mood suddenly changes.

Andy calls Opie in from the backyard. As Andy waits for Opie's arrival, the camera pans downward from his troubled face to the candle and matches inside the box. The scene fades out, signaling the end of the episode's first act.

"When it comes to the end of an act, we have a thing in our business called 'the hook,'" says Jack. "This means a 'hook' to keep the viewers from switching to another channel during the commercial break. That's why we thought this act one ending was perfect. How would Andy handle this problem that Opie has brought about? The viewer is 'hooked' to find out."

Act two opens with a close-up of Opie. Opie looks at Andy, who is questioning him about the box's contents. Opie answers that he has the candle for light when he goes out at night. Andy reminds Opie that he is not allowed out at night. Opie, thinking quickly, responds that when he is allowed, he wants to be ready.

"All of us who have had children know they're a lot smarter than we give them credit for," says Jack. "Opie is right on top of the 'smart' list and has no trouble explaining the need for a candle."

Andy tells Opie that there was a fire at Jubal Foster's place and questions Opie about the Wildcats meeting in the barn. Opie, remembering the club vows he made, feels he can't answer. He does, however, admit he didn't start a fire.

Andy sends Opie up to his room. He tells Aunt Bee that Opie has been playing with matches and "he's got to get a whipping."

"If we were writing the show today, even the thought of Andy whipping Opie would be a no-no," says Jack. "The whipping would be considered child abuse. When I came across the punishment while rereading the script, I was jarred by it."

The script directions and dialogue for the scene reflect Jack Elinson's disapproval of physical punishment. *Andy leaves on a mission (whipping Opie) that he does not relish.* Later, Andy tells Barney he hated to whip Opie. (The dialogue was deleted from the filmed episode.)

The Wildcats call an emergency meeting. (The meeting is held in a garage.) Tom, the leader, looks directly at Opie and announces that a club member is weakening. Opie denies the accusation but confesses he wanted to tell Andy the club was not responsible for starting the fire. Opie is reminded of his vow of secrecy and forbidden to talk with his father. (This scene was deleted from the script.)

Later, Andy tells Barney, that as a parent he is responsible for Opie's actions and will have to pay for the burned barn. In response, Barney says he would like to "have a go at Opie." Barney feels he is a "pretty good interrogator" and can get to the truth.

To prove his point, Barney reminds Andy how he recently got Otis to confess he was drunk. Andy is not impressed. He recalls that Otis crawled in on his hands and knees, hollering, "Close the door, there's an elephant behind me."

"As a writer, it was satisfying to know we could write dialogue about a character who never appears in the episode," says Jack. "The audience knew Otis and could easily imagine him doing what Andy recalls."

Undeterred by Andy's remark, Barney insists on questioning Opie. He believes it would be best to distract Opie and then casually ask questions about the fire.

Opie enters, and Barney, realizing this is the perfect time to put his plan into action, shoos Andy out of the office. Barney coaxes a reluctant Opie into a game of checkers. As the game proceeds, Barney casually begins the interrogation. Barney keeps prodding for answers as Opie single, triple, and double jumps his opponent's checkers.

Opie admits the Wildcats were inside the barn but are not responsible for the fire. Barney, distracted by Opie's gameplay, is barely listening. Opie continues to talk and assault Barney's checkers. Eventually, Barney's remaining checkers are trapped. Barney, completely forgetting the interrogation, blames Opie's nonstop talking for breaking his concentration and causing his defeat.

This wonderful scene was deleted from the script. (Perhaps to shorten the episode's run-time.) The scene, however, was not discarded. It appears, with slight changes, in the season four episode "Opie and His Merry Men."

That night, Opie *is in bed with hands clasped behind his head as he stares broodingly.* (The script directions give insight into Opie's thoughts and emotions.) Andy enters and asks if Opie has said his prayers. He has.

Andy sits on the edge of the bed. He tells Opie he will go to Jubal Foster's place in the morning and pay him the money needed to build a new barn. Opie thinks this over and reaffirms that he didn't start the fire.

Opie affirming that he has said his prayers, in response to Andy's earlier question, helps the audience believe that Opie is telling the truth. A praying boy is not likely a lying boy. Andy, however, is not convinced the truth has been told.

The time has come for a straight answer. Andy asks Opie if he was at Jubal Foster's barn the day of the fire.

Opie bites his lip mindful of the Curse of the Claw. He hesitates. Opie makes his decision. His allegiance is to his Paw. He admits he was there.

Andy responds, "You're looking at the man who's gonna have to pay for that barn." Andy leaves Opie *no better off for having told the truth.*

"It's a tough spot for Opie . . . knowing his dad is going to pay Jubal for something he didn't do," says Jack. "I'm sure the viewers were touched by that. After Andy leaves, Opie is in the same situation as when the scene began . . . brooding with hands clasped behind his head."

The next morning, Foster is busy filling mason jars from a moonshine-filled bucket. He sees the squad car in the distance, stops what he is doing, and hides the jars in a nearby shed.

Andy and Barney emerge from the squad car. Andy tells Foster he has come to pay for the barn. Foster, enjoying himself, begins figuring in his head what the total cost will be.

While Foster and Andy are negotiating, Barney, feeling the heat of the morning sun, takes out his handkerchief and mops the sweat from his brow.

Andy and Foster continue to bicker over the barn's replacement cost. Barney sees a bucket sitting on a bench beside a shed. Hoping the bucket contains water, he walks to it.

The script directions describe what happens next. *Barney takes a dipper, scoops into the bucket, and takes a long drink. He drains the dipper and immediately his eyes bug, he clutches his throat, sniffs dipper, then bucket . . . then on instinct goes into the shed.*

Barney emerges from the shed and walks over to Andy. The cost negotiations are entering their final stages. Barney, waiting for an opportunity to report his discovery, begins to sway as he bides his time.

Barney, growing impatient, interrupts. He has something to report. Andy hushes him up. Barney begins quietly playing with his holster. He grins, rolls his eyes upward, and places his chin on Andy's shoulder.

Andy turns, catches a whiff of Barney's breath, and realizes . . . Barney is gassed!

Andy quickly puts the pieces of the puzzle together. Foster is running a still and set fire to his own barn.

Foster protests. Barney, in response, shakes his head "no," and repeats Jubal's name five times in a reprimanding tone. Jubal Foster is guilty!

Andy and Barney take Foster by the arm and start walking toward the squad car. Barney weaves, stumbles, and almost falls. Foster, seeing this, changes positions. Andy and Foster resume the journey, holding Barney securely between them.

"It's funny to see a person who doesn't drink accidentally take a sip," says Jack. "Barney, after sipping the moonshine, becomes an instant drunk. Don Knotts played it beautifully. No wonder he won five Emmys."

"Barney being helped to the car by Andy and Jubal was the perfect ending," says Jack. "The scene was easy to write. It fell naturally into place."

The epilogue, one of the best in the series, is set in Opie's room. Opie is painting with watercolors when Andy enters. (In the script, Opie is working on a model plane.)

Andy apologizes for not trusting Opie's "word." He admits that he pronounced Opie "guilty" and then went looking for evidence. Andy confesses that he should have known better.

Andy and Opie agree to "consider the case closed."

Before leaving, Andy brings up "one other thing." He tells Opie that when he was a boy, he too was a member of a secret club. His job in the club was Keeper of the Flame.

Andy's father was fearful of his son handling a lighted candle. In response, he came up with "an outstanding idea." He replaced the candle with a flashlight and renamed Andy the Keeper of the Flashlight!

Andy presents Opie with a flashlight, *a flat kind that can serve as a lantern.*

Andy affectionally pats Opie on the shoulder and exits.

Opie *admires his gift, then looking after his father, says (thoughtfully, with a touch of surprise), "He ain't so dumb."*

"Andy revealing that as a boy he too belonged to a secret club and was the Keeper of the Flame might be a bit too convenient, but it led to the great line 'He ain't so dumb,'" says Jack. "The payoff was well worth the setup."

"Another memory I have is the same one I have for all the other scripts," says Jack. "We wrote them, handed them in, then got them back. We rewrote them and handed them back in. After that, a lot of talented people made the show work."

"The Manicurist"

"We never knew that manicures would turn out to be such a rich subject for humor. Lucky us!"—JACK ELINSON

Episode 48

First Broadcast on
January 22, 1962

Written by
Charles Stewart
and Jack Elinson

Opening Directed by
Bob Sweeney

Barbara Eden
Guest Stars as
Ellen Brown

"The Manicurist" begins in Floyd's Barbershop. Barney is getting a haircut, Andy is waiting his turn, and Mayor Pike and two other men are sitting around enjoying the usual "cracker-barrel session."

This will be the last on-screen appearance of Mayor Pike. Dick Elliot, the actor playing the role, passed away from natural causes thirty-seven days after the production of "The Manicurist" was completed on November 15, 1961.

The mayor complains that the "world is moving too fast." Floyd turns toward the mayor, jesters with his scissors to punctuate his agreement, and afterward, with scissors in hand, turns back toward Barney.

Barney pulls back in alarm. He feels Floyd is carelessly attacking him with the scissors. Floyd's scissor assault is repeated three times during the haircut. Floyd ends the trim with an overabundant brushing of talc. Barney protests and tells Floyd he is not "a diseased crop."

"This was our favorite kind of scene," says Jack. "Before starting the story, the small-town guys are just talking about life in general and how the world is moving too fast. All the scenes like these, to me, were always a highlight. We delayed the story for a moment of plain old small talk typical of a small town."

"It's rare when you can get two sources of comedy in one scene," says Jack. "In this opening scene, source one is the everyday discussion about the world in general. Source two is Barney trying to keep Floyd from cutting his head off."

The Nashville bus arrives across the street. (In the script, the bus is arriving from Miami.) Barney sees the bus through the front window. A passenger exits. Barney's eyes bulge!

The passenger, Ellen Brown, *a well-endowed, lovely thing, is stepping off the bus, suitcase in hand. She is a bit flashier than Mayberry is used to.*

"Just as Alan Hale Jr. was perfect for 'The Farmer Takes a Wife,' Barbara Eden was perfect for 'The Manicurist,'" says Jack.

The men join Barney at the front window. They admire Ellen Brown and are momentarily stunned speechless by her beauty.

Speech returns. "Ring a ding, ding," "That's what I call a female," and Andy's, "That is definitely not a boy," are spoken.

Barney is asked if he could handle a gal like Ellen. With a cocky attitude, Barney answers that he knows just what to do. Barney *struts, twirls a whistle on a chain, is the picture of the Sporting Life.* (This script-directed behavior was deleted from the filmed episode.)

Barney says he would "be inclined to treat a gal like that a little rough. They kind of expect it . . . let her know right off who's boss. Rough 'em up." (These lines are often edited out in reruns.)

"I am amazed that Barney's lines are edited out of the reruns," says Jack. "We wrote the lines because we felt they fit what the character was all about. Barney thought of himself as John Wayne as a law officer and as Clark Gable as a lover.

~~Anyone who would~~ think he'd ever be rough ~~with a woman didn't get it. Obvi-~~ ~~ously, all the rough talk was simply a setup to have him freeze~~ when ~~this beauti-~~ ~~ful woman walks in."~~

Andy ~~tells Barney~~ he ~~may get~~ the ~~chance~~ to demonstrate his ~~way of treating a~~ ~~woman. Ellen is walking toward them!~~

~~The scene's script direction reveals Barney's true self.~~ . . . ~~all bravado and no ac-~~ ~~tion. Barney quickly looks out and grows numb with terror. He practically plasters~~ ~~himself against the wall.~~

~~Ellen enters.~~ She is ~~looking for the proprietor. All the men, except for Floyd and~~ Andy, ~~quickly~~ retreat ~~out the door.~~

The ~~script~~ describes Ellen ~~as a girl with the ability to talk nonstop seemingly~~ ~~without taking a breath.~~

~~Ellen~~ explains that her boyfriend, Pierre, has repeatedly asked her to marry him. ~~Ellen needed~~ time ~~to think~~ over the ~~proposal,~~ so she got on a bus ~~in hopes~~ of ~~finding a friendly town~~ that would ~~provide~~ her with the ~~unpressured opportu-~~ ~~nity to think~~ through her ~~future.~~ The ~~sign marking the city limits read,~~ "Welcome to Mayberry, the ~~Friendly Town."~~ Mayberry ~~seemed~~ like ~~what~~ she was ~~looking~~ for. Ellen's ~~chosen profession~~ is a manicurist. She is hoping for a job in ~~Floyd's barber-~~ ~~shop. Ellen explains this~~ in ~~many words.~~

"There ~~are many fast-talkers~~ in this world," ~~says Jack. "Ellen is one of them.~~ She ~~never bothers~~ to ~~put a period between sentences. She just rolls on,~~ going from one ~~subject to another at full speed. Having~~ Ellen talk this way complemented the ~~comedy. Given the fact that~~ Ellen was a ~~knockout beauty,~~ Andy and Floyd don't care ~~how much she talked~~ . . . they just keep staring at her, hoping that this could go on forever."

~~Floyd~~ is ~~stunned~~ by the ~~employment inquiry. Andy doubts there'd be "much~~ ~~call for fingernail doing in Mayberry."~~

"I'm ~~sure that 'fingernail doing' came from Andy Griffith,"~~ says ~~Jack. "A New~~ ~~Yorker, sophisticated as I am,~~ could ~~never have come up with that."~~

~~Ellen~~ agrees to work ~~on commission.~~ She ~~continues talking as she moves a~~ ~~table~~ and ~~two chairs~~ into ~~position~~ by the ~~window.~~ She leaves ~~to settle in at the~~ hotel.

~~After Ellen's departure, Floyd,~~ in a ~~state of shock, passes~~ the ~~situation to Andy.~~ ~~Andy, amused that~~ he has been given the ~~problem to solve,~~ reassures ~~Floyd~~ that it ~~will not take Ellen~~ long ~~to find out there is no work~~ for a manicurist in ~~Mayberry.~~ In ~~the meantime, having~~ Ellen ~~to look at~~ will be ~~like seeing a calendar picture of~~ a pretty girl ~~come~~ to life.

~~"This~~ was such a simple ~~idea,"~~ says ~~Jack.~~ "In a small and ~~sleepy town~~ like ~~May-~~ ~~berry,~~ what would be funnier than ~~having~~ a ~~manicurist in a town where none of~~ the men ever had a manicure? ~~This was one of the easiest scripts we wrote. Every-~~ ~~thing fell into place,~~ and ~~we knew where we were going."~~

"Floyd handing the problem to Andy is in perfect character for him," says Jack. "Floyd gets flustered easily. Andy's line about Ellen being like a calendar come to life belongs to Charles and myself."

Later, Barney, the mayor, Art Crowley, and hardware store owner Sam Lindsay are surprised when they see the "Manicurist on Duty" sign displayed in the barbershop's front window. Ellen comes out of the back room and takes a seat at the manicure table.

Floyd invites the men inside. The men file in, keeping their distance from Ellen. She welcomes them and asks if anyone would like a manicure. There are no takers.

The script directions narrate what follows. *Ellen registers disappointment at the lack of interest. She sets about puttering as manicurists do, putting a hundred little things in order. The moment she turns away from them, the men all look at her, covertly, enjoying all the moving parts . . . in a nice TV way, of course.*

The men never take their eyes off Ellen as they discuss rabbit hunting, fishing, and business at the hardware store. Sam, the owner of the store, says he is thinking about running a sale to boost business. Barney asks what items will be on sale. At this point, Ellen bends over to repair a run in her stocking. Sam answers, "Legs." Barney acknowledges "that's always a good household item."

"This was a fun scene to write," says Jack. "Once we got the idea of how oblivious the guys were, we wrote the scene in minutes."

The script direction continues the narrative. *Ellen, having done all the little things she can think of to occupy her time, picks up her tray and takes it into the back room. The men follow her with their eyes and sit transfixed, waiting for her reappearance. But, instead, the front door opens and Andy enters.*

Andy, not seeing Ellen, reaffirms his earlier prediction that she would not last long in Mayberry. Ellen emerges from the back room. She overheard Andy's statement. In response, she says Mayberry isn't a very friendly town after all. Near tears, she announces she will get back on the bus and leave.

"It was good for a change to have Andy put his foot in his mouth instead of Barney," says Jack. "It shows that Andy wasn't perfect . . . in other words, only human."

The episode's second act begins in the barbershop. Ellen emerges from the back room carrying her suitcase and is obviously ready to leave. Andy enters, sees the suitcase, and tells Ellen he would like a manicure.

Floyd maneuvers Ellen into the back room to get her tray. Floyd and Andy quickly set up the table and chairs. Floyd pats Andy on the shoulder and acknowledges that he is a "real prince of a fellow."

Ellen, in a cold professional manner, begins the manicure. Andy, attempting to break the ice, warns that his nails are a mess and explains that he normally cuts them with dressmaking scissors, poultry shears, or hedge clippers. Ellen can't help but laugh. Andy, continuing the humor, requests that she not file his nails too short . . . he needs a little bit left for scratching.

"We went a little over the top about Andy's previous nail-cutting methods, but we're comedy writers and couldn't resist," says Jack. "The request to 'leave a little bit for scratching' actually makes good sense."

Barney walks by, sees Andy getting a manicure, waves, and continues toward the sheriff's office. After a few seconds, what he has seen registers and he rushes back to the barbershop. Barney can't believe what he is seeing. Andy explains that he wants to look sharp right down to the fingernails. He orders his deputy to look the same.

Barney is pushed into the chair, and his manicure begins. The scene's script directions give insight into what Barney is feeling. *Barney has the expression of a child left to face a tonsillectomy . . . or two weeks at camp. Barney looks upwards and says, 'Wyatt Earp, forgive me.' Barney pulls his hand back and shudders. Barney has a stricken look as he watches every move of the operation.*

Barney instructs Ellen not to file his trigger finger and explains that if the finger gets damaged, he might as well quit the law business.

"It's amazing how often we were able to refer to Barney's trigger finger," says Jack. "It was like Jimmy Durant's nose . . . you could always get a laugh with it. I worked with Jimmy for many years."

Barney eventually grows accustomed to the manicure and allows Ellen to "do" his trigger finger.

Outside, the mayor and Sam are watching Barney's manicure through the window. Andy joins the two and shows off his attractively manicured fingers. He says the best part of the manicure is having a pretty girl like Ellen hold your hand. It's also a pleasure to breathe her pretty perfume. The mayor and Sam are persuaded.

Before long the barbershop is jammed full of customers. Ellen is convinced that Mayberry is a friendly town, but trouble is brewing.

The script directions explain. *Across the street a storm gathers for our heroine in the persons of Emma Watson, the mayor's wife, and one other woman who are peering with much sniffing and snorting at the activity inside Floyd's Barbershop. This is too much. The women look at each other and grimly nod in agreement on what has to be done about this scandalous state of affairs.*

Later, Floyd visits Andy with "awful news." Customers have been canceling manicure appointments "left and right." The cancelations were caused by wives who do not want their husband's hands held by "a pretty young thing like Miss Ellen."

Floyd, uncomfortable with the situation, makes a request: Would Andy talk with Ellen?

Ellen enters and tells Floyd that something very important has come up. Floyd hurries out the door. *Andy sighs and prepares to perform the onerous task Floyd has thrust upon him.* (The writers may be writing comedy, but they do so with a literary flair.)

Ellen is puzzled by Floyd's reaction. Andy begins an explanation. He tells Ellen that nature has been good to her. "I mean real, real, real gooooood! I can't remember any time when I've seen nature spend so much time on any one person!"

"Most men looking at Ellen would say 'You're to die for,'" says Jack. "Andy, being Andy, eases into it with the understatement 'nature has been good to you.' He gets to the point gently."

Andy explains that due to her beauty, she has become a worrisome thing to Mayberry's married women. He suggests it would help if she was married.

A warm smile spreads across Ellen's face. She replies, "Oh, Sheriff Taylor! That is the sweetest proposal I have ever heard!"

Andy is struck dumb.

Ellen turns the proposal down with many words. (Barbara Eden delivers the lengthy dialogue exactly as is written in the script. She never misses a word!)

Ellen explains that she has decided to marry her boyfriend Pierre and will be leaving Mayberry. She cannot marry Andy.

"Here's where Ellen's personality, with her nonstop talking, makes it easy to give us our resolution," says Jack. "She's always on the fence. 'Should I marry Pierre? Should I have come to Mayberry?' She's ditsy. Poor Pierre is going to have a tough life with this woman."

Ellen kisses Andy on the cheek, and Barney, who has just arrived, gets a goodbye kiss as well.

Ellen makes a grand exit. As she walks away, accompanied by a sexy soundtrack melody, all her perfectly moving parts confirm that nature has indeed been good to her.

"All we indicated in our script was *Andy and Barney go out on the street and look after her,*" says Jack.

"Sometimes the epilogues were easy to write and sometimes they were hard," says Jack. "This was especially the case when we'd said everything there was to say. 'The Manicurist' was one of the broadest scripts we wrote . . . just a fun thing all the way with no moral messages. Now we had to squeeze in one or two more pages for the ending."

The episode concludes with Andy and the mayor discovering that the "Manicurist on Duty" sign is back in the barbershop's front window. The mayor rushes in and takes a seat at the manicure table.

The mayor is shocked when elderly Emma Watson emerges from the back room dressed in a manicurist uniform. This time Floyd has made sure he will not have any further trouble with jealous wives!

"The Jinx"

Episode 49

First Broadcast on
January 29, 1962

Written by
**Jack Elinson and
Charles Stewart**

Directed by
Bob Sweeney

John Qualen
Guest Stars as Henry
Bennett, the Jinx

"Cryin' out loud, Andy, he pulled out the hat size!!!"—BARNEY FIFE

"The Jinx" begins with a man and woman walking by the front window of the barbershop. The brief shot introduces the location of the first scene. ("The Manicurist" opened with the same exact footage of the walking couple.)

Inside the barbershop, Barney and Floyd are playing a game of checkers. Several men are watching, including Henry Bennett. Henry stands behind Barney. Barney starts to make a move but stops.

He turns around and asks Henry to stand somewhere else. Barney believes it is bad luck for someone to stand over a player's left shoulder.

"Superstition, hard to believe, is still alive and well," says Jack. "'Don't ever walk under a ladder. Don't ever let a black cat cross your path' . . . and on and on. We thought it would be a good topic for an episode."

Barney moves a checker. Floyd responds by jumping three of Barney's checkers in succession and wins the game.

Barney blames his loss on Henry. Henry protests and tells Barney that his loss may be the result of carelessness rather than bad luck.

Barney recalls that Virgil Hush was pitching a beautiful game of horseshoes during last year's Labor Day celebration until Henry patted him on the back, and Virgil lost the game.

Andy enters and is told by Barney that Henry hexed his checker playing. Henry tells Andy that because of this he has been labeled a jinx.

Floyd, justifying the label, recalls that Henry once caught a foul ball at a little league game and threw it back into play. The next batter hit a fly to Floyd's son who dropped the hexed ball.

Andy defends Henry. Barney, however, is convinced Henry is a jinx.

Henry has heard enough. He calls Barney "a great big sap" and angrily walks out. After Henry is out of earshot Barney yells after him, "Who are you calling a sap?" (In the filmed episode, Barney closes the barbershop's door to assure that Henry doesn't hear his response.)

Andy is disgusted with Barney's behavior. He tells the men they are acting like a "bunch of superstitious schoolboys." (Andy Griffith marked out "schoolboys" on his script and replaced it with "young'uns." Later, Andy calls the men barbershop clowns. This too was deleted from the script.)

Andy departs and finds Henry outside. He tells Henry that the men were only joking. Henry, however, doesn't find being called a jinx funny.

"Andy tells Henry the men are just joking," says Jack. "The reality is that it's not a joke to Barney and Floyd. They really believe there is something to it, and if that's hurtful to Henry, so be it. That's what the episode is all about . . . how damaging it can be to give someone a label. It's the whole point of the story."

Andy has an idea. He invites Henry to join Barney and himself on the opening day of the fishing season. The two always do "extra good" because they know the location of a special fishing hole. A successful day of fishing would prove Henry is not a jinx.

Henry is concerned about what Barney will think. Andy tells him not to worry—once you explain something to Barney, "he gets real sensible."

"Sensible" Barney is upset when he learns Andy has invited Henry to join them for the opening day fishing sweepstakes. Andy and Barney have caught the biggest fish three years in a row, but with Henry in their boat, Barney believes they have no chance of repeating their wins.

Barney is disappointed that he and Thelma Lou will have nothing to celebrate. They had planned a "entime dinner." The two had planned a dinner featuring the prize-winning trout accompanied by candlelight, wine, and the music of Cole Porter. Barney regrets that he will not be reaping the benefits of *the certain effect Porter's music has on Thelma Lou*.

"There are two reasons for Barney's planned celebration plans," says Jack. "First, to establish how much he's looking forward to it. Second, to remind the audience of Barney's and Thelma Lou's romantic relationship."

Andy jokingly dismisses Barney's concerns. In response, Barney says, "You're funny, you are! Why don't you put a flower in your lapel and squirt water?"

"It was fun writing Barney's comeback," says Jack. "The comebacks became a staple for the series . . . like the single bullet."

Later that afternoon, Opie stops by the sheriff's office. He finds Barney in the backroom *engrossed in a large volume with old-fashioned binding*.

The book, borrowed from Barney's grandma, is full of "valuable information."

Barney reads aloud two examples. "Do not trot the horses across a bridge going to a funeral. Never bury a chicken with his mouth open. The first person who leaves the grave after a funeral will be the next to die." (These superstitions are deleted from the filmed episode.)

The *idea of being left alone to mull over these macabre items is not too appealing to Barney*, so he invites Opie to stick around and keep him company.

Barney thumbs through the book and finds what he is looking for. "To ensure good luck before a coming event . . . rub the head of a redheaded man. If a man with red hair cannot be obtained, a boy will do."

"I believe we made up the stuff in Barney's grandmother's book to ward off bad luck," says Jack. "I'm sure that there are books like that around, but we didn't want to take the time to find one."

Barney looks at Opie and receives permission to give his "carrot top" a good rub.

Andy enters and is asked by Opie if he would like to rub his head as a precaution against a jinx. Opie, thinking about superstitions, repeats two of the warnings Barney read to him earlier. "Don't never run across a bridge when you're going to a funeral and never bury a chicken with your mouth open." (This joke, based on a child's jumbled memory, was deleted from the filmed episode.)

Andy tells Barney to stop the superstitious nonsense. Barney nods in agreement while rubbing Opie's head.

The next day Andy, Barney, and Henry are fishing from a boat and not catching anything. Barney is busy rubbing a rabbit's foot and muttering incantations. "Come fish come. Come fish come. Sam's at the gate with a frosted cake. Come fish come!" and "Fly away buzzard; fly away crow, way down South where the wind don't blow. Rub your nose and give two winks and save us from this awful jinx."

"It was fun to write the rhymes," says Jack. "Sometimes, they take longer than writing dialogue, but it's worth it. Now, in addition to our credit as comedy writers, we can add 'poets.'"

Andy's fishing line begins "whirring out" and his pole bends. He has hooked a big one!

The script directions narrate what happens next. *Water is pouring into the boat. Andy grabs an oar and hands it to Barney. As he does so the fish escapes. Andy looks at the lost pole, the lost fish, the rapidly filling boat . . . then, to add insult to injury there is a sudden clap of thunder. They all look up at the sky. Andy's eyes slowly settle on Henry. Henry looks back at him, and the single thought between them is "Could it be? Could it really be?"*

In the filmed episode, the boat sinks completely beneath the water leaving the occupants wet from the waist down. (The clap of thunder, which the writers planned to reference later in the episode, is omitted from the soundtrack.)

The next day, the barbershop gang discusses the fishing incident. Floyd suggests hiding the lake the next time Henry decides to go fishing. (This line was deleted from the script.)

Andy enters and is asked if he still believes Henry is not a jinx. Andy doesn't feel that the bad day of fishing can be blamed on Henry. The boat sinking is more the fault of Earl Gilley, the boat's owner. Earl was too "blame cheap" to seal the boat with quality caulking.

The scripted name of the boat's owner was Fred Evans. Andy Griffith marked through the name on his copy of the script and changed it to Earl Gilley. Earlie Gilley was a longtime friend and married to Andy Griffith's cousin, Lorraine Beasley.

Barney accuses Andy of "flying" in the face of science and brings up Buzz Fluehart's discovery of the effect that atmospheric rays have on bodily action. Scientific fact proves Henry is a jinx because he creates static that jars a successful atmospheric ray into an unsuccessful motion.

"I'm sure we all have a friend who pretends to be an expert on just about everything," says Jack. "Barney was a know-it-all. There isn't anything he doesn't know better than anyone else . . . and that includes Albert Einstein."

Aunt Bee enters. She is selling raffle tickets for the church social. The prize is a portable TV.

Floyd recalls that last year's raffle prize was a transistor radio "without the earplug."

"We loved coming up with lines like 'a transistor radio without an earplug,'" says Jack. "That kind of line helped get across the image of a small town and small-town people who don't have all the modern conveniences, like earplugs, they have in the big cities."

Barney spies Henry coming toward the barbershop. He hurriedly touches everyone with his rabbit's foot and tells them to hold their left earlobe with their right hand. Barney recites, "Winken, pinken, Noddamus Rex, protect us from the man with the hex."

"This was where we really went crazy," says Jack. "Having established Barney's superstitious nature, the sky was the limit."

Henry enters, sees the group protecting themselves from a jinx, and realizes he will be blamed for every bad thing that happens in Mayberry.

Henry makes an announcement. He has decided to leave Mayberry. He plans to put his farm up for sale and move upstate near a brother. (The details of the plan are deleted from the filmed episode.)

The men are surprised by the announcement and humiliated for having caused the proposed move.

After Henry leaves, the men decide they must show him his luck has changed. Floyd suggests that Henry winning the church raffle would likely do this, but how can his winning be guaranteed?

Andy suggests cheating. All the numbers on the raffle tickets will be the same. No one will answer when the winning number is called, except Henry.

The plan is approved. Floyd, in response, tells Andy he "sure is a good sneak."

"I don't remember any problem coming up with Andy's plan to ensure that Henry wins the raffle prize," says Jack. "There didn't seem to be any other way to assure that Henry would win."

The script gives the next scene's location and action. *INT. SOCIAL HALL— NIGHT: A square dance is in progress. Andy holds a derby hat, which he hands to Aunt Bee.*

The filmed episode inserts an important scene between the square dancing and the passing of the hat. A little cowboy is shown standing with one hand propped against the wall, the other hand placed on his hip, and his legs crossed. The character, played by Clint Howard, will later be given the name "Leon" and make four more appearances in the series.

Ronny Howard was usually accompanied to *The Griffith Show* set by his father, Rance. Younger brother Clint stayed at home with his mother, Jean. Occasionally, Clint and Jean would visit.

The two visited *The Griffith Show* soundstage on either Tuesday, December 5, or Wednesday, December 6, 1961, when the filming of the interiors was scheduled. Seeing Clint dressed as a cowboy, director Bob Sweeney decided to include him in the opening of the social hall scene.

"I don't remember Clint Howard being part of the crowd at the church social," says Jack. "I'm sure we must have spotted his addition when we saw the finished show broadcast. His presence provided the scene with a laugh."

Later in the evening, Andy is asked to draw the winning raffle ticket. The script includes detailed instructions on how this is to be done. *Andy reaches into a fishbowl with some numbers in it and, putting on a large act of not looking at the numbers, he turns completely away and gropes into the bowl until he brings out a number.*

The winning number is forty-four. As planned, no one answers—not even Henry. Andy prods Henry to look at his number. Henry double-checks his number. It is six and seven-eighths. Barney inspects the ticket and discovers Henry picked out the hat's size!

"We felt we needed just one more funny beat before the revelation of the rigged plan," says Jack. "That's when we came up with the six and seven-eighths cap size."

Henry feels he has jinxed himself and starts to leave. Andy stops him and explains that the raffle was rigged. Henry is "flabbergasted" to learn that all the tickets had the same number. Aunt Bee tells Henry that everyone wanted him to win the TV and hoped that doing so would convince him that he was not a jinx.

Andy points out that the luckiest thing a person can have is friendship. A person with friends "can't ever be a loser."

"It was definitely our purpose to teach a lesson," says Jack. "We did this on many of the episodes."

Aunt Bee suggests that the TV be awarded to Henry by unanimous consent. (In the script this is Barney's idea.) Everyone agrees.

Andy asks Barney to drive Henry home. In response, Barney looks around anxiously. On the way out, he spies a man with red hair. With a smile of relief, Barney quickly massages the puzzled man's head.

"Having Barney rub the head of a red-haired man before getting into the car with Henry made the point that Barney was and would always be a big believer of bad luck happening if you don't ward it off somehow," says Jack.

The next day Andy and Opie are waiting for Barney. The three are going fishing. Andy and Opie pass the time playing a game of checkers.

Barney enters, stands behind Andy, and watches as Andy makes a move. In response, Opie makes *about six jumps in a row, sweeping the board.*

Opie shouts, "I won, and I never did before in my whole life! Didja see that, Uncle Barney?" (The dialogue in the filmed episode was changed to "I beat Paw! Did you see that, Barney?")

Andy sees an opportunity to do a little picking at Barney and claims Barney hexed him.

Barney does not want to hear it and changes the subject. He reminds Andy that they had planned to go fishing. He strides to the door as a clap of thunder rumbles in the distance.

Earlier in the script, during the fishing sweepstakes, a clap of thunder was proof that Henry is a jinx. A storm is coming because Henry is present! The sound of thunder was deleted from the filmed episode.

The thunder rumbling outside the sheriff's office is the result of Barney, the new Mayberry jinx. The relationship of the two thunderclaps was defeated by the deletion of the thunder from the soundtrack in the earlier scene. The thunder rumble without earlier reference is a weaker proof that Barney is a jinx.

Andy, hearing the thunder, says, "Bad Luck Barney, you've done it again!" He rubs Opie's "carrot top" as a precaution.

Barney angrily stomps out and says to Andy, "You're a riot! Why don't you go someplace and happen?"

"Barney's parting line just popped into our mind," says Jack. "It's sort of like the line that's going around right now . . . 'Get a life.'"

"I often join Aaron Ruben and a group of comedy writers for breakfast," says Jack. "Recently, Aaron and I were talking about 'The Jinx.' He recalled that Don and Andy were disappointed in the way this show turned out. In reading this script again after forty years, it kind of fell flat as I went through it. Don and Andy never mentioned their feelings to us. I'm glad they didn't. In those days, I could get depressed really easily."

"Jailbreak"

Episode 50

First Broadcast on
February 5, 1962

Written by
Harvey Bullock

Directed by
Bob Sweeney

Allan Melvin
Guest Stars as
Clarence "Doc"
Malloy

"We were all hungry freelance writers, pitching story ideas to as many different shows as we could but happiest when it was *The Andy Griffith Show*. Every writer in town wanted an assignment there, knowing the performers were magic and the production/direction was flawless. The friendly atmosphere on the set gave it the sweet smell of success."
—HARVEY BULLOCK

"'Jailbreak' was my first 'Barney' show," says Harvey Bullock. (Harvey's two previous *TAGS* scripts, 'Opie's Hobo Friend' and 'The Pickle Story' had not featured Barney prominently.) "My reaction to getting the assignment? Pure joy. I had, of course, watched Don Knotts perform other scripts and marveled at his magic. That gifted man was a writer's very best friend; he made us look good.

"The storyline for 'Jailbreak' developed from inevitable chuckles while watching Don do other episodes. It also involved long hours of staring at the ceiling, making false starts, then finally getting a few notions in good enough shape to present them verbally to *TAGS* producer Aaron Ruben. To me, getting a story idea was by far the hardest part of writing. But when you finally molded and shaped the idea, and the outline worked, then it became interesting, and the fun began. I couldn't wait to give Barney some transparent tough-guy lines and all the other business at which Don was so masterful."

The filmed episode begins with Barney reading a book out loud to himself. The word "silenc-er" is separated by the turning of a page. "The title of Barney's book, *Penitentiary*, was named in my script," says Harvey. "The page-divider joke was not. It may have been added from Andy's recollections of the opening scene from *No Time for Sergeants* in which Will Stockdale reads a page-divided word."

Barney's reading is interrupted by the arrival of State Inspector Horton. Horton, who is looking for the sheriff, refuses to explain the reason for his visit to Barney. Hoping to impress the inspector, Barney stands in front of a framed newspaper clipping that reports one of his arrests. Barney asks Horton if the frame is straight. The headline of the clipping reads, "Deputy Sheriff Barney Fife Cracks Walker Case."

"In my script the headline reads, 'Barney Fife Makes Heroic Capture' and underneath, 'Commended for Excellent Police Work,'" says Harvey. "The script directions were *framed, large headlines, large clear picture of Barney.*"

By referring to a previous crime from a first-season episode ("Andy the Matchmaker"), this minor change adds realism to the episode and establishes a sense of continuity with Mayberry's "on-screen" past.

Barney gets a call from the grocery store while Horton is waiting for Andy. The grocer tells Barney he has captured "Sam," a dog belonging to Floyd "that's been barking every morning and waking up the whole neighborhood." Again hoping to impress Horton, Barney says he'll "take the big brute single-handed." Horton still refuses to explain the reason for his visit. Instead he asks directions to Andy's house.

Harvey's guidelines for Sam's physical appearance were given primarily through a joke omitted in the filmed episode. Barney was originally supposed to say, "Looking at him, you'd never guess he belonged to a barber, would you?" The line was followed by the script instructions, "Close on dog—featuring long hair over eyes."

The inclusion of a grocery-store scene required the hiring of an additional actor and the decorating of a grocery-store set. Both increased the total production cost of the episode. Although it was easier and cheaper to simply show Barney taking the call in the courthouse, Harvey explains why the short scene was necessary: "The grocery set was very small, what is called a 'fragment.' It was vital that the grocer set all the lines for Barney's listening, and the 'feed' lines from the grocer had to be clear. If Barney was just listening, it would bog down, and any words from the grocer that Barney heard might also be overheard by State Police Inspector Horton. Yes, the inclusion of the scene was a small decision, but a very good one."

When Horton finds Andy, he tells Andy that one of the fellows who robbed the furniture-factory payroll, Clarence "Doc" Malloy, is in Mayberry. Horton feels that Malloy will eventually lead him to Malloy's partner and the stolen payroll. Horton wants Andy's agreement to stay clear of the operation.

Soon afterward, Malloy gets "wise" and "makes a break for it." Horton arrests Malloy and brings him to the courthouse to be locked up. Malloy is locked in the cell where Barney has been holding Floyd's dog Sam. Sam has been shedding, so the cell's cot is covered with dog hair.

Barney gets excited when he learns that Malloy is in the Mayberry jail. Barney feels this is a "golden opportunity to interrogate this bird."

The comic spotlight shines brightly on Barney as he prepares to be "planted" as a stool pigeon in Malloy's cell. Don Knotts brings Harvey's directions for the scene magically to life. The directions were as follows:

Barney appears from the back room. He has changed into his street clothes, suit, and tie. Barney walks over to the mirror to check his appearance. Not too happy, he loosens his tie, that's better—still not right. He musses his hair a little—better and better. Now he tries a hard, bitter expression, checks it full face and profile—adds a bit of a meaner leer and goes into the cell.

The sleeping Malloy is awakened when Barney enters the cell. Playing the role of a fellow prisoner, Barney tells Malloy that he's going to "pick the lock, get that 'gat' [the gun hanging on a rack beside the framed newspaper clipping], and bust out."

When Malloy looks at the gun, he sees Barney's picture in the framed clipping. Malloy asks Barney, "Who are you?" Barney replies, "Puddingtame." Playing along, Malloy questions Barney about his ability to "spring out of here." Barney answers, "They don't call me 'Fingers' for nothing."

Barney tells Malloy that after they break out they'll need some "dough for a hideout until we cool off." Barney asks Malloy if he has a partner or any money. Malloy says he is hesitant to answer because he feels Barney may "tell the cops." Barney assures Malloy that he "has been called plenty, everything from 'Chopper' to 'Mad Dog.' One name they never call me is 'Tattletale.'"

After Barney picks the lock and opens the door, he and Malloy say in unison, "So far, so good." Barney insists that they lock little fingers and say, "needles/pins." While Barney's back is turned, Malloy gets the gun. He then locks Barney in the cell and escapes.

"Barney's progression of nicknames (Fingers, Chopper, to Mad Dog, but never Tattletale) helps set up his lock picking," says Harvey. "They were just a mish-mash in Barney's style. 'Puddingtame' is an old wheeze, funny when used by an adult. 'Needles/pins' is an example of another child's routine from a desperate adult."

Horton is upset when he learns of Malloy's escape. He again orders Andy to "stay out of this." Andy feels otherwise. However, Barney has no desire to get involved further. Instead, he plans to take the suit he wore while in the cell with Malloy to the cleaners. The suit is "just full of dog hairs."

While stopping by the dry cleaner's to drop off Barney's suit, Andy and Barney learn from dry-cleaner H. Fred Goss that "this is the second suit in a row to come in here with dog hairs." Goss's comment captures Andy's attention. Andy questions Goss further and learns a lady brought the suit in. Goss points out the lady's car, which is still parked across the street. The car has a trailer hitch on the back bumper. From this, Andy figures out that Malloy is hiding at the trailer camp.

"I don't know where I got the name 'Goss,'" says Harvey, "but for once I did have a source for the character. When I lived in New York City, my hearing was getting bad, and my family doctor sent me to an ear doctor, evidently a very unfashionable, but very talented, older man. I went to his office in a stuffy, crammed house, and he pulled up a stool to put the 'flashlight' in my ears. His vest was covered with cigarette ashes, and he was smoking the whole time I was there, seemingly unaware of his ashtray vest and the constant fresh ash dropping."

After going to the trailer camp, Andy and Barney split up. While searching for Malloy, Barney comes across a trailer with a "Just Married" sign. He sees the sign, walks away, but then goes back for a look. The newlywed couple, the Franklins, sensing Barney's presence, stop kissing and look up. Harvey explains the thinking behind Barney's actions: "Barney's instructions were to search every vehicle, and the sign could have been a ruse. He decided that he must check them all and, with some apprehension and embarrassment, looked in the Franklins' window."

Andy and Barney reunite and spot the car Malloy's partner was driving. Barney looks inside the attached trailer and sees Malloy, his partner, and Horton, who is being held prisoner. After Andy goes to get some help, Malloy decides to leave. While Malloy is inside the trailer, Barney jumps in the car and drives away. Pulling the trailer, Barney drives the car to the courthouse, where the shaken Malloy is recaptured.

As Malloy exits the trailer, Barney points to his gun and says, "This baby's loaded with six bullets this time."

There is no previous mention in the episode that Malloy was aware of only one bullet or that the one bullet was a factor in his escape, so the line seems unnecessary.

"Yes, Malloy was never told about Barney's single bullet," says Harvey. "It is not important to the story that Malloy knows what Barney means. It is just Barney being excitable and delighted with the extra artillery and telling the world—and Andy."

In the epilogue, Andy, Barney, and Opie are looking at the disguises in a toy detective set. The Franklins stop by the courthouse to report a peeping Tom at the trailer camp. The complaint is given to Andy. Barney turns his back to the couple. Andy asks Barney if he will take down the information about this peeping Tom. When Barney turns around, he is wearing a fake nose and glasses from the toy detective set. He gives an excuse (which is unclear because of the laugh track) and makes a hasty departure.

"I don't think I introduced the Franklins earlier in the episode just to set up the epilogue," says Harvey. "I concentrated on the main story. Then when that was finished, I looked for some loose ends or a funny setup—and bringing back the Franklins seemed to do it."

"On my script, Barney's last line reads, 'I can't now, Andy, Opie and I are going out for a soda,'" says Harvey. "I guess the laugh at his disguise covered the line, but it wasn't a gag line. It was just a production line. A gag line together with the disguise would have been trying for a 'double' joke, which can be tricky and confusing."

Harvey adds, "I was told that the crew seemed to enjoy shooting 'Jailbreak.' This is oddly pleasing to a writer. That millions would view it with approval was a fuzzy distant possibility, but if two-score working professionals—who had seen it all—if they approved, then the long hours of ceiling-staring were all worthwhile."

"Barney and the Choir"

Episode 52

First Broadcast on
February 19, 1962

Written by
Charles Stewart
and Jack Elinson

Directed by
Bob Sweeney

"John Masters has welcomed Barney aboard. [Looks upward prayerfully] 'Now I just hope the ship makes port!'"—ANDY

"Barney and the Choir" was filmed on a different schedule from the regular *Andy Griffith Show* routine. Friday was normally rehearsal day. Monday, Tuesday, and Wednesday were filming days.

The filming of "Barney and the Choir" began on Friday, December 22, 1961. The Christmas and New Year's layoff began the next day, Saturday, December 23, and ran through Monday, January 1, 1962. Filming of the episode resumed on Tuesday, January 2, and ended on Wednesday, January 3.

The script direction narrates the episode's opening. *Andy is working at his desk. Barney is working at the bulletin board. As Barney works, he sings a song such as "Juanita." He thinks he is the second coming of Sinatra, but Andy doesn't share this opinion. Andy is suffering. Every off-key note . . . and they are the ones Barney holds longest . . . causes him to wince and roll his eyes in pain.*

"I don't exactly know why, but there's something funny when you hear a person singing off-key," says Jack. "My wife sings off-key, and I laugh every time she does so. I'm color-blind, and people laugh at me whenever I can't see color correctly. There's just something amusing about not being perfect."

"I believe Juanita was mentioned on other episodes," says Jack. "I think she was a waitress at a diner on the edge of town. I don't think she was ever seen. We knew Barney was interested in her. It seemed natural that he would express his interest in song."

Andy attempts to engage Barney in conversation instead of song. He asks about the new wanted posters. Barney, however, has music in his heart and resumes his "Juanita" serenade.

Aunt Bee arrives at the sheriff's office with a lunch tray. Barney exits into the back room to wash up. While he is absent, Andy confides in Aunt Bee.

Aunt Bee advises Andy to be tolerant of Barney's singing. Barney returns in song. Aunt Bee, forgetting her advice, immediately hands Barney a sandwich to shut him up.

At this point, John Masters, the choir director, enters. He is upset and shares the news that the choir's first tenor is dropping out. The choir had planned to participate in an upcoming state choral contest. This is a serious matter!

Barney listens with eager anticipation. The wheels are turning.

Barney casually recalls a saying of his old music teacher: "A choir without its tenor is like a star without its glimmer."

"The old music teacher's catchy saying was an original line we came up with," says Jack. "Charles and I felt that Barney never had a voice teacher. He was misleading John Masters."

John, learning that Barney is a trained first tenor, welcomes him "aboard." Andy and Aunt Bee are horror-stricken. Barney is ecstatic.

Barney can't wait to share the news with Thelma Lou. He is certain she will be thrilled.

Later, Thelma Lou is not thrilled. The news is unbelievable. Barney can't sing a lick!

"Thelma Lou says Barney can't sing . . . wait until they get married and she finds out he also snores," says Jack. "We knew her comment about Barney's singing deficiencies would get a laugh. Human frailties are sometimes funny."

That night at rehearsal, John presents Barney and thanks him for "coming to the rescue." The choir applauds and gathers around Barney to welcome him.

While Barney is occupied, Andy sidles over to John and reminds him that it is customary to audition new choir members. Andy is concerned that John has never heard Barney sing.

In response, John points out that it is a blessing to have a trained singer like Barney step forward in a time of emergency.

The audition dialogue points out an obvious question. Why would a conscientious choir director like John Masters give Barney the solo without first hearing him sing? John's decision was based on Barney's word, not his singing talent.

The audition dialogue was deleted from the script. The deletion weakens the realism of the story. Andy voicing the obvious question and John Masters's "emergency" situation response are never heard.

John Masters begins the rehearsal with a run-through of 14A, "Welcome Sweet Springtime." It doesn't take long for Barney's lack of talent to emerge. He hits a clinker on the word "song."

"'Welcome Sweet Springtime' wasn't our selection," says Jack. "Most likely it came from Earle Hagen, our musical director. We did come up with '14A.' I haven't the faintest idea why we threw in the 'A.'"

John Masters detects the flat note and stops the choir. Barney volunteers to move around and see if he can spot the culprit.

Barney's plan works in reverse. As he moves through the choir each person becomes aware it is Barney's "not-so-golden" voice that's off-key.

After the rehearsal, Andy, Aunt Bee, Thelma Lou, and John Masters gather for an emergency meeting. John has decided to tell Barney to get out of the choir. Andy feels it is wrong to dismiss Barney so soon.

The group cannot agree on how to deal with Barney's lack of talent. Aunt Bee suggests that Barney's singing may improve. The others give her an "Oh come on now" look.

Aunt Bee's suggestion is deleted and replaced with Andy's solution: "Maybe he'll fall down and break his mouth."

A week before the choral competition, John Masters calls a secret rehearsal at his home. The choir needs to practice without Barney.

The choir sings 14A. The doorbell rings. They have been discovered. Hazel, the pianist, stops playing and with a hand covers her mouth in the surprise of getting caught in the act.

"We never dreamed that Hazel would do so well without saying a word," says Jack. "We didn't even give her a name. I think she was later named in honor of script consultant Hazel Hall. I'm sure the actress playing the role was hired as an extra and faked the piano playing."

Barney enters. He was unaware that the meeting place had been changed but happy that he "turned down Elm Street and heard the singing." The choir returns to 14A. Barney joins in. Another practice is ruined!

Two days before the concert, John Masters meets with Andy and Thelma Lou. John cannot let the choir's performance be ruined by "that caterwauling tenor."

Andy feels it would be best if he and Thelma Lou gave Barney the news of his dismissal. Andy suggests that she and Barney come by the house that evening. After supper, the two will sit Barney down, "talk to him, reason with him, explain it all to him, then tie him up and put him in the closet."

That evening Andy, Aunt Bee, Opie, Thelma Lou, and Barney adjourn to the living room after supper. The time has come to broach the subject. Andy wants to talk about the choir. Before he can continue, Barney voices Andy's concern. The way 14A has been sung "leaves a lot to be desired." Barney suggests the adults "get in a little practice."

Barney escorts Thelma Lou to the piano to "tickle the ivories." Andy. Aunt Bee, and Opie gather around. Barney takes the role of choir director.

The mini choir begins singing 14A. At Barney's first clinker, Opie comments, "Someone sounds terrible." The music and the clinkers continue. Opie, "the little big mouth," comments, "I think it's Uncle Bar . . ." Andy claps a hand over Opie's mouth. (This is Jack and Charles's second consecutive script in which Opie refers to Barney as "Uncle." "Uncle" is deleted.)

Barney hits a long high note. Andy has an idea. He stops the music and examines Barney's throat. Andy reports that his throat is red, swollen, and lumpy. Barney will have to forget about the concert. He should go home and rest.

Later, as Andy is getting ready for bed, the doorbell buzzes. Barney enters with great news. He visited the doctor who found nothing wrong. The lump Andy detected was a uvula. Barney explains, "All God's children got a uvula." Andy dully responds, "Hallelujah."

"As Barney said, 'All God's children got a uvula,' that's how we knew," says Jack. "When Andy said, 'Hallelujah.' It wasn't said with joy. As writers, we needed to keep Barney in the choir, and this was a funny way to do it."

The next day, the whole choir, except Barney, discusses what to do next. Andy, sharing his thoughts, says aloud, "It's a shame Barney can't talk his part."

Barney enters. Andy, putting his thought into action, tells Barney the group has decided that he should recite rather than sing the lyrics of "Welcome Sweet Springtime." Andy explains that Barney's dramatic voice will be effective in the middle of all the singing.

Andy moves Barney to the side as the choir begins 14A. After the opening verse, it is time for the recitation. The spoken word, however, doesn't last long. Barney, unable to stop himself, breaks into song. Like a bird, he was born to sing!

The next day Andy meets with John Masters. He has worked out a plan. Barney will be on stage singing into a dead microphone. The live microphone will be backstage with someone else singing into it.

"Andy was getting desperate as one plan after another wasn't working, and that led us to the dead microphone idea," says Jack.

John asks, "Why go to all that bother? Why not just throw Barney out?"

Andy explains, "I got to work with Barney. I see him every day. This way he doesn't get hurt and we don't get hurt!"

John's questions, which may be the viewing audience's questions as well, are deleted. Andy's explanation was also discarded.

The deletions weaken the story. Without them, the attempts to protect Barney's feelings seem noble but unjustified. Andy's deleted dialogue explained why Barney cannot be hurt.

The next day at the final practice, Andy tells Barney he will be singing into a solo microphone. The microphone is very sensitive and will amplify his voice a thousand times.

Andy instructs Barney to sing "real low." Barney begins softly singing. Andy guides him with a downward motion with his hands. Barney sings "softer and softer until, finally, he is just mouthing the words."

A male choir member is positioned behind Andy and Barney. His facial expressions perfectly respond to Andy softening Barney's voice to a whisper. The man's expressions underscore the humor of the situation and enhance it. The accompanying laugh track audibly does the same.

The script does not have a man standing behind Andy and Barney. The placement was likely the idea of director Bob Sweeney.

The big event arrives! The script direction narrates, *In the back row of the choir, Glen Cripe ducks behind a curtain. Andy gestures to Barney, a palm-down gesture reminding him to keep it low. Barney nods that he has received the message. The moment arrives, John throws Barney his solo cue, backstage Glen Cripe gets ready, and Barney opens his mouth to sing ever-so-softly, breathing into the microphone like a tired Mel Tormé . . . but, instead of a velvet fog, we HEAR a glorious baritone voice.*

Barney is startled. He looks at Andy as if to say, "By gosh, you were right!"

Barney is enjoying himself. Andy nods encouragement and the old pro really spreads himself with large gestures to emphasize his vocal prowess. The song comes to an end. Barney, the Artist Who Has Given His All, drops his head wearily as the APPLAUSE thunders past his ears and we FADE OUT.

"Everything Don Knotts did was scripted, but as he always did, he lifted it up to hilarity," says Jack. "With Don, you knew it was always going to be funnier than it read in the script."

"The ending was a stretch, more like 'I Love Lucy' than *The Griffith Show*," says

Jack. "And why Glen Cripe wasn't asked to sing the solo from the start was a big gaping hole in the story. Having said that, I thought it was one of the funniest shows we did . . . if not the funniest."

Back in Mayberry, Barney reflects on the previous night's performance and says he is going to enjoy singing with the choir in the future.

Andy is prepared. He reminds Barney of the ten-dollar merchandise certificate he won as the concert's outstanding performer. Barney receiving remuneration makes him a professional singer and makes him ineligible to perform with an amateur choir.

Barney reflects on the situation and realizes it could be a blessing in disguise. If the deputy business ever falters, he can move over to show business.

Barney bursts into his old favorite, "Juanita," *and as Barney hits the inevitable sour note, Andy quietly dies.*

"Guest of Honor"

"Oh, what a tangled web we weave, when we practice to deceive."
—ANDY quoting a line from nineteenth-century writer Sir Walter Scott's epic poem "Marmion: A Tale of Flodden Field"

Episode 53

First Broadcast on February 26, 1962

Written by
Jack Elinson and Charles Stewart

Directed by
Bob Sweeney

Jay Novello
Guest Stars as
Sheldon Davis,
the Guest of Honor

"Guest of Honor" begins during a meeting of the Chamber of Commerce. Andy, Barney, Floyd, hardware store owner Sam Lindsay, and butcher Art Crowley are discussing how to increase outside interest in Mayberry's Founders' Day celebration.

Andy suggests making an outsider the celebration's guest of honor. The idea if correctly promoted could attract folks from the whole state.

Barney, relaxing in Andy's chair with his legs up, claims that he had the same idea. Barney's laid-back position was not scripted. It may have been the idea of either Don Knotts or director Bob Sweeney to visually communicate that Barney is not alert and his claim of having the same idea is untrue.

Andy suggests that on the morning of Founders' Day the committee go out to the city limits and stop the first car driven by an out-of-towner.

Barney claims he was about to make the same suggestion. He contributes his idea for a banner welcoming the outsider, with a band present and a police escort into town.

Andy, mocking Barney's earlier behavior, claims he was thinking the exact same thing.

"This narrative came up as all stories do from scratching our heads trying to think of the next story," says Jack. "Having a thief come into Mayberry and marrying that with the Founders' Day celebration seemed like a new twist to a similar idea we used in 'The Woman Speeder' episode. We always had luck with a city slicker coming into sweet, innocent Mayberry."

"We wrote the beginning with the 'that was my idea' runner already in mind," says Jack. "It was all set up in the original story outline."

On the morning of Founders' Day, Andy swears in Floyd, Art, and Sam as temporary deputies. The script has Art wearing his butcher's apron and Floyd *wearing his usual costume.* This direction was dropped, and the three men are dressed in suits.

Andy explains that their primary duty is to welcome people and answer any questions they may be asked.

Andy tells the men to wear their deputy caps for easy identification. The caps are ill-fitting and swapped back and forth for a better fit.

Andy dismisses the men, but they are stopped by Barney. He has "something to say."

Barney reminds the deputies that the badge they are wearing "means something." Barney instructs the trio to nip any Founders' Day trouble "in the bud."

Barney is asked if the deputies will be armed. Barney laughs at the question. He takes out his weapon and says only someone educated "in the proper use of firearms" ~~should carry a gun.~~ He shoves ~~the gun back into the holster,~~ and it ~~goes off.~~

Barney gathers his composure and ~~explains he fired the gun to show~~ what ~~could happen. He assumes the role of drill~~ sergeant and marches the deputies ~~out the door.~~

~~"When we came up with the temporary~~ deputy idea, we knew it would be ~~funny,"~~ says Jack. ~~"Barney playing it like a marine drill~~ sergeant couldn't miss."

"Word that it took twenty takes to film the scene reached us," says Jack. "The actors and crew kept laughing and ruining every take. We loved hearing about it, but I'm sure the director was looking at his watch, panicky about getting behind schedule."

The next morning, two motorcycle patrolmen are escorting a car. They all stop at the Pierce County line. One officer dismounts and walks over to the car. The car is driven by Sheldon "The Dip" Davis, a prominent pickpocket and sneak thief.

The patrolman orders Davis out of the car for a final frisk. A watch belonging to the Pierce County chief of police is found, and Davis is ordered out of the county.

"This kind of scene is always fruitful," says Jack. "The audience knows the truth about Mr. Davis, but the Mayberry characters off-screen don't. Once that's set up, the writing is a breeze."

"Sheldon Davis in our minds was executive producer Sheldon Leonard," says Jack. "Sheldon would have been great in ~~the role. Sinister,~~ yet perfect, like when he played ~~the tout (a person~~ who makes a business of selling tips on racehorses) on *The Jack Benny Show.* ~~We would~~ have loved it if Sheldon himself would have ~~done the role,~~ but he was ~~too busy running~~ his empire."

A ~~Founders'~~ Day welcoming group has gathered on the edge of Mayberry's city limits. Barney spies a vehicle approaching. The group gets ready to welcome the guest of honor, but it turns out to be a pickup truck driven by Frank Robbins the milkman. Frank is told to keep going. (This scene is deleted from the filmed episode.)

A car, driven by Sheldon Davis, approaches and is stopped. Andy and Barney step up to the driver's side. The script has Davis sticking his head out the window. The car used in the scene, however, was changed from a hardtop to a convertible to allow easier camera access.

Andy believes he has found a stranger passing through. Davis decides to hide his identity and tells Andy he is Thomas A. Moody, a traveling salesman.

This is Thomas A. Moody's lucky day! He is invited to be Mayberry Founders' Day guest of honor. As such, he will be welcomed in all the stores in town and given free gifts. Davis accepts the honor and is given a token key to Mayberry.

Davis is escorted into town. He is cheered by a gathering of townsfolk. In his acceptance speech, Davis acknowledges that Mayberry has been "given" to him, and he cordially agrees to "take it."

Davis shakes hands with Andy and several others before going inside the hotel to freshen up. After his departure, Andy goes over the planned schedule and checks the time. His watch is missing. The other persons who shook hands with Davis look for their watches. One after another discovers an empty wrist.

Andy slowly realizes the guest of honor is a thief!

Later in the day, Andy follows up his suspicion. He makes a call and learns that Davis is known "up and down the Eastern Seaboard" as a thief and pickpocket.

Barney enters, is told the bad news, and says Davis should be run out of town.

Andy responds, "After we picked him as our guest of honor? Had pictures taken for the papers . . . all that publicity . . . now wouldn't the Mayberry police force look real sharp if we had to turn around and admit we picked a thief?"

This dialogue is crossed out on Andy Griffith's script. In the left margin, written in a female hand, probably belonging to Hazel Hall who oversaw script continuity, is the dialogue heard in the filmed episode.

Andy decides the best thing to do is to keep an eye on Davis.

Floyd enters and reports there is "nothing to worry about in Mayberry today." Davis has received his free shave and is currently freshening up at the hotel.

Andy and Barney hurry to the hotel and stand watch outside Davis's room. While the two wait, Barney tells Andy that he has read about fellows who steal in a police magazine. Persons who steal because they can't help it are called "kleptomeneriacs."

"In our script, the word 'kleptomaniacs' was spelled correctly," says Jack. "We never intended it to be a malaprop. Don Knotts must have come up with that."

Barney explains a rehabilitation program for fellows who steal. The thieves are talked to a lot, given books to read, and allowed to make baskets. The program teaches that stealing is wrong.

Barney is interrupted by Floyd who has come to tell Andy the reception committee would like to meet with him. Before leaving, Andy reminds Barney to keep an eye on Davis.

With Andy absent, Barney sees an opportunity. He says aloud, "I think I'll have a little talk with him," and knocks on Davis's door.

"We knew the rehabilitation approach by Barney would make for a funny scene," says Jack. "There's always talk about rehabilitating prisoners, so Barney's actions were based upon the truth that rehabilitation is not just punishment."

Barney enters Davis's room and begins a long discourse about "rotten men disappointing their mothers" and "fellows who take the wrong road because nobody trusts them."

Barney illustrates the point. He shows the ring of keys he carries to Davis. They are the keys to every store in Mayberry. The store owners trust Barney.

Davis confides that he wishes someone would trust him.

Barney takes the bait. Eager to display his trust, he indicates his wristwatch. He points out that the watch has twenty-one jewels and a pure gold band. The band, however, pinches his wrist. Barney removes the watch to give his wrist "some air" and lays it on a table.

Barney turns his back to Davis and continues to "philosophize." As he speaks, he turns around and discovers the room is empty. His watch remains on the table. Davis has been rehabilitated!

At the sheriff's office, Andy is finishing up his meeting with the reception committee. He reminds the committee to "get the words right" when they sing the Mayberry song at the Founders' Day Ceremony. Andy recites the lyrics as a reminder.

"We enjoyed writing the 'Mayberry Song,'" says Jack. "'Mayberry will shine when the moon comes up and the sun goes down.' I don't think it'll ever top 'God Bless America.'"

Barney enters. He is whistling a happy tune and twirling his key chain. Andy asks about Davis's whereabouts.

Barney explains that he talked with Davis about "truth and honesty," then placed his watch on a table and turned his back. Barney points to the watch on his wrist as proof that Davis has been cured of his stealing ways.

During the explanation, Barney continually twirls his key chain. Andy looks down and sees the keys are missing!

Andy and Barney rush out the door to find Davis.

Davis is busy at work inside a jewelry store, filling his pockets with loot. Both of his arms are covered with watches. Andy and Barney walk by the store and see Davis preparing to exit through the back door.

The script directions narrate what awaits Davis outside. *Ext. Back door of shop—Alley on Stage. There is a sign posted reading: No Parking—Barclay's Jewelry*

Store. (The "Alley on Stage" direction tells the crew that the alley behind the jewelry store, though an exterior setting, was to be built inside the studio. The alley scene would not be shot on location.)

The door opens and Davis tiptoes out. Takes cigarette out of his pocket, puts it in his mouth, fishes for a light. HAND comes in with light. ANGLE WIDENS to reveal Andy lighting his cigarette, Barney standing by.

"The shot showing Andy's hand lighting the cigarette was scripted," says Jack. "Usually, the director comes up with a shot like that, but we called for that close-up because we knew it would be effective."

Andy places his hand on Davis's shoulder to affirm that the capture has been made. The laugh track accompanying the on-screen action changes to applause as *we FADE OUT.*

In the epilogue, Barney locks Davis in a cell as Andy goes to his desk with the pickpocket's suitcase. Barney stands outside the cell and informs Davis that he isn't dealing with "a bunch of hicks."

Barney walks over to Andy who is opening the suitcase. The suitcase is full of watches, jewelry, and wallets. Andy notices that another item was been stolen . . . Barney's badge is missing!

"As for the epilogue, we thought the only thing we could do to top the stealing of Barney's keys was having his badge stolen," says Jack. "Hey, I just thought of something better. Instead of the badge, Davis steals Barney's gun . . . and escapes!"

"Aunt Bee the Warden"

Episode 55

First Broadcast on
March 12, 1962

Written by
**Charles Stewart
and Jack Elinson**

Directed by
Bob Sweeney

"I do believe you missed your calling. You shoulda been a warden."
—ANDY, speaking to Aunt Bee

"The inspiration for this story was simply to give Aunt Bee her turn at bat," says Jack. "The writers brought in many stories featuring Barney (everybody's favorite) or Andy or Opie. Frances Bavier was low on the totem pole, and we tried hard to correct that. Frances was too good an actress to ignore. Hence this story where she's the funny one for a change."

The episode opens with footage of the squad car speeding down a dirt road with a siren blasting. The scene switches to Barney, responding to the approaching siren and looking out the front window of the sheriff's office.

The scripted opening of "Aunt Bee the Warden" was different.

Barney is at the desk, feet up, cap tilted back, reading a newspaper. He shakes his head and *clucks disgustedly.*

Opie enters and asks the whereabouts of his "paw." Barney answers "out" and clucks some more. Opie is curious.

Barney explains the clucking is in response to an article he is reading about overcrowded conditions in a jail up north. Barney resents the fact that the Mayberry jail rarely gets a customer.

Barney tells Opie that he is a man of action, and he gets restless if action doesn't come his way.

Barney pulls out his gun and gives it a rueful look. He admits that he hasn't "slapped leather to this old baby in some time." It "frosts" Barney to see the cells empty, and he sorrowfully says to the gun, "Poor baby, all dressed up and no place to go."

Barney shoves the gun back into the holster, gives it a slap, and yawns.

Opie sees something out the window. The squad car, siren silent, is pulling up. There are prisoners inside!

Barney bolts toward the front door to get in on the action and nearly runs Opie over.

Outside Andy is removing his prisoners, the four Gordon boys, from the car. He looks "roughed up" and has a cast on his right hand. Andy explains to Barney that he had "a little trouble" making the capture and stopped at Doc Zack's on the way in to get fixed up.

"I don't remember Andy breaking his hand," says Jack. "There's nothing in our script indicating a cast and no reference to it. The injury explanation must have been put in prior to filming."

Andy Griffith was a door puncher. Andy pounded his fist through a door, suffering several broken bones, sometime between the conclusion of the filming of "Guest of Honor" on the evening of January 17 and the beginning of the filming of "Aunt Bee the Warden" on January 22, 1962.

Andy was forced to wear a cast for three weeks. The "official" cause of the injury was reported in the March 12, 1962, edition of *TV Guide*. "Andy shows up in this episode with a bandaged hand—which is covering a very real injury he suffered while building a toy garage for his son Sam."

Barney is overcome with excitement at the prospect of having a full jail. The prisoners are moonshiners who have been operating a still in Franklin Canyon. Franklin Canyon Reservoir was the location of the site where Andy and Opie were photographed in the series' opening credits. (The site of the still is changed to Franklin Hollow in the filmed episode.)

Barney locks the Gordons inside the cells with a "flourish," hangs the key on the wall peg between the cells, and informs the prisoners that they are in a maximum-security prison.

Andy suggests the "prison" would be more secure if the key was moved out of the prisoners' reach.

Barney is momentarily embarrassed by this oversight but regains his confidence. He is soon strutting back and forth in front of the cells, a happy deputy.

"Barney's behavior was right in character," says Jack. "Barney is always a bit pompous. Barney thinks of himself as Clint Eastwood. Whenever he realizes he's blundered, it's not for long; in a minute, he's Clint Eastwood again."

The front door opens, and Otis Campbell enters. He is intoxicated and singing the "Dipsy Doodle."

Barney plans to put Otis in a cell with the Gordon Brothers. The brothers accuse Otis of telling his "pal" Andy the location of their still and are eager to get their hands on him.

The brothers believe Otis has been out to get them ever since they raised their prices. Otis denies the accusation and explains that he has taken his business elsewhere because the brother's moonshine is lacking quality. He also found someone who delivers.

"We didn't have Otis singing when he makes his entrance," says Jack. "That was added when the scene was being filmed. We had fun writing this scene. Otis complains about the Gordon Brothers' moonshine like it was a fine wine from France. Our favorite line was 'I found somebody who delivers.'"

The Gordon boys continue to *yammer for Otis's scalp.* Barney blows his whistle for quiet. (The whistle blast was not scripted.)

Andy and Barney walk over to the desk to talk over the situation. The Gordons immediately reach through the bars, grab Otis, and start pummeling him. Andy and Barney come to the rescue.

Andy decides to place a call to the Elm City police to see if they have any room for Otis. Barney stops him and says sending Otis to another jail would be like giving away your child.

Otis can't believe Andy would consider giving him away and points out that he is the Mayberry jail's steadiest customer.

Andy realizes that he can solve the problem by dismissing Otis's case and sending him home.

Otis however refuses to be set free. He doesn't want to go home to his wife, Edith. (In later episodes, Otis's wife is named Rita.) Otis reasons that Edith would kill him, and he doesn't want Andy to "have blood on his hands." (The idea of sending Otis to Elm City is deleted from the filmed episode.)

Andy comes up with a solution. He will take Otis to the Taylor home. Otis can serve his sentence there.

Otis is pleased with the idea and anticipates a "fun" imprisonment.

Andy drives a happy and singing Otis to his house. Andy decides to take Otis in through the back door. As the two pass the kitchen window they hear women's voices. Andy realizes Aunt Bee has company and reroutes Otis to the front of the house.

"Otis singing and staggering was in the script," says Jack. "We had Andy leading Otis to the porch and into the house, but the details of Otis's behavior were not described in the script."

Hal Smith portrays Otis as extremely intoxicated. Otis has a difficult time stepping up onto the porch and must be pulled by Andy. Otis walks past the front door and into a corner. Andy pulls him backward. Otis spins halfway around and walks away from the house. Andy grabs Otis by the back of the coat and redirects him into the house. Otis sees a vase by the front door containing flowers and sticks his nose among them.

Aunt Bee comes out of the kitchen and learns that Otis will be "incarcerated in her domicile." Aunt Bee is not happy.

Andy explains that he has run out of space at the jail. He had no other choice than to bring Otis home with him. Otis will be put in the guest room and released after his twenty-four hours is up.

While Andy and Aunt Bee talk, a thirsty Otis picks up the flower vase, removes the flowers, and drinks the vase's contents. Andy takes the vase from him. Otis picks a few petals from the flowers and sticks his nose in the bouquet for a sniff. Andy hands the vase back. Otis takes another sip to quench his thirst.

"When Otis drinks the water in the vase, he hopes by some miracle that it's moonshine," says Jack. "At this point, he is thirsty enough to settle for rubbing alcohol . . . or water."

Andy maneuvers Otis into the guest room. He starts to undress him for bed. Otis makes the task more difficult by refusing to put down the flower vase.

"When Andy tells Otis to 'pull' his arm out of the sleeve, it's precisely like undressing a child," says Jack. "In this case, it happens to be a drunk, childlike adult."

After getting Otis settled, Andy joins the ladies in the kitchen. The ladies are preparing cakes for an upcoming church social. Icing and cake decorations are on the table. Andy picks through a bowl of jelly beans, looking for black ones, which are his favorite.

"When you're writing a show about real people, small details come naturally," says Jack. "Personally, I don't like jelly beans. What I like are chocolate-covered nuts and chews. Andy Taylor liking black jelly beans seemed right for the character."

Meanwhile, upstairs, a thirsty Otis is on the prowl. He makes his way down the hall with the flower vase. He stops at a *special lamp* that sits on a table. The writers requested a lamp with a barrel and spigot base. Otis attempts to draw water from the spigot. When no water is dispensed Otis makes a verbal note "to call the plumber in the morning."

The *special lamp* was acquired and placed on the set. Otis's interaction with the lamp was likely filmed and later edited out to shorten the episode's run time.

Otis continues downstairs and into the kitchen where he announces to Andy, Aunt Bee, and the ladies of the church that he has come "to fill my vase."

The next morning Andy gives Aunt Bee a breakfast order for Otis. Aunt Bee is "miffed" that she is responsible for the prisoner's care. Andy leaves to get a few things done. On his way out, he asks for permission to give the "warden" a goodbye kiss.

At the sheriff's office, Barney begins a rehabilitation program for the Gordon boys. Barney plans to assign constructive activities "designed to bring out hidden talents." Barney passes out a wood-carving set, a leather-craft set, a metal-craft set, and a Mr. Potato set.

"This is the funniest scene in the show," says Jack. "We did this type of scene in 'Guest of Honor' when Barney was trying to get the thief to change his way and become an honest citizen. I don't know if this 'rehab' angle was ever used again in the series. It had the potential to become a funny 'runner.'"

At the Taylor home, Aunt Bee attempts to serve Otis his breakfast. Otis wants to sleep longer and gives instructions to keep the food hot and the coffee simmering.

Aunt Bee protests. Otis points out that he is a prisoner with rights and demands to be treated like one.

The comment sets Aunt Bee off in a different direction. She enters the guest room, sees the flower vase on a bedstand, picks it up, and pours water over Otis's head. Otis must get up and get to work. The warden has spoken!

Otis's work assignments are revealed in a series of vignettes. The scripted chores were lawn mowing, window washing, carrying out buckets of ashes, and additional mowing. The filmed montage shows Otis mowing, washing windows, and chopping wood.

"Our script doesn't have a scene of Otis chopping wood," says Jack. "Obviously it was added at a later time to the sequence."

Otis chopping wood led to a rare ad-lib during filming. Aunt Bee walks by Otis, who is sitting on a stump resting with axe in hand. Hal Smith raises the axe and pantomimes using it on Aunt Bee. The spur-of-the-moment ad-lib was included in the filmed episode.

"As for Otis ready to go at Aunt Bee with an axe, that was funny," says Jack. "Startling, but funny."

Otis attempts to take numerous breaks as he works. Every attempt is forbidden. Aunt Bee snaps her fingers in Otis's face and motions for him to get back to work.

"Aunt Bee snapping her fingers was in the script," says Jack. "Like Barney so often does, she's become a marine drill sergeant. Aunt Bee is just as tough on Otis as Barney ever was, but in her own way. For Otis, it's turned into a living hell."

Andy returns home and finds Otis on his knees scrubbing the kitchen floor. Otis pleads with Andy to get him out of "this." "Bloody Mary" is about to work him to death.

Andy is amused by the situation and goes to find Aunt Bee. Otis alone in the kitchen thinks through the situation and realizes he has "made a mess" of his life. He decides to "crack" out of Aunt Bee's jail.

The escape attempts are shown through a series of vignettes. Otis tries to silently sneak out the front door, attempts to gain his freedom by climbing out a window, and hides in the back of a laundry truck with the hope of an undetected liberation. Each attempt is discovered by Aunt Bee and dismissed with a snap of the fingers and an order to get back to work.

Later that evening, Andy returns home. Otis has served his twenty-four-hour sentence and can be released. Andy calls Otis to the living room to give him the news.

Otis enters. He is neat and clean. His clothes have been pressed. Otis explains that Aunt Bee made him do it. Aunt Bee has also put him on probation. Any further drinking will result in a return to "the Rock."

Andy and Otis step outside. Otis takes a deep breath and cries, "Freedom! Oh, it smells good!"

"The whole situation was so funny, every line from Otis was a zinger," says Jack. "Otis played this whole thing like he was in San Quentin. 'Freedom, oh it smells good,' was more of the same. It was hilarious."

Barney drives up and runs up on the porch. He sees Otis all clean and scrubbed and is incredulous.

Barney asks for a private word with Andy. He reports that the Gordon boys have escaped. The brother who was given the metalcraft set made a pass key and unlocked the cell doors.

"Here, again, we borrowed from ourselves," says Jack. "Namely, 'Guest of Honor' when the thief stole Barney's ring of keys during rehabilitation. The metalcraft pass-key was the result of another rehabilitation attempt."

The epilogue begins with the squad car pulling to a stop at the Taylor home. The recaptured Gordon boys get out and are escorted into the annex jail.

The script directions provide excellent narration: *Barney and Andy literally shove the four toward the house, the prisoners all the while whimpering and protesting: "No, no ... not the Rock!" They reach the porch, and the door opens. There stands Aunt Bee with a broom in one hand and a mop in the other. She greets them with a sweetly sinister smile.*

"This was a perfect ending," says Jack. "By now, Aunt Bee has become Attila the Hun ... sweet, gentle Aunt Bee. We were happy to give Frances Bavier such a good script to work with."

"Looking back, I don't think there was such a thing as a bad script during the entire series," says Jack. "Aaron Ruben, a great writer, had his hand in every single script that went through the assembly line. Then the work that was done, starting with the first reading of the scripts when everyone around the table gave their contribution ... the director, the actors, and of course executive producer Sheldon Leonard. It takes a lot of people to turn out a weekly show."

"The County Nurse"

Episode 56

First Broadcast on
March 19, 1962

Written by
**Charles Stewart
and Jack Elinson**

Directed by
Bob Sweeney

Julie Adams
Guest Stars as
Mary Simpson,
the County Nurse

"He died before his time so that others might live."
—EPITAPH FOR RAFE HOLLISTER

"The County Nurse" was filmed one week prior to the first layoff of 1962. The layoff changed the normal production schedule.

The episode's exterior locations were filmed on Monday, January 29. The first day of soundstage interior filming was Tuesday, January 30. The next day, Wednesday, January 31, was a layoff day.

The cast returned to the studio on Thursday, February 1, for a script read-through of the upcoming "Andy and Barney in the Big City" episode (Episode #57).

On Friday, February 2 the filming of the remaining "The County Nurse" interiors resumed on the Desilou Studio's lot. The multiday layoff officially began on Monday, February 5, and concluded on the morning of Friday, February 9, with the rehearsal for "Andy and Barney in the Big City."

"After Ellie Walker exited, this script was an attempt to test the waters with a new lady," says Jack. "As we all know, Andy was single when the series started, and he was single when it ended. My guess is it was Andy Griffith himself who called the shot on that."

Script directions narrate the episode's beginning. *While consulting a book in his left hand, Barney is swiping at the air with his right hand, his fingers curled like a claw of a wild beast. As he does so, he snarls ferociously. Andy enters but stops abruptly at the sight that greets his eyes.*

"It's obvious what inspired Barney's interest in karate," says Jack. "Barney is a daydreamer, fantasizing that he's Gary Cooper in 'High Noon.' He now pictures himself as an icon of martial arts. Don't mess with this man—he's mean."

Barney demonstrates several animal-inspired karate moves. The moves are based upon the deadly attack of a hawk's talons, the hoof strike of the bull elk, and the prestrike motions of a rattlesnake. Andy incorrectly guesses the rattlesnake move is inspired by a mad worm.

Barney gets carried away with the demonstration and smashes his "hand of

steel" into the desktop. The pain is immediate. Barney holds his breath to keep from screaming.

"It's always wonderful to write a scene when you're laughing as you write it," says Jack. "Charles Stewart and I couldn't contain the giggles. Chuck, who did the typing, was laughing so much, he made a dozen typo errors."

Mary Simpson, the county nurse, enters. She is on her way to Rafe Hollister's place. Mary explains that she is participating in a drive to get everybody inoculated for tetanus. Rafe is a leader of the farmers. Mary hopes that if Rafe gets his shot, the others will follow his example. Barney warns that Rafe "doesn't hold much with doctoring."

Andy's interest gradually moves from what Mary is saying to how she looks. He gives her a head-to-toe once-over.

"Andy's look of interest at Mary was not scripted," says Jack.

Andy volunteers to drive Mary to Rafe's farm and agrees to help convince Rafe to get his shot.

Mary is delighted and *plants a kiss* on Andy's cheek.

"The tetanus shot story was actually the 'A' story," says Jack. "That same story could have been done with a male doctor. Andy's romantic feelings about Mary were the 'B' story. I frankly can't remember which story came to us first before we blended them together."

Mary exits to get supplies at the drugstore. Andy, carried away in the moment, announces his feelings aloud: "Mary is a fine girl!"

Barney, realizing this is a rare opportunity to tease Andy, begins singing, "For it was Mary, Mary. . . ." (Ironically, Jack and Charles give Barney a pleasant singing voice only two scripts after Barney can't sing a lick in "Barney and the Choir.")

"It was nice for a change to have Barney putting on Andy," says Jack. "Andy usually does the teasing."

Andy and Mary arrive at Rafe Hollister's farm. Andy suggests that he be allowed to "carry the ball" when they talk with Rafe. It will be best if Rafe is approached "slow and easy." Andy believes they must gain Rafe's trust before talking about the shot.

Andy asks Mary to tell him about tetanus so he will be better informed. Andy moves close to Mary and gazes longingly into her eyes.

Mary begins a scientific lecture about the toxin of Bacillus tetani. Andy is happy to gaze into Mary's eyes.

Mary's explanation of bacilli is deleted from the filmed episode. Her discussion of tetanus begins with the symptom of "stiffness in the back of the neck."

Andy asks about the location of the stiffness. Mary reaches over and places a hand on the back of Andy's neck. Andy reaches up and places his hand over Mary's.

Mary sees Rafe Hollister in the distance. Andy wishes she hadn't.

"This might have been the only time in the series that Andy gets this romantic," says Jack. "I'm not familiar with all the episodes done in later years, but in this one, Andy has definitely been shot by Cupid."

Andy and Mary approach Rafe. Andy introduces the county nurse. Rafe responds, "Nobody needs a nurse. We don't get sick up here."

Rafe amends this. There was old Minnie. She had the shakes all winter. Mary sympathizes with "the poor woman." Rafe explains that Minnie isn't a woman; she's a hen.

The "hen" dialogue is deleted from the filmed episode. Instead, Rafe tells Mary that he has never been to a doctor in his life. When he was born, he had his mama; when he dies, he'll have an undertaker. No sense in cluttering things up in between.

"One of the prerequisites in being a writer is to have an ear for the way different people speak," says Jack. "Rafe's manner of speech is very colorful. His explanation of why he's never been to a doctor is right to the point. He doesn't waste words."

"We pictured Rafe as a mountain man," says Jack. "We always envisioned 'the hills' beyond Mayberry. Especially when someone was caught in possession of a still. We always assumed that it was mountain men who had stills."

Rafe refuses to be "jabbed" by a needle and sends Andy and Mary on their way.

Andy and Mary return to the sheriff's office. Mary is disappointed and fearful she will look like a fool after promising she would get one hundred percent cooperation on the shots. Barney, busy changing a light bulb in one of the cells, overhears.

The telephone rings. Andy is summoned to the mayor's office. He departs and Barney takes over.

Barney volunteers to drive Mary back to Rafe's farm. He explains that Andy failed because he is too "soft." Barney plans to be tougher. He will order Rafe to take his shot.

At the Hollister farm, Barney demands that Rafe stop acting like a child and take his shot. Rafe answers with a rifle shot near Barney's feet. Frightened out of his wits, Barney retreats.

Barney grabs Mary and escorts her to the squad car. Rafe shoots the hat off Barney's head. Barney gets into the car and informs Rafe he is in "big trouble."

"This is a typical Barney scene," says Jack. "Barney plays it large to impress Mary. He is totally confident that when he confronts Rafe, the mountain man will shake in his boots. When Rafe fires the first shot, Barney gets out of there fast. Clint Eastwood flops again."

Barney and Mary return to the sheriff's office and report the incident. Andy can't have Rafe shooting at people. Rafe will have to be brought in.

Barney reaches for the bullet in his pocket. He plans to be properly armed when Rafe is apprehended. Andy advises Barney to keep his bullet where it is. He is confident Rafe can be brought in without any trouble.

Andy and Barney arrive at Rafe's farm. Barney remains in the squad car. Andy gets out and reaches to open the barnyard gate. He is greeted by a bullet.

Andy, like a schoolteacher vexed with a naughty child, starts for the barn. He is warned by Rafe to stay back. Andy walks up to Rafe, reaches out, and snatches the rifle away. *Now Blood and Guts Barney rushes up, with gun drawn.*

Back in Mayberry, the door of the sheriff's office opens, and Mary enters carrying her nurse's bag. Rafe, locked in one of the cells, protests. Andy assures him that nobody is going to force him to take a shot against his will.

Mary explains to Rafe that the shot is important and may prevent future deaths. Rafe still refuses to be inoculated.

Mary frowns and is told by Andy that if she "frowns like that, her face will grow to it." He touches Mary's forehead and gently rubs her wrinkles away.

"Andy's 'permanent frown' line was scripted," says Jack. "His romantic rubbing away of Mary's wrinkles was not. That likely came from Andy Griffith."

Mary exits. Rafe asks for a cup of coffee. Andy goes to the back room and returns with two cups of coffee. He enters the cell, hands Rafe a cup, sits down, and takes a sip from his own cup.

"In this scene, Andy was the spider and Rafe was the fly," says Jack. "Slowly, but surely, Andy lures Rafe into the web, convincing him that his days are numbered."

Andy explains to Rafe that refusing the tetanus shot will eventually make him a sacrificial hero. Andy predicts that someday Rafe will cut himself with a rusty saw or get bitten by an animal. This will likely lead to death since Rafe refused to get his shot. The death will serve as a lesson for Rafe's family and neighbors not to neglect theirs.

Andy predicts that Rafe's funeral will be a grand occasion. He would like to "sing a song over Rafe" if he is able to control his emotions.

Andy gets his guitar and begins singing a sad song. Rafe falls into the web of sorrow the song weaves.

"All we had in the script was *Andy sings a most mournful song*," says Jack. "I'm sure there is a song called 'Dig My Grave with a Silver Spade' and Andy Griffith knew of it."

The lyrics to Andy's mournful song were included as a revision to the script.

The song was not given a title. The grave is dug with a gold spade instead of a silver one, and the final line was originally "place me in the ground," not the "tell my wife to marry again" that Andy sings in the filmed episode.

Rafe realizes he doesn't want to die a preventable death. He asks Andy to "fetch" the County Nurse. He is ready to take his shot!

Later, Andy and Barney watch as Mary *pulls out the needle* and swabs Rafe's arm with rubbing alcohol. Mary starts to wipe away the excess alcohol but is stopped by Rafe. He likes the smell.

"Rafe's request not to rub off the alcohol was our favorite line in the script," says Jack. "You can be sure Rafe has a moonshine still up at his place. We were thinking the smell of rubbing alcohol would be a welcome reminder of the aroma of the drinking kind."

Mary opens her record book to check Rafe's name off the "Haven't Received a Shot" list.

Barney reprimands Rafe for "making a big to-do over a little thing like getting a shot."

"After Barney chides Rafe about being frightened of a little shot, I'm sure the viewing audience knew what was coming next," says Jack. "We didn't have to tell them, but unashamedly we did."

Mary has discovered something in her record book. Barney hasn't received his tetanus shot!

Mary readies the shot. Andy rolls up Barney's sleeve. Barney protests and rolls his sleeve back down.

The script directions describe the inoculation. *Andy rolls up Barney's sleeve once more, and this time, before Barney can roll it down, Mary darts in with a bit of cotton and swabs Barney's arm with alcohol. Barney stiffens at the touch, his eyes roll, and he slumps against Andy.*

Barney thinks the shot has been administered but is informed "that was just the alcohol."

As Mary jabs in the needle we mercifully: FADE OUT.

"Another typical Barney routine," says Jack. "Barney almost fainting when the alcohol was rubbed on actually happened to me when I got into the army and received the first of many shots."

"Andy and Barney in the Big City"

Episode 57

First Broadcast on
March 26, 1962

Written by
Harvey Bullock

Directed by
Bob Sweeney

Allan Melvin
Guest Stars as
Detective Bardoli

"The 'Barney Fife, MD' [Mayberry Deputy] bit was written for this script.
I don't recall any other episodes in which Barney used it. Perhaps it was
best as a one shot."—HARVEY BULLOCK

"I cannot remember whether Aaron Ruben suggested the idea for the script,
or whether I brought the notion in," says writer Harvey Bullock. "It probably just
accumulated slowly in our minds that a trip to the big city might be interesting
because it would give the show a different look in set and wardrobe."

Though primarily set in the "big city," Harvey's finished script begins in the
familiar Taylor home. Andy is departing on a two-day business trip. Barney arrives and notices Opie's front tooth is missing. Barney has Opie repeat a tongue-
twister to test how the missing tooth affects his pronunciation. Aunt Bee packs
Andy and Barney "a brown paper sack full of sandwiches to eat on the bus" and
reminds the two "to step out with your right foot, so all will go well."

"I had no idea Ronny had a missing tooth," says Harvey. "Once I dropped off
the second draft of a script I did not hang around the set. I guess Ronny showed
up with a missing tooth, and Aaron reshaped the script to use it. Andy and Barney's 'stepping out on your right foot' was also not in my script and is another
example of an addition by either Aaron or Andy.

"Aunt Bee's preparation of 'a sack of sandwiches' was my idea and grew out of
my understanding of the character. Aunt Bee's response to almost any happening is to cater it. She's totally convinced that 'you are what you eat,' and the more
the better. If a twister hit Mayberry, Aunt Bee would immediately start handing
out slices of pie, and Andy's trip definitely called for a movable feast."

After arriving in "Capital City," Andy and Barney check into their hotel. While
standing in the lobby, Barney notices a lady claiming her emeralds from the hotel's safe. While the lady places the jewels in her pocketbook, Barney observes
that she is being watched very carefully by a man.

Later that day, Andy and Barney visit the state commissioner with a request for
new equipment. The commissioner is not optimistic about the request. He feels

there have not been enough arrests in Mayberry to justify new equipment. Barney believes "that one good felony" would get them everything they want. Andy suggests they go back to the hotel, eat supper, and "forget about our problems."

Andy and Barney have supper in the hotel's French restaurant. The menu is printed in French, which neither Andy nor Barney can read. Andy asks the waiter for a steak. Not wanting to appear to be a hick, Barney points randomly to items on the menu, which turn out to be snails and brains.

"What we have here is a variation on the so-called 'Fish Out of Water' sketch," says Harvey. "Ordering fanciful food by mistake is a basic comic staple. It's a minor tweak, but in my script, Barney ordered frog legs and snails."

Barney sees the "emerald lady" leaving the restaurant. The man Barney observed earlier departs immediately afterward. The suspected "crook" makes a telephone call in the lobby and identifies himself during the conversation as Bardoli, the hotel detective.

"Allan Melvin, who played Bardoli, was a wonderfully versatile type and a 'great face,'" says Harvey. "He was a close friend of Aaron's from the early Sergeant Bilko/The Phil Silvers Show days. But there was no favoritism here. Allan was a scrupulous professional and totally reliable. It didn't matter that Allan was cast as Bardoli after portraying 'Doc' Malloy in 'Jailbreak' [Episode 50]. Television audiences are most amenable. They can absorb all kinds of cast changes without being disturbed, as long as the laughs keep coming."

"We came up with the last name for the hotel detective, Bardoli, after putting together a few syllables which sounded Italian. Aaron may have suggested it. He was a giant Italophile. He even took lessons in Italian from TAGS director Peter Baldwin and got pretty good before Peter left and there were no others to practice his new language on."

The next day, Andy tells Barney he is "going down to police headquarters and browse around." Barney decides to stay at the hotel and watch "his man." On his way out of the lobby, Andy bumps into a man. Bardoli suspects that the man, C. J. Huffman, is a thief. After Andy leaves, Bardoli tells Huffman to "keep his hands in his own pockets."

"Writers were not consulted on casting but occasionally would suggest the type of performer needed," says Harvey. "My scripted description for C. J. Huffman was 'a pleasant Rotarian type.' Actually this doesn't fit Les Treymayne [who was cast in the role], but the character wasn't written finitely, so many different types could play it equally well. Les, by the way, was great in the role."

Huffman takes a seat in the lobby and is joined by Barney. Barney warns him to be careful about talking to strangers. Barney then informs Huffman that Bardoli is a jewel thief. Barney also tells Huffman about the "emerald lady." Huffman identifies himself as the owner of a newspaper and agrees to help Barney catch the jewel thief.

Barney and Huffman follow Bardoli upstairs to the emerald lady's room. Bardoli checks to see if the door is locked and departs. Huffman and Barney decide to see if Bardoli has already stolen the jewels. After Huffman pries open the door, he and Barney search the room. Barney searches the outer room while Huffman looks in the bedroom. Huffman finds the jewels and places them in his pocket. Bardoli returns while Barney and Huffman are in the room. When Bardoli enters the room, Barney pushes him into a closet and locks the closet door.

Meanwhile, Andy's visit to police headquarters included a look around the file room. While thumbing through a book of mug shots, Andy spots a picture of the man he bumped into in the hotel lobby.

Accompanied by a policeman, Andy returns to the hotel. He sees Bardoli in the lobby and is told by the policeman that Bardoli is the hotel detective.

Harvey's carefully constructed story enables the audience to view the episode from an informed viewpoint. Part of the viewer's satisfaction is gained from knowing the truth about Bardoli and C. J. Huffman while Barney does not. Harvey lets the audience in on the deception/joke.

"There are two main types of drama, the 'open' and the 'closed,'" explains Harvey. "The open lets the audience in on 'who done it.' In a closed format the guilty party is not revealed until the end, and both the audience and 'good guys' have to work to figure it out. Would the story benefit from being open or closed? That is a difficult decision to make when fashioning a story. You run the story through your head endlessly, both open and closed. Sometimes it seems to work both ways equally well—and sometimes it doesn't seem to work either way!"

Barney and Huffman encounter Andy in the hotel lobby. Barney tells Andy the "fellow I spotted took the emeralds, and C. J. and I locked him in a closet." Andy immediately recognizes Huffman "from his likeness at police headquarters," and Huffman is arrested.

Following the arrest, Andy explains the situation to the baffled Barney. The explanation and Barney's reaction to it are presented in pantomime. An audible explanation would have been somewhat repetitious, since Harvey has already let the audience in on "who done it." Barney's exaggerated reaction, accompanied solely by *TAGS* musical director Earle Hagen's musical sound effects, is more comical and satisfying.

The episode concludes with Detective Bardoli asking for Barney in order to commend him for his arrest of Huffman. Mistaking Bardoli's intentions, Barney hides in a closet in his hotel room. By taking an earlier situation and reversing the circumstances, Harvey cleverly creates a comic ending.

"Wedding Bells for Aunt Bee"

"I remember as a child, slipping out to the shed behind our house, crawling up on top of a table, and falling asleep to the tapping of my father's manual typewriter. I still love to hear that sound."—COURTNEY BULLOCK

Episode 58

First Broadcast on April 2, 1963

Written by
Harvey Bullock

Directed by
Bob Sweeney

"The 'Wedding Bells' storyline began where most of the storylines originated, my office ceiling where I did my major heavy-duty staring," recalls writer Harvey Bullock. "The office was actually a shed behind our home. I would stare at the ceiling, juggling half notions, seeking to find a story problem. That was the magic word which helped me get started—the problem. Who could handle it? What was its progression? What was at stake, and what is the solution? I'd have a constant circus of thoughts dancing through my head, but I didn't always come up with anything.

"So I'd give up and go in the house to raid the fridge. Often nothing worked until after nightfall when there were no distractions. My wife would tell our three small daughters, 'Don't disturb Daddy, he's thinking.' And I'm out in the shed, praying for an interruption.

"Aaron Ruben tried to rotate scripts to give each cast member a prominent role in upcoming episodes. Oddly enough, the one character most difficult to find stories for was Andy himself. The reason for this was that he had no pesky little foibles. So when it came time for an Andy story, we found it could be someone else's problem that he is dragged into."

Harvey's "Wedding Bells" script begins with Aunt Bee, Clara Johnson, and Otis Campbell in the dry cleaner's. Aunt Bee has stopped by to pick up Andy's suit. When the owner of the dry cleaner's, H. Fred Goss, invites Aunt Bee to attend a dance with him, she declines the invitation.

H. Fred Goss first appeared in "Jailbreak" (Episode 50). "I can't recall the exact circumstances of selecting Goss again," admits Harvey. "It might have been that Aaron and I, knowing what we wanted, mutually made suggestions during the early discussions of the story. The character we had in mind had to be a contemporary of Aunt Bee's and a solid citizen who was a known commodity in

Mayberry, so viewers wouldn't suspect an outsider was working a scam. Fred Goss fit both these requirements and, moreover, could do the boring speeches on his sole interest in life—the honorable cleaning profession."

After leaving the dry cleaner's, Otis stops by the courthouse to leave his suit in case he "gets out in time to go to church on Sunday." While at the courthouse, Otis tells Andy about Goss sweet-talking Aunt Bee. As the two talk, a rare thing happens—Otis and Andy become equals, two adults. (Otis is usually childlike in relation to Andy.)

"Otis's scene in the courthouse was written straight, adult-to-adult," says Harvey. "I knew Otis had to be dead sober to give credence to his observation that Goss was sweet-talking Aunt Bee."

Aunt Bee and Clara return to the Taylor home after leaving the dry cleaner's. As the two put up groceries, Clara tells Aunt Bee that she shouldn't be so quick to turn down Mr. Goss. Clara feels Andy needs to be married, but he "can't bring a wife home" with Aunt Bee living in the house.

While conversing at the kitchen table, Clara confidently helps herself to a cookie from a jar on the table. Clara's behavior visually reinforces the character's boldness and authority.

"This bit of business was not in the script," says Harvey. "Clara's behavior was probably one of the many suggestions offered by Bob Sweeney, the director, to make the scene flow. Clara is an authoritative character without props, but I think the 'cookie' thing was a very nice corroborative touch."

Andy and Opie enter the kitchen while Aunt Bee and Clara are talking. Aunt Bee asks Andy who he's taking to the dance. She names several possibilities. Andy answers that he's not going to the dance. He thinks he'll just spend "a nice, quiet evening at home."

"Near the end of the kitchen scene, Aunt Bee is eagerly asking Andy if he's going to the dance," says Harvey. "She asks who he's taking and volunteers a few names. Well, I just typed in whatever names and then the name of a girl I had worked with on *The Today Show* popped into my mind, and I routinely added it to the list. The lady in question, Estelle Parsons, went into performing and did that marvelous role in *Bonnie and Clyde*."

Acting on Clara's advice, Aunt Bee invites Goss over for dinner. As a result, Andy postpones taking the family to Mt. Pilot for a Chinese dinner.

"This idea grew out of a childhood memory," recalls Harvey. "As kids, we loved going to The Grotto, a Chinese restaurant where it was all spooky, like a darkened cave. Dinners were eighty-nine cents, and little paper parasols came with the rice."

Mr. Goss accepts Aunt Bee's invitation and joins the Taylors for dinner. During the meal, Goss talks about cleaning chemicals and the hardships of removing spots and stains.

"I went to the local cleaner and found out some cleaning tips and vexations of the cleaning business when working up the character of Fred Goss," says Harvey. "It was worth all the effort just to find the word 'perchloroethylene.'"

Aunt Bee dislikes Mr. Goss but continues to see him for Andy's sake. Thinking Aunt Bee is interested in Goss, Andy encourages the relationship.

After Aunt Bee and Goss leave for a picture show, Andy goes to check on Opie. Opie is exiting the bathroom as Andy enters the upstairs hallway. Andy asks if Opie's brushed his teeth. Opie replies, "Just feel how wet the toothbrush is." Andy tells Opie the story of a boy who thought it was funny to wet his toothbrush instead of brushing his teeth. Andy says, "To him, it was a right-funny joke. Every time he thought about it, he'd smile. And then one day, he quit smiling; never smiled again the rest of his days—he couldn't, he didn't have any teeth." Upon hearing this, Opie immediately goes back into the bathroom to brush his teeth.

"In general, it is nice to open an Opie scene with a light touch before getting into the more serious stuff," says Harvey. "The wet-toothbrush scene affirmed the warm, fun relationship between father and son, so Andy wasn't just into preachments. I tried to use the phony, wet-toothbrush evidence when I was a child, and I think Andy's story about the 'boy who quit smiling' was original."

As Opie brushes his teeth, Andy tells him, "It looks like Aunt Bee might be getting married pretty soon." Hearing this, Opie asks, "Why do people get married, Pa?"

Andy's explanation is photographed in three separate sequences. The first is filmed with the camera positioned in the hallway, looking past Andy into the bathroom where Opie is standing in front of the sink. In the scene's master shot, the wall with the mirror has been removed. The camera is positioned behind the sink, looking past Opie at Andy. The third camera position photographs Andy's close-ups. The three sequences, which are edited expertly in the finished film, flow together flawlessly.

After Opie brushes his teeth, he continues to question Andy about love as the two enter Opie's bedroom. Andy explains "the marrying kind of love" as he tucks Opie into bed. The dialogue reflects the serious side of childhood and is very special.

OPIE: Did you and Mom have that deep-down kind?
ANDY: Yes, son, we did.
OPIE: And does Aunt Bee have that kind now?
ANDY: Yes, she does.
OPIE: Then, it's alright, ain't it?
ANDY: Yes, son, I s'pect it is.

"I didn't realize at the time that this was the first and last reference to Opie's mother in the series," says Harvey. "I'm uncertain why she wasn't referred to again. It might have been that Aaron preferred to emphasize Andy as the eligible bachelor rather than as the grieving widower."

Aunt Bee returns from her date later in the evening. Opie wakes up and comes downstairs. Andy invites Opie to join him and Aunt Bee on the porch for a piece of berry pie.

After the pie is finished, Andy and Aunt Bee discuss the advantages of her marrying Mr. Goss. Andy says, "all in all, I'd say there's every reason in the world for you to get married." Opie has been listening carefully to what has been said and comments, "Pa, you left out one of the reasons—that Aunt Bee's getting married because she's got that special deep-down type of feeling."

Reflecting on Opie's comment, Andy realizes that Aunt Bee doesn't have the marrying-kind-of-love for Mr. Goss. Andy explains to Aunt Bee that "among folks that love each other, like we do, nothing can be best for us unless it's best for you."

The impact of the scene lies in the audience's identification with what Andy is saying. Andy's dialogue expresses concisely and beautifully the universal appeal of giving love to someone else.

Aunt Bee decides to end her relationship with Mr. Goss immediately. The next day, Andy breaks the news to Mr. Goss. The Taylor family, free of the dry cleaner, happily heads to Mt. Pilot for a Chinese dinner.

"Three's a Crowd"

Episode 59

First broadcast on
April 9, 1962

Written by
**Charles Stewart
and Jack Elinson**

Directed by
Bob Sweeney

Sue Ann Langdon
Guest Stars as
Mary Simpson

"Phantom Fife strikes again!"—ANDY

"I mentioned earlier in my comments on 'The County Nurse' that it was possibly the only show that dealt with romance other than the one with Ellie," says Jack. "Imagine my surprise when I started reading 'Three's a Crowd.' I forgot completely that we did another script with the Mary character. I also have no memory of why there was a casting change from Julie Adams to Sue Ann Langdon."

Julie Adams was unavailable for a second appearance on *The Andy Griffith Show*. She made several television guest appearances in early 1962. It is likely that she was committed to appear in the *Dr. Kildare* series episode "The Horn of Plenty" when "Three's a Crowd" was scheduled for production.

The episode begins with County Nurse Mary Simpson entering the sheriff's office. Andy is at his desk. Barney is crossing from the cells with a broom and dustpan. Barney's chore is changed to painting the bars in a cell door in the filmed episode.

"At the opening in our script, we had Barney using a broom and dustpan," says Jack. "I have no idea why they changed it to painting."

Mary is planning to drop off some medication at the Powell place and has stopped by to see if Andy knows if the road construction up that way has been completed.

Andy reports that the roads are fine and quietly asks Mary if he could come over to her place that evening. Mary suggests they can watch television, play some records, and make a pizza pie.

Barney is busy painting and listening. He invites himself and Thelma Lou to Mary's that evening. Barney plans to bring his new set of bongo drums. He has just learned "Cumina" and would like to perform it.

"Cumina" or "Kumina" is Jamaican music that features drums. The song Barney plans to perform was changed to "La Cucaracha" in the filmed episode.

That evening the foursome gathers at Mary's. The script directions narrate the scene. *Andy, Barney, Thelma Lou, and Mary are indulging in a songfest, with Andy*

169

accompanying on the guitar. At the finish, Barney turns to his bongo drums and raps out a big crescendo. The others stop and look at him a little stunned at the unusual accompaniment. Barney finishes with a flare, feeling every beat and seeming to talk to himself as drummers do.

"Continuing with my forgetfulness, I have no memory of Barney playing the bongo drums or whether it was our idea or somebody else's," says Jack. "Maybe the drums were suggested by Don Knotts himself and the script directions written by Aaron Ruben."

Thelma Lou makes a request. She asks Barney to take her home.

Andy helps Barney to the door. Andy hands Barney his coat to speed up the departure. (Andy Griffith marked out the word "jacket" on his script and replaced it with the more southern-sounding "coat.")

Barney is surprised when he realizes that Andy isn't leaving as well.

Andy says he plans to stay a little longer and explains that Mary is going to show him some slides through her microscope.

The Essential Mayberry | 1961–1962

Thelma Lou purposely leads Barney out. Barney can't believe looking at germs could be any fun.

"The fact that Mary was a nurse led us to the microscope idea," says Jack. "Looking through a microscope isn't exactly 'party time,' which is what made it funny."

A little later, Mary returns to the living room with the pizza pie she promised Andy. A phonograph record plays softly in the background. Mary casually sits down on the end of the coffee table.

Julie Adams and Sue Anne Langdon bring a different persona to Mary Simpson. Adams's Mary is beautiful and mature. Langdon's Mary is sexy and girlish. Sitting on the coffee table seems right for Langdon's Mary but would be out of character for Adams's Mary.

Andy suggests a future picnic date. Mary approves and suggests taking Opie along. Mary, like Barney, doesn't seem to understand that Andy wants to be alone with her.

At this point the music ends and Mary gets up to shut off the phonograph. In the filmed episode, Mary restarts the record. While her back is turned, Andy slyly rearranges a pillow, making room for Mary on the sofa beside him. Mary sits down in the prepared spot and reaches for her coffee cup. Andy, seeing an opening, slips his arm across the back of the sofa. He starts to embrace Mary but is rudely stopped by the doorbell buzz.

Mary answers the door and discovers Barney! Barney has taken Thelma Lou home and returned because he is too wide awake to sleep. He helps himself to the pizza and asks Mary to get her microscope out so the trio can look at germs.

The next day, Andy is secretly talking on the telephone with Mary while Barney is in the back room. Andy sets another date for that evening.

Barney overhears the conversation and invites himself and Thelma Lou on Andy's date. Andy reminds Barney that he promised to straighten up the files that evening and will not be able to "make it."

That night at Mary's, Andy performs "He's Gone Away." (The song is changed to "I Wish I Was a Red Rosy Bush" in the filmed episode.)

Andy's song lasts fifty seconds. Earlier in the episode, the group singing of "Bringing Nellie Home" lasted twenty-five. The two musical performances along with the slower-paced romantic scenes required fewer lines of dialogue and thus fewer script pages. The "Three's a Crowd" script is twenty-eight pages long. "The County Nurse" script numbered thirty-three pages.

Mary asks Andy if it is hard to play the guitar. Andy sees an opportunity. He moves closer to Mary, hands her his guitar, and positions her fingers on the fretboard. His arm goes around Mary and directs her hand toward the strings.

The telephone rings, interrupting the intimate lesson. It is Barney. He needs Andy's help in locating a letter from the state attorney's office. The lesson resumes. The telephone rings. Barney needs more help. The lesson resumes. The telephone rings . . . Barney again. *Andy is a study of frustration.* The lesson resumes but quickly concludes with the breaking of a guitar string.

"Andy is smitten with Mary," says Jack. "Andy teaching Mary how to play the guitar was his sneaky way of putting his arm around her like a guy teaching a girl how to play golf. When Mary asks, 'Is it hard to play a guitar?,' Andy jumps at the chance. We had never gotten that physical in romantic scenes before. The guitar string breaking was another way to show that nothing's going right even without Barney being there at that moment."

The script direction narrates what happens next. *FIFTEEN MINUTES LATER— Andy is on the sofa alone and Mary enters from the kitchen with coffee."* Andy suggests letting the coffee cool. *"He pats a place next to him and waits for her to sit. But this little maneuver is thwarted by a doorbell ring. Mary must answer it. She opens the door to admit guess who . . . ol' Barn.*

Barney has found the missing letter. He celebrates by helping himself to a cup of coffee. He volunteers to go out and get some pizza in preparation for an extended visit.

The presence of a takeout pizza restaurant in a small southern town in the early 1960s was rare. A pizza would likely be difficult to find in Mayberry.

"We didn't realize that pizza places were rare in the sixties," says Jack. "The obvious question is, 'How come Andy Griffith didn't tell us?'"

The next day, Barney tells Andy he had a good time at Mary's the night before. Andy decides to "take the plunge." He points out that he and Barney have been spending a lot of time together. It's been Mary and Andy and Barney and Thelma Lou, or it's been Mary and Andy and Barney.

Andy suggests they (meaning himself and Mary) ought to spend some time alone.

Barney understands. He telephones Thelma Lou and cancels a planned visit to Mary's that evening—the reason being he and Andy would like to spend some time alone.

Andy is stunned. He tells Barney that's not what he had in mind at all.

"At this point in the script, we wanted just one more beat of Barney driving Andy crazy other than constant interruptions and we came up with the 'misunderstanding' scene," says Jack.

Andy explains to Barney that he would like to talk to Mary. There are a few things he would like to say to her in private.

Barney understands.

Andy leaves to get a haircut. Barney voices the understanding aloud, "He's gonna pop the question. Our sheriff's gonna get himself hitched."

Later, Barney shares the news with Thelma Lou. Barney admits that Andy's wedding will be like watching his own kid getting married. Barney hopes he won't cry during the ceremony.

"As we progressed in the series, each story kicked us into another aspect of Barney's character," says Jack. "Calling Andy 'the kid' as though he was Andy's father is a prime example. That wouldn't have come about if we didn't have the imagined wedding to open the door for it. Each year, Barney grew and grew."

Barney also shares the news with Aunt Bee. Aunt Bee gets emotional reflecting on the marriage. She hopes she doesn't cry at the wedding. Barney hopes so too. If Aunt Bee starts crying, he will be certain to join her.

Later in the day, Thelma Lou sees Andy coming up the street. She calls to him.

The script direction narrates the scene. *Andy waits for Thelma Lou to come over to him. As she approaches, she has a warm, happy-for-him smile. He is slightly puzzled. But then he is thoroughly mystified when Thelma Lou reaches up and gives him a quick kiss on the cheek, sniffs, dabs at her nose and eyes with a handkerchief, and walks away. Andy looks after her a moment, shrugs, then enters the courthouse.*

Aunt Bee brings lunch to the sheriff's office. Without a word, she kisses Andy on the cheek, gets out a hanky and wipes away tears of joy, and hurries out.

Barney enters next. He has a sly "I know what's going on" smile. Andy suggests going across the street for some root beer to go with their lunch. Barney starts on the errand, stops, and approaches Andy with his hand extended. Andy figures Barney must want to shake hands.

Barney is all business. He takes Andy's hand and solemnly shakes it. Barney sniffles and goes out to get the root beers.

Andy reflects on the three encounters and concludes that Thelma Lou, Aunt Bee, and Barney are all coming down with colds.

That night, Andy and Mary enjoy a candlelit meal. Afterward, they move into the living room by the fireplace. The two finish their coffee and celebrate "a whole evening alone together."

Meanwhile, at the Taylor house, an excited Barney is announcing "the plan" to a group of Andy's friends. Barney figures Andy and Mary have had time to finish their supper. He would like to give Andy time to pop the question and then go over to Mary's house. The group will march in unannounced and yell, "Surprise!"

Back at Mary's house, Andy is enjoying the "nicest, quietest evening" he has spent in a long time. Mary notices a beautiful full moon out the window and suggests the two go for a drive in her convertible with the top down.

The caravan of partygoers, led by Barney driving the squad car, arrives at Mary's. The group slips quietly across the front porch, Barney opens the unlocked door, everyone bursts inside, yells "Surprise," and discovers the "newly engaged" couple is missing.

"Unlocked doors have always been used as 'theatrical license,'" says Jack. "Even shows that take place in New York City, where there are ten locks on each door, have done it. Unlocked doors take less time and save the trouble of searching for a key. We felt a town like Mayberry would never have had locked doors. There are no thieves in Mayberry. I don't think there are many keys in Mayberry other than for the jail cells and handcuffs in Andy's office."

Meanwhile, Andy and Mary have parked beside a secluded lake. Andy adjusts the radio to a station playing romantic music. The two settle back and gaze up at the full moon. It seems like they are a million miles away from everyone.

The script directions narrate. *They regard each other. This is the moment. Andy starts to put his arm around Mary, and both lean in for the long-awaited kiss when she stops short, startled.*

Voices are heard in the distance. Barney and the "mob" descend upon the car. "Phantom Fife strikes again."

"In hindsight, it would have been wise if early in the script there was some mention of a lookout point where lovers went," says Jack. "A reference to a popular lover's destination may have helped explain how Barney knew exactly where Andy and Mary were."

"Similarly, it would have been wise if we explained where Opie was in this episode," says Jack. "Like he's at a sleepover at a friend's house. We blew that, too."

Andy and Mary remain seated in the car. Everyone else is eating, drinking, and enjoying themselves.

A musician is seated by a fire playing a guitar. The script directions called specifically for a banjo, so the sound of a banjo rather than a guitar is heard on the soundtrack.

Barney carries around a large bowl of potato salad and attempts to serve what's left in the bowl so it will not have to be thrown away.

"Barney's dialogue about the potato salad being thrown away is typical 'picnic' talk," says Jack. "In my family, my mother used to say, 'Eat everything up. People are starving in Europe.'"

In the epilogue, Andy asks for Mary's permission to court her in public. Mary, aware that no one is paying them any attention, agrees.

Andy puts his arm around Mary, and they finally kiss.

In the background, Barney can be heard still hawking the leftover potato salad.

"Epilogues, or tags as we used to call them, weren't really necessary, since the whole story had already been told," says Jack. "The end business of Andy and Mary courting in public was included so the sponsor could squeeze in one more commercial before the end credits."

The first three seasons of *The Andy Griffith Show* included commercials featuring the cast in character selling General Food products.

The commercial for "Three's a Crowd" has Mary serving a "special" treat instead of pizza. She brings a hand from behind her back revealing a box of Post Toasties.

Mary reminds Andy of the cereal's merits. He agrees and says anyone who serves Post Toasties deserves a kiss.

Andy and Mary are about to kiss when Barney marches in and sits down in front of a bowl of cereal.

Andy repeats his belief that Mary deserves a kiss for serving Post Toasties. Barney quickly jumps up and gives Mary a kiss on the lips.

Even in the commercial, Andy can't get a romantic break!

"The Bookie Barber"

Episode 60

First Broadcast on
April 16, 1962

Written by
**Ray Saffian Allen
and Harvey Bullock**

Directed by
Bob Sweeney

Howard McNear
Is Featured as
Floyd the Barber

"The Bookie Barber," Scene 4, INT Floyd's Barbershop. Andy is encouraging Floyd to hire a second barber, telling Floyd he could put a sign in the window—"Two-Chair Shop—No Waiting." Floyd nods, wide-eyed in thought, and delivers his all-time classic line: "Uh-huh—and I got enough magazines to swing it."

"The late Ray Saffian Allen hired me for my first true writing job at CBS, where he was head writer for a daily variety show," says writer Harvey Bullock. "Ray had other writers who did most of the work, giving me a chance to fail and fail—which meant learn and learn. After a year of that, a friend of Ray's asked him to come to London to write a sitcom [*Dick and the Duchess*]. Ray asked if I would like to go with him as his partner, and I jumped at the chance.

"After completing the sitcom, I wanted to return to the States, but Ray wanted to stay in London and develop some ideas there. So we agreed that we would each do what we wished, and we could reunite at the first opportunity.

"I worked solo in New York (*The Johnny Carson Show*) and then went to Hollywood, where I got jobs as a freelancer on various shows. The time on my own proved very valuable. Hitherto, I wasn't sure if I was depending too much on Ray. After I had worked alone and was reasonably successful, I had total confidence, but I knew I preferred working with Ray.

"Ray eventually returned to the States and came west. By this time, I had written for *TAGS*, and Aaron gave me the supreme vote of confidence—a twelve-story commitment. Ray and I started working on them, 'The Bookie Barber' being the first. I did the bulk of the writing, and Ray assisted."

In the opening scene of the completed script, Opie is trying to talk his way out of a haircut. Opie feels he doesn't need a haircut because "he can still see." He dreads "the little hairs that itch your back." In response to Andy's suggestion that he can get rid of the hairs by taking a bath, Opie replies, "A bath too! This is turning out worse than I thought."

"My children (I have four) all think of me as a 'kid' person," admits Harvey.

"I've always enjoyed the honesty of the small ones, before terminal sophistication sets in. In my younger days, I worked summers as a leader at a YMCA camp. My charges were eight years old. Spending two months in the same little cottage with seven of them, you get a hint of how their minds work."

Andy accompanies Opie to the barbershop. To photograph this scene, the mirrored wall in the shop has been removed, and the camera is positioned in its place. The camera films past the freestanding sink. Barney is also in the barbershop, getting a haircut. The shop is full of customers, and Floyd is rushing to finish.

When his haircut is finished, Barney walks over to the camera. A close-up shows Barney carefully scrutinizing his sideburns. Barney comments that just once he'd like "them sideburns to come out even."

"Barney's complaining about his sideburns was inspired by a personal observation I have made," says Harvey. "Somehow, customers never pass up a chance to air disapproval of their haircuts. The easiest target to disapprove is the sideburns. They are a true index, used by the knowledgeable, as to the value of the haircut. Sideburns are never even, because if they are, a tilt of your head, and they're out of alignment. Barney has been having his sideburns adjusted regularly for years. They're still not exactly right and never will be."

Andy leaves Opie at the barbershop. Bill Medwin enters as Floyd is finishing Opie's haircut. Medwin introduces himself and says he too is a barber. He then asks Floyd if he would be interested in "taking on another man."

When Andy returns to pick up Opie, he meets Medwin. Andy encourages Floyd to take on the new man. Andy reminds Floyd that a two-chair shop is something he has always wanted. Andy tells Floyd that he could put a sign in the window saying "Two-Chair Shop—No Waiting."

The possibility of owning a two-chair shop with no waiting has a dramatic effect on Floyd. He begins speaking in unfinished sentences and anxiously fumbles with a comb as he thinks the situation through out loud. At one point, he gets so flustered that he sits on Opie, who is seated in the barber's chair.

"Floyd's animated behavior was not caused by nervousness," explains Harvey. "He has decided to take on the other barber, and the idea of having a two-chair shop is so delicious, he backs onto the chair (and Opie) in sheer wonderment."

The new barber immediately attracts customers. The new customers are a "smart-looking" clientele. They all seem to be well dressed and stern faced.

"We didn't include a detailed description of the new barber's clientele because there were really no hard specifics needed," says Harvey. "They were described in the script simply as 'mug-like customers.' Aaron worked ahead on all scripts, and he knew what type of cast was needed. In this case, an easy cast, just three rough-looking guys."

The mug-like customers' frequent patronage of the barbershop arouses Andy's suspicions. His suspicions are confirmed as it becomes evident that Floyd's barbershop has become a front for a booking operation.

Andy shares the information with Barney. Barney wants to make an immediate arrest. Andy tells him that a hasty arrest won't work because the bookie would just "hide the evidence and play innocent." Andy suggests they use a plant to place a bet. When the bookie takes the bet, they can then make an arrest. Barney thinks a sweet little old lady like Emma Watson would be the perfect plant. Andy disagrees because he feels the situation is too dangerous to involve a private citizen.

Andy leaves to attend to other business. Before departing, he tells Barney that they'll think of something when he gets back. Barney, however, cannot resist the opportunity. He decides to become a plant himself and dons the disguise of a little old lady.

The scripted directions for the scene in which Barney first appears in disguise were as follows:

HOLD ON DOOR a moment, then door slowly opens, and Barney peers outside. Door opens wider, and Barney steps out into the street, looking furtively. He is dressed something like Emma Watson.

The directions were expertly photographed and edited to heighten the scene's comedy. The forty-five-second scene is visually presented on-screen in the following manner: The courthouse door cracks open. Barney is shown in extreme close-up. As the door opens further, the camera pans backward for a heightened shot, revealing a woman's hat on Barney's head. As Barney steps out to the sidewalk, the camera pans backward for a medium shot, which shows Barney putting on gloves before proceeding toward the barbershop.

Medwin and his clients are stunned by Barney's appearance. They become suspicious when Barney talks about a daughter-in-law who disapproves of his gambling and his need to place a quick bet. Barney then spots a black bag on the floor that contains "the names of the horses and things." He, Medwin, and the other clients all dive for the bag at the same time.

Meanwhile, Andy has returned. Opie tells him that Barney "looks like a little old lady." Suspecting what Barney is up to, Andy rushes to the barbershop. He arrives just in time to break up the scuffle over the bag. The needed evidence is scattered on the floor, and Medwin is caught red-handed.

In the episode's epilogue, Floyd is unaware of Medwin's arrest. He believes the barber has been receiving calls from numerous girlfriends and had to leave because of a romantic conflict. The problem has thus been resolved without Floyd ever "having to know the awful truth." This reaffirms a basic *TAGS* premise—bookie barbers and other problem-causers may invade Mayberry, but the town and its residents are never permanently threatened or changed.

Harvey Bullock Talks about Howard McNear

I never met Howard McNear. Writers seldom visited the shooting set. We just plain weren't needed. We had already done our part, the rewrite completed and slid under the producer's door. Any small fix-ups could easily be done by the director or actors. And the economics would not let us indulge. We had to be constantly beating the bushes, trying to sell stories.

So, I never met Howard McNear. But we share a very special, mutual friend. That fey and wispy, wide-eyed barber of Mayberry, Floyd Lawson.

Howard/Floyd was a magician. His signature "oohs" and "ahs" lent his lines a whimsical touch which defies analysis. He would suddenly switch to sing-song, then to an unconvincing, stern authority, then whispered amazement—all the time wheezing, gasping, and rolling his eyes. All of which busied him so he never got to finish a sentence. It was very funny, and viewers never thought he was acting!

When we wrote for Floyd, we couldn't wait until that episode was shown to see how he had immeasurably improved the dialogue with his stop-and-go delivery, his breathlessness, his awe, and his pained disapproval.

TAGS cast members were very close to Howard. When his health worsened, you could sense a palpable sadness on the set. Scenes were restaged so he could do his lines seated in his barber's chair. And he did them as fresh and funny as ever.

When the end came, he was mourned on every soundstage in Hollywood where he had done his quiet, wondrous wizardry.

Yes, I sure wish I had met Howard. But at least I knew Floyd. And now, up in that 'Great Barbershop in the Sky,' perhaps Floyd is finally speaking complete sentences—but I hope not.

"Andy on Trial"

Episode 61

First Broadcast on
April 23, 1962

Written by
**Jack Elinson and
Charles Stewart**

Directed by
Bob Sweeney

Ruta Lee
Guest Stars as
Jean Boswell

"The people of this town don't have a better friend than Andy Taylor."
—BARNEY FIFE

"Stories about city slickers versus Andy worked well for us," says Jack. "'Manhunt,' 'Andy and the Woman Speeder,' and the Danny Thomas spin-off all fell into this category. This one was basically the same formula. Audiences love to see Andy outsmart the big shots. Opening the show in a large city office was a nice change of pace."

"Andy on Trial" begins with an exterior shot of a multistoried office building. The shot dissolves into an office interior. Andy, dressed in a suit, enters and says to a *smart-looking secretary right out of Central Casting* that he would like to see Mr. J. Howard Jackson.

The secretary buzzes Mr. Jackson on the intercom and tells Jackson the sheriff of Mayberry would like to see him. Jackson asks the reason for the visit. Andy answers that he has come to arrest Jackson.

Jackson, hearing Andy over the intercom, opens the door of his office.

Andy reminds Jackson, an eminent publisher, that he was given a speeding ticket coming through Mayberry about two weeks ago. Jackson was on his way to an important meeting, so Andy let him go with the condition that Jackson would come back and stand trial. Jackson failed to do so.

Jackson charmingly invites Andy into his office to straighten the matter out.

Jackson's sumptuous office impresses Andy. Jackson directs Andy to a huge chair. Andy sits down and almost sinks out of sight.

The chair in the filmed episode is average-sized. Andy sits down and leans back a considerable distance. He is uncomfortable and frowns. He repositions himself on the front edge of the chair.

Jackson takes a position of power behind his desk. He insults Andy. The sheriff, in his opinion, should be running down chicken thieves and curfew breakers instead of in a big city. Andy responds with a mechanical smile.

Jackson offers Andy a cigar from a desktop humidor. Andy declines but says he would like to take one for his deputy. Barney likes to smoke a cigar when he's feeling 'specially sporty.

"In the first draft of the script, we wrote 'sporty,'" says Jack. "I think Andy added the 'specially.' It wasn't a phrase we'd ever heard."

Andy returns to the subject of the speeding ticket. Jackson is ready to draw a check for the fine. Andy, however, feels Jackson's failure to attend to his hearing changes things. He must return to Mayberry.

Jackson informs Andy that he is the head of a big business and has responsibilities that prevent a trip to Mayberry. He reaches for his wallet to settle the matter.

Andy informs Jackson that Mayberry takes a dim view of bribery.

Jackson leaves his wallet in his pocket. He shouts into the intercom and informs his secretary to have his lawyer meet him in Mayberry.

Later in Mayberry, Andy is seated at his desk. Barney stands by the door. Jackson and his lawyer, Fred Krim, are waiting for the hearing to begin.

The script direction explains why Barney is positioned by the door. He is there to prevent Jackson from making a "break" for it. This explains to Don Knotts why Barney is standing by the door. The audience doesn't know this and likely doesn't give Barney's position a second thought.

Andy turns the sign on the desk from "Sheriff" to "Justice of the Peace." Jackson pleads guilty to get the hearing over with. Andy charges a fifteen-dollar fine.

Jackson is outraged to have been dragged to Mayberry for such a small fine. Andy explains that Jackson can't flaunt the law and perhaps the inconvenient trip to Mayberry will teach him a lesson.

Jackson accuses Andy of "trying to be a big man" and promises that "one of these days Andy will be pushed down to size."

"Andy's a cool cat," says Jack. "If some bad guy insults him, he has control and just smiles respectfully . . . which drives the bad guy absolutely crazy."

Later, back in the big city, Jackson meets with Jean Boswell, *a very attractive newspaper reporter.*

Jackson gives Boswell an assignment. He wants her to investigate Sheriff Andy Taylor. Boswell is to look for anything that "can be twisted into an article" that will "pulverize" Andy's good image.

Jackson visually demonstrates his desire to destroy Andy by elaborately crushing out his cigarette.

"The crushing out of the cigarette was not scripted," says Jack. "Roy Roberts, who played the role, was evidently a smoker and he probably asked the director if he could use a cigarette in the scene. In the sixties, smoking wasn't such a no-no. Everybody on TV and in the movies smoked."

The script directions set up the next scene with *stock footage of the squad car pulling up at the sheriff's office—set EXT.—Stage.*

In the filmed episode, the audience sees the stock footage of the squad car's arrival. The footage was filmed at Culver City, the site of Mayberry's exterior locations. The next shot is of Jean Boswell standing in front of the barbershop. The shot was photographed inside the soundstage on a recreated Main Street set.

"Andy on Trial" required no exterior photography. Exteriors were either stock footage (like the opening shot of the multistoried office building) or Main Street buildings recreated inside the soundstage.

The script direction narrates, *Our reporter, Jean Boswell, walks over. We see she now wears the garb of a college girl with coiffure to match. Barney straightens himself at the sight of the attractive stranger.* Andy goes inside the office, leaving Barney to welcome Ms. Boswell.

Boswell flatters Barney by mistaking him for the sheriff. She asks about the location of a good hotel and explains that she is a college student come to Mayberry to research a thesis on small-town administration. Barney volunteers his assistance.

The script direction concludes the sidewalk meeting with *Barney pats the old holster, his specter of authority. Boswell smiles, thanking him. She has quickly found the pigeon to work through.*

"Barney's enthusiasm sets up another classic 'Barney' scene," says Jack. "Enough said."

Inside the sheriff's office, Barney tells Andy about *the new girl in town. The door opens and Ms. Boswell shyly enters.*

Barney introduces Boswell to Andy and takes her on a tour of "headquarters."

Barney points out and lectures on the "confines of the office and jail." The tour highlights are the cells, the bulletin board, and the gun rack.

Andy suggests that the tour should include the back room where Barney takes his afternoon nap. Barney dismisses the suggestion.

Barney has run out of highlights but picks up steam again by mentioning "things to come." A crime lab, a new wing of cell blocks, a dispensary, a rec hall, and a chapel are currently in the blueprint stage.

Andy is amused by Barney's imagination. Barney, aware that Andy may discredit what he has said, quickly ushers Boswell out the door to show her around town.

Barney concludes the around-town excursion with a stop for refreshments at the "coffee shop." He and Ms. Boswell share a booth. Boswell thanks Barney for the assistance he has given her.

Boswell takes control of the conversation. She begins by praising Barney's professional appearance. She contrasts it with the fact that Andy doesn't even wear a tie. Barney agrees that appearance is "one of Andy's weak points."

Boswell points out that Barney is a "progressive, forward-thinking, dynamic man."

Barney, stroking his own ego, admits there are certain things he would do differently if he was "running the show." Barney admits that he likes to run a "taut ship."

"The actual phrase would be 'I like to run a tight ship,'" says Jack. "How it got to be 'taut' I have no idea. Maybe my partner, Stewart, typed it wrong."

Andy, in Barney's opinion, is a "little lax." He mollycoddles Otis, the town drunk, who is allowed to arrest and release himself. Crimes go unpunished. Andy tears up the jaywalking tickets Barney issues to chronic jaywalker Emma Watson. Andy also uses the squad car for unofficial business, such as delivering groceries and driving Emma home.

Barney asks if Boswell has enough information to write her thesis. Ms. Boswell assures him she has.

"All the bravado from Barney about being the big shot and inferring that Andy was a little too lenient on the job was written with the trial referred to in the episode's title in mind," says Jack.

Sometime later, Andy is seated at his desk. Opie and Barney enter laughing from the back room. Opie asks Andy if he would like to hear a joke. Opie begins the joke but quickly falters. Barney whispers the opening line in Opie's ear. Opie delivers the "missing bath" joke and gets a big laugh from his audience. Barney admits that the preacher told him the joke.

"In our script, Opie knew the opening line to his little joke without any help from Barney," says Jack. "This change happened during filming. Also, Barney's reference to the preacher was not in our original script."

The front door opens and a well-dressed stranger, Deputy State Attorney Roger Milton enters. Milton hands Andy a newspaper article and asks for an explanation.

Andy reads the article's headline aloud, "Does the Sheriff Run the Town, or Does the Town Run the Sheriff?"

"It didn't take any great effort to come up with the article's headline," says Jack. "The phrasing was modeled after President Kennedy's 'Ask not what your country can do for you; ask what you can do for your country.'"

The article accuses Andy of malfeasance of public funds and disintegration of law enforcement. Milton informs Andy that he will have the opportunity to deny the charges at a hearing scheduled for the next day. In the meantime, Andy is suspended from office. Barney will be the active sheriff until the matter is resolved.

Milton exits. Andy and Barney are stunned. *Opie is particularly bewildered by it all.*

Andy assures Opie that the charges are "some mistake that will all be cleared up."

"Opie overhearing what's happening to his dad is a touching moment," says Jack. "You can feel for a child when his father is threatened."

Andy takes off his badge and pins it on Barney. *Barney looks at the badge as though a tarantula has been placed on him.* (Andy, pinning his badge on Barney, was deleted from the filmed episode.)

On the day of the hearing, Barney is sitting at the sheriff's desk pondering the situation. Andy enters dressed in a suit and tie.

Andy greets Barney, "Hi, Sheriff." Barney rises and asks if Andy has any further information on who is behind the newspaper article.

Andy moves behind the desk and starts to sit from force of habit. He stops and asks Barney if he minds if he (Andy) sits in the sheriff's chair. Barney responds, "That's your chair. Always was and always will be." The clock shows the hour is eleven o'clock. (This scene was deleted from the filmed episode.)

The script directions set the scene. *INT. SHERIFF'S OFFICE—CLOSEUP— CLOCK now showing one o'clock. CAMERA PANS DOWN to show the sheriff's office has now become a hearing room. The sheriff's desk is sort of a judge's bench, at the moment unoccupied. Elsewhere in the room are several townspeople, Andy and Barney and Roger Milton.* (The spectators are deleted from the filmed episode.)

The remainder of the episode is written as a drama. No laugh track will be heard on the soundtrack.

The door opens and Jackson enters. *J. Howard Jackson is smug as the proverbial cat that got the cream.*

Jackson's presence answers a lot of questions. Andy now realizes that the accusing article was in one of Jackson's publications. Jackson assures Andy that the charges will be substantiated by a key witness. Barney, angered, labels the witness that will testify against Andy "a low, crawling snake."

The commissioner enters, takes his place at the desk, and starts the hearing. Milton assures the commissioner that there is a witness who will verify the charges against Andy. The commissioner asks who the witness is. Milton answers, "Deputy Barney Fife."

The script directions describe the deputy's reaction. *Barney has been looking around, watching for the rat witness to reveal himself. He does a double take as he realizes his name has been called.*

"We purposely dragged out the time it took to announce the name of the main witness," says Jack. "The delay created drama."

Barney takes the witness chair. Milton reminds Barney of his statement about Andy being "a little lax" and not running "a taut ship." Barney denies the accusation. Milton, to help jog Barney's memory, calls for "the young lady."

Jackson goes to the door and beckons. *To Barney's horror the newcomer is Jean Boswell, although no longer dressed as a coed.*

Barney is outraged that Boswell fooled him. He calls Boswell a "sob sister" and labels her tactics a "dirty trick." A "sob sister" is a journalist who specializes in witty sob stories. (Andy Griffith crossed out the phrase on his script.)

Milton attacks Barney with rapid-fire questions about Otis releasing himself from jail, crimes that go unpunished, and Andy's misuse of the squad car. Barney is only allowed to answer "yes or no."

"The questioning of Barney was shot in every way possible," says Jack. "The director used close-ups, reaction shots of Andy, shots of the people present, but mostly shots of Barney, who is in such pain at the moment."

Milton finishes his questioning. Barney is told by the commissioner to "step down."

The script directions give insight into what Barney is feeling in the moment. *Barney doesn't move. He looks at Andy, almost with tears in his eyes. He says with a tremor in his voice, "Gee, Andy."*

Barney refuses to "step down." Instead, he demands an opportunity to say more than "a bunch of yeses." The commissioner concedes.

Barney admits that sometimes he gets carried away with himself. He confesses that he bragged about himself before Ms. Boswell and made Andy look bad. Barney then comes to Andy's defense. He states that Andy is the best sheriff in the world and a friend to all the citizens of Mayberry. Barney points out that Andy conducts himself "not so much by the book but by the heart."

"Barney's speech wasn't difficult to write because everything he said was the truth," says Jack. "The way Andy runs a town like Mayberry is the only way it should be. Andy took care of everybody and kept them safe."

The commissioner asks if there is any other evidence outside of the newspaper article. There is not.

The commissioner apologizes for any embarrassment the hearing may have caused and reinstates Andy as sheriff.

Upon hearing the decision, Barney rises from the witness chair, walks over to Andy, and extends his hand. Andy shakes it with a smile. Andy is proud of Barney. Nothing needs to be forgiven.

The script direction narrates what happens next. *At this point, Otis comes weaving in humming to himself as he goes through the ritual of locking himself in a cell, much to the onlookers' amazement and amusement.*

Otis's arrival was wisely deleted. His appearance would have undercut the dramatic tone of the hearing.

In the epilogue, Barney orders Andy to punch him in the nose for being a blabbermouth. Andy instead praises Barney for his fine job of "explaining" on the witness stand.

Barney makes Andy promise to do something to stop him if he ever blabs again.

The telephone rings. It is Thelma Lou calling to learn the outcome of the hearing.

Barney can't help being "Barney." He answers that he made the prosecutor look like a fool and "pulled Andy out of the mess."

Andy, remembering the promise he made, pulls Barney's cap down over his face and shuts off his blabbing.

"In the discussion of 'Three's a Crowd,' I pointed out the unimportance of epilogues," says Jack. "I said they were unimportant because the story had been finished by the end of act two. But in this story, I feel that what was the epilogue should have been the last scene of act two. It was so important to show how terrible Barney felt and how apologetic he was. It's a shame this became the epilogue, which is now cut out of every repeat."

Season 2 Wrap-Up

"After the second year of *The Griffith Show*, Charles Stewart and I continued our work on *The Danny Thomas Show*," says Jack. "We stayed until that series ended. Stewart and I worked on that show for eight of its eleven years. After the *Thomas Show* wrapped up, we decided to split and go our separate ways. Stewart became the producer of *Petticoat Junction*, and I moved over to *Gomer Pyle, U.S.M.C.*, During that period, I also did five more *Griffith Show* scripts. Four alone and one with my brother Izzy."

The production of *The Andy Griffith Show*'s second season concluded on March 28, 1962. The series ranked number seven in the A. C. Nielsen year-ending ratings.

1962–1963

"Andy and Opie, Bachelors"

Episode 65

First Broadcast on
October 22, 1962

Written by
**Jim Fritzell and
Everett Greenbaum**

Directed by
Bob Sweeney

Joanna Moore
Appears as
Peggy McMillan

"Even though Jim died seventeen years ago, I still dream that we are meeting at the typewriter every morning to get on with an overdue script."
—EVERETT GREENBAUM

"I'm amazed at the length of time between 'Quiet Sam,' our first *TAGS* script, and this one," says writer Everett Greenbaum. "After nearly forty years, which is half of my lifetime, I can't remember why there was such a long period between our first and second *TAGS* scripts.

"My reaction to seeing our names as writers in the 'Bachelor' episode's closing credits is to say to myself, 'Jim and I never wrote that one.' But sure enough, I found it in one of the bound volumes of my past scripts.

"I think the reason I can remember so little about this one is because it was likely my least favorite of the twenty-nine *TAGS* scripts we wrote. Joanna Moore didn't seem to me to belong in a small town and didn't bring with her an inborn sense of comedy like so many of our cast. Also, the story didn't provide enough 'meat' to fill a half hour. It seems to me that we did a lot of padding to stretch out its length."

"Joanna Moore was cast as Peggy McMillan after the script was written," says producer Aaron Ruben. "The script called for an attractive woman, and Joanna was certainly that. The relationship between Andy and Peggy, however, didn't seem to gel. We wanted to get the right actress for the role, so Joanna appeared in only four episodes."

Jim and Everett's "forgotten" script begins at the Mayberry sidewalk bus stop. Andy, Opie, and Aunt Bee are preparing for Aunt Bee's departure to visit her Aunt Louise for three or four days. As they await the bus's departure, Peggy McMillan walks up. Aunt Bee asks Peggy if she will look in on "these two helpless creatures" while she's gone.

After boarding the bus, Aunt Bee tells Andy and Opie to be sure to change their underwear. "Opie's bottom is ripped." She also wants the two to be "clean on the inside and the out." Andy is embarrassed by Aunt Bee's instructions because

Peggy overhears them. Aunt Bee also reminds Andy to take Opie for a haircut on Friday and to make sure that Floyd does not "cut him so naked at the back of his neck. Last time, he looked like a baby bird." These instructions are excellent examples of comedy presented through everyday conversation.

After the bus departs, Andy, Peggy, and Opie walk toward Floyd's barbershop. At this point, Peggy offers to help out while Aunt Bee is gone.

Floyd overhears Peggy's offer. After she leaves, he compliments Andy "on the pretty little housekeeper who is coming in to take over for Aunt Bee." Floyd explains that "it starts here and ends with your mailbox." He predicts that Peggy "will want to come over to the house to make supper. Then she'll kind of hint around that she wants to do this all the time. And then it happens. You'll be out changing the card on your mailbox to read, 'Mr. and Mrs. Andy Taylor.'"

Later that evening, Opie asks Andy what they're having for supper. Opie suggests they "chew tar." Opie says that his friend, Johnny Paul Jason, says that "chewing tar is real good for the teeth."

When Andy puts a chicken in the oven, Opie gives him a pencil, so he can figure out what time to take the chicken out. Opie warns Andy "to be sure and not lick the point—it's an indelible pencil." Johnny Paul has told Opie that "if you lick indelible pencil lead, you die in a minute and a half." Opie tells Andy that Johnny Paul learns his facts from "reading in bed with a flashlight."

The wisdom of Johnny Paul Jason is introduced in this episode. Jim and Everett drew upon past memories when writing Johnny Paul's sayings. "Johnny Paul's words of wisdom were based on folklore from my childhood, and Jim recognized it as part of his," says Everett. "Opie's telling Andy that Johnny Paul knows so much because 'he reads in bed with a flashlight' came from another childhood memory. Reading under the covers with a flashlight, preferably Tom Swift books, was something the two of us had done as children."

Despite their best efforts, Andy burns the supper. Arriving just as Andy examines the charred chicken, Peggy offers to "fix something." She prepares an elegant table setting and serves a delicious meal that is "pure gala."

After the meal, Andy, Peggy, and Opie sit on the front porch. Andy plays his guitar as he and Peggy sing "Down in the Valley." The simple and harmonious singing, the set's shadowy lighting, and the peaceful sound of chirping crickets combine to create a serene Mayberry evening. The realistic squeaking of the screen door, as Opie enters the house, ends the scene on a perfect note.

"We didn't include the song to highlight Joanna Moore's singing talents," says Aaron. "The song simply seemed to fit the scene, so we used it."

The next day, Opie asks Andy when Barney will be coming home from his vacation in Raleigh. Opie's questions lead into Andy's hilarious description of Barney's idea of a good time in the big city.

"Andy's telling Opie about Barney's life at the Raleigh YMCA—wearing a pongee shirt, seeing a movie or hearing a lecture on cleanliness, and concluding his evening with tapioca pudding and a cup of hot chocolate—is typical Fritzell and Greenbaum," says Everett. "It was the sort of thing we wrote together that we couldn't write apart.

"What one missed, the other one could provide. I knew nothing about sports, or cared. Sports was one of the main concerns of Jim's life. While I knew all about science, machinery, flying planes, literature, and music, Jim knew how to play cards, what people drank, and the slang of fighters, jazz players, and factory workers."

Meanwhile, back at the courthouse, Peggy brings lunch. After she leaves, Opie asks Andy if "Miss Peggy is practicing for when you and she might get married."

When Peggy offers to come over that evening, Andy rejects her offer. Instead, he prepares burnt weenies and beans. After the meal, he and Opie sit on the front porch. When Opie suggests that they talk, neither can think of anything to say. Opie asks Andy to play his guitar, but Andy says he doesn't "feel much like playing."

Peggy stops by while Andy is washing dishes. Opie tells her that they had a "terrible supper," and Peggy offers to cook. At this point, Andy asks her quite frankly why she is doing all of this. Peggy answers that she just feels sorry for "two helpless bachelors. Besides, I enjoy it."

Andy accepts the sincerity of Peggy's reply, and the joyous atmosphere created when good friends get together is instantly restored.

Opie is puzzled about what has happened and asks Andy for an explanation. Andy simply replies, "There's a woman in the house. We're just going to have fun, and that's all there is to it."

Jim and Everett humorously conclude the scene with a final reference to Opie's wise friend. "That's all there is to it," Opie ponders aloud. "I'll have to ask Johnny Paul about that."

"Mr. McBeevee"

Episode 66

First Broadcast on
October 1, 1962

Written by
**Ray Saffian Allen
and Harvey Bullock**

Directed by
Bob Sweeney

Karl Swenson
Guest Stars as
Mr. McBeevee

"Yes, the 'bedroom' scene is one I am proud of."—HARVEY BULLOCK

"I vividly remember the storyline origination for this script," says writer Harvey Bullock. "Ray Saffian Allen and I were attending one of *TAGS* executive producer Sheldon Leonard's legendary two-day story seminars, along with some other writers, plus Andy and Aaron Ruben. We tossed notions haphazardly in the air, and often someone would grab one and suggest an embellishment.

"Someone tossed up a notion about Opie having an imaginary friend. Another writer suggested that Opie might thus be having trouble separating the real from the fanciful. Then Sheldon offered, 'And Andy has to lecture Opie sternly about telling the truth.'

"At that moment, I got a quick, urgent flash like nothing I had ever experienced," says Harvey. "As Sheldon was trying to figure out whether to proceed with the story, I stood up and said, 'There's a better way.' Already this was strange, because no one ever stood up at those meetings. But I suddenly had a picture in my mind of Andy and Opie in the bedroom. I continued, slowly, feeling my way, still under some unreal impetus. 'After Opie makes seemingly outrageous statements, Andy does go to punish him, as you suggested. But Andy then realizes Opie wouldn't lie, and preposterous as the statements were, he owes it to Opie to believe the boy, since so many times Opie has blindly believed him.' Sheldon loved it immediately. 'Yes, that's the story! Go write it!'

"The episode was originally named 'Mr. McTeevee,' but we were later told this title was not available—I presume for legal reasons. So Aaron changed it to 'Mr. McBeevee.' The role was played by veteran actor, Karl Swenson, a most able and versatile performer. Aaron thought so much of Karl he even hired a double (Thurston Holmes) to do the scenes of climbing down from trees or poles. The 'climb downs' were pretty tame. Karl always said he could have done them himself, but I suspect he was happy to have a stunt double take over."

Early in the episode, Opie delivers mail to the courthouse that was wrongly delivered to the house. When Andy asks Opie to take out the trash, Opie says

he can't because he told Mr. McBeevee he'd be right back. Opie tells Andy and Barney that Mr. McBeevee is "new around here." Opie says he met Mr. McBeevee in the woods and describes him as a man who "walks around in the treetops and wears a great big shiny silver hat."

Later that day, Opie returns home with an unsharpened hatchet. Opie says the hatchet is a gift from Mr. McBeevee. At this point, Andy thinks Mr. McBeevee exists only in Opie's mind. Andy explains to Opie that somebody probably left the hatchet in the woods, which means he'll be coming back to pick it up. Andy tells Opie to return the hatchet to the place where he found it.

As instructed, Opie returns the hatchet to Mr. McBeevee. At this point, the audience sees that Mr. McBeevee is actually a lineman for the telephone company. Upon the return of the hatchet, Mr. McBeevee agrees that "perhaps it is too dangerous." He cheers Opie by showing him how the "heathen cannibals" taught him how "to make smoke come out of me ears." In place of the hatchet, McBeevee gives Opie "an old, old quarter that's just begging to be turned into gum and ice cream."

"The 'smoke from the ears . . . learned from heathen cannibals' idea came from a childhood memory of a favorite black-sheep uncle who used to visit my family," says Harvey. "He did the smoke-from-the-ears trick over and over. We were enchanted, and he appreciated our enthusiastic reception because it was his only trick. I decided to include an on-screen performance of the trick without hesitation. I figured if my beloved, but inept, uncle could do the trick, any good actor could too."

After carefully thinking the matter through, Barney believes there really is a Mr. McBeevee. He decides that an eyewitness identification by Opie will confirm his belief.

"We wanted a casual device, which would justify Opie giving lots of answers, so we could get maximum mileage out of his seemingly fanciful description," says Harvey. "We felt we could have more fun with a relaxed boy helping Barney out than with Opie, a suspected faker, being sternly admonished by his father, so we came up with the idea of Barney's eyewitness identification test."

When Opie returns to the courthouse, Barney casually talks him into identifying Mr. McBeevee. Opie answers questions about McBeevee's height, weight, eye color, and hair color. Barney is pleased with Opie's answers until Opie tells him that Mr. McBeevee "sort of jingles" when he walks. Opie then adds that the jingling comes from the "twelve extra hands that hang from his belt." Opie also mentions that Mr. McBeevee can make smoke come out of his ears. Opie ends his description by saying, "And, he's a real nice man. He even gave me this quarter."

"Opie's description of McBeevee was fashioned by staring at that spot on the ceiling in contemplation and testing and retesting mentally crazy things that described McBeevee and also had a second solidly sane meaning," says Harvey. "I visualized all the tools, and how colorful McBeevee would describe them, which led to his 'twelve hands,' etcetera."

After Opie shows the quarter, Andy asks him where he got it. Given the description that Andy has just heard, Andy does not think Mr. McBeevee is the source for the quarter. To settle the issue, Opie suggests they go and ask Mr. McBeevee about it.

When Andy and Opie arrive at the woods, Opie calls to Mr. McBeevee, but his calls are not answered. Unbeknownst to either Andy or Opie, Mr. McBeevee has left the site to pick up another worker.

Andy then takes Opie home and sends him up to his bedroom. Andy believes Opie has gotten in the habit of "stretching the truth a little out of shape" and thinks it's time "for a whipping."

Ray and Harvey's script directions for the next scene were quite simple. They read: *INT. OPIE'S BEDROOM—DAY Opie is sitting in the window seat. Andy enters, sits next to him.*

Director Bob Sweeny followed those script directions exactly. Andy and Opie are seated by the window, but instead of photographing the scene from inside the house, the scene is photographed looking into the bedroom from outside. The window effectively frames the scene, and the simulated sunlight filtering through the trees dramatically lights the set.

At this point, Andy wants the truth. He expects Opie to admit that Mr. McBeevee is just make-believe.

The scene's climax was scripted as follows:

Opie makes a decision. He shrugs, speaks in a weary monotone.

OPIE: Mr. McBeevee . . . is only make- . . .

ANDY: Say it.

Opie makes a difficult decision.

OPIE: I can't, Paw. Mr. McBeevee isn't make-believe. He's real.

Andy looks at the boy's upturned face. Now comes the fateful question.

OPIE: (continuing) Don't you believe me?

Andy pauses. He wants to postpone facing the all-important question.

OPIE: Don't you, Paw?

It's the moment of decision. Andy is troubled. He looks at the earnest face. Then the answer is there. Andy's sternness relaxes. He finds a strange peace within him as he reaches out to take Opie's hand.

ANDY: I believe you.

"Ronny's picking at the window sill, his trembling lower lip, and the cue for the tears in his eyes were carefully worked out during rehearsals," says Rance Howard, Ronny's father. "Nothing you see on screen was improvised. Andy and Ronny knew exactly what they were going to do before the cameras started filming."

"Ronny and his father went over the lines repeatedly," says producer Aaron Ruben. "Ronny's attitude in the scene was established by the director and Andy."

After leaving the bedroom, Barney questions Andy about what happened upstairs. In response to Barney's question about whether Andy believes in Mr. McBeevee, Andy replies, "No, no, but I do believe in Opie."

"Earlier in our careers, Ray and I worked in New York for a daily variety show," says Harvey. "At Christmas one year, we wrote a 'Santa interview' bit. We ended the interview with Santa saying sadly, 'I don't know why people don't believe in me. I believe in them.' I remembered that line while working on the McBeevee script, changed it some, and gave it to Andy."

Harvey continues, "One of the decisions a writer always makes is whether to write a show open or closed. This episode is half-closed, half-open. It is closed right up to the end of act one, where McBeevee is first seen by the audience. The second act is open—the audience now knows Opie isn't faking it—and the scene where Andy believes him is made even more solid."

After his talk with Opie, Andy drives to the woods. He calls out, "Mr. McBee-vee." A voice answers, "Hello, somebody call?" At that point, Andy realizes Mr. McBeevee is real and is overjoyed!

Andy returns to the courthouse and tells Barney he just met Mr. McBeevee. Barney feels Andy has been working too hard and needs to let his "mind go blank." When the telephone rings, Barney answers. It is Mr. McBeevee calling to confirm a supper date at the Taylors'. This leaves Barney speechless.

"By the episode's end, the only principal player not knowing McBeevee actually exists is Barney," says Harvey. "So we felt we could continue the double entendre one more time in the epilogue. We tried to make the scene believable by Andy initially trying to tell the truth, but Barney just overrides him. So Andy, as he so often does, goes along with it a bit and lets him run on."

"Andy's Rich Girlfriend"

"I loved Barney's speech about how rich people grow up. I recall how Jim and I laughed as we wrote it."—EVERETT GREENBAUM

Episode 67

First Broadcast on October 8, 1962

Written by
Jim Fritzell and Everett Greenbaum

Directed by
Bob Sweeney

Joanna Moore
Returns as Peggy McMillan

In the opening scene of Jim and Everett's third *TAGS* script, Andy, Peggy, Barney, and Thelma Lou are out on a date. After eating at Mom's Diner, the foursome decides to go for a ride. Barney takes Andy aside and asks him to drive. Barney plans to sit in the back seat with Thelma Lou. In an effort to accommodate Barney, Andy rushes everybody into the car. In the confusion, Barney ends up in the front seat with Andy.

"Barney's scheme about how to get together with his date in a car without mentioning anything about it goes back to the puritanical mores my generation grew up with," says writer Everett Greenbaum.

As the episode continues, Andy drives the group to a beautiful lake. Andy and Peggy walk toward the lakeshore. Barney and Thelma Lou remain in the back seat, kissing.

As Andy and Peggy walk, a hawk calls out. Andy asks Peggy if she'd like to hear him "talk" to the hawk. Andy places a blade of grass between his thumbs and blows.

"Jim and I always loved writing one-way dialogue between a character and an animal," says Everett. "In one of the shows we had written for, *Mr. Peepers*, Wally Cox's character talked to small creatures, crustaceans, and even microbes numerous times. So, we decided Andy would talk to the hawk, making the noise with a blade of grass just as we had done in our childhoods."

Thelma Lou and Barney eventually join Andy and Peggy. Thelma Lou suggests they take off their shoes and go wading. Barney is reluctant. He doesn't want to take his shoes and socks off in front of the girls.

"The concept that Barney would not want to appear barefoot in front of the girls also harks back to my puritanical early years," says Everett.

Andy and Peggy skip stones across the water and have a wonderful time. At the date's conclusion, Andy walks Peggy to her door and asks for another date the next night. Peggy tells him that she is on duty at the hospital the next night, but she will be available the night after. With the next date set, Andy kisses Peggy good night.

The next morning, Andy stops by Peggy's house to return a compact that she left in the squad car. Andy notices a new car parked in front of Peggy's house and asks about the car. Andy learns that the car is a gift from Peggy's father, who owns the R and M Grain Elevators in Raleigh.

"In my hometown of Buffalo, New York, grain elevators were a common sight," says Everett. "Tall cylinders of concrete were all along the lakes, getting grain from the ships. When we were thinking of a business for Peggy's father, the Buffalo grain elevators came to mind."

Andy tells Barney about Peggy's new car and her father's wealth. Barney then tells Andy that his relationship with Peggy won't work. Barney explains that Peggy is "one of the rich, and they are different." He advises Andy to "give Peggy up. Nip it in the bud."

"I started using Barney's trademark phrase after I got married," says Everett. "My wife Deane (a girl who grew up in a cabin in Arkansas) was not at all familiar with machinery, especially cars. I remember the two of us were out driving, and I had put my new Thunderbird into low gear as we went down a steep hill. It produced a high whining noise. At the bottom of the hill, I shifted back into drive. When the sound stopped, Deane said, 'Well, you sure nipped that in the bud.' By the way, my Thunderbird was the same model as Peggy's."

Barney then "spells out" the ways of the rich for Andy—"they are born with a silver spoon in their hand," a rich kid's bike is "solid chromium with six or seven reflectors," and after the bicycle age they go off to a "refinishing school."

Barney's two-minute-fifty-second description of the wealthy is filmed in one long, sustained shot. Two reaction close-ups of Andy were edited in later. The scene ends when Andy stands and walks out of the back room. The next shot is photographed with the camera positioned outside the courthouse. Both courthouse doors are propped open, and Andy is seen exiting out the door toward the camera.

The next day at the courthouse, Andy makes final preparations for his date with Peggy. Barney advises Andy to cancel his out-of-town date. Barney reminds Andy of their shared experiences: "We made second-class scout the same month," and "I was second to your first in the county penmanship contest." Barney then warns Andy, "Don't get hurt."

"The scouting remark and the penmanship award were Barney's way of showing Andy how close and intertwined their lives were," explains Everett. "Hence, his advice to give up Peggy was given out of concern for Andy's well-being."

On their date, Andy takes Peggy to a fancy restaurant in Raleigh. Peggy orders a "New Orleans" drink and asks Andy if he has ever been to New Orleans.

Andy tells Peggy that he and Barney once drove to New Orleans in a Model T and wound up selling the broken-down car for twelve dollars.

"Andy's story about the car breaking down was based upon something that actually happened to my cousin Calvin and me," says Everett. "The two of us were driving to New York City in a 1934 Pontiac. The car broke down, and a junkman took the car as compensation. We completed the trip by bus."

During the course of the evening, Peggy orders escargot for herself and Andy, mentions a trip that she made to Paris when she finished high school, and asks Andy to dance. In declining the invitation to dance, Andy says he can "two-step a little, but when they start in on the cha-cha, I generally sit down." In general, Andy has a miserable time on his date.

The next day, Andy avoids Peggy when she drops by the courthouse. He also refuses to take her calls when she telephones his house.

Eventually, Peggy finds Andy in the courthouse and asks him what is going on. Andy denies Peggy's accusation that he is avoiding her, but he immediately cancels a future date the two had planned.

Andy and Peggy's reconciliation occurs when both discover each other later that night skipping stones at the lake. Peggy tells Andy that he is a snob. She says, "Just because my father's rich, you're snubbing me. I want to go out with you, but you don't want to go out with me. You think that nothing can ever measure up to Paris, New Orleans, wherever. The other night when we came out here with Thelma Lou and Barney, that was one of the nicest evenings I've had in a long time."

Andy realizes that Peggy is sincere. He picks up a stone and skips it across the lake before the two walk off arm in arm.

"We always had to balance believability with a quick resolution to the problem," says Everett. "Sometimes, as in this episode, the solution comes too easily to be credible, but we were writing a half-hour show which didn't allow the luxury of fully developing a solution. Our attention was always focused foremost upon the comedy."

"Andy and the New Mayor"

Episode 69

First Broadcast on
October 15, 1962

Written by
**Ray Saffian Allen
and Harvey Bullock**

Directed by
Bob Sweeney

Parley Baer
Appears as Mayor
Roy Stoner

"Capture the fragrance of Riviera rose petals and the passion of the Mediterranean moon in a rugged he-man scent. Caution: User should wear gloves."—Nuit de Paris (Paris Night) bottle label

Ray and Harvey set the opening scene of their "New Mayor" script in the courthouse. Barney is calling Juanita, who is working the breakfast shift at the diner. Barney explains his morning call by saying that he wanted to call to ask for a date that night. He then adds that "the early bird gets the worm." Realizing what he's said, he adds, "No, I didn't mean it that way—honest."

"Barney just bulges with common sayings and laces his talk with them," says writer Harvey Bullock. "Barney perceives himself as a smooth conversationalist. He loves a reassuring phrase, but he can also foul them up mightily. In this instance, he has to undo an embarrassment, 'No, I didn't mean worm.'

"In the early going, it was tempting to cast Juanita in a script. But *TAGS* producer Aaron Ruben realized that Mayberry was already well populated and having a character talked about but never seen would stimulate the audience's imagination. Everyone could fashion their own version of Juanita however they liked. As long as the character remained unseen, no one could prove their 'Juanita' was incorrect."

Barney tells Juanita he would like to bring a new Ted Weems record over to her place for a late-night listen. When describing Ted Weems's music, Barney says, "It soothes the savage in me."

"Ted Weems was a bandleader in the thirties," says Harvey. "He was popular but very unexciting. His appeal was his dreamy style, which was perfect for slow dancing. It's easy to see why Weems was one of Barney's favorites. You could 'dip' to his music, which was Barney's favorite dance-floor maneuver."

In anticipation of his upcoming date with Juanita, Barney picks up a bottle of "Paris Night" shaving lotion. When Andy enters the courthouse, he stops and asks Barney if he's been painting. The fact that the fragrance of Barney's aftershave smells like paint is a running gag throughout the episode's first act.

"The idea for and the name of Barney's lotion originated from a childhood memory," says Harvey. "Way back when I was just a little older than Opie, I went downtown to buy my mother her Christmas present. I always bought her the same thing, a tiny bottle of perfume called 'Evening in Paris,' which I had heard advertised on the radio. It cost thirty-five cents. My mother would enthuse mightily over it, and I would boast importantly, 'They talk about it on the radio.'"

Later in the episode, the newly elected mayor, Roy Stoner, has arranged to meet with Andy. Andy is late for the meeting because he has taken Opie fishing and "it got late on us." At the meeting, the mayor makes recommendations for improvements in the sheriff's department.

When the new mayor complains that Andy does not carry a gun, Andy responds that "over in the old country, in London, England, policemen carry sticks."

The old-country reference sounds like a line from one of Andy Griffith's early comedy monologues. "The old-country line does not appear in my script," says Harvey. "I think Andy did contribute that.

"The events surrounding the creation of the new mayor are difficult to remember. I can't recall whether Parley Baer was in place and we wrote with him in mind, or if we wrote just for a generic, fussy bureaucratic type."

Andy and the mayor conclude their meeting with a look around the courthouse. While the mayor is looking around, Mrs. Morgan stops by to pick up her husband, Jess. Andy is holding Jess for moonshining. Jess has not served his full sentence, but Andy allows him to split his sentence so he can harvest his crops before they spoil.

"I know Andy contributed the idea to let the prisoner, Jess Morgan, out of jail for three days so he could bring in his crops," says Harvey.

"While Andy did not actually write a complete script, his comments and suggestions were invaluable," says *TAGS* producer Aaron Ruben. "Andy would not leave the table where we would be doing a final rewrite until he was satisfied that not just his lines were exactly right, but that of every other character in the script as well. I honestly don't know how successful the series would have been without his input and the authenticity he brought to it."

The mayor tells Andy he wants the prisoner to serve his "full time." After the mayor departs, Andy releases Jess. Jess gives Andy his word that he will return in three days.

On the morning of the third day, Barney encourages Andy to go pick up Jess. Andy refuses. He told Jess he had until five o'clock. Andy explains to Barney that "if we go running out there ahead of time, it'll show that we don't think Jess's word means a thing. A guy like Jess Morgan ain't got too much more than his word. Take that away from him, and he's really got nothing."

Andy's desire not to take away Jess's word is very "noble" and a wonderful example of how the show taught some of "life's little lessons."

"*TAGS* was a show which liked to point out life's little lessons," says Harvey. "We were constantly seeking comedy story ideas with implied or explicit morals.

It was always a challenge. Comedy was central, and overdone moralizing can be worse than none at all."

The mayor stops by the courthouse while Andy is at home eating lunch. Barney is lying on the jail cot with a blanket pulled over his head. The mayor thinks Barney is the unguarded prisoner. The mayor immediately drives to Andy's home and confronts him about leaving prisoners alone. Unaware of the mistaken identity, Andy explains that nobody is at the jail because "the best interest could be served by letting Jess go home for three days."

The mayor then orders Andy to "go get Morgan." The mayor threatens Andy by saying, "After this, somebody else may be wearing that badge." The mayor then angrily taps Andy's badge with his keys to make his point.

"Yes, the mayor flicking Andy's badge was scripted," says Harvey. "Sometimes these touches were included if we felt strongly about them—which we did in this case. Otherwise, the directors added 'business' where needed."

Andy refuses to pick Jess up early. Andy, Barney, and the mayor wait for Jess's return until twenty-five minutes after five. Andy tells the mayor that something must have happened to keep Jess from keeping his word and suggests that they drive out to Jess's house together.

After Andy parks the squad car by the road, he suggests they take a shortcut through the woods. When Barney spots Jess up in a tree, the mayor believes Jess heard them coming and "crawled up in that tree to hide." When Andy orders Jess to come down, he refuses. The mayor then decides to go up and get him.

As the mayor approaches the tree, the camera reveals a bear sitting at the bottom of the tree that Jess has climbed. The bear then attacks the mayor. Although his clothes are torn, the mayor is not hurt. When the mayor joins Jess in the tree, the bear turns its attention on Andy and Barney. Andy and Barney seek refuge on top of the squad car, and the bear climbs into the car's back seat.

"We never thought the bear would be difficult or dangerous to work with when we were writing the ending," admits Harvey. "But the particular bear doing this show was a real ornery cuss. We were told it chased Don Knotts all the way back to the squad car, where the gasping Don actually climbed up on the car roof!"

Harvey adds, "Sometimes we teased production chief, affable Frank Myers, by sneaking a page into a script he was analyzing for location, props needed, etcetera. Our insert would call for an elephant stampede or a bridge collapsing, and we could hear poor Frank scream from way down the hall."

The episode concludes with Jess in his cell. Barney is in the courthouse making his final preparations for his date with Juanita. Andy enters and tells Barney the mayor wants "no parking" signs put up at the duck pond because the site has turned into a "regular lover's lane." Andy gives the assignment to Barney.

Barney had planned to take Juanita to the duck pond himself, so he takes the signs from Andy, places them under his arm, and angrily storms out.

"The Cow Thief"

"This script was a good detective story."—AARON RUBEN

Episode 70

First Broadcast on
October 29, 1962

Written by
**Ray Saffian Allen
and Harvey Bullock**

Directed by
Bob Sweeney

Malcolm Atterbury
Guest Stars as
Luke Jenson,
Ralph Bell as
William Upchurch,
and **Parley Baer** as
Mayor Roy Stoner

"For once I know with absolute certainty where a story came from," says writer Harvey Bullock. "During one of Sheldon Leonard's seminars, Andy mentioned that back home a fellow once stole some cows by putting shoes on them. The thief was then able to lead the cows away without leaving hoofprints for the owner to follow. All the writers present shouted their appreciation. Andy's recollection was a guaranteed good story.

"At the close of the seminar, Sheldon assigned the various story notions we had worked on, and I got the 'Cow Thief.' I was very pleased. An episode with a strong plot element is often easier to make funny. But Andy's notion was also a bit wacky, so it had to be made credible."

Ray and Harvey's completed script quickly introduces the mystery—someone is stealing cows. In its opening scene, farmer Tate "Fletch" Fletcher tells Andy that his cow has been stolen—just like Weddie Huff's cow.

As Andy talks with Fletch, Barney examines the fence beside the barn. Fletch warns Barney to keep away from the gate because "I just put my big bull in there. Since the police ain't giving me no protection, maybe he can."

"I named one of the farmers whose cow was stolen Weddie Huffman," says Harvey. "Weddie was a North Carolina classmate of mine at Duke University—actually just a nodding acquaintance, but a neat guy. His name just popped up when I was writing the script. I thought Weddie was a good southern name. How his named popped into my typewriter I'm not quite sure, and quite possibly he has never known about it either. Somehow in making the episode, Weddie's last name shrank to just 'Huff.' It's a total mystery why, but somehow a 'man' is missing."

The mayor arrives to console Fletch on his loss. The mayor assures Fletch that his administration will see that Fletch gets "proper protection." Because the mayor feels Andy isn't doing enough, he plans to "phone down to the capital and have them send up a man who really knows something about solving crimes."

This is the second consecutive *TAGS* episode that uses Mayor Stoner as an antagonist. (The character's first appearance was in Episode 69, "Andy and the New Mayor.")

"Scripts were processed by the producer and then scheduled for shooting, but incoming scripts were not necessarily shot in the order received," explains Harvey. "Aaron would juggle the scripts to give each of the top performers an episode in which they were a dominant part. Mayor Stoner may have appeared in two consecutive scripts, written by two different writers, at two different times, which happened to be juxtaposed and filmed one after the other."

After returning to the courthouse, Barney tells Andy that they can handle this case without "any nosey parker coming up here from the state capital." Barney feels they should make it clear to the outsider that he is not needed. He proposes that they "stand together and turn on the big freeze."

While Barney is talking, Andy looks out the window and sees Luke Jenson, who has a reputation of being a "bad penny," crossing the street to the hardware store.

Ray and Harvey's script directions for the character's initial appearance were as follows:

Display tables have been set up outside the store, stocked with hardware miscellany, tools, kerosene lanterns, hangs of rope, paint cans. One table has various sizes of cast-iron skillets, cheap tableware, etc. A hand-lettered sign over the items says, 'SERVE YOURSELF.' Luke Jenson wanders by and stops. He is shabby, grim, withdrawn. He is nearsighted and squints continually. His mongrel hound stays close by his side. Luke surveys the street, squints toward store to see if he is being watched. Then he casually picks up a skillet and inspects it.

"Luke's glasses were not in the original script," says Harvey. "Instead Luke's nearsightedness was, hopefully, brought to the audience's attention by his constant squinting. It may be that Aaron wanted to make sure Luke's poor vision was remembered by the audience, so he brought in the glasses."

Malcolm Atterbury, the actor who portrays Luke Jenson, fit the role well, but a mistake was made in the selection of Luke's dog, Mac. The dog is too clean and polished looking—not at all the stray mutt that Jenson would have.

"I haven't seen this episode for thirty years and don't remember my reaction to the dog's appearance," says Harvey. "We just wrote his description as 'a mongrel hound.' If indeed a clean and polished dog was cast, it was a goof."

Luke Jenson's menacing presence is heightened audibly by *TAGS* musical director Earle Hagen's score. The character's on-screen appearance is accompanied by deep bass notes, which signify evil.

"We never had to suggest music," says Harvey. "Earle Hagen was a resident genius, and all could be left to him. Occasionally, a comedy bit might require a definite piece of music, and we would so specify in the script. But mostly, we just sat back and enjoyed Earle whistling away."

Andy walks over to the store and greets Luke. He advises Luke not to take the "serve yourself" sign too seriously. After Andy walks away, Luke turns to Mac and says, "Everybody knows poor old Luke ain't got any money." At that point, Luke takes a wad of bills out of his shirt pocket and continues his conversation with the dog by saying, "Everybody but you and me."

William Upchurch, the crime expert, arrives from the capital that afternoon. At first, he mistakes Barney for the sheriff. He tells Barney that he remembers when Barney made a special report about safety procedures on country roads. Upchurch especially remembered the jingle Barney used: "Walk on the left side after dark, or you'll wind up playing a harp."

Upchurch wins Barney over immediately, and Barney forgets all about the "big freeze."

"The special-investigator character, William Upchurch, was named after an administrator at Duke University," says Harvey. "He was a small man, ever neat, and totally in command. I liked the sound of 'Upchurch' and brazenly appropriated it. Oddly enough, the real Mr. Upchurch always wore a bow tie. Although we had not requested it in any way, Ralph Bell, the actor cast as Upchurch, turned up with a bow tie."

Andy, Barney, Upchurch, and the mayor visit the Fletcher farm so Upchurch can begin his investigation. Upchurch notices footprints on the ground and asks Andy if he made a moulage (a plaster cast of the prints).

Upchurch joins Barney by the footprints and says, "The sheriff tells me you've decided not to make a moulage." Barney responds, "That's right, we decided not to make a moulage. We told a few people, but we decided it didn't make any sense upsetting folks—running around blabbing, making a big moulage out of it."

"I am uncertain where I heard about moulage," says Harvey. "Obviously, it had stayed for years in the dusty files of my mind. Somehow, when I was writing the script, the word just popped up, and I knew instantly it was right for Barney. The word moulage was a godsend. The perfect bit of exotica for Barney to at first misunderstand and then revel in using."

Upchurch speculates that the footprints were made by a gang of three fellows. The mayor feels they are finally getting somewhere and rushes the group off to find the culprits.

After they depart, the barn door creaks open slowly. Luke Jenson emerges with a cow in tow. The cow has a shoe on each foot.

When Andy, Barney, and Upchurch return to the farm to make a moulage, Andy becomes suspicious about the way the footprints line up. He notices that "number two walked right through a mudhole."

The three return to town and set the plaster prints up in the courthouse for "extended data analysis." As Upchurch explains his investigation to the mayor, Andy looks out the window. When he sees Luke Jenson, Andy comes up with a plan.

Acting on Andy's instructions, Fletch brings a prize cow to town in his truck. As Luke walks by, he sees the prize cow and overhears Andy telling Fletch he will be working late in the office that night. After Fletch leaves with his cow, Luke decides that night will be an appropriate time for the cow thieves to pay Fletch's farm another visit.

That night at the farm, Andy presents his theory to the others. He has figured out what Luke is doing because there were not any footprints for the stolen cow. Since he believes Luke or his dog would spot them outside, Andy suggests they hide inside Fletch's house until they can catch Luke with the evidence.

The mayor feels Andy's theory is implausible, so he, Upchurch, and Barney depart.

A short time later, Barney returns to stand watch with Andy and says, "I was almost out in the car, and I remembered another time a few years back when another mayor of our town accused you of having a hairbrained idea—when you had the idea of making me your deputy."

"Whenever a story gave an opening for a touching, heartfelt scene, we tried to fulfill it," says Harvey. "The 'Andy and Barney' scene fit in nicely and reminded the audience of the true strength of the show, which was the caring that existed between the leading characters."

As Andy and Barney wait inside the house, they hear Luke Jenson yelling, "Help, get away!" They rush outside and capture Luke with shoes in hand. Andy explains that Luke got more than he bargained for when "a nearsighted man tries to put shoes on an ornery old bull."

In the epilogue, Andy and Opie are taking items to the street that Aunt Bee has cleaned out of the attic. When Opie finds a discarded elephant-foot umbrella stand, he asks if he can play with it. When Barney arrives, he sees the hoofprints that Opie has made with the stand and jumps to the conclusion that an elephant is loose in Mayberry.

"The elephant-hoofprint hoax was actually pulled off by students at Colgate University," says Harvey. "It was after a deep snow, so the prints made four at a time were deep and clear. But just because something really happened doesn't mean it is a good story. I have always preferred to make up my own stories. I believe truth isn't important as long as you can make the false plausible."

"The Mayberry Band"

"My favorite memory of this episode is the beatific smile on Floyd's face as he marched."—AARON RUBEN

"Andy Griffith played the sousaphone and the guitar and always loved it when an episode included a musical sequence," says *TAGS* producer Aaron Ruben. "This may have given Jim and Everett the idea to write an episode featuring the Mayberry Band."

As the episode opens, Andy is getting a haircut. The barbershop is full of members of the town band because all the band members need haircuts for their annual trip to the band festival.

Barney rushes into the barbershop to tell Andy he's got something at the courthouse to show Andy. Andy joins Barney outside, and the two see that Freddy Fleet's band is in town. Freddy introduces Andy and Barney to Phil Sunkel, "his new horn."

The same band made its initial *TAGS* appearance in "The Guitar Player" (Episode 3), but that band was led by Bobby Fleet, not Freddy Fleet.

"At the time we wrote this script, Jim and I were just trying to make a living," says writer Everett Greenbaum. "We didn't know we were making history and never dreamed the episodes we wrote would be watched and analyzed for years to come. If we had, we would have looked at old scripts once in a while to verify a name or two.

"Aneta Corsaut, who would be cast later as Helen Crump, was a good friend of ours. Aneta had a musician friend in New York and wanted to give him a thrill by having us use his name in the script. So, we named Fleet's 'new horn' Phil Sunkel. The real Phil Sunkel sued us for twenty thousand dollars. Aneta was devastated and made many long-distance phone calls trying to get Sunkel to 'call off the dogs.' The show finally got him to settle for five thousand dollars."

Freddy Fleet asks Andy's permission to leave his bus parked on the street for an hour while he goes into the diner "to make the food scene." Andy and Barney proceed to the courthouse.

Episode 72

First Broadcast on
November 19, 1962

Written by
**Jim Fritzell and
Everett Greenbaum**

Directed by
Bob Sweeney

Parley Baer
Guest Stars as
Mayor Roy Stoner

Caught up in the excitement of the Mayberry band's annual trip to the capital, Barney purchases a pair of Andre Kostelanetz marching cymbals, which are pure brass with leather straps. Barney asks Andy to "sit there with your back to me" while he auditions for a position in the band. Barney then quietly walks up behind Andy and presents a loud audition. After this performance, Andy agrees that Barney can be a "stand-by cymbalist."

"Andre Kostelanetz was a big conductor of concert music," says Everett. "There were no cymbals of that name. It just sounded comical."

Following Barney's audition, Andy meets with the town council. Andy requests the approval of funds to "send the town band to the capital." Mayor Roy Stoner refuses to give his approval because he feels "we have the worst town band in the entire state. The band is a disgrace to the town of Mayberry. There will be no trip this year."

"We had seen Parley Baer's two previous *TAGS* appearances and thought he was very, very good as the mayor," says Everett. "He was a grouchy type of character and the perfect antagonist, so we decided to use him."

Andy pleads with the mayor to hear the band one more time before making a decision. After Andy promises "to rehearse the boys real good and real hard," the mayor reluctantly agrees.

When Andy gathers the band for rehearsal, Barney calls the group to attention with a cymbal crash. He orders the band to "Cool it! Let Andy make the scene." Floyd explains to Andy that Barney got his new slang from Phil Sunkel.

"Jim adored baseball players and swing musicians to distraction," says Everett. "He picked up their speech easily. The musician's slang used throughout the script, such as Barney's, 'Cool it! Let Andy make the scene,' was written by Jim."

When the mayor arrives, Andy instructs the band to turn to "number twelve in the brown book and play it like you never played it before." The band's performance is terrible! Despite this performance, the mayor admits, "They sound better than they did last year, but they are still the most disgusting band I have ever heard in my life—no trip."

"Because the storyline involved music, *TAGS* musical director Earle Hagen played a prominent behind-the-scenes role in the episode," says *TAGS* producer Aaron Ruben. "Earle scored the episode and worked out all the arrangements for the musical performances. He even wrote in and carefully arranged the town band's sour notes."

Later in the afternoon, Andy has an idea. He wants Freddy Fleet's boys to play with the town band. Fleet refuses because he's "got to get going." Andy then threatens to hold Fleet's bus for an interstate pest-control inspection because it is bug month. In order to avoid the inspection, Fleet agrees to go along with Andy's plan.

Andy asks the mayor to listen to the band "while we're marching." Andy explains that the band didn't sound good during the previous performance because they were sitting down. He explains that they are a marching band, so they need to keep moving. The mayor agrees to listen one more time.

Andy has the band members change uniforms with Freddy Fleet's boys. After the exchange, the band consists of Freddy Fleet's boys and a few members of the original Mayberry band. Andy instructs the Mayberry band members not to play their instruments.

"Two of the episode's best visual gags came from director Bob Sweeney," says Everett. "Bob came up with the idea to have a giant piccolo player exchange band uniforms with a very short man. During the marching scene, the second gag includes a wonderful close-up of Floyd playing his horn in a comical manner."

"Bob Sweeney was also involved in all areas of preproduction planning," says Aaron Ruben. "The first meeting of the week was the production meeting in which Bob met with the heads of all departments. During the meeting it was decided what was needed in the way of sets, props, wardrobe, etcetera, for that week's episode. Bob would also lay out the schedule for the week's shooting, which actor he would need and for how long, and how much time was needed for getting the seven or eight pages of script shot that day. It was an early morning call, but when the production meeting was over, everyone knew his or her task for the week, and the week's work was properly organized."

As the episode continues, the town band marches down the street and plays a rousing rendition of "Stars and Stripes Forever." The mayor can't believe how good they sound. He agrees to allow the band to go to the capital.

After Andy announces that they can go, he pats the mayor on the shoulder and says, "Much obliged, mayor. You won't regret this." This dialogue, photographed with the camera facing the actors, is immediately followed with a shot photographed behind Andy and the mayor. Andy repeats the two lines of dialogue a second time and pats the mayor's shoulder again.

"I don't think the repetition of Andy's dialogue was in our script," says Everett. "Most likely what happened was that the 'much obliged' line and the shoulder patting were used as a starting point for photographing the scene from a different angle and should have been edited out in postproduction. It was a small mistake that was overlooked."

"Convicts at Large"

Episode 74

First Broadcast on
December 10, 1962

Written by
**Jim Fritzell and
Everett Greenbaum**

Directed by
Bob Sweeney

**Reta Shaw,
Jean Carson,
and Jane Dulo**
Guest Star as the
Escaped Convicts

"I loved writing this episode, and it has always been one of my favorites to watch."—EVERETT GREENBAUM

"'Convicts at Large' was an attempt to do a satire on a popular movie, *The Desperate Hours*," says writer Everett Greenbaum. "Before the movie was made, *The Desperate Hours* was a Broadway play based on the kidnapping of the Hill family in Philadelphia. We got the idea for our script from the play and movie and turned the kidnappers into women, which seemed funny.

"Our idea got Jim and me into a lawsuit. Another writer sued, claiming that he had submitted a similar idea to Jim Fritzell's agent. *TAGS* finally agreed to pay this guy some small fee, which was cheaper than going to court."

The "convicts" script begins with a prison escape. Searchlights scan the prison walls, and sirens sound the alert that an escape has occurred. Three women convicts are shown emerging from heavy underbrush. The three are looking for a hideout.

Andy hears a news bulletin about the escape on the courthouse radio. The alert warns that the women are unarmed but possibly dangerous. The leader of the group is named Big Maude Tyler. She is accompanied by Naomi Conners and Sally (no last name is given).

"We created Big Maude Tyler with Reta Shaw in mind," admits Everett. "Jim and I had previously written for Reta on *Mr. Peepers*, and we knew what we would get out of her. She was a wonderful actress and a personal friend of my family."

"I assume that *TAGS* producer Aaron Ruben knew our work from New York theater and live television," says Jean Carson, who portrayed escaped convict Naomi Conners. "I had known Reta for years in New York and always wanted to work with her. She was a brilliant actress. I had seen Jane work as a stand-up comic several times in New York supper clubs."

As Barney and Floyd return from a fishing trip, they discover Floyd's car is out of gas. The two decide to go to the O'Malley cabin to borrow some gas. They do not know the convicts are hiding there while Mr. O'Malley is in Detroit. As they

approach the house, Barney notices smoke coming from the chimney and calls out. Barney explains that they would like to borrow some of Mr. O'Malley's gas for their car.

Big Maude invites Barney and Floyd inside. Barney quickly realizes from the prison uniforms that the women are "cons." The convicts grab Barney and Floyd, steal Barney's gun, and take the two prisoner.

"You can't work with better actors than Andy Griffith, Don Knotts, and Howard McNear," says Jean. "They were total professionals. The only problem I had was breaking up on camera. I wanted to laugh anytime I had to look Howard or Don in the face. *TAGS* was ensemble work all the way. It was a marvelous experience working with all that talent and, most of all, niceness."

Barney reminds Sally of "Al at the old Cascade Club in Toledo." Barney has "that same dumb face, weak chin, and round shoulders." Sally begins calling Barney "Al," and the bit becomes a running gag throughout the episode.

"The 'Al' gag was inspired by a line from Al Jolsen's 'Buddy, Can You Spare a Dime' song," says Everett. "The line was 'Call me, Al.' To my knowledge, there is no Cascade Club in Toledo."

As instructed by the convicts, Barney phones the courthouse to tell Andy that he and Floyd are at O'Malley's house. He tells Andy that they are tired and plan to spend the night.

The convicts grow bored waiting for a chance to escape. The cabin has a record player, so Big Maude tells Sally to put on some music. The song on the record player reminds Sally of "that old Cascade Club," so she asks Al to dance. Barney refuses but is told by Big Maude, "If Sally wants to dance, you dance."

"We figured that one of the great differences between male and female convicts is that the female convicts would want to dance," says Everett. "It was a funny idea that had great potential."

Sally decides "to play something dreamier," so she changes the record. Naomi has a strong reaction to the new music and breaks a vase over Floyd's head. Big Maude explains Naomi's behavior by saying, "Naomi and her husband—that was their song."

"At that time, I had been involved in several mishaps in live television, such as a gun misfiring and the bullet flying into my face and hitting an actor with a breakaway bottle that didn't break," says Jean. "I was petrified that I might hurt Howard McNear. I checked and double-checked to make sure he had good protection under his hat but was still very uneasy about hitting him with the vase."

As the episode continues, Big Maude sends Floyd and Sally to town for supplies. Floyd is told if he "tries any funny business, Big Maude will let Al have it."

When Andy spots Floyd in Mayberry, he notices Sally sitting in Floyd's car and thinks, "O'Malley is having a little party up there." Floyd and Sally quickly depart.

Andy sees the bus arriving soon after Sally and Floyd drive away. When Mr. O'Malley greets Andy as he gets off the bus, Andy realizes "something sure is fishy somewhere" and offers to drive O'Malley out to his place.

After Floyd and Sally return to the cabin, Big Maude sends Sally "out for some water" and tells Naomi "to cook." Naomi constantly scratches as she fries hamburgers.

"Naomi's constant scratching was my idea," says Jean. "Naomi was a nasty, mean little character, and I somehow thought that the scratching would imply a nasty habit for a woman. The intention was to indicate that she might have lice. The scratching ended up creating a lot of extraneous movement. Every time I see it, I cringe. In defense of director Bob Sweeney, you must remember it was Floyd's show, and I'm sure a lot of Sweeney's focus was on Floyd's character. Then in the women's scenes, the focus was definitely on Big Maude. I've always suspected Sweeney's failure to point out the distracting scratching was an oversight, because nobody knew more about what was right—what worked and what didn't work—than Sweeney."

When Andy and O'Malley arrive at the cabin, Andy sneaks up to an open kitchen window and looks in. When Naomi turns away, Andy reaches through the window and pours the bucket of water that Sally had placed on the counter down the sink.

232 The Essential Mayberry | 1962–1963

Nixon—The Mayberry Connection

Y ears ago, I had a friend, Leonard Garment, who was a clarinet player studying law, *Life* magazine did a story about the Hill kidnapping, which offended the family. The Hills sued *Life*. When the Life *v. Hill* case went to the courts, my friend Leonard and Richard M. Nixon worked together on it. Eventually, they became law partners, and Leonard played a large part in Watergate. So in a roundabout way, Richard Nixon has a connection with Mayberry.—EVERETT GREENBAUM

Naomi discovers the empty bucket and decides to get the water herself. She steps outside to the pump and is captured by Andy and O'Malley. When Big Maude sends Sally outside "to see what's keeping Naomi," she too is captured.

Big Maude orders Barney into the kitchen to tend to the hamburgers. Andy gets Barney's attention through the open window and tells him to "get the big one to come outside."

Barney asks Big Maude to go outside with him to get some water. Big Maude refuses. Instead, she puts on a record. The music gives Barney an idea. He looks at Big Maude with steely passion and says, "Let's you and me dance—you're beginning to get to me."

Barney dances over to the door and opens it. He explains that he "can't stand crowded ballrooms." As Barney and Big Maude dance back and forth across the room, Andy, who is out of view, swipes at Big Maude's wrist with a pair of handcuffs each time Barney leads her through the doorway. On the third pass, Andy cuffs Big Maude. After a struggle, she is apprehended.

Oblivious to the capture, Floyd runs to the door and shouts, "Maude, Al, if those hamburgers are ruined, I won't be responsible!"

"The physical action in the capture was suggested in great detail in our script and executed brilliantly on the set," says Everett. "When I first saw the scene on the air I fell apart. Reta and Don played the scene even funnier than I had imagined it would be.

"The idea that kidnap victims may eventually identify themselves with the kidnappers seemed funny with Floyd. We used that idea throughout the episode and, especially, in the end when Floyd is more concerned about burning the hamburgers than anything else."

The epilogue is set in the courthouse. Barney recalls the experience with the convicts and tells Andy that Floyd was "helpless in the face of grave danger." When a knock is heard at the door, Barney opens the door and retrieves the newspaper. He looks at the front-page headline and yells, "For crying out loud!" The headline reads: "LOCAL BARBER CAPTURES ESCAPED CONVICTS."

"Shortly after the completion of 'Convicts at Large,' Howard McNear suffered a stroke," says producer Aaron Ruben. "We were all devastated by the news. The stroke was obviously not a minor one, but Howard's spirits never flagged, and he triumphantly returned to work with us again fifteen months later."

"The Bed Jacket"

"'The Bed Jacket' has always been one of my favorites."—HARVEY BULLOCK

Episode 75

First Broadcast on
December 17, 1962

Written by
**Ray Saffian Allen
and Harvey Bullock**

Directed by
Bob Sweeney

Parley Baer
Guest Stars as
Mayor Roy Stoner

"A writer gains an appointment to pitch brief story ideas to the producer," explains writer Harvey Bullock. "If an idea captures the producer's fancy, the writer is given the green light to write a very detailed outline of the projected episode. Fashioning the outline was time consuming and exhausting but, without question, the most vital step in writing the episode.

"I made a long, complete road map of every story before writing one word of dialogue. My endings were always totally worked out before I started—as was the middle break, etcetera. This was hard labor, but I was very dependent on a thorough outline, and it made fleshing out with dialogue more relaxing—more attention could be focused on the fun words when you didn't have to worry about writing yourself into a corner.

"Upon completion, the outline was sent to the producer who studied it carefully, then summoned the writer to discuss changes. This was the crucial moment when all snags and problems had to be perceived and resolved before the actual script was written. Sometimes the story was changed completely, sometimes the outline was accepted almost 'as is.'"

Producer Aaron Ruben is listed as story consultant in the closing credits of "The Bed Jacket." "The story-consultant title was part of my duty as the producer of the show," explains Aaron. "I believe it was done to give me credit as a Writers Guild member and, therefore, as a writer. As story consultant, I did just that. I was consulted as to the theme of the play, how it was to be constructed, what the act break would be, the conclusion, etcetera."

"The Bed Jacket" opens with Andy and Opie fishing. Opie says to Andy, "We sure are catching them today, huh, Pa?" Andy replies that his fishing rod, "Eagle-Eye Annie," is "doing herself proud."

At this point, Mayor Stoner walks up. He tells Andy, "They're not biting today—fishing is a waste of time." Andy casts his rod and immediately catches a fish. Andy asks the mayor if he would like to try Eagle-Eye Annie. The mayor takes the rod and catches "a fish that is a fish." The mayor then offers to buy Annie, but Andy refuses.

"The location lake shoots were not difficult to set up," says Aaron. "However, if it was an overcast morning, we would often have to wait for the sun. And, of course, rain cancelled it all.

"Whenever we had an episode dealing with an animal—whether it was a dog, a bird, or a fish—we had an animal trainer who would come in with the species called for. In this episode, the trainer brought a bucket of live fish. Just before the scene was to be shot he hooked a fish on the line. We then went to a close-up of Opie and Andy, showing their reaction as we went to a wider shot, showing the line tightening as the fish was flapping around."

Mayor Stoner was a one-dimensional character and served primarily as a problem-causer. "This did not make the character difficult to write for," says Harvey. "His was, I suppose, a clichéd role. It would be nice to give all characters full dimension, but ofttimes we just needed a single note from them and couldn't indulge in filling them out at the expense of air time more usefully spent filling out roles for major characters. Making the lesser characters more dimensional would be distracting and disproportionate to their story importance."

After the mayor leaves, Andy tells Opie they need "to scoot on home—we got to do some shopping for Aunt Bee's birthday."

Andy and Opie take Aunt Bee with them when they drive into town to do their shopping. Aunt Bee tells Andy she is going to be very upset if he does anything foolish about her birthday. She makes him promise to be "sensible."

Andy parks the squad car in front of Lukens' Style Shop. When Andy and Opie leave to shop for Aunt Bee's present, Aunt Bee stays behind. When she looks in Lukens' front window, she sees a beautiful bed jacket on display.

When Aunt Bee looks at the jacket, the camera is positioned on the sidewalk, looking in through the store window. In contrast, the close-ups of Aunt Bee are filmed with the camera placed inside the store, looking outward. After entering the store, there is no audible dialogue between the salesclerk and Bee, just background music.

"The no-dialogue scene was the writers' idea," says Aaron. "We know exactly what Aunt Bee has gone into the store for, and it would have been somewhat dull to hear what we can guess by the pantomime. It also seemed to be dramatically more interesting. The camera angles used were included in the writers' script directions."

The script directions for the scene were as follows:

Aunt Bee stands transfixed, her eyes wide with appreciation. Slowly, she leans a little to one side to get another angle. Then she leans the other way for a different perspective. She stares again and sighs. Determined, she breaks the spell and averts her gaze and starts walking briskly away, but her steps gradually slow until she stops. She turns and goes back and looks again in the window. She repeats by turn-ing and walking away. As she passes the shop door, her steps falter. She stops, gives up, and goes in. The CAMERA MOVES OVER to the window. In a second, a saleslady picks up the jacket carefully. She holds it up near Aunt Bee and nods approvingly at the size. The saleslady asks another question; Aunt Bee shakes her head. The bed jacket is replaced in the window. The saleslady leaves. CAMERA MOVES IN as Aunt Bee reaches over and fingers the jacket lovingly.

Meanwhile, Andy has decided to buy Aunt Bee two dozen glass preserving jars. Opie selects salt-and-pepper shakers.

After making the purchases, Andy joins Aunt Bee in front of Lukens' Style Shop. Aunt Bee hints that the store has "some awfully nice things" in their front window and remarks that "they're so nicely displayed." Andy looks at the window and sees the mayor inside the shop making a purchase. Andy is reminded that he is supposed to have some papers ready for the mayor, so he rushes off to the courthouse.

The mayor comes out of the shop and explains to Aunt Bee that his wife has been away visiting her sister for a month, so he was purchasing some guest towels for a coming-home present. Knowing that the mayor will be talking with Andy, Aunt Bee points out the bed jacket and remarks that it would make "an ideal gift for almost any occasion."

After the mayor checks Andy's reports, he tells Andy he has another meeting in his office in five minutes. Before leaving, the mayor asks Andy to do him a favor. The mayor wants Andy to exchange the guest towels for the bed jacket.

Aunt Bee and Clara Johnson are standing across the street from Lukens' store, so they see Andy making the exchange. Aunt Bee tells Clara, "Tomorrow I'm going to have a birthday I'll never forget."

The next morning, Andy and Opie give Aunt Bee her presents. Aunt Bee's hands shake as she opens Andy's present. She removes the wrapping paper and discov-ers preserve jars. She thanks Andy and goes upstairs to hide her disappointment.

The doorbell rings. It is Clara Johnson. She couldn't "wait another second to see how Bee liked her birthday present. How'd it look on her? I was with her yes-terday when she saw you take the bed jacket out of Miss Lukens's window."

Andy then realizes his mistake. He goes to Lukens' shop to buy another bed jacket, but there are no more in stock.

Andy goes to the mayor's house, wakes him up, and asks to buy the bed jacket. Andy explains that "Aunt Bee's got her heart set on it." The mayor thinks "perhaps we can work something out. You sell something to me, and I'll sell something to you. You want the bed jacket. I want your fishing rod."

Andy returns home and tells Aunt Bee she needs "to finish opening up her presents." Aunt Bee opens present "number three" and finds the bed jacket.

Aunt Bee calls Clara to tell her about her present. While Aunt Bee is on the telephone, Opie enters the room and tells Andy, "If we're going fishing, Pa, we better hurry." Opie reaches for his fishing rod and notices Eagle-Eye Annie is missing from her usual place.

Andy explains to Opie why he sold Annie. Andy's explanation, which is beautifully written, reads as follows:

> OPIE: You sold it! But, you said you'd never sell it.
> *Aunt Bee can be heard in the background talking excitedly on the phone.*
> ANDY: No, not quite. I said I kept it because it gave me so much enjoyment and that I wouldn't sell it for money. And, I didn't sell it for money. I kind of swapped it for a different kind of enjoyment. So old Eagle-Eye Annie's doing just what she did before. Even right now she's giving me pleasure—real, heartwarming pleasure.

"I don't recollect this scene being difficult to write," says Harvey. "The whole thrust of the story fostered this revelation of feelings involved and discovered."

In the epilogue, Andy and Opie watch Aunt Bee blow out the candles on her birthday cake. After successfully blowing the candles out, Aunt Bee victoriously shakes hands with Opie.

"The handshake was not scripted," says Harvey. "It was either the suggestion of the director, or Frances Bavier came up with it."

The doorbell then rings. It is the mayor, who is desperate. His wife was in Lukens' store and found out that he bought a bed jacket. She thinks he gave it to some other woman while she was away. The mayor wants Andy to call his wife and explain things.

Andy thinks the situation over and says, "Perhaps we can work something out." Andy agrees to straighten things out if the mayor will sell him Annie. The mayor agrees.

"Most episodes were written with the plot all wrapped up at the end of the second act," says Harvey. "Being unnecessary to the story, the epilogue was just an added fun decoration. However, this story is different from most. I feel this epilogue is vital. The difference is that there are actually two stories in the episode. One, 'The Gift for Aunt Bee,' the second, 'The Fishing-Rod Finagle' or 'Getting Even with the Mean Ol' Mayor.' However, I could not work the fishing-rod denouement at the end of the second act, because Aunt Bee's gift story was primary, and it would be anticlimactic at that point to continue and add the fishing-rod climax. So, I had to take a chance, give the gift ending the full treatment—and hope the epilogue would always be included.

"After we completed the 'Bed Jacket' script, Ray admitted he would rather not do any more. He just didn't have the feel for small-town life, and Aunt Bee was a total mystery to him. Ray was a supremely gifted big-joke writer and did well on other sitcom stories, but he felt unable to contribute to Mayberry stories. So I went to Aaron to say we wouldn't be doing more *TAGS* scripts.

"Aaron stunned me. He said, 'Why don't you do them yourself?' I suddenly realized I wanted very much to stay with *TAGS*. I told Ray about Aaron's suggestion, and he said I should do whatever pleased me. There was never a better understanding between two men than there was between us. So I used nights and weekends to do *TAGS* and collaborated with Ray during the day on all other mutual projects. Ray never gave it a second thought. We were together thirty-one years. I miss him."

"Man in a Hurry"

Episode 77

First Broadcast on
January 14, 1963

Written by
**Jim Fritzell and
Everett Greenbaum**

Directed by
Bob Sweeney

Robert Emhardt
Guest Stars as
Malcolm Tucker,
The Man in a Hurry

Note: This episode
was actually written
after episodes 78 and
79, but it was aired
before them.

"This is one of Andy's favorites."—EVERETT GREENBAUM

The storyline for "Man in a Hurry" is a variation of the theme in which an outsider gets "stuck" in Mayberry and is transformed by the experience. This theme was also used in the earlier episodes, "Andy and the Woman Speeder" (Episode 35) and "Bailey's Bad Boy" (Episode 47).

"The storyline for the episode came out of a meeting between Aaron Ruben, Jim Fritzell, and me," says writer Everett Greenbaum. "I don't think the 'stranger stuck in Mayberry' theme was consciously repeated."

"We were never concerned that a theme had been repeated if it had a variation," says producer Aaron Ruben. "Each episode stood on its own, and each new character had his or her own tale of woe."

Jim and Everett's script begins with Malcolm Tucker, a businessman, driving through the outskirts of Mayberry on a Sunday morning. After Tucker experiences car trouble, he parks his car and walks into town to find help. Tucker has urgent business in Charlotte, so he must get the car fixed.

"Tucker was the typical, well-fed, no-nonsense, impatient, successful businessman," says Aaron. "He was probably a workaholic with no time for the civilities and pleasantries that make life more bearable. Robert Emhardt was perfect casting for the role."

Mr. Tucker arrives in Mayberry just as the congregation is leaving the Sunday morning worship service. Andy, Barney, Aunt Bee, and Opie are among the worshippers. Opie meets his friend Johnny Paul in the churchyard and trades a horsehair from the lapel of his suit for a penny that's been run over by a train. According to Johnny Paul, if you put a horse hair in stagnant water it'll turn into a snake.

"When I was a kid, we used to observe long, slender worms in stagnant pools," recalls Everett. "The popular belief was that they were horsehairs come to life. We also believed that a penny flattened on the train track would become magical and bring you luck."

Mr. Tucker asks Andy for help. Andy tells Tucker he will drop the family off and take him to Wally's filling station. Andy warns Mr. Tucker that the station is just barely open because Gomer Pyle's in charge.

Told of Mr. Tucker's car problem, Gomer offers to fill his car with gas. Andy explains that Gomer is not a mechanic and that Wally, the owner of the station, "is the man you're gonna have to see." Andy suggests that Tucker plan to stay in town overnight because "it's nigh impossible to get anything done here on Sunday."

"Jim and I created Gomer Pyle for this script," says Everett. "The character was inspired by an actual experience. I was having car trouble, and the guy at the service station could think of no cure except to put more gas in the tank. I never dreamed at the time that such an incompetent would provide the inspiration for a character that would eventually find his way into the dictionary."

Andy agrees to drive Mr. Tucker over to see Wally. As the two are leaving the filling station, Mr. Tucker refers to Gomer and asks why "they leave a boy like that in charge?" Andy responds, "It's just a part-time job. He's saving up to become a doctor."

"Andy's response to Mr. Tucker's question is typical of Jim Fritzell's humor and was inspired by the Miss America beauty contest," says Everett. "Jim was always amused at the Miss America contestants who were going to be brain surgeons or bring peace to the world and gave a similar aspiration to Gomer."

Wally tells Mr. Tucker that he will repair his car in the morning. Frustrated by the delay, Mr. Tucker returns to the filling station to ask Gomer who else might be able to fix his car. Gomer suggests that his cousin Goober might be able to because he knows about motors. Gomer relates that Goober "hopped up an old V-8 engine and put it on his rowboat. That thing'll do eighty. That's fast on water." Gomer then tells Mr. Tucker that Goober is not available on Sundays because "he's always out on his boat."

"As teenagers, my gang was not into parties or dates," says Everett. "We bought old motorcycles or cars for a few bucks and tried to get them running. We always talked about putting a V-8 engine in a boat. You'd say, 'She'll probably do thirty. That's fast on water!'"

Mr. Tucker is so desperate that he jumps in Wally's truck and drives away while Gomer is helping a customer. Andy catches up with Tucker and suggests that he "come on home with me 'fore you get in any more trouble." Mr. Tucker reluctantly agrees.

Mr. Tucker then tries to use Andy's telephone, but he is unable to place a call because the line is tied up by Maude and Cora Mendlebright. The sisters visit by phone for three or four hours every Sunday afternoon. When Mr. Tucker overhears the sisters talking about "their feet falling to sleep," he wants to know how "a public utility would be tied up with such drivel."

"The script included two memorable off-screen characters, the Mendlebright sisters," says Everett. "We wanted two elderly sisters to talk endlessly about the most boring thing we could think of—why their feet hurt."

That evening, Barney joins the Taylors for supper. He and Andy are still dressed in their Sunday-morning white shirts and ties.

"I was raised in the reformed temple of the Jewish religion," says Everett. "They believe the Sabbath was Sunday, not Saturday. I had to go to Sunday school wearing my Sunday suit. Then for the rest of the day, I was in tie and white shirt, having doffed the jacket. There were a lot of horsehairs on the lapels of that jacket, by the way."

After supper, Andy and Barney retire to the front porch. Andy plays his guitar as he and Barney sing "Church in the Wildwood." Mr. Tucker steps out on the porch and is momentarily transformed by the singing. For the first time that day, he is at peace.

"The front-porch shadows were carefully set up for maximum effect," says Aaron. "The singing scene was lengthy [three minutes, thirty seconds] because we knew it would hold, plus the fact that there were two dramatically arresting things going on—the lovely singing of Andy and Barney and the noticeable effect it was having on Tucker."

"I'm sure Andy chose whatever hymn they sang," says Aaron. "He is a great gospel fan." Everett concurs, "Andy knows every hymn ever written. He picked 'Church in the Wildwood.'"

At this point in the episode, Gomer rushes up and breaks Mr. Tucker's serenity. It turns out that Goober is back, and he's going to fix the car.

As Mr. Tucker paces back and forth across the porch, Barney shares with Andy what he's going to do—"Go home, take a nap, then go over to Thelma Lou's for TV. That's the plan." Barney repeats the "plan" three times. Exasperated by the repetition, Mr. Tucker tells Barney, "For the love of Mike, do it!"

"I may have been responsible for the repetitive 'that's the plan' dialogue by Barney," says Aaron. "To me it is typical of a person who is stalling for time, not ready to give up the comfort of just sitting, and trying to convince oneself that leaving is the thing to do. It may be boring, but it's funny."

After Barney leaves, Mr. Tucker waits with Andy and Aunt Bee on the front porch. Andy peels an apple without breaking the peeling and proudly holds the peeling up for Mr. Tucker to see.

Gomer returns with Mr. Tucker's car and says, "We just blowed out the fuel lines, and she runs as good as new. Goober deemed it a real honor to get under that fine a machine, so there's no charge."

Aunt Bee comes to the screen door and asks Andy if he would give her a hand. She was planning to make ice cream and is disappointed when she learns Mr. Tucker is leaving.

Opie runs up as Mr. Tucker is getting into his car. He too is disappointed that Mr. Tucker is leaving. Opie says, "Oh rats, if you was staying I was going to get to sleep on the ironing board between two chairs—that's adventure sleeping."

"The idea for Opie's adventure sleeping came from Jim," says Everett. "Jim was

Sing Along with "Barn"

I am often asked to do programs about *TAGS* for church groups. Several years ago, I did a program for a United Methodist church in Charlotte. The program was held in the sanctuary, and I showed "Man in a Hurry." The lights were turned off, and during the front-porch scene a wonderful thing happened. As Andy and Barney were singing, I noticed a few voices, confident in the anonymity of the darkness, joining them. The singing was very reverent and sincere. Gradually, as the scene progressed, more and more of the audience joined in—just like Malcolm Tucker—until everyone was singing.—NEAL BROWER

Swedish and half Norwegian. I guess Scandinavians don't give warnings before they come to visit. Jim spent many nights sleeping in bathtubs and, he claimed, on ironing boards."

Aunt Bee prepares chicken legs and cake for Mr. Tucker to eat on the road. Opie gives Mr. Tucker his lucky penny that was run over by a train. After Mr. Tucker starts the car, he hesitates as he contemplates what he is leaving behind.

Mr. Tucker jumps out of the car and says, "Listen to that motor. Sounds like it's falling apart. Don't you think I should wait until morning and let Wally look at it?" Andy agrees.

The epilogue is set late in the evening. Barney has returned, and he, Andy, and Mr. Tucker are seated on the front porch. Andy suggests to Barney that they all "go uptown and get a bottle of pop." Andy asks Mr. Tucker if he'd like to go along. There is no answer. Mr. Tucker is asleep—in his hand is an apple with a long peeling hanging down.

"Andy came up with the apple peeling," says Aaron. "It was very homey and just the sort of bit that Andy was so fond of—what he refers to as the 'humanity.' The closing zoom on the apple had to be the director's choice, since the script direction calls for a dolly in on Tucker asleep.

"I am not at all surprised that 'Man in a Hurry' was voted the favorite episode by TAGSRWC [*The Andy Griffith Show* Rerun Watchers Club—the show's fan club] members. More than any other episode, it symbolizes what the show was all about and why it endures to this day. *The Andy Griffith Show* is every grown-up's Oz. Imagine a town where one could live peacefully, securely, and happily with one's family and neighbors. No drugs, no gangs, no violent crimes. If this was a dream back in the sixties, think what a longed-for dream it is in today's world."

"Man in a Hurry" | Episode 77   255

"The Bank Job"

First Broadcast on
December 24, 1962

Written by
**Jim Fritzell and
Everett Greenbaum**

Directed by
Bob Sweeney

"Bank Hold-Up Foiled Here."—*Mayberry Gazette* headline

The opening scene of Jim and Everett's "Bank Job" script is set in the courthouse. Barney is reading a newspaper and sharing with Andy the details about several robberies that have taken place in nearby Marshal County.

"We made up the names of places as needed," says writer Everett Greenbaum. "Sometimes we used names of towns in Arkansas, my wife Deane's home state, or upstate New York, where I was raised. Our scripted names were sometimes changed by Aaron Ruben when he wanted to match up a town or county with a name used in an earlier show."

Barney grows concerned about the crime wave and tells Andy, "Today it's happening over in Marshal County, tomorrow it's us. This town is a piece of cake. A crook could come in here and walk off with the place. Why? There's no security."

Andy tells Barney he is "awful police this morning." After questioning Barney about his date with Thelma Lou the previous night, Andy learns that the two saw the Glenn Ford movie *G Men*.

"There was no actual movie *G Men* with Glenn Ford," admits Everett. "Barney was the type who could get all worked up after seeing a B-grade police picture and *G Men* sounded like the typical title given that type of film."

Inspired by the movie, Barney decides to do a security check of the Mayberry bank. Barney finds the security guard, Asa Breeney, asleep with a cash drawer and the vault open and Asa's gun in need of repair.

Barney is convinced that the bank is a "cracker box." When Andy enters, Barney reports his finding. Andy tells Barney that he's "getting all steamed up over this." In an attempt to calm him down, Andy suggests that Barney "take a walk over to the Grand and watch them change the marquee. Then, go over to the drugstore for lunch and order the businessman's special."

"In my hometown, the Grenada theater was next door to Woolworth's," says Everett. "When I was a child, my friends and I used to enjoy watching the guy climb a ladder to change the signs on the movie marquee. This was a regular ritual, and afterward we would go into Woolworth's for a soda. That's how I remembered the drugstore's lunch specials. It was a leisurely way to pass an hour and inspired Andy's advice to Barney."

Barney complains to Andy that for four years Asa has been walking around "without any screws in his gun." In response, Andy shares a fond childhood memory he has of putting Asa's gun in his belt. The gun slipped through the belt, tearing the buckle off his knickers.

"Andy's story about Asa's gun was the result of a childhood memory," says Everett. "Out in front of School 54 in Buffalo, a policeman was on duty at the beginning and end of the school day. We used to beg him to show us his gun. The world wasn't so violent then, so seeing the gun was a big thrill."

After leaving the bank, Andy drives Barney to Mrs. Kelsey's house. Mrs. Kelsey had to go to Mt. Pilot, and Andy promised to take her laundry off the line. As Barney takes down the clothes, he is joined by Leon, a sandwich-eating boy dressed as a cowboy. Barney confides in Leon that the bank is in such a "sorry state" that he wishes they'd get held up once to see what an easy mark they are. As Barney looks at a dress he has just taken off the line, he has an idea.

"We had the idea that Barney would disguise himself and go back to the bank to attempt a fake robbery," says Everett. "During the actual writing of the script, we had to go back and put in something which would foreshadow this development. That's why we wrote the scene where Barney takes down Mrs. Kelsey's laundry."

"We knew Ronny Howard had a little brother, Clint, who had made one previous *TAGS* appearance. It was his character's peanut-butter-and-jelly sandwiches that initially got us interested. As we thought about the scene, we decided we needed some way to communicate to the audience Barney's thoughts about disguising himself. Having Barney talk to Leon as the idea formed in his mind was the answer."

Barney enters the bank disguised as the cousin of Mrs. McGruder, the regular cleaning lady. Barney explains to Harriet, the bank teller, that Mrs. McGruder is not coming because she has a "fungus of the knee." Barney begins mopping the floor. He works his way over to the open vault and slips a stack of money into his mop bucket.

Harriet is suspicious, so she watches the old woman carefully and discovers it is Barney Fife. Harriet gets the bank president, Mr. Meldrim. Meldrim tells Harriet to "watch this" as he yells, "Stop, thief!" Startled, Barney grabs the vault door and slams it shut behind him. The vault is locked and "won't open again until eight o'clock tomorrow morning." Mr. Meldrim sends Asa over to the filling station to get an acetylene torch.

Gomer returns with Asa and attempts to cut through the vault. Meanwhile, Barney has escaped by kicking his way through the vault's back wall into the adjoining beauty shop.

"One of my favorite movies of the time was *The Big Deal on Madonna Street*," says Everett. "It was an Italian picture in which an incompetent group of gangsters dig their way into a kitchen, which they could have reached by walking through a doorway. This inspired the idea to have Barney get locked inside the bank vault and kick his way into the beauty shop. By the way, the beauty-shop customer, Mrs. Rodenbach, who calmly witnesses Barney's escape, was named after Jack Rodenbach, a grammar-school friend of mine."

Barney enters the bank through the front door while Gomer is still working on the vault. Barney explains his escape and complains "that there's not a bank in the whole world that has less security than the Mayberry Security Bank." Barney's remark is overheard by a criminal who is waiting in line to pass a bad check.

After Barney and Andy leave, Mr. Meldrim tells Gomer that he'll pay half of the charge for the torch because the sheriff's department ought to pay the rest. A scream is then heard off camera. Gomer remarks, "Oh, I forgot to tell you—that door is still hot."

"Audiences love to 'get' a joke from an offstage sound," says Everett. "They have to think to understand the joke, and the laugh is a tribute to their intelligence."

The criminal decides to forgo passing the bad check. Instead, he rejoins his partner, and the two drive off to formulate a plan to rob the bank.

The next day, one of the criminals holds up Mr. Meldrim as he opens the bank. On her way to work, Harriet sees Mr. Meldrim and the criminal through a window. Thinking it is Barney "at it again," she gets Andy. Meanwhile, Asa has entered the bank. The bank robber tells Asa and Mr. Meldrim to get against the wall.

Andy enters the bank with Harriet. Thinking the robber is Barney, Andy casually takes the robber's gun away. The bank robber then crosses the room, grabs Asa, takes his gun, and points it at Andy. He then orders Andy to throw the gun down. Andy complies. Asa breaks away, and the robber pulls the trigger of Asa's gun. The gun, still without screws, falls apart, and the bank robber is apprehended.

Andy rushes outside to check the getaway car and finds Barney writing the bank robber's partner a ticket for overtime parking.

In the epilogue, Andy is shown holding a newspaper with a front-page story about the foiled bank robbery. Barney is on the telephone complaining to the newspaper editor that his name was misspelled. This is somewhat reminiscent of the epilogue for "Convicts at Large." In both episodes, a newspaper headline is featured.

"A newspaper headline had played a prominent role in the 'convicts' epilogue," admits Everett. "But if we had a story with a beginning, middle, and end, we were so happy that we weren't worried that something similar had been done—especially if it wasn't the week before."

"One-Punch Opie"

"The script copy I have of 'One-Punch Opie' is a first draft that was rewritten subsequently either by myself or others. I do have a recollection of writing material not seen in this draft but represented in the finished film."
—HARVEY BULLOCK

Episode 79

First Broadcast on
December 31, 1962

Written by
Harvey Bullock

Directed by
Bob Sweeney

"When I think of this script, I am reminded of a *TAGS* anecdote," says writer Harvey Bullock. "I once found myself in Aaron Ruben's office with a superb writer, Frank Tarloff. Aaron, Frank, and I were pitching some story ideas, and Aaron finally came up with a story he really liked. I didn't think much of it, but hey, if the producer wanted it, it would be an immediate assignment. But before I could say anything, Frank spoke up, 'That story will never work—never.'

"The meeting broke up soon after. Frank walked out with me, stopped, and asked, 'You really wanted to write that story, didn't you?' I had to admit I truly wanted that assignment. Frank said, 'You'll take that story home, work on it all night and find out what we already know—it won't work. You'd have wasted your time and would have had ulcers by breakfast.'

"The moral of that story is just because a producer is ready to buy doesn't mean the material is right. Take no assignment unless you can sell it to yourself, or else you'll find yourself at three in the morning trying desperately to make a silk purse out of a sow's ear.

"The 'One-Punch' story had a rocky course of many changes, which was to be expected when you juggle 'don't ever fight' and, more importantly, 'never start a fight' with 'there are times when you have to fight for what's right.' Aaron and I labored to get an acceptable approach for Opie to take the challenge and fight the new boy. Using the title 'One-Punch Opie' might have helped by establishing the fight was a one-time-only event. I'm not certain we were able to deliver both messages, but I know we made sizable changes as it went along."

The script introduces a new boy in town, Steve Quincy. The boy is more athletic and muscular in Harvey's script than in the finished film. Steve's father, a college professor who is taking time off to write a book about wildflowers, is featured prominently in the draft's storyline.

The original draft of the script provided the basic storyline for the filmed episode. The episode begins with Opie asking Andy to allow him "to go fishing with the gang." Andy gives his permission.

Opie's friends have met Steve Quincy. Steve asks the guys what they want to do. One of the boys answers, "Well, we were planning on going fishing." Steve says fishing is "stupid" and suggests the group "go swipe some apples."

Opie arrives and introduces himself to Steve. "What did you say your name was?" Steve asks, "Opie or Dopey?" Opie doesn't like this but backs down when Steve asks him what he's going to do about it. Following Steve's lead, the boys decide "to go get some of those apples."

Meanwhile, Andy has learned that "people from out-of-town have rented a house on Grove Street." When Barney asks who they are, Andy tells Barney that anything they want to know they can learn from Aunt Bee. Aunt Bee is in the back room of the courthouse picking up some dirty laundry, so Andy gives Barney a made-up description of the new people. When Aunt Bee overhears Andy's description, she tells him that he's got it all wrong. Aunt Bee then describes the newcomers in detail: "The name is Quincy, and they have a child—a boy named Steve, age nine." Mr. Quincy "is a salesman selling farm implements of some sort, and she was married once before to someone in the service, and just before she came here, she had an operation on her foot."

Aunt Bee leaves the courthouse as Opie enters. Opie asks Andy if there is any way he "can stop being sheriff for maybe just ten or fifteen minutes?" It turns out that Opie feels as long as Andy is sheriff, he can't fight. Opie explains that somebody already started a fight and "I just want to get in on it."

Barney decides he should give Opie a "few pointers on how to handle rowdies." Barney believes bracing yourself for the first punch is extremely important. He demonstrates this by "making himself hard all over." He asks Opie to hit him in the stomach "as hard as you can." Opie gives the punch "all he's got," and Barney's eyes bulge out in pain.

The segments in which Aunt Bee shares her knowledge about the Quincys and Barney points out how to handle bullies were included in Harvey's original draft and required only slight revisions.

While Barney is recovering from Opie's punch, Andy asks, "Who is this boy you want to fight, Ope?" Andy learns it is the new boy in town. Andy tells Opie he can't fight just because the boys went off with Steve Quincy. Andy feels Opie should "go out there and see if you can't find something you like about this new boy."

Opie follows Andy's suggestion and finds Steve with his friends. Steve challenges Opie to hit a streetlight with an apple. Opie throws an apple and misses. Steve belittles Opie by saying, "You call that throwing? Try it again, and this time—more like this." Steve throws an apple and shatters the streetlight. Andy drives up, and the boys take off, leaving Opie behind.

Barney is upset when he learns about the broken streetlight. He feels when you see the "first sign of youngsters going wrong, you got to nip it in the bud."

"There's a strange history to 'Nip it in the bud,'" says Harvey. "It appeared almost simultaneously in several scripts, each writer evidently thinking of it independently. I was sure 'nipping' was first written in 'One-Punch,' but now I'm not so sure.

"I didn't try to include Barney's trademark phrase whenever possible, even though it was perfect for him and would probably fit into almost every story. Overuse would have left the audience sated, and they were entitled to fresh material. I hated to give the phrase up, but I did. I think I used it only one more time in thirty-one scripts."

All the boys come to the courthouse to have a meeting with the sheriff except Steve Quincy, who said "he didn't have to come." Andy gives the boys a warning but adds, "If I catch any of you doing any more of this, I'm going straight to your daddies."

Before the boys leave, Barney offers to add "a word or two" to what Andy said. Barney warns that if you "keep on getting into trouble and breaking the law, it can only lead to one thing—incarceration." Barney steps over to the cells and says, "This is where convicted persons are incarcerated. A man confined to prison is a man who has given up his liberties—no more carefree hours; no more doing what you want, whenever you want; and no more peanut-butter-and-jelly sandwiches." As Barney steps into the cell, he adds, "It definitely is no fun when that iron door clangs shut on you." Barney clangs the door shut to make his point—locking himself inside the cell.

It appears that Barney's speech was added after the first draft of the script. "There is no trace of Barney's 'incarceration' speech in my script," says Harvey.

The next day, Andy decides to take Opie and his friends fishing. While Opie is getting ready, Mr. Foley from the grocery store comes into the courthouse and reports "that them boys came by my store, marked up my window, then grabbed some tomatoes and ran." The new boy started throwing tomatoes at Mr. Foley.

In the filmed version, Andy goes to talk to the boys' daddies. The filmed episode is drastically different from the original script. In the script, Andy meets with Mr. Quincy, Steve's father, who has some interesting insights. He tells Andy that sports have always been an important part of his life. He tells Andy that he won a football scholarship that got him through college. He also boxed professionally to pay his way through graduate school. When he raised his boy, he wanted the boy to be strong. He adds, "I seem to have made a mistake—a bad mistake." Mr. Quincy feels he has taught his son to be strong, but the boy misinterpreted what it means to be tough. Andy suggests that Steve might learn a lesson from another boy.

In the original script, Steve's father follows Andy's suggestion and teaches Opie how to take advantage of his son's one fighting weakness—Steve drops his left and is a sucker for one punch, a right cross.

With his new knowledge, Opie decides to confront Steve. He puts up his fists—ready to fight. At this point, the original script is the same as the filmed version. When Steve dares Opie to "step across this line," Opie does. When Steve places a piece of wood on his shoulder and tells Opie to knock it off, Opie does. Opie continues to accept Steve's dares until Steve finally gives up and "goes home."

"All the dares and rites Steve Quincy goes through with Opie as he builds up to a challenge and fight were as I remembered them from my school days," says Harvey. "The local bully, talking tough, put a piece of wood on his shoulder and challenged, 'All right, knock it off.' If you accepted the challenge, you knocked the piece of wood off, and the fight was on. There were variations of the challenge such as 'step over this line' or 'step inside this circle.' In the script, I worked the gambit in reverse with Quincy, the bully, not wanting to fight and continuing a list of challenges in hopes of wearing down Opie's resolve."

After Steve leaves, the boys celebrate Opie's heroics and decide to go fishing.

In the epilogue, the boys stop by the courthouse. Barney is cleaning a cell. The cell door is open. Leon, the little sandwich-eating cowboy, follows the boys inside and remains behind after their departure. The departing boys do not close the courthouse door, so Barney asks Leon to close the door. Leon walks over to the cell and clangs the door shut, locking Barney inside. Then, Leon offers Barney his sandwich. Andy makes the most of the situation by commenting, "He can't have that, Leon. No more carefree hours; no more peanut-butter-and-jelly sandwiches. Right, Barn?"

"The reference to the incarceration speech in the epilogue was obviously another addition to the script," says Harvey. "In my script, Mr. Quincy has donated some used exercise paraphernalia and is moving it into the courthouse. Barney comes in, ready to help. Quincy casually tosses Barney a weighted medicine ball, and the impact projects Barney backward, right out of the room.

"I imagine these additions were the work of Aaron Ruben. Aaron did a masterful job as producer, and he was the supreme homogenizer who tailored the input from dozens of us neurotic writers. He kept the series from farce, deleted obviously intrusive jokes, made knife-edged character delineations, and (with all respect to Nashville) avoided *Hee Haw*. In many, many respects, *TAGS* is *The Aaron Ruben Show*."

"High Noon in Mayberry"

Episode 80

First Broadcast on
January 21, 1963

Written by
**Jim Fritzell and
Everett Greenbaum**

Directed by
Bob Sweeney

Leo Gordon
Guest Stars as
Luke Comstock

"Yes, this story was inspired by the Gary Cooper picture, *High Noon*."
—EVERETT GREENBAUM

Jim and Everett's "High Noon" script begins with a humorous encounter involving the mailman, Billy Ray. The mailman blows a whistle to announce his presence but will not hand Andy the mail because Andy is not "an authorized receptacle." Responding to the situation, Barney comments, "Put a mail sack on some people, and it goes right to their head."

"Mailmen used to blow a whistle when they delivered the mail," says writer Everett Greenbaum. "I guess Jim and I came up with the mail dialogue because we used to relish writing scenes with Andy and Don together. The mailman provided a nonthreatening adversary the two could respond to in a comical manner. As I start to read the script, I realize that we were so young when we wrote it that we refer to Billy Ray Belfast, the mailman, as 'an old codger in his sixties,' and here I am almost seventy-eight."

Billy Ray delivers a letter to Barney that contains a dividend check from Amalgamated Oxidation and Aluminum Corporation of America. The twenty-seven-cent check represents the earnings from one-eighth of a share of stock.

"The name of the company was made up, but it does sound real," admits Everett. "The ideas for the bit and the small amount of the dividend were inspired by the residual checks that writers and actors often get for a few cents."

In the same delivery, Andy receives a letter from Luke Comstock, an ex-convict who was shot in the leg by Andy during a gas station holdup. Comstock writes that he has been wanting to see Andy for a long time "to set things straight between us." Andy is not sure of Comstock's intentions. When Andy shows the letter to Barney, Barney thinks Comstock intends to come to Mayberry to "gun you down for revenge. Everything about that letter says just one thing—r-e-v-e-n-g." Barney suggests that Andy leave town for a week, but Andy refuses. He prefers to see what Luke wants.

"Barney was a wonderful character to write for," says Everett. "The letter from Comstock gave him the opportunity to cleverly analyze its implications and then reveal his lack of knowledge by misspelling *revenge*. Much of Barney's comedy comes from pretending to have knowledge and then immediately blowing that perception."

Andy takes a telephone call from Mrs. Peterson. After hanging up the phone, Andy tells Barney that "Mrs. Peterson's Fluffy is on the roof again." Barney disgustedly asks, "This is a time for pussycats with a killer on the loose?" Andy answers, "Well, Fluffy's got kittens, and you know how you'd feel seeing your mother on the roof?" As Andy leaves to rescue the cat, Barney offers his gun as protection against Comstock. Andy replies, "I won't need it, Barn. Fluffy and I've been friends for years."

"Mrs. Peterson's call about her cat was inspired by my childhood memory," says Everett. "My cat's name was Fluffy, and she was my pet during the fifteen years I spent growing up."

While Andy is away, Barney deputizes Otis and Gomer to give Andy some protection. Otis is worried "that somebody might get hurt." Gomer wants to know, "Are we going to get guns? Do we get to ride in the patrol car?" When Barney offers the two the opportunity to leave if they feel the "mission" is too dangerous, Otis and Gomer head toward the door. Barney then tells them they are going to be deputies whether they want to be or not.

"This episode is the first time Jim and I wrote Otis Campbell into one of our scripts," says Everett. "He worked well paired up with Gomer in the temporary deputy role and provided a continuous comedic presence throughout the episode. We always liked writing for Otis because we knew that Hal Smith would give it all he had as an actor."

When Barney explains to the deputies that they will be plainclothes operatives, Gomer answers that he has a brown suit "that's pretty plain" and a dark gray one that "might even be better." Barney explains that he doesn't want Andy to know he's being protected, so the deputies should just "happen to be where he is."

That night, Barney plays dominoes with Andy. When he leaves, Otis and Gomer take the second shift and spend the night outside Andy's house.

The next day, Andy tells Barney he doesn't need bodyguards. Andy says he appreciates the protection, but he's not sure Comstock will show up.

At that moment, Luke Comstock steps off the bus. The first shot of Comstock is photographed from the waist down, so his face is not shown.

"Seeing Comstock only from the waist down as he exits the bus was included in our script directions," says Everett. "Bob Sweeney cleverly copied the approach used in the Gary Cooper picture *High Noon* by not showing Comstock's face until near the end of the episode. [The face of the villain in *High Noon* is not revealed until the movie's climactic confrontation.] His decision heightened the audience's feeling of suspense."

That evening, Barney interrupts the Taylors' supper. He tells Andy that Otis saw Comstock carrying a leather shotgun case as he got off the bus. Barney says that he doesn't care what Andy does, but he and the boys are going to "be on our toes." When Andy protests, Barney responds that he won't discuss it further and tells Andy to "tick a lock."

"'Tick a lock' was something my teachers used to say to the class," says Everett. "If teachers wanted kids to be quiet, especially during fire drills or visits to museums, they would make a gesture of locking the lips and say, 'tick a lock.' The phrase seemed right for Barney."

After Barney leaves, the telephone rings. It is Luke Comstock, saying that he wants to come over. After thinking the situation over, Andy suggests that Aunt Bee and Opie go over to Clara's for "a little bit." Before leaving, Opie asks Andy if he is scared. When Andy admits that he is nervous, Opie asks if it is the first time he's ever been nervous. Andy answers that he has been scared many times, to which Opie responds, "Really, Pa? Gosh you sure couldn't tell it." Opie then looks at Andy with an expression of concern before departing.

"Andy and Opie's discussion is somewhat unusual for our writing style," admits Everett. "Jim wrote most of that scene. One of my many failings is a fear of sentiment, or at least of expressing it openly. In all of our scripts, I wrote only one sentimental scene between Andy and Opie."

As the episode continues, Andy takes a gun from the top of the china cabinet. He starts to load the gun but changes his mind and places it back on top of the cabinet.

The suspense of the situation is heightened by camera angles, sound effects, and *TAGS* musical director Earle Hagen's ominous score. As Comstock's footsteps are heard crossing the Taylors' front porch, two piano chords chime the hour of confrontation. As Comstock is shown pressing the doorbell, the musical score diminishes to one bass note that is sustained for twenty seconds. The note fades to silence as Andy puts his hand on the knob and opens the door.

When Comstock enters the house, the audience gets its first look at his face. Comstock then explains that he reviewed his life while he was recuperating from the "shooting scrape we had." During his reflections, he came to the conclusion that he was wasting his life and decided to change his ways. He began to educate himself and, as a result, he is now leading "the good life."

Comstock announces that he has come to Mayberry to bring Andy a shotgun as a "a little gift of appreciation." Comstock pulls the gun out of its case and holds it in front of Andy.

Meanwhile, Barney, Gomer, and Otis are watching through a front-porch window. Surveying the scene, Gomer says, "It's too late. He's got the drop on him." On the other hand, Barney has an idea. He crosses the porch and throws a breaker in the fuse box, causing the house to go dark.

When Andy and Comstock step out on the porch to check the fuse box, Barney, Gomer, and Otis enter from the back.

As Andy restores power, a commotion is heard inside the house. After the power returns, Andy and Comstock enter the house and find Barney, Gomer, and Otis on the floor bound together with rope. Andy explains to Comstock that this is "our Mayberry knot-tying class. It meets here every Tuesday."

"The Loaded Goat"

Episode 81

First Broadcast on
January 28, 1963

Written by
~~Harvey Bullock~~

Directed by
Bob Sweeney

"I suppose ~~Barney~~ could have said ~~'kaboom,'~~ but 'blooey' just ~~happened to come to mind first. It seemed~~ right for the character, ~~and there was~~ no reason to ~~replace~~ it. Besides, *blooey* ~~rolls well on the~~ tongue."
—HARVEY ~~BULLOCK~~

"Producers ~~once had all~~ the ~~power,"~~ says writer ~~Harvey Bullock~~. "They could ~~make~~ you ~~write~~ and rewrite ~~ceaselessly~~ for no ~~extra money~~. The studios encouraged ~~speculative~~ writing, which ~~paid~~ nothing unless a script was produced, and then the ~~actual~~ money the writer was paid was often less than what was originally ~~agreed~~ upon.

"The ~~Writers Guild finally~~ developed ~~clout~~ and ~~set out a rigid~~ new ~~procedure.~~ First, the ~~writer~~ made ~~an appoint~~ment with the ~~producer~~. At this ~~meeting,~~ you ~~orally pitch~~ed new ~~story notions~~. If the ~~producer didn't~~ find any of your ~~notions~~ to his ~~satisfaction, you left to cook~~ up ~~more ideas, and~~ no ~~money~~ changed hands. ~~However,~~ if ~~the producer~~ ~~indicated~~ there was one of ~~your notion~~s he ~~thought~~ might ~~work, he was then officially~~ committed to ~~buy~~ that ~~notion~~ and at that ~~time paid you 'story money,'~~ which ~~was close~~ to a ~~third of the total~~ ~~contracted~~ ~~$3,500.~~ ~~For this~~ ~~story~~ ~~money,~~ you ~~agreed to~~ deliver a full treatment within a prescribed ~~time~~. Next you ~~delivered~~ a ~~full~~ written ~~treatment, which~~ the producer could ~~either discard~~ or ~~elect~~ to ~~go forward~~ with. If he decided to ~~proceed~~ with the story, he ~~would~~ then ~~have to pay~~ the writer the ~~remainder~~ of the ~~contracted~~ fee.

"The ~~scripts~~ I wrote for *TAGS* all varied in one way or ~~another~~. Some had to ~~endure massive~~ changes, and ~~some sailed right through~~. '~~Mimeograph~~' was the sweetest word ever ~~heard when~~ you called Aaron Ruben after ~~dropping~~ off the ~~first draft~~ and asked ~~for~~ an ~~appoint~~ment with him to ~~discuss changes~~—to which ~~dear Aaron respond~~ed, 'It ~~doesn't need~~ any ~~changes~~. We're ~~putting~~ the first ~~draft~~ ~~right into mimeograph.'"

"The ~~Loaded Goat~~" ~~episode begins with Andy~~ and the ~~mayor~~ waiting for Floyd ~~to return to the barbershop after lunch~~. As they ~~await~~ Floyd, ~~dynamite blast~~s at the ~~construction site~~ of a new ~~underpass~~ are ~~heard in the distanc~~e.

Cy "Hudge" Hudgins comes into the barbershop for a haircut. Hudge brings his goat, "Jimmy," into the shop with him. He explains that he has been promising Jimmy that he would "bring him to town."

When he learns Floyd is still at lunch, Hudge decides not to wait. He ties Jimmy to a sidewalk bench while he runs errands. Hudge instructs Jimmy to wait there until he returns.

"Farmer Hudgins talks to Jimmy the goat as if he were a person," says Harvey. "This, of course, is very common with owners of any kind of pet. There is a constant conversation, and it's possible that some little bit of the owner's chatter does really register with the pet. But mainly, it is probably just comforting to the owner. I envisioned Hudge as a loner—someone who would treat his goat as an equal."

As it turns out, Jimmy pays little attention to Hudge's order. He chews on the rope until he is able to free himself. Jimmy then walks to the courthouse, nudges the door open, and enters. Barney is inside practicing on his French harp. Startled by Jimmy, Barney shoos the goat outside.

After Jimmy's departure, Andy enters the courthouse. He hears Barney playing his French harp and compliments his performance. At this point, Hudge comes in to report that Jimmy is missing. Barney responds that Jimmy was in the courthouse a few minutes previously. Andy teases Barney that the goat came to the courthouse because he liked Barney's harp playing. Barney, Andy, and Hudge then go looking for the goat.

Meanwhile, Jimmy has wandered into a shed where dynamite is stored. Jimmy, "who will eat anything he can get his teeth into," stuffs himself with the explosive.

"I'm uncertain about the development of the storyline for 'The Loaded Goat,'" says Harvey. "But when I was fleshing it out, a goat seemed a natural as something unique to stuff with dynamite.

"Animal handlers are very resourceful, so it never occurred to me that they couldn't come up with a goat to do the scenes as written or, if not, substitute other behaviors the goat had mastered to get the same result."

Andy and Barney learn from Opie that a goat was in the shed behind the hardware store, so they go to investigate. It is dark inside the shed when Barney enters, so he lights a cigarette lighter. When he holds the flame up to a wooden box labeled "Dynamite High Explosives—Dangerous," he realizes the shed is full of dynamite.

Shaken by his discovery, Barney exits and leans against the shed to catch his breath. When Andy goes in the shed to investigate, he finds a piece of Jimmy's rope on the floor. He tells Barney, "Jimmy's been here all right, and what's more he had lunch."

Hudge sees Jimmy entering the courthouse and runs after him, intending to teach Jimmy a lesson by giving him "a good kick." Andy and Barney tell Hudge not to kick the goat because "that goat ate himself full of dynamite. One swift kick and blooey."

Hudge responds, "Ain't that the way it always is. First time he comes to town, he figures he's got to do everything."

"The line about Jimmy coming into town for the first time was developed, just like the rest of the dialogue, by writing and rewriting scenes or just endlessly running them through your mind," says Harvey. "It always helped me to close my eyes, project what the set looked like, and mentally move the characters about, while imagining in my mind what they might say."

As the episode continues, Andy sends Barney to find the engineer with the highway crew. While waiting, Andy decides to place Jimmy in one of the cells. He and Hudge spread straw on the cell's floor and pad the wall with a mattress.

Barney returns with the blasting engineer, Mr. Burton, who advises that it is possible for Jimmy to explode. He explains that he has worked with explosives for twenty years and the one thing he has learned is that "there's nothing you can be sure of."

"I included Mr. Burton, an experienced blasting engineer, in the script to strengthen the possibility that Jimmy could indeed blow up," says Harvey. "Burton responds to the question the audience is asking, 'Is it really possible that Jimmy is a loaded goat?' I knew the audience had been patiently waiting for someone to tell them there was, in fact, a chance that Jimmy could go 'blooey.' Although I felt I couldn't quite quote Burton as firmly believing it, he could say truthfully that you can never be sure what will happen with explosives. His guarded opinion was good enough to maintain the possibility."

After Mr. Burton leaves, Andy and Barney decide to get more hay and pillows to pad the cell.

After they leave, a drunken Otis comes into the courthouse. He opens Jimmy's cell and enters. Otis sees the mattress attached to the wall and attempts to get into bed. He falls to the floor and says, "Wow! This is a new one. First time I ever fell off a bed onto a wall."

"The 'pillows and mattress on the wall' scene evolved when I needed an interesting device for the loaded Otis," says Harvey. "Hal fell off the wall perfectly."

"I hurt my back when I tried to jump on the mattress, and it took me about a week to get over it," says Hal Smith. "The cell floor was hard cement. The abundant amount of straw you see me scrambling under near the end of the scene was added later—after I had fallen off the wall. Originally, they had about an inch of straw spread out. I remember getting my feet up, hitting the mattress, falling back onto the cement floor, and hearing my back pop.

"The TAGS crew was wonderful. If you did something that was unusual or funny, they would wait until the scene ended, and then they would applaud, scream, whistle, and holler. My fall got a big response from the crew, and their approval momentarily made my injury seem less painful."

After his fall, Otis spots Jimmy and asks, "Uncle Nat, what are you doing here?" Otis eventually realizes that the goat is not Uncle Nat and wrestles him out of the cell. When this happens, Jimmy becomes angry.

By the time Andy and Barney return, Jimmy is furious. Andy and Barney are forced to seek refuge on top of Andy's desk. Andy then suggests that Barney play his French harp. This calms Jimmy enough to allow Andy and Barney to ease off the desk and slip a rope around Jimmy's neck.

The scene concludes with a shot of Andy and Barney leading Jimmy down a deserted dirt road. The mournful sound of Barney's harp accompanies the exodus.

"For the end of the second act, I wanted to conclude on a plaintive note," says Harvey. "This would be a distinct change of pace after all the explosions and frantic reaction to the loaded goat. I brought Barney's French harp back to add a soulful background and placed the performers in a desolate setting. The versatility of the performers made writing for them a pleasure, and I know they enjoyed playing this different scene. This was my first try at making an atmospheric no-dialogue ending, and I was extremely pleased with the on-screen result."

"Class Reunion"

Episode 82

First Broadcast on
February 4, 1963

Written by
**Jim Fritzell and
Everett Greenbaum**

Directed by
Bob Sweeney

Peggy McCay
Guest Stars as
Sharon Despain

"Barney beloved—The tears on my pillow bespeak the pain that is in my heart."—NOTE TO BARNEY from Ramona Wiley

"The idea for a class-reunion show was stock material in those days [the early 1960s]," says writer Everett Greenbaum. "Jim and I did it on almost every series we wrote for."

The opening scene in the "reunion" episode is set in the Taylor garage. Andy and Barney are storing a trunk of Barney's belongings. To store the trunk, Andy cleans off a shelf positioned against the wall.

Barney tells Andy that his landlady, Mrs. Mendlebright, insisted that he move the trunk from the cellar because she is planning to grow mushrooms there. Barney says that she saw a magazine ad that said "Grow Mushrooms at Home for Fun and Profit."

Barney relates that Mrs. Mendlebright is full of ambition. The previous year she sent away for "a machine that tore car tires into long shreds of rubber. She weaved them into floor mats, and purses, and seat covers, and other attractive items."

This scene offers an excellent example of a "cheat shot"—a camera angle that cheats reality. As Andy and Barney talk about Mrs. Mendlebright, the two are seen from a viewpoint on the wall behind the shelf. The actual wall has been removed, giving the viewer the feeling of being part of the scene.

"During the Depression, there were always ads in magazines from outfits selling equipment to grow mushrooms, grow orchids, or shred old tires to earn money," says Everett. "The tire shredders could also get other machines which wove the shredding into sandals, purses, and other useful objects. Sometimes the ads promised to buy all of these products from the makers. Of course, they never bought anything from the poor sucker who is now broke having gone into hock to buy the machine. By the way, one of those shredding-machine people is my next-door neighbor. He served five years and thinks I don't know about it."

As the scene continues, the bottom of the trunk falls out when Andy and

Barney lift it to the shelf. As they examine the trunk's contents, they find a tennis racket, an "old" rock Barney used to strike kitchen matches on and hold them to his daddy's pipe when he was "a little fellow," and an old high-school yearbook.

One of the strengths of *TAGS* was its believability. Mayberry seemed like a real town populated with real residents. A technique used by the writers to create believability was to give the characters a personal history.

The discovery of the yearbook opens the door to a wonderful glimpse into the pasts of Andy and Barney. The minor details surrounding their pasts were inspired in part by the lives of the episode's two writers.

Andy thumbs through the yearbook (*The Cutlass*) and finds their class pictures. As Andy continues thumbing through the book, Barney stops him at a picture of Ramona Wiley. Beneath her picture is the inscription: "Always, Ramona." Barney explains that Ramona was "crazy about me. It was all one-sided. I wasn't interested." Barney, however, will never forget one note Ramona wrote: "Barney beloved—The tears on my pillow bespeak the pain that is in my heart."

Andy's high-school sweetheart was Sharon DeSpain. He and Sharon were voted "Couple of the Year" two years in a row. Barney wonders where Sharon is now. This gives Andy the inspiration to organize a class reunion.

"*The Cutlass* was the name of the yearbook in Jim Fritzell's high school in San Francisco," says Everett. "I think Ramona Wiley came from a list of names my wife made for me of some of the people she knew in Arkansas. Sharon DeSpain went to school with Jim."

"In grade school I was, as yet, quite unformed—really a fetus in sneakers. But the whole school knew I had a crush on a girl named Jane Clark. Another boy, Fred Remington, thought this was hilarious. I once put a little ring on Jane's desk. Fred Remington got hold of a tiny ivory elephant, wrapped it in a gift box, and put it on my desk with the note 'The tears on my pillow bespeak the pain that is in my heart' and signed it 'Jane.' I think we were all in high school when I finally learned that I had been tricked. Small wonder those words should be burned in my mind years later."

Andy's idea is approved and invitations are sent to the members of Mayberry Union High School's Class of 1945.

Sometime afterward, Mary Lee, a classmate of Andy and Barney, rushes into the courthouse and announces, "We sent out thirty-five invitations, and so far we got twenty acceptances!" When Mary Lee says Sharon DeSpain is not one of the respondents, Andy is clearly disappointed.

In an effort to cheer Andy, Barney says, "Even if she don't come, we're in for the time of our lives. It's going to be great. Yeah, the old orange and blue."

After a moment's reflection, the three former classmates begin singing the Mayberry Union High School song.

"The lyrics for the Mayberry Union High School song were mostly the lyrics from the song of my high school, Bennett High in Buffalo," says Everett. "Orange and blue were Bennett's school colors."

The night of the reunion finally arrives. The auditorium is decorated with balloons and streamers. Carl Benson's Wildcats provide the music.

Andy and Barney struggle to identify names and faces. After the two meet Harry Becktoris, Ramona Wiley's husband, Harry goes to get Ramona. At this point, Barney panics. He doesn't "want to wreck a marriage." Barney decides he will wash the punch glasses. He grabs an armful of glasses, but Ramona walks up before he can make his getaway. Although Ramona remembers Andy, she mistakes Barney for the bartender, which deeply offends Barney.

As the evening progresses, Andy is disappointed that Sharon DeSpain didn't show up. Just then, Mary Lee walks by and says, "Uh, uh, Andy," and points toward the door. Barney turns Andy around so he can see that Sharon has arrived!

The episode takes a dramatic turn after the arrival of Sharon DeSpain. Andy and Sharon dance. Watching the couple, Barney comments, "Look at that. It was one of the great natural romances of all time, and it's still going on."

After dancing, Andy and Sharon step outside and quickly rekindle the passion of their former love. But as the two talk, they quickly remember their differences—Andy likes Mayberry, Sharon prefers the big city. The possibility of reviving "one of the great natural romances of all time" is lost.

In the background, Carl Benson's Wildcats begin playing "Good Night, Sweetheart," and Andy delivers the bittersweet line, "How about a couple of old friends having that last dance?" Sadly, the two former sweethearts realize they will forever be just "old friends."

The episode's epilogue is equally as poignant. Andy and Barney remain after everyone else has left. They sing the school song one last time and reflect upon the departure of their youth. As the epilogue ends the "tears" truly "bespeak the pain that is in their hearts."

"I was very pleased with the 'Class Reunion' show, although I was always nervous when I saw a show we had written for the first time on the screen," says Everett. "In those days, Jim and I never felt we had the time to thoroughly hash a script over in our minds because we were always late with the next one, and the one after that, and the one after that."

But Everett need not have worried. "Class Reunion" strikes a universal chord. The audience identifies with Andy and Barney as they reminisce about high school, sing the school song, experience the pain of lost love, and acknowledge the passing of time. Andy and Barney's feelings are real to the audience because most members of the audience have felt them firsthand through their own personal experiences. The human feelings projected through their characters enable Andy and Barney to come alive in a powerful way.

"Rafe Hollister Sings"

"I don't think Harvey wrote this script with a specific actor in mind. The Rafe Hollister role required someone with a fine voice, and Jack Prince fit the bill perfectly."—AARON RUBEN

"Rafe Hollister Sings" begins with Barney loosening up his voice for tryouts for the Ladies League Musicale. Rafe Hollister, a local farmer, stops by the courthouse to drop off "a mess of fresh-picked string beans." When Rafe hears Barney "practicing up on his singing voice," he asks Andy how long Barney has been "ailing."

"When a writer creates a character, he automatically develops a picture of that person in his mind," says writer Harvey Bullock. "However, when the script is shot, the writer will often see an actor who looks entirely different. At first look, Jack Prince didn't seem to be quite the same as my mental image of Rafe Hollister. Not that Jack wasn't right for the role, it was simply that the casting director, Ruth Birch, had her mental picture too. The differences I perceived were all minor things, and when Jack got into the role, the differences disappeared."

"I think *TAGS* director Bob Sweeney may have suggested me for the Rafe Hollister role," said Jack Prince. "Bob directed a second-season episode I appeared in called 'The County Nurse.' I didn't sing in that episode, but during the week we worked together, he learned that I was a professional singer."

As Barney continues his practice session, he brings Andy's guitar out of the back room and asks Andy to play a "C" chord so he can check his pitch. When Andy asks Barney what he plans to sing at the tryouts, Barney answers, "I thought I'd do something from the light classics—sort of a toss-up between 'Tico Tico' and 'The Umbrella Man.' I might even go all the way with 'The Moon of Manicura.'"

"All the titles Barney mentions as possibilities for his Ladies League Musicale audition were actual songs," says Harvey. "'Tico Tico' was played endlessly by every accordion player big enough to strap on a keyboard. It supposedly showed off their fast finger work. 'The Umbrella Man' is 'a one-a and a two-a' trite little

Episode 83

First Broadcast on February 11, 1963

Written by
Harvey Bullock

Directed by
Charles Irving

Jack Prince
Guest Stars as
Rafe Hollister

ballad. 'The Moon of Manicura' was crooned by Bing Crosby to Dorothy Lamour in one of their 'road' pictures and had a slow and syrupy style. These songs were selected because each one had fame for a second, then a complete fade-out. I always enjoyed using quaint, old remembrances in my scripts."

Andy suggests that Barney warm up with "Believe Me If All These Endearing Young Charms." As Barney begins the song, Rafe interrupts by saying, "Barney, that ain't the way it goes." Andy suggests that Rafe "join along and sing with Barn." Rafe does, and his voice is beautiful.

Andy suggests that Barney take Rafe along to the tryouts. Barney feels doing so would be a mistake because they might ask questions that "only a trained musician would understand." To make his point, Barney asks Rafe, "Suppose they was to ask you, can you sing 'a cappella'? Would you know what to do?" Andy asks Barney, "Supposing they was to ask you, can you sing 'a cappella'? What would you do?" Barney answers with a short rendition of a song.

"Barney constantly thinks he knows something when he really doesn't," says Harvey. "When Andy asks if he can sing a cappella, he assumes a cappella to be the name of a song. Since the song seems to be Latino, he gives it the music of 'La Cucaracha.'"

Despite Barney's apprehensions, Rafe decides to try out. After the tryouts, Barney tells Andy that his audition was "one of those electric moments in the theater."

John Masters, the choral director, enters the courthouse and tells Andy he "has discovered a truly outstanding voice." John then thanks Andy for sending Rafe Hollister.

Barney rationalizes that he was not chosen because he had the "wrong selection. I picked something from the light classics, 'Ciribiribin,' and it was just over their heads."

"'Ciribiribin' was a crazy polka," says Harvey. "It was a song that someone like Barney would enjoy."

When he learns that Rafe Hollister will be the representative at the musicale, Mayor Roy Stoner is upset. Mrs. Jeffries, the head of the Mayberry chapter of the Ladies League, feels Rafe is not "presentable." Since sending Rafe to the tryout was Andy's idea, the two feel Andy should "march himself right out to Rafe's place and tell him he will not be needed."

Andy goes to visit Rafe and realizes that singing at the musicale means "too much" to Rafe and his wife to disappoint them. He says nothing about the mayor and Mrs. Jeffries's opposition.

The mayor is upset when Andy confesses he didn't tell Rafe. The mayor holds Andy "personally responsible for Rafe's appearance."

On the day of the musicale, Rafe shows up dressed in bib overalls, a coat, and a tie. Andy asks Rafe to come back to the courthouse in an hour because he's got some work to do before they go over to the town hall to practice.

When Rafe returns, Andy gives him a suit. Andy explains that he forgot to give Rafe the government clothes when he was "turned loose for moonshine about a year ago."

After Rafe puts on his suit, he and Andy go over to the town hall. When Rafe steps on stage in his new suit, Mrs. Hollister compliments him on his appearance.

"I remember walking on stage in that new suit, and seeing Rafe's wife sitting in the auditorium," said Jack Prince. "I was stunned by the expression of love and pride communicated by Isabel Randolph, the actress cast as the wife. I thought to myself, 'My God, this is an actress.' I never felt her performance was completely captured in the finished film."

Sitting in the back of the hall, Mrs. Hollister overhears Mayor Stoner and Mrs. Jeffries as they agree that Rafe's appearance is all right as long as "he doesn't associate with anyone."

When Andy realizes that Mrs. Hollister has overheard the comment, he takes another tact. On the night of the musicale, Rafe steps on stage dressed in bib overalls. Accompanied by Andy on guitar, Rafe sings beautifully.

"The song Harvey originally scripted for Rafe's musicale performance was 'I'm Coming Back,'" said Jack. "Director Charles Irving, Aaron Ruben, and I kicked around a number of songs. 'Lonesome Road' and 'Ridin' That New River Train' were ultimately chosen because they fit the character, and the copyright on both had expired.

"All my vocals in the episode were prerecorded, and I lip-synced the filmed performances. I remember cringing the first time I saw my performance in the finished film, because I thought my lip movements didn't correspond correctly with the vocals heard on the soundtrack."

"Aaron Ruben would stopwatch a script reading and trim or add as needed," says Harvey. "When a song was included in a script, it was timed as well. Most of my *TAGS* scripts were thirty-six pages, but this script, which included several musical performances, had only thirty pages.

"I was concerned about holding the audience's attention throughout the musicale performance, so I included directions in the script that numerous camera shots of the audience be shown with Rafe's singing over them. This enabled Rafe to get in more of the song without being the focus of the picture endlessly."

At the end of the musicale, Rafe is asked to perform an encore. After the encore, Mrs. Dennis, the president of the Ladies League, says to the mayor and Mrs. Jefferies, "Oh, he's really wonderful, isn't he? And what a perfectly marvelous idea having him appear dressed that way. It made his selection so much more authentic."

In the epilogue, Andy and Opie enter the courthouse and find Barney getting ready for next year's tryouts. Barney tells Andy that this time he's "got the perfect selection—'The Crawdad Song.'" Barney hands Andy his guitar and asks for accompaniment.

Harvey's script directions were as follows:

Andy reluctantly takes guitar and accompanies Barney on "Crawdad Song." In the midst of the song, Opie enters, listens a moment, and frowns. They stop. Opie sings last part of song. Barney watches, chagrined. Barney gives Andy a smoldering look and storms out. Andy amused, Opie puzzled as we: FADE OUT.

The epilogue was refined during production and extended a few seconds longer. By repeating the action of the scene in which Rafe is "discovered" by Andy, the audience understands that Barney feels Andy may get the idea to suggest Opie try out at next year's auditions. After Barney storms out, Andy reprises the "Crawdad Song" with a lively guitar accompaniment. Opie joins in, and the joy of song, as well as the harmony of Andy and Opie's relationship, is captured on screen.

"Opie and the Spoiled Kid"

> "It was always more difficult to write for child actors. Their characters don't have as much history, lore, or aspirations to draw on."
> —EVERETT GREENBAUM

"Opie and the Spoiled Kid" begins with Andy and Barney walking down Main Street. When they see Mrs. Tarbocks, Barney notes that she is "getting gray for a woman her age." Andy agrees and tells Barney that she's been having trouble with her husband. Barney wants to know what kind of trouble, so Andy explains that her husband wants them to move out of town because people in town gossip too much.

Their discussion is interrupted by a boy riding his bike on the sidewalk. The boy nearly runs over a woman coming out of Foley's Grocery. As Andy and Barney help the woman pick up her scattered groceries, they question her about the boy's identity. The woman has no idea what the boy looked like. She says, "It was just swoosh, and he was gone." Barney tells the woman that a trained professional, like himself, "has a photographic mind." The boy on the bike rides down the sidewalk a second time, nearly running over Barney. Despite the close call, Barney has no idea what the boy looked like. He comments, "It was just swoosh, and he was gone."

As it turns out, the boy on the bike is Arnold Winkler. After his ride through town, Arnold pedals over to visit Opie. Opie is impressed with Arnold's new bike, which is an Intercontinental Flyer.

"Jim Fritzell and I once took two years off from one another to work on separate projects," says writer Everett Greenbaum. "During that time, I moved to California to work on *The George Goble Show* with another writer named Harry Winkler. Harry was a wonderful friend who, unfortunately, died young. Arnold was a name I always thought was kind of ugly. So, when I was thinking of a name for the spoiled kid, the ugly first name and the last name of a former good friend came to mind."

Episode 84

First Broadcast on February 18, 1963

Written by
Jim Fritzell and Everett Greenbaum

Directed by
Bob Sweeney

"We wrote that Arnold Winkler should be 'nicely dressed.' The wardrobe department followed our description perfectly. Arnold's button-up shirt, sweater, slacks, and dress shoes gave him the look of worldliness and sophistication we wanted.

"The name we gave Arnold's new bicycle, 'Intercontinental Flyer,' was made up. We thought the name sounded expensive and appropriate for the bike a spoiled kid would have."

Arnold offers to take Opie for a ride. Opie can't because he has to clean the garage or he won't get his "quarter this week." Arnold can't believe Opie works for his allowance. According to Arnold, "allowance is money a kid is allowed to have—and without working for it. It's for being a kid."

Opie decides to talk this over with Andy.

Back at the courthouse, Barney is sorting through a group of wanted posters. The names on the posters are Henry "Shopping Bag" Leonette, Max "the Tongue" Rassmussen, and Benjamin Schuster. Holding the posters, Barney notes that he has "$8,500 American silver cartwheels right in my hands. There's only one small hitch—we don't know where they are."

"We always knew we could get fun out of something like a bunch of wanted posters," says Everett. "So, we used them here to give the scene a humorous beginning. Barney refers to the total reward money on the posters as '$8,500 American silver cartwheels.' I remembered that silver dollars were sometimes called cartwheels, and the phrase, which seemed like something Barney would say, went into the script."

Opie enters and tells Andy he wants to have a talk. Opie then asks Andy if there are rules about how a pa should treat his son. Barney thinks Opie's question "takes the cake." When Andy tells Barney that he and Opie "usually keep these little talks to ourselves," Barney gets the message and steps into the back room.

After Barney leaves, Opie asks Andy whether Barney's feelings are hurt. Barney steps back into the room when he hears Opie say he is "kind of sensitive." Barney explains that he is "spirited, not sensitive."

"I think Barney's feelings had been hurt in some of the previous scripts we had written, but this was the first time his sensitivity was discussed," says Everett.

Andy tells Opie there are no rules for "pas and sons." Each parent raises his child the way he thinks is best. Andy explains that he thinks it's best for Opie to get a quarter and work to get it because "when you give something and get something in return like a quarter, that's the greatest feeling in the world." Opie admits that after working he feels "good and tired." Andy continues to explain that as you get bigger you will do more work for more return and that will make the good feeling even bigger. Opie capsules this philosophy by saying, "The bigger you get, the tireder you get—that makes me kinda sad."

"Andy and Opie's conversation appears in the finished film pretty much like we wrote it," says Everett. "However, Opie's 'The bigger you get, the tireder you get—that makes me kinda sad,' was not in our script. Most likely, it was an addition written by Aaron Ruben."

After Opie leaves, Barney emerges from the back room and tells Andy, "This time you really muffed it." Barney has been reading about child-rearing in the magazine section of the Sunday paper. According to the magazine, there is a definite trend toward stronger discipline. Andy asks Barney if his father ever hit him. Barney answers, "Well, he couldn't. I was a lot bigger than he was." Andy replies, "I thought as a child you were sickly." Barney responds, "Well, he was sicklier."

Barney then begins to tell Andy "the way I'd talk to a child of mine," but Andy interrupts. He doesn't want to hear any "imaginary child" theories.

"Barney picked up a lot of information and misinformation, about raising children and other subjects, from the magazine section of the Sunday paper, but in his mind, it was an authoritative source," says Everett. "And the bit about Barney's father never physically disciplining him because Barney was bigger, was a deliberate attempt on our part to get a laugh. We felt we needed one on that page of the script.

"Barney's advice to Andy about raising Opie was inspired by Jim Fritzell's annoying habit of telling Bob Sweeney and me how we should raise our daughters. Jim had no children of his own. In fact, he never even got married, but he was always full of parental advice."

Opie shares with Arnold the result of his man-to-man talk with Andy. After listening to Opie, Arnold explains that "talking is a waste of time. You have to take action—temper tantrums, holding your breath, kicking a table leg, rolling around on the floor, pretending you can't stop crying." Opie is not sure about Arnold's advice. To demonstrate the effectiveness of his technique, Arnold starts crying. When Opie rushes to comfort him, Arnold looks up from his fake crying and says, "It works every time."

The boys' two conversations both take place in front of the Taylors' garage. In the first conversation, Opie stands in front of a barrel. During this conversation, Opie sits on the side of the open barrel.

"Jim and I didn't put it in our script that Opie was to sit on a barrel during his second conversation with Arnold," says Everett. "This type of action, though minor and probably unnoticed by the majority of the audience, was the input of Bob Sweeney and was done in an effort to prevent the two conversation scenes from looking exactly alike."

Later in the day, Barney warns Arnold about riding on the sidewalk. Arnold promises not to do it again. He rides across the street and immediately gets back on the sidewalk. Andy then stops Arnold and impounds his bike.

Barney takes the bike away, and Andy proceeds to the courthouse. Before entering, Andy stops and watches a man who is sitting on the sidewalk bench while he whittles a stick. Andy asks, "How's it coming?" After carefully examining the stick, Andy says, "When you're finished with it, tell me what it is, and I'll give you fifty cents for it."

"The whittler and his nondescript handiwork were our ideas," says Everett. "His presence on the courthouse bench seemed like the sort of thing you'd see in a town where people had a lot of spare time."

Acting on Arnold's advice, Opie stops by the courthouse and tells Andy that he doesn't want to work for his allowance anymore. Andy says, "Fine, you don't have to—no work, no allowance." At this point, Opie yells, "That's not fair!" and throws a temper tantrum. He holds his breath, cries, and lies on the floor kicking uncontrollably. Andy casually reminds Opie not to "get your clothes all dirty."

"Andy's casual reaction to Opie's temper tantrum is the result of his knowing that the tantrum is fake," explains Everett. "Andy suspects that Opie picked it up from Arnold, so he more or less ignores it."

Arnold and his father enter the courthouse. Mr. Winkler demands that Andy return Arnold's bike. Andy informs Mr. Winkler that if he is not going to take responsibility for his son's actions, perhaps he should be locked up. Upon hearing this, Arnold encourages Andy to put his dad in jail. He then pounds Andy's desk and yells, "I want my bike!" Mr. Winkler now understands his son's priorities. He asks Andy for the bike, saying he plans to sell it.

"The scene with Arnold and his father was shot exactly as it was scripted," says Everett. "Jim and I included Arnold's yelling, crying, and desk-pounding in our script directions."

In the epilogue, Opie wonders if Andy "needs someone to clean the garage and do odd jobs." Opie apologizes to Andy for "the way I acted." Andy acknowledges the effort it took for Opie to apologize and agrees to raise his allowance to twenty-seven cents a week.

The epilogue's master shot is photographed where the wall behind Andy's desk would usually be. The scene begins with the camera positioned behind the wall's corner file cabinet. Andy, who is filing papers, turns as Opie enters. The camera pans left with Andy as he moves to his desk chair. The camera is thus perfectly positioned to photograph the special encounter between an apologetic son and his forgiving father.

"The Great Filling Station Robbery"

Episode 85

First Broadcast on
February 25, 1963

Written by
Harvey Bullock

Directed by
Bob Sweeney

"I respected the audience's knowledge of mythology and used the Trojan horse idea without any hesitation."—HARVEY BULLOCK

"The Great Filling Station Robbery" begins in the courthouse where Barney is setting up an intercom system. As Andy and Opie enter, Barney is busy wiring a speaker in one of the cells.

Barney tells how he plans to use the intercom to communicate with the prisoners. Andy interrupts Barney to ask him to take the squad car to get a new carburetor put on. Although Barney agrees to do that task, he still continues to talk about the intercom. He explains that the intercom works both ways, so he will be able to hear what the prisoners are saying. Barney calls the intercom his own "little spy in the sky." To demonstrate its effectiveness, Barney enters the cell and imitates a prisoner by saying, "All right Lefty, you and me's busting out tonight." Andy can hear Barney plainly, even though the intercom is turned off. Barney then tells Andy to turn the intercom on so he can show him how it will even pick up whispers. Barney gets Opie to sit on the cell cot and whisper, "All right Lefty . . . " Andy can't hear Opie because he is too far from the speaker. Barney moves Opie closer two times, but the sound "is still no good." Barney finally holds Opie up to the speaker, and the sound is perfect.

"Writing the opening scene with Opie doing his 'All right Lefty, you and me's busting out of here tonight' line four times was taking a chance we might make that scene overlong," says writer Harvey Bullock. "But knowing how skillfully Opie and Barney interplayed, I took the chance, hoping the repetition would build the joke. This scene was also important because it helped set up the bit with the surveillance camera used later in the episode."

Since Barney is busy with the intercom, Andy decides to get the carburetor put on himself. Before leaving he signs off, "This is Mercury Control, over, a-OK, and out."

"I always regarded the show as set in the thirties, even though it played in the sixties," says Harvey. "Barney's 'spy in the sky' line had been used in military lingo for decades, but it is also identifiable with NASA rocket missions. And Andy's 'mercury control' reference is definitely a catchword of the early space program. I don't think the audience was too concerned about precisely nailing down the show's era. The main thing in their minds was whether the show's characters delivered the stories.

Gomer greets Andy when he arrives at the filling station. He tells Andy that Wally is away for the week, and he is the one who will need to attach the carburetor. Gomer informs Andy that he doesn't do engine work, "just gas and oil, water and air."

"'The Filling Station' script was the first time I had written for Gomer Pyle," says Harvey. "I enjoyed writing for Gomer. The fact that the character was created by Everett Greenbaum and Jim Fritzell didn't disturb me in the least. A writer constantly had to write for characters created by other writers, and we felt great satisfaction that we could write for any character the story called for.

"One reason I enjoyed working with Jim Nabors is that he's really such a nice guy. Jim had previously been a film-cutter at NBC and performed his big opera tunes nightly at The Horn tavern in Santa Monica. Someone saw him and told Andy. Andy saw Jim's show, called his manager, Richard Linke, and Linke grabbed Jim up. Jim was so grateful and polite, we kept asking him if he had turned into a 'scummy' star yet, and he'd just get more bashful.

"He never did become a monster—just the opposite. Jim was and is a delightful guy who somehow survived the showbiz pressure cooker. And he's very bright. Jim was an overnight sensation, a true star, yet he still called me 'sir' until I threatened to wreak extreme bodily harm upon him."

As the episode continues, the Hanson brothers, who have been parking their car inside the filling station during Wally's absence, stop by while Andy is talking to Gomer. They promise to "see" Gomer later that day.

Before Andy leaves, a local businessman named Mr. Carter brings Jimmy Morgan, a teenager he has hired to make deliveries, to the station. Carter accuses Jimmy of stealing the battery out of his truck. Jimmy claims he just borrowed the battery to connect it to a starter motor he built. Because the battery was greasy, Jimmy dropped it and broke it.

"My only script description of the Jimmy Morgan character was almost no description at all," says Harvey. "Here it is. 'Teenager Jimmy Morgan.' The role didn't call for any special wardrobe or physical characteristics, so that was all the description needed."

While Andy and Carter are talking, Jimmy inspects the carburetor Andy wants installed. Jimmy tells Gomer that the carburetor will really boost the power. He tells Andy to "put on dual points, advance the timing, switch the manifold— that would really hop her up."

Jimmy's obvious knowledge of cars gives Andy an idea. He asks Jimmy to install the carburetor. Then, Jimmy can buy Mr. Carter a new battery with the money he will earn. Gomer agrees to let Jimmy work at the station while Wally is away.

"I know nothing about cars, so I asked the local garageman a few valid terms to help me with Jimmy's mechanical dialogue," says Harvey. "He found out I was with *TAGS*, so I was stuck there while he expounded enthusiastically about the *TAGS* episodes he had seen and the great ideas he had for others.

"I take it as a compliment that *TAGS* was so deceptively simple and its characters so real and engaging that many fans felt confident that they could come up with a good episode or two themselves.

"It was not at all uncommon to encounter fans who were eager to make suggestions. It even happened to me once in the barbershop. Sal, the barber, knew I wrote for the show and greeted me with 'I'm glad you came in today. I got a great idea for an Andy Griffin [sic] episode. It just came to me out of nowhere, and boy, is it a beauty.' Then Sal turned to the other barber, 'Charley, is it a great story, or isn't it?' Charley says, 'Yeah.' Then Sal continues, 'What a real winner—a knockout! Boy, oh, boy, you will love it. Got everything? You ready, you want to hear it?'

"How could I say no? I nodded. Sal takes a stance, 'You ready? Now get this: THE KID WON'T EAT HIS SUPPER.' That was it in its entirety! Naturally, I told him it had promise, and I'd see what I could do with it. He asked again if I got the idea and repeated it all the way through the haircut."

The next morning, Barney telephones Juanita, a waitress at the Bluebird Diner. Barney calls during the breakfast shift and greets Juanita, "Good morning, cocka-doodle-doo." Andy walks in and overhears the conversation.

"I had Barney sweet-talk Juanita twice in this episode," says Harvey. "Barney, of course, considers himself a knowing Romeo. His 'cocka-doodle-doo' line was a little flourish to remind Juanita how cute and clever a rascal he was.

"I enjoyed writing for Barney immensely. It was intriguing to start writing a Barney scene and to become aware of how many different words and actions could be given him, and Don Knotts would knock your socks off with any of them. It was also fun to come up with a word or moral for Barney to explain."

After Barney hangs up, Gomer rushes into the courthouse to report that the box with all of Wally's brand-new tools is missing. He tells Andy that Jimmy worked late and was the one who locked up.

When Andy and Barney go to the station to investigate, they find that none of the locks have been tampered with. While they are looking around, one of the Hanson brothers stops by to pick up their car.

Because Andy believes that the robber is taking advantage of the fact that Wally is out of town, he is sure the culprit will be back, so he plans an all-night stake-out.

Barney feels there is something additional they can do, so he sets up a surveillance camera in the filling station. He rigs the front door so that anyone who opens it will trigger the camera and get his picture "took." To test the camera, Barney opens the door and waves to the camera. Gomer is amazed by Barney's idea and remarks, "Shazzam, Captain Marvel wouldn't think of that, Barney."

"Gomer's 'Shazzam' appears in this script, but I don't think I originated its use," says Harvey. "I was pleased to see how perfectly it fit the character in the 'surveillance camera' scene. Whoever did introduce the phrase helped all the writers who followed afterwards."

That night, Barney and Gomer stake out the station. Inside the station, one of the Hanson brothers quietly emerges from the trunk of their car. As Barney and Gomer stand in front of the station, a hand can be seen through the window in the background lifting merchandise off the counter.

The next morning, Gomer discovers the missing merchandise. Andy realizes that whoever stole the merchandise "didn't bust in, they got in quiet-like with a key." All the evidence points toward Jimmy, so Andy goes to pick him up.

After Andy leaves, Barney learns from Gomer that Jimmy's key fits the front door. Barney remembers the surveillance camera and says excitedly, "Gomer, we got ourselves a picture!" Barney removes the film from the camera, and Gomer takes it to the drugstore to be developed.

A short time later, Andy brings Jimmy in for questioning. Jimmy says he knows nothing about the missing merchandise. Barney tells Jimmy that he'd better "come clean" because he was under "high-speed surveillance." Gomer arrives soon afterward with the developed photo. Barney pulls the picture out of its envelope only to discover himself waving hello to the camera!

Jimmy escapes while Andy, Barney, and Gomer look at the picture. Andy goes after him, leaving Barney and Gomer behind. Gomer admires Barney's picture and suggests he have "a whole bunch of wallet sizes printed up."

"The inspiration for the wallet-sized prints line goes back to when my high-school class picture was being taken and some wise guy called out he'd like a few wallet-sized prints," say Harvey. "The expression tickled us all and stayed in my memory."

Andy is unable to find Jimmy. That night, he and Barney receive a call from Gomer saying that someone is moving around inside the filling station.

Andy and Barney arrive at the station and find Jimmy hot-wiring the cash register. Jimmy has attached one end of a wire to the register and the other to a group of batteries that will send a charge through anyone who touches the register. Andy approaches Jimmy to make an arrest. At that moment, a painful scream comes from inside the station. Andy and Barney rush in to find Prothro Hanson attempting to rob the cash register. He is being shocked by Jimmy's trap.

Andy realizes Prothro has been hiding in the trunk and refers to the situation as "a regular Trojan horse."

The crime's solution comes almost too quickly to be credible.

"If you reexamine the story, you will find the solution to the crime didn't really come so easily and quickly as to be incredible," says Harvey. "Prothro Hanson (named after the football coach Tommy Prothro, by the way) is shown coming out of the car trunk way before the second act's conclusion. The audience now knows the perpetrator, but Andy and Barney's gradual solution of the crime continues right to the end of the second act. This keeps the audience's attention, since they are now in the know and able to see both the miscues and the developing solution. The possible guilt of Jimmy is thus a working subplot."

In the epilogue, Barney telephones Juanita. Barney tells her that he has finished the poem he has been working on. He asks if she wants to hear it. Barney then reads the poem. As Barney is reading, Andy quietly walks up behind him and begins to read the poem along with Barney. Upon hearing Andy's voice, Barney slams the receiver down and musses up his hair in frustration.

"The love poem was further evidence to Barney of his high-powered 'animal magnetism,'" says Harvey. "He was positive Juanita would be swept off her feet by all the special attention (and more than likely she was.)"

"The Darlings Are Coming"

Episode 88

First Broadcast on
March 18, 1963

Written by
**Jim Fritzell and
Everett Greenbaum**

Directed by
Bob Sweeney

**Denver Pyle,
Maggie Peterson,
and The Dillards
(Doug Dillard,
Rodney Dillard,
Mitch Jayne, and
Dean Webb)**
Guest Star as
The Darlings

"Back in our hometown of Salem, Missouri, all the activities stopped on the night 'The Darlings Are Coming' was shown, and the local National Guard meeting was called off so everyone could watch."—MITCH JAYNE

"Andy knew about the Dillards and wanted to use them. We didn't know if they could act and thought it would be funny if they were silent. As it turned out, they were wonderful!"—EVERETT GREENBAUM

"To the best of my knowledge, the Darling family was one of the many brain-children of Jim Fritzell and Everett Greenbaum and was a concept before they furnished it with characters," says Mitch Jayne. "The Dillard audition for Andy occurred when Andy's manager, Dick Linke, knowing that *TAGS* producer Aaron Ruben and Andy liked the Darling concept, read about Elektra records signing a bluegrass group from Missouri. Dick then called Elektra, who referred him to our manager, Norman Malkin.

"Norman took us over to the Desilu lot, and we carried our instruments onto the first soundstage any of us had ever seen. We were introduced to Andy, Aaron Ruben, Dick Linke, and Bob Sweeney. Andy asked us to do a couple of songs—just whatever suited us. We played several things, and I was comfortable enough to talk about where we were from, just like I did in our stage act. Andy walked off a way to listen and look, exchanging comments with Bob Sweeney and Aaron Ruben.

"Andy always liked to weave music into the show and had previously used the Golden State Boys (a California-based bluegrass group) in two shows. For one reason or another, he and Bob Sweeney had definite types in mind for the Darling boys. It wasn't just musical ability. They wanted to go in a different direction.

"On that first meeting, Andy used us to perpetrate what would be our first of a long line of running jokes on Bob Sweeney who, like Barney in the 'choir' episode, 'couldn't sing a lick.' Bob asked us if we knew 'Big Rock Candy Mountain' and said it was his favorite song. Andy said, 'Of course these boys know that, Bob, and they'll probably do it if you'll sing.' I, for one, didn't know the song and was petrified. (I had been playing bass for only four months and only knew our material.) Andy borrowed Rodney's guitar, hit a cord, and insisted that Bob sing the first verse, and then we realized the joke. It was the first and most comforting thing we could have found out about Andy—that his good nature and sense of humor was never far from his professional side."

Jim and Everett developed the "Darling" concept into a well-written comedy script. Their script begins with the Darlings driving into Mayberry. Briscoe Darling stops their truck in front of the "David Mendlebright Memorial" water trough because the truck's radiator is boiling over.

The script instructions introduced the Darlings as follows:

A vintage flatbed truck is coming down the street. The radiator is boiling, and the motor is missing a little. On the flatbed are the Darlings: long, gangly, mountain-type boys. Driving the truck is the father of the clan, Briscoe Darling. Seated alongside Briscoe is the daughter, Charlene Darling. The truck stops at a watering trough alongside the curb.

"A canister of dry ice and water hidden under the hood caused the Darling truck radiator to boil," recalls Mitch. "The truck's standard Model A transmission, used in the episode, was later replaced by an automatic. That wild ride into town, with its stops and starts, damn near flung us out the back of the truck and came close to wrecking our instruments."

Briscoe uses his hat to fill the radiator with water from the trough. Charlene gets out of the truck and joins Briscoe. As Andy walks up, Charlene looks at Andy with approval and calls him "a pretty man."

Briscoe orders Charlene to get back in the truck and tells Andy that "she's promised—Private First-Class Dudley A. Wash, USA Army, honorably discharged."

The Darlings are in town to meet Dud, a boy from the mountains who is coming in on the next day's bus. It seems that Dud and Charlene have been betrothed since Charlene was five. Briscoe warns Andy not to "go making any fancies for her."

Andy informs Briscoe that he is breaking two city ordinances: parking in front of the trough, which is for horses only, and dipping his hat into the water. Andy gives Briscoe a warning instead of arresting him. Before driving away, Briscoe asks where he and his family "might bed down." Andy suggests the Mayberry Hotel.

Briscoe enters the hotel lobby alone and requests "a room as far back as I can get." The rest of the family sneaks into the room soon after he settles in.

The Darlings decide to play some music while "that clerking fellow" is gone to supper. When John Masters, the hotel clerk, returns, he hears the Darlings "raising the roof in there." He summons Andy. Andy tells John he knows who they are and remarks that he had "warned them earlier today on a 907—Dipping your hat in a horse trough."

"I believe Don Knotts's contract allowed him a week off now and then," says writer Everett Greenbaum. "The city-ordinance number was more characteristic of Barney than Andy, but we needed a joke there. Due to Don's absence, we gave it to Andy."

When Andy knocks on Briscoe's door, the music stops. When Briscoe opens the door, he is the only person in the room. Andy spots a rope tied to the room's radiator and leaves.

Andy then steps outside the hotel and stands beneath the window of Briscoe's room. The music resumes, so Masters knocks on the door again. The four Darling boys and Charlene shimmy down the rope into Andy's arms.

Later that evening, as Andy and Aunt Bee relax on the front porch, Aunt Bee asks Andy if he liked the white beans he had for supper. Andy grunts his approval. Aunt Bee comments that he didn't say anything about them at dinner. Andy responds, "Well, I ate four bowls. If that ain't a tribute to white beans, I don't know what is."

As Andy and Aunt Bee sit on the porch, the Darlings can be heard playing their instruments in the distance. Andy goes to see what "they're up to."

The front-porch scene is photographed in one long, sustained sequence (one minute and fifteen seconds in length). The sustained shot, which eliminates the editing together of numerous camera angles, gives the scene a relaxing visual presentation and assists in the on-screen creation of a tranquil Mayberry night.

The scene also shows an excellent way to present humor by using everyday conversation. Andy and Aunt Bee's discussion of "white beans" is comically realistic. The humor results from what they say to each other, rather than from a joke followed by a punch line.

When Andy finds the Darlings inside an abandoned store, he informs them they are in violation of "317—Occupancy of private property without permission of the owner." Andy offers to put the Darlings up for the night in the courthouse cells.

After a supper of Aunt Bee's white beans, the Darlings and Andy play two songs, "Tearin' Up Your Old Clothes for Rags" and "Salty Dog."

"'Salty Dog' is a real song," says Everett. "The rest of the stuff, the mountain dialogue and the song titles, we made up. Briscoe's 'More power to you' was a saying of my father-in-law, Tom Ward, who was from Arkansas. Jim suggested the first song title, 'Tearin' Up Your Old Clothes for Rags,' and that got us into the style or rhythm for them."

"Everett and Jim loved those ridiculous gag-song names, and, of course, we did too," says Mitch. "Briscoe delivered the outrageous titles straight-faced, and the excuse for us to play something from our own material was that the gag song made Charlene cry.

"We were always allowed to play our own stuff as long as it fit. I remember Andy was delighted that we had written most of our own material, and he talked to us about that. He wanted original material and a new look at this very old music. Incidentally, knowing that we would make royalty money on our own songs, Andy encouraged us to come up with our own music. That piece of thoughtfulness has paid wonderful dividends over the years, and all of us are grateful. Whereas the actor's screen residuals ran out, in most cases long ago, the Dillards are paid as musicians each time a Darling show is rerun.

"All the musical numbers done on the show were prerecorded at Glen-Glenn Sound studios and synched to the live performance. All of the music on the series was done that way. Andy wanted the music to be studio quality, which made all of us appreciate the respect he had for our work."

Prominently featured in all of the episode's musical performances is the sound of Briscoe's jugging. The jug sound, however, somewhat dominated the presentation of the music.

"After the first show, Rodney objected to the jug," remembers Mitch. "He was nice about it but very alarmed at the way the overdone sound took away from the music. Andy agreed that, though the jug was a necessary prop for Denver, thereafter it would be only that. The jug notes had been done on a separate track by a studio jug player, if you can believe such a thing. In the following shows, the jug sound was left up to the viewer's imagination."

The next day, the Darlings walk to the bus stop to meet Dud. Five minutes before the bus's arrival, Briscoe realizes that Charlene is missing. The boys are sent to find her.

Charlene is inside the courthouse chasing Andy. She wants to "snuggle up a little." Briscoe enters and accuses Andy of "egging" Charlene on. He tells Andy that he and Dud will have to "fight it out" to see who gets Charlene.

The Darlings and Andy walk to the bus. After Dud steps off, he gives Charlene a gift—"a tiger-eye ring right out of Spokane, Washington." Dud reveals that he carries Charlene's letters, her hair ribbon, and "the remainders of that mountain gladioli you gave me the day I departed to fulfill my country's needs" around his waist in a money belt. This impresses Charlene. She hugs Dud, and the two kiss.

Briscoe consoles Andy, now that he's lost Charlene. Andy responds by saying, "Well, some got it, and some ain't."

In the epilogue, Andy performs Dud and Charlene's wedding ceremony. Instead of the usual two-dollar fee, Andy is paid with a song.

"'The Darlings Are Coming' was an important show for more reasons than we knew at the time," admits Mitch. "It was the Dillards' first appearance on television and gave us national recognition as bluegrass musicians. The immense impact that first show had on bluegrass music itself is hard to guess, coming at a time when only Flatt and Scruggs had ever managed to get prime-time exposure on a top-rated television show. Even with our following appearances, nothing jarred the bluegrass world as much as that first Andy Griffith show, because so much of it was devoted to our music, and the Darling family was such as outrageous concept.

"Of all the shows we did, 'The Darlings Are Coming' is easiest to capture in memory because we met three people who were to change our lives considerably: Andy, Denver, and Maggie. It was also our first exposure to television on what we would later learn was known as a 'happy set,' a set where the star's disposition determined the attitudes of the cast and crew. In later years, after dozens of television shows, we were to understand how fortunate we were to have been initiated into that grueling business by the kindest and most understanding of professionals—Andy Griffith."

"Andy's English Valet"

"In 1957 Ray Saffian Allen was asked to come to London to write a new series, *Dick and the Duchess*, for CBS," says Harvey Bullock. "Ray asked if I would like to be his partner, and I leapt with joy. We went to London and wrote twenty-six episodes. Working with talented British actors was a delight. Thus, we met Bernard Fox.

"After *Dick* was completed, I returned to America, but Ray stayed on to try his hand at producing sitcoms. He worked with Bernie, and I believe he was instrumental in convincing the talented Mr. Fox to come to the States. More pressure came from a pretty American girl, Jackie, whom Bernie later married."

"A fellow by the name of Ray Saffian Allen produced a TV series in England titled *Three Live Wires*," says Bernard Fox. "I was one of the stars playing a Malcolm-type of character. When Ray returned to America, he told me that if I came to Hollywood he would write me into something. That turned out to be one episode of *The Danny Thomas Show*."

"Back in California, Ray and I were writing *Danny Thomas* shows," says Harvey. "We convinced Danny to use Bernie and then wrote an episode for him, 'Danny's English Friend,' in August 1962. Bernie was great playing the part of a totally fouled-up waiter in Danny's night club.

"Bernie did a follow-up episode as the same character in Danny's 'Girl Shy' episode the next year. I recall Danny admiring Bernie's gifts. He once said, 'That man is sprinkled with star dust.'"

"I evidently caused something of a sensation because I was asked to do a pilot for a series," says Bernard. "Sadly, to save expense, Danny Thomas and Sheldon Leonard decided to do a spin-off instead. Danny appeared at the beginning and again at the end, which left me about fifteen minutes to develop a character and very little time for a storyline.

Episode 89

First Broadcast on March 25, 1963

Written by
Harvey Bullock

Directed by
Bob Sweeney

Bernard Fox
Guest Stars as
Malcolm
Merriweather

"At the script reading, I ventured to suggest that it wasn't going to work. Naturally, I was overruled, but it was an abysmal flop and nothing came of the series. Happily for me, *The Andy Griffith Show* was shooting on the same lot, and they were anxious to utilize my talent."

"Andy's English Valet" begins with Aunt Bee making final preparations for a trip. She is worried that Andy and Opie will not be able to care for themselves in her absence and is hesitant to leave. As the two walk down the driveway, Aunt Bee reminds Andy that Mrs. Edwards is leaving her car, and Andy is free to use it. Aunt Bee returns to the house to get a scarf.

As Andy waits, a man on a bicycle rides up and asks Andy if he is the constable. The man, Malcolm Merriweather, is an Englishman from Heckmandyke [script spelling] who is touring America. Malcolm asks for directions to Route 43.

"I thought an elegantly mannered but affable character would make an interesting contrast with the honest and uncontrived Mayberry folk," says Harvey. "Producer Aaron Ruben agreed, so I wrote the story—the 'fish out of water' genre, an English valet bicycling across America."

"In the script reading, when I was asked where Malcolm might have come from I remembered the name of a village in Derbyshire called Heckmonwyke, which was always turning up in the Boy Scout magazines as having a particularly inept troop of scouts," says Bernard.

"I think I devised the name Malcolm Merriweather, but I know Bernie added immensely to the episode," says Harvey. "I remembered such colorful terms as 'bubble and squeak' (which I think was corned beef and cabbage) and a few others from my London writing venture. But Bernie came up with almost all the 'Englishisms.'"

While pedaling through Mayberry's business area, Malcolm reads his road map and recklessly rides his bicycle into the path of a truck, causing the driver to run into a pile of packing crates.

Barney sees the accident happen. He untangles Malcolm from the scattered crates and takes him to the courthouse. Andy estimates that Malcolm will have to pay "upwards toward forty dollars" to repair the damage to the wrecked truck.

Malcolm doesn't have the money, so Barney wants to lock him up. Andy, however, sympathizes with Malcolm and suggests he might be able to help around the house to work off the debt. A grateful Malcolm responds, "Aren't you kind?"

Malcolm begins working off the debt by repairing an upstairs window at Andy's house. When Malcolm adjusts the height on the ladder, he catches his head between the rungs.

The script gave the following directions for the scene in which Malcolm gets entangled with the ladder: *Malcolm lies where he fell in the shrubbery, his foot through the bottom of the bushel basket, the ladder almost on top of him. He struggles to his feet and walks with his foot still through the basket.*

The filmed version is simplified, but still comically effective.

"Quite a lot of the comedy stuff was suggested by me," says Bernard. "The ladder business was my idea."

"Bernie added all the grace notes that made this episode work," says Harvey. "He has infallible comic instinct honed by his work on music-hall stages. He has the rare ability to do farce, which I think is the most difficult style of comedy."

After Malcolm adjusts the ladder, Opie walks up and introduces himself. As Malcolm continues the repair, he accidentally breaks the window pane when he raises the ladder.

Just then, Andy drives up. He looks at the broken window but doesn't complain. Andy simply says he's going inside to fix lunch. At this point, Malcolm offers to prepare the meal because it is a bit more "in my line." It turns out that Malcolm worked in England as a gentleman's gentleman.

That evening when Andy comes home, he is greeted by Opie, who is "dressed for dinner" in a suit and bow tie. The table is elegantly set.

The next morning, Malcolm, acting in the capacity of a gentleman's gentleman, offers to help Andy put on his pants. Andy refuses.

Malcolm then prepares breakfast. He even draws a face on Opie's boiled egg. Malcolm delivers Andy's morning paper to the table, reports the weather conditions, and brushes Andy's cap.

Another of Bernard's ideas was to have Malcolm draw a face on Opie's egg. The idea resulted in an interesting response from *TAGS* sponsor, General Foods, the manufacturer of Sanka Coffee and Post cereals.

"I had been reading how American sponsors interfered with shows—you couldn't have a person commit suicide in a gas oven if the sponsor was a gas company," says Bernard. "So I mentioned to the prop man, Reggie Smith, that I was surprised that nobody had complained about having a boiled egg in the show. He said, 'Are you kidding?' He then pulled open his desk drawer that held a stack of letters detailing what had to be in evidence on the table around the egg—all General Food products."

Malcolm's attention makes Andy uncomfortable. When Malcolm steps into the kitchen, Andy quietly sneaks out the front door. He carefully crosses the front porch, turns, and walks into Malcolm, who is waiting for him beside Mrs. Edwards's car.

Flawless editing of a variety of camera angles presents Andy's attempted escape in an effective manner. The fifty-second scene begins with a shot of Andy getting up from the table and walking to the door. A second shot shows Andy crossing the front porch. The action continues with a third shot of Andy and Malcolm standing beside the open car door. The fourth camera angle is a close-up of Andy and Malcolm. The scene concludes with a shot of Andy sitting in the back seat, a shawl pulled over his legs. This scene is filmed with the camera positioned inside the car.

"I didn't really notice how camera angles and musical backgrounds were effective," admits Harvey. "While watching an episode, I was tuned to the words and storytelling. The fact I don't remember all those goodies is the supreme test—they were so good they weren't evident."

Andy tells Barney that Malcolm makes him uncomfortable. Barney suggests that Andy just tell Malcolm how he feels. When Andy comes home, he overhears Malcolm telling Opie how much he enjoys taking care of Andy and Opie. After hearing this, Andy decides he will wait for the right moment to talk to Malcolm.

During the course of the evening, Malcolm overhears Barney telling Andy that "the guy is just making a grade A pest of himself." Malcolm overhears this front-porch conversation through an open window. With this realization, Malcolm leaves a note saying he had to "leave on urgent business."

When Andy finds a glass of milk that Malcolm was taking up to Opie by the open window, he realizes that Malcolm left because he overheard Barney's comments. Andy then goes looking for Malcolm.

"The idea for the telltale milk in the window was worked out by hopscotching back and forth in scripting—planting and then reaping," says Harvey. "The word is 'construction,' not much in vogue today, but to me one of the fun things in writing. I truly enjoyed flipping about, stitching in small unifying bits of dialogue or business."

When he finds Malcolm pedaling out of town, Andy says he doesn't care what Malcolm overheard, but he'd better get back to work. Malcolm replies, "Right away, sir" and pedals back into town.

The theme that musical director Earle Hagen composed for Malcolm is excellent and adds to the overall presentation of the character. The theme is used to highlight the emotions that the character experiences—a slower tempo to express sadness when Malcolm overhears the front-porch conversation, a faster tempo to communicate the joy he feels as he pedals back to Mayberry.

Harvey initially saw the finished version of his script when the episode was broadcast by the network. "There were no special screenings for the writers. Time and economics did not permit them," says Harvey. "We pitched stories, then wrote and polished them, after which the script became the producer and director's sole property—and we were off rushing about to seek other assignments. However, when *TAGS* came on the air I was right there at home in front of the set with my four kids. We loved it!"

Bernard Fox had a very different experience. "I had just finished watching myself on *The Andy Griffith Show*," says Bernard. "At that time I was very, very new to Hollywood. There was little money in the bank and no signs of immediate work. So, I was sitting there thinking that the future looked fairly bleak when the phone rang. It was Andy, full of praise for my work. He mentioned that it was one of the best shows they had done, and that they were definitely going to do more—my spirits soared."

"Barney's First Car"

Episode 90

First Broadcast on
April 1, 1963

Written by
**Jim Fritzell and
Everett Greenbaum**

Directed by
Bob Sweeney

Ellen Corby
Guest Stars as
Mrs. Myrt
"Hubcaps" Lesh

"I was not surprised at all when 'Barney's First Car' won the Writers Guild of America award. This script was Jim and Ev at their funny best."
—AARON RUBEN

"'Barney's First Car' was a good show," says Everett Greenbaum. "The storyline grew out of the fact that cars are so important in our lives. I had forgotten that we won the Writers Guild award for this script even though the brass award plaque, with the script's title engraved on it, is hanging in my office."

Jim and Everett's award-winning script begins with Barney happily entering the courthouse. Barney has withdrawn three hundred dollars from his bank account to buy a car. He announces that he will soon be "Mr. Independent Wheels."

Barney reads some of the ads in the newspaper. One describes a "fixer-upper —a 1949 Hudson Terraplane. Was fallen on last Saturday by a thirty-ton semitrailer. Lots of miles left in the rubber. Cash or swap for twelve good laying hens." He finally finds an ad that "looks right up my street," which describes "a beautifully maintained low-mileage 1954 Ford sedan."

"The wording in the car ads was just basic comedy writing," says Everett. "The reason we selected a 1954 Ford sedan for Barney to purchase was that we wanted the car to be commonplace, and that model fit that description perfectly."

Barney arranges to have the owner drive the car to Mayberry so he can "give her a once-over." While waiting impatiently for the car's arrival, Barney tells Andy about another major purchase he once made—an all-steel, reinforced septic tank given to his parents on their anniversary.

"Many of the gifts Jim and I included in our scripts were very basic—like giving an aunt electrolysis treatments to remove excess facial hair," says Everett.

"The acting in the 'septic tank present' scene had to be very sincere in order for the scene to work. Don and Andy did a great job and felt the scene was so successful that they performed it at parties for years.

Two blasts from the car's horn, followed by swelling harps and trumpets, dramatically announce the arrival of Barney's car.

286

The car's owner is Mrs. Lesh. A harpsichord soundtrack reinforces Mrs. Lesh's "little old lady" demeanor.

Mrs. Lesh says she never drives "the machine" over twenty-five miles an hour. She also says that her late husband Bernard "loved and cherished the machine," so she wants to be sure it finds a good home.

"My ancestors, including my father, called the family car 'the machine,'" says Everett. "I remembered this and gave the line to Mrs. Lesh."

Although Barney is eager to purchase the car, Andy advises him to take it on a test drive. He also advises Barney to take it to the filling station and have Wally look it over, but Barney refuses because he doesn't want to insult Mrs. Lesh.

Barney makes "the deal right here and now." Mrs. Lesh sadly hands over the keys. She then lovingly caresses the machine's door handle, takes a few steps, and hesitates. Barney advises, "Don't look back."

"The line 'Don't look back' was a phrase used in a lot of corny 1930s movies," says Everett. "It seemed like something that sentimental Barney would say to the departing Mrs. Lesh."

As the episode continues, Mrs. Lesh is picked up a few blocks away by her "nephew." After getting into the car, the man inquires, "How did you do, Myrt?" Mrs. Lesh replies, "Unloaded another one, Jake. Three hundred easy clams from the sucker of the world."

Barney then takes Andy, Aunt Bee, Opie, Thelma Lou, and Gomer on his new car's maiden voyage. He assigns each person a seat, so the weight will be distributed evenly. Gomer is assigned the middle position in the back seat. After learning that Gomer might get carsick, Barney reassigns him to a seat near a window.

As Barney drives through the countryside, everyone is enjoying the ride—even Gomer, who announces, "I'm sick as a dog but having the time of my life."

"One of the lines of dialogue I always liked was Gomer's line, 'Sick as a dog but having the time of my life,'" says Everett. "Jim and I decided to further develop the character, so we emphasized Gomer's pleasant personality to offset his lack of intelligence. Only the sweetest person on earth would say the 'sick as a dog' line."

Barney's face beams with satisfaction as he drives along. His satisfaction, however, is soon shattered when something that looks like a snake starts lifting the steering column. Gomer sums up the situation when he says, "It looks to me like you got too much grease in your steering column."

"The inspiration for the grease coming out of the steering wheel came from something that happened to a very good friend of mine who worked in a gas station while attending medical school," says Everett. "He once had trouble getting the grease to go into the fitting in the steering of a Packard convertible. The boss told him to force it, so he did. When the owner, who was wearing a white suit, drove away, the car hit a bump, and a snake of grease arose, taking the horn button with it. The grease held together for a second and then flopped down on the white suit."

"The scene inside the car was very special because it showed Barney's hilarious reaction to the rising steering column, his mood change, and his bewilderment over the situation," says producer Aaron Ruben. "The car was stationary and photographed inside the studio. The passing scenery, which is seen through the windows, was done with rear-projection shots."

When Barney stops the car, the motor begins "boiling but good," and Andy, Gomer, Opie, and Aunt Bee wind up pushing the vehicle as Thelma Lou steers. Barney is so heartbroken he can neither push nor steer.

The next day, Wally checks the car and finds sawdust in the car's deferential and transmission.

"Sawdust in the transmission used to be a trick of used-car dealers," says Everett. "It made the gears run smoothly for a couple hundred miles and seemed like the kind of scheme Mrs. Lesh would pull on an unsuspecting buyer."

Andy tells Barney that the sawdust "is all the evidence we'll need. Let's take that car right back to the little old lady in Mt. Pilot."

The car breaks down on the way to Mt. Pilot. Andy leaves Barney with the car and walks to a telephone to call Gomer to come give them a tow.

When Andy returns to the car, he and Barney crawl in the back seat to take a nap. The two are awakened sometime later by the car's movement. Andy notices that the tow truck that is pulling them does not belong to Wally. He tells Barney to stay hidden so they can see where the tow truck is taking the car.

"We decided to put Andy and Barney in the car's back seat because there was more room for napping that way, and, of course, it makes them invisible to the tow-truck driver, which helped our story," says Everett.

The car is towed into a garage. After the tow truck stops, Andy and Barney quietly get out of the car. Barney puts his bullet in his gun. Mrs. Lesh, who is inside the garage, inspects the car and recognizes it "as that clunker I sold that boob in Mayberry."

At that point, Andy and Barney emerge from their hiding place and arrest Mrs. Lesh and her gang. Mrs. Lesh tries to bribe her way out of the arrest by offering them a deal on a "sweet 1958 custom sedan."

Although Barney is interested, Andy doesn't let him make the same mistake twice.

"The Rivals"

Episode 91

First Broadcast on
April 8, 1963

Written by
Harvey Bullock

Directed by
Bob Sweeney

"Opie's question, 'Just what can you do with a grown woman?' is one of the best lines—and that's covering a lot of ground."—HARVEY BULLOCK

"The Rivals" begins with Opie seated on the steps of the Mayberry Hotel. He looks down the sidewalk and sees someone coming. He licks his palms and slicks down his hair just before Karen Burgess, one of his classmates, walks by. Opie begins walking beside her. As they near the courthouse, Opie asks her if she would like to see the inside of a real jail. Karen is interested.

"This script deals with Opie at that wondrous age before sophistication," says writer Harvey Bullock. "Most of us experienced the same sweetness and utter confusion of first love and asked the same disarming questions that Opie asks.

"I opened the episode with Opie seated on the hotel steps, waiting for Karen to pass by. In my script Opie does all that's indicated except for licking his hand and slicking down his hair. This adolescent behavior sounds like a touch the director, Bob Sweeney, added.

"The name of Opie's girlfriend, Karen Burgess, was taken from a girl named 'Karen Birch,' who was best friends with one of my daughters."

Opie introduces Karen to Andy and then shows her "the layout"—the file cabinet, the gun rack, the cells, and "the door I go through when I empty out the trash baskets."

After the tour, Opie offers to carry Karen's books, but Karen turns down the offer.

That night, Opie talks to Andy about "liking someone a whole lot." Opie asks Andy how he can get Karen to like him. Andy suggests that Opie treat her "as nice as you can."

The next day, Barney and Thelma Lou see Opie sitting on the hotel steps. He looks depressed. When Barney sees Andy, he asks Andy, "What's wrong with Opie? He's moping around out there like he doesn't have a friend in the world." Andy explains that Opie has a crush on Karen.

Opie's crush reminds Barney of an experience he had when he "wasn't no bigger than Opie." He met a girl named Vickie Harmes at the ice cream parlor. He describes his reaction, "I stepped outside one day with my raspberry snow cone, and there she was." Barney knew it was love because "icy chills just ran all over me." Vickie was stuck up because "her daddy was in civil service." She also used to do one thing that really irritated Barney. When Barney offered her a bite of his snow cone, Vickie would bite off the end, sip out all the syrup, and leave him with "nothing but the ice." Knowing what he knows now, he would do things differently. If he had a date with Vickie Harmes today, he would ring her doorbell, bite off the end of his snow cone, sip out the syrup, and hand her the ice.

"Vickie Harmes, the name of Barney's former heartthrob, was taken from my niece of that exact name," says Harvey. "Barney's snow-cone problem was inspired by the strict procedures we boys all used to keep an ice cream cone from melting too quickly. Different theories were ardently advocated—lick around the edge, bite with your teeth, or wrap a paper napkin around the cone for insulation. The latter theory was seldom used by boys because the paper napkin smacked of sissyhood. Also ice cream was never ever ordered in a cup, always in a cone. Cups and spoons were for elders who dripped a lot.

"Girls who wanted boys to like them would always order cones. Girls who asked for cups were definitely snooty because boys saw no point in having a nonedible, such as a cardboard cup, between them and the ice cream. A similar protocol existed with snow cones, just as Barney elaborates. Draining the syrup immediately was world-class ignorant behavior."

That afternoon, Opie waits in front of the grocery for Karen to walk by. When she arrives, Opie does a handstand to impress her, but she is unimpressed.

Thelma Lou comes out of the grocery after Karen leaves. She needs someone to carry her packages, so Andy volunteers Opie. Thelma Lou plans to make some fudge brownies when she gets home. She needs a "test pilot" to sample the brownies along with her homemade peach ice cream.

"Fudge brownies were the mainstay goodie at our home, which was the social center for all the kids in the neighborhood," says Harvey. "My daughter Diana had devised a super-satanic recipe for fudge brownies by adding chocolate pudding to the already extra-chocolate mix.

"Earlier in my career, I had written for a daily variety show in New York. In one of our skits we talked about peaches from South Carolina. The South Carolina Peach Growers Association caught it, enjoyed the publicity, and sent me a bushel of their finest. We invited all the neighbors over, got thick whipping cream, processed those glorious peaches, hand cranked the freezer, and produced the most magnificent ice cream devised since the earth began to cool. That was almost fifty years ago—and I remain ruined for any other.

"Fudge brownies and homemade peach ice cream were minor details that seemed right for Mayberry. Sometimes a minor detail wasn't quite satisfying, and I would spend hours tweaking and changing. I actually enjoyed the rewrite process. You have the whole story finished, then if time permits before the script-due deadline, you can go back and make improvements. The trap, of course, is you start deleting a word or two, and soon you are rewriting the whole scene.

"My writing partner on some of the *TAGS* scripts, the late Ray Allen, was amused, but realistic, about my tendency to rewrite. He would occasionally come to my desk when I was agonizing over a change, pull the paper out of the typewriter, and call out, 'Good enough—next!' Mostly he was right. I was micro-polishing."

Opie agrees to accompany Thelma Lou. Barney walks up while Opie is retrieving Thelma Lou's packages. He invites Thelma Lou to go get a cup of coffee, but Thelma Lou explains she has "made some plans with Opie."

As Thelma Lou and Opie walk away, Karen Burgess is standing around the corner of the courthouse. She silently watches as the two pass by.

When Barney enters the courthouse later that afternoon, Andy is painting a partition. Barney decides to telephone Thelma Lou and "invite her to go for a little ride tonight. There's going to be a moon. Maybe we'll just go up to the duck pond and park."

"Andy did no painting in my script," says Harvey. "I imagine the painting was added just to have something different happening in the scene and to place Andy in the background while Barney calls Thelma Lou."

Thelma Lou's telephone rings. She asks Opie to answer it. When Barney asks to speak to Thelma Lou, she asks Opie to just relay the message because she's busy. Barney tells Opie to ask Thelma Lou if she would like to go for "a little ride tonight to the duck pond." Opie asks why Barney would want to go to the duck pond at night when "you can't see the ducks." Thelma Lou enjoys the situation, so she encourages Opie to ask Barney again why he wants to go to the duck pond. Barney hangs up in frustration.

"In the kitchen scene, Thelma Lou is tickled by Barney's embarrassment when the duck pond is mentioned," says Harvey. "She manipulates him marvelously by using the oblivious Opie. The script's inclusion of the duck pond is as close to my heart as fudge brownies and homemade peach ice cream. In my upstate New York home, there was a duck pond with a scandalous reputation for being where lots of kissing was going on. As soon as you got a driver's license, the first stop you made, with any luck, was the duck pond. Even if you went there very properly and left quickly, it was still considered absolute big-time."

The next day, Opie waits on the hotel steps for his girl. Barney sees Opie and sits down beside him. Barney then gives Opie some "fast tips" that will get his girl back.

When Opie sees his girl coming, he follows Barney's advice. He walks up to Thelma Lou and says, "Well, here I am, you lucky girl. You play your cards right, maybe I'll let you walk with me." Thelma Lou tells Opie that she'll take him "up on that." When Barney realizes that Opie has become his rival, he is upset.

After Opie and Thelma Lou depart, Karen walks by the hotel. She stops, looks around, and realizes Opie is not in his usual place.

On Saturday, Barney eagerly prepares for a date with Thelma Lou. Opie enters the courthouse and announces to Andy that he hardly thinks of Karen anymore, "now that Thelma Lou's my girl." When Opie tells Andy that he plans to spend the whole day with Thelma Lou, Barney storms out.

After Barney leaves, Andy asks Opie what he and Thelma Lou plan to do. Andy suggests that they ride bikes, climb apple trees, or go see a cowboy "shoot-em-up picture." After making these suggestions, Andy observes that none of these activities would appeal to "a grown woman."

Opie then asks, "Pa, just what can you do with a grown woman?"

Andy answers, "Sometimes they take you shopping with them. You set around while the woman tries on dresses and hats. Then you set around her house while the woman gets dressed up. And then you go over to visit the woman's mother— so, it's a fun day."

"As a habitual theatergoer (Suburban Theater on Main Street, Saturday afternoon, ten-cent admission) I always called the cowboy pictures 'shoot-em-ups,'" says Harvey. "The other Saturday activities suggested by Andy—going bike riding and climbing apple trees—were mostly taken from personal childhood memories.

"Andy's description of a day with a woman was the sort of explanation which would occur easily to Andy on his way to wrapping up with, 'So, it's a fun day.' The scene also illustrates what Andy does extremely well. He doesn't voice stern disapproval to Opie. Instead he assumes a seemingly enthusiastic and helpful acceptance of Opie's fun day with Thelma Lou and slides in the negatives very smoothly."

Andy looks out the window. When he sees Karen standing outside, he rushes Opie out the door.

As Opie exits, Karen comes up to him and asks, "Are you going to the movies?" This invitation interests Opie. He steps back inside the courthouse and asks Andy if he will explain things to Thelma Lou. Andy agrees.

Opie and Karen walk off hand in hand. Opie starts out on Karen's right but switches over to her left, walking closest to the street.

"In the script, the second-act fadeout does not have the Opie/Karen cross-overs," says Harvey. "It seems like a very nice touch—boyhood chivalry at work."

In the epilogue, Andy looks out the window and sees Thelma Lou walking toward the courthouse. He tells Barney. Barney decides he is going to show Thelma Lou that he was not just sitting around waiting for her while she spent time with Opie.

Barney picks up the telephone and holds down the receiver with his thumb. As Thelma Lou enters, Barney says, "I'm sorry, Sally. I really can't say yes or no about going to the movies tonight." As he is supposedly talking on the telephone, it rings. Because Barney is closer, Andy suggests he take the call. After Barney hangs up, Thelma Lou says, "I'm sorry you're going to be busy at the movies, Barney. I was hoping we could drive up to the duck pond."

"Ray Allen and I used the 'holding down the telephone and pretending to be talking to someone' gimmick in a sitcom we wrote in London in 1958 or so," says Harvey. "I have seen it used occasionally on other shows, but it never seemed terribly effective. The gimmick popped into my head while writing for Don Knotts, and I used it in the epilogue of this show. Don cast his magic with the scene, his ruse all smoked out, and it was tastier than anyone else has ever done it.

"'The Rivals' has always been one of my favorite episodes because its structure gave each of the four main characters time enough to get into a role instead of just making short appearances. Barney has a lot of funny dating experiences to talk about, Opie has lots of screen time, Andy is the clever and humorous arbitrator, and Thelma Lou, portrayed by the wonderful Betty Lynn, works throughout. It was a team experience with all four at the top of their game."

"Dogs, Dogs, Dogs"

"The script was a real departure for the series and fun to do."
—AARON RUBEN

"I believe *TAGS* director Bob Sweeney suggested a story with dogs overrunning the town," says producer Aaron Ruben. "I liked the idea and gave Jim and Everett the assignment. They wrote a great script, although it was something of a departure for the series. Believability was always a concern, since Mayberry was a real town with real people, flaky as they might be. The storyline's need for an ever-increasing number of dogs may have pushed the limits of reality."

Jim and Everett's script begins early in the morning. Aunt Bee has left "a nice big breakfast" at the courthouse for Otis Campbell. After a night of drinking, Otis feels bad, so Andy prepares him a "fixer-upper"—a raw egg, hot sauce, etcetera. Otis drinks the mixture reluctantly and instantly perks up.

"The opening scene in which Otis wakes up appears on-screen exactly as it was scripted," says writer Everett Greenbaum. "In those days drunkenness was still considered funny, and we felt having Otis drink a morning-after elixir would be a good comedy gag. Jim and I suggested the ingredients for the mixture, as well as we could remember, from seeing it prepared in movies."

The humor of the gag is enhanced by Earle Hagen's musical sound effects. Music comically traces the mixture's journey from the glass to Otis's stomach and perfectly accompanies Hal Smith's hilarious response.

"I actually drank the mixture that Andy prepared in the episode," said Hal Smith, who portrayed Otis Campbell. "The raw eggs Andy put in the drink were not mixed thoroughly and one of them stuck in my throat on its way down. My reaction to the drink was partly the result of the momentary choking I experienced from the egg."

In the day's mail is a response to an application Andy made for additional funds for the office and jail. The letter announces that a state investigator will be coming to Mayberry to see if the funds are necessary.

Episode 93

First Broadcast on April 22, 1963

Written by
Jim Fritzell and Everett Greenbaum

Directed by
Bob Sweeney

Otis asks Barney what they need money for. Barney answers that one of the things they need the money for is to have a charge account at the diner so they can pay for Otis's meals instead of having Aunt Bee fix the meals at Andy's expense. On hearing this, Otis threatens to "take his business somewhere else" because the food at the diner is "too spicy." Otis claims the food is bad for his liver. Barney then yells at Otis, "If you can drink anything, you can eat anything. Otis, you got a pickled liver."

"This was the first script in which we verbally pitted Otis and Barney against one another, and it worked very well," says Everett. "A writer learns little tricks along the way. For instance, it's very easy to drift into the habit of writing dialogue between two actors in a straight question-and-answer format. But people don't talk that way. There are infinite ways of making a scene more effective by using pauses, answering a question with another question, or changing the subject and turning defensive rather than informative. The dialogue between Otis and Barney reflects their personalities and, thanks to Hal and Don's great talent, is delivered in a natural way with pauses and agitation."

At this point in the episode, Opie enters with a dog in tow. Opie wants to feed the dog because it looks hungry. Over in his cell, Otis quickly finishes his breakfast so he will not have to share. Andy gets Barney's lunch bag from the desk and gives the dog a sandwich and a Mr. Cookie bar.

After the dog eats, Barney suggests that they get it out of the office because the state investigator is coming. Opie begs to keep the dog, and Andy reluctantly agrees.

Later in the day, Opie tells Andy and Barney that the dog got away. When the three enter the courthouse, they find Opie's dog and three new dogs.

Barney emphasizes the need to get rid of the dogs before the investigator comes. He comes up with the idea that Otis should take them home.

Otis returns a short time later and announces that the dogs are gone again. As he turns to leave, he opens the door and is stampeded by eleven dogs.

Andy, Barney, Otis, and Opie discuss what to do with the dogs. Otis suggests taking them to the dog pound, but his idea is rejected. Andy wants to think about it, so he takes Opie to the filling station to get a bottle of pop.

Meanwhile, Barney tries to think of a place eleven dogs would be happy. He suddenly has an inspiration, so he rounds up the dogs, herds them into the squad car, and drives away.

When Andy and Opie return to the courthouse, the dogs are gone. Just then, Barney walks in. He proudly tells Andy and Opie that he took the dogs to "a nice, big field out in the country." Opie is not convinced the dogs will "be fine."

"Whenever we had an episode dealing with an animal we called a company, and they would send over a trainer with the requested animal," says Aaron Ruben. "All the dogs used in this episode were well trained. We had no problem getting them to follow Otis when he left the courthouse or with their jumping into the squad car after Barney decided to drive them to the country. The trainer would simply give a command, and the dogs eagerly responded."

Andy sends Opie home. As Opie opens the door to leave, thunder crashes in the distance. Since a storm is coming, Andy decides it would be better for Opie to stay at the office awhile.

Opie begins to worry about the dogs' welfare. Barney reassures Opie that a dog can't be struck by lightning because it is too close to the ground. He adds that "if they was giraffes out there in that field—then we'd be in trouble."

Still trying to convince Opie (and himself) that the dogs will be fine, Barney continues to talk. The thunder crashes again. With every flash of lightning, Barney's discourse loses assurance. Barney continues, "Dogs are short. They take care of their own. Giraffes don't. No, giraffes don't at all. Boy, giraffes are selfish."

"My copy of the script must be a shooting script because Barney's 'giraffe' speech is included," says Everett. "I remember that Aaron either created it or made additions to our original speech, and I was very pleased with the final results.

"There were very few monumental script changes on *The Griffith Show*. The stories had been so carefully detailed in outlines and drafts that not many changes were needed. And if changes were made, Aaron, also a superb writer, would only improve the scenes."

"Jim and Ev give me credit for the giraffe speech," says Aaron. "The speech just seemed to fit the character and the story. The line, 'Boy, giraffes are selfish,' was Barney's inflated idea on a subject he knew very little about."

When another crash of thunder booms, Barney asks Andy, "Are you just going to sit there or are you coming with me to get them dogs? Are you coming with me?"

After retrieving the dogs, Barney responds to Andy's comment that he's "all heart" by reciting the lines, "The quality of mercy is not strained. It droppeth as the gentle rain from heaven."

"Jim and I thought it would be a nice surprise to have Barney quote Shakespeare," says Everett. "After all, he isn't a jerk, you know!"

Although Barney is sympathetic to keeping the dogs in the courthouse, he still fears they can "kiss that application for new funds goodbye." The telephone rings. State Investigator Somerset is on his way over.

Opie takes the dogs out back.

When Somerset arrives, he is all business and somewhat negative. He looks around and announces that everything seems to be "adequately supplied."

As Somerset walks into the back room, the dogs rush in and knock him to the floor. His demeanor changes instantly. It turns out that he is a dog lover. The requested funds are cordially approved.

Some viewers think Somerset's dramatic change and the solution to the problem caused by the dogs' presence seem to come too abruptly to be credible and somewhat hurt the story.

Everett concurs, "Yes, the ending of this show is too quick, too easy, and very sitcom-like by Mayberry standards. This may be why I disowned the episode in my memory bank."

In the epilogue, Andy and Barney wearily enter the courthouse. They have just finished finding homes for the eleven dogs. Just then, a man comes to the office looking for his eleven dogs. Andy and Barney exit wearily—to retrieve the dogs.

"Mountain Wedding"

"Ernest T. grew out of interest in the Darlings and their environment."
—EVERETT GREENBAUM

"When the William Morris Agency contracted to handle the Dillards after our first appearance on ~~TAGS~~, one of the first things our assigned representative told us was, 'You guys act ~~like~~ every job you get is the only one you'll get,'" says Mitch Jayne, the ~~Dillards'~~ bass ~~player~~. "He, of course, hit the nail on the head. We were so new to the ~~Hollywood~~ scene that each job was a once-in-a-lifetime chance to us. When you consider th~~at five~~ months prior to our first *Griffith* show we had been watching *~~Andy Griffith~~* at home in the Ozarks, never dreaming we would even meet these people, much less be ~~part~~ of the show, it isn't hard to imagine our excitement at being asked to come ba~~ck~~ for a second one."

~~Jim and Everett's second Darling script~~ begins on the sidewalk in front of Foley's Grocery. Andy and Barney are watching a sign painter. The painter is painting an advertisement on the grocery window, which Barney calls "a delicate piece of artistic work." Barney questions Andy about the painter's spelling of "chicken." Andy reminds Barney that the rule is, "*i* before *e* except after *c*, and *e* before *n* in *chicken*."

"The chicken sign was not in our script," says writer Everett Greenbaum. "We began with a routine about Barney's fingerprint kit. The routine was either replaced during rewrite or on the stage."

Andy looks down the street and sees Briscoe Darling's truck parked in front of the courthouse. He and Barney walk to the office and find Briscoe inside. Briscoe has come down out of the mountains because there is trouble. Briscoe explains that "there's this fellow up home, Ernest T. Bass, he just don't take to Dud and Charlene being married." It seems that Ernest T. keeps bothering Charlene because he doesn't believe she is really married. Since he doesn't recognize her marriage, Ernest T. wants to court her himself. He comes to the cabin during the night and yells at Charlene and throws rocks through the windows. Briscoe

Episode 94

First Broadcast on April 29, 1963

Written by
Jim Fritzell and Everett Greenbaum

Directed by
Bob Sweeney

Howard Morris
Guest Stars as
Ernest T. Bass

asks Andy if he will come to the mountains and "straighten this thing out." Andy agrees.

Barney decides to sleep at the courthouse so he and Andy can get an early start. The next morning, Andy comes by to pick up Barney but has difficulty waking him. Yelling "wake up," ringing an alarm clock, and blowing a whistle in his ear all have no effect. When Andy finally snaps his fingers, Barney awakes instantly.

Andy and Barney arrive sometime later at the Darlings' mountain cabin.

"The Darling cabin was set in Decker Canyon, the same location I believe for most of the outdoor shots," says Mitch. "The cabin interior was shot, as usual, on the Desilu set. This was interesting to us four boys, learning for the first time how interior shots had to be filmed in entirely different locations, even when conversation had to be spliced as someone went out the door. Like most *TAGS* watchers, we supposed that the action happened linearly, and we were amazed when things happened totally out of sequence, a fact that the actors, of course, took for granted. Someone would walk out the door on Monday and maybe continue that action, or complete that sentence thirty miles away on Wednesday, when the set moved to location."

The Darlings are playing their instruments when Andy and Barney arrive. The two enter the cabin and are warmly welcomed by Briscoe, Charlene, Dud, and the boys.

Briscoe asks Dud if he told Ernest T. Bass the sheriff was looking for him. Dud was unable to find Ernest T. because he "went off into the woods to kill a mockingbird."

"We thought it was clever to use 'to kill a mockingbird' in the script," says Everett. "It was the title of a hit movie that year."

Dud advises Andy to stay at the cabin. He explains that Ernest T. "is a pestilence, and a pestilence will find you." Briscoe suggests they play some music while they wait for Ernest T. to come along. The Darlings, with Andy playing guitar, break into "Dooley."

"One of the songs we performed early in the episode was 'Dooley,'" says Mitch. "We didn't write the song for the show, but it fit in perfectly. I'd known a few moonshiners and made up the lyrics. Rodney Dillard wrote the tune and sang the song in the episode. Rodney's inspiration for the tune came from a song that had the words 'Do Lord' in it that a black group sang at some club we played. That sounded like 'Dooley' to me, and that's what we called the song."

At the conclusion of "Dooley," Andy compliments the boys on their playing. The compliments are interrupted by the breaking of one of the cabin's windows. Andy, Barney, and Briscoe step outside and confront Ernest T. Bass.

"The second show gave us an opportunity to meet and work with Howie Morris," says Mitch. "Watching Howie was a wonderful way for the Dillards to be introduced to this business of being with actors. This educated, camera-wise pro plunged into the Ernest T. role with complete abandon. It made us more comfortable with the oafish roles we were playing. He let us understand that any role you play is as good as you choose to make it, and that acting was its own reward. One example of this impressed me: Howie hates guns and told us so. But he knew that Ernest T. would have a mountaineer's knowledge of handling them. I am still struck when I watch 'Mountain Wedding' by how well and easily he handled that .30-30 in the scenes where he carried it and shot it. He looked as if he had packed the thing through the woods all his life. It was the same way with the voice he invented for Ernest T. It was almost menacing and in anyone less bizarre it might have been feminine—a perfect foil for the wildness of this crazy little man who threw rocks."

Andy explains to Ernest T. that he is a justice of the peace. He goes on to tell Ernest T. that he performed Dud and Charlene's wedding ceremony and has a copy of the marriage license with him. Ernest T. is unimpressed. He doesn't believe

Dud and Charlene "are rightly married" unless the ceremony is performed by a preacher.

Ernest T. refuses to leave Charlene alone, so Andy comes up with a solution that will keep anyone from getting hurt. The circuit preacher will come by on Sunday to marry Dud and Charlene again. Ernest T. is overjoyed because he still has twenty-four hours "to sweet-talk, woo, and charm" Charlene.

If you look closely, you will notice a continuity error in the scene. Andy, Barney, and Briscoe are shown facing the camera with Andy on the left, Briscoe in the middle, and Barney on the right. The scene's concluding shot, following a cut-away of Ernest T. retreating into the woods, has Andy and Barney in reversed positions.

That night, Andy, Barney, and the Darlings all bed down in the cabin. Andy and Barney can't sleep because the Darlings are all snoring loudly.

"I think the snoring scene that opens the second act was the single funniest thing Denver Pyle, who portrayed Briscoe Darling, ever created on that show," says Mitch. "It was intended to be ridiculous, of course, with Andy and Don trying to sleep through this Darling racket, but Denver was the one who invented that incredible maelstrom of noise and directed the Dillards like some sort of insane Leonard Bernstein. It was so unbelievably colorful that it created an ambience more like a hog killing than anything else; a cacophony of all the best snores each of us had heard, piled onto one another car-wreck style, until you couldn't believe it was human. Neither Don nor Andy could handle it. Each time we would try a take, the two of them would slide out of their chairs onto the floor, helpless. Of course, that would free us up to laugh, and I remember Rodney laughed so hard he fell out of bed. Director Bob Sweeney was too weak from laughing to do anything but just wave his hands like flippers, and I personally was so cracked up that I had to lie with my arm over my face and mash on it to get any kind of control.

"To the best of my memory, we shot that scene for half an hour trying to get it right. Don and Andy would do pretty good until they looked at each other. Andy's eyes would start to squinch up, his mouth would get grim. Don would see that and just collapse. Oh Lord, that was fun and still is today when I see the reruns and remember the sound crew, the grips, the light men, and the entire cast, just down pounding the floor or hanging over something, wiping their eyes, helpless with the outrageousness of it all, wondering if we were going to make this scene. It's the only time I ever saw Andy Griffith lose it."

The Darlings' snoring is interrupted by the breaking of a window. Ernest T. Bass is paying another visit. In response, Barney yells, "You listen to me out there. I'm armed. If you don't go away, I'm just liable to take a shot out this window." Ernest T. answers with a flurry of rocks.

"The cabin windows Ernest T. breaks in order to wake the family and get Charlene's attention were made of candy glass, which doesn't make much noise, so the breaking-glass sound effects had to be added later," says Mitch. "You'll notice that when the stagehand tosses the rocks through the windows no one is directly in the line of fire. The rocks themselves were furnished by the prop department and were lava rock, which weigh almost nothing."

At this point, Andy suggests that if they let Ernest T. "speak his piece" he might go home. When Charlene steps to the window, Ernest T. "declares" for her. He serenades her while accompanying himself by tapping on a gas can, chins himself on a tree limb, and asks if he can "come over there and kiss you on the jaw."

At this point, Dad steps in and denies Ernest T's request to kiss Charlene. He tells Ernest T. that they are "having a preacher wedding" the next day just to satisfy him. Ernest T. is not so sure.

"Ernest T. serenades Charlene with the poem, 'Aunt Maria,'" says Everett. "I got the poem from my wife Deane. It was a jump-rope song she recalled from her childhood days in Arkansas."

The next day, Briscoe and the boys are dressed for the wedding. Charlene steps out from the back room in her wedding gown.

The scene begins with a shot of the Darling boys. Mitch reaches in his pocket for a match, doesn't find one, then stands and walks left toward the kitchen. The camera, following Mitch, stops on Briscoe and Andy as Mitch passes behind them.

"My move was simply to direct the eye across the kitchen set to the principal actors so the viewer can see where everybody is without posing them," explains Mitch. "I didn't feel any special notice doing the shot, I was just the only one moving—a Bob Sweeney trick. I noticed that Bob often used crossing shots like this to get the most coverage with the one camera before resetting it. Since this was the first TV I had ever seen filmed, I took these shots for granted, supposing all TV was done this way. I seem to remember that we were the only sitcom being filmed at that time with only one camera. I also remember hearing that it was Andy's decision. He liked the intimacy of one-camera shots and hated the way two or three cameras interfered with the actor's attention.

"I don't remember any special reaction to Maggie Peterson's first on-screen appearance in the wedding dress, but that's probably because we all told her how nice she looked off set. By the time we had done a half-dozen light settings, rehearsals, walk-throughs and all the standing around inherent in that process, we had all seen the dress and what the effect would be. Denver's line, 'You look just like your ma,' and his expression says it all. One of Maggie's charms is that she shone like a new penny regardless of what she had on."

Before the ceremony begins, Ernest T. Bass throws a rock through the window

A Wreath of Smoke

I always smoked a pipe on stage, so it was more of a Dillard prop than a Darling one, I started out smoking a pipe, using it as a storyteller's tool, to make myself comfortable with these strange California audiences. When someone broke a string on stage, which happened all the time, I would use it as an excuse to light my pipe. It was a physical sight thing that helped me start a story that kept the audience's attention away from string repairs and tuning. Finding that it worked wonders with an audience who enjoyed the look and the laid-back nature of the pipe, I used it to audition for *The Griffith Show*. Apparently, Andy thought it was part of the charm too. Bob Sweeney never told me when to light it or how to do anything with it. Because Bob considered every detail, I think he thought the more natural I was with it, the more natural the boys would be. And sure enough, the wreath of smoke that followed me when I moved the bass around worked for us.—MITCH JAYNE

with a message attached. The note reads: "Maybe you going to have a preacher, and maybe you going to have an altar, but maybe you not going to have a bride. You ever think about that?"

After considering how to foil Ernest T., Andy has an idea. Barney dresses in Charlene's bridal gown and stands in for Charlene.

The ceremony proceeds through the first hymn without interruption. As the preacher starts the wedding vows, three rifle shots ring out. Ernest T. emerges from the underbrush and kidnaps the bride.

As soon as Ernest T. is out of sight, Charlene comes out of her hiding place. The preacher quickly performs the ceremony.

After the ceremony, Barney emerges from the woods and runs toward Andy. He is hotly pursued by Ernest T. Bass.

"The idea of Barney dressing up as the bride came from the movie *Some Like It Hot*," says Everett. "Fleeing from gangsters, Jack Lemmon and Tony Curtis were disguised as women, and Joe E. Brown tries to marry Lemmon."

In the epilogue, Ernest T. reluctantly shakes Dud's hand. The Darlings play a song so Dud and Charlene can dance. Ernest T. enjoys the music, gets an idea, and asks the "lady sheriff," who is still dressed in a wedding gown, to dance.

"Looking back on it, 'Mountain Wedding' was a major show for us," says Mitch. "We met Don Knotts and saw firsthand the magic interaction between him and Andy—two pros who really got off on each other's work. We got to meet Howie, who was always on and full of stories, and we experienced that raw energy he exudes. We were accepted by the cast and crew as good guys who were no trouble to work with and who took direction instantly. Even the pragmatic assistant director, Bob Saunders, who was always pinned to the clock and the budget, seemed to like the way we did things and took time to share some of his Hollywood humor and behind-the-scenes jokes with us.

"With 'Mountain Wedding,' the Dillards became comfortable with the whole idea of representing our music this way. The first show had bothered Rodney, since some people said we looked like a family out of *Deliverance*. In the good-natured and forgiving climate of *TAGS*, however, we were more like idiot savants, letting Briscoe interpret us as we played our instruments with incredible expertise but acted like blocks of wood. It was fun along the lines of Harpo Marx, and we got into it—the stunned and stuporous look of boys who had only one means of expression, their music.

"The most important part of that show for the Dillards was the friends we made on the set. We were treated as professionals. We were part of the overall plan, important to the development of ideas and direction. Both George Lindsey and Jim Nabors came by to see the filming of that show. *TAGS* executive producer Sheldon Leonard dropped in too, and we began to be aware that the *Andy Griffith* set was basically a friendly, successful place where everybody felt at home and wanted to see what was happening. People felt involved in the show, curious and interested in this rural phenomenon that had captured the number-one spot in the TV ratings. Most significant, the Darlings, whatever they represented, had been approved and would be seen again."

"The Big House"

Episode 95

First Broadcast on
May 6, 1963

Written by
Harvey Bullock

Directed by
Bob Sweeney

Rule #1: Obey all rules.
Rule #2: Do not write on the walls, as it takes a lot of work to erase writing on the walls.—"Rules at the Rock"

"The Big House" begins with Barney, Gomer, and Opie listening to a news bulletin on the radio. Four bandits have pulled off "a daring holdup." The bulletin goes on to say that two members of the gang have been captured and will be held temporarily in the Mayberry jail.

After hearing that the two criminals are coming to Mayberry, Barney tells Andy, "Those two hoods are in for a big surprise when they get here. They're going to come in here expecting some small-town, two-bit lockup. Well, they're going to find out different."

Barney suggests hiring an extra deputy and takes it upon himself to find "his assistant."

When Andy returns to the courthouse later in the day, Barney proudly introduces "our number-three man." Dressed in a deputy's uniform, Gomer marches from the back room.

"The details for Gomer's appearance in his deputy's uniform were not spelled out in the script," says writer Harvey Bullock. "Gomer was simply described as *having on an ill-fitting uniform, a peaked hat like Barney's, a gun in a holster, and a badge.* That's all the description I felt was needed. I knew that the director Bob Sweeney would work out the details.

"Generally, a three-character story is more effective than a two-character story. More angles can be covered without the continuous 'talking-head' shots of the same two people. Gomer Pyle was an extremely useful character with his colorful twangy speech and guileless good nature. In 'The Big House,' both Barney and Andy play off him effectively.

"I enjoyed including Gomer in this script because I knew Jim Nabors would bring an engaging and very likable performance to the story. Jim was open, energetic, and a most dependable, talented guy."

306

Andy is hesitant about having Gomer around the jailhouse. Barney insists that Gomer has "learned a lot from me already" and assures Andy that he is putting Gomer through a crash program. Barney pleads with Andy to give Gomer a chance.

The two prisoners arrive. Minutes after they are jailed, Barney tells them the "Rules at the Rock." The two prisoners listen stone-faced, but Gomer is spellbound.

"Having Barney proclaim the 'Rules at the Rock' is a prime example of his unmatchable comic character," says Harvey. "Barney is so transparent, assuming importance, and emulating the behavior he thinks proper for a big-time lawman. Don Knotts is a true magician. His performance made the rules speech sound better than I imagined it would."

Four different camera angles are used to photograph Barney's speech. The speech begins with a wide-angle shot of Andy, Gomer, and Barney standing in front of the jail cells. As Barney begins to recite the rules, the camera is repositioned inside the cell, so Barney is seen from the prisoner's point of view. Two medium shots of Andy and Gomer bookend a wonderful close-up of the spellbound Gomer. The speech then concludes, as it began, with a wide-angle shot.

"I wrote camera directions only when I felt they were critical to the story and might have escaped the director's attention in the hectic pace of doing the series," says Harvey. "The shooting and cutting to 'singles' [one person in a shot] is fairly routine, and I had great confidence in Bob Sweeney. I knew Bob would be sure to shoot effective coverage as the scene required.

"A typical scene is first shot from a slight distance to contain most of the characters. This is the master shot. Then the scene is shot again with the camera on one character for his lines and reactions. Then, if warranted, a third take is made on another character. Often the single takes are mostly reactions to lines being read off camera. Lots of film was thus shot, giving the director all kinds of dramatic/comedic ammunition.

"The film cutters (editors) made a tremendously important contribution to the finished film. It is amazing how they can take the most disparate footage and make a final cut that flows seamlessly."

"In one-camera photography, the director shoots the master shot, the close-ups, the over-the-shoulder shots, and then the editor puts it together the way he sees it," says Jay Sandrich, assistant to the producer. "On *TAGS*, Bob Sweeney was directing most of the shows, so he didn't always have time to sit in the editing room and work with the editor. Bob would usually get a rough cut of the editor's work, view it, and then give the editor notes to change this or to use a close-up instead of a wide-angle shot. Then the producer, who has the final authority, would view the corrected cut and say, 'Yeah, that's good,' or 'Let's make some changes.' So editing was a collaborative process.

"An episode's postproduction time would sometimes vary, but it usually would take two weeks to edit a show and another week to add the music and the laugh track. After all that was done, the film would have to go to the laboratory to make sure it really looked good. Postproduction thus averaged about four to six weeks per episode."

At the conclusion of Barney's speech, Andy leaves to look for the two criminals who are still on the loose. He returns sometime later and learns that things at the courthouse have "gone as smooth as clockwork." To demonstrate, Barney announces that "it's time for mealtime formation." When Barney blows a whistle, the prisoners jump to attention and march to the adjoining cell.

Andy inquires about Gomer's whereabouts. Barney says he has Gomer "stationed outside, manning the blockhouse lookout." He and Andy step outside. Andy looks up and sees Gomer's feet hanging over the side of roof of the courthouse.

When Barney yells, "Attention," Gomer drops his gun over the side of the building.

Andy and Barney go up on the roof to return Gomer's gun. The roof is cluttered with decorations left from a past Christmas. Andy reminds Barney that he was supposed to have cleaned this up. Andy then gives the cleanup assignment to Gomer.

"The 'courthouse roof' scene was written after I finally came up with a way for one man, with no regular weapons, to fool four hardened would-be escapees," says Harvey. "The discarded decorations explained the presence of the Christmas lights, which play a prominent role in the episode's conclusion, and the rooftop setting was a nice change."

Meanwhile, the two prisoners agree to let the "hick deputy think he's a big shot. Lead him on far enough and that hick deputy is going to be our free pass out of here."

Andy gets a call that two men, who may be the two other members of the holdup gang, have been spotted around Mayberry. He leaves to investigate.

After Andy departs, the prisoners, in Barney's presence, talk about the similarities between the Mayberry jail and the state pen. They note there is one major difference. The Mayberry jail has not had a "shakedown." They say that all prisoners are taken out of their cells while "the screws make a surprise inspection of the mattresses for guns and knives." Barney immediately yells, "Shakedown" and flings open the cell door.

"I was looking for a routine the prisoners might devise that would get them out of their cell," says Harvey. "The prisoners had Barney sized up as loving to play warden so much that they could out-think him by saying the Mayberry jail wasn't as highly regarded as other 'big houses,' which had shakedowns."

While Barney is busy "shaking down" the cell, the prisoners walk out. When Barney realizes they are gone, he picks up the phone and frantically yells, "Mayday" to Sarah, the telephone operator.

"Sarah was very helpful," says Harvey. "For one thing, having a phone operator who knew all the numbers in town (instead of a soulless dial) was a constant reminder we were in a small town."

While Barney is still on the telephone, the door to the courthouse opens. The two prisoners walk in, followed by Andy. Andy tells Barney that it was a good thing he was still outside the office.

After Andy leaves, Barney exhibits his anger. He walks over to the cell and tells the prisoners that there will be "no more Mr. Nice Guy." As he routinely does, he hangs the cell keys on the wall peg and goes into the back room to get a cup of coffee.

While Barney is out of the room, one of the prisoners reaches through the cell bars, takes the keys off the wall, and unlocks the cell.

Andy enters the courthouse at this point and thwarts the prisoners again.

Once again Andy leaves. He returns later in the day with two plainclothes policemen. The two want to use the Mayberry jail as "a trap." The policemen believe the other two gang members will try to free their buddies.

Andy doesn't tell Barney about the two plainclothes policemen or their plan. Instead, he sends Barney up on the roof with Gomer.

Andy rejoins the two policemen and is assigned a position on the other side of the street.

As anticipated, the other two gang members arrive, but they decide to "case the joint" before attempting to spring their buddies. Meanwhile, Gomer is placing Christmas lights in a basket. Barney senses that something is amiss. He looks into the alley and sees the two policemen. Mistaking them for the missing gang members, he disarms them and locks them in the jail.

Meanwhile, the real missing gang members enter from the back room. They then force Barney into the cell with the two policemen, and all four gang members escape through the back room.

Andy sees the escape and yells for Gomer to assist. Gomer drops his gun over the side of the building, knocking Andy's gun out of his hands. As Gomer looks over the side of the building, he knocks over the basket of Christmas lights. The lights fall to the street in rapid succession. With their backs turned, the gang members think the breaking bulbs are machine-gun fire, so they give up.

After locking the four criminals in a cell, Andy unselfishly gives Barney the credit saying, "Great work, Barn. Your scheme worked."

"The 'Christmas-light, machine-gun-effect' capture was carefully detailed in the outline before a word of the script was typed," says Harvey. "The outline was broken into actual scenes to be written. This helped me to make sure all the prominent points were in order, and ensured that the story came to a logical conclusion."

In the epilogue, Barney and Gomer are taking steps to keep themselves "razor sharp for the next emergency." When Andy enters the courthouse, Barney asks Gomer to show Andy what he's learned. Gomer draws his gun and accidentally throws it through the glass of the bookcase. Barney reprimands him, saying, "If you don't know how to handle one of these things, you got no business carrying one." At this point, Barney places his own pistol back in its holster and accidentally fires it into the floor. Andy then extends his hand, and Barney hands over his pistol.

"The scripted epilogue does not have Barney accidentally firing his pistol," says Harvey. "Instead, Gomer gives Barney a bill. Gomer wants to pay to cover the cost of all the light bulbs he broke. Barney generously tears up the bill, throws it away, and Gomer promptly writes Barney a ticket for littering."

1963–1964

"Briscoe Declares for Aunt Bee"

"Andy always wondered how a Swede from San Francisco and a Jew from Buffalo were able to write *The Andy Griffith Show*. I should have told him that God wanted it that way because I can't explain it otherwise."
—EVERETT GREENBAUM

Episode 96

First Broadcast on October 28, 1963

Written by
Jim Fritzell and Everett Greenbaum

Directed by
Earl Bellamy

Denver Pyle
Guest Stars as
Briscoe Darling

"We were never told by Aaron Ruben that our two previous Darlings scripts were a success," says writer Everett Greenbaum. "We were just tickled not to be fired, and that was all the praise we needed."

Jim and Everett's third Darlings script begins with Andy responding to a call from Nick's cafe. As Andy arrives, Briscoe Darling and the boys are exiting the cafe. When Andy questions Briscoe about the trouble, Briscoe explains he was taking "normal safeguards for eating in a strange place." He just wanted to sit in the kitchen to watch while his meal was cooked. As a result, Nick refused to serve Briscoe and the boys.

"Jim Fritzell was a large, raw-boned man, always worried about his company manners," says Everett. "He was somewhat like Briscoe and served as a model for the character. Although Briscoe's language did not really exist in life, it mysteriously poured out of Jim. I often thought it was because he watched every western movie ever made. He would have loved to have been a cowboy (except for his fear of horses)."

Andy invites Briscoe and the boys to have supper at his house. Before supper, Andy and the boys pass the time playing a bluegrass instrumental.

"The first bluegrass instrumental we performed in the episode was 'Mockin' Banjos,' our arrangement of 'Dueling Banjos,' originally written by Arthur Smith," says Mitch Jayne, the Dillards' bass player. "We retitled it because our version featured the mandolin and banjo, but we wanted to keep the tune recognizable. We were allowed to pick our own music for the episode, unless the script called for a tune familiar to Andy. We selected 'Mockin' Banjos' because it was so fast and showy."

Aunt Bee prepares the supper under Briscoe's watchful eye. Impressed by what he sees, he remarks, "That's the cleanest cooking woman I ever did see."

When the meal is served, the bread is passed first. The boys each take a piece. By the time the plate gets to Briscoe, it is empty. Briscoe yells to Aunt Bee in the kitchen, "Bread!"

The potatoes are passed next. The boys each help themselves. By the time the bowl gets to Briscoe, it too is empty. Briscoe yells, "Taters!"

When the meat is passed, Briscoe gets the dish first. By the time the plate gets to Opie, it is empty. Opie yells, "Meat!"

"The gag that begins the first act's dining scene developed gradually," says Everett. "We started with the line, 'Bread,' then with 'Taters' we began to see what we called a routine develop. A routine is like a little plot. In this case, the payoff was Opie following Briscoe's example and yelling, 'Meat.'"

Aunt Bee eventually finishes in the kitchen and takes a place beside Briscoe at the table. From the supper conversation, Aunt Bee learns that since Charlene got married, Briscoe and the boys have been cooking for themselves. Briscoe says the boys are "just about the worst cooks they is."

"This story was clearer without Charlene, so we did not include her in the script," says Everett. "Her absence freed us to aim all the female attention toward Aunt Bee.

In response to Briscoe's comments about the poor meals he has eaten since Charlene's marriage, Aunt Bee gives him special attention. She serves Briscoe extra butter, more pot roast, and pearly onions. Briscoe takes note that she "specializes on him" and gives Aunt Bee an appreciative wink.

The supper scene's master shot was photographed with the back wall of the dining area removed and the camera positioned in the place normally occupied by the china cabinet. This shot is supplemented with close-ups, especially during the interaction between Briscoe and Aunt Bee.

"To the best of my memory, all extraneous cast members and settings were moved for the close-ups," says Mitch. "The single camera dictated the place the Darling boys occupied in the wide-angle shot."

After supper, the Taylors and the Darlings gather for some entertainment. Accompanied by Andy on guitar, the Darlings play "Doug's Tune." Opie and Andy sing "Old Dan Tucker." After some coaxing, Aunt Bee recites the poem "A Fading Flower of Forgotten Love" by Agnes Ellicott Strong.

"Jim and I usually handed in forty pages per script and let Aaron Ruben figure out what was to be cut out if the episode ran too long," says Everett. "In this case, because of the after-dinner music and poetry recitation, we turned in five pages less.

"Several years ago, a woman wrote to me. She was trying to locate Agnes Ellicott Strong, the author of 'A Fading Flower of Forgotten Love.' This is the poem

Aunt Bee recites. I had to tell her I was Agnes Ellicott Strong. By the way, Briscoe calls the poem 'rose poetry' because a rose is mentioned in it."

Briscoe is awestruck by the recitation. He feels Aunt Bee's heart "talking" to his heart. In response, Briscoe says, "I want you to be my bride."

Andy and Aunt Bee are dumbfounded and immediately protest the declaration. Briscoe tells Aunt Bee, "You get your clothes, and your sewing, and your pot holders packed, and I'll be by for you the first thing in the morning."

When Briscoe realizes that Aunt Bee is upset by his boldness, he decides her negative reaction is because the courtship is too speedy. He says he'll "put on my square wheels so things won't get to rolling too fast."

Later that night, Aunt Bee is awakened by Briscoe's singing. Following a "life-long custom" of his people, Briscoe is serenading his beloved.

"Dean Webb, the Dillards' mandolin player, is the one who supplied 'Low and Lonely' for the serenading scene," says Mitch. "Denver had asked us to find him a suitable courting song. Dean came up with 'Low and Lonely' after finding it in an old Roy Acuff songbook and taught it to Denver. I don't remember any particular difficulties with the serenading scene. It was filmed on an interior set. Because the vocals and music were prerecorded, it was a fairly simple scene."

Aunt Bee is not impressed by Briscoe's caterwauling and slams her bedroom window shut. In response, Briscoe decides "to think this thing out."

The next day, Opie rushes into the courthouse to report that Aunt Bee is missing. When he went home for lunch, Opie found a note that said, "She's with me—Briscoe Darling."

Andy immediately heads to the mountains to get Aunt Bee.

Andy arrives at the Darling cabin and finds Aunt Bee unharmed. Although Aunt Bee and Andy again decline Briscoe's declaration, he refuses to give up.

Andy has an idea. He asks Aunt Bee to step outside so the two can have "a little talk." When they return, Aunt Bee accepts Briscoe's declaration.

Briscoe is overjoyed. When he hugs Aunt Bee, Andy warns him, "Easy, Mr. Darling. You might break her. You're pretty strong, you know."

Andy's comment leads Briscoe to show off his arm muscle. He lifts the bed so his muscle will "bug." Aunt Bee can't see because the light in the cabin isn't very good, so Briscoe and the boys take the bed outside.

This gives Aunt Bee an opening. She says, "As long as we have the bed out here, why don't we clean that part of the floor?"

The floor cleaning turns into a complete house scrubbing. The scrubbing is followed by baths.

Later that evening, Aunt Bee prepares and serves supper. The potatoes are served first. Briscoe is instructed to take one and pass to the left. Briscoe takes his fork, gets one potato, and passes the potato on the fork to the left. He is immediately corrected by Aunt Bee, who tells him to put one on the plate and pass the bowl to the left. Briscoe informs her that they don't do things "that way here." Aunt Bee responds that they "do now," and whacks Briscoe on the back of the hand with a wooden serving spoon.

"Jim and I decided to begin the cabin dinner scene by having Briscoe incorrectly pass a potato around the table," says Everett. "We liked the potato-passing gag so much we used it again with Ernest T. in the episode 'My Fair Ernest T. Bass.'"

When Briscoe places his elbows on the table, Aunt Bee hits his elbow with her spoon and says, "No elbows on the table."

When Briscoe places his napkin under his chin, Aunt Bee removes the napkin with one swift wave of her spoon and says, "Napkins go in the lap."

When Briscoe reaches for the salt, Aunt Bee whacks him on the back of the hand.

"The dinner scene with the wooden spoon was a joy to watch," says Mitch. "My favorite part of the scene was Aunt Bee's work with the spoon, and in particular, her expertise at lifting the napkin from Briscoe's bib and putting it in his lap, which was a good trick that she managed three times for the camera, laying it in exactly the same place each time. The spoon had a thick Styrofoam pad, cut to spoon shape, and she handled that thing like a baton. It hurt to watch her whack Briscoe with it, and it was always hard not to laugh. But we usually learned to get that out of our systems when we rehearsed the scene, so we could play the filming as solemn as owls."

Aunt Bee's spoon gets the best of Briscoe. He jumps up from the table and calls off the declaration, saying, "This has gone just far enough. I can take some manners, and I can take some cleaning up, and I can take a bossy mouth, but I ain't about to be beat to death with no spoon."

In the epilogue, Andy and Aunt Bee are preparing to return to Mayberry. Aunt Bee calls Briscoe over to the car, kisses him on the cheek, and thanks him for "wanting" her. Briscoe appreciates the gesture and replies, "Well, Miss Bee, your kisses are awful nice and highly valuable, but to be perfectly honest with you, it just ain't worth the pain."

"Earl Bellamy directed this episode instead of Bob Sweeney," says Mitch. "As far as I could see, Earl directed with the same level of competence that all directors of *TAGS* seemed to assume when they did that show. It was almost as if Mayberry was larger than the sum of its parts. The director was merely moving pieces around to get a nice camera angle, while the place itself set the movements and happenings. I know this sounds dumb, and probably is, but I can't imagine a directing talent that wouldn't be able to do a good job of holding the magic of something that Bob Sweeney and Andy Griffith had already captured and frozen in time."

"Gomer the House Guest"

ANDY: Do you know anything about cutting meat?
GOMER: Do you think they'll ask me that?
—Dialogue after Gomer tells Andy he is applying for
   an experienced butcher position

Episode 97

First Broadcast on
November 4, 1963

Written by
**Jim Fritzell and
Everett Greenbaum**

Directed by
Earl Bellamy

"The structure of this script could have resulted in a very ordinary sitcom," says writer Everett Greenbaum. "But we hoped to avoid that flavor by featuring Gomer, who was a fresh new face on the small screen."

"Gomer the House Guest" begins as Andy pulls up to the gas pumps at Wally's Service Station. Gomer, who is waiting on Jake, tells Andy that he will get to him "in a couple of shakes." Since Andy is in no hurry, he gets a bottle of pop and listens as Gomer tells about a recent fishing trip with "Birdy" Blush. Gomer tells how he caught a fish after baiting his hook "with a dab of Limburger cheese and a slice of onion." He goes on to say he dropped his hook at the base of Lover's Leap Rock and relates the legend behind the naming of the rock. Legend has it that "a Confederate colonel plunged to his everlasting calling there after being spurned by a Yankee woman."

"'In a couple of shakes' was a very popular phrase in the time of my childhood, and it seemed right for Gomer," says Everett. "We then had Gomer tell his 'Birdy Blush' story in detail to get the point across that he was in no hurry to wait on the station's customers. The story and its details, such as using Limburger cheese and onion to catch a trout and the legend of Lover's Leap Rock, came about from letting our imaginations roam and using things resting in our subconscious."

Another customer drives up as Gomer tells the story. This customer gets "testy" because of the wait. When Wally, the station owner, arrives, he notices the testy customer and tells Gomer to finish up.

Gomer continues to talk with Jake. He explains that the trouble Jake was having with his car was caused by corrosion on his battery terminals. Gomer took soda pop and "cleared it right up."

"Soda pop will, in fact, clear up corrosion," says Everett. "I was a mechanic in my younger years. I later attended MIT for three years but flunked out. (The Boston theaters and the airport were too tempting for me.) At the age of twenty, I received a patent for an automatic-flush rivet countersink, which I worked out when I was a riveter at Bell Aircraft. The countersink was made by a company in Boston who lost their shirts. By that time I was in naval pilot training. All of this is to explain how I knew about soda on the battery terminals. Not to brag, because I can't do any sports, and I don't understand anything about business."

The testy customer angrily drives away. Wally is furious and warns Gomer that he had "better start snapping to."

Gomer eventually waits on Andy and begins to retell the Birdy Brush story. Another customer drives up to the gas pumps, but Gomer is in no hurry and continues the story.

Later that day, Opie stops by the courthouse to collect his allowance. Andy compliments Opie on not "having to be reminded one time to do your chores." Opie replies that he didn't have to be reminded because he wrote his chores on his wrist.

"As a naval pilot trainer, I learned that World War II pilots often wrote important time settings, radio frequencies, headings, and altitudes on their wrists," says Everett. "This knowledge inspired the idea to have Opie remember his chores by writing them on his wrist."

As Opie leaves, Gomer enters. He tells Andy that he's been fired. His firing also means that Gomer had to give up the room he had in the back of the station, so he doesn't have anywhere to sleep. Gomer asks Andy if he can sleep in a cell until he "can settle on my feet someplace." At this point, Andy invites Gomer to stay at his house, and Gomer accepts.

That evening after supper, the Taylors and Gomer gather around the television to watch the *Shep and Ralph Show*. Gomer, who sits on the floor with his legs extended beneath the coffee table, talks throughout the program.

"Gomer's floor posture fit the character perfectly," says Everett. "The idea to sit on the floor must have come up on the set, because it was not included in our script."

After the program, the Taylors go to bed. Gomer, however, *sits up a spell*. Before the family retires, Gomer asks if he can do some chores to pay for his board. Although Andy feels it isn't necessary, Gomer insists.

Later that night, Gomer decides to saw some firewood. Awakened by the noise, Andy asks him to stop.

A few hours later, Gomer gets out Andy's vacuum cleaner. He notices the toggle switch is loose, tightens it, and accidentally locks the switch to on. The noise again wakes the Taylors.

Andy encourages Gomer to go to bed. Gomer agrees, even though he is not really tired.

Gomer, however, does not go to bed immediately. He walks loudly across the floor, slams the bathroom door, gargles, and sings "No Account Mule" as he looks at himself in the mirror.

Due to lack of sleep, Andy can't concentrate on his work the next day. When he leans back in his chair to take a short nap, he is interrupted by Gomer. When Andy explains to Gomer that he couldn't sleep last night due to all the racket, Gomer promises to be "quieter tonight."

That night, Andy turns off the house's lights before going upstairs to bed. The scene is interestingly photographed. Director Earl Bellamy positions the camera outside the Taylor house. Andy is shown in silhouette against the closed curtains. The camera then pans left across the front porch and through the closed front door as it follows Andy up the stairs. Positioning the camera outside the house presents the scene in a unique and interesting way.

This night, Gomer also goes to bed. He is quietly reading a comic book when the quiet is interrupted by one of Gomer's former customers. The man parks his car outside Andy's house and revs the engine so Gomer can analyze its problem. Gomer diagnoses the problem immediately and advises the man to pull out his choke.

Gomer goes back to his reading but is interrupted by a second customer who stops by with squeaky shocks.

The next morning, the Taylors are all irritable because no one has had enough sleep. Andy decides to ask Gomer to leave.

Gomer enters the kitchen enthusiastically, unaware that he has caused the Taylors a second night of sleeplessness. Aware of Gomer's good mood and innocence, Andy puts off asking him to leave.

Later in the day, Andy stops by Wally's Service Station. Wally tells Andy that he is "the first customer in here all day."

When Andy returns home, he finds his driveway overflowing with "folks needing some repairs." Andy orders everyone into their cars. Accompanied by Gomer, Andy leads everyone to Wally's.

Back at the station, the customers huddle around Gomer as he retells the Birdy Blush story. As Gomer tells the story, Andy says to Wally, "See that fellow there?" Wally answers, "Yeah, that's Gomer." Andy replies, "That's more than Gomer. That's your business." After Wally thinks the situation over, he rehires Gomer "with pleasure."

"Jim and I hoped no one would notice Gomer's varying mechanical ability between 'Man in a Hurry' and this show." says Everett. "In the earlier episode he knows nothing about engines, only how to pump gas. The resolution to losing his job depended upon Gomer's mechanical expertise and his likable personality, so we increased Gomer's mechanical skills to fit the story. We felt we could get by with the change because we thought the audience would have forgotten the earlier show by the time this story aired."

Some viewers think the conclusion of the second act in which Andy leads everyone back to Wally's is not well developed. "The solution was very, very important in comedy writing," says Everett. "Sometimes a perfectly good story had to be discarded because we couldn't think of a credible solution. This was nearly the case with this script. Even after much thought, the solution we came up with arrives too quickly and flaws the story."

"The Haunted House"

Episode 98

First Broadcast on
October 7, 1963

Written by
Harvey Bullock

Directed by
Earl Bellamy

"I think the cast enjoyed filming this episode because it had the hint of special effects, a bit of suspense, and a different setting than most other stories."
—HARVEY BULLOCK

"The Haunted House" begins with Opie and a friend walking down the road that runs in front of the deserted Rimshaw house. Opie is carrying a baseball bat, and his friend has a baseball and glove. The two are discussing Whitey Ford's pitching and Mickey Mantle's hitting. Opie's friend, who imitates Whitey Ford, gets ready to pitch to Opie, who imitates Mickey Mantle. Before the pitch is thrown, Opie uses the bat to knock the dirt off his tennis shoes.

"The scene in which Opie knocks the dirt off his shoes before hitting the ball was scripted," says writer Harvey Bullock. "This action grew out of the fact that young fans adopt the mannerisms of their heroes and emulate anything their favorite players do—even if their shoes have no cleats."

Opie hits the baseball through the window in the front door of the Rimshaw house. The boys are reluctant to retrieve the ball because they fear the house is haunted. Opie assures his friend that there won't be any "spooks" in the daytime. As the boys slowly approach the house, they hear a wail coming from within and run away.

"I decided to write this script because haunted houses are fixtures in small towns, and ghosts and spooks catch an audience's attention," says Harvey. "Stark fear oddly can be comic if the audience feels nothing really fearful will happen.

"When I wrote the script, I did not have a Halloween broadcast date in mind and never bothered to suggest it. Haunted-house stories can be aired anytime. A few others, like the wonderful Christmas story that features Ben Weaver, are better screened during the holidays. Aaron Ruben did the scheduling, shifting scripts to fit actors' availability and also to evenly distribute shows starring specific cast members."

Meanwhile at the courthouse, Andy is releasing Otis. Barney enters as Otis is unlocking his cell. Barney doesn't think Otis is sober yet, so he suggests they give him a sobriety test. Barney steps into the back room and returns with a rope. He reasons that if Otis is "steady enough to jump rope, he's steady enough to be turned loose."

Otis is reluctant to take Barney's sobriety test. Barney agrees to forgo the test if Otis will tell where he has been getting his moonshine, but Otis refuses.

Barney has Otis and Andy turn the rope as he demonstrates the test. As he jumps the rope, Barney recites, "Call for the doctor. Call for the nurse. Call for the lady with the alligator purse."

After Barney's demonstration, Otis prepares to jump into the turning rope. As he watches the rope carefully, he recites an improvised rhyme, "Slow it down and let me in, or I'll go out and get some gin." This infuriates Barney.

"The idea of Barney giving Otis the rope-jumping sobriety test was the result of going through the script backwards and forwards and rewriting over and over," says Harvey. "The jump-rope idea eventually came to mind. It seemed funny and could be used in the epilogue. I got the notion from my wife's Girl Scout troop, which met in our garage and played with jump ropes after their meetings. The rhyming verses the girls recited while jumping were hilarious. I especially liked 'Call for the doctor.' I could envision Barney doing that chant and felt it was a perfect fit. Having Otis do his own verse seemed like a natural topper."

At this point, Opie and his friend burst into the courthouse. They tell Andy about hitting the baseball into the Rimshaw house and the ghostly sounds they heard. Andy is surprised that "great big boys like you" would be talking about ghosts. He explains that the sound was "probably just the wind blowing." Barney agrees and adds, "There's nothing to fear but fear itself."

Andy tells the boys to stay away from the Rimshaw house because it's not safe. He promises to get the baseball and tells the boys to "run along."

After the boys leave, Barney tells Andy that he should have sent the boys back to the Rimshaw house to get the ball. He says, "That would cure them of the squidgets."

"I don't know where *squidgets* originated," says Harvey. "I suspect it was just a word I made up that sounded right coming from Barney."

When Andy suggests that Barney go to the Rimshaw house and get the ball for the boys, Barney is hesitant. He thinks the situation over and then realizes that he can't leave because he has to finish administering Otis's sobriety test.

When Andy asks Barney if he's "shying away from going to the Rimshaw place," Barney responds angrily that he's going.

Gomer enters to deliver a car battery as Barney walks toward the door, so Barney invites Gomer to "go for a little ride." Gomer agrees.

Gomer is surprised when Barney parks the squad car in front of the Rimshaw house. Barney sends Gomer inside to retrieve the ball. As Gomer starts toward the house, he stops and asks Barney if he's coming. Barney stalls by saying he has to check the timing on the engine. When Gomer volunteers to check the engine, Barney replies, "I'll check the engine. I said it first."

"Barney's 'I'll check the engine' is a variation of a formula line for spooky stories where the self-styled brave man uses outrageous excuses not to tangle with possible ghosts," says Harvey. "When Gomer contests the order, Barney says, 'I said it first.' Again, a timeless recognizable phrase with children, and hence a good line for Barney."

Gomer continues to balk at going into the Rimshaw house alone, so Barney reluctantly agrees to go with him. The two slowly approach the house. As Barney opens the door, a moan is heard coming from inside the house. Barney and Gomer make a hasty retreat.

Barney bursts into the courthouse and tells Andy, "When Old Man Rimshaw died, he said he didn't want that place disturbed, and I think we ought to respect the wishes of the dear departed." Andy asks Barney about his "nothing to fear but fear itself" speech. Barney answers, "Well, that's exactly what I got—fear itself."

"Reading this script for the first time in thirty-some years, one small line doesn't seem right," says Harvey. "Barney's 'Well, that's exactly what I got—fear itself.' This open admission by Barney that he's afraid after he's gone to great lengths to conceal it doesn't seem consistent. I probably fell in love with Franklin Roosevelt's famous line and didn't realize it went somewhat counter to the character and scene."

Otis is still at the courthouse. He agrees with Barney's suggestion to stay away from the Rimshaw place. Otis says that he has heard that "the walls move, pictures with eyes follow you all around the room, and axes float in the air."

Andy suggests that he, Barney, and Gomer go over to the Rimshaw house to get the baseball.

After they retrieve the ball, Andy suggests they look around a bit. Andy walks to the rear of the house while Gomer and Barney remain in the front room.

When Andy returns, he notices that the wallpaper beside the fireplace is torn. He examines the tear and discovers that the wall around the tear is warm.

Barney looks above the fireplace and sees a portrait of Old Man Rimshaw. According to local legends, Rimshaw put chains on his hired man and killed him with an ax. Barney then notices that the "eyes in the painting are staring at us."

The script directions for Old Man Rimshaw's portrait were as follows: *On the wall adjacent to the fireplace hangs a commanding, forbidding portrait of a man. The features are sinister, the picture weird, the eyes strangely alive.*

"I had no concern about any problems with the props when writing the ghost scenes," says Harvey. "I knew that Aaron Ruben could tone down the effects if the props became too complicated or costly."

Barney brings Rimshaw's moving eyes to Andy's attention and suggests they leave. By this time the eyes have changed, so Andy doesn't see anything strange about the portrait. He suggests that it is probably just the way the light strikes the portrait.

Andy feels that perhaps some tramps are staying in the house and decides to look upstairs. Barney and Gomer check the cellar.

As the two proceed toward the cellar, they notice the eyes in the portrait are following them again. Barney consoles Gomer by saying, "It's just the lighting, like Andy said."

They open the cellar door and see an ax attached to the inside of the door. Gomer now consoles Barney by suggesting that the ax is "probably just the lighting."

"The running gag is a part of the writer's comedy kit, but it required careful handling so it wouldn't be just repetitive and dull," says Harvey. "The repetition of 'It's just the lighting, like Andy said' seemed to work because it progressed. The line gave comfort and was used by Barney and Gomer as they clung to the hope that it was the light."

Andy returns, notices the ax, and asks if everything is all right. Barney answers, "Just fine, knock on wood." When Barney knocks on the wall, three knocks answer! Andy knocks three times on the fireplace mantel, and three knocks reply! In a loud voice, Andy says, "You're right. This is no place for us. Let's get out of here."

Barney and Gomer retreat out the front door.

After the room is cleared, Otis and Big Jack Anderson, a local moonshiner, emerge from their hiding place. Big Jack is ecstatic. He believes he's found a place to run his still for twenty years.

Big Jack and Otis celebrate with a "snort." After the drink, Otis looks up and sees an ax floating in the air. Then what appear to be footsteps are heard coming down the stairs.

"Andy starts the hint to the audience that he's on to something by saying in an extra-loud voice, 'Let's get outta here!'" says Harvey. "Andy's scheme to uncover the truth continues with the floating ax and the baseball bouncing down the stairs. I realized that some of the audience may not have caught on to Andy's discovery and ruse yet, so I had Big Jack and Otis come out of the paneling to explain everything."

Meanwhile, Barney and Gomer realize that Andy is not with them. Barney believes Andy is still inside and courageously goes to get him.

"The audience knows about Otis and the moonshiner's presence in the house before Barney," says Harvey. "It was absolutely vital that Barney swallow his fear and go in the house to rescue Andy. He had avoided any direct contact with the spooks, but when Andy might need him, Barney, shaky knees and all, will respond. It was important for Barney to overcome his fear because I didn't want him to be a nondimensional figure who goes through the whole story just being scared."

After seeing the floating ax and hearing the footsteps, Big Jack and Otis make a fearful retreat out the front door. As Barney enters the house from the back, he sees the floating ax and the moving eyes of Old Man Rimshaw's portrait and almost faints. Andy calls out, "Barney, wait. It's okay, it's me."

"Barney does get a bit faint when he sees the floating ax, but I would never have him actually faint," says Harvey. "It's a matter of degree, but if Barney really fainted it would be much too broad and unbelievable. Barney is affected by the happenings but not to the nth degree. Besides, I wanted Barney conscious. I needed his lines and presence to make the remainder of the scene work."

Andy pulls down the ax that he strung to the ceiling and tells Barney they now have to bust up a still. Barney then takes the stance that he thought it was "something along them very lines." The two then head toward the cellar to bust up the Rimshaw "spirits."

"Ernest T. Bass Joins the Army"

Episode 99

First Broadcast on
October 14, 1963

Written by
**Jim Fritzell and
Everett Greenbaum**

Directed by
Richard Crenna

Howard Morris
Returns as
Ernest T. Bass

"My late brother worked for a movie-titles producer named Saul Bass. On *Mr. Peepers*, Jim and I called the football coach Frank T. Whip, and that's where the T came from. Ernest had the proper rhythm."
—EVERETT GREENBAUM

"Ernest T. Bass Joins the Army" begins with Andy and Barney sitting in the squad car. As the townspeople walk by, Andy and Barney discuss each one. It seems the doctor made Mrs. McKnight lose weight because "her ankles were too skinny to hold up all that heft." Mrs. Devereaux "is just as ugly as homemade soap." Cecil Gurney "has two sets of false teeth." When Barney sees Viola Slat walking toward them, he drives away because she "is the biggest gossip in this town. Once she gets started, you never hear the end of it."

"My script does not open with Andy and Barney gossiping about the towns-folk," says writer Everett Greenbaum. "The dialogue about Mrs. McKnight, Viola Slat, and the others must have been written by either Andy or Aaron."

As Barney drives down the street, he and Andy see a group of men scuffling on the sidewalk. The two break up the scuffle and discover Ernest T. Bass at its center. Ernest T. caused the disturbance when he tried to break into the "soldiering" line of potential enlistees waiting outside the army recruitment office.

Ernest T. tells Andy he wants to "soldier." Andy suggests that Ernest T. go on home because the army's "no place for you." An army sergeant who has come outside to see what the ruckus is all about encourages Ernest T. to stay. He announces that they will take all able-bodied men.

Before leaving, Andy and Barney warn the sergeant about Ernest T. Andy believes the sergeant would make a mistake to take him, while Barney simply says, "He's a nut."

"I don't remember how we came about doing this one," says Everett. "We knew that Andy and Aaron Ruben loved Howard Morris as Ernest T., so we knew a funny storyline featuring him was likely to be approved.

"Andy informs Ernest T. that he is in the soldiering line. *Soldiering* was a real word used in England. I thought it sounded right for Mayberry."

Ernest T. stays in the soldiering line and eventually gets his physical examination. The doctor begins the exam by probing inside Ernest T.'s mouth with a stick. Ernest T. tells him that the inside of his mouth will be nicer after he gets his gold tooth. Ernest T. explains that he plans to knock out his three front teeth and "put the gold one right in the center—leave a space on each side." He explains that it will stand out better that way, "especially when I'm dancing."

The doctor tests Ernest T.'s hearing by having him repeat numbers. The doctor says a number and slowly walks away as he says the other numbers. The doctor is unaware that Ernest T. is following right behind. The sergeant informs Ernest T. that he is supposed to remain standing where he was. Ernest T. tells the doctor that if he did that, he might not hear him.

"We realized that lots of funny physical-examination scenes had been done previously in movies and on TV, but we decided to write an examination scene because we knew that Ernest T. would bring a wildness to it that had not been seen before," says Everett.

The sergeant has seen enough. He tells Ernest T., "Boy, was that sheriff ever right about you. Okay, buddy, out. We're turning you down."

Ernest T. becomes angry when he realizes he's "not going to get my uniform" and swears revenge on everyone—especially Andy.

After lunch, Andy and Barney return from the diner and discuss the eighty-cent meal they have just finished—"three Vienna sausages, heavy on the tomato purée, a slice of bread, and a pat of butter on a paper dish." During the conversation, Andy and Barney discover that they both left Olive, their waitress, a quarter tip. Barney suggests that he go back to the diner and put his hat down on one of the quarters to retrieve it.

"Every morning for thirty years I had to listen to Jim tell me what he had for dinner the night before," says Everett. "The idea to have Barney and Andy discuss their meal was inspired by this. Jim and I also enjoyed describing awful meals and jumped at the chance to work it into the script.

"Barney's concern about the abundant tip grew out of our memories of when having a quarter was like owning a treasure. So, the Depression played its part in *The Griffith Show*."

The sergeant enters and warns Andy about Ernest T.'s sworn revenge. Moments later the front window of the courthouse is shattered.

Andy, Barney, and the sergeant step outside and see Ernest T. retreating down the street. Referring to Ernest T., Barney again comments, "He's a nut."

"Sometimes we would repeat a short sentence throughout a script," says Everett. "It usually had a humorous effect and was called a reprise. Barney's 'He's a nut!' description of Ernest T. is an example of this, and we used it several times for a laugh."

Later that day, Andy gets several telephone calls about broken windows. From the calls, he realizes Ernest T. is coming their way. Andy goes to the back and Barney goes to the front to wait for Ernest T.

When Ernest T. meets Barney in front of the office, he says, "If I'd a seen you coming, I'd knowed what to do. I'd a-riz both arms, and I'd a-wove at you." Barney then orders Ernest T. to "stand still." Ernest T. replies, "If a duck stands still, you can catch him by the bill."

"Ernest T.'s rhyme, 'If a duck stands still, you can catch him by the bill,' is in my script, but 'If I'd seen you coming' isn't," says Everett. "Howard Morris made up some of the rhymes, and the second one was his creation."

Andy quietly sneaks up behind Ernest T. while he is taunting Barney. After a struggle, Andy locks Ernest T. in a cell.

The next morning, Barney has breakfast at the diner. The customer sitting beside him at the counter is reading a newspaper. Barney asks the fellow to pass the sugar. As the man lowers the newspaper, Barney discovers that it is Ernest T. Bass. Barney marches Ernest T. back to the courthouse and locks him in the cell.

Barney calls Andy to ask if he let Ernest T. out of the cell to get breakfast. Andy says he did not. Barney then goes to pick up Andy.

While Barney is away, Ernest T. escapes again. Andy and Barney chase Ernest T. all over town but are unable to recapture him. Andy spots the deliverymen bringing a new window for the courthouse. Andy and Barney follow the two men delivering the window, well aware that if Ernest T. is still in town, he won't be able to pass up the opportunity to break the new window.

As the two men near the courthouse, Ernest T. jumps from behind a storefront with a rock in hand. Barney orders Ernest T. to stand back and says, "Now you drop that rock, and you get over here." Emphasizing the command with a backward gesture of his pistol, Barney shatters the new window.

The gesture is the end result of the serious thought given to how Barney would break the window in a natural and credible way. "Barney's breaking the new window was another addition to our script," says Everett. "It's a very good idea and was either added in a rewrite or worked out on the stage during rehearsals."

As the episode continues, Ernest T. takes off down the street. His route leads Andy and Barney back to the courthouse. The two enter and find Ernest T. relaxing on his cell bunk.

The fact that Ernest T. can get in and out of the locked cell is making Andy and Barney nervous and angry. Ernest T. tells Andy that he will continue to escape until Andy gets the army to give him a uniform. When Andy tells Ernest T. that it won't work if he joins the army, Ernest T. reveals that he had no intention of joining the army. He just wanted a uniform for "girls and love." He had noticed how the girls "flit around Jelsick Sturman when he come back home with his uniform. 'Jelsick, walk with me. Jelsick, dance with me. Jelsick, kiss my mouth.'"

"By this time we had learned what Howie Morris could do with certain words, so we tried to find them," says Everett. "The name 'Jelsick Sturman' and the line 'Kiss my mouth' contained some great sounding words and were perfect for Howie's unique pronunciation."

Pondering Ernest T.'s problem out loud, Andy wonders where they could find a small-size uniform. When he looks at Barney, Barney protests that he had his uniform made in Raleigh and that it's "genuine whiplash cord."

A short time later, Ernest T. exits the courthouse proudly wearing a uniform. He is followed by Andy. As Ernest T. marches away, Barney emerges dressed in a raincoat and white panama hat. He watches Ernest T. depart and says, "There goes a happy nut."

"The idea for Barney's 'genuine whiplash cord' uniform came from Jim's army life," says Everett. "After giving the uniform to Ernest T., we put Barney in a raincoat. The white hat that he wears in the filmed episode was added on the stage during rehearsals."

In the epilogue, Barney is searching Ernest T.'s cell. He finds a fork under the mattress and calls Andy into the cell. Barney slams the cell door shut, sticks the fork into the lock to demonstrate how Ernest T. unlocked the door, and turns the fork—nothing happens. Andy and Barney are now locked inside. The keys are in the filing cabinet. When Andy asks, "What do you suggest we do now?" Barney answers by yelling, "Help!"

"We always thought the audience loved to see 'here we go again' epilogues, so we concluded this script with the boys locking themselves in the jail cell," says Everett. "Aaron never asked us to repeat a gag, like this one, which had been used successfully in previous episodes. I think he was always hoping we'd write a new one."

"Opie the Birdman"

Episode 101

First Broadcast on
September 30, 1963

Written by
Harvey Bullock

Directed by
Richard Crenna

"The script was a gem from the start."
—AARON RUBEN

Wynken, Blynken & Nod one night
Sailed off in a wooden shoe
Sailed on a river of crystal light—
Into a sea of dew.
—EUGENE FIELD

"'Opie the Birdman' is one of my favorites," says writer Harvey Bullock. "Despite that, my memories about its origin are unclear. I'm uncertain whether or not the story originated at *The Griffith Show* seminars in which a half-dozen writers would meet two or three days in the offseason with Aaron Ruben, Sheldon Leonard, and, sometimes, Andy to collectively pitch story ideas. Or it may have been an individual story idea I pitched to Aaron. However, I know it was one of Aaron's favorites, and he scheduled it to open one season."

The episode begins with Barney tutoring Opie in the history and shooting technique of slingshots. In his younger days, Barney asserts that he was "a pretty good shot." He could perform numerous tricks—"Over the Mountain," "Behind the Barn," "Under the Bridge"—but his best shot was the "Tail Gunner." Barney's lecture concludes with a visual demonstration. Against Andy's protests, he performs the "Tail Gunner" and accidentally breaks the glass in the bookcase.

"Someone off camera threw a stone, or perhaps even used a slingshot, to break the bookcase on cue," explains producer Aaron Ruben.

Andy warns Opie to be careful with the slingshot. In his front yard, Opie shoots into a tree and accidentally kills a bird. The bird falls to the ground. Opie walks over to the bird, gently picks it up, and begs it "to fly away." When there is no response, Opie becomes upset. He drops the bird and runs into the house.

On the way into the house that evening, Andy stops to pick up the newspaper

and notices the dead bird. He hears chirping overhead, looks up, and sees a nest containing baby birds.

Opie has no appetite at supper. During the meal, Andy says to Aunt Bee, "Next time you see Mrs. Snyder, tell her to keep her cat at home. That thing killed one of our songbirds today." Aunt Bee responds that it couldn't, because Mrs. Snyder is visiting her sister and took her cat with her. Opie immediately gets up from the table and runs upstairs. Andy now realizes what happened to the bird.

One of the strengths of *TAGS* was its attention to realistic detail. During the supper scene, numerous cooked foods (sweet potatoes, rolls, etc.) are visible.

"The property department with its own kitchen, complete with pantry, stove, and refrigerator, usually prepared the food," says Aaron. "Nothing was ever thrown away. After the scene was over and the food was no longer needed, there were plenty of volunteers to polish off the leftovers."

Andy enters Opie's bedroom and finds Opie on his bed. Opie admits that he killed the bird and gives his slingshot to Andy. When Opie says he's sorry, Andy replies that "sorry" won't bring the bird back: "*Sorry* is not the magic word that makes everything right again."

Opie asks if he is going to get a whipping. Instead, Andy walks to the window and raises it. The chirping of baby birds fills the room. Andy says, "That's those young birds chirping for their mama who's never coming back. You just listen to that for a while." Andy then walks out.

One interesting aspect of the background in this scene comes when Andy opens the window. The curtains fluttering in the breeze add a realistic touch. This was an interior studio set, and an off-camera wind machine was used to make the curtains move.

"During production I realized that 'Opie the Birdman' was special because it had so many outstanding elements: death, guilt, redemption, humor, and, most importantly, the wise and judicious way Andy handled the situation—sparing the rod but teaching a child how to solve his own problems," says Aaron.

"The fact that Andy does not whip Opie is the most vital treatment of the story," concurs Harvey. "Physical punishment would have reduced the situation to a trite, single-dimension, two-party standoff, an unequal confrontation between angry adult and guilty boy. It is far more interesting that Opie has to be his own punisher while Andy is the enlightener."

The next morning, Opie is up early. Andy walks onto the front porch and finds Opie fixing breakfast for the little birds. Opie has decided that he is going to feed them since it is his fault that their mother won't be coming back. Opie names the three birds Winkin, Blinkin, and Nod.

"A writer's mind is like a huge, cluttered attic," says Harvey. "If you seek to write, become an eclectic reader to help stuff your attic with word toys. Not necessarily formal knowledge but all sorts of neat nonsense.

"The names for the motherless songbirds, Winkin, Blinkin, and Nod, were inspired by a prowl through the attic. Seeking a fun-named threesome, those names popped into mind. I liked the sound and rhyme, so in they went—by the way, Wynken and Blynken are misspelled in the script. The names come from a lullaby poem by Eugene Field."

A few days later, Mrs. Snyder returns from visiting her sister. During breakfast, Mrs. Snyder's cat cries out. Andy, Opie, Barney (who has stopped by to pick up Andy), and Aunt Bee realize that the cat may be attacking the birds and rush outdoors.

The birds are put in a cage for safety and placed on the Taylor front porch. After they admire the birds in their new cage, Andy warns Opie that he will soon have to let them go.

A few weeks later, Barney stops by to pick up Andy and give Opie a lift to school. While Opie is upstairs getting his books, Barney mentions how much the birds are growing. Andy tells Barney that "we both know them birds are big enough to be off on their own."

Andy decides to talk with Opie about the birds when he comes down. When Andy mentions that the birds have been flopping around in their cage, Opie answers that "maybe we should get a larger cage. They need a bigger place." Andy agrees, but Opie suddenly realizes Andy is referring to turning the birds loose. Opie feels he "just can't." Andy reminds Opie that he took over for the bird's ma, and she would have let them go "to be free like they was intended to be."

Opie knows what he must do. He removes the cage from its stand and walks to the front yard. One by one he sets his birds free.

The script directions following the release were as follows: *Opie pauses, looks up at the trees. Cut to tree—shooting over Opie and Andy. High lift shot. The chorus of songbirds is heard.*

"It seemed dramatically fulfilling to end the scene with a high lift shot," explains Harvey. "I indicated the camera angle because it was ultraimportant to the action. In rereading the ending scene, I see my script called for Barney and Aunt Bee to appear at the screen door. In the filmed scene they were not used—a wise decision, probably made by the director."

In the epilogue, Andy is talking on the telephone. He tells Otis that Otis forgot his pocket transistor radio. Andy says he will keep it until Otis comes back. Andy places the radio in the top drawer of his desk.

Barney enters with a fishbowl. He has bought Opie some goldfish. Andy asks Barney if fish talk to one another. Barney answers, "Of course they do. They've made recordings of fish talking to one another down on the bottom of the ocean." Andy secretly opens the desk drawer and turns on Otis's radio.

As Barney leans over the bowl to feed the fish, he hears voices. He asks Andy if he hears talking and proudly nods that his statement is confirmed. At that point, Andy pulls the radio out of the drawer and says he'll turn it off if it "bothers you."

"The epilogue was shot as a continuous scene [two minutes in duration] because there were no dramatic moments that needed highlighting, no need for close-ups for reactions," says Aaron. "It was just a closing joke and needed no stops or interruptions."

The epilogue is somewhat flawed by an omission. It was probably shortened because the episode was running too long. After hearing a voice coming from the direction of the fishbowl, Barney was to say, "I gotta get away. I've been under strain." This dialogue implies that Barney questions what he is hearing. The dialogue is omitted, however, from the filmed scene, and it hurts the character. Barney would not unquestioningly believe that fish communicate in human voices.

Overlooking this minor weakness, "Opie the Birdman" is an exceptional *TAGS* episode. There is a magical quality to it that leaves the viewer with the feeling that the writer, production crew, and actors got everything exactly right.

"From the first, I felt the story was solid, and watching it grow was delightful," says Harvey. "And it typed fast, which is usually an indication the script flows well.

"Sometimes words or expressions just spring into existence on their own, totally unbidden. It's one of the most awesome and joyous experiences in writing when the paper suddenly comes to life. It seems to push you aside and, for a brief moment, the story takes over and literally writes itself.

"I have one keen memory of this. I was completing the final scene in which Andy and Opie go out in the front yard to release the young birds Opie has raised. I was typing away. I got them outside, and Opie released the birds. Suddenly, I stopped, unsure of exactly what to say. But the typewriter kept going. I looked in amazement at the words being typed out. I was only a spectator; the story was writing itself."

The following words were typed on the paper:

Opie looks upward. Then he turns and looks at the empty cage, its door open.

OPIE: (wistfully) Cage sure looks awful empty, don't it, Pa?
ANDY: Yes, son, it does. But don't the trees seem nice and full.

"I never rewrote even a comma," says Harvey. "It went right into production just like it was. It was without doubt the best ending of any of the shows I did, and I'd gladly give proper credit to the real writer—if I only knew who he was!"

"Up in Barney's Room"

"I enjoyed directing *The Griffith Show*. The scripts were terrific, and the cast was great. We had a good time, and I think it shows."—~~JEFFREY HAYDEN~~

"I'd been directing *The Donna Reed Show* for three consecutive seasons when I received a call from Aaron Ruben," says Jeffrey Hayden. "Bob Sweeney had left, and Aaron needed someone to direct. I directed eight episodes and left at the end of the season to work on one-hour dramas.

"The atmosphere on *The Griffith Show* was the best. Everyone was very loose and pleasant, which was very conducive to good work. There were a lot of laughs in between the hard work of rehearsing and shooting the script."

"Up in Barney's Room" begins with Barney outside the Mendlebright Park Apartments. He has been grocery shopping, but the sign outside the apartments states "No Cooking." Barney looks around to be sure the coast is clear. He hides his groceries in his pockets and under his shirt.

Inside the house, Mrs. Mendlebright is talking to Mr. Fields. Mr. Fields has recently moved to Mayberry and is pleading with Mrs. Mendlebright to give him a room. According to Fields, part of the appeal of the Mendlebright apartments is Mrs. Mendlebright herself because she is nice.

Barney enters the house and is stopped by Mrs. Mendlebright. She introduces Barney to Mr. Fields. When Barney shakes Fields's hand, the handshake causes a bottle of milk, which Barney has hidden under his shirt, to slip. As Barney adjusts ~~the bottle, Mrs. Mendlebright asks if something is wrong with his back. Barney~~ answers, "It's just that dampness and humidity kinda work on my disks sometimes." Mrs. Mendlebright is concerned and tells Barney to go lie down awhile.

"~~Barney's land~~lady, ~~Mrs. Mendlebright~~, was based on my landlady in a rooming house in New York," says writ~~er Everett Greenba~~um. "Enid Markey was a perfect ~~Mrs. Mendlebright.~~ By the ~~way,~~ in sil~~ent mo~~vies she was the first Jane in a *Tarzan* film."

Barney goes to his room, removes his groceries from his clothing, sets a hot plate on Mrs. Mendlebright's dresser, and prepares a pot of chili. When Andy

Episode 104

First Broadcast on December 2, 1963

Written by
Jim Fritzell and Everett Greenbaum

Directed by
Jeffrey Hayden

Enid Markey
Guest Stars as
Mrs. Mendlebright

drops by to bring Barney's paycheck, Barney offers Andy a little chili and a glass of sweet cider. Andy declines the offer.

The master shot of Barney's room is photographed with the camera positioned behind Mrs. Mendlebright's dresser. "I would roughly work out the master shot and the other camera angles at home the night before a scene was shot," says Jeffrey Hayden. "These would then be adjusted and readjusted after rehearsing the scene with the actors."

Andy looks around Barney's room and notices that Barney has made a lot of changes since Andy's last visit. Barney proudly points out that he has "picked the room right up" with a "set of bound copies of *True Blue Detective* magazine that go back to 1959." Barney's walls are decorated with his old Mayberry High School pennant and framed copies of newspaper clippings.

"The appearance of Barney's room was important in bringing the script to life," says Everett. "Several items were added to our description of the room's decor. In my copy of the script, I don't have the magazines. In place of the bound volumes, we had a hunk of driftwood, which Barney considers great art because he thinks it looks like a horse. The Mayberry High School pennant and the framed newspaper clippings were the proud contribution of the set decorator."

The chili begins to burn! Mrs. Mendlebright knocks on the door, and Barney quickly hides the hot plate in the top drawer of the dresser.

Mrs. Mendlebright enters the room, discovers the hot plate, and becomes very upset. She notes that the dresser "came by bus all the way from Fort Lauderdale."

"People always bragged about items of furniture which had come with them from Europe," says Everett. "We gave this a comic twist and placed a dresser in Barney's room that came all the way by bus from Fort Lauderdale."

Mrs. Mendlebright also removes Barney's seventy-five-watt light bulb from its socket. She reminds Barney that "the rule is no bulbs over forty watts." Mrs. Mendlebright has seen Barney sleeping with the light on and accuses him of being afraid of the dark. This angers Barney, so he calls Mrs. Mendlebright a "snoop and a bulb-snatcher."

"Jim and I both lived in rooming houses during our struggling days," says Everett. "Forty-watt light bulbs and cooking on a hot plate were part of that experience, and we included them in this script."

Mrs. Mendlebright asks Barney "to kindly leave my house. There is someone [Mr. Fields] who is a real gentleman who can use this room."

Barney agrees to do so "with pleasure." He gathers his belongings and leaves.

Barney decides to temporarily live in the back room of the courthouse. He moves his belongings in and decorates the room.

Barney proudly shows the back room to Thelma Lou. He offers Thelma Lou some sweet cider before dinner, but Thelma Lou declines. Barney plugs up the hot plate and begins cooking dinner.

Later that evening, Andy and Opie are walking home after a movie. The movie starred Gregory Peck. As the two walk, Opie comments that Gregory Peck "has an accent." Andy explains that's because "he's a northern person." Opie mentions that the last time they had seen Gregory Peck in a movie, "he talked like you." Andy explains, "That's the actor of the man."

"The movie Opie is referring to was *To Kill a Mockingbird*," says Everett. "I can't explain how we invented the speech patterns such as Andy's 'actor of the man.' You just picture a character in your mind and let him or her talk."

As Andy and Opie approach the courthouse, they notice the lights flickering off and on. Barney and Thelma Lou are still inside. Barney has Thelma Lou cornered against the wall. Every time he turns off the lights and sneaks a kiss, Thelma Lou playfully turns the lights back on.

Andy and Opie enter. Barney quickly opens the filing cabinet and hides his lipstick-smeared face. Opie walks over to the filing cabinet and begins telling Barney about the movie. Barney mumbles a reply, but Opie continues to talk.

Barney finally becomes aggravated and pulls his face out of the filing cabinet. When Opie sees the lipstick, he thinks Barney's face is bleeding.

Andy returns from the back room and quickly ushers Opie out. Before walking out, Andy sternly whispers to Barney, "You better get yourself a room."

"The scene in which Andy and Opie walk in on Barney and Thelma Lou in the midst of a passionate moment was fun to write," says Everett. "When you come up with a natural comic setup, like Barney hiding his lipstick-covered face in the filing cabinet, the writing begins to flow."

Barney's efforts to find a room are unsuccessful. He and Andy discuss the situation. Andy suggests that Barney apologize to Mrs. Mendlebright, but Barney feels it won't do any good because she's already rented the room. Andy still thinks it's worth a try.

Andy and Barney drive over to Mrs. Mendlebright's. Although Barney agrees to talk with Mrs. Mendlebright, he insists that he'll "bend a little but no crawling."

Barney and Mrs. Mendlebright apologize to each other, and Barney pleads to have his room back. Mrs. Mendlebright then tells Barney that she is giving up the rooming business and selling her house because she's getting married.

In response to the news, Andy proclaims, "No you're not!"

Andy Griffith's timing, tone of voice, and expression are perfect. His response is an example of an actor taking a simple line and making it special.

"We wrote simply 'no,'" says Everett. "Andy improved it with a little bit of the way he himself speaks. He is, after all, a man of great talent."

Mrs. Mendlebright says she plans to marry Mr. Fields. Andy wishes the couple well, but Barney later tells Andy he "doesn't like it. I hope it ends in a quickie Mexican divorce."

"Mexican divorces were common in California at the time but wrong for Mayberry," admits Everett. "We decided to use it in the script anyway because the phrase contained good words for Don Knotts to pronounce."

The next day, Barney is standing outside the bank. Mrs. Mendlebright comes out and tells Barney she and Mr. Fields are going to buy a house in Raleigh. Mrs. Mendlebright has just drawn out her savings to help make the down payment.

Barney decides Fields is up to no good and rushes to the courthouse. When he gets to the office, he bumps into Andy, who is standing beside the watercooler. Barney causes Andy to spill a cup of water.

The watercooler is located beside the bookcase near the back room. Earlier in the episode, when Barney is moving his belongings into the courthouse, the cooler is positioned in its normal location between the jail cells. The spilled water helps communicate Barney's urgency. So the cooler, an important prop, was repositioned to simplify Barney's movement.

Barney tells Andy about Mrs. Mendlebright's withdrawal and his suspicion that Mr. Fields is attempting to "pull the old take-her-money-and-run game."

Andy decides the best thing to do is to call the state police and get a rundown on Fields. The state police agree to call Andy as soon as the rundown is completed.

Barney drinks a cup of sweet cider while waiting for the telephone call and explains the logic behind his suspicions: "(A) A guy moves into town. (B) He has no job. (C) He wants to marry Mrs. Mendlebright."

The cider brings back pleasant memories of Mrs. Mendlebright and life at the rooming house. Barney tells Andy that he and Mrs. Mendlebright used to have a glass of cider together every evening. "We'd go out on the porch and sit, drink cider, count cars."

Mrs. Mendlebright reminds Barney of his mother. He reflects that "she's a good soul" and "the most faithful member we got at church." Barney recalls the time Mrs. Mendlebright received a white Bible.

"Sitting on the porch and counting cars was a pastime in my hometown of Buffalo," says Everett. "A white Bible was a common award in Sunday schools."

While Andy is listening to Barney, he is seated at his desk. He picks up the gavel and begins marking on it with a pencil.

"Andy's wonderful business with the gavel was not scripted. It was his own input," says Everett.

Barney continues to drink cider. He repeats the logic behind his suspicions: "(A) A guy moves into town. (B) He has no job. (C) He wants to marry Mrs. Bendlemight."

Hearing the illogical numbering and mispronounced name, Andy looks carefully at Barney and proclaims, "Barney, you're gassed!" Andy takes Barney's cup, smells its contents, and realizes the cider has turned hard.

"I can't explain the creation of Barney's 'A - 2 - C,'" says Everett. "It's just comedy writing. And yes, you can get drunk on hard cider."

Meanwhile, Mr. Fields is getting Mrs. Mendlebright gassed on the cider left by her former tenant.

The telephone call from the state police finally comes. Fields is indeed a con artist—"a bunko man all the way."

Andy and Barney hurry to Mrs. Mendlebright's. They arrive in time to catch Fields running off with Mrs. Mendlebright's purse.

Andy explains the situation to Mrs. Mendlebright. Barney comforts her and the two embrace and have a tearful reconciliation.

"A Date for Gomer"

Episode 105

First Broadcast on
November 25, 1963

Written by
**Everett Greenbaum
and Jim Fritzell**

Directed by
Richard Crenna

Mary Grace Canfield
Guest Stars as
Thelma Lou's Cousin,
Mary Grace Gossage

"I remember the 'guys' really enjoying this episode."
—AARON RUBEN

"This was one of our favorites. It was one of the wonderful times in the business when the writing and the casting came together perfectly."
—EVERETT GREENBAUM

"As time went by, we realized Gomer Pyle was becoming a big hit," says writer Everett Greenbaum. "This script was written after Aaron Ruben called us wanting a new show featuring Gomer. We met Aaron and suggested a couple of story ideas. Aaron decided which one to use. We then went back to our workplace, made a two-page outline, got it approved the next day, and got to work writing.

"This was the way we worked most of the time. Early on in the show, before the season began, there were daily conferences with Andy, Sheldon Leonard, Aaron Ruben, and the writers in attendance. For a week we came up with story ideas and by week's end it was decided who would write which shows. This practice was later ended by the Writers Guild because the writers were actually working that week for nothing."

The filming of the completed script was overseen by director Richard Crenna. "Dick Crenna was one of the stars on *The Real McCoys*, with which Sheldon Leonard was associated," says Aaron Ruben. "Sheldon was also executive producer of *The Griffith Show*. Maybe Dick asked Sheldon for a chance to direct, or maybe Sheldon saw some potential in Dick as a director. Dick was fine as a director. Actors, for the most part, make good directors since they enjoy a kinship and sympathy with the performers they are directing."

"A Date for Gomer" begins as Andy and Opie are exiting the barbershop. Andy has just gotten his hair cut for the Chamber of Commerce dance on Saturday night. Through the shop window, Floyd can be seen readying the barber chair for his next customer. A close viewing of the scene reveals that an extra, rather than Howard McNear, is portraying Floyd Lawson.

"The reason Howard McNear does not appear in the episode could be due to the fact that he might have been too ill," explains Aaron. "Or, since there wasn't anything of substance for Howard in the piece, we just used the barbershop locale. It was a neat way to set up the Saturday night dance."

Opie asks Andy to give him a ride home, but Andy can't. It seems Barney is using the squad car for "a very important mission."

Barney is actually making an ice-cream delivery to Thelma Lou's house. The ice cream, "West Indian Licorice Mocha Delight," was purchased at "Murphy's House of the Nine Flavors."

"Murphy's House of the Nine Flavors was a combination of two local firms— International House of Pancakes and Baskin Robbins Thirty-One Flavors," explains Everett.

The telephone rings while Barney is at Thelma Lou's. It is Thelma Lou's cousin, Mary Grace Gossage. Mary Grace is coming to Mayberry for a visit.

"Jim and I had used Mary Grace Canfield in New York on *Mr. Peepers*," says Everett. "We knew she was going to play Gomer's date, so we named her character Mary Grace Gossage."

Mary Grace's visit causes a problem. Thelma Lou can't go to the dance with Barney and leave Mary Grace all alone. Thelma Lou tells Barney they'll have to get her a date or Thelma Lou won't go.

Barney remembers meeting Mary Grace previously. He recalls that Mary Grace was not very attractive. In fact, he describes her as "a dog." Barney doesn't think he can get her a date, but Thelma Lou insists that he ask Andy to take Mary Grace to the dance.

Andy declines because he's taking Helen Crump. Andy and Barney discuss other possibilities, but the bachelors they think of are either unavailable (Nate Bushy is taking his mother) or not right for Mary Grace (Luke Taft hits the sauce). Barney feels "we've got to get a guy who's not been around too much. Some guy with not too much upstairs—in other words, a real dope." Just as he finishes his statement, Gomer Pyle enters the courthouse.

Andy asks Gomer if he's given any thought to the dance, but Gomer hasn't. Barney then asks if he'd like to "come along with us in the company of a young lady?" Barney tells Gomer he knows a young lady who is dying to go but doesn't know anybody in town because she's a stranger. Gomer asks if she's pretty, to which Barney and Andy respond that "she's so nice."

"'She's so nice' was dialogue used in our time when friends tried to convince you to take a blind date with a girl unknown to you," says Everett.

Gomer agrees to take Mary Grace to the dance.

Thelma Lou is not enthusiastic about Barney's selection. Barney assures her that if she "took the trouble to get under all that oil and gasoline smell, you'd find a heck of a human being." Thelma Lou reluctantly agrees.

After Mary Grace's arrival, Thelma Lou and Helen tell her about the dance and her date. At first, Mary Grace is hesitant, but she eventually agrees to go to the dance with Gomer.

Thelma Lou telephones Barney at the courthouse to tell him that the date is set. Barney is ecstatic. He hangs up and demonstrates his dance steps.

The scene in which Barney demonstrates his dance steps begins with the camera positioned behind the corner file cabinet. The camera pans left and stops at the map that hangs on the wall behind Andy's desk.

"The decision to use this camera angle was made by the director," says Everett. "Ordinarily, cinematographers and directors do not like the writers to suggest camera angles, unless it is necessary to understanding the story."

Gomer comes by to show Andy and Barney the "whole new set of accessories" he has purchased. Gomer proudly shows off a pair of yellow nonporous socks, a brown belt with a horseshoe buckle on it, a purple tie with acorns on it, and a pair of eight-dollar shoes.

"Gomer's accessories were typical of Jim Fritzell's stuff," says Everett.

Gomer feels the money he spent on the "matching things" is worth it because "this Mary Grace could be Miss Right." Andy advises Gomer not to "over-expect." Barney explains, "What Andy is trying to say, Gomer, is during our life-time we travel many roads. There are big roads and little roads, rocky roads and smooth roads . . ." Andy interrupts and says, "Gomer, do me a favor. Just don't overexpect."

"Barney's 'we travel many roads' monologue arose from his love to preach now and then, especially when he was talking to someone more ignorant than himself," says Everett.

Andy, Barney, and Gomer meet at Andy's house before the dance. Aunt Bee insists on ironing Andy's pants because no nephew of hers is going to a dance with "wrinkled knees." Opie asks Gomer if this is the first time he has been out with a girl. Gomer asks if cousins count, but Opie doesn't think it does. Gomer replies, "Then this is the first time."

"Seeing Aunt Bee help Andy get ready added to the importance and suspense of the big date," says Everett.

"Aunt Bee's and Opie's appearances added some color and a human touch, along with providing us with some pleasant jokes," explains Aaron.

Gomer is nervous and asks Barney what they will talk about. Barney assures Gomer that "a million things will pop into your mind, you'll see."

Gomer replies, "It's easy for you, Barney, you're so 'swave' and worldly. And you've been out with waitresses and even a registered nurse."

"The importance placed on dating a nurse came from dirty boyhood talk. The hottest women were nurses, preferably registered," says Everett.

Andy, Barney, and Gomer drive to Thelma Lou's to pick up their dates. The couples sit and talk before leaving for the dance. Andy comments on the weather, and everyone agrees the evening is perfect. The conversation lags. Andy recalls an incident from earlier in the day. He says a shaved collie dog walked into the grocery, and Al Becker was standing there. Andy stops and asks if anyone knows Al Becker. No one does. Andy stops his story and says, "It doesn't mean anything if you don't know Al Becker."

"I don't remember the shaved collie dog, but Al Becker lived across the street from me in Buffalo," says Everett. "The device of Andy's unfinished story is a surprise to the audience, and we used this technique a lot."

At this point, Gomer jumps up from the sofa, says, "Would you folks excuse me, there is something I got to do," and walks out the door.

Mary Grace claims she has a headache and insists that the others go on to the dance without her. Thelma Lou and Helen reluctantly agree.

One of the funniest moments in the episode occurs as Andy, Helen, Barney, and Thelma Lou are departing for the dance. Barney ~~escorts the~~ angry Thelma Lou to the back seat of the squad car and proceeds to "have a little fun." The camera immediately cuts to Andy and Helen in the front seat, and a sharp off-screen punch is heard. The camera pans from front seat to back, revealing Barney holding a handkerchief to his wounded nose.

"The ~~off-screen event~~ that leads to a laugh is a higher form of humor, which pleases the audience because they've figured out what happened on their own," says Everett.

~~A short time later, Mary Grace answers a knock on the door.~~ It is Gomer with "~~your flowers—your cor-sage.~~" Gomer explains that he noticed the other girls had one and she ~~didn't. Gomer left to get the flower because it wouldn't be right for Mary Grace~~ "to go to the dance ~~unadorned.~~" Mary Grace invites ~~Gomer~~ in.

"We wanted ~~Gomer~~ to be loved," says Everett. "And so, he was ~~good.~~" Gomer's goodness is beautifully expressed when he gives a corsage to the "~~unadorned~~" ~~Mary Grace.~~

Thelma Lou refuses to get ~~out~~ of the car at the dance because she has a headache. Helen ~~thinks it's best if she~~ stays in the ~~car with Thelma Lou.~~ Barney doesn't want to ~~go inside and~~ "stand in no stag line with old M~~r.~~ Perkins and ~~a bunch of slumped-over~~ teenage boys," s~~o~~ Andy ~~decides to drive~~ everyone ~~back home.~~

The two couples are surprised when they return to Thelma Lou's and ~~hear loud music coming from inside~~ the house. They open the door and find ~~Gomer and Mary Grace~~ dancing. The couple~~'s concluding dance~~ is a celebration of ~~two "nice"~~ people set~~ting physical appearances~~ aside and enjoying one another's company. Gomer ~~prances~~ over and says ~~to Andy and Barney,~~ "You know something? She's ~~just like you said.~~ She's nice. She's real nice."

"For the closing scene, we included the script directions *they are doing a wild jazz dance*, hoping Jim Nabors could dance," says Everett. "And he was terrific!"

"Gomer had instant popularity," says Aaron. "It wasn't long before Andy was urging me to come up with something for Jim. Happily for all, that turned out to be *Gomer Pyle, U.S.M.C.*"

"Citizen's Arrest"

Episode 106

First Broadcast on
December 16, 1963

Written by
**Jim Fritzell and
Everett Greenbaum**

Directed by
Richard Crenna

"By this time, we knew how Jim Nabors would say, 'Citizen's arrest!'"
—EVERETT GREENBAUM

"Citizen's Arrest" begins with Andy and Barney sorting through some old files. The two sing as they work.

"The singing that opens this episode was not scripted," says writer Everett Greenbaum. "Andy and Don loved to sing together on the set, and sometimes on camera. I imagine Andy selected the song after it was decided that singing would be a good way to begin the episode."

Barney comes across "some of old Sheriff Pinkley's stuff" and asks Andy if he should keep it or throw it out. Andy sees that the paper is a record of the arrest of Purcell Branch for riding down Main Street in a Reo Flying Cloud with the cutout open.

"The Reo Flying Cloud was an actual car built, I think, in the thirties," says Everett. "The cutout was a switch that bypassed the muffler. When the switch was turned on, the car made more noise and went faster."

Barney asks Andy if he took over after Pinkley. Andy lists the names of all the sheriffs who proceeded him. Barney asks where Frieberger, a name Andy had not mentioned, fit in. Andy answers that Frieberger was a sewer inspector. When Barney says that Frieberger once gave his father a speeding ticket, Andy jokingly remarks, "Maybe your daddy was speeding through a sewer."

"The name of the overzealous Mayberry sewer inspector was borrowed from Freddie Frieberger, a fellow writer and friend at the time," says Everett.

Andy continues sorting through papers and comes across the custody receipt for the first revolver Barney was issued. According to the receipt, it has been ten years and one month since Andy swore Barney in. Andy tells Barney, "I owe you a lot, Barn. I really do. We been through a lot together. You been a fine deputy. A true public servant. You can feel right proud of yourself." Barney is overcome with emotion and becomes teary-eyed.

"Jim and I enjoyed exploring facets of the Mayberry characters," says Everett. "After all, we were with them for years. We ended the opening scene with Barney getting emotional over Andy's praise for the fine job he has done as deputy. We enjoyed developing Barney's sentimental side because it made the character multidimensional, and Barney's emotional displays were usually comical."

Later that day, Barney is sitting in the squad car observing traffic. He sees Gomer walk out of the post office, get into his truck, and make a U-turn. Barney immediately turns on the car's siren and pursues Gomer. When Gomer stops, Barney demands an explanation for the U-turn. Gomer answers that he's in "an emergency vehicle." Barney makes the point that the vehicle is not on an emergency run by reaching into the truck and examining Gomer's mail—"a postcard and a copy of *Mechanics Monthly*." Barney takes out his ticket book and writes Gomer "a ticket for committing a 911."

"The idea to use a U-turn in the story came about because I had gotten tickets for two illegal turns that year," says Everett. "The 911 code number Barney cites for the violation was made up. We never verified any of the numbers we gave the various violations with an actual code book."

As Gomer protests the ticket, a crowd attracted by the commotion begins to gather.

When Barney hands Gomer the ticket, Gomer mumbles a response. Barney asks, "What was that?" And Gomer answers, "You just go up an alley and holler *fish*."

"'You just go up an alley and holler *fish*,' was one of my mother's sayings," says Everett. "It meant 'hush up' and came from the vendors who sold food in the alleys of her Philadelphia childhood."

Barney explains to Gomer that the law must be upheld. He says if he was just "plain John Doe, an ordinary citizen" and saw someone making a U-turn, he'd have to make "a citizen's arrest."

At this point, Barney gets into the squad car, backs up, pulls away from the curb, and makes a U-turn.

Gomer immediately yells, "Barney, stop! Citizen's arrest! Citizen's arrest!"

Barney stops the car and explains to Gomer that "this little black-and-white baby here [the squad car] is a real emergency vehicle." Gomer points out that Barney wasn't on an emergency call and orders Barney to write himself a ticket. The crowd gathered around the two cheers.

Attracted by the cheering, Andy comes over to investigate. When the situation is explained, Andy asks Barney to write himself a ticket. Then they can go to the courthouse and settle everything in private.

Andy repeatedly asks Barney to write out the ticket. Barney finally complies but becomes furious while doing so.

In the courthouse, Barney explodes in anger. He refuses to pay his five-dollar fine and will not allow Andy to pay it. Barney removes his badge, places it on Andy's desk, and locks himself in a cell. He says he prefers to serve five days in jail rather than pay the fine. Barney tells Andy that "when word gets out that your deputy, and ex–best friend, has been jailed for a minor offense, you'll be the fool."

That night, Andy returns to the courthouse to check on Barney. Barney has started smoking during Andy's absence. As Andy approaches his cell, Barney marks off a day on his cell calendar and asks, "What did you come back for, bed check?"

"All of Barney's in-jail behavior (his smoking, marking off the days on the calendar, and asking Andy if he would like to make a bed check) was inspired by Edward G. Robinson and James Cagney gangster movies," says Everett.

Andy asks Barney if he is going to stay in the cell all night. Since Barney is determined to remain in the cell, Andy walks toward the door. A drunken Otis enters.

Otis sees Barney behind bars and becomes confused. Otis thinks Barney is out and he's the one locked in the cell. He then looks at Andy, standing beside him, and realizes Andy wouldn't be in a cell. Otis panics and says, "I ain't in, and I ain't out. I'm in the twilight zone."

"Otis's dialogue in response to seeing Barney behind bars was an acknowledgment of the popularity of the series created by Rod Serling," says Everett. "By the way, Rod used to follow Jim and me around New York before he got started."

Andy explains to Otis that Barney is in—he's a prisoner. Andy escorts Otis into his cell and Otis begins to sing, "I'm Sorry I Broke Your Heart, Mother." The singing irritates Barney, so he yells, "Pipe down, Otis!"

Otis can't resist taunting Barney. He taps on his cell bars with a tin cup and chants, "Barney's in jail. Barney's in jail."

"We used Otis as a comic antagonist for Barney in this script," says Everett. "The song Otis sings was specifically requested in our script. The idea to have Otis tap the cell bars with a tin cup (the jailhouse code for 'Barney's in jail') was borrowed from gangster movies. Having Barney and Otis fight was funny, but only in short doses."

The next morning, Barney comes out of his cell and hands Andy a letter of resignation. Andy accepts the resignation calmly and tells Barney he'll take it to the town council the first chance he gets. Andy then walks out.

Surprised by Andy's reaction, Barney walks slowly back into his cell and closes the door behind him. The clang of the door startles him. He looks back at the door and realizes that perhaps he is also closing the door on his work as a deputy.

The renewal of Andy and Barney's personal and professional relationship is set in motion when Opie stops by Wally's Service Station. Opie tells Gomer that Barney quit. He tells Gomer that it all started with the citizen's arrest. Gomer is stunned by the news. Opie continues his story, saying, "Barney gave Pa his resignation and then he went to sleep. Pa said to Aunt Bee, 'He made his bed, let him sleep.'" As Opie leaves, Gomer says his famous line, "Tell your Aunt Bee Gomer says, 'Hey.'"

"Opie's misinterpretation of a statement or a situation was a comic approach we seldom used," says Everett. "A little use of childish misunderstanding was okay, but at the time, Jim and I felt it was overused in radio and TV.

"We concluded the scene with the phrase 'Gomer says, "Hey."' We somehow thought that 'so and so says "hey"' was widely used in the South. Maybe we were wrong, but the phrase was right for Gomer."

After talking with Opie, Gomer decides to take action to get Andy and Barney back together. He telephones the courthouse to report a robbery. Because Andy is not in the office, Otis, who is still sleeping in his cell, answers the telephone. Otis tells Barney that there's been a holdup at Wally's. Otis runs out, yelling for Andy, but Barney remains locked in his cell.

Andy learns of the holdup and rushes to the station. Upon seeing Andy, Gomer immediately asks if Barney came with him. Andy tells him to forget Barney and explain what happened. Gomer explains that since he was the one who got the two apart, he thought he'd try to get them back together. He tells Andy he faked the robbery hoping "you and Barney would come together."

Just then, Barney comes running up. He knew Andy would need someone to cover him. Andy tells Barney that Gomer turned in a false alarm. This angers Barney, and he decides to "throw the book at Gomer." Barney writes out several tickets.

After issuing the tickets, Barney walks to the squad car, tells Andy to "come on," and drives away—making a U-turn. Gomer runs after the departing car, yelling at the top of his lungs, "Citizen's arrest! Citizen's arrest!"

"We always enjoyed writing for Gomer and loved watching Jim Nabors perform the role," says Everett. "However, I'm sad to say, we never got to know Jim very well. As soon as *Gomer Pyle, U.S.M.C.* became a hit, Jim became very popular and very social. I recall years later, while being interviewed by Maureen Reagan, President Reagan's daughter, she bragged to me that she was friends with Jim long before President Ford's daughter even met him."

"Barney and the Cave Rescue"

"The differences between this script and the film are sizable. Andy's telling the legend of Lost Lovers' Cave, Barney's dialogue about bats/moths 'flying in your hair,' and Gomer's 'skunk' story were not in the original script. Each was likely the work of Aaron Ruben and was added in the rewrite."
—HARVEY BULLOCK

Episode 109

First Broadcast on January 6, 1964

Written by
Harvey Bullock

Directed by
Richard Crenna

"When Ray Saffian Allen and I were writing *Dick and the Duchess* in London, we were constantly in search of stories," says writer Harvey Bullock. "Somewhere along the line we mulled over a possible rescue story, but it didn't fit the show, so we never developed it. But the idea stuck in my mind and eventually led to the 'Cave Rescue' script."

Harvey's script begins with Andy talking to Helen on the telephone. Helen tells Andy she is taking an apple crumb pie to the town picnic. Andy informs her that Gomer will take care of things at the office while he and Barney attend the picnic.

At this point, Barney and Gomer come out of the back room. Barney is familiarizing Gomer with the layout of the courthouse. Barney points out cell number 1 and cell number 2.

"I began the script with Barney giving Gomer his final instructions: 'Cell number 1 is on the right, number 2 is on the left,'" says Harvey. "I had no way of knowing whether the cells were numbered 1 and 2 in previous episodes by other writers. I was only trying to load Barney with extraneous information to pontificate to Gomer. All of the *TAGS* writers were freelance, working alone and remote from the studio. We did not collaborate with one another or even know what stories others were doing."

Gomer is dressed in a deputy's uniform. The uniform's shirtsleeves are too short, the shirt's cuffs and collar are unbuttoned, and the narrow end of Gomer's tie is longer than the wide end.

"Gomer's appearance in his deputy's uniform was not described in the script," says Harvey. "My guess is that the wardrobe people simply duplicated his tie (with the narrow end longer than the wide end) and his ill-fitting uniform from his previous appearance as a deputy."

As Andy leaves the courthouse, he is surprised to see Mr. Meldrim, the bank president, opening the bank on Saturday morning. Meldrim explains that he has a bank examiner coming, so he has been working long hours to prepare for the audit. As a result of the stress, he has a terrible cold and frequently wipes his nose with a handkerchief. Meldrim has trouble unlocking the door because the lock sticks.

The inclusion of Mr. Meldrim in the script has some problems with consistency in his appearance in previous episodes. In the episode, "Up in Barney's Room," originally broadcast two weeks earlier, the name of Meldrim's bank is "Mayberry Bank." In this episode, the name of the bank is "Mayberry Security Bank."

"I don't know if the name 'Meldrim' was purposely written by me," says Harvey. "More likely, Aaron Ruben had done a previous script using the character and changed the name I had scripted for consistency. There is no name of any sort on the bank building in my script. I imagine the name change was just an oversight by the prop department."

The bank examiner arrives, and Andy departs.

Meanwhile, Barney and Gomer are walking down the street. Barney is instructing Gomer to walk through the business district every once in a while to check what's going on. As Barney looks toward the bank, he sees Mr. Meldrim, but his face is covered by his handkerchief. The man is struggling with the locked front door. The bank examiner is standing with him. Barney deduces that the bank is being robbed.

Barney puts his bullet in his revolver and bravely crosses the street to apprehend the thieves. Barney sneaks up behind the two men only to catch Mr. Meldrim trying to get into his own bank.

Two of the town's loafers see the incident. After Meldrim is identified, they find the situation hilarious. They laugh at and taunt Barney.

Barney returns to the courthouse. He is embarrassed by his mistake. He wants to avoid anyone who might laugh at his error, so he tells Andy that he may not be able to go to the picnic because the paperwork in the office has "been piling up something awful."

Andy asks if his decision has anything to do with "that ruckus over at the bank." Andy tells Barney he did exactly the right thing. "A good lawman can't afford to take chances. Not when he's protecting others."

Barney reconsiders and decides to attend the picnic.

Just then, Opie runs into the courthouse and asks Andy if it's true that Barney pulled a gun on Mr. Meldrim at his own bank. As Opie says that everyone is laughing about it, Andy quickly ushers Opie out the door.

Andy tells the dejected Barney that at the picnic, they will get off by themselves and have their "own private picnic."

At the picnic, Andy, Helen, Barney, and Thelma Lou go off by themselves. The two couples set up their picnic a short distance from "the old mine cave." Andy suggests they explore the cave before eating. Barney doesn't like the idea, so Andy and Helen leave Barney and Thelma Lou at the picnic site and go exploring.

As the two enter the cave, Andy tells Helen that the place was called Lost Lovers' Cave when he was a boy. Andy says the story was that two Indian lovers went into the cave, got separated, and never did come out again. He then adds that even now, if somebody calls out, a voice will answer. Andy yells, "Where are you?" An echo answers.

"The exterior scenes in this episode were shot at Franklin Canyon, where we photographed the opening credits with Andy and Opie walking by the lake," says producer Aaron Ruben. "We only spent one day shooting the exterior scenes, even though a large part of the episode centers around the cave. We reduced the time spent on location by rehearsing many of the exterior scenes on the stage at the studio.

"The cave, made of synthetic material painted with earth colors, was constructed on a stage. The sound engineers easily duplicated Andy's echo."

Thelma Lou eventually talks Barney into exploring the cave. As the two enter the cave, Barney tells Thelma Lou that he never liked caves. He says, "You know what you find in caves? Bats! You know what they do? They fly in your hair and get tangled up in there and lay their eggs, and you go crazy." When Barney hears a noise overhead, he covers his head. Thelma Lou points out that the noise was only a moth. Barney replies, "Well, you don't want a moth in your hair either. They lay these moth eggs. You go crazy from that too."

Further inside the cave, Andy hears a rumble. It turns out to be a rockslide, and Andy and Helen are trapped.

Barney and Thelma Lou also hear the rumble and rush out. Moments later they realize that Andy and Helen are still inside. Barney says, "They're buried alive."

"The roof of the cave was scored in advance and gave way easily to pressure," says Aaron.

Inside the cave, Andy checks the debris left by the slide and realizes the passageway back to the cave's entrance is blocked. He suggests they go a different way, so they head deeper into the cave.

Outside, Barney sends Thelma Lou to the picnic grounds "to round up every able-bodied man." Barney goes back to town to get the emergency equipment.

Andy and Helen find a tunnel that leads to the other side of the cave. When they finally emerge from the cave, they are both covered with dirt. Helen doesn't want anyone to see her, so they decide to hitchhike back to town to clean up. Andy warns Helen that they will have to hurry "before some of them start missing us and worrying." Andy stops a passing motorist, and they ride back to Mayberry.

Back at Helen's house, Andy listens to the radio while he waits for Helen to change. He hears a news bulletin that announces that an earth slide is believed to have trapped two people in a cave. The announcer reports that Deputy Barney Fife has organized the entire town in a "mammoth rescue operation."

Helen picks up the telephone to call the courthouse to report they are not trapped, but Andy stops her. He realizes how embarrassed Barney will feel "if we pop up. That ribbing he took at the bank this morning won't hold a candle to what he's in for now." Andy and Helen agree there has to be somebody in the cave for Barney to rescue.

"I agree with many viewers that the rescue story seems to have questionable timing and validity," says Harvey. "But I feel even stronger that, upon close inspection, elements in the story, although borderline, are in order and plausible.

"Andy and Helen escape from the cave and flag down a truck, but neither thinks anyone else is involved. Even though Andy says, 'We better hurry before some of them start missing us and worrying,' this does not imply an overwhelming need for speed. What some viewers forget is that Andy is not in a real rush. He has no idea that, at that moment, Barney is trying to save them."

Meanwhile at the courthouse, Barney is removing the emergency equipment from the back room. While Barney continues to gather the equipment, Gomer tells "about the time my cousin Goober got himself lost in a cave. He was tracking a skunk." When Gomer finishes the story, Barney says to him, "Two people are trapped in a cave, and you stand there yakking about your stupid cousin Goober." Gomer thinks this over and replies, "My cousin Goober ain't stupid. He's ugly, but he ain't stupid."

A short time later, Andy and Helen reenter the cave through the back entrance.

Outside the cave's front entrance, Barney uses a megaphone to orchestrate the rescue. He calls out that "now is the time for all good men to come to the aid of their neighbor."

"As always, Barney takes pride in his pronouncements while instructing the crowd with the megaphone," says Harvey. "If there's a loose cliché around, he'll nab it. Professing authority is his favorite stance. Somewhere he's heard someone say, 'Now is the time for all good men to come to the aid of their party.' It pops into his mind, with the switch of the last word to 'neighbor,' and he's happy with it."

Andy and Helen take their places near the slide just minutes before Barney digs through. Andy and Helen are rescued!

Outside the cave, Andy tells the townsfolk, "It sure was a close call. I don't know what we'd have done if it hadn't been for Barney. It could have been any of us in there. I'd say we're pretty lucky to have a fellow like Barney Fife around." The townsfolk all agree.

As Thelma Lou and Helen stand in the crowd, Thelma Lou says to Helen, "That Barney's really quite a guy." Helen answers, "You're right, he certainly is. As a matter of fact, they both are." These simple lines speak of the close friendship between the two men and acknowledge the audience's awareness that Andy and Helen returned to the cave in order to be rescued by Barney.

"Thelma Lou and Helen's lines were not difficult to write," says Harvey. "As a writer you imagine what has occurred in the story and have the characters react to the situation. The hard part was manufacturing the story in an outline before one word of dialogue was written.

"Primarily, my intent was to tell an interesting story, but when Andy and Helen work to save Barney from humiliation, it teaches an important lesson in friendship. There is another more subtle moral as well—that lawmen sometimes have to chance appearing ridiculous. A call might be laughable, but it could also be a major crime in progress. The man with the badge can't take the chance of not responding to what may subsequently prove to be a false alarm."

"Andy and Opie's Pal"

Episode 110

First Broadcast on
January 13, 1964

Written by
Harvey Bullock

Directed by
Richard Crenna

David A. Bailey
Guest Stars as
Trey Bowden

"This script is the simple tale of a boy who feels his father shares too much affection with another boy."—HARVEY BULLOCK

"Andy and Opie's Pal" begins with Opie walking down the street. He is dressed in a football jersey and carries a football. When Opie passes a boy sitting in a front yard, he stops and asks if the boy is "new around here." When the boy answers, "Uh-huh," Opie tells the boy that his football is "a genuine, full-size, regulation football they played with at a state college game." The boy shows little interest. When Opie asks, "You want to be friends," the boy answers, "Okay." When Opie says his father is the sheriff, the boy immediately becomes interested.

At the courthouse, Barney is taking a complaint from Gomer by telephone. When Barney hangs up, he tells Andy that Gomer has just come from Pierson's Sweet Shop and is "all riled up again." It seems that the sweet shop is running a giveaway contest. If you purchase a peppermint that has a pink center, you get a free peppermint. If you get a green center, you win a flashlight. On Thursday Gomer bought ten lucky peppermints, all with white centers. Today, he bought twelve more; again all had white centers. Barney says that Gomer is not saying he expects to get a green center right away, but he does think he should have had at least one pink center out of the twenty-two peppermints he bought. Andy responds that he can't believe that Jesse Pierson would ever "run a fixed peppermint box."

"The idea for Pierson's Sweet Shop peppermint contest grew out of my early addiction to gambling," says writer Harvey Bullock. "The neighborhood store kept a box of chocolate mints on the counter for sale at a penny apiece. After you bought one, you immediately bit it in half and checked the color of the filling. Most of the centers were white, but every once in a while you'd hit it big and bite into a colored center. If it was pink, you won a free mint. But if it was green, hold tight, you won a flashlight!

"I don't recall ever seeing a flashlight awarded, but I did see some pinks—enough to keep me coming back for more. It was exciting, the lure of something for nothing and the admiration of your gang who somehow thought winning a free peppermint was huge proof of masculinity. To have Gomer claim that Pierson runs a fixed peppermint box seemed funny, juxtaposing a gambling term on a most insignificant item."

As the episode continues, Opie enters the courthouse accompanied by his "brand-new friend," Trey Bowden. Opie introduces Trey to Andy and Barney.

Opie explains that Trey is his nickname. His real name is Frederick Bowden the Third. Opie says, "Since he's the third, that's why they call him Trey."

"The new boy in Mayberry, Frederick Bowden III, a.k.a. Trey, was named after a neighborhood boy who was a friend of my son Andrew," says writer Harvey Bullock. "The boy's actual first name was Robert, but no one ever called him that. We all called him Trey, because both his father and grandfather were also named Robert Bowden. I liked the sound of Trey for a boy's name and filed it away in my cluttered brain."

When Andy asks Trey about his father, Opie answers that "he ain't got a pa. He's dead." When Andy asks Trey how he likes "our little town," Opie again answers for Trey.

"Having Opie do all the talking when he introduces Trey to Andy was just a comedy bit to show Opie's initial wild enthusiasm about having a new friend," says Harvey. "It's not that Trey is the quiet type, it's just that he's in a strange room with a real sheriff, and he doesn't get the chance to talk with Opie bubbling over. Opie's enthusiasm contrasts nicely with the later quiet despair he suffers when he feels Trey has supplanted him in Andy's affection."

Before going out to play, Opie asks Andy if Trey can come fishing with them on Saturday and stay at their house that night. Andy says it will be all right with him.

Opie and Trey's new friendship causes Andy and Barney to reminisce about their own relationship. Their discussion reminds Barney of "a little set-to" concerning a visit by the queen of the State Apricot Festival.

The queen of the State Apricot Festival visited Mayberry, and Barney thought he was going to be her escort. Instead Andy met her "at the city line and took her around." Andy had nearly forgotten "that little mix-up." Barney agrees, "That's all it was—a little mix-up" and continues talking. He recalls the actual date—"June 23, 1952, on a Saturday afternoon." Barney reflects momentarily on what happened and adds, "Patterson's, three ninety-five. Three ninety-five, that's what I paid at Patterson's for a brand-new shirt to meet her while you were off squiring her around." The more he thinks about it, the angrier he becomes. He says, "I stood out on that corner under a blazing sun for two hours waiting, while you two were off gallivanting around. Why should you take the Apricot Queen around? Who eats all the apricots around here anyway? I do, that's who."

"The term 'set-to' means a disagreement or fight," says Harvey. "The June 23 date for the visit of the Apricot Queen was picked at random. The date had no significance except to Barney, who will remember that date as the day that Andy took the Apricot Queen away from him."

After Barney calms down, Andy decides to go on patrol. Before leaving, he reminds Barney that he's invited to the Taylor house for supper that night.

That evening, Opie and Trey quickly finish their supper and rush upstairs to Opie's room. Andy, Barney, and Aunt Bee remain at the table. Aunt Bee picks up the bread basket and says, "One roll left." When she asks Barney if he would like it, he responds, "Okay, but I hate to be the old maid."

"I would often include words or phrases in common usage when writing dialogue," says Harvey. "An example of this is when Barney eats dinner with the Taylors and reluctantly takes the last roll. He says in explanation, 'I hate to be the old maid.' That expression was frequently said by anybody who took the last of any dish."

After hearing Trey and Opie bumping around upstairs, Andy recalls how he and Barney used to do the same thing whenever they spent the night together. The two would stay up most of the night, and Barney would "make up for it the next day by sleeping in Sunday school."

"Andy's dialogue about sleeping in Sunday school was inspired by a childhood memory," says Harvey. "As a child, my Sunday school classes were taught by one of the dads. These men were not teachers or public speakers, so often the class was deadly dull and the room overheated. If you had been out late the Saturday before, you were weary, and sleep would overtake you."

When the bumping gets louder, Andy goes upstairs to investigate.

The boys hear Andy coming, quickly jump into bed, and turn off the lights.

Andy tells the boys they have to get some sleep, so one of them will have to come in Andy's room. Opie gets up, but Andy chooses Trey to go to his bed. Andy explains to Opie that he'll bring Trey back as soon as he dozes off.

Opie gets back in bed. Opie overhears Andy asking Trey out in the hallway if he would like a glass of milk and a piece of pie. He lies in bed and thinks the situation over intently before falling to sleep.

The next morning, Trey is up early. When Trey joins Andy and Barney on the front porch, Barney notices that Trey is interested in the "old roscoe." Trey doesn't understand what Barney is talking about, so Barney explains: "Roscoe—revolver. That's what the civilians call it. We refer to it as a roscoe, or a heater, or an old persuader, or a rod."

Barney tells Trey that the important thing with any firearm is safety. Then Barney demonstrates a safe draw and accidentally fires the revolver into the floor.

Andy holds out his hand, and Barney places the revolver in it. Andy tells him to wait in the car.

"Barney's reeling off slang names for his revolver is not in my script, but the accidental firing of his weapon was," says Harvey. "I felt this gag had to be used judiciously, so it wouldn't wear out, but it proved to be hearty stuff, and all the writers got a lot of mileage out of it."

After Barney leaves, Andy checks the revolver to be sure it is empty and allows Trey to hold it. Opie watches the two through the screen door.

Later that day, Opie visits the courthouse and asks Andy if he, Andy, and Barney can go fishing without Trey. Barney enters the office through the back room. He has returned from putting gas in the squad car. As Andy steps into the back room, Opie sees Trey through the front window and goes outside. Trey asks if Andy is inside, but Opie tells him that Andy is busy. Opie tells Trey that he has to go to football practice. Since the team will be practicing secret plays, Trey can't come. Opie waits until Trey walks away and reenters the courthouse.

Trey walks around the corner of the courthouse and finds Andy getting into the squad car. Andy is going on lake patrol and invites Trey to come along. When Andy asks Trey where Opie is, Trey says he's at football practice.

Inside the courthouse, Opie asks Barney where Andy is. Barney says he's about to leave for lake patrol. Opie rushes outside just in time to see Andy and Trey driving away.

The mechanics of Opie missing out on the lake patrol provide an example of the careful attention given to detail. Barney enters the courthouse from the back room and parks the squad car on the side street. This allows a logical setup for Andy and Trey's out-of-sight departure when Opie enters the courthouse from the front door.

"My script does not have Barney entering the courthouse from the back room," says Harvey. "This detail was an important addition, however, because it explained why the car was parked on the side street instead of in its usual place in front of the courthouse."

After returning from lake patrol, Trey walks by the yard where Opie and his friends are practicing football. Opie and Trey argue and begin shoving each another. As Barney drives by, he sees Opie and Trey fighting and stops. He breaks up the "little tiff" and warns Opie that if his father found the two had been fighting, it would be "the end of you and Trey."

Barney returns to the courthouse, and Opie enters a short time later. He is covered with bandages and tells Andy that he and Trey have been fighting. He adds, "Guess I can't play with Trey anymore." When Andy lifts a bandage, he sees that there is no injury.

"I decided to have Opie put on fake bandages to convince Andy that he has had a fight with Trey, even though it could be argued that Opie was smart enough to know that his scheme wouldn't fool Andy," says Harvey. "I felt Opie might wishfully consider the bandages plausible. Also, Opie's not thinking too clearly because the possible alienation of Andy is bedeviling him."

Opie then says, "Well, I guess Trey can't come fishing with us tomorrow, uh?"

Andy says he doesn't think so. Opie then responds, "Oh, well he's always horning in anyway. From now on, it'll be just you and me, Pa."

Andy agrees and adds, "Just you and me will go fishing. Barney was coming, but just me and you will go off together."

When Barney hears that he won't be going along, his feelings are hurt. He storms off into the back room.

Opie questions Andy about excluding Barney. Andy points out that Trey was probably hurt just like Barney when Opie "pushed him off." Opie walks to the entrance of the back room and invites Barney to come fishing with them. Opie then walks to Andy's desk, looks at his father, and proceeds out the door.

After Opie leaves, Andy apologizes to Barney and explains that "the whole thing was just a pretend job. See, I had to show that young'un that you don't drop your friends just like that. It seemed like the only way I could get it across to him was to give him an example."

"My intention with this script was to tell a good story and give it dimension by centering on a pertinent moral," says Harvey. "This episode does deal with friendship. 'Barney and the Cave Rescue' had a similar moral, but of course, the story was sufficiently different so as not to seem redundant."

That night, Opie stops Andy in the upstairs hallway. Opie tells Andy that he and Trey are friends again and that they can all go fishing tomorrow. Andy says they can call Trey first thing in the morning, but Opie says they won't have to. He leads Andy into his bedroom where Trey is asleep in Opie's bed. He is clutching the "genuine, full-size, regulation" football that Opie has given him. Andy tells Opie that Trey has "gotten something even better. Now he's got a genuine, full-size, regulation friend to match."

"I was very pleased with Andy's ending lines," says Harvey. "The constant mental shuffling of dialogue and ideas helped arrange their placement and later play-off. Sometimes, somehow, the muses take pity on a writer and whisper things like 'genuine, full-size, regulation' in your ear, and you realize what a gift it is—perfectly describing the football—and the boy."

"Barney's Sidecar"

Episode 112

First Broadcast on
January 27, 1964

Written by
**Jim Fritzell and
Everett Greenbaum**

Directed by
Coby Ruskin

"At the age of fourteen, I bought the remains of a World War I Harley Davidson motorcycle in bushel baskets for four dollars. I actually got it running, and memories of that motorcycle inspired this episode."
—EVERETT GREENBAUM

"Barney's Sidecar" begins with Mrs. Beggs entering the courthouse. She explains that she has "just had the most frightening experience" of her life. While driving on Highway 6, a speeder almost ran her off the road. She says that "a woman was driving that car. She was wearing a green hat trimmed with pink baby roses, and a beige cloth jacket with buttons with furry middles like my sister Tilley has on her jacket." Mrs. Beggs goes on to tell Andy that "Tilley is a tall woman with long teeth. In school Tilley was called 'the Beaver.'"

"The humor in the Mrs. Beggs scene derives from the fact that a woman pays attention to completely different details from a man," says writer Everett Greenbaum. "Jim Fritzell was the inspiration for the comment about the sister, Tilley. Her long teeth were Jim's teeth."

Andy ushers Mrs. Beggs out of the courthouse as Barney enters. When Andy tells Barney about "the speeder up on Highway 6," Barney offers to take the squad car out to the highway and "take a look-see." Andy declines the offer because he needs to use the squad car.

Then Barney suggests they set up a "checkpoint chickie" to "nip this speeding in the bud." Andy reminds him that they only have one car. Barney complains that police departments are the "lowest budgeted public servants of them all, but it's thank you, Johnnie Shaffto, when the guns begin to shoot."

"Barney's 'checkpoint chickie' came from the World War II phrase 'checkpoint Charlie,'" says Everett. "'Thank you, Johnnie Shaffto' was a line from a Rudyard Kipling poem."

Andy returns later in the day and finds Opie in the office. When Andy asks where Barney is, Opie says he doesn't know. He adds that Barney has not been there since he arrived. During this conversation, Opie is writing his name on a

board using a woodburning set that he got for his birthday. Andy asks him to take his woodburning work home.

As Opie walks toward the door, he says "Abyssinia," to which Andy replies, "See ya Somoa."

"In the thirties it was considered clever to say 'Abyssinia' for 'I'll be seeing ya,'" says Everett. "The reply was 'See ya Somoa' for 'See ya some more a.' That farewell exchange came to mind as we were writing this scene, and it seemed to me that a young boy might say this to his father instead of goodbye."

As Opie leaves, Barney enters. He puts goggles, gloves, and a helmet on Andy's desk. Barney announces that he has been to the war-surplus auction in Mt. Pilot. Barney then asks Andy to come outside so he can show Andy something. Andy complies.

Parked in front of the courthouse "is a mechanically perfect RJ 300 motorcycle"—with sidecar. Barney believes the motorcycle will be the answer to their problems. He can cover Highway 6 with the motorcycle while Andy is using the squad car. Andy asks what the sidecar is for. Barney answers, "Are you kidding? That's to carry fire-fighting equipment, guns and ammunition, room for another deputy in case of a raid, going back and forth to the store. Besides, that's the way it came."

"We made up the RJ 300 model number of Barney's motorcycle," says Everett. "The motorcycle, however, was based on the World War I Harley that I built as a teenager.

"I always thought sidecars were amusing. As a child, I was fascinated by one that was in my father's tire store. Jim and I agreed that a sidecar attached to Barney's motorcycle would be a wonderful prop and could be developed into some wonderful gags."

The next day, Barney marches into the office wearing a helmet, goggles, and leather gauntlets. Andy greets him by saying, "How you doing, Baron Von Richthofen?"

"Baron Von Richthofen was the leading German ace of World War I," says Everett. "In the comic strip *Peanuts*, Snoopy the dog fantasizes that he is the Baron—so he lives today."

Barney is upset by Andy's kidding. He takes off his helmet, sets it on the desk, and turns his back to Andy. Andy picks up the helmet, puts it on his head, and asks Barney what he thinks. Barney turns around. His eyes get big, and he says, "Don't wear my hat. I can't stand to wear a hat after it's been on somebody else's head. My mother was the same way."

"Barney's not wanting to wear a hat after it's been on somebody else's head and the comment that his mother was the same way, just bubbled up while Jim and I were writing," says Everett.

Andy apologizes and offers to take Barney to lunch to show there are no hard feelings. Barney wants to drive them to lunch in the new motorcycle. He says, "Big fellow, you're going sidecar express to the diner." Andy reluctantly agrees.

As Andy and Barney walk outside, a group of the "boys" are lounging around the door to the courthouse. Andy gets in the sidecar. Barney mounts the motorcycle and fires up the motor. Barney revs the motor, looks at Andy, and asks if he is ready. Andy answers, "Let her rip." Barney rides away, leaving Andy and the sidecar behind.

"I must confess, the joke about the unattached sidecar was not original," admits Everett. "We stole it from the Marx Brothers."

"We had a laugh machine that would take a laugh and cycle it," says Jay Sandrich, who was the assistant to the producer. "The machine had a small laugh with five or six people, a bigger laugh with ten or twelve people, and a really large group laugh. We never wanted the laughs to get too big since the laugh track's purpose was simply to help the audience sitting at home enjoy the show.

"One of the sound editor's responsibilities was to be sure there weren't too many laughs, that they weren't too big, and that the laughs fit the gag. Don Knotts was so funny that it was easy to insert a laugh at every single thing he did, but then there would be too many laughs. So, we tried to include a laugh only when there was something that was very funny.

"There was never any question about inserting a laugh as Barney rides away without the sidecar. In fact, it was one of the few times the large-group laugh was used on *TAGS*."

Andy laughs at the incident, but Barney is furious. Andy warns Barney that if he keeps the cycle, he is probably in for a lot more problems. Andy asks why Barney doesn't just make his life easier and get rid of it. Barney responds that "every thinking pioneer and inventor has suffered the same kind of ridicule. It's right there in your history books. Take Alexander Graham Bell. People laughed at him over the telephone. Wilbur and Orville, people practically laughed them right off Wright Air Force Base."

"The dialogue about how people laughed at Alexander Graham Bell because of the telephone and how people practically laughed Orville and Wilbur Wright 'right off Wright Air Force Base' grew out of Barney's tendency to pick up a lot of information and only retain some of it," says Everett.

Andy agrees that Barney can keep the motorcycle if he doesn't spend too much time in town. Andy tells him to patrol "way out on Highway 6."

Barney sets up a "checkpoint chickie" and begins stopping trucks on Highway 6. He stops a truck driven by Edgar J. Masters. Barney tells him, "Well, Eddie, I watched you doing forty miles an hour in a thirty-five-mile zone." Edgar Masters explains, "We've always had an understanding about it. We need that extra five miles an hour to get over Turner's grade." Barney gives him a warning and tells him to "move her [the truck] out."

"The scene in which Barney stops the truck driver, asks his name, and then calls him 'Eddie' was inspired by the fact that we had heard that New York City cops did the same first-name thing," says Everett.

At the end of the afternoon, Barney checks in with Andy. Barney tells Andy that "if you ride into the wind with your mouth open and you put your tongue up on the roof of your mouth, it's impossible to pronounce a word that starts with the letter *t*."

"Barney's dialogue about 'riding into the wind with your mouth open' is not in my script," says Everett. "It sounds to me like Aaron Ruben's writing."

Barney tells Andy that he gave out eleven speeding warnings. When Andy asks who was doing all the speeding, Barney answers, "El truckos."

"The Spanish stuff gave Barney a man-of-the-world pose," says Everett.

That night, the truck drivers protest Barney's warnings by loudly revving their engines and keeping the whole town awake.

During the next few days, Barney patrols the town on motorcycle. He gives out a number of tickets and warns motorists about reckless driving. As Aunt Bee exits the grocery, Barney rides by and frightens her. When she drops her groceries, Barney warns her about jaywalking.

The townsfolk complain to Andy that Barney is making "our lives miserable since he got that darn motorcycle." Even Aunt Bee tells Andy that he has to do something about Barney.

Andy helps Aunt Bee carry the groceries home. At home, Aunt Bee says, "You know, I saw this war picture once. These Nazis were riding around on motorcycles, and these guerrillas strung wire across the road so high, and when these Nazis came roaring through on their motorcycles—phfftt." As she says this, Aunt Bee passes her hand across her throat. Andy responds, "Aunt Bee, we don't want to kill him—maybe hurt him a little, but we don't want to kill him."

"The Nazi suggestion was not in our script, and I don't like it for Aunt Bee," says Everett.

As the episode continues, Andy notices a "familiar smell." Aunt Bee tells him that Opie is burning a new house number with his woodburning set.

Andy goes to investigate and finds Opie burning the number right into the house.

"Jim and I committed many of Opie's mistakes, such as burning numbers into a house, so that is how we knew about them," says Everett.

Andy stops Opie and takes the wood-burner from him. When Barney roars by on the motorcycle, Andy looks at the wood-burner and gets an idea.

The next day, Andy brings some oilcloth to work. He wants Barney to fix up the torn cushion in the sidecar. He removes the cushion and hands it to Barney. Beneath the cushion, Andy finds a wooden plaque with an inscription. The inscription reads: "First motorcycle to cross the Marne River—Battle of Chateau-Thierry, 6-12-18. Passenger: Black Jack Pershing. Driver: Corporal Nate Jackson, A.E.F."

"The battle of Chateau Thierry, the Marne River, and Black Jack Perishing all existed, but we fictitiously bunched them together for the inscription on the plaque," says Everett.

Andy guesses the plaque was "probably done right in combat with a heated bayonet."

"Jim and I ran into a problem after we came up with the sidecar storyline," says Everett. "We didn't know how to finish the story. Then we thought of placing a fake plaque under the sidecar's seat and went back to the beginning and put in Opie and the woodburning set."

Andy tells Barney, "You don't have an ordinary cycle there, Barn. You got a monument on your hands." Barney responds, "You know, it probably ought to be on display someplace—like there in that Smith Brothers' Institution in Washington, D.C." Andy agrees. Barney realizes that Andy means he should give the motorcycle to them. Andy tells Barney, "Your first loyalty is to your town. We got a lot of World War I veterans right here—Al, Bert Stevens, the Milo boys. Actually this cycle belongs over at the National Guard Armory between the Civil War cannon and the World War II jeep."

"I don't remember where the names of the Mayberry World War I veterans came from," says Everett. "But 'Al, Bert Stevens, and the Milo boys' sounded just right."

Barney understands he must give up the motorcycle. He can't, however, bring himself to drive the motorcycle over to the armory. He asks Andy to do it. As Barney turns away, he starts to look over his shoulder. Andy simply says, "Don't look back."

"My Fair Ernest T. Bass"

"You know, if you wrote this into a play nobody would believe it."
—BARNEY FIFE

"It was always fun doing an Ernest T. show. Howie was always 'up' and fun-loving, and there was never a dull moment when Howie was around."
—AARON RUBEN

Episode 113

First Broadcast on February 3, 1964

Written by
Jim Fritzell and Everett Greenbaum

Directed by
Earl Bellamy

Howard Morris
Guest Stars as
Ernest T. Bass

"The origins of the Ernest T. Bass character are somewhat hidden," says producer Aaron Ruben. "Apparently, we had talked about introducing a wild mountain character into the quiet and placid town of Mayberry. When the mountain character was decided on, we then looked for someone who could play this untamed and zany guy. I was familiar with Howie's talents, having worked with him on *Caesar's Hour*. Remembering how outrageous and funny Howie could be, both on and off camera, I thought he'd be an ideal choice."

"Aaron Ruben was one of the writers on *Caesar's Hour*," says Howard Morris. "*Caesar's Hour* was one of the biggest variety shows, and the cast played all kinds of things—every kind of situation there was. As a member of the cast, I was involved in hundreds and hundreds of sketches.

"Aaron remembered the kind of talent and abilities I had brought to *Caesar's Hour*. I hadn't worked with him in some time, and I had never worked *The Griffith Show*. Out of the blue, he called me and said, 'We have a character in an episode, and we don't know quite what to do with it. Would you look at it?' He sent me a script, and I looked at it. I called him up and said, 'I think I can fool around with this.' And he said, 'Okay, we'll hire you then.' I came in, the cast read the script, then we did it, and they loved it so much they eventually wrote four more episodes.

"I don't know exactly where my portrayal of Ernest T. came from. Here I was, a guy born and raised in the Bronx of New York City with little or no connection with the South. I was, however, drafted before World War II and sent down to Wilmington, North Carolina, where I spent seven or eight months. I met people there, and I listened and watched. I apparently have a pretty good ear, and I picked up a lot.

"The character developed as I performed. *The Griffith Show* producer and directors were very good to me. They allowed me to write the kind of poetry that I did—the rhyming thing. There were times when they didn't use it, but pretty much they gave me a great deal of creative freedom."

Howard's input was acknowledged and appreciated by the writers. "Howard Morris played Ernest T. perfectly," says Everett Greenbaum. "He added a lot to it in the way of pronunciation and physical moves.

"In 1963, the Broadway musical *My Fair Lady* was a hot ticket," says Everett. "I've always considered it the best American musical comedy, so Jim Fritzell and I decided to do it. We followed the plot of the show—the coaching and educating of Ernest T. and finally the big event, the ball, or, in this case, the party at Mrs. Wiley's. But it didn't seem right to have Ernest T. make a big success of his new persona, so we had him go nuts, ruin his chances. But the episode ended on an up-note due to Ramona. By the way, when Mrs. Wiley says, 'He's from Back Bay Boston,' it is the same beat the Hungarian linguist uses in *My Fair Lady* when she says, 'She's royalty.'"

The episode begins with a close-up of Ernest T.'s arm lifting a rock to throwing position. The camera pans backward to show the breaking of Mrs. Wiley's window.

"The windowpanes were made of candy set in a mold," says Howard. "It was called candy glass because it looked like real glass but broke harmlessly."

When Andy and Barney arrive, Mrs. Wiley tells the two that a man burst into the house uninvited and started acting in the "most peculiar manner." The man stuck his hand in the punch bowl, ate every bit of the watermelon rind, soaked the paper napkins in the punch, and threw them at the ceiling. The man also demanded "to meet a woman." Mrs. Wiley gives Andy and Barney the rock that the man threw through the window, thinking they "can study it for fingerprints." From Mrs. Wiley's description, Andy is positive the man is Ernest T. Bass.

Andy and Barney look for Ernest T. "on every street, in every store and restaurant, and even under two houses." They return to the courthouse. Andy parks the squad car, and he and Barney discuss what to do next. Andy tells Barney he wishes there was some way they could straighten Ernest T. out. Barney replies that nobody can. "The man's hostility is ingrained. It's carved in the deepest recesses of his subconscious id. I wouldn't touch his id with a ten-foot pole."

Throughout its production, *TAGS* was filmed with one camera. The scene in which Andy and Barney discuss Ernest T.'s id provides an excellent example of how this technique worked. Preparations for filming the scene began by positioning the camera alongside the driver's door of the squad car. This camera position provided the "master" print of the scene. The actors' performances were photographed by looking into the car over Andy's left side. After this shot was completed, the camera was repositioned alongside the passenger's door for the required secondary shot. The actors repeated their performances and were photographed by the camera looking into the car over Barney's right side. The on-screen version of the scene is the end result of carefully combining the two separately photographed viewpoints.

When Andy and Barney go inside the courthouse, Barney's old uniform, which was given to Ernest T. Bass the last time he was in town, is on Andy's desk. Ernest T. is sitting in one of the cells.

Ernest T. explains that the uniform did not have the effect on girls that he had anticipated. He says the girls "gazed right on through me" when he wore Barney's uniform. Ernest T. tells Andy and Barney he tried "courtin'" old Hog Winslow's daughter, Hogette. He wrote Hogette a love note, tied it to a rock, and tossed it through her front window. The rock "caught" Hogette on the head. The cut required seven stitches.

Andy suggests Ernest T. "give it another chance with Hogette." Ernest T. explains it's too late because Hogette married the "taxidermist what sewed up her head." Ernest T. feels the best thing to do would be "to find myself a cave and hermitize myself."

"After thirty-two years, all I remember about the Hogette Winslow story is that we had a name, Hog Winslow, and when Jim suggested his daughter be called Hogette, I laughed all day," says Everett.

Andy offers to help Ernest T. get a woman. Andy plans "to clean him up, teach him a few manners—maybe he'll even quit throwing rocks."

Andy begins by inviting Ernest T. over to his house for supper. Ernest T. joins Andy, Aunt Bee, and Opie at the table. Opie asks, "Mr. Bass, will you pass the bread, please?" Ernest T. picks up a piece of bread and throws it to Opie. Aunt Bee reprimands him, and Andy explains, "You pass it. You don't throw it."

Andy asks Ernest T., "Would you pass the potatoes, please?" Ernest T. picks up a potato and hands it to Andy. Andy explains, "You don't pass one. You pass the whole thing." Ernest T. picks up every potato in the bowl and hands them to Andy.

After supper, Barney stops by to find out "how the big experiment with Ernest T. is coming." Ernest T. is upstairs cleaning up. Andy tells Barney that Ernest T. is "showing progress." Andy plans to keep working with him and try to pass him off at Mrs. Wiley's upcoming party.

Ernest T. stomps down the upstairs hallway, leaps over the banister, and jumps into a chair. Andy decides it's time to talk with Ernest T. about how to come into a room. Andy asks Barney to show Ernest T. the proper way to come into a room.

Andy points out that Barney "is a perfect example of a young man-about-town." Ernest T. compliments Barney by saying, "You can afford to be mighty proud of yourself."

The colorful words and phrases that Ernest T. uses, such as "hermitizing" and "you can afford to be mighty proud of yourself," arose from the freedom the writers felt when creating dialogue for fictional characters.

"No one ever spoke the way our mountain people talked," says Everett. "It was just something that happened when Jim and I got into a room with a pile of yellow paper and a typewriter."

Barney agrees to show Ernest T. "how to come into a room." Before doing so, he quizzes Andy about what type of an affair he is supposed to be attending and the number of people present. Andy asks, "Are you gonna enter, or are you planning on bringing the sandwiches?" Barney angrily replies, "If you're gonna do something, do it right. There are different entrances for different affairs." He walks toward the door to make his entrance and mutters, "Jiminy Christmas."

"In middle America, my generation had many euphemisms for curse words," says Everett. "One was Jiminy Christmas."

Barney enters and silently mouths his amenities. Ernest T. and Andy are both thrown off by Barney's "mouth work."

"We had once written a scene for a show on *Mr. Peepers*, in which Tony Randall taught Wally Cox how to sell encyclopedias door to door," recalls Everett. "It was a case of the naive teaching the naive—only the first naif thinks he is the sharpest living human on earth. It worked well and fit the Barney and Ernest T. characters perfectly."

The night finally arrives when Ernest T. is ready to attend Mrs. Wiley's social. He is dressed immaculately. Barney stops by to drive Andy and Ernest T. to Mrs. Wiley's and doesn't even recognize him. This is one night Barney would "just love to be a wall at Mrs. Wiley's." Andy suggests that Barney join them at the social.

At the party, Andy introduces Ernest T. as Oliver Gossage, his cousin from Raleigh. Mrs. Wiley takes Oliver aside. She wants to get better acquainted. After hearing Ernest T.'s accent, Mrs. Wiley arrives at the conclusion that he must be from "Back Bay Boston."

Barney arrives while Ernest T. and Mrs. Wiley are talking. He is greeted by Andy. As Barney looks around the room, he comments that "Ernest T.'s sure got slim pickin's here. Dogs. Nothing but dogs. If you flew a quail through this room, every woman in it would point."

"The line 'If you flew a quail through this room . . .' was suggested by a writer friend who had once gone away for a weekend at a popular resort back East," says Aaron. "It was a spot where unmarried young ladies went in search of husbands. On the weekend he was there, he walked into the dining room and looked at the many females at the tables who were, unfortunately, not very attractive. And like Barney he said, 'Dogs, all dogs,' followed by the 'quail' line."

Andy tells Ernest T. that he's "coming off like a million dollars." Andy suggests that Ernest T. "get a girl and dance a little." Andy points out Ramona Ancrum. Ernest T. gets the rhythm by bobbing up and down to the music and walks over to Ramona. She is "delighted" to dance.

Mrs. Wiley stops the music and announces that the next dance will be a tag dance. "When you're tagged, you give up your partner." Ernest T. and Ramona begin the dance together. When Ernest T. is tagged and another man takes his place, he doesn't like it. He tags Ramona's new partner and is ignored. Andy tells Ernest T. "to give it [the tag] to him firm." Ernest T. tags the man and is again ignored. He walks to a table, picks up a flower vase, and breaks it over the man's head. At this point, Ernest T.'s cover is blown. Mrs. Wiley yells, "Oh no, it's him. That animal, that creature."

Andy and Barney wrestle Ernest T. out the door. Ernest T. eventually calms down and thanks Andy for trying to help. He decides to "give up his thoughts of femaling."

As Andy and Barney lead Ernest T. away, Ramona comes out on Mrs. Wiley's front porch and yells, "Mr. Gossage, wait. Wait for me." She runs to Ernest T. and asks, "You're not leaving, are you? I was hoping we could spend some more time together."

Ernest T. joyfully lifts Ramona off her feet and carries her across Mrs. Wiley's front yard. After he puts her down, the two leapfrog a stump and scamper away.

"We wrote that Ernest T. and Ramona leapfrog a hydrant," recalls Everett. "I guess there was a stump on the set but not a hydrant."

The stump that the couple leapfrogs was located one house away from the exterior set that served as the front of Andy's home. The familiar set can be identified by its oblong front window and twin-support porch columns that are present in the scene's background.

"Sets were often used a number of times with some minor changes to suit the locale," says Aaron. "It never concerned us that the audience would remember a set. We always felt the story was more meaningful than trivia."

"'My Fair Ernest T. Bass' began production on Thursday, November 21, 1963. The second day's production was interrupted by startling news," Howard recalls. "We were reading around the table and in came the assistant director Robert Saunders. He said, 'I have a very sad announcement to make. President Kennedy has been shot and killed.' Boy, were we upset! It delayed the production schedule for a day, but the show must go on, and it did."

"I remember coming out of my office onto the studio street to walk to the stage, having just heard the news," recalls Aaron. "And there was Howie wandering aimlessly, it seemed, a stricken look on his face. He was repeating loudly, to no one in particular, 'They killed him. They killed the president.' That evening many of the people connected with the show gathered at one of the actors' homes. We tried to console one another and read some meaning into this senseless tragedy. Like the rest of the country, we were in shock."

"I have no other specific memories of working on 'My Fair Ernest T. Bass' or any of the other episodes," says Howard. "They kind of run together as a very happy and joyful experience. It was a remarkable place to be, with these wonderful people, back in a better time for the United States and culture in general."

"Andy Griffith enjoyed this total departure."—AARON RUBEN.

Barney turns to look back toward the angel in the cell to make sure the vision really exists.—Directions from the "Prisoner of Love" script

"Prisoner of Love" begins with Andy and Barney talking outside the courthouse. It is early evening. A train whistle is heard in the distance. Barney tells Andy, "Know what I just might do tonight? Go home, change, drop by Thelma Lou's, and watch that George Raft movie on TV." Barney repeats the statement three times. Andy remarks that he might go over to choir meeting "because they're voting on new robes for next year."

"*TAGS* was the only show on television that could spend three or more minutes with just two men on a porch casually rocking and neither saying much of a thing—pure artistry," says writer Harvey Bullock. "I had previously seen a *TAGS* episode that had Barney repeating over and over what he planned to do later in the day. I thought the scene was wonderful and patterned the opening dialogue in this script after it.

"George Raft was a popular actor in the thirties and forties who performed in a zillion B movies. Whatever his part, he always played it the same way. He would stride into a room, hair slicked back, camel's hair coat draped over his shoulders, glossy patent leather shoes, and tell the gorgeous blonde, 'Grab your stuff. We're leaving.'

"Andy's remark about the pending crisis at the choir meeting over the color of the robes underscored to me the casual, laid-back, affable, small-town atmosphere of Mayberry."

The evening's tranquility is interrupted by the ringing of the telephone. Andy answers the call and learns the state police have captured a criminal. They would like to "park" their prisoner in the Mayberry jail. The unexpected "guest" means that either Andy or Barney will have to stay overnight. Andy eventually agrees to

Episode 114

First Broadcast on February 10, 1964 (To Coincide with Valentine's Day)

Written by
Harvey Bullock

Directed by
Earl Bellamy

Susan Oliver
Guest Stars as
The Prisoner

do so because he wouldn't "feel right having Thelma Lou spend a whole evening alone in a dark room with George Raft."

Andy asks Barney to stay just long enough for him "to run over to the drugstore and get a magazine." The state police arrive while Barney is waiting for Andy's return. Much to Barney's surprise, the prisoner is a beautiful woman.

When writing the script, Harvey had a vivid image of the prisoner. He described her in his script as *breathtakingly beautiful. There is nothing of the criminal about her, nothing cheap or brassy. Her beauty is classic, soft, beguiling, feminine. The room, upon her entrance, pulsates with sex appeal.*

"I named the prisoner 'Angela Carroll,'" says Harvey. "Oddly, as the writing progressed, I realized there didn't seem any need to mention her name. It wasn't a plot point or an enhancement to her extraordinary femininity.

"I wanted the prisoner's crime to be elegant, with high stakes but no violence. Grand larceny for stealing jewels seemed to me the type of crime someone like Angela, who was all charm and breathless beauty, would be charged with.

"I didn't know who would be cast in the role while I was writing the script and had no real nominees after the script was finished. But I had infinite faith in *TAGS* casting director, Ruth Burch. The actress she selected for the role, Susan Oliver, was the perfect, absolute perfect Angela Carroll."

"Susan Oliver was indeed a joy to work with," says producer Aaron Ruben. "She was a fine actress and fit everyone's image of the prisoner."

"Whenever Barney was flustered, it was always solid stuff," says Harvey. "When it is in connection with a beautiful woman like Angela, he is rendered helpless. When Angela asks his name, Barney momentarily forgets. This gag was somewhat predictable, but again, Don Knotts made everything seem new."

Barney lights a cigarette for the prisoner. According to the script directions, *she blows smoke toward Barney, which he drinks in like perfume.*

"Barney's lighting the cigarette for Angela was a typical romantic gesture of the sixties," says Harvey. "The smoke emanating from that Venus would be delightfully intimate, and Barney revels in it. If I wrote this script today, there wouldn't be a cigarette in sight. It would be a no-smoker script and just as effective."

After Barney's departure, Andy has his first conversation with the prisoner, which is interestingly photographed. A close-up shows Andy saying, "Evening." A second close-up shows Angela with no cell bars visible. She answers, "Evening." Andy then asks, "Are you the prisoner?" Angela replies, "That's what they tell me." As Angela rises from the bed, the camera pans backward. For the first time, the bars around her face become visible.

From the audience's point of view, nothing separates Andy and Angela in the preceding close-ups. They are simply a man and a woman meeting each other. When the camera pulls back, revealing the cell bars, the true nature of their relationship is visually established.

Barney eventually returns and tells Andy that he "has checked in the paper about that movie, and it is one I have already seen." Andy and Barney decide they will both "guard" the prisoner. They make final preparations for the night by giving Angela an extra pillow and hanging a sheet in front of her cell. Both the pillow and sheet are taken from the other cell.

When the lights are turned off, the prisoner, silhouetted behind the sheet, prepares for bed under Andy and Barney's watchful eyes. The evening's quiet, however, is abruptly interrupted by the arrival of Otis.

"When the smashed Otis barged into the jail, it added some physical comedy to a conversational script and gave the story a bit more dimension," says Harvey. "Back in the sixties, the drunk was a standard character who could get laughs with his stupor. Writers would bring a staggering Otis into a scene without batting an eye. Over the past thirty years comedic drunks have gotten scarce. Too many families, blighted by alcoholism, don't find the drunk fool amusing."

Upon seeing the pillow and sheet missing from his cell, Otis says, "What happened? Hey, where's everything? There's been a drunk in this cell."

"Otis's speech makes sense only if he suspects crooks, not drunks," says

Harvey: "How did this ~~get by~~? In my script, ~~the~~ line is, 'There's been a crook in this cell.' ~~Possibly~~ this scene was the last shot of the day, or they were running behind time, or ~~perhaps the~~ director ~~automatically~~ associated ~~Otis~~ with a drunk and didn't catch the mistake."

Andy tells ~~Otis~~ they ~~can't take him tonight. He must go~~ ~~home~~. Otis objects and demands to ~~be locked up~~. Andy and ~~Barney~~ physically force him outside. Barney loses the flip of a coin to see who drives ~~Otis home~~.

Andy and ~~Angela~~ have a friendly conversation while Barney is away. At the end of the conversation, Angela asks Andy if he will help her open a troublesome lock on ~~her case~~. ~~Andy~~ enters the ~~cell~~, works on the ~~lock~~, but becomes distracted by the proximity of ~~Angela~~. The two look at each other ~~longingly~~, but the possibilities of ~~the moment~~ are shattered when ~~Barney~~ is heard ~~returning~~ in the squad car.

~~Somewhat shaken by his attraction to Angela~~, ~~Andy~~ decides to go home and let ~~Barney~~ take over.

"This episode has ~~become~~ the subject of ~~much~~ argument with ~~some~~ viewers ~~who say~~ the story wasn't right for *TAGS*. Some say the characters acted differently from ~~their usual roles~~, the attraction of upright Andy to a female stranger was ~~distasteful~~, the show seemed dark, etcetera," says ~~Harvey~~.

"I did want this episode to be a ~~little~~ different by showing Andy involved and intrigued (if only ~~slightly~~) ~~with a Venus~~ such as ~~Mayberry~~ had never produced. I had never before brought him face to face with a mind-numbing angel. And understandably, she did affect him. He found her company appealing—but so would the Pope!

"I guess from the start Angela tried instinctively to size up the rural jail for a means of escape. But more telling, she found herself for once with people who were not judgmental but genuinely friendly. The steady, upright Andy finds an attraction for the beautiful Angela—she's fun, appealing, and vulnerable. Nevertheless, Andy remains in control. He senses her loneliness and talks to her softly but never makes the slightest improper move. Andy shows a glimpse of his personal side. He is not totally cold steel, but he isn't foolish either."

Later that evening, Andy is edgy at home because he senses that Barney is no match for Angela. If Andy goes back to the courthouse, it might crush Barney who would feel he wasn't dependable and had to have every move double-checked.

Andy finally returns to the courthouse. He walks up to the door, reaches for the knob, then pauses, filled with self-doubt. He asks himself one more time if he really should vex Barney by checking on him. He is torn because he also feels the proper conduct of his job is paramount. He decides to chance the vexation and make sure that all is under control. Just as the decision is made, the door opens, and the escaping Angela walks out.

Andy escorts Angela back into the office and finds Barney locked in her cell. His earlier suspicion that Barney is no match for Angela is confirmed, and luckily the prisoner's escape has been prevented.

The train whistle heard in the opening scene foretold the episode's poignant epilogue. On her departure the next day, the prisoner says to Andy and Barney, "You both are kind of 'specially nice guys. I really mean it. And if things were different, well . . . " This is indeed a rare and bittersweet moment in Mayberry—a place where most often things are as they should be.

"Hot Rod Otis"

Episode 115

First Broadcast on
February 17, 1964

Written by
Harvey Bullock

Directed by
Earl Bellamy

We shall meet, but we shall miss him
There will be one vacant chair . . .
We shall linger to caress him
When we breathe our ev'ning prayer.
—"The Vacant Chair"

"I began this script with Andy and Barney playing a game of gin rummy because it was a typical jailhouse pastime," says writer Harvey Bullock. "The game also provided the opportunity to have Otis advise Barney which card to play. Otis's poor advice results in an argument between the two and prevented what could have been a wordy opening scene from becoming terminally bland.

"Otis is somewhat unstable even when sober, so Hal Smith could play the character as broadly as he wished, at times even childlike. When Barney scraps with Otis this childlike attitude rubs off on him, and he ends up arguing on Otis's terms and vernacular.

"I ended this scene with Barney saying to Andy, 'He [Otis] sure does soak up the sauce, doesn't he?' If Andy had responded with an easy reply, he would have answered, 'He sure does.'

"This would have been dialogue standing still. Instead, I wanted to move away from having Andy's reply being nothing more than just a colorless agreement with Barney. I tried a new tack rather than the predictable and had Andy respond with mock reproach, 'Now, Barney, is that any way to talk about your card partner?'

"This is a minor illustration of dialogue construction. Not a big thing, but a very helpful maxim for writing interesting dialogue. And Andy Griffith made the most of it. He was always superb at twisting lines, pulling off repetition with the correct spin, admonishing with the right twinkle, and closing out scenes with finality."

After the card game, Andy leads Otis to his cell. Before going to sleep, Otis asks to be "called at 8:00 in the morning."

The next morning, Barney wakes Otis at 8:00 a.m. Surprisingly, Otis is pleased. He asks Andy for a sip of his coffee as he exits his cell. Otis explains that today is the day he is going to buy something he has always had his heart set on. Andy and Barney question Otis about his purchase, but Otis wants to surprise them and refuses to say any more.

"Otis's request for a sip of Andy's coffee was scripted," says Harvey. "The request and Andy's compliance were intended to show how close Andy, Otis, and Barney were. The bond between the threesome explains why Andy and Barney went to such lengths to help Otis later on.

"Barney speculates that Otis's big purchase may be a vacation to 'the Natural Bridge in Virginia' or to 'an alligator farm in Florida.' Both spots are among the most familiar and, to be frank, possibly the least exciting destinations to anybody but a Mayberrian."

Later that morning, Andy and Barney's speculation is interrupted by the honking of a car horn. The two step outside and find Otis seated in a newly purchased car.

"The prop department got an old, outdated car for Otis's 'hot rod,'" says producer Aaron Ruben. "The car stood out and seemed funnier than having a new sleek vehicle."

Barney feels Otis is now a "mechanized drunk," and he cannot "just stand by and do nothing while this town gets creamed off the map." Barney decides to call Otis in for a driving test. He gives the test using toy cars.

"Taking a driver's test with toy cars had many advantages," says Harvey. "An outdoor test with a real car would necessitate Otis actually driving and would have required hours of production time, drivers, and stunt drivers, etcetera. With toy cars, I got a comic effect without all the production woes and had a greater ease of dialogue between Otis and Barney than if they were in an actual car. With a real car, if Otis didn't pass, the story would be over. On the other hand, if he did pass, Barney's spying on Otis later in the episode would be weakened because Otis has already demonstrated his driving ability. All of these problems were avoided with toy cars, which would never convince Barney that Otis could drive."

At first Otis protests the test. After seeing the toy cars, he tells Barney he "ain't never going to get in that thing." Barney warns Otis to not get "facitious." Otis eventually consents and good-naturedly imitates a car motor so the test will be "more authentic."

"Barney's mispronunciations were always funny," says Harvey. "In the written script *facetious* was spelled correctly, and no directions were given how it should be mispronounced. It is a likely word to twist, and Don Knotts or the director may have come up with it.

"The motor sounds Otis made were requested in the script and grew out of the fact that when any red-blooded American picks up a toy car, he will make a motor sound without realizing it. The sound will sometimes be loud, sometimes faint, depending on the person's sophistication. A mute reaction when a toy car is picked up labels the picker-upper indelibly and absolutely as a poseur of questionable birth with not a trace of wonder."

The driving test ends with Barney being totally frustrated by Otis's performance. After Otis leaves, Andy tells Barney, "If it will make you feel better, why don't you watch him for a while?"

"Barney's surveillance of Otis triggered many possibilities, such as Barney's camouflaged hat," says Harvey. "I also toyed with flashlight codes, Barney holding a glass to the side of Otis's house, the use of a flash camera, and Barney hiding in Otis's car."

Returning from his surveillance, Barney walks down Main Street, stops at a gumball machine, gives it a shake, and takes out a free gumball. Barney's behavior surprises the audience and is comical because it is so unexpected.

"In the script, Barney pauses briefly by the gumball machine to fish for any gum which might be accidentally left in the chute," says Harvey. "Then he continues ambling along. Whoever changed this to Barney actually shaking down the machine and getting a freebie gumball made a distinct improvement."

Barney relates the results of his surveillance. He discloses that Otis was "spotted over at the County Line Cafe buying himself a bottle of the old red-eye." Otis then went over to "Charlie Varney's place to get himself gassed." After Barney shares this information with Andy, the two go over to the Varney residence to check on Otis.

Soon after their arrival, Otis staggers out of the house and passes out beside his car. Barney asks Andy if he can imagine what would have happened if Otis had gotten behind that wheel. After a moment's reflection, Andy comes up with "a way to fix it so Otis will never want to drive again."

Andy and Barney take Otis back to the courthouse, place him in a cell, and douse him with water. When Otis comes to, he finds Andy and Barney reacting to his "driving through the railing, into the river—drowned."

"The fake death story is an ageless standby," says Harvey. "I don't recall any concern from Aaron Ruben even though 'The County Nurse' [Episode 56] had a similar scene. I never saw that show, incidentally, and my approach must have varied enough that it didn't seem repetitive.

"The script stated that the speeches in Andy and Barney's staged 'Otis is dead' performance were to be delivered in 'a wooden, overdone, innocent voice.' Andy and Barney's amateur acting status was important to the scene. If their performance had been too polished it would have reminded the audience that the characters were in reality being portrayed by actors.

"I specifically requested that Andy and Barney sing 'The Vacant Chair.' It was a song I had used when writing hero/villain melodramas for an off-off Broadway dinner/drama house back in the fifties, and it fit perfectly into the scene. 'Chair' is what I asked for and 'Chair' is what I got—sung, by the way, in great harmony."

Otis is so moved by Andy and Barney's performance that he joins them in singing. Eventually, he is overcome with grief and collapses on the bed. Taking advantage of the moment, Andy douses him again with water and tells the startled Otis that he must have been having a nightmare.

Otis promises Andy and Barney he "ain't never going to drive another car again as long as I live—you can get drowned that way." When Barney asks Otis if his "nightmare" was a factor in his decision, Otis explains that he sold his car to Charlie Varney before he took his first drink. Otis continues, "The dream didn't have anything to do with that. Just another of those nutty nightmares. I have them all the time."

"The epilogue for this episode was more serious than most, and the humor arises from Barney's personality," says Harvey. "I had Barney tearful about Otis. Even though the scheme worked, and Otis is hale and hearty, Barney is still carried away. All the theatrics reecho, and he can't shake it off. He goes in the back room to have a cry over a tragedy which he knows never happened!"

"The Songfesters"

Episode 116

First Broadcast on
February 24, 1964

Written by
**Jim Fritzell and
Everett Greenbaum**

Directed by
Earl Bellamy

"Me they, me they, I-O-U, I-O-U..."
—**BARNEY'S voice-box calisthenics**

"I first heard the word songfester from *TAGS* director Alan Rafkin," says writer Everett Greenbaum. "I liked the word and thought it would be a good title for a script that featured music."

Jim and Everett's "Songfesters" script centers on the Mayberry choir's preparation for a concert. Barney, the only tenor, is a featured soloist. During choir practice, however, director John Masters comes to the realization that Barney's "terrible." Mr. Masters calls Andy aside at the end of the practice and tells him that he is going to look for a "decent" tenor. If one is found, he will replace Barney.

Barney has been taking voice lessons to prepare for his solo. After practice, Barney wants to begin his next lesson while his "voice box and muscles are still loose."

"Barney's voice teacher, Eleanora Poultice, was named after Eleanora Duse, a dramatic actress in the early American theater," says Everett. "Jim and I created the character with Reta Shaw in mind. We felt she always gave a great performance, and both of us were pleased when we learned she had been cast in the role."

Before beginning his lesson, Barney proudly tells Miss Poultice that he did his solo today and "knocked them dead." In response, Miss Poultice predicts that Barney is "going to be another Leonard Blush." We learn that Mr. Blush walked in off the street one day and "two years later he sang the 'Star Spangled Banner' at the opening of the county insecticide convention." His rise to the "big time" was "meteoric." For a while he had to wear a black mask while singing to cover a skin condition, which was "probably emotional." At this point, Mr. Blush has a radio program, the third Tuesday of every month on station YLRB in Mt. Pilot.

"I began my writing career in New York City," says Everett. "For a while, my only New York friends were the Schactel family. Irv Schactel was a young lawyer, who at age thirty became the president of Sonotone Corporation. But he loved show business. At three p.m. every Wednesday afternoon, he would get into a cab, put on a black mask, and go to a radio station where he was 'the masked crooner' for fifteen minutes. Mayberry's 'masked singer,' Leonard Blush, was inspired by this memory."

After returning to the courthouse after his lesson, Barney announces that he may be another Leonard Blush. Andy isn't familiar with Mr. Blush, so Barney explains that Leonard Blush "used to sing all the vocals on the Ethel Page organ recital shows." Andy doesn't recall ever hearing "any human words on the show— only a canary singing." Barney replies that the "canary hasn't sung with her since she performed on Sunday afternoons at the Pot O' Honey restaurant."

"The dialogue about Ethel Page and the canary was inspired by radio shows I remembered from the thirties where an organ played and canaries sang," says Everett. "This was before radio stations were allowed to broadcast recorded music. Ethel Page was named after Ethyl Shutte, who was a famous organist. The name of the restaurant, Pot O' Honey, came from the Bit O' Honey candy bar."

Andy warns Barney that he's "pumping up his heels too fast." If John Masters can find another tenor, Barney will be replaced.

Andy's warning becomes a reality during the next practice. Gomer is outside the auditorium repairing a flat tire. When he overhears the choir singing, he joins in. Gomer's voice is wonderful! Following an audition, John Masters decides that Gomer Pyle will be the new soloist.

"After Gomer Pyle's appearance in the 'Man in a Hurry' episode, we realized the character had potential," says producer Aaron Ruben. "We decided to develop the character slowly and didn't want to immediately overload him with talents. That is why we waited awhile before introducing Gomer's singing ability."

"Andy Griffith first heard Jim Nabors sing at The Horn, a coffeehouse that was a spawning ground for new talent," says Everett. "Andy told us that the really odd thing about Jim's singing voice was that it was completely different from his speaking voice. So we decided that if Jim Nabors could talk one way and sing another, Gomer could too."

"Andy Griffith's wife, Barbara, was a gifted musician, so we cast her in this episode," says Aaron. "She appears as Sharon, a member of the Mayberry choir. A wordless role would have made her no more than an extra, so we gave Barbara one line of dialogue: 'I'm sorry, Mr. Masters.'"

"Ric Riccardi supervised all of the episode's choral music. Ric was a gifted musician and the owner of The Horn, where Jim Nabors was discovered. The song the choir sings, 'Santa Lucia,' was probably Andy Griffith's selection. Andy taught choir for a time before becoming an actor and was very knowledgeable about choral music."

Before breaking the news to Barney, Andy reminds him of advice he once gave Gomer. In the episode "A Date for Gomer," Barney gives his "life is like a road" speech after learning that Gomer had high expectations for his blind date with Mary Grace Gossage.

"Jim and I didn't mind referring to a previous show," says Everett. "We liked Barney's 'life is like a road' advice and felt that having Andy use it showed how concerned he was about hurting Barney's feelings. Andy also realized he was speaking in a way that Barney, having previously given the advice, would understand."

Barney is devastated by the news and seeks solitude in the back of the darkened auditorium. The sorrow he feels is communicated powerfully in the script:

In the last row of the hall we see a figure. We TIGHTEN to reveal Barney slumped down in a seat. He gets up slowly—his face very sad—and walks toward the stage. He mounts the stage a forlorn, defeated figure.

He looks around, thinking how it could have been. He runs his hand caressingly over the piano and spots the sheet of music left by Gomer. He picks it up and looks at it sadly. GOMER COMES BACK—UNSEEN.

The lonely figure of Barney stands center stage looking at the sheet music. In a small, weak voice he sings the solo that might have been his. He doesn't get through it. He puts the music down almost in tears and leaves.

The scene's impact is enhanced by Don Knotts's brilliant dramatic performance and Earle Hagen's poignant musical score. Both Gomer, watching from the auditorium's entrance, and the audience are touched by Barney's sense of loss.

Gomer responds to Barney's sorrow by pretending to lose his voice, thus giving Barney his chance to sing. Right before the concert begins, Gomer enthusiastically reveals the truth by shouting, "Sing it good, Barney!" The scene then concludes with the comic dilemma of who will sing the solo—Andy, Barney, Gomer, or all three.

"The Shoplifters"

Episode 117

First Broadcast on
March 2, 1964

Written by
**Bill Idelson and
Sam Bobrick**

Directed by
Coby Ruskin

"We submitted this script to the Writers Guild of America and were totally surprised when it won an award for episodic comedy writing. It was a big thrill."—SAM BOBRICK

"Bill Persky and Sam Denoff, producers of *The Dick Van Dyke Show*, suggested Bill Idelson and I team up," says writer Sam Bobrick. "Soon afterward, Bill suggested an idea for a script. The idea was based on a sketch he had written years earlier about a clerk in a department store who volunteered to catch a shoplifter by posing as a mannequin."

"Bill Idelson pursued us for an assignment," says producer Aaron Ruben. "He and Sam Bobrick came in with a funny idea for an episode. I liked their idea, gave them the assignment, and they wrote an excellent script."

"Aaron Ruben and Sheldon Leonard helped us work out the story," says Sam. "It was my first attempt at writing situation comedy. I had previously written mostly for game shows and *Captain Kangaroo*.

"After the first draft was completed, Aaron read through it and gave us some notes, which we incorporated into the finished script. 'The Shoplifters' was a joy to write, and Aaron was the best producer I ever worked with. He knew exactly what he wanted, which made the writing easier."

"I remember there was a lot of laughter around the table when the actors first read Bill and Sam's script," says Aaron Ruben. "The idea of Barney posing as a mannequin was hilarious, and everyone agreed that the script worked well."

"I was always a big fan of *The Griffith Show* and knew most of the characters," says Sam. "Asa Breeney, the night watchman, and Ben Weaver, the store owner, were written into the script because I remembered them from previous episodes. I also remembered Leon, the little cowboy with the sandwich, and knew he would be perfect interacting with Barney in the mannequin scene.

"Barney was always easy to write for because you instinctively knew what his actions would be in any situation. An example of this is his reaction when he first hears about the robberies at Weaver's Department Store. He immediately pulls

out his gun and wants to line the customers up against the wall. I knew instinctively the reaction fit Barney as soon as we wrote it."

After learning about the robberies, Barney decides to "stake out" the store. He telephones Thelma Lou to call off their date. "The movies are out," he says. "Something big has come up." After a brief pause, he adds, "No, it has nothing to do with trash cans!"

Thelma Lou has assumed that a crime involving trash cans, perhaps a vandal turning them over, could be the "something big that has come up." Barney's response requires that the audience figure out what Thelma Lou has said over the telephone. Her assumption reflects the status of crime in Mayberry. Vandalism of trash cans rather than shoplifting is the norm. Her statement also shows her awareness of Barney's tendency to make a minor crime sound important.

"Barney's telephone dialogue was based more on our understanding of the character than on joke construction," says Sam. "Bill and I never tried to write a joke simply for the sake of a joke. Our goal was to have the humor arise from the personalities of the characters and the situations they were involved in."

Sky Pilot

Bill Idelson is a curmudgeon. I am very fond of the man, but he takes a bit of understanding.

All through my youth, and his, he played the son Rush on a wonderful radio show from Chicago—*Vic and Sade*. So he has been in showbiz longer than any of us and is rather casual about it.

It isn't generally known, but Billy was quite a war hero in World War II. He was a night fighter pilot on aircraft carriers. He was highly decorated, having shot down several planes right over Tokyo. Unlike me, who loved flying, he hated it, which makes it even more heroic.

He will never mention this except to me, since we both wore the navy wings of gold. I was mostly an instructor.

But he is an eccentric, which we all allow him to be.

Incidentally, he is a wonderful teacher of comedy writing. Many of his students have found employment in the industry.—EVERETT GREENBAUM

Barney stakes out Weaver's Department Store later that evening. Ben Weaver also suspects a nighttime robber and is inside the store with Asa Breeney. Barney and Ben, each unaware of the other's identity, scurry through the store's aisles in pursuit of the "robber." The pursuit and the accidental interaction with the store's merchandise (a talking toy clown, a glassware display, etc.) are carefully choreographed. *TAGS* musical director Earle Hagen's score effectively accompanies the stakeout. The sound effects (a ringing cash register, clanging glass, etc.) bring the scene to life.

The episode's second act begins with Barney explaining his theory that Ben Weaver is stealing from himself. In Weaver's defense, Andy says, "Weaver is one of our best churchgoing members. He knows every hymn in the book." Barney replies, "Oh, that's just a front. You watch him sometime when we're singing 'Leanin' on the Everlasting Arms.' He don't even know the words. He just moves his lips."

"Individual bits of dialogue, such as Andy and Barney's discussion about Weaver, are born in exactly the same way for all comedy writers," says writer Bill Idelson. "The process goes like this: Two partners sit in a room, create the scene for themselves, and then improvise, sometimes assuming one character, sometimes another. It's kind of a stream-of-consciousness thing. The writers probe and investigate the working of the minds of their characters. Naturally, a lot of garbage emerges, but when something seems funny, believable, and right, they seize it and write it down."

Andy disagrees with Barney's theory and assures him that what they are looking for "is a plain, ordinary shoplifter." Andy sends Barney over to Weaver's store to give Ben "the feeling that we are giving him a little cooperation."

Andy arrives at Weaver's store a short time later to relieve Barney and is unable to find him. Andy causally walks around the store and discovers Barney, disguised as a mannequin. Barney tells Andy, "I have my eye on our bird right now." Afraid that Andy will blow his cover, Barney quickly shoos him away.

Barney continues to watch his suspect but is repeatedly interrupted by the store's customers. Aware that his cover is "blown," Barney decides "to make his move." He approaches his suspect—a little old lady. The woman is outraged, and no shoplifted merchandise is found in her possession.

After the suspect appears to be innocent, Andy and Barney step outside. Andy explains to Barney that you never arrest a shoplifter inside a store. Andy then says he has a line on a suspect himself and adds, "There's our man now." The dialogue keeps the audience guessing. The scene immediately cuts to a shot of Barney's "little old lady."

Andy sends Barney into the store for a bathroom scale. After Barney returns, Andy asks the little old lady to step on the scales. Her weight is a surprising 163 pounds! Andy unbuttons her coat. The coat is lined with "a traveling pawnshop" of stolen merchandise.

"*TAGS* was always a wonderful writing experience," says Sam. "But a show is only as good as those in control of it. Aaron Ruben, Sheldon Leonard, Andy Griffith, and Don Knotts were not only brilliant in what they did but were the nicest people you could ever work for. As a young writer, I was very lucky. Billy Idelson was also a great partner. I owe him a lot."

"Andy's Vacation"

"I've had it! I'm sick of sheriffing! I'm sick of this room! I'm sick of this town!"
—ANDY TAYLOR

Episode 118

First Broadcast on
March 9, 1964

Written by
**Jim Fritzell and
Everett Greenbaum**

Directed by
Jeffrey Hayden

Jim and Everett's "vacation" script begins with Barney bringing in a couple for fighting. Andy has repeatedly warned the couple and angrily fines them "ten dollars or ten days in jail." Barney is shocked by the severity of the fine.

Andy explains that he's just "beat to the socks." Barney encourages Andy to take a vacation and suggests a trip to Miami. Andy agrees to take some time off. He plans to "lay around home, read the *Geographic*, and just take it easy."

"Early in the episode we established Andy's need for a vacation and had Barney advise him to go to Miami Beach and 'take in one of those rabbit girl clubs,'" says writer Everett Greenbaum. "Of course, Barney meant the 'Bunny' clubs. The suggestion grew out of the image Barney has of himself as quite a man of the world.

"It seemed that everyone got the *National Geographic* and saved all the copies. However, no one ever read it. Everyone said, 'One day, I'm going to catch up on my *National Geographies*.' This fact inspired Andy's comment about reading the magazine during his vacation."

Barney summons Andy back to the courthouse soon after his vacation begins. He wants Andy to inspect Gomer, who is serving as a temporary deputy.

"Jim and I first used Gomer as a temporary deputy in 'High Noon in Mayberry' and liked the results," says Everett. "Andy's absence set up the perfect opportunity to use Gomer in the position again, so we did. We were well aware that Barney's supervision of Gomer would lead to some good comedy."

Barney and Gomer interrupt Andy's vacation again when they stop by to get a set of handcuff keys. They are standing on the Taylors' front porch, talking to Andy through an open window. While waiting for the keys, Gomer requests an apple. When he reaches through the window to get the apple, Gomer reveals that he and Barney are cuffed together.

"We originally set the handcuff scene outdoors where Andy was pruning an apricot tree," says Everett. "Gomer asks for an apricot and reveals his cuffed wrist. We later changed the setting to the interior of the house and used the window and apple. This decision saved the production a half day outdoors."

Andy eventually comes to the realization that if he is to have any peace he "has to get away from here." He decides to go to the mountains for a week.

"The mountain exteriors were shot at Coldwater Canyon in Beverly Hills," says director Jeffrey Hayden. "We traveled to the end of the canyon road, and they would unlock a gate for us. We then proceeded to the reservoir above. The area had no homes and was very rustic."

After Andy's departure, the state police bring an escaped convict to the Mayberry jail. The convict is to stay overnight. Gomer feels Andy should be contacted, but Barney disagrees. The two discuss the situation with their backs turned toward the cells. Unnoticed by Barney and Gomer, the convict reaches for the key hanging outside the cell, unlocks the door, and escapes.

The convict heads to the mountains and stumbles on Andy. Tipped off by the convict's prison shoes, Andy apprehends him, ties him to a tree, and goes off for help.

"I was never crazy about this episode," says Everett. "I worried that the audience might feel that the escaped convict coming across Andy in the mountains was too much of a coincidence. But the encounter paid off in fun and moved the story along, so we went with it."

Barney and Gomer arrive a short time afterward. They have come to find Andy. Gomer suggests they "make animal noises in case they get separated."

"Gomer's suggestion that he and Barney make animal noises to stay in contact was one of Jim Fritzell's ideas," says Everett. "Using an animal noise as a warning was often used in movies—especially westerns, which were Jim's favorites."

Barney begins the search by looking through a set of binoculars. Gomer wants to take a look too and reaches for the binoculars strapped around Barney's neck. He lifts them to his eyes, momentarily strangling Barney, and spots a man tied to a tree.

"The binoculars were included in our script," says Everett. "But Gomer wanting to see and almost strangling Barney with the strap was inserted on the set."

Barney and Gomer come to the aid of the tied-up convict. The convict hides his face and disguises his voice. He explains that an escaped convict jumped him and tied him to a tree. Barney and Gomer free the man and allow him to leave.

Barney and Gomer continue their search. They come up on Andy. Because Andy's back is turned toward them, Barney mistakes him for the convict. Barney courageously sneaks up on the "convict," jumps on his back, and is overtaken by Andy.

"We felt it didn't hurt to see Barney being truly brave once in a while, so we had him mistake Andy for the escaped prisoner and courageously attack him from behind," says Everett. "We did, however, temper his courage by having him repeatedly ask Gomer, 'Are you ready?' before making his advance."

As the episode continues, Andy, Barney, and Gomer split up to search for the convict. Andy soon finds the convict and apprehends him. Meanwhile, Barney and Gomer stalk each other.

"While Barney and Gomer search for the prisoner, we used the old visual gag of having them circle a tree, each thinking the other is the prisoner," says Everett. "This was a very tired routine and the weakest part of the show."

In the epilogue, Barney is reading a newspaper article that reports the arrest of the convict. Barney discovers that his name is misspelled.

"We repeated the gag of misspelling Barney's name in the epilogue. We first introduced it in 'The Bank Job.' Barney constantly thirsted for publicity. When the paper misspelled his name, Fisk-e, it always worked.

"We concluded the epilogue with Andy suggesting to Barney that he take a week off and 'get a corner room at the Y in Raleigh.' Staying at the Y enabled young fellows with little money to travel. That's how I got to see New York City in my teens. I never, however, stayed in a corner room—that's a writer's embellishment."

"Andy Saves Gomer"

Episode 119

First Broadcast on
March 16, 1964

Written by
Harvey Bullock

Directed by
Jeffrey Hayden

"I'm sure the average viewer has no concept of the effort required to put together a thirty-six-page script—nor should they. I would rather have them join us in Mayberry and enjoy the doings than have them dissect it. Perhaps the best stories are those where the viewers forget they are watching a written play and are completely caught up with the characters and action."
—**HARVEY BULLOCK**

"Andy Saves Gomer" begins with Opie rushing into the courthouse with a letter from Barney. Barney and his cousin Virgil are vacationing in Raleigh.

"I have no recall why Don Knotts wasn't in this script," says writer Harvey Bullock. "Maybe he had another show to do, or a trip, or an illness. I was told he wasn't available, so I knew ahead of time and fashioned whatever I could without him."

Andy reads the letter to Opie and Floyd.

"This was the first episode Howard McNear appeared in following his stroke," says producer Aaron Ruben. "We wanted to make Howard feel he was still part of the series despite his handicap and invited him back for this scene. His reactions to the contents of Barney's letter were hilarious."

Barney writes:

"Last night was really wild. We went to the arcade and played four games of Skee-Ball. Then we went in a booth where you get four pictures taken for a quarter. I was going to send you one, but it turned all brown later. After that, we had supper at a waffle shop where the waitresses all dress alike in peekaboo blouses. Have to close now. Having fun, but money sure doesn't last. Been here only three days and already gone through ten dollars."

"In my script, most of the first three pages are devoted to Andy reading Barney's letter," says Harvey. "Some of the highlights of Barney's vacation were taken from my own recollections, especially the photo booths where you got four prints, which all turned brown later, for a quarter."

Andy decides to show the letter to Gomer. When he arrives at Wally's Service

Station, he finds Gomer asleep. The trash can inside the station is smoking. Andy wakes Gomer and puts out the fire, which "was more smoke than anything else."

"The trash can in the filling station contained some inflammable material, like film, that would only smoke and not flame up," says Aaron.

Gomer thanks Andy for saving his life. He is very appreciative and offers Andy free gas and oil, but Andy declines.

The next morning, Andy joins Opie at the breakfast table. Opie's hair is slicked down and neatly combed in preparation for school.

"The slicked-down hair was not included in the script," says Harvey. "If every detail of wardrobe, props, makeup, camera location, and actor's intonations were in the script, it would have been a hundred pages long and too cluttered to follow. So I wrote directions only when they were critically important. All of the production crew knew their jobs, knew the script, and each contributed his particular expertise without being told. The slicked-down hair was probably the suggestion of the director or Andy."

Gomer enters the kitchen with "a mess of fish." He got up "special early" to catch the fish for Andy's breakfast. Gomer feels it "is little enough for the man who saved my life." He dramatically describes the rescue to Aunt Bee and Opie.

Gomer has already washed and polished the squad car. He offers to fix Andy's fence, trim the back hedges, sweep out the garage, and clean out the "ease" troughs.

"Gomer says ease troughs for eaves troughs," says Harvey. "He occasionally slurs words and phrases to make them phonetic soundalikes."

That afternoon, Andy returns home and finds Gomer "setting him up with some firewood." Stacked firewood covers the front porch. Inside the house, firewood is stacked up to the ceiling. A stunned Andy observes that "there's enough wood there for seven winters."

"The load of firewood Gomer cuts was acquired by the prop department, who were masters at getting anything a script required," says Aaron.

Andy tells Gomer that he's done enough. Andy says he will see Gomer at the station on the weekend, and "we'll have a bottle of pop." Andy ushers Gomer out the door.

"There is interesting and endless speculation among many of *TAGS* viewers as to whether bottle of pop is right or whether we should have said Coca-Cola, or dopes, or dranks," says Harvey. "It seems to vary from place to place, so any one name could be justified. When I was a kid in New York state, it was always bottle of pop, so that's what I put down without a second thought."

After Gomer leaves, Aunt Bee comes down the stairs. Gomer insisted on straightening the attic. She has spent the past hour "putting things back where I can find them." Aunt Bee tells Andy that Carter Finch called. He said, "They're having a boiled dinner down at the firehouse and cribbage afterwards."

"Aunt Bee's line about 'a boiled dinner down at the firehouse and cribbage afterwards' was probably a total mystery to most southerners," admits Harvey. "I can only plead attrition in my Dixie roots which allowed me to think that Yankee phrase was universal. After all, I left North Carolina when I was only three and hadn't absorbed much of a decent vocabulary."

On his way to the boiled dinner, Andy bumps into Gomer. Gomer tells him that he will not forget the good deed Andy has done for him. He says, "If I live to be a hundred, I intend to be by your side to help you out every day of my life. Goodbye, lifesaver man."

"'Lifesaver man' was a made-up phrase that comes from mentally running a scene over and over through your mind, putting yourself inside the character, and then letting your thoughts run amuck until something seems to work," says Harvey.

The next morning at breakfast, Aunt Bee tells Andy she is going to do some baking. She asks him which he would prefer—applesauce cake or angel food cake. "You choose which. You can have your favorite." Andy chooses applesauce cake. Aunt Bee immediately replies, "I think I'll make angel food. I have a lot of egg whites."

"Asking what kind of cake Andy would like for supper and then deciding on another kind was right out of the Bullock household," says Harvey. "As I was leaving for work in the morning, my wife Betty would often ask what I'd like for dinner and then usually give me a choice. I might pick lamb chops. All day I would be salivating all over the typewriter in anticipation—LAMB CHOPS!

"Then I'd come home, zoom into the kitchen, and she'd say offhand, 'ready in ten minutes. We're having meat loaf.' She had found some ground beef in the freezer and decided to make a meat loaf, completely oblivious to the fact that my whole system was crying out for the promised lamb chops."

Gomer comes into the kitchen while Andy is having breakfast. He offers to cut Andy's grass. Andy declines because that's Opie's job. Instead, Gomer trims the hedges. Afterward, he takes Opie roller-skating.

Later that day, Opie comes to the courthouse to complain about Gomer. Andy is working on the gas line to the heater. Opie tells Andy that Gomer puts on his skates for him and picks him up when he falls down. Opie is upset because "all the guys laugh." Opie looks out the window and sees Gomer walking toward the office. He hides under Andy's desk.

Gomer enters, asks about Opie, and decides to wait until Opie comes by. Andy tells him that Opie will probably be heading home because Aunt Bee is baking, and he likes to be "close by when there's any cake baking." Gomer rushes off to help Aunt Bee.

That evening, Andy, Aunt Bee, and Opie hide in one of the cells. They drape a blanket over the cell's bars and have supper. When Aunt Bee leaves, Andy tells her that he may be late because he has to fix a leaky heater.

Opie asks if they are going to have to eat in the courthouse all the time. Andy assures him that things will return to normal once Gomer figures he's done enough. Andy adds, "Course, with him, he may not figure we're even until he saves my life for me." This statement gives Andy an idea, and he tells Opie to run along.

Andy telephones his house and asks Gomer to bring his jacket to the courthouse. Andy explains that the gas heater is broken, and it's chilly in the office. He adds that there is no real problem unless the gas should start to leak. Then it would "asphyxiate whoever was here. But you would smell the gas if that was happening."

After hanging up, Andy opens the valve on the gas line, lies down on the floor, and closes his eyes.

"The idea for the gas leak in the courthouse came from pondering what prop would work best to make Andy a possible victim," says Harvey. "Drowning and a fake car wreck were considered, but the gas line seemed by far the most acceptable and easiest to understand. It also didn't require a lot of production time."

Before Gomer arrives, Opie enters through the back room. He walks over to Andy and asks, "Pa?" Andy immediately starts doing push-ups.

"I used Opie's walking in on the passed-out Andy to further frustrate Andy while he waits for Gomer's arrival," says Harvey. "It would have been too pat to have Gomer enter the scene immediately. Opie's interruption left Andy concerned that the fakery wouldn't work and created more story tension."

Opie has come to the office because he needs Andy's help. His skate is stuck in the sidewalk grate. Andy agrees to free the skate. As the two walk out, Opie remarks that he smells gas.

Gomer enters moments later. He smells gas too and attempts to turn it off. The gas, however, overcomes Gomer, and he passes out. Andy returns, sees Gomer, shuts off the gas, and wakes Gomer up. Andy says, "It's just lucky I came back," then realizes this will simply mean another debt.

Gomer is still drowsy, so Andy leans back against the cell and tells Gomer, "Thank heavens you come by when you did. Fast thinking, Gomer, to turn the gas off like you did and pull me away. No two ways about it, Gomer, you saved my life. And if I live to be a hundred, I'll never forget it. I'll be by your side every day."

Gomer replies, "Oh, you don't have to do all that." Andy then suggests that they're even for saving each other's lives. They can now go back to "being what we were before."

In the epilogue, Aunt Bee asks Andy if turning on the gas was taking a chance. Andy answers, "Not really. All's well that ends well . . . Happy days are here again." This sounds somewhat strange, since Andy doesn't usually use clichés.

"I suppose some more colorful phrases could have been devised, but it was important that Andy reveal his exact feelings," says Harvey. "These two old standbys are right on target. Also colorful terms sometime divert attention away from the story point the scene needs to make. I felt Andy was needed as a complete straight man in this scene, so I felt the obvious clichés were okay."

At this point, Gomer enters and tells Andy that he's noticed that Andy is accident prone. Gomer says, "There's no question about it. You need somebody around to keep an eye on you." Gomer has decided to be that person.

"This episode is a rare instance in which the problem is not completely solved," says Harvey. "Gomer feels Andy is accident prone and vows to stay by his side, but his attention will soon wane as other problems and puzzles intrigue him. I plead guilty, however, to using the 'here we go again' finish. I tried not to use it. I experimented with alternates and wasn't thrilled by them. Time was short, so I succumbed. I promised to never do another 'here we go again'—unless time got short, and I wasn't thrilled with alternates."

"Divorce, Mountain Style"

"You can't explain how the details arise. You just sit down together with the typewriter and usually things just bubble up. On bad days, nothing bubbles."
—EVERETT GREENBAUM

Episode 121

First Broadcast on
March 30, 1964

Written by
Jim Fritzell and
Everett Greenbaum

Directed by
Jeffrey Hayden

"Divorce, Mountain Style" begins with Andy and Barney in the courthouse. Andy asks what Barney and Thelma Lou did after the movie the night before. Barney tells Andy that they dropped by Nelson's Hardware Store. Barney says, "He's got a new window display—bicycle accessories. He's featuring a transparent plastic tool kit. They're really practical, you know that? Say you got a pair of pliers, a screwdriver, a wrench, and half a candy bar. Well, you know at a glance what you got." Andy responds that he prefers the solid black kits because "what I got in my bicycle kit is my business."

Mitch Jayne, the Dillards' bass player, offers some observations on this opening scene: "Denver Pyle, who had sort of taken us under his wing, went to great lengths to explain just what an actor did. He urged us to see what Don and Andy did with a script, not altering the words so much as interpreting them and letting the characters take over. This was particularly impressive in the little intro things they would do, usually on the bench in front of the courthouse. Just the two of them with a few ridiculous lines like this episode's 'bicycle tool-kit' bit, which they would transform into a marvelous comedy sketch. I have the feeling Everett and Jim relished these little character vignettes, which played so lovingly with the premise.

"Since the little introductory bits were part of each show, we usually got to see these filmed. I had always loved the short introductory things. Even watching them back home (without an inkling that we would soon be a part of it all), I realized that this was a supremely clever way to center a viewer who had been elsewhere in TV-land and needed a chance to adjust to Mayberry. These, I think, were the keys to the time machine that Mayberry was, and of course, still is."

"Before I met Jim Fritzell he had been a writer on a radio show starring *TAGS* director Bob Sweeney and his partner Hal March—*Sweeney and March*," says writer Everett Greenbaum. "The tool-kit bit was inspired by a joke written for that show by a comedy madman named Jack Douglas."

Andy and Barney are interrupted by the arrival of Charlene Darling Wash. Charlene is alone. The rest of her family is "still up in the mountains." Andy asks how Charlene made the long trip. In response, Charlene sticks up her thumb and whistles.

"Charlene responds to Andy's question by sticking up her thumb and whistling," says Everett. "In the script, we wrote that Charlene replies, 'I can herd a T Model with the best of them.' The thumb and whistle, which fit the character perfectly, came up on the set.

"When we first introduced Charlene in 'The Darlings Are Coming,' we described the character as 'about seventeen, voluptuous, blonde, etcetera.' The casting of Maggie Peterson was a surprise to Jim and me. We just never pictured Charlene as long, tall, and thin, but Maggie made the part hers and was excellent."

Charlene has come to town to complete "a tiny errand." She asks Andy if he could help her out, and Andy agrees to do so. Charlene wants Andy to drive her somewhere, but she is mysterious about where she wants to be driven. She will only say, "I'll tell you when we get there."

Andy and Barney drive Charlene out of Mayberry. Charlene has Andy stop the car by an oak tree and asks if there is a shovel in the back of the car. Charlene then digs a hole, buries a sack, motions for Andy to stand by her side, recites an incantation, draws a circle in the dirt, and says to Andy, "Now I can be yours." Charlene has just completed "divorce proceedings. From now until the moon comes full is the waiting period."

"While writing this script, I got several books on superstitions from the library," says Everett. "By altering or combining many of them, we were able to catch the flavor and make up our own."

"Even though we were familiar with the culture of the Ozarks, the Dillards had no input about the script's mountain folklore," says Mitch. "We figured the scripts weren't seeking accuracy, and, for sure, we didn't think they needed our help."

When asked why she is divorcing Dud, Charlene says he went "fox hunting with Hasty Buford and they didn't come home till Wednesday week." According to Charlene, the two "sit around drinking hard cider, punch each other on the arm, and holler, 'flinch.'" Andy tries to offer a defense for Dud by saying that he might have been "getting you the makings for a fox pie."

"Andy's line about the fox pie grew out of a comedy routine of a friend of mine, Eddie Lawrence, in which he offers advice to avoid anyone eating a fox pie," says Everett.

Andy, Barney, and Charlene return to the courthouse. Barney decides to go over to the library to get a book on mountain folklore. He tells Andy that he's going to get him "out of this." When Andy and Charlene enter the courthouse, Briscoe Darling and the boys are waiting inside.

Briscoe learns from Charlene that Andy stood at her side for the divorce incantation. Briscoe accuses Andy of leading Charlene on "since day one." Briscoe doesn't go along with the divorce, "but the fact is that the ritual's been performed right and proper. The deed's been done. So, come the next full moon, we's going to have ourselves a ceremony."

Later that evening, Barney returns from the library with a book on mountain folklore. Barney has found an antidote in the book for the divorce proceedings: "If the intended should dig up the proceedings before the moon comes full, the divorce proceedings are null and void." Barney suggests they dig up the proceedings. He justifies this action by saying, "If there's a peaceful way, take it." Andy wants no part of this solution. Digging up "that stuff would mean I believe in all this hocus-pocus."

Dud Wash barges into the courthouse and accuses Andy of being a "homewrecker." Dud wants to "fight it out" with Andy. Andy responds by grabbing Dud by the seat of the pants and ushering him out the door.

"We were all appalled when Hoke Howell, who originally played the role of Dud Wash, was replaced by Bob Denver, even though Bob was a great Dillards fan and a good actor," says Mitch. "Bob just wasn't Hoke. In our brief Hollywood experience, Hoke was like family. It was almost as if all of our characters could be replaced if they could replace Maggie's husband so offhandedly. The only explanation we heard was that Hoke was making a picture and was unavailable. I think we patterned our reaction to Maggie's and Denver's—that's showbiz. But I remember that basically this just reinforced my belief that every show was probably our last. You have to remember that in the year this show was made, no one, including Andy, dreamed that it would last as long or have as lasting an impact as it did."

"The reason I didn't appear in 'Divorce, Mountain Style' was because CBS wanted to give Bob Denver some prime-time exposure," said Hoke Howell. "The network had just decided to go with *Gilligan's Island* for the following season, and they felt it was important to give Bob, who starred in the series, some advance publicity."

As the story continues, Andy reluctantly agrees to dig up the divorce proceedings. When he and Barney return to the oak tree, Andy begins digging. As he throws aside a shovel of dirt, a shovelful of dirt is immediately thrown back. The Darlings walk up with guns drawn. This frightens Barney, and his hands tremble. Briscoe suggests that Andy "just go on home and forget all this nulling and voiding."

The "digging up the divorce" scene is photographed in part from ground level. When the dirt is thrown back into the hole, Andy is shown from the knees down. Then the legs of Briscoe and the boys enter the frame.

"This camera angle was not mentioned in the script," says Everett. "Another addition to this scene was Barney shaking fearfully when he and Andy are confronted by the Darlings. We just wrote Barney was scared, no shaking. I think this works better, since the Darlings were never a real physical threat, even with their guns drawn."

Later that night, Barney takes another look in the book. He reads aloud the following passage: "If a rider dressed in black rides east to west on a white horse in the light of a full moon and passes a bridegroom, the bridegroom is cursed, and the union is cursed." Andy realizes "that's it." Barney agrees, "All we need is somebody willing to dress up in a black outfit and ride a white horse—some patsy." At this point, Andy looks at Barney.

"The rider dressed in black was an enlargement of something I found in one of the library books on superstitions," says Everett.

The next night, Andy and Barney prepare to "curse the union." Dressed in black, Barney meets Andy at a stable. A white horse is saddled and ready. Barney complains that he feels "like a real idiot. Black makes me look so thin." He begins sneezing. It seems Barney is allergic to horse hair. He says to Andy, "Remember when we were kids? We all had our pictures taken on a pony. Well, not me. I had mine taken sitting on the hood of my uncle's Hudson Terraplane."

"Having Barney ride the white horse opened the door to numerous comic possibilities," says Everett. "His line, 'I feel like a real idiot. Black makes me look so thin' grew out of Barney's concern with his appearance, which was always funny. Barney's comment about his childhood picture was inspired by the memory of a photographer coming around to the neighborhood with a pony, which was a staple in Jim and my childhoods. Using the Hudson was a way of turning the memory into comedy."

The Darlings pass the time prior to Andy and Charlene's wedding by playing "Shady Grove." Charlene dances and whistles during the song's instrumental break.

"Maggie's whistling during 'Shady Grove' was her own touch," says Mitch. "She has a nice tomboy feel for these things and can whistle up a coon hound (or a cab) if she has to."

Andy joins the Darlings. He tells Briscoe that he has decided to go along with "this marriage idea." Andy, Charlene, and the Darlings proceed "down to the preacher's house."

Meanwhile, Barney is having difficulties getting the white horse to travel east to west. The horse walks into Floyd's front yard. Floyd is sitting on the porch and greets Barney by saying, "You seem to be on a horse. The reason I was so surprised—I just wasn't expecting it."

"We didn't get to see any of the horse scenes being filmed, much to my dismay," says Mitch. "I didn't get to meet Howard McNear, who played Floyd the barber either, which was a disappointment because everyone loved him and talked about his incredible sense of humor. I still ache over missing that. I have an idea that Andy added the scene with Howard because it's the kind of thing Andy would have done to ease him back into work."

"Floyd was added later," concurs Everett. "We always loved Howard McNear on screen and off. He was a welcomed presence in this script."

Barney eventually gets the horse to move from east to west. He rides past Andy, Charlene, the Darlings, and Dud (who was waiting for Charlene at the preacher's house). Charlene immediately recognizes "the curse of the white horse." The Darlings back away from Andy, and Charlene and Dud are reunited.

"In the epilogue, Barney dances to the Darlings' music (some very fancy footwork by the way)," says Everett. "There was no music, however, in our epilogue. I'm sure that Andy, with the Darling family present, wanted to do some music, so it was added. Barney's wonderful dancing, which grew out of Andy's suggestion, is just another example of Don's comic genius."

"A Deal Is a Deal"

Episode 122

First Broadcast on
April 6, 1964

Written by
**Bill Idelson and
Sam Bobrick**

Directed by
Jeffrey Hayden

"Cures poison ivy, athlete's foot, prickly rash, complexion, and spring itch."
—The label on Miracle Salve

"If I thought up a story idea for *TAGS*, I would call Aaron Ruben for an appointment. He would give me a date and time he'd be available," says writer Harvey Bullock. "These appointments were granted mostly to seasoned writers whose work the producers knew. A novice writer occasionally could crack in, but mostly the veteran writers had the edge because the producer knew they would deliver a script on time, it would be shootable, and the characters would be consistent. However, when a new writer who showed talent came on the scene, the word got around very quickly, and he was sought after."

"Our first script, 'The Shoplifters,' was well received, and Aaron Ruben agreed to meet with Bill and me so we could present an idea for another story," says writer Sam Bobrick. "The idea we presented was one I thought up about boys who are Opie's age selling salve on consignment. Aaron liked it and gave us the go-ahead to write the script."

Bill and Sam's completed script begins with Opie and Johnny Paul arriving at a potential customer's residence at the same time. The boys decide who will make the sales pitch by matching "odds or evens." Opie wins. He rings the doorbell. When the door opens, Opie begins the pitch by saying, "Madam, would you like to buy a jar of . . ." The door slams shut.

"The 'odds or evens' idea was inspired from memories of our childhoods," says Sam. "A lot of our own realities went into each script. I don't remember what inspired the name Miracle Salve and the list of ailments the salve was supposed to cure, but the dilemma the boys faced of not being able to sell the stuff was very real to me. For one week in college, I tried to sell Amana freezers door to door, so I knew the plight of a salesman firsthand. Thank God I failed, and the experience was soon behind me."

"The prop department had the boxes printed up with Miracle Salve and Mt. Pilot on them," says director Jeffrey Hayden. "I don't recall how many boxes were

printed, but the prop department had the time-consuming job of folding and taping each one together. There was nothing inside any of the boxes, so I showed the boys how to hold them so they would appear to be filled with jars of salve."

Opie dejectedly enters the courthouse after a day of poor sales. Opie tells Andy he is thinking about sending the salve back. When Barney enters, Opie tries to sell him a jar of salve. Barney refuses. He has already purchased a jar and is dissatisfied with the product. He tells Opie that it's supposed to be good for crow's feet, but "I put it on my crow's feet a week ago, and they're still there. See that crease in my cheek—nothing."

Barney thinks Opie's problem may be poor salesmanship. Opie shows Barney his technique. Opie repeats the opening line of his sales pitch and stops. He explains, "That's as far as I get. Then they slam the door in my face." Barney suggests that's his problem. "You can't give them a chance to cut you off like that. You got to get your foot in the door and start talking and never stop."

Barney demonstrates. He takes a jar of salve and says to Andy, "Hello, little girl, may I see the lady of the house?"

"Barney's demonstration of a proper sales technique was inspired by my freezer-selling spiel," says Sam. "We gave the speech a comic twist by having

Barney say to Andy, 'Hello, little girl, may I see the lady of the house? Oh, you are the lady of the house,' etcetera."

One of the boys, Trey, decides to return his unsold jars of salve. A short time later, he receives a letter from the Miracle Salve Company. Trey tells Opie and his friends that the manufacturer wrote they were "real disappointed in him as a salesman and are putting him on a blacklist."

None of the boys know what a blacklist is. They rush to the courthouse to have Andy explain it to them. Andy, however, is away, so Barney is consulted.

Barney explains that a blacklist means "you can't get a job." Trey shows Barney the letter. Barney thinks the situation over carefully and asks, "How do you fight fire?" One of the boys answers, "With a hose?" Barney replies, "No, with fire! You fight fire with fire. They scared you with a letter. We'll scare them back with a letter—a lawyer letter."

The master shot for the first part of this scene, from its beginning through Barney's question, is photographed from behind Barney's desk. The wall, on which the gun rack is mounted, is removed, and the camera is positioned in its place.

"Much of the action in this episode takes place in the courthouse," says Jeffrey Hayden. "It was my responsibility as the director to select camera angles that would present the action in an interesting way. Placing the camera behind Barney's desk was perfect for photographing the beginning of the scene when Barney is napping. The audience also sees the action from a point of view that was rarely used, which made the scene visually interesting."

Barney dictates a letter to Opie. The letter opens with, "From the office of Bernard P. Fife, attorney-at-law." Opie stops writing after the first few words, but Barney continues a long discourse.

After Barney finishes, one of the boys immediately says, "I don't think fighting fire with fire is going to work."

At this point, Andy enters. When he is told that Trey has been blacklisted, he reassures the boys that the salve company is just trying to intimidate them. He says, "It's their way of getting you to sell more salve." Andy tells the boys "to run along and don't worry about it."

After the boys leave, Barney tells Andy they ought to figure out a way of getting back at the salve company. He suggests that they go to Mt. Pilot to visit the company. Andy cuts him off. He doesn't want to hear Barney's idea. His "mind is closed."

After Andy walks out, Barney immediately telephones Wally's Service Station. When Gomer answers, Barney asks if he would like to "take a little drive with me over to Mt. Pilot."

Barney and Gomer visit the Miracle Salve Company in Mt. Pilot. The two are dressed in suits, and Barney wears wire-rim glasses. When they enter the Miracle Salve office, Gomer introduces himself to one of the owners as Opie Taylor Sr. He says, "My little boy sent away for some of your salve. Well, he got to experiment-ing with it, you know like kids do sometimes. So he put some on his dog. You see, Junior's dog had the mange. Well, that mange cured up overnight. So I took some of the salve over to Dr. Pendyke here [Barney]. Dr. Pendyke is a veterinarian."

In a high-pitched voice, Barney confirms what Opie Sr. has said and tells the owner that they decided they would like to buy the salve and sell it to other veter-inarians, or even drugstores.

The owner steps into the back room to get his partner. While the man is away, Gomer asks Barney what is wrong with his voice. Barney explains that it is just part of his disguise. Gomer is amazed. He remarks, "That's good. I wish I could do my voice like that."

When the two owners return, Gomer introduces himself, in a deep voice, to the other man. Dr. Pendyke is told the company has "four or five gross" of Miracle Salve on hand. Pendyke replies, "That's good for a starter, but don't you think you could get some more back from those boys in Mayberry?" The owners agree to try.

"We knew immediately that the idea to have Barney and Gomer visit the Miracle Salve company incognito would work beautifully," says Sam. "Jim Na-bors and Don Knotts were wonderful in the scene, and each one's reaction to the other's disguised voice made the scene even better than we had imagined."

After leaving the Miracle Salve office, Barney tells Gomer, "They're on the phone right now, calling every veterinarian and drugstore in the county telling them they got a new mange cure."

A few days later, the company collects all the salve Opie and his friends have been unable to sell.

Assuming their scheme was a success, Barney and Gomer enter the court-house triumphantly. Barney confidently takes a seat on the edge of Andy's desk, crosses his legs, folds his hands smugly in his lap, and starts to explain the scheme to Andy. Gomer shows his admiration for Barney by mirroring Barney's actions in childlike fashion.

"Gomer's copying of Barney's actions was not suggested in our script," says Sam. "It was probably the idea of the director or one of the actors. Gomer's won-derful pronunciation of *salve* was likewise not in the script. I imagine it was the idea of either Jim Nabors or Aaron Ruben."

The telephone rings just as Barney is about to begin his explanation. It is Aunt Bee, who is "awful upset." Andy tells her to "just take it easy, and I'll come right home." Barney and Gomer accompany him.

When Andy arrives at home, he finds 946 jars of Miracle Salve billed to Opie Taylor Sr., with payment due in seven days. Gomer turns to Barney and says, "It didn't work the way you said it would, Barney." Andy is now very interested in hearing all about the scheme.

An important element in most *TAGS* episodes is the resolution of the problem on which the storyline is based. "A Deal Is a Deal" twists this premise somewhat. The original problem is solved, but a bigger problem takes its place.

The epilogue centers on Barney's efforts to get rid of the boxes of salve. He has Gomer round up Opie and his friends and bring them to the courthouse. Upon their arrival, the boys are seated. Barney begins a speech to persuade the boys to once again sell the salve.

As he talks, the close-ups are photographed with the camera positioned so it looks up into Barney's face. This camera angle draws the audience into the action and allows the viewer to see Barney through the eyes of the seated boys.

The boys listen for a short time, then silently walk out. Without saying a word, Andy rises from his desk, picks up several boxes of the salve, and hands them to Barney and Gomer. The two exit the courthouse yelling, "Salve!"

"The Return of Malcolm Merriweather"

"Frances Bavier was a vastly underrated actress."
—HARVEY BULLOCK

Episode 124

First Broadcast on
April 20, 1964

Written by
Harvey Bullock

Directed by
Coby Ruskin

Bernard Fox
Guest Stars as
Malcolm
Merriweather

"I met Bernard Fox while I was in London working on some British sitcoms," says writer Harvey Bullock. "I knew his style and strong points, so it was no problem coming up with a second storyline for his character, Malcolm Merriweather. In pitching the idea to Aaron Ruben, I mentioned showing how foreigners often know more about our country than we do. Another point I emphasized was that the properly dignified, well-mannered Englishman was an interesting contrast with local Mayberrians. Malcolm's accidental friction with Aunt Bee, who feared she would be replaced, made it all come together."

"I was, of course, very happy to learn that there was to be another episode of *TAGS* for me," says Bernard Fox. "Working with Andy, Don, and Ronny Howard was indeed a pleasure.

"I found Andy outgoing and charming, and it seemed to me that he kept a very firm hand on the way the show was headed when we sat and read the script round the conference table. Don was nice, friendly to the newcomer, and, of course, brilliant. I remember young Ronny getting quite enthusiastic when he learned that I was keenly interested in fencing, and we had some long conversations on the subject.

"I didn't get to spend much time with Frances Bavier. She tended to keep to herself in her dressing room, and we only met when rehearsing or when actually filming the scene.

"The director, Coby Ruskin, was a darling man. I knew him vaguely from England, where he was directing a TV series. It was some sort of show with guest entertainers. I was in a comedy at the Garrick Theater London, and a segment from the play was to air on this show. The actors all trooped in for rehearsal with Coby, who was directing the segment. He was just marvelous. When he finished, the segment was better than anything else in our play, and we all wished that he had directed the whole thing. I will never forget it. His talent, his understanding and warmth just enveloped you, filled you with confidence, and made you as steady as a rock. Coby, you were great!"

Harvey began the script for "The Return of Malcolm Merriweather" with Barney impatiently waiting for Aunt Bee to bring lunch to the courthouse. Verbalizing his impatience, Barney comments that he has a clock in his stomach that tells him it is past time to eat. Barney adds that his mother was the same way. Andy responds by asking, "Hey, Barn, these clocks you and your mother have in your stomachs. Did the ticking keep your father awake at night?"

"This opening scene was just an extension of an old wheeze—'I bought one of those Venus de Milo statues with a clock in its stomach, but I'm too embarrassed to wind it,'" says Harvey. "It's an American icon, and I used it here because I always found it personally amusing."

Aunt Bee arrives with lunch and apologizes for being late. She says she had to get her wash hung out. Andy compliments her on the lunch and gives her the title, "Miss Luncheon Tray." Aunt Bee has no time "to listen to such blarney." She has "a cake in the oven, and ironing to do, and supper to get."

After Aunt Bee leaves, Andy wonders aloud to Barney if Aunt Bee knows how much they appreciate everything she does. Barney's mouth is full. He starts to answer Andy but can't resist another mouthful of sandwich.

"Because Barney has a mouthful of food, he has to just nod for an answer," says Harvey. "This was scripted. In the script Aunt Bee hasn't left the courthouse when this part of the scene takes place. The script repeated the business of Barney's mouth being too full to talk three times."

The lunch is interrupted by the honking of car horns. The two walk outside to investigate and discover that Englishman Malcolm Merriweather, who is somewhat of a traffic hazard, has returned to Mayberry. Malcolm greets the two with his trademark—holding a hand out for a handshake and changing it instantly to the tipping of his hat when the other person reaches for his hand.

"Malcolm's disappearing handshake and hat-tipping were Bernard's contributions," says Harvey. "He also contributed many expressions to flavor the story such as 'Aren't you kind?' and 'proper Bobby Dazzler.'"

"'Aren't you kind?' originated in the north of England somewhere," says Bernard. "I borrowed it from the actress Dame Thora Hird, who used it frequently as a gag."

After learning that Malcolm is traveling through America, doing odd jobs along the way to finance the trip, Andy asks if he would like to work at the Taylor house for a while. Andy explains that Aunt Bee's got "a way yonder too much to do. You'd be a big help." He also adds that it would be more than a position. Malcolm would be staying with friends. Andy's proposal beautifully expresses the spirit of Mayberry.

"Andy's offer reflected my desire to make Malcolm's hiring more than a completely business relationship," says Harvey. "I wanted Malcolm's employment at the Taylors to be informal, so they could sup together and be relaxed."

That evening, Malcolm prepares supper and cleans up afterward. While Malcolm is in the kitchen, Aunt Bee tells Andy that she's not sure about "having a man around the house all day." Andy responds with some very humorous dialogue: "With Malcolm here you'll have more leisure time to watch TV. You know that show you like where everybody is sick and in the hospital. You can watch the whole thing instead of peeping at it through the kitchen door. Sit right there and watch every operation without missing a single stitch."

"Andy's reminder to Aunt Bee that with Malcolm around she can watch all of her soap opera was a powerful enticement," says Harvey.

When Malcolm finishes in the kitchen, he tells Opie that it's past his bedtime. Before going to bed, Opie asks Malcolm to show him a magic trick.

Malcolm pulls a folded sheet of newspaper out of his sleeve. He makes a simple tear in the newspaper, has Opie hold the ends, says the magic words, and lifts the newspaper, revealing a paper ladder!

"The ladder-tree trick was another idea of mine," says Bernard. "I think Harvey asked me if there was anything I could do in the way of magic that would astonish Ronny. I had a whole paper magic act I was taught as an eleven-year-old boy working the fit-ups in Ireland (six plays a week, with a matinee Wednesday and Saturday), so I suggested a paper trick for Malcolm."

The next morning, Aunt Bee oversleeps. When she comes downstairs, she asks Malcolm if Andy and Opie have had their breakfast. Malcolm informs her that they have had breakfast and gone. He then seats Aunt Bee at the table, serves her coffee, hands her the morning newspaper, and goes into the kitchen to get her eggs. Holding the newspaper, Aunt Bee looks at the perfectly set table and seems at a loss.

Later that day, Barney waits impatiently for lunch. Andy notices Barney's restlessness and asks, "Clock in your stomach bothering you? Your tummy going tick-tock?" Barney replies angrily, "Now don't start up with me, Andy." When Andy starts to speak, Barney sings, "ra-bop-bop-bop" to drown out Andy's voice.

"Andy mentions Barney's inner clock again because it really tickles him," says Harvey. "Barney sings to prove he is not listening to Andy. He wants Andy to know that he is wasting his time teasing."

Aunt Bee enters the courthouse. She has just finished attending a club meeting. When she offers to bring Andy and Barney some lunch, Andy declines.

As Aunt Bee is walking toward the door, Malcolm enters with a "little high tea." He has prepared Cornish pasty. After listening to Andy and Barney's enthusiastic remarks about the lunch, Aunt Bee says, "You boys won't be satisfied with tuna-fish sandwiches anymore, will you?"

"Cornish pasty was not my first choice for the main dish Malcolm serves Andy and Barney," says Bernard. "At one script conference, I was asked by Harvey for a typical English dish. I suggested spotted dick, but Harvey didn't think a British dish called 'spotted dick' was appropriate for *TAGS*, so I disappointedly suggested Cornish pasty. By the way, I must say the prop man did a nice job of it— meat and potatoes in one end, plum pudding in the other."

"The next night's after-supper scene on the Taylor front porch was written to show the serenity of Mayberry after dark," says Harvey. "Andy is idly picking his guitar, Barney is stretched out on the wicker love seat, rubbing his stomach contentedly, and Aunt Bee is playing solitaire."

After finishing in the kitchen, Malcolm joins the three on the front porch. Barney asks Malcolm about his plans to visit Gettysburg and says, "See, that's famous because that's where Lincoln made his famous Gettysburg Address speech. See, Lincoln, he was what we call a pres-e-dent. And Washington, you see, was our first president and Lincoln, now he didn't come along till later. He was fourteenth or fifteenth—somewhere along in there." Malcolm immediately replies, "sixteen" and names the fourteenth and fifteenth presidents.

"I definitely wanted Malcolm to be knowledgeable about American history," says Harvey. "This illustrated one of the script's selling points—that our foreign visitors often know more about us than we know ourselves. I felt it was important that Malcolm's knowledge be low-key so as not to seem patronizing. The serenity of the Taylor front porch provided the perfect setting to have Malcolm demonstrate his knowledge.

"Barney's pronunciation of *president* was scripted, as was the follow-up where Barney isn't sure of Lincoln's number, and Malcolm helpfully spews names of all the early presidents—finally getting to Lincoln at number sixteen."

Before going back into the house, Malcolm makes a play in Aunt Bee's game of solitaire. The play takes her "out." He then places her sweater upon her shoulders, which she pushes off moments after his departure.

"Malcolm is really trying to help Aunt Bee with her cards, but she resents it— especially after all the attention Malcolm has been getting," says Harvey. "Naturally, Aunt Bee is far too well-mannered to lay out any of her personal problems or to betray her anguish over being replaced.

"This script required an extraordinary attention to detail in its progression. It was important that the audience understood that Aunt Bee has a cherished fatigue from doing housework, which in fact gives a center to her life. She is also fearful that Andy and Opie might benefit from having Malcolm around. But she must not seem to be whiny or petulant. Her feelings of apprehension about being replaced have to grow at the right pace. Her feelings are communicated in part from the placement of her close-ups, which convey much, even when she has no lines."

Opie joins Malcolm in the kitchen for a glass of milk before going to bed. Malcolm sings as he cleans a pot. Opie asks him if he always sings when he does the dishes. Malcolm answers affirmatively and explains that "you're happiest when you're working because it makes you feel useful." Opie agrees and says, "When Aunt Bee was working, she'd sing all the time." Malcolm thinks about what Opie has said and replies, "I don't think I've heard your Aunt Bee sing."

"I needed a device for Malcolm to realize Aunt Bee's distress and understand that she actually enjoyed keeping up the house and depended on it for her worthiness," says Harvey. "I achieved this by having Opie and Malcolm discuss how Aunt Bee used to sing when she worked. When Malcolm explains that 'you're happiest when you're working because it makes you feel useful,' he arrives at the realization that this likewise applies to Aunt Bee. So he does a bit of self-destruction to bring things back as before."

Malcolm sets up the circumstances for his dismissal by serving Sunday lunch drunk. He pulls the drawer of the china cabinet out and spills the silverware on the floor. He then serves the soup cold right out of the can.

"Malcolm's drunk scene was constructed from waiter's goofs," says Harvey. "In fact, Ray and I had given Bernard a similar but longer scene as an errant waiter in an episode of *Make Room for Daddy*. In that episode, Bernard was truly a goof, not pretending as in this script."

"In order to give myself a slight feel for the drunk scene, I asked the prop man if he had any ideas. He produced a shot of scotch," says Bernard. "He did give me a very old-fashioned look when I asked for a second! As a matter of interest, the assistant prop man was a lad from Liverpool."

Andy, Barney, and Aunt Bee hear a crash in the kitchen. The three go to investigate and find Malcolm sitting on the floor. Barney notices an empty bottle of cooking sherry on the counter and brings it to Andy's attention. He tells Andy that he has no choice but to fire Malcolm. Barney says, "The guy's a wino. Get rid of him." Malcolm overhears and agrees to "pack up my things and leave."

After Malcolm leaves the kitchen, Andy examines the bottle, which Malcolm supposedly emptied. He smells the kitchen sink and realizes the bottle's contents were poured down the drain.

Before leaving, Malcolm tells Opie to try being "a little more help around here, young man." Andy opens the kitchen door to enter and stops. He then overhears Malcolm telling Opie that "when your Aunt Bee starts singing around the house, and she will soon, you just join in and have a regular sing-along."

Opie leaves and Andy enters. He acknowledges what Malcolm has done by observing that he "sobered up mighty quick." Malcolm looks around the kitchen and apologizes for the mess. Andy tells him not to worry, that Aunt Bee will take care of it.

Malcolm then tells Andy goodbye, and Andy responds by saying, "Thanks, Malcolm, for everything."

"I made the decision to have Andy realize Malcolm's sacrifice and to thank him obliquely without forcing an admission, which might be uncomfortable for them both," says Harvey. "Having Andy tactfully talk around the subject was very effective and provided a satisfying ending."

"The Rumor"

"What a dumb trick. Don't ever call me dumb again."
—GOMER talking to Barney

Episode 125

First Broadcast on
April 27, 1964

Written by
**Jim Fritzel and
Everett Greenbaum**

Directed by
Coby Ruskin

The situation in this episode is somewhat different from Fritzell and Greenbaum's usual storylines. Instead of a motorcycle or the purchase of a first car causing the problem, the problem in "The Rumor" results from Barney's misinterpretation of Andy and Helen's intentions.

"This is one of the few times that Jim and I stole from ourselves," says writer Everett Greenbaum. "We had done this story with almost the same complications on *Mr. Peepers*. We enjoyed including Aneta Corsaut, who portrayed Helen Crump, in the script. Jim Fritzell was dating Aneta at the time and had encouraged her hiring on *The Griffith Show*. Aneta was a wonderful person and a close friend."

"The Rumor" begins with Andy walking through Mayberry's business district. He looks into the window of Sterling's Jewelry Store and sees Helen. Andy enters and asks Helen about a bracelet she is holding. Helen tells him it's a charm bracelet for her niece's graduation.

The jeweler steps into the store's back room. While he is away, Andy and Helen kiss.

Barney, who is patrolling the street, walks by the jewelry store and notices Andy and Helen inside. Barney sees the kiss and immediately jumps to the wrong conclusion.

A short time later, Barney tells Thelma Lou that Andy and Helen are "up to something." When Thelma Lou asks why they couldn't just happen to be in the jewelry store together, Barney replies, "Put two and two together. Read the handwriting on the wall. Blow away the smoke and look at the fire." In response to his clichés, Thelma Lou says, "Barney, you're always throwing your education in my face."

Barney responds, "I can't help myself. I'm just a student of the humanity. I guess that's the difference between a sharply honed lawman and just an ordinary jerk wearing a badge."

"It was always fun to write Barney's bull," says Everett. "Barney's dialogue flowed out of us—since the two of us were naturals at doing the same thing."

Barney eventually tells Thelma Lou that he thinks Helen and Andy are getting engaged. He points out that Andy wouldn't kiss anybody "out in public unless he had been hit by a transport of emotion."

"The 'transport of emotion' line was taken from old novels," says Everett.

When Barney tells Thelma Lou to keep the engagement a secret, he says, "I know it's tough on you being a woman, but for heaven's sake don't tell anybody."

Barney's statement is immediately followed by a close-up of Aunt Bee crying over news of the engagement. The camera pulls back, and Barney is revealed as the one who has told the secret.

"This visual joke was included in the script," says Everett. "We set it up with Barney's request for silence from Thelma Lou. The director's decision to begin the next scene with a close-up of Aunt Bee, before showing Barney sitting beside her, made the joke even more effective."

Still emotional over Barney's news, Aunt Bee cries while serving supper later in the evening. When she steps into the kitchen, Opie tells Andy that he thinks "she's got one of those allergies." When Andy asks what he means, Opie explains, "You see, at a certain time of the year bumblebees stand on the flowers, and they get a lot of this flower dust on their legs." Opie points out that the bees spread the dust, and people with "allergies" breathe the dust. He goes on to say, "I guess 'cause they just don't know any better. Well anyways, they get all puffy and their eyes run water."

When Aunt Bee comes back into the room, she starts to take her place at the table but is overcome with emotion and returns to the kitchen.

In response to Aunt Bee's crying, Opie observes that he doesn't think "that's allergic." Aunt Bee's sobs get louder. Opie responds, "I just don't understand it. I washed my hands and face. I emptied all the dirt out of my pants cuffs. My lizard is outside in the lizard house."

Andy explains that things sometimes "set women off." He alludes to certain sounds, smells, music—"a song on the radio reminds them of a rowboat ride or a dance." After listening to Andy, Opie says he doesn't understand. Andy replies, "Well, when you grow up, you won't understand it either, so don't worry about it."

"Opie's bumblebee and flower-dust theory is his way of explaining things—just as Barney has his way," says Everett. "I can't remember how the lizard house came up, but I clearly recall the inspiration for the dirt in the pants cuffs. In Buffalo I had a radio show called *Greenbaum's Gallery*. A man named Ray Wander wrote it with me. We wrote at Ray's house. As I typed, he brushed out the cuffs of all his pants.

"A lot of Andy's talk about women sprang from Jim Fritzell. To him, women were a race apart—very hard to understand. On the other hand, I was a bit better with them.

"We wrote a brief scene in the first act in which Helen is walking one of her students home. Helen tells the student to remember to have her mother put something on her sty. We included this scene because we wanted to show that Helen was not only a good teacher but deeply concerned with the well-being of her students."

Thelma Lou sees Helen on the sidewalk in front of the student's house. She hugs Helen and tells her how happy she is. Thelma Lou invites Helen to walk downtown with her and do some shopping. Helen replies that she does need some stockings but she can pick them up when she goes to the jeweler's on Friday. She excuses herself from the shopping spree by saying she has papers to grade.

As the plot continues, Barney decides to surprise Andy and Helen with a party. At the planning session for the party, the food is discussed. Aunt Bee asks if Lillian should be asked to bring her meatballs. Barney answers, "They're always terrible—1 percent meat and 99 percent bread crumbs. She puts them in the oven, and they vulcanize."

"Vulcanization was the baking of crude rubber, sulfur, and other chemicals to make commercial rubber," explains Everett. "Barney thought it was a clever way to comment on the toughness of the meatballs."

Aunt Bee suggests that the perfect gift for Andy and Helen would be to fix up Andy's bedroom, which "is like an elephant's nest." The room needs fresh paint and wallpaper, new curtains, and a canopy bed "like in the Errol Flynn movie *The Dashing Prince*."

"Aunt Bee's description of Andy's bedroom was inspired by my brother-in-law's father," says Everett. "He said when his sons were boys their room looked like an elephant's nest. The name of the movie with the canopy bed in it was made up."

After the party plans are made, Barney goes around town collecting money to pay for the new decorations in Andy's room. Barney has each person write in a little book their name and the amount given.

The painter and wallpaper hangers are hired. When Barney stops by to see the room, he tells Aunt Bee that everybody will arrive for the surprise party "at eight bells" that night. "Thelma Lou and I will make like we're taking Andy and Helen out to dinner, see. Then we're going to stall them until it's time to get here."

By eight o'clock Andy's room is ready. Aunt Bee proudly shows it to one of the party guests and says that it is her "dream room."

Meanwhile at the courthouse, Barney can't decide where to go for supper. No place suits him. Andy eventually tells Barney to drive him to the market, and he'll get a loaf of bread and some baloney. Barney finally agrees to drive over to Andy's and "get something out of the icebox."

The party guests decide that everybody will go into the kitchen. When Aunt Bee gives the signal, they will come out and yell, "Surprise!" Gomer volunteers to go outside to "do my hoot owl" when he sees them coming.

Andy, Helen, Barney, and Thelma Lou arrive at the Taylors'. Gomer is eating a piece of cake when the squad car drives up. His mouth is full, so he is unable to hoot.

Andy and Helen enter the house. Gomer enters behind them and does his hoot owl. At this point everyone yells, "Surprise!" When Andy wants to know what the surprise is for, Barney says, "Oh, come on, buddy. It's not a secret anymore. We all know." When Helen asks what they know, Thelma Lou answers, "That you're engaged, and you picked up the ring today."

Aunt Bee ushers the speechless Andy and Helen upstairs to see Andy's room. Everyone follows. Aunt Bee announces, "This is your present."

Andy gets everyone's attention and tells them that there has been a mistake. He tells the group that they aren't engaged and have not even discussed the topic. When Barney asks about seeing the kiss, Helen says they were just buying a bracelet for her niece.

At this point, everyone begins to yell at Barney. Andy speaks up and says, "Folks, hold it! A party's a party anyway. And you're all here. There's plenty of food and pop here and everything, so why don't we all go downstairs and have a good time." Everyone leaves the room except Andy and Helen.

The two discuss the possibility of "getting together" in the future.

"The scene between Andy and Helen was difficult to write," says Everett. "The dialogue had to express their immediate feelings of not wanting to get married and the possibility that someday they might. We ended the scene with the couple kissing, which I'm sure Andy Griffith enjoyed—he was always ready to do some kissing."

When Andy and Helen join the party, Andy announces that everyone will get their money back, and Aunt Bee will get the room she's "always dreamed of."

"In the epilogue, Barney loses the book in which he wrote down the amount each person contributed to fix up the bedroom," says Everett. "The scene would have been nothing without the conflict the lost book caused. The discussion about who owes whom and how much each gave is not only conflict but a way to work some of the other characters into the end of the show."

"Barney and Thelma Lou, Phfftt"

"Believe me, I'm not worried. I got that little girl right in my hip pocket."
—BARNEY FIFE

This was the first episode written by Bill Idelson and Sam Bobrick in which the storyline's problem results from difficulties that arise in a relationship. In their two previous *TAGS* scripts, the problems resulted from a shoplifter and jars of salve.

"An episode which dealt with relationships was actually easier to write," says writer Sam Bobrick. "The characters gave better guidelines for developing the story than in our first two scripts where the narrative centered on a comical situation."

The episode begins with a wonderful scene in which Barney and Thelma Lou are window shopping. The two stop in front of a furniture store and fantasize about decorating their future home. Momentarily carried away in their dreaming, the couple speak as if their marriage is a certainty. Barney, however, makes it clear that marriage is at best a distant possibility.

"By the time we started actually filming a scene, Don Knotts was ready, and you really believed whatever he said or did when he looked at you," says Betty Lynn, who portrayed Thelma Lou. "Don's performance always came from the bottom of his heart. Whenever I was in a scene, I played it for real too.

"I felt that Barney was the love of Thelma Lou's life. She adored Barney. I think Thelma Lou was kind of hurt at times that Barney didn't say, 'Well, let's get married.' She kept hoping, and it never quite happened. It was like 'You're my girl, and somewhere off in the future we might get married, but we don't have to talk about that now.' In a way, there was a longing for Barney in Thelma Lou's heart that was never really satisfied."

The following day, Andy and Barney are busy with monthly reports. Thelma Lou telephones Barney and asks if he can drive her to Mt. Pilot for a dental appointment. Gomer drops by while Barney is on the telephone. He tells Andy that the squad car, which is in the garage getting fixed, won't be ready until that

Episode 126

First Broadcast on
May 4, 1964

Written by
**Bill Idelson and
Sam Bobrick**

Directed by
Coby Ruskin

afternoon. Gomer offers Barney the use of his pickup. Barney, however, can't drive the pickup. Nobody can except Gomer, so Gomer volunteers to drive Thelma Lou to Mt. Pilot.

After Barney hangs up, Andy begins to tease him about going along to chaperone. Andy says, "You mean you're sending your girl on a long trip all alone with a handsome fellow like Gomer here? You're liable to lose your girl."

In response, Barney tells Andy and Gomer, "There are a lot of things in this world I might be worried about, but losing Thelma Lou is not one of them. I got that little girl right in my hip pocket."

"The message in this show," says Sam, "was 'Let's look at relationships. Are they fair and the same for all parties?' Obviously, most of the time, they aren't.

"One way we demonstrated the difference in Barney's and Thelma Lou's feelings about their relationship was to have Barney tell Andy that he had Thelma Lou in his hip pocket. We repeated the line several times in the episode, but when we first wrote it, that was not our intention. The line just worked well as a connector, which is a word or phrase that can be comically repeated. We liked to have connectors, but only when it was natural—like Barney's line was in the context of this story."

After Gomer leaves, Barney refers to Gomer and says, "Sheik."

"This was an example of Barney's tendency to mispronounce words," says Sam. "The word Barney had in mind was *chic*, which is French for sharp, current, or stylish."

During their drive to Mt. Pilot, Gomer asks Thelma Lou when she and Barney are getting married. He tells Thelma Lou that people say "you hardly ever hear one name without the other one." Thelma Lou is pleased. Gomer continues, "If he don't hurry up somebody's going to come along and steal you away." He goes on to add that Barney said "he had you in his hip pocket." Thelma Lou is no longer pleased.

"Gomer and Thelma Lou's conversation during their trip to Mt. Pilot was photographed inside the studio," says producer Aaron Ruben. "The camera was placed in front of the stationary truck. A cloth was placed behind the truck's back windshield to eliminate the need for a rear projection shot of the passing scenery. The shadows that were cast on the truck's hood were done with lights and a cut-out that simulated the shadows that would be cast on the vehicle."

After returning from Mt. Pilot, Gomer shares with Andy and Barney the details of his outing with Thelma Lou. He says, "She bought me lunch—sausages and three eggs, six flapjacks. It must have set her back over seventy cents."

After Gomer leaves, Barney tells Andy that in all the years he's known Thelma Lou, she's never bought him lunch. They've always gone "dutch treat."

"Barney's response to Thelma Lou's buying Gomer's lunch showed an endearing sort of pettiness and insensitivity on his part," says Sam.

Thelma Lou decides to teach Barney a lesson. She breaks their standing Tuesday night date. Barney goes to the courthouse and dejectedly explains to Andy that he was "all dressed up—tie, coat, the works." He called Thelma Lou to tell her he was on his way over, but she acted surprised, "like it completely slipped her mind that it was Tuesday night." Thelma Lou told Barney that she was busy. Barney is amazed because every Tuesday night for as long as he can remember "we're sitting on that couch, a pan of cashew fudge between us, watching that doctor show on TV. Now all of a sudden, it slipped her mind."

"We painted a situation in which the viewer would know instantly that a great date for Barney was not what anyone would consider to be a great date—for Thelma Lou or any other person," explains Sam.

Barney accompanies Andy on his nightly check of Main Street. As the two walk down the street, they see Thelma Lou and Gomer going to the movie.

The next day, Barney tells Andy that it's all his fault that Thelma Lou went with Gomer to the movie. Andy responds by telling Barney he is "acting like a kid. There's nothing serious going on between Thelma Lou and Gomer. So they went to the movie. As far as that goes, you've stepped out a few times yourself." Andy then asks Barney about Juanita who works at the diner. Barney says that's different. When Andy pushes him for an explanation of the difference, Barney says, "Well, if you don't know how it's different, I ain't going to tell you."

"Barney's response to Andy showed the narrow concept of fairness he had," says Sam. "Barney was a very chauvinistic fellow."

Andy advises Barney to go see Thelma Lou. He tells him to take her some flowers and see what's wrong. Barney insists that "she ought to come to me with flowers. I'm the stood-up party."

When Gomer enters, Barney walks out. Andy asks Gomer how he came to take Thelma Lou to the movie. When Gomer replies that Thelma Lou asked him, Andy asks what the two talked about on their way to Mt. Pilot. Gomer answers, "We talked some about Barney . . . and how he thought he had her in his hip pocket."

Andy begins "to get the picture. Thelma Lou is playing a little game with Barney, trying to make him jealous." Gomer is upset when he learns that Barney's feelings are hurt. Andy tells him not to worry. The two of them will get over it, but it was a good thing Thelma Lou picked Gomer because sometimes a "thing like that could backfire, you know." When Gomer doesn't understand, Andy explains, "Suppose she had this date with another fellow. This fellow got to liking it, got to liking her, and wanted her to be his steady. I expect she'd drop her game pretty fast and go running back to Barney."

After hearing this, Gomer decides to "scare Thelma Lou back into Barney's arms." He visits Thelma Lou. Soon after his arrival, he asks for a cup of coffee. While Thelma Lou is out of the room, Gomer telephones Andy. He tells Andy he is fixing to "backfire on her." But Thelma Lou overhears Gomer.

Meanwhile, Barney is outside Thelma Lou's house. He has decided to follow Andy's advice and bring Thelma Lou some flowers. When he starts to ring the doorbell, he hears Gomer's voice and stops. Barney walks over to the window and looks in.

Inside, Gomer asks Thelma Lou to "be his steady." Thelma Lou answers, "Gomer, I'd love to," and kisses him on the cheek.

After seeing the kiss, Barney goes to Andy's house. He tells Andy that they were "kissing—hugging and kissing. You couldn't have gotten a piece of tissue paper between them. They were that close."

The doorbell rings, and it is Gomer. Barney immediately raises his fists and tells Gomer to "put 'em up." Andy has to separate the two.

"What we were going for in this scene," says Sam, "was to have Andy come across as an adult trying to separate two children."

Gomer tells Andy that something went wrong with his plan. "She kissed me right flush on the jaw. And you know what that means, don't you? There's only one thing I can do now, only one honorable thing. After she kissed me like that, I got to marry her."

Andy decides "this thing has gone far enough" and takes them all over to Thelma Lou's house.

Barney remains in the squad car while Andy and Gomer talk with Thelma Lou. Andy explains to Thelma Lou that Gomer comes from a family with a very strict code of conduct. When a girl kisses a fellow "it's marrying time." Thelma Lou tells Andy it was all a joke. Andy asks Gomer if it is a joke when a "girl kisses you like that." Gomer says, "It ain't no joke to me. When a fellow and a girl kiss, it means they got to marry. Shoot, my mama and daddy just shook hands on their deal."

"This dialogue grew out of the character," says Sam. "It communicated Gomer's innocence and the fact that absolutely nothing happened between him and Thelma Lou. This also helped explain Barney's warped look at relationships—in his mind, one kiss implied there was something going on between Thelma Lou and Gomer."

Andy asks Thelma Lou if she would "take the kiss back." Thelma Lou kisses Gomer, taking the first kiss back.

After Andy brings Barney inside, Thelma Lou apologizes to Barney and asks him to "please don't ever say you've got me in your hip pocket." The two are reconciled.

In the epilogue, however, the original cause of the misunderstanding is not resolved—Barney once again confidently tells Andy, "I've got that little girl right in my hip pocket."

"Comedy writing is delivering a message in a clear and easy-to-take way," says Sam. "More than being concerned with solving any problem, we were always more concerned with dealing with the message."

"Back to Nature"

"I just patched some bird words together and came up with web-footed, red-crested lake loon."—HARVEY BULLOCK

Episode ~~127~~

First Broadcast on
May 11, 1964

Written by
Harvey Bullock

Directed by
Coby Ruskin

"Back to Nature" begins with a conversation between Andy, Barney, and Floyd about modern gadgets. Barney is upset because the new automatic cutoff on the filling-station gas pump has caused a scratch on the squad car. After listening to Barney's complaint, Floyd goes off on a tangent and says he dislikes the new, electric lather makers. He prefers the sound the shaving brush makes in the mug when it goes "klep."

"The script copy I have begins with the scene in the courthouse in which Andy tells the boys about the impending overnight camping trip," says writer Harvey Bullock. "Perhaps producer Aaron Ruben wrote the scene with Howard McNear, who portrayed Floyd Lawson, to add length or variety.

"All writers have a proprietary interest in what they write. I would occasionally feel twinges when I saw changes to my script. Most of the script changes on *TAGS*, however, enriched the story, and I always felt comfortable with writer-friendly Aaron Ruben at the helm."

The next day, the boys who are going on the camping trip meet with Andy at the courthouse. Andy gives the boys instructions about the trip.

One of the boys is Opie's friend Trey Bowden. ~~Trey first appeared in the~~ episode "Andy and Opie's Pal" and was named ~~after a friend of Harvey's~~ son, Andy, who lived up the street from the Bullocks.

"The real Trey Bowden was one of ~~the boy campers in this show~~," says Harvey. "For some reason I can't recall, my son Andy was not used. I was seldom on the set, but I think it was a rare occurrence when friends were used as extras."

After the boys leave, Gomer enters and tells Andy he has decided not to go along on the camping trip. He says, "There's this movie on the TV tomorrow night with Preston Foster I wanna see."

"Preston Foster was a prominent movie star in the 1930s," says Harvey. "He was a leading-man type who played rugged outdoorsy roles—Mounties, rangers,

419

woodsmen, etcetera. Gomer felt watching a Foster movie would make up for his not going on the camping trip."

The next morning, Andy, Barney, Gomer (who was finally persuaded to come along), and the boys arrive in the woods and set up camp.

Later that night around the campfire, Barney leads the boys in their request for a ghost story. Andy agrees to tell one. He asks the boys to "be real quiet." An owl hoots in the distance. Andy says the hoot owl reminds him of a story and starts with "a long time ago, right in these very woods, there lived an old hermit."

"As a child, I spent three summers at YMCA Camp Arrowhead in Binghamton, New York," says Harvey. "The experience definitely left memories. What we kids loved best were the ghost stories—either when the whole camp was around a fire or when they were told by individual leaders at bedtime in the cabins. Later I worked at the same camp, in charge of entertainment, and told ghost stories, using moans, groans, and staring eyes. The campers would buy it all, huddle closer, and walk back to their cabins in tight groups with sweeping flashlights.

"As I remember, I told a story like Andy's 'The Hermit with the Golden Arm' early in the summer. Then one of the camp counselors would dress up as the hermit and allow the campers to get a fleeting glance of him. This put the kids in a tizzy, which they loved. We kept up the deception for weeks, even sending search parties after the apparition. Then, finally, we had the hermit walk nonchalantly into the mess hall. I can still hear the kids screaming. The hermit story naturally came to mind when I needed a ghost story to include in the script."

After the story, Barney tells the boys that it was just a story and that there is "nothing to be frightened about."

Later that night, Andy wakes up. He looks from side to side and sees Barney and Gomer. The two have placed their sleeping bags next to Andy and are wide awake.

"Barney and Gomer's fearful reaction to the story is somewhat ingenious and possibly stretched credibility a little," says Harvey. "But they were out in a strange foreboding place and had just gulped down a horror story told effectively by Andy. And the two were somewhat unsophisticated and impressionable."

The next morning, Trey tells Andy, Barney, and Gomer that Opie's gone. His sleeping bag is still there, but he isn't anywhere around.

Andy goes out searching for Opie. After he leaves, Barney decides he and Gomer will "comb the north slope."

A short time later, Andy returns to camp with Opie. Opie left camp without telling anyone because he wanted to surprise Andy with some berries he picked.

Meanwhile somewhere on the north slope, Barney tells Gomer, "Opie isn't anywhere around here or these old baby blues would have spotted him." He suggests they work their way back to camp. Barney starts back, but Gomer thinks camp is in the opposite direction. Barney insists he knows the way back. As they start walking, a handkerchief in Barney's back pocket gets snagged on a branch and is left behind.

Fletch, a friend of Andy's, arrives in camp. Fletch has brought up a "little archery equipment." Fletch also brought along two roasted chickens, which Aunt Bee sent in case they got "tired of hot dogs." Andy asks Fletch if he has seen Barney and Gomer, but he has not.

Fletch takes the boys "to have some fun with the bows and arrows." While the boys are occupied, Andy decides to go look for Barney and Gomer. He takes Aunt Bee's roasted chickens and leaves camp.

Barney and Gomer continue wandering in the woods. When they stop "to take a breather," Gomer tells Barney that he's starved. He says, "We didn't have no breakfast, and it's already past noon." Barney responds that normally he would make a snare and catch a pheasant or wild bird, but "you can't make a decent snare without a piece of string. If I had a piece of string, I'd catch you a bird dinner you'd never forget." At this point, Gomer pulls a pair of extra shoelaces from his shirt pocket.

"The extra shoelaces are a stretch that I missed," admits Harvey. "It would have been infinitely better if Gomer volunteered the shoestring from his high-top sneakers. Then he could have flopped around with one open sneaker to add to the comedy."

Barney builds a snare and sets it up. He and Gomer then leave, so they won't scare the pheasants away.

Gomer suggests they will need a fire. Barney agrees and asks for a match. While Gomer is searching his pockets, Barney bends over, picks up two sticks, and says, "Course, we could start one just as quick by rubbing two sticks together. You know fire by constriction."

"I reveled in giving Barney word miscues—*constriction* for *combustion*, for example," says Harvey. "I tried not to overdo it, but the occasional miscue was tasty."

When Gomer can't find a match, he looks at Barney and says, "I guess you better use those pioneer sticks."

When Barney sits down beside a fallen tree, Gomer observes that the place looks like the same place where they started. When he suggests they are lost and walking in circles, Barney replies, "This is not the same tree, and we are not lost."

Barney sends Gomer "to keep an eye on the snare while I get a fire started." Barney places one of the sticks on the fallen tree and twirls it back and forth between his hands.

Andy finds Gomer while he is checking on the snare. Gomer asks Andy what he's doing there. Andy explains that when they didn't come back to camp, he thought he'd come out to look for them. Gomer tells Andy that he thought they were lost, but Barney had said they weren't. He adds, "Are the boys back at camp going to have fun with this! The laugh is really going to be on him."

Andy explains to Gomer that he's afraid that kind of laugh will "hurt him pretty bad." After a moment's reflection, Gomer observes that Barney was only trying to help. He wishes there were something they could do.

"When Andy explains to Gomer that Barney will be ridiculed for getting lost, he is telling the audience as well to back up their understanding and emphasize the importance of all which follows," says Harvey.

Andy decides there is something they can do. He gives Gomer some matches and tells him to break them off and put the heads in Barney's "fire maker." Andy promises "to watch the snare and get you a pheasant." Gomer then rejoins Barney.

While Barney is away gathering twigs, Gomer puts the match heads in Barney's fire maker.

When Barney walks a short distance away, he finds his handkerchief hanging from a branch and realizes he has been walking in circles. He accepts the realization that he is lost.

Barney walks dejectedly back to Gomer. He is about to admit he is lost when Gomer interrupts and insists that Barney "show me your twirling again." Barney twirls the stick, and a flame shoots up. Barney gets excited and runs off to "get some firewood."

While Barney is away, Andy hands Gomer one of Aunt Bee's roasted chickens and tells him to hold it over the fire. Andy tells Gomer that when he and Barney finish eating, Gomer should listen for a loon call that Andy will make. If Gomer and Barney follow the call, Andy will lead the two back to camp.

Barney returns and is surprised to find Gomer roasting a bird over the fire. He asks incredulously, "You mean that snare worked? And [the pheasant's] done and everything?" Barney reasons that the "pheasant" cooked so fast because "any fire started pioneer-style is bound to be hotter than fire started with just ordinary matches."

"I spent some mental time seeing how Barney could accept a cooked bird without being suspicious," says Harvey. "A fire seemed a good idea since Barney had claimed expertise in building one and the match heads Gomer put in the fire maker gave Barney all the credit without much suspicion. Barney's question about how the pheasant cooked so fast was an intelligent question which he would ask almost without thinking. Then Barney answers his own question— 'pioneer fire is hotter.'

"The viewer has to put themselves in Barney's place. He's lost, apprehensive, and a bit confused. He wants desperately to have caught and cooked that bird and is willing to come up with almost any explanation—especially if it backs up his pioneer moxie. Remember, Barney doesn't question that they caught the bird.

He is not aware of any other person or thing involved. The actual bird proves he's on the right track, and no other explanation of the cooking comes to mind—so he accepts it."

Barney and Gomer enjoy the meal. Barney observes that "there's a taste you can't match with anything you'll ever find in the city. Even Aunt Bee couldn't have cooked up anything that good."

Just then, a bird cries out. Gomer asks, "Hear that? That's a lake loon, and it come from that direction." When Barney ignores him, Gomer continues to drop hints that the loon is probably headed toward the lake. Barney still ignores what Gomer is saying until he begins to think out loud, "Probably a web-footed, red-crested lake loon. Where would a web-footed, red-crested lake loon be headed? Toward the lake. We just follow that sound, and it's a shortcut home."

Barney and Gomer follow Andy's bird calls back to camp and triumphantly share their story of survival. As the story is told, Gomer shows the boys the snare Barney made. Interestingly, as the two walked through the woods, neither Gomer nor Barney was carrying the snare. Nevertheless, Gomer has it with him when he emerges into camp.

"Details of continuity were watched by the script supervisor and the director," says producer Aaron Ruben. "The missing snare was simply an oversight that no one caught."

"A lot of pencil plotting went into the structuring and sequencing of this story," says Harvey. "If you have a movie screen in your head, that helps. Close both eyes. Be there in the scene on the screen. Watch where everyone else is, and how it progresses. Then stop and do it another way. Sometimes any approach to the scene seems inadequate. In that case, toss the whole scene away, study the story again, and reset the scene and characters somewhere else. This sounds glib, but consciously or unconsciously that is what most writers do. And here's where a writing partner is so very helpful. Two people bouncing ideas off each other is far more fruitful than one person bouncing ideas off the wallpaper alone."

"'Back to Nature' was Jim Nabors's final *TAGS* episode," says Aaron. "The 'Gomer Pyle, U.S.M.C.' episode, which was broadcast the following week, was actually filmed much earlier in the season. I recall Jim being elated when 'Nature' was completed. He was about to star in a series of his own and was already eagerly anticipating the future."

1964–1965

"Barney's Bloodhound"

Episode 128

First Broadcast on
October 26, 1964

Written by
**Bill Idelson and
Sam Bobrick**

Directed by
Howard Morris

"This episode and 'The Case of the Punch in the Nose' were my two favorite scripts."—SAM BOBRICK

"Our first two *TAGS* scripts were well received," says writer Sam Bobrick. "As a result, Bill and I became part of the group of writers who met with executive producer Sheldon Leonard at the beginning of the year to work out storylines for the new season.

"Every morning for about two weeks, the writers met in Sheldon's office and pitched stories until late in the afternoon. During the two weeks, we would come up with ten to twelve stories. 'Barney's Bloodhound' was one of the stories that came out of the seminar."

By the fall of 1964, Howard Morris had directed *The Dick Van Dyke Show*, *The Bill Dana Show*, and dozens of other shows on different networks. "I was getting known as a director," says Howard, "and *TAGS* producer Aaron Ruben asked me if I wanted to direct *The Griffith Show*. I said, 'Sure,' and I did. It fell together quite well."

"Barney's Bloodhound" begins with Barney rushing down the sidewalk to get to the courthouse in time to hear *The Leonard Blush Show* on the radio. The show is interrupted during Leonard Blush's first song by a special news bulletin. The news bulletin reports that a convict, Ralph Neal, has escaped from the state penitentiary.

"The script called for a radio announcer to introduce *The Leonard Blush Show* and then interrupt the program to make the announcement about the escaped convict," says Howard. "I was there on the set, they needed a voice for Leonard Blush and the announcer, so I did them both."

Barney turns off the radio as soon as the news bulletin is completed. He gets excited over the possibility that Neal may be heading for Mayberry and feels he and Andy should be prepared to assist in the capture of the convict. Andy is unconcerned because the state prison is "a long ways from here." Barney is frustrated by Andy's nonchalance and storms out.

That afternoon, Barney asks Andy if there have been any more reports on Neal. Andy answers that a motorist thought he saw him near Mt. Pilot, but "he's probably just imagining." Something pulls Barney away from the doorway where he is standing. When he returns to the doorway, he is pulled away a second time. At this point, Barney announces that he wants to show Andy something.

Barney struggles to enter the courthouse. He is holding a rope. On the other end of the rope is a dog. According to Barney, the dog, who is named Blue, is part bloodhound. Barney says Blue is going to "lead us right straight toward that criminal." Barney then demonstrates Blue's responsiveness to a dog whistle. When Barney blows the whistle, Blue snarls. This causes Andy to comment, "I don't think he likes that."

"The dog cast as Blue fit my image for the animal perfectly," says Sam. "The name Blue was a cliché. We chose that name because we felt it was one that Barney would come up with."

Andy doesn't believe "that dog could find his own food dish." Barney then threatens to make Andy "eat those words. I'm going to give you a little demonstration." On the way to the courthouse, Barney had stopped at the barbershop and picked up one of Floyd's handkerchiefs. Barney has Blue sniff the handkerchief and encourages him to track Floyd. Barney pushes Blue out the door, nudges him down the sidewalk, and guides him into the barbershop.

Floyd watches the dog's work with great interest. Blue eventually walks to Floyd. Floyd responds that "he's probably looking for some more of that candy." When Barney had brought Blue into the barbershop earlier, Floyd gave the dog a lollipop.

"This was the first time Bill and I wrote for Howard McNear, who portrayed Floyd Lawson," says Sam. "Floyd was a very easy character to write for, and we always enjoyed Howard McNear's performance."

"The dog was just wonderful," say Howard Morris. "The trainer would say, 'Show the left side,' and the dog would turn around and show his left side. Or the trainer would say, 'Now do a take. When Barney does a take, you do a take,' and he would. The dog's long gone now but working with him is a memory that I cherish.

"Howard McNear was a lovely man. I'd say, 'Show your left side,' and he would. Howard had had a stroke by this time and was unable to walk around, so he remains seated throughout the scene in the barbershop. In another episode I directed, Howard had to pretend to cut Andy's hair. We built a kind of seat for Howard behind the barber chair, which couldn't be seen. It made Howard appear to be standing. Howard was a lovely, lovely man and a wonderful actor."

Andy tells Barney that the dog will probably lead them straight to the criminal, "providing he's traveling around with a pocketful of lollipops." Barney is not amused. He calls Blue to leave, but Blue does not respond. Barney takes the dog whistle out of his pocket and blows it. Blue snarls angrily and chases Barney out of the barbershop.

Later in the day, the state police visit the courthouse and confirm Barney's suspicion that Neal is in the vicinity. They ask Andy to check out the area north of Mayberry.

After the state police leave, Andy calls Barney into the office. He has been outside, working with Blue. Barney tells Andy that the manhunt couldn't have come at a better time. He is convinced that the dog is going to be "such a help to us."

When Andy protests the use of Blue in the manhunt, Barney offers to show how much the dog has learned. Barney calls Blue, but the dog is asleep on the cot in the back room. Looking at Blue, Andy tells Barney that he'd better leave the dog at the office. "He looks like he needs the rest."

An angry Barney says, "You want to see that dog move?" He then pulls out his gun and says, "All right Blue, there's a man out here with a gun. Get him." Blue continues to sleep. When Barney blows the dog whistle, Blue bounds out of the back room and knocks Barney to the floor.

Andy, Barney, and Blue travel north of Mayberry to assist in the manhunt. Before beginning the search, Barney shows Blue a picture of Neal and talks to the dog as if he were a person. Barney gives Blue his instructions: "That's your man. Now you go get him."

"The idea to have Barney show Blue the wanted poster and then talk to the dog as if it were a person was inspired by the fact that most people talk to their pets," says Sam. "Barney, of course, always pushes a normal situation a little bit farther."

After looking at Neal's picture, Blue takes off. When Andy and Barney decide to split up, Barney follows Blue.

Blue leads Barney to a man who is fishing. The man is dressed in jeans and a dark shirt. As Barney approaches, the man takes off his hat and hides a gun beneath it. Barney warns the man that there's a convict on the loose. As Barney describes Neal physically and shows Neal's picture, he realizes he's talking to Neal.

The first act, which concludes with Barney's capture by the convict, is unusually long (fifteen minutes and twenty-nine seconds).

"We were never concerned with the first act's length or the spacing of the commercial breaks," says Sam. "That was not a writer's problem."

Neal takes Barney to a cabin where he is held hostage. Neal plans to keep Barney at the cabin until dark. He is going to take Barney along for "a little insurance. Cops don't shoot so quick when you got a hostage."

Meanwhile, Andy has discovered Barney's hat and the picture of Neal at the site where Barney was captured. He walks to the cabin, sees smoke coming from the chimney, and carefully works his way closer to look inside.

Inside the cabin, Neal is asleep. Barney quietly rises from his chair and slowly walks toward the door. Barney is almost at the door when Blue barks. Neal wakes up and orders Barney back to the chair. Neal leaves Blue in charge and goes back to sleep.

By this time, Andy has worked his way to the cabin. He motions to Barney through a window, and the two silently mouth a plan of escape. Barney runs toward the door. As he reaches the door, it opens. Barney runs out, and Andy steps in. Now Andy is the hostage.

Andy warns Neal that he'd better give himself up. He says, "This place will be surrounded by police in a matter of minutes. My deputy is getting a posse right now."

Upon hearing this, Neal decides to leave. He orders Andy to open the door. When the door opens, Barney is standing outside and is recaptured.

Neal puts on Barney's uniform and leads Andy and Barney, who is now dressed in Neal's clothes, to the squad car. Before getting in, Neal asks, "Where's the mutt? Hey, Blue."

Andy explains that the dog's a "little hard of hearing, but you got a whistle in your pocket there. If you blow that, he'll come right to you." Neal blows the whistle. Angered by the annoying whistle, Blue rushes up and jumps on Neal, enabling Andy and Barney to capture him.

The epilogue is extremely well written and uses a *TAGS* trademark—Andy and Barney locking themselves in a cell—in a clever way. Excited by Blue's capture of Neal, Barney continues to work with the dog. He attempts to have Blue pick the cell-door keys off the floor on command. Andy, who is straightening up a cell, asks Barney for help. Barney enters the cell and shuts the door, locking it behind him. Blue, holding the keys in his mouth, now becomes the center of attention as Andy, Barney, and the locked-up Neal all call his name. Remembering the dog whistle and its effect on Blue, Andy instructs Barney to blow it. The keys are quickly delivered to the cell.

"'Barney's Bloodhound' was an easy script to write," says Sam. "It worked extremely well, and Don Knotts, as always, was a comic genius."

"Family Visit"

Episode 129

First Broadcast on
October 5, 1964

Written by
**Jim Fritzell and
Everett Greenbaum**

Directed by
Howard Morris

"I remember that Andy's house was crowded."
—HOWARD MORRIS, DIRECTOR

"I don't think Don Knotts's contract obligated him to be in every show," says writer Everett Greenbaum. "Producer Aaron Ruben would tell us who was going to be in each script. We wrote 'Family Visit' knowing Don wasn't available."

The opening scene of Jim and Everett's completed script begins with Andy, Aunt Bee, and Opie sitting on the front porch on a Sunday morning. The three have already been to church and are greeting folks who are passing by on their way to the second service. Johnny Paul Jason, one of Opie's friends, walks by, and Opie tells him, "Good sermon today—about Cain and Abel. You see it's about these two brothers, and they had all this trouble." Andy interrupts and tells Opie to hush, but Opie continues, "That's all I can tell you, Johnny Paul, but don't be surprised if somebody gets killed." After Johnny Paul walks off, Andy tells Opie that "Bible knowledge is a fine thing, but don't flaunt it."

"The episode's opening scene was inspired by a childhood memory," says Everett. "When I was growing up in Buffalo, my family lived next to Saint Mark's Catholic Church. In summer, we could sit on our front veranda and watch the congregation get out of their cars and walk to Saint Mark's. There was an early service and a later service. We didn't know any of the people personally, so there was no conversation, but that didn't matter. It still was a peaceful way to spend a Sunday morning.

"Opie's line, 'Don't be surprised if someone gets killed,' was the Greenbaum way of spoiling the ending of a movie or a novel for another family member."

Andy, Aunt Bee, and Opie see the Beamon family on their way to church. Four generations of Beamons—Claude Sr., Claude Jr., Plain Claude, and Claudette—are walking together. Opie asks why they call Mr. Beaman "Plain Claude Beamon." Andy answers, "Because he's not a Senior, and he's not a Junior, so they call him Plain Claude Beamon." Aunt Bee says she thought they called him Plain Claude because he was so homely. Andy replies, "He's not homely. He's just got the Beamon overbite, but that's more of a characteristic."

"I remember very little about this one," admits Everett. "I don't even remember seeing it in reruns. I can't recall how the Beamon dialogue originated. But if it hadn't bubbled out, we never would have been paid."

Seeing the Beamon family stirs up Aunt Bee's desire to see her baby sister Nora and her family. After a brief discussion, Andy and Aunt Bee decide to invite Nora, her husband, Ollie, and their two sons for a visit.

Ollie, Nora, and the boys arrive the next weekend. Andy helps Ollie unload the car. Ollie tells Andy about how many miles-per-gallon he got on the trip to Mayberry while he hands Andy the luggage. Andy carries four suitcases into the house, while Ollie carries a sack, a pair of shoes, and a small valise.

"Andy's Uncle Ollie was based roughly on Jim Fritzell's cousin Ivor," says Everett. "Ollie's annoying habits of talking about his gas mileage and driving victories were inspired by a routine that had worked well for us on *Mr. Peepers*. One of the characters on that show, Aunt Lil, always enjoyed telling her adventures about driving in her Reo. The idea to have Ollie load Andy down with all the heavy luggage came from my memories of my Uncle Arthur. He somehow always avoided carrying in the luggage whenever my family visited him in Philadelphia."

During supper Aunt Nora mentions a friend of hers, Racine Tyler, who she feels would be a good match for Andy. Nora tells Andy that Racine's deceased husband owned Tyler Bakery. Nora adds that Racine recently collected four thousand dollars on his life-insurance policy. Echoing his wife, Uncle Ollie sums up the situation concisely. "Pretty good deal, Andy. Skinny widow, four thousand dollars, three-year-old bakery truck with the original paint."

"Jim and I felt that Nora had been trying to make a match between Andy and this Racine for some time," says Everett. "Nora felt that the insurance payout was an important selling point for Racine. Ollie's summation of the situation demonstrated what a shallow materialist he was—another of his many annoying attributes."

Following supper, Andy takes his guests for "a little spin around town to see the sights." He stops the car at the Mayberry Gas Works and points out the new blacktopped parking lot.

"My dad's idea of showing visitors a good time was to drive around Buffalo, pointing out new stores, or better yet, stores having tire sales," says Everett. "My father owned a tire store and was always interested in tire prices. We wanted Andy to show off something even more boring—blacktop."

Due to limited space, Opie must share his bed with Ollie's two sons, Roger and Bruce. Before going to sleep, Opie complains to Aunt Bee "that Roger has his foot in the pit of my back." Aunt Bee tells Opie she will "rub it down with witch hazel in the morning." Opie continues to complain that "witch hazel makes my eyes water." Aunt Bee responds, "Well, you won't see as well, but you'll feel better."

"I've always been fond of witch hazel," says Everett. "I love the way it smells and still use it constantly for fleabites, since we have pets. Sleeping in a crowded bed was a memory from childhood, and as the gag developed, witch hazel fit in perfectly."

Andy and Ollie share a bed. Before going to sleep, Ollie and Nora get into an argument. According to Ollie, Nora forgot to bring his goose-down pillow. Nora replies that she thought he had it. "After all, you're the one who uses it." When Ollie admits he forgot the pillow, Nora says, "You forget everything. You forgot my birthday. You forgot our anniversary." Ollie explains that he forgot their anniversary because "the foreman sent me around looking for a spindle wrench just at quitting time."

"After I flunked out of MIT, I was obliged to go to work at Bell Aircraft as a riveter," says Everett. "It seemed to me that parts chasers always had the best job. The job seemed to fit Ollie."

Ollie is upset by the argument. He tells Andy that he won't sleep "a wink. She's got me all on edge." Andy suggests that Ollie read a little bit. He says, "I always find that when I can't sleep, if I read a little piece out of a magazine, I just doze right off." Andy reaches for a magazine from the nightstand. He hands the magazine to Ollie, but Ollie is already asleep.

The next morning, Andy and Aunt Bee are in the kitchen before Nora and Ollie wake up. Andy tells Aunt Bee that "half the night Ollie had his arm in my mouth. The other half, he was dreaming he was riding a bicycle. All in all, I'd say it was one of the most active nights I ever spent." Aunt Bee assures Andy that everything will work out because they are only visiting for the weekend. Andy replies, "I guess we can stand our loved ones that long."

When Ollie and Nora join Andy and Aunt Bee, Nora talks about how wonderful the visit has been. Aunt Bee and Andy agree. Andy says, "We were just saying what a fine visit it's been, and what a shame it has to be so short." In response, Nora and Ollie decide to stay for a whole week.

During the breakfast scene, Aunt Bee is seated with her back to the stove. The close-ups of Aunt Bee show the wall behind her. This wall is rarely seen in the series, since the kitchen is normally photographed with the camera positioned behind the stove with the wall removed.

Later that morning, Ollie visits Andy at the courthouse. Ollie takes a rifle from the gun rack, cocks it, aims toward the door, and pulls the unloaded rifle's trigger. Andy takes the gun away from Ollie and returns it to the gun rack.

When a man stops by to pay a traffic ticket, Ollie reprimands the man.

Wanting to get rid of Ollie, Andy suggests that he go fishing. Ollie follows Andy's suggestion and drives off in the squad car. Andy runs out onto the sidewalk and tries to stop him but is too late.

Floyd is sitting outside his shop. Hoping to catch Ollie, Andy asks if he can borrow Floyd's car. Floyd tells Andy that his car is at Wally's. In reference to his car, Floyd adds, "Oh, the poor dear's in terrible shape. Her transmission, her second gear had a whine like a crying child. Wally opened up her gearbox and took one look and closed her right up."

"Using Floyd's comments about his sick car was our way of satirizing the older generation's medical gossip," says Everett. "We took a comment such as 'Dr. Phelps took one look inside her abdomen, found it incurable, and closed her right up' and applied it to Floyd's car. Floyd was always fun to write for, and here, as always, Howard McNear delivered Floyd's lines as only he could."

Andy rushes back to the office to use the telephone. Nora is on the telephone talking to Racine Tyler. She insists that Andy talk with Racine. Andy reluctantly complies. After a short conversation, Andy hangs up the telephone and calls Harry's Pond. Andy tells Harry to send "his uncle right back with the squad car."

Later that evening, Andy and Ollie hear a news bulletin over the radio that three convicts have escaped from a South Carolina prison. Ollie tells Andy, "Good thing [the escapees] are not headed this way. We'd take care of them in two winks."

Andy leaves to "make his rounds." Sometime later, he receives a call at the courthouse that the escapees have been caught. After hanging up the telephone, Andy gets an idea. He telephones his house and tells Ollie that he has great news. "You know those two convicts we heard about on the radio? They've been seen in this area. I'm going after them, but I'm going to need some help. I'll throw an extra rifle in the squad car and come by for you. I'll be there in a few minutes."

This scene has a continuity error. This passage of the script mentions two convicts, while the earlier news bulletin reported three.

Ollie suddenly remembers that he left the gas on at home and makes a hasty departure.

"The resolution of the problem in this episode was typical sitcom and kind of ordinary," says Everett. "I was not very satisfied with it, but we needed an ending. Time was a factor, so we decided it would do."

The episode's epilogue is set on the Taylor front porch. It is evening, and Andy and Aunt Bee are enjoying the peacefulness of life without company. The two-minute scene, photographed in one sustained shot, opens with a close-up of Andy playing his guitar. The camera then pans back, revealing Andy and Aunt Bee. The two comment on Nora and Ollie's visit. When the telephone rings, Aunt Bee rises. The camera pans left and follows her as she enters the house. The camera then pans right and stops on Andy, who listens to Aunt Bee talking on the phone.

The decision to photograph the scene in one sustained shot adds to its peaceful atmosphere. The sustained shot enables the camera to float around the porch and is more visually relaxing than having various camera angles edited together.

"The epilogue in my script is different," says Everett. "It is set in the dining room, and Andy is not playing his guitar."

The change in setting gives the story a sense of symmetry. The episode opens on the front porch. After the relatives leave and peace is restored, it ends there.

"Aunt Bee's Romance"

Episode 130

First Broadcast on
October 19, 1964

Written by
Harvey Bullock

Directed by
Howard Morris

Wallace Ford
Guest Stars as
Roger Hanover

"'Everybody complains about the weather, but nobody does anything about it.' Know who said that? Calvin Coolidge."—FLOYD LAWSON

"I have a mental blank about this classic 'Floyd' scene. I really can't recall whether it was my contribution or not."—HARVEY BULLOCK

"Aunt Bee's Romance" begins around the breakfast table. Andy compliments Aunt Bee on "a fine breakfast" and whispers to Opie, "That girl's going to make somebody a fine bride one of these days." Opie asks Andy if he will write "a permission for school, so I can go on a field trip. The whole class is going on a bus to a bakery in Mt. Pilot to see how donuts are made."

"I recall the opening scene of this episode vividly," says writer Harvey Bullock. "The reason I do is because I went on a similar field trip when I was a Boy Scout. Our scoutmaster announced that we would be going to the big Spaulding Bakery. Their huge donut-making machine made a lasting impression on me. Dough was extruded in donut shapes, which dropped onto a pan of gas-heated oil. Then as they drifted along, a paddle turned them over to fry the other side, after which they were deposited into wire baskets moving several times to the ceiling and back on an endless chain to cool them off before they were packaged.

"Then, the highlight—the bakery manager said we could stand at the end of the cooling line and eat as many donuts as we wanted—heaven! We cleaned out basket after basket hurriedly, fearing the miracle would be recalled. The bakery man just smiled, but soon our scoutmaster, seeing we were all desperately and deliciously on a life-threatening donut binge, dragged us away. That's why I selected that field trip for Opie."

While Andy is writing the permission note, the mail is delivered. Several of the letters are addressed to "Occupant," and Opie questions Andy about this.

"Opie and Andy's 'occupant' discussion was of minor importance to the storyline," says Harvey. "I actually guided scripts onto little plateaus of idle conversation such as this. The idle conversation emphasized the relaxed relationships that existed among the people of Mayberry."

One of the letters is for Aunt Bee. Aunt Bee is curious about the identity of her letter's sender, but she doesn't open the envelope immediately. Instead she looks at the Raleigh postmark and holds the letter in front of a light. She makes several guesses (Mrs. Deacon, Donna Forbes, or Rita Aiken) before opening the letter and learning it was sent by Roger Hanover, "a boy I used to keep company with."

"I've known folks who try everything to guess who has sent them a letter, including holding a totally opaque envelope up to the light," says Harvey. "Postmarks, blurred mostly, suggest other possible correspondents. It can be maddening, but it's funny to see someone try everything but opening the envelope. Writing the gag for Aunt Bee gave Frances Bavier, who portrayed the character, an acting moment and a chance to do some comedy.

"The names of the ladies Aunt Bee mentions as possible correspondents came from many sources. I needed several names quickly and just wrote down whichever names came to mind. Mrs. Deacon was a friend of my parents and the mother of comic actor Richard Deacon who played Mel Cooley on *The Dick Van Dyke Show*. Veeda Aiken, whose first name was later changed to Rita, was a neighborhood friend whose husband was a sheriff. Gertrude Turner, the name of a lovely woman my widower father tried to marry, was changed to Donna Forbes. The legal department would often change a name, or Aaron Ruben would have one that was better, so I tried not to waste time naming characters."

Aunt Bee answers Roger's letter and invites him to come to Friday night supper.

Friday arrives. Aunt Bee dresses up in preparation for Roger's visit. Andy, returning home with some ice cream, responds to her appearance with some wonderful dialogue. He tells Aunt Bee: "You must be the teenage babysitter. Aunt Bee, you look good enough to take to Chinatown. New hairdo, red lining in your jacket, peach ice cream." Andy whistles and turns his head.

"Andy's whistle and head turn were not scripted," says Harvey. "He once told me this was something his father did, and he got it from him."

Aunt Bee tells Andy that "Roger phoned and what's more he said he might be able to stay for a few days." Andy asks if he needs to "get out my old shoes and rice." Aunt Bee ignores the remark and reminisces aloud, "Oh, it's so good to hear his voice again." Andy responds, "Try to control your passion, Aunt Bee. You're melting the ice cream."

"The idea of an enticing female melting ice cream has been used in many forms for many moons," says Harvey. "I was always quite comfortable finding old clichéd descriptions and dressing them up a bit to fit a scene or a character."

When Roger arrives, he looks at Aunt Bee and says, "Just as pretty as ever."

Aunt Bee introduces Andy and Opie to Roger. Roger holds out his hand to shake, pulls it back at the last second, sticks his thumb up, and says, "Hang it on the wall." Aunt Bee comments, "I told you he's full of the devil."

Aunt Bee offers to show Roger to his room. Roger moans, steps over his suitcase, and says, "I'm just a little weak. I just got over the grippe." Roger then points out the suitcase he stepped over.

"Roger Hanover, who is really annoying, was modeled after an insurance salesman of equal likability," says Harvey. "The salesman was also named Roger. I would give his last name, but he'd probably read this and show up here again. The guy knew all the ancient gags and practical jokes, was overbearingly authoritative, and a real nuisance.

"Roger's jokes are old creaky routines that someone like him would persistently use. His attempts at comedy were inspired by my father, who also spewed old jokes and groaners. But my father was affable about it and, happily, didn't know too many.

"Wallace Ford's portrayal of Roger was wonderful. In fact, I still have viewers tell me how much they disliked the character—which proves that Wallace was an able and convincing actor."

The next morning at breakfast, Roger continues his joking. He emerges from behind the newspaper he is reading wearing a mask and says to Andy, "Take me to your leader." Roger asks Opie if he knows why people have thumbs and answers, "Because if they didn't have thumbs, and you shook hands with somebody, the other fellow's hand would go right up your sleeve and hit you right in the nose." Roger shoves Opie in the nose.

Andy invites Opie to join him for breakfast at the diner. As the two leave the kitchen, Opie asks if Roger is really going to be "our new uncle?" Andy thinks over Opie's question and its implications carefully.

Later in the day, Andy joins Floyd outside the barbershop. It is hot. The temperature is ninety-two degrees. Andy comments, "Well, like Mark Twain said, 'Everybody complains about the weather, but nobody does anything about it.'" Floyd remarks that he thought Calvin Coolidge had said that.

Aunt Bee and Roger walk up. After a brief conversation, the two depart. After their departure, Andy confesses to Floyd that he can't stand Roger.

That evening after supper, Andy decides "to fix the cord on that lamp." Roger takes the cord away from Andy and says, "Don't mind me showing you how to do this, do you, boy?" Roger twists the ends too tightly and ruins the cord.

When Aunt Bee asks Andy if he has the plug fixed, Roger responds that he "tried to help the boy." Referring to Andy, he adds, "Funny thing, these electrical gadgets. You have the knack for them, or you haven't."

"I found it was easier to write for a loud brash character like Roger Hanover than for a mild-mannered, polite person," says Harvey. "A brash character produces more friction and energy as he interacts with others, which is good for the story. I simply wrote dialogue that I felt fit Roger's personality."

Roger takes Aunt Bee "on a little stroll." After the two depart, Opie asks Andy, "You don't much like Mr. Hanover, do you?" Andy refuses to give a direct answer and instead tells Opie, "I've tried to bring you up teaching you there's some good in everybody. Now, the same goes for Mr. Hanover."

"Andy's statement seemed like an apt moral," says Harvey. "Also, in stating it to Opie, it helped explain to the audience why Andy has been so patient with Roger, instead of ushering him on his way."

The next morning, Andy is potting petunias before he goes to work. Roger comes outside. He is "down to half a cigar" and is "going to the store to get a few more." Roger offers to show Andy how to pot petunias, but Andy refuses his help. Andy says, "Roger, I know we don't see eye to eye on electricity, but when it comes to potting petunias, I'm a giant." Roger replies, "Just wanted to be helpful, boy."

Roger starts to the store but returns a short time later. He says he left his money in his other pants and asks Andy for a half-dollar. Andy asks Roger what his future plans are. Roger answers, "My original plan was Florida, but things are running along so nicely here I sort of hated to think of leaving."

Roger eventually tells Andy that he needs four hundred dollars to fund a trip to Florida. If he doesn't get the money, he plans to marry Aunt Bee and move in permanently. Roger tells Andy, "Four hundred dollars and I'd be right there on that noon train. Otherwise, I'd say you got yourself a new uncle." Andy tells Roger he can find Aunt Bee in the kitchen. Roger sarcastically responds, "I never expected to have such a grown-up nephew. I might have a hand in those petunias yet, Andy."

A short time later, Roger and Aunt Bee join Andy on the porch. Roger says, "Andy, I just had a little talk with Bee." Aunt Bee tells Andy that Roger is leaving on the noon train to Florida. She then goes back inside to make Roger some sandwiches. Roger remains behind.

Roger asks, "Sheriff, you ever play poker?" Andy answers, "Yeah, Roger, I used to play. I used to be pretty good at it."

As this scene develops, Roger addresses Andy in a progression—boy, Andy, sheriff. "Boy" places Roger in a superior position. When the showdown comes, and it's man to man, "Andy" is used. After Roger's bluff is called, it's the respectful "sheriff."

"Roger's request for the needed funds is a shakedown," says Harvey. "Roger will keep moving if Andy gives him four hundred dollars, but Andy never offers to go along. Both men have hidden cards. Andy seemingly takes a chance when he sends Roger into the kitchen to propose to Aunt Bee. Andy is hoping she has gotten over her crush by now. Roger, however, is confident the starry-eyed Bee will grab at his proposal. It's poker, pure and simple. Labeling it so helps the audience be aware of the drama and tension as the two men match wits."

In the episode's epilogue, Aunt Bee comes back into the house after seeing Roger off. She confesses to Andy that "a little of Roger goes a long way. All those tricks and jokes—they're fun for a while, but you wouldn't want to live with them for the rest of your life, would you?"

Andy answers that he "certainly wouldn't." Aunt Bee then adds, "Fun is fun, but there's a limit to everything." Andy replies that he'll go along with that. "In fact, I'll just shake on it. Hang it on the wall."

"The epilogue serves to restore Aunt Bee to her previous nongullible status," says Harvey. "She has come to recognize Roger and his annoying habits—and has had more than enough of his jokes. Andy sensed this when he took the big chance of telling Roger to go ahead and make his play for Aunt Bee. The reuse of Roger's trademark, 'Hang it on the wall,' was just a light comic flip to button up the epilogue."

"The Education of Ernest T. Bass"

"I had fun doing this episode. It was great comedy to fool around with. Jim and Everett wrote some wonderful stuff. They were the best."
—HOWARD MORRIS

Episode 133

First Broadcast on October 12, 1964

Written by
Jim Fritzell and Everett Greenbaum

Directed by
Alan Rafkin

Howard Morris Guest Stars as Ernest T. Bass

"It was always difficult to sit down and produce an outline for a new script," says writer Everett ~~Greenbaum~~. "In the case of Ernest T., it wasn't as painful because we knew we would have fun with it eventually."

Jim and Everett begin their script with Andy and Barney discussing where they will eat lunch. Andy suggests the diner. Barney has checked the diner's special on the way in—"chicken wings, rice, and mixed vegetables." He observes that the cook "gives you two wings and usually from a chicken who's done a lot of flying." The discussion is interrupted when Ernest T. Bass throws a rock through the window of the courthouse.

"We did a lot of scenes about eating in everything we wrote," says Everett. "Eating is a very basic life activity, and having Barney and Andy discuss lunch seemed like a good way to begin this episode."

Ernest T. enters the office, drops his bag of rocks on Barney's hand, and explains that he has returned to Mayberry to get an education to please his girl-friend "Romeena." (We were introduced to Ramona Ancrum in "My Fair Ernest T. Bass." Ernest T. calls her Romeena.) Ernest T. tells Andy and Barney he has tried to attract Romeena in other ways, including getting a gold tooth. He tells them he didn't go to a dentist to get his gold tooth. Instead he "had it did at the sign company. Gold leaf, they call it." All his efforts have been unsuccessful.

"Having Ernest T. drop his bag of rocks on Barney's hand was not scripted," says Everett. "It came up on the set. Ernest T.'s gold tooth was inspired from observing unsophisticated people who considered it fashionable to have a gold tooth flashing at the world."

Ernest T. wants Andy to help him "get some schooling." If Ernest T. can't get an education, he intends to "bust every window in town."

Andy decides to help Ernest T. and enrolls him in Helen Crump's fifth-grade class. Ernest T. joins the class and immediately causes a disruption with his comments about a sentence written on the blackboard. The sentence reads, "The possum hid under the rock."

When Helen asks the class who can point out the preposition, the object, the subject, and the verb, Ernest T. jumps to his feet and asks, "Why don't we break down that rock and find out what that possum's doing under there?" The class laughs.

When Helen calls on Sharon, Ernest T. comments, "Ain't no little girl going to tell you nothing about a possum under a rock. If you want to really find out about a possum under a rock, you find a boy with dirt under his fingernails." Helen responds with, "Mr. Bass, that's quite enough!"

"I've forgotten most of this script," says Everett. "As I read through it, it seems as if it were written by a strange hand. I can't recall how the possum sentence entered our heads, but it is funny."

Ernest T. is upset after his first day in Helen's class and shares his feelings with

Andy. He complains that Helen "ain't teaching me nothing." Andy comforts Ernest T. and agrees to help him study.

Andy begins by having Ernest T. read from Opie's first-grade reader. When Andy opens the book, Ernest T. points at the page and says, "I know that word. *Cat*." Andy asks Ernest T. if he figured out the word from the picture on the page. Opie tells Andy to "turn to a page without any pictures." Ernest T. tells Opie to "have more respect for your elders." Andy explains to Ernest T. that Opie was just trying to help. Ernest T. then says apologetically, "Well, I take off my humble hat to you, boy." Opie then goes upstairs and says, "Good night, Ernest T. Bass." Ernest T. replies, "Good night, Opie Taylor."

"Ernest T.'s 'humble hat' line grew out of an expression I once heard, 'He's the button on the cap of kindness,'" explains Everett. "We used the expression in many variations. Ernest T. says, 'Good night, Opie Taylor' because he is trying to fit in and do as the Romans or, in this case, as Opie does. Opie used Ernest T.'s complete name when he bid him good night, and Ernest T. does likewise."

While working with Ernest T., Andy discovers that he can already read several words. Ernest T. puts the words into a sentence, "No hunt, beware, open and close, no credit."

The next day at school, Ernest T. wants to write his sentence on the blackboard, but Helen tells him to wait until after arithmetic. Ernest T. refuses, and Helen punishes him by slapping his hand with a ruler. This disciplinary action stirs up strong feelings in Ernest T., and he immediately declares his love for Miss Crump.

That evening, Ernest T. throws a rock through Helen's window with a note attached to it. The note says, "I love you." Andy arrests Ernest T.

The next day, Barney explains to Andy that Ernest T.'s reaction to Helen is psychological, that she has become his "mother figure." Barney tells Andy, "Sigmon Frued wrote a lot about that. Old Sig had this thing pegged years ago."

"I can't remember how the 'mother figure' thing came up," says Everett. "But 'Sigmon Frued' was an example of Barney's tendency to mispronounce words. We always enjoyed writing these and worked them in whenever we could."

Later that evening, Andy comes home from work and finds Ernest T. sitting in an easy chair. Ernest T. has escaped from jail. Andy questions Ernest T. and learns that his mother used to hit him. Andy explains to him that all of his feelings for his mother came back when Helen hit him with a ruler. Andy goes on to say that Ernest T. is just putting Helen in his mother's place, and Helen has become his mother figure. Ernest T. thanks Andy "for clearing up the whole thing" and invites him to be his "brother figure."

Ernest T. feels "a good son is supposed to help his mother." The following day, he sees Helen coming out of the grocery store and offers to carry her groceries.

Helen declines the offer and hurries down the sidewalk to Andy. Andy is sitting with Mr. Schwump on the bench outside the courthouse.

"Mr. Schwump was not scripted," says Everett. "The guy probably could have used a day's pay, so they put him in."

Andy ushers Helen inside the office. Andy, Helen, and Barney discuss how to deal with Ernest T. and eventually decide the best thing to do is to get him an education as soon as possible. Andy quickly prepares Ernest T. for a final exam in geography, arithmetic, reading, and writing.

Ernest T. demonstrates his knowledge of geography by reciting "boundaries— Mexico, Canada, Atlantic Ocean, Pacific Ocean, Kelsey's woods, Kelsey's creek, Kelsey's ocean."

"We tried to imagine what the world looked like to Ernest T.," says Everett. "These boundaries reflected his worldview."

One of the best visual jokes in the entire series occurs as Ernest T. demonstrates his mathematical skills. Ernest T. counts out two and two by stamping his foot on the floor like a trained horse. The joke would have been great if it had ended there, but it is brilliantly taken one step further by having Ernest T. do a harder problem—twenty-five and twenty-five. The humor comes when he stands and frantically stamps out the answer.

"In the script, Ernest T. pounds on the wall to answer the math problem," says Everett. "Of course, stomping the floor like a horse is much better and must have been added on the set. Whoever thought it up should be commended.

"Another addition to the script was Ernest T. timidly shaking hands with Andy and Barney after receiving his diploma. His humility was a nice counter to his normally wild behavior."

The epilogue repeats the episode's opening. Andy and Barney are discussing where they will eat lunch. Andy suggests the drugstore, and Barney replies, "I don't like to eat at the drugstore—everything tastes like medicine." The two decide to go to the diner instead. Barney thinks aloud, "I wonder how old Ernest P. Bass made out over at Ramona's. I guess everything turned out all right, or we would have heard from him." A rock breaks the front window of the office, and the problem with Ernest T. starts over.

"The epilogue in my script is completely different," says Everett. "More than likely either Aaron Ruben or Andy rewrote it. The rewrite follows the 'here we go again' format and is much better than the original."

"Barney's Uniform"

"It's perfect for dancing, hangs just right for the dip."
—BARNEY FIFE, talking about his "salt-and-pepper" suit

Episode 135

First Broadcast on
November 9, 1964

Written by
**Bill Idelson and
Sam Bobrick**

Directed by
Coby Ruskin

Allan Melvin
Guest Stars as
Fred Plummer

"This episode had a different type of story than our previous *TAGS* scripts," says writer Sam Bobrick. "It was more serious and taught an important lesson about respect for the law. Even though it was different, Bill and I didn't find it any more difficult to write. We never had trouble with any story that Don and Andy were in together. Their relationship was so good it made writing for them a pleasure."

The episode opens with Andy taping a poster on the window of the courthouse. The poster announces an upcoming charity dance. Barney approaches and is so mad he can hardly see straight because Fred Goss, the dry cleaner, has misplaced his "salt-and-pepper" suit. Then, Barney notices Fred Plummer, an employee at Foley's Grocery Store, sweeping trash into the street. Barney has warned Plummer previously about littering and decides to "go over there and cut him down to size."

Barney confronts Plummer about "sweeping trash right into the street" and writes him a ticket for littering. Barney makes note of the time, place, weather, and traffic conditions on the ticket.

"We were always looking for ways to insert humor into a script," says Sam. "I enjoyed writing little details, such as Barney's 'weather clear, traffic light' observations as he is writing the ticket. Barney always went a step or two farther than the norm. In this case, he felt his observations should be included on the ticket."

Fred Plummer is angered by the ticket and tells Barney that he is "gonna take this ticket, see, but you and me are gonna meet sometime when you're not wearing that uniform, and I'm going to beat you to a pulp."

In response to Plummer's threat, Barney not only wears his uniform while on duty, but also to church and on his day off.

Unaware of Plummer's threat, Andy questions Barney about wearing his uniform. During their discussion, the two are sitting on the bench outside the courthouse. Fred Plummer steps onto the sidewalk in front of the grocery and glares at

Barney. When the telephone rings, Andy goes inside to answer it. He is followed closely by Barney.

The telephone call is from Fred Goss. Barney's suit has been found and is waiting for him at the cleaner's. In response to the news, Barney tells Andy, "I figured on wearing something else." When pressed by Andy, Barney starts coming up with excuses for why he can't wear his favorite suit. He doesn't think the suit will fit him anymore. He has been "gaining weight like crazy lately."

When Fred Plummer comes into the courthouse to pay his ticket, Barney leaves.

The master shot for the scene inside the office is photographed from the wall behind Andy's desk and the adjacent wall where the gun rack is usually mounted. Both walls have been removed. The camera is positioned in the corner usually occupied by the filing cabinet. The camera pans right to photograph the conversation between Plummer and Andy.

During the conversation, Andy learns that Plummer threatened Barney.

Andy later questions Barney about the situation, and Barney explains that he has resumed his judo class in Mt. Pilot and is wearing his uniform to protect Fred Plummer. Barney feels his knowledge of judo would be an unfair advantage if the two were to fight.

Andy decides to visit Barney's judo school. As Andy exits his car, Earle Hagen's musical score switches to an Asian theme that audibly identifies the school.

Andy learns from Mr. Izamoto, Barney's teacher, that Barney is an excellent student. Mr. Izamoto says, "He try very hard." Andy asks for Mr. Izamoto's professional opinion about how Barney would fare if he were to get into a fight. Mr. Izamoto asks how much the other fighter would weigh. When Andy answers two hundred pounds, Mr. Izamoto replies, "You a friend of Barney's? Then you stop that fight. That man kill Barney. Around here we call Barney the 'chicken.' He got bones like chicken, weak bones, they snap. You stop that fight. I like Barney very much. Not want him to get hurt."

As Andy walks toward the door, he gets an idea. He asks Mr. Izamoto what size suit he wears.

Andy puts his plan in motion. After warning Plummer that Barney knows judo and is dangerous, Andy tells him that Barney will be out of uniform when he attends the charity dance that night. Andy also mentions that Barney's suit is in the courthouse. He tells Plummer that Barney plans to change into his civvies for the dance around a quarter to eight.

As he speaks with Plummer, Andy helps himself to some fruit from a stand outside the grocery. Taking the fruit is mildly devious and helps to communicate visually the fact that Andy is sharing some "inside" information while conspiring with Fred Plummer.

Acting on Andy's tip, Plummer confronts the person he thinks is Barney at the designated time on the dimly lit street. Plummer is actually fighting Mr. Izamoto dressed in Barney's suit, and he is no match for the judo instructor.

After Plummer's defeat, Andy decides to teach Barney an important lesson. A good visual joke occurs when Andy knocks on the door to Barney's room. Rushing to get into his uniform, Barney puts his shirt on backward.

"We were allowed to write whatever we felt was good," says Sam. "Aaron Ruben was a great producer and gave the writers a lot of freedom. Aaron encouraged us to trust our instincts about what would work in a scene. So whenever we felt a visual gag, such as Barney putting his shirt on backwards, would work, we didn't hesitate to include it."

Andy has brought over Barney's suit. Barney, however, hasn't changed his mind about wearing it to the dance. He intends to wear his uniform. Andy tells Barney that he is going to have to face Fred Plummer sooner or later because of "what you are." Andy reminds Barney that they are "symbols of the law. When people look at us they just don't see Barney Fife and Andy Taylor, they see the law. And more than that, they have respect for the law. We've worked a long time to get that respect, and I don't think we should give it up . . . We're lawmen no matter what we're wearing."

Barney comes to the realization that he must confront Fred Plummer. Barney's courage to do so is admirable, even though his behavior during the confrontation expresses the fear he still feels.

Barney walks past Foley's grocery and finds Plummer sitting in an alley. In a weak voice, Barney tells Plummer, "Whether I'm wearing my uniform or not, it doesn't make any difference because I'm a symbol of the law, and you got to have respect for the law." A beaten and bruised Plummer says, "You know that judo is something awful. You could kill a person with that."

After realizing that Plummer is afraid, Barney's demeanor suddenly changes. He becomes confident and cocky. (So much so that it somewhat ruins the humanity displayed by his bravery and willingness to learn from Andy's advice.)

"A good rule for this show is that the human spirit must triumph," says Sam. "I think we showed Barney's courage and vulnerability as he confronts Plummer. Perhaps Barney's drastic change in demeanor, after he sees he has the upper hand, was a mistake. Sometimes we were wrong."

In the epilogue Andy helps Barney practice his judo. This scene highlights the wonderful rapport that existed between Don Knotts and Andy Griffith. Barney gives Andy a ruler to use like a knife and instructs him "to try to run me through." As Andy attacks, Barney stops him. He needs another look at his judo manual. Barney studies the manual and goes through the motions of blocking the attack. Once again, he is ready. Andy attacks Barney and overpowers him.

After being "let loose," Barney tells Andy, "You didn't do it right." Barney tells Andy that he was holding the ruler wrong. Barney suggests they practice in slow motion. Andy attacks. This time, Barney successfully defends himself. Now Barney is ready. Andy attacks at full speed. He overpowers Barney and gently lowers him to the floor.

Don Knotts and Andy Griffith genuinely seem to be enjoying themselves. Their acting is excellent. Although they remain in character, it is evident they love working together.

"The Pageant"

"Eventide
The gentle rustling of the leaves
The birds seeking their nests
O, my Happy Valley."
—LADY MAYBERRY'S SOLILOQUY

Episode 138

First Broadcast on
November 30, 1964

Written by
Harvey Bullock

Directed by
Gene Nelson

"In my ceiling-staring sessions, when I was seeking a story to write, it crossed my mind that many towns celebrate their lineage, however modest, with a pageant," says writer Harvey Bullock. "My hometown (Binghamton, New York) once had a centennial pageant showing the fine work of Mr. Bingham, who brought the settlers and Indians to a peaceful coexistence. And I was in the cast!

"Staged at the high school, the pageant ran for three nights and was a sellout—a full-blown costumed fantasy with early settlers, Indians, and pioneers. I had a very minor ten-second part as a settler's son who runs across the stage in near panic and announces, 'The Indians are coming.' That was it. Despite it being such a quickie, I experienced the heady elixir of audience approval. The memory of the experience stayed with me and inspired 'The Pageant' script."

Harvey's script begins with Andy, Barney, and Opie discussing the celebration of Mayberry's centennial. The centennial pageant is mentioned, and Barney, who plans to attend the tryouts, demonstrates his elocution by reciting several tongue twisters.

"For some reason, my mother decided my sister should have elocution lessons," says Harvey. "When my sister graduated from high school, it fell to me to continue the lessons. Once a week, I went to Mrs. Merchant's and sat in an overstuffed parlor, spieling off tongue twisters. My mother was determined I should become a better speaker even though the full-hour, single-student rate cost a not inconsiderable fee—fifty cents.

"The tongue twisters 'Peter Piper Picked' and 'How Much Wood Would a Woodchuck Chuck' were too ordinary for Mrs. Merchant's taste. She preferred 'She Sells Seashells' and 'With Sturdy Threats and Loudest Boasts.' She is totally responsible for searing them into my limp brain. I jumped at the chance to have Barney recite them and was very pleased to have found a place to use them after all these years. The 'Rubber Baby Buggy Bumpers' twister that stumps Barney was an audience warmup routine that the emcee used with contestants on a quiz show that I once wrote for."

When Aunt Bee enters the courthouse, Andy reminds her not to forget the tryouts that night. Aunt Bee answers that she won't be attending the tryouts because she sews the costumes. Andy points out that there's "a real good woman's part, Lady Mayberry, founding mother of the town." Aunt Bee is sure Mr. Masters has decided to use Clara Edwards for that part.

At home, Aunt Bee tells Opie she is certain she could play the part of Lady Mayberry. She tells him that she was in a church play years ago, and her mother and father both said she was "the best one in it." She shows Opie a review of the play, which was called *The Little Princess*, that appeared in a church publication.

"I had always taken part in school plays and essay readings," says Harvey. "One of the plays I performed in was *The Princess Marries the Page*. It was a two-part play and inspired the name of the play Aunt Bee appeared in."

That night, Andy and Barney try out for the pageant. Andy reads for the James Merriweather role, and Barney reads for Chief Noogatuck.

"The name of Andy's character was James Meredith in my script," says Harvey. "The name of Barney's character, 'Chief Noogatuck,' was conjured up as a correct-sounding but goofy sort of Indian name."

Barney's performance during the tryouts is a classic. He loses his place in the script and delivers his first line, "How," too fast. As he and Andy step down from the stage, Andy says, "Hey, Barn, I know how you can learn your part real good." Barney asks, "How?"

"I was not troubled by using this venerable wheeze," says Harvey. "I thought viewers familiar with it would enjoy hearing its resurrection.

"The scene of the tryouts worked very well. Of course, the material had an edge. The performers were so skilled and comfortable in their roles that they could make any reasonable situation come to life. And a pageant for a friendly town like Mayberry seemed totally believable."

The script directions were artistically interpreted by the director and photographed in one sustained shot. The shot begins with Andy and Barney stepping off the stage. The camera follows the two toward the back of the auditorium. Aunt Bee is seen in the background, seated on the far side of the auditorium. Andy and Barney exit from the frame, and the camera moves with Aunt Bee as she rises from her chair and walks to the stage to speak with John Masters about trying out for the role of Lady Mayberry.

John Masters doesn't give Aunt Bee an opportunity to express her interest in the role. When Aunt Bee mentions Lady Mayberry, Mr. Masters tells her that the costume she makes for Lady Mayberry will be almost as important as the words Lady Mayberry speaks. He then says Clara Edwards will play the role.

"In the filmed episode, Clara is called to tend to her sick sister in Saberton," says Harvey. "In the script I wrote 'sick sister in Mebane,' which is a real North Carolina town. I selected it because a freshman friend of mine at Duke University came from Mebane, and I always liked the sound of it."

In Aunt Bee's presence, Andy, Barney, and Mr. Masters discuss finding someone else to play Lady Mayberry. Throughout their discussion, Aunt Bee drops hints about her theatrical experience and interest in the role. Andy eventually notices and asks her why she doesn't play the part. Mr. Masters thinks it over and gives Aunt Bee the role.

That night at play practice, Andy, wearing a coonskin hat, and Barney, dressed in an Indian headdress, smoke a peace pipe while rehearsing a scene. Barney coughs after he takes a puff and delivers his lines in a high-pitched voice.

"Barney's high-pitched voice was not scripted," says Harvey. "Don Knotts was masterful with high voices and probably felt it worked well in the scene.

"When Barney and Andy are reading lines, Barney stops to ask the director if they can change his last line, 'Paleface is not a man of his word.' He says that the line is 'just not Noogatuck.' This is an echo of a supposedly true story of an actor who, when playing a role of a Martian in a sci-fi story, asked the director in all seriousness to change his lines because 'a Martian wouldn't talk like that.' Here Barney is stating that he knew how the mind of an Indian worked—even though a hundred years has passed."

After Andy and Barney finish their scene, Mr. Masters calls on Aunt Bee to practice "the opening of the second act, your soliloquy." While Aunt Bee is getting into place, Mr. Masters tells Andy to have the "faintest smile" when Noogatuck calls him "laughing face."

"Having the director ask for a faint smile, which Andy summons up, grew out of my memories of directors who have to make their contribution to everything," says Harvey. "Andy smiles because he, like most cast members, actually wants to be given directions—it's cool."

Aunt Bee walks past the wings and runs back and forth behind the backdrop before eventually making her entrance. Her performance is terrible.

"Frances Bavier actually isn't called upon to do much physical activity," says Harvey. "The stage is small, and it's not very demanding to ask her to change directions to get to the proper side. The running behind the curtain was probably done by a crew member.

"Writing a script calls for absolutely no obligatory interaction between the writer and the performers. In the process of doing thirty-some scripts, however, it was inevitable that I might occasionally run into the actors in the studio commissary. So I met Andy, Don, Ronny Howard, Jim Nabors, etcetera, and we knew each other. Frances Bavier was never in sight. I heard she was a very private person and quite a disciplinarian on the set. At times she even had Andy tiptoeing about if she was annoyed. Andy was aware of Frances's minor personality quirks and was very deferential, diplomatic, and supportive. Above all, she was a superb actress and totally Mayberry."

After working with Aunt Bee for three hours the previous night, Mr. Masters insists that Andy tell her she is not right for the Lady Mayberry role.

That evening, Aunt Bee complains to Andy that she doesn't think Mr. Masters understands the Lady Mayberry role. Andy replies, "If you don't see eye to eye with him, why don't you just forget it?" Aunt Bee says she won't give up the part for "anything in the world."

As Aunt Bee rushes off to practice, she remembers supper. Andy tells her that they'll pick up something at the diner. Aunt Bee feels she is neglecting Andy and Opie, but she can't "seem to find the time."

After Aunt Bee leaves, the telephone rings. Mr. Masters is calling to say the problem with Lady Mayberry is solved because Clara is back in town. Mr. Masters insists that Andy tell Aunt Bee.

Andy asks Mr. Masters not to say anything to Clara yet. While Andy ponders what to do, Opie mentions that he'll be glad when the pageant is over because he's "getting tired of eating at the diner." Opie's comment gives Andy an idea.

The next day, Aunt Bee is busy planning her day around play practice. Clara comes over because Andy asked her to help out while Aunt Bee is "busy with the pageant." Clara is delighted to help and says she's looking forward "to having someone to cook for."

As Andy and Clara talk, Andy reminds Aunt Bee that she'd "better run along if you expect to get that stuff done." Aunt Bee agrees and mentions that she "still has to work on that opening speech." Clara fondly recalls the opening speech and recites it beautifully.

Aunt Bee leaves reluctantly. As Clara goes into the kitchen, it appears that the plan didn't work.

However, Aunt Bee goes out the front door, walks around the side of the house, and enters the kitchen through the back door. She insists that Clara "take back the part." Clara joyfully accepts, and Aunt Bee willingly prepares Andy and Opie's supper.

In the epilogue, Andy and Barney watch Clara practice the opening speech. She is wonderful. Barney tells Andy, "Well, Aunt Bee tried, but it's just one of them things. Either you got it, or you don't." Barney looks up on stage and sees someone dressed in Chief Noogatuck's headdress. He yells at the man, jumps up from his chair, and rushes the stage. Mr. Masters stops Barney and takes him aside "to speak privately."

"The epilogue might have been more effective in mime," says Harvey. "Just a slight change is needed. After Barney states that 'either you got it or you don't,' it might have been better to have an actor walk by in Indian headdress. But perhaps it's too late to change the script."

"The Darling Baby"

Episode 139

First Broadcast on
December 7, 1964

Written by
**Jim Fritzell and
Everett Greenbaum**

Directed by
Howard Morris

"In my more positive moments I like to think of *The Andy Griffith Show* **as a sort of modern Charles Dickens oeuvre. After all, most of his work was first published as serials in newspapers."**—EVERETT GREENBAUM

"I don't remember how this story first originated," says writer Everett Greenbaum. "As far as I can remember, Jim Fritzell and I were the only ones to write Ernest T., the Darlings, and, at first, Gomer stories. Then the other writers began writing for Gomer. It wasn't any more difficult to think up a new reason to have the Darlings return to Mayberry than to come up with new ideas for other stories."

Jim and Everett begin their "Darling Baby" script with Andy and Opie in the courthouse. Andy is inspecting a glass jar with an egg inside. Opie shows Andy a rubber wishbone he made by "soaking it in vinegar." Opie learned how to do the tricks, which he calls "facts of science," from the book, *Twenty Scientific Tricks a Boy Can Do at Home* by Seymour Shreck. Opie's interest in magic and one of his tricks, the use of disappearing ink, will later play a prominent role in solving the episode's problem.

"Opie's interest in magic and the title of his book were inspired by my own childhood interest in magic," says Everett. "As a kid I got a lot of magic tricks from library books with titles like *Twenty Tricks a Boy Can Do at Home.*

"The construction of this story was the same as 'Barney's Sidecar.' In the 'Sidecar' episode, we resolved the problem caused by Barney's motorcycle by having Andy place a fake plaque, which he had inscribed with Opie's woodburning set, under the sidecar's seat. We then had to go back and insert the woodburning set into the beginning of that script. This script came later, so this one starts right off with Opie's magic trick, which we reprise for an ending. We remembered the sidecar episode, followed its structure, and had the disappearing ink in mind before we ever began writing this script."

Andy steps outside with Opie and finds Barney sitting on the bench. Although

Barney is asleep, when Andy wakes him, he claims he "was watching traffic." He says his eyes were "squinched up so they couldn't see me looking."

At this point, the Darlings' truck comes down Main Street. The Darlings are welcomed warmly by Andy and Barney. Charlene proudly shows off her three-month-old daughter Andelina. Charlene acknowledges that they named her after Andy, since he "done so much to help us."

"Jim and I made up the name Andelina," says Everett. "It was our version of the feminine form of Andy."

While admiring the baby, Barney tries to get Andelina to take his finger, but the baby refuses. Later in the episode's epilogue, Jim and Everett cleverly reprise this gag with a twist—after taking Barney's finger, the baby won't let go.

Andy, Barney and the Darlings go inside the courthouse to "get that baby in here where it's cool." Briscoe tells Andy, "This ain't a to-show trip. It's got purpose. It's a betrothal."

It seems the Darlings have come to Mayberry "to find a young boy to pledge his hand and heart to Andelina." Briscoe informs Andy that "the young fellar that gets Andelina comes in to a pretty good dowry—an eight-by-ten cottage on the back twenty. All it needs is a roof, some fresh mud on the floor. It'd be a real paradise. And a cow comes with it, and two acres of side hill with good strong boulders." Andy and Barney both agree that it sounds like a good deal.

"Andelina's dowry and Briscoe's dialogue were pure Jim Fritzell and are examples of the rapport he had for characters like the Darlings," says Everett.

The Darlings spend their first day in Mayberry looking for a husband for Andelina. Their search is unsuccessful. They came "across one young'un, but he had a big wart on the end of his nose."

That evening the Darlings drop by the Taylor house to "pick with Andy a little bit." After Charlene sings a love song, Opie comes downstairs to tell Andy good night. Opie takes Andy aside and asks if it would be okay if he doesn't kiss Andy in front of company. Andy understands, and the two shake hands.

"Opie's concern about giving Andy a good-night kiss in front of company grew out of my own experience with my father," says Everett. "My father considered it an insult if you didn't kiss his cheek on arriving, leaving, or going to bed. The older I got, the more embarrassing it became. As an adult, it didn't bother me."

After seeing Opie, the Darlings decide that he would be a perfect match for Andelina. Andy protests, but Briscoe pays no attention. He takes out the betrothal papers for Andy to sign. When Andy refuses, Briscoe thinks that Andy is all "choked up," so he decides "to leave the signing until tomorrow."

The next day Andy tells Barney about the Darlings' intentions for Opie. The situation reminds Barney of an experience he had with a girl named Halcyon Loretta Winslow. Barney describes in detail the experience, which he says was like "*A Tale Out of Two Cities*." It all began when Halcyon's father, who owned a prune-pitting factory, saw Barney's picture in the newspaper after he had won four free haircuts in the church raffle. The father wanted Barney to meet Halcyon, so he set up a date for the three at Klein's Coffee House for lunch. Barney tells Andy, "You know me. When opportunity knocks, Old Barn's got to a least take a peep and see if there is anybody on the stoop." During the lunch, Halcyon's father offered Barney one-third interest in the family business, full use of the company car, and a beautiful hillside plot in the Mt. Pilot cemetery.

Halcyon, however, was "Beasto Maristo," and Barney turned down the offer. Barney ends the story by telling Andy that Halcyon later went off to finishing school but is still "ugly, single, and pitting prunes."

During the conversation, Andy gets up from his desk without saying a word and goes into the back room. He returns a short time later with coffee for Barney and himself. This action seems exactly like something someone would do while enjoying a good story. Intent on hearing the story, but also wanting a cup of coffee, Andy quietly gets up without disturbing the storyteller and returns quickly.

"I knew a girl in Buffalo named Halcyon," says Everett. "As for the rest of the stuff about her—it was what happened with Fritzell and Greenbaum and a typewriter on a good day. It was not scripted for Andy to get coffee. This was probably worked out on stage.

"Andy and Don were perfect in the scene. I think they gave the most relaxed performances of their careers, and I often think the best—except for Andy's performance in the movie *A Face in the Crowd*."

After Barney finishes his story, Opie enters the courthouse dressed in a new suit. Opie tells Andy he was walking down the street when Briscoe and Charlene took him into Weaver's Department Store. The next thing he knew he was in a suit that they said was his to keep. With this new development, Andy decides to stop the Darlings.

Andy, Barney, and Opie find the Darlings at Andy's house, where they are having an engagement party. Mr. Darling admires Opie's egg in a bottle. He observes that he "ain't never seen it fixed like that before. I think I'll pass it up for the time being." Briscoe hands the bottle to Andy.

When Barney becomes wrapped up in the celebration and helps himself to the sandwiches, Andy tells him to sit down. Barney sits down in a chair that has a jug of "mulberry squeezings" beside it.

When Charlene hands Andelina to Opie, Opie tell Andy he doesn't want to marry Andelina. When Andy tries to object, Briscoe interrupts by saying, "Don't they make a nice-looking couple. They's matched together like a racy team of buggy mules." As Andy starts to put the egg in a bottle down, he gets an idea. He hands the bottle to Opie, whispers to him, and sends him upstairs.

After Opie leaves, Andy sees Barney sipping from the jug of squeezings. He points out that Barney is still on duty, but Barney replies, "The boys said this was just mulberry squeezings." He takes a sip, coughs, and says in a strained voice, "That's all it is—mulberry squeezings."

At this point, Andy seems to have accepted the betrothal and "joins the boys in a number." After the song, Opie returns with a pen and the bottle of disappearing ink. Andy and Opie seem eager to sign the betrothal papers. Somewhat inebriated by the squeezings, Barney attempts to stop the proceedings. When Briscoe gives Barney a threatening look, Barney returns to his chair.

Andy and Opie prepare to sign but are interrupted by Barney again. This time, Andy sends him into the kitchen.

"We thought it would be a good idea for Barney to get a little drunk," says Everett. "Otherwise, he may never have allowed the signing of the agreement."

Before signing the papers, Andy recites, "Ebum, Shoobem, Shoobem, Shoobem" and explains to Briscoe, "That's just something we say." Andy and Opie sign the papers. Moments later their signatures disappear. The Darlings see the signatures vanish before their eyes. Suspecting "witchery" in Andy's family, they call off the betrothal and depart quickly.

"The idea for the 'witchery' came from Jim, but 'Ebum, Shoobem' was not scripted," says Everett.

In the epilogue, Andy and the Darlings reunite and play a song. Afterward, Briscoe explains that he and the boys got to talking and decided "since there's some witches that lives up around our place that we visit with and talk to and everything—even go to church with—there ain't no reason we can't associate with you." Andy and the Darlings "seal" their friendship with another song.

"If memory serves me, we felt a little written out on *The Griffith Show* during the time we were writing 'The Darling Baby,'" says Everett. "We had also been offered a high-budget movie, *Good Neighbor Sam*. The offer ultimately proved to be too much to resist, and our Mayberry days came to an end."

"Andy and Helen Have Their Day"

Episode 140

First Broadcast on
December 14, 1964

Written by
**Bill Idelson and
Sam Bobrick**

Directed by
Howard Morris

"Howard Morris was a fine director. Most actors are. They have empathy for the artist."—GEORGE LINDSEY

"Goober was invented in 'Man in a Hurry,' but we didn't see him. Gomer mentioned him. I named him after a teacher my wife had in Arkansas—Old Goober Mouth."—EVERETT GREENBAUM

Bill and Sam begin their script with Barney explaining to Andy why he looks tired. Barney explains that he was out late the night before. He says, "I don't think my head hit the pillow before a quarter to eleven." Barney had taken Juanita from the diner to Morelli's and "then over to her house for a little 'quote' TV."

"Bill and I enjoyed writing the details of Barney's date with Juanita," says writer Sam Bobrick. "Barney's expectations of a good time are always hilariously low, so he's very seldom disappointed. A meal at Morelli's and an evening of TV is his idea of an exciting time."

Barney asks Andy if he had a date with Helen the night before. Andy says he plans to take Helen to the movies tonight.

During this conversation, Helen enters the courthouse and tells Andy she will have to break their date because she has papers to grade. As they attempt to re-schedule the date, they both have conflicts. Andy promises Helen that "one of these times, I'll take you off somewhere, and we'll spend the whole day."

Overhearing their conversation, Barney agrees to make Andy and Helen "a present of Saturday." He will take care of all their responsibilities, so the two can spend the whole day together at Myers Lake. Barney will not take no for an answer. He tells Andy, "Saturday, you, Helen, picnic, the whole day alone together, the birds and the bees."

"The storyline for this script centered on the relationships of the characters more than upon a situation," says Sam. "I always felt it was easier to write character than contrivance-centered stories."

A Set of Threads

T he suit Goober wears to the wedding was originally owned by Howard McNear, who portrayed Floyd the barber. The story I was told was that Howard had sent the suit to a funeral home so a friend of his could be buried in it. The suit wouldn't fit, so the funeral home returned it to the studio. Jim Nabors was then given the suit to wear. After Jim left, it was handed on to me. Eventually moths got into the suit, and it had to be thrown away. By then, however, it had become a Goober trademark, so wardrobe made a replica of the suit before discarding the original.—GEORGE LINDSEY

Barney has Goober drive Andy and Helen to the lake. After their arrival, Goober interrupts Andy and Helen's day by hanging around to eat. This begins a pattern that will continue throughout the episode.

"I read the part for 'The Man in a Hurry' script and was told I was going to be Gomer," says George Lindsey, who portrayed Goober Pyle. "At the last minute a change was made, and Jim Nabors got the part. I was later offered the role of Dud Wash in the first Darlings episode but turned it down. I just knew I was going to be on that show, and I figured if I took the minor role of Dud I would never become a regular. It was a decision made in heaven. Jim Nabors eventually left to start his own series, and I was called in to play Goober."

"It was not much different to write for Goober instead of Gomer," says Sam. "The characters were very similar. With both, there was a thin line between dumbness and innocence."

While Goober is eating with Andy and Helen, Barney arrives at the lake to get the key to Helen's house. The television repairman is coming over to work on her TV, and Barney has volunteered to oversee his work. Helen tells Barney that she had left the key under the mat. As Barney leaves, he orders Goober to return to town.

After lunch, Andy and Helen relax by the lake. Andy has his head in Helen's lap, and Helen strokes his hair affectionately. The two start to kiss but are interrupted when Barney yells, "Andy!" and walks up with Opie. Barney wants Andy's permission to take Opie to the movies. When Andy gives his consent, Barney responds, "Let's go, Ope. Let's get out of here, and let them get back to whatever they were doing." Barney then adds, "What were you doing?"

After Barney leaves, Andy suggests that they take a walk. The two find a boat and row to the middle of the lake. Andy tells Helen, "Well, at least nobody can walk right in on us." Andy puts his arm around Helen, and the two start to kiss. The kiss is interrupted by Barney yelling, "Andy!" He is standing on the lake shore with George, the television repairman. It seems Helen's set will have to go into the shop, and Barney wants to be sure she will approve the repair.

"We had no difficulty thinking up reasons to have Barney return to the lake repeatedly," says Sam. "Almost any reason was legitimate from Barney's viewpoint, and this gave us a lot of freedom."

"We were sitting around the table reading the script and came to the part for George the repairman," says director Howard Morris. "They had not yet cast an actor in the role, so I read the part. As I read, I used a nasal voice. They liked what I did and asked me to play the role."

After Barney leaves, Andy and Helen finally have some time alone and decide to go fishing. Andy catches several fish and is stopped by the game warden, who asks to see Andy's fishing license. Andy has left the license in his wallet, which is in the pocket of his uniform back in Mayberry. The unsympathetic game warden escorts the couple to the justice of the peace to set Andy's fine.

"Colin Male was cast as the game warden," says Howard. "Colin was a tall, handsome guy. He had a great voice and was the announcer who introduced the show in the opening credits. I was not privy to the casting people, but I imagine his wonderful voice and appearance are what got him the role."

After arriving at the justice of the peace's office, Andy calls the Mayberry courthouse. Goober answers the telephone, and Andy asks him to tell Barney that "Helen and I are over at the justice of the peace in Siler City. I was fishing, and I didn't have a license. Tell Barney to get over here as fast as he can with twenty-five dollars." When Goober relates the message to Barney, it becomes, "They are at the justice of the peace in Siler City, and he said something about a license, and he wants you to bring twenty-five dollars as fast as you can."

Barney jumps to the conclusion that Andy and Helen have decided to get married. Barney goes by the Taylor house to pick up Aunt Bee and Opie. The three, plus Goober, head to the "wedding" dressed in their Sunday best.

Barney's conclusion that Andy and Helen are getting married is very similar to the storyline of the fourth-season episode, "The Rumor." In that episode, Barney thinks Andy and Helen are getting married after he sees the two kiss in the jewelry store.

"Sometimes we would put a character in a similar situation and see where it would lead us," says Sam. "Apparently, producer Aaron Ruben felt this episode was far enough away from the previous script. He never expressed any concern about repeating a storyline."

The four arrive at the justice of the peace. Goober "gets busy" tying shoes and cans to the bumper of the squad car. Barney, Aunt Bee, and Opie rush inside. Aunt Bee embraces Helen, and Opie asks, "Pa, are you really getting married?" Barney gives Andy the twenty-five dollars and says, "You don't have to worry about paying me back. Just take your time." Andy looks at the money and says, "This is for a fishing fine. We're not getting married. You beat anything." Goober enters and begins throwing rice.

In the epilogue, Andy and Helen are relaxing at Helen's house. Andy has sent Barney and Thelma Lou "out into the woods." As Andy hugs Helen, the moment is interrupted when Barney bursts in. He has dropped his fishing pole in the lake and wants to borrow Andy's. Barney apologizes for "barging in," and then asks Andy, "What were you doing?"

"Barney Fife, Realtor"

"If you're selling something, you should tell the people the truth about it, or else it ain't honest."—OPIE, repeating Andy's rule of fair dealing

Episode 143

First Broadcast on
January 4, 1965

Written by
**Bill Idelson and
Sam Bobrick**

Directed by
Peter Baldwin

**Dabbs Greer and
Amzie Strickland**
Guest Star as Harry
and Lila Sims

"I don't really remember what inspired the storyline for this episode," says writer Sam Bobrick, "but when I first came to Los Angeles everyone was in the real-estate business. We may have gotten the idea from that. I do recall that I enjoyed writing this script."

Bill and Sam begin their script in the courthouse. Andy enters and finds Barney on the telephone. Barney is talking with Mr. Clark about moving the iron bed out of his garage. Barney hangs up the telephone and begins figuring on a piece of paper. Andy says, "Boy, you sure are doing a lot of figuring. What you doing, buying a house?" Barney answers, "Not me personally. I'm in the business."

Barney explains that he recently talked to Mr. Slummer, the real-estate man. According to Barney, all Mr. Slummer does is "sit around in his office all day long, smoking a big fat cigar, and never stirs unless somebody wants to buy something. Then he takes them out in that old rattletrap car of his, and if they buy he collects 5 percent." Barney thinks "a younger guy with some drive" could make some money.

Barney tells Andy he has been in the real-estate business "less than twenty-four hours" and has already learned that "everybody wants to sell their house."

During the conversation, Andy goes into the back room to get a cup of coffee. The coffeepot is covered with a plate instead of a lid. The plate lid is a realistic detail that captures the feel of everyday life.

Andy remarks that he is completely satisfied with the house he's living in. Barney asks, "What if I told you the Williams house was available?" Barney reminds Andy that he always points out the house every time he and Barney drive by it. Barney tells Andy he could put him in "that little unit," if Andy would sell his place and get a mortgage for the difference. Andy eventually asks, "Well, what are we doing? Is this a real-estate office or a sheriff's office?"

Barney replies that the real-estate business is strictly a sideline. The words are just out of his mouth when the phone rings. Without hesitation, Barney answers, "Fife Realty."

"Jokes like this were easy to write," says Sam. "You just had to be sure they fit the character and didn't come off as a joke just for the sake of a laugh."

Later that day Andy returns home and finds Opie and a friend, Howie Williams, examining Opie's bicycle. Opie has decided to sell the bicycle to Howie. Andy asks Opie if he has told Howie that the bicycle's coaster brake slips, the chain comes apart, and the inner tubes are covered with patches. Opie asks Andy if he should have told Howie about the defects. Andy answers, "I think so, Ope. If you're selling something, the buyer's got a right to know everything that's wrong with it, otherwise it's not quite honest."

"I don't remember that Bill and I intentionally set out to teach a lesson," says Sam. "The importance of fair dealing to the storyline and the interaction between Andy and Opie just developed as we wrote the script."

During supper, Opie tells Andy that he ruined the deal on the bike by being honest. Andy responds, "Ope, let me give you a little talk on fair dealing." Opie asks if he can get a glass of water first. When Opie goes into the kitchen and turns on the water, the plumbing begins to rumble. Andy tells Opie to turn the faucet all the way open.

The rumbling sets Aunt Bee's "teeth on edge." Andy asks her if she would like to move and explains that the Williamses might want to sell their house. Andy says Barney has told him they could afford the Williams place.

After supper, Barney surprises the Taylors by dropping by and asking if he can bring in prospective buyers, the Simses, to look at the house. The Taylors reluctantly agree and quickly "straighten up the place" while Barney goes to the car to get the Simses.

While showing the house, Barney whispers to Mr. Sims, "There is a little work to be done, but with your imagination, you folks could really do something with this place." Andy overhears this and responds with a grimace.

"Andy's grimace grew out of the fact that most people think they live in a perfectly decorated house," says Sam. "People quickly become incensed if someone should think differently."

During the visit, Opie points out that the kitchen ceiling is cracked, that there is a "noise" in the faucet, and that the roof leaks. After hearing about these problems, the Simses quickly lose interest in the house.

"The Griffith Show always was a friendly set," says Amzie Strickland, who portrayed Lila Sims. "During breaks, Andy liked to go into his dressing room and play his guitar. Quite often I would go in and sit down and talk. My husband and I knew Andy from his early days in New York. After we moved to California, Andy was kind enough to recommend us for jobs.

"TAGS casting director Ruth Burch would call my agent if they wanted me for an episode and ask if I was free. I was never told what kind of a role it was or anything about it because in those days I was one of a group of actors who played different parts every week. We were very versatile, so the type of role was not important."

"If I was available, they would send over a script a couple of days ahead of time," says Amzie. "In those days, the writing was so good that very few rewrites were required. The scripts were ready in advance, and there were few changes when you got on the set. Once you had a script, you knew that maybe you'd have one line changed but never anything else because the writers knew what they were doing.

"If you were good the first time you were on, they would give you other opportunities to work. If you didn't work in with the show, then they kind of eased you out. The next time a role came up, they wouldn't call you."

After the Simses leave, Andy asks Opie if he pointed out the house's defects just to get even. Opie answers that he was just thinking about what Andy had said about the rule of fair dealing. Andy responds with, "Well, bikes are bikes, and houses are houses." Andy says when he bought the house, the crack was already in the ceiling, and the previous owner had just painted the kitchen so the crack wouldn't show. Andy tells Opie that one owner passes the things wrong with a house on to the next owner.

Opie then asks, "You mean, kids should be honest but the grown-ups don't have to be?" This observation leaves Andy at a loss for words, and he sends Opie to bed.

The next day, Barney is angry because Opie prevented him from making a sale. When the telephone rings, Barney answers it curtly. When Barney realizes it is Mr. Sims, his demeanor changes instantly. He pleads frantically with Mr. Sims for one more chance to show Andy's house. After Sims agrees, Barney says, "Thank you, thank you, and bless you, bless you."

"'Bless you' grew out of Barney's relief that Mr. Sims will give him another chance," says Sam. "A desperate Barney is also relieved that God has not forsaken him."

At the second showing, Barney tells the Simses that there is nothing really wrong with the place. "It's just the boy said those things last night, and we know how kids exaggerate." Andy admits to the Simses that kids do tend to exaggerate, but in this case everything Opie said is true. Opie responds to Andy's honesty with a look of deep admiration.

"Opie's admiration of Andy was called for in the script," says Sam. "The decision to show Opie's face in close-up, however, was the call of the director."

Thinking Andy has got another buyer, Mr. Sims immediately offers to buy the house. Before Andy can sell, however, he must decide if he wants to purchase the Williams house. Barney quickly calls the Williamses, and Andy and Aunt Bee go to look at the house.

Andy and Aunt Bee are greeted by Howie at the Williamses. Howie's feet are wet. He explains that he has "been down in the basement sailing the boat. There's about a foot of water down there. It's great. Sometimes after a heavy rain there is a lot more." Howie turns to his father and says, "The crack in the furnace is getting a lot bigger, and you can see the flame real clear."

"It never concerned us that the audience might wonder where Opie was while Andy and Aunt Bee were at the Williams house," says Sam. "But it could have given the viewer something to think about. Maybe it was late, and Opie had to study or go to bed. After all, Barney stayed with the Simses at Andy's house. Or perhaps Opie stayed out of sight, down in the flooded basement, sailing a boat."

After thinking over the situation, Andy decides that the best thing would be for everyone to stay where they are. He uses the telephone to "warn Barney." Barney is irate when he learns Andy has decided not to buy the Williams house. Andy lays the telephone down and walks out. Thinking Andy is still listening, Barney continues to protest his decision.

The next day, Barney is busy figuring. Andy asks if he has another real-estate deal. Barney tells Andy he is completely out of that business. When Andy asks what the figures are all about, Barney replies, "Ange, you been wanting a car, haven't you?"

"Goober Takes a Car Apart"

"I won't set foot outside that courthouse, Andy, I promise."
—GOOBER PYLE

"This was another script that was fun to write."
—SAM BOBRICK

Episode 144

First Broadcast on
January 11, 1965

Written by
**Bill Idelson and
Sam Bobrick**

Directed by
Peter Baldwin

The opening scene of "Goober Takes a Car Apart" finds Andy seated on the bench in front of the courthouse. He is reading a letter when Goober drives up in the squad car. Andy asks how the squad car is going. Goober responds, "Running like a scalded dog." When Goober asks Andy what he's reading, Andy tells him that it's a letter from Barney. "He's up in Raleigh. Took his vacation up there." Goober sits down on the bench, and Andy reads Barney's letter out loud.

"Bill Idelson was always great with phrases," says writer Sam Bobrick. "Goober's 'scalded dog' description of the squad car came from him. I don't remember anything in our script about a letter from Barney. I imagine it was added later and written by either producer Aaron Ruben, Andy Griffith, or Don Knotts."

The office telephone rings as Andy finishes reading. A man named Shorty tells Andy he will not be able to answer the sheriff's phone while Andy is attending the Sheriffs' Safety Conference in Mt. Pilot. Goober eagerly offers to take Shorty's place. He tells Andy, "I really would enjoy it. You know how I love to hang around the courthouse." Andy reluctantly accepts Goober's offer. Goober gives Andy his word that he'll be at the office early on Wednesday morning.

"This was the first script that featured Goober," says George Lindsey. "I remember that the script seemed to have miles and miles of dialogue to memorize. I wasn't overly excited when I saw that I had a major role in the script. I was just very pleased that I was getting a job—a good job."

On the day of the conference, Goober fails to show up. Andy goes to Wally's Service Station in search of Goober and finds him working on Gilly Walker's carburetor. Goober imitates different carburetor noises as he explains to Andy the trouble Gilly is having with his engine.

467

"Goober was a natural mechanic and knew cars so well he could talk their language," says Sam. "In my mind, he was the kind of mechanic who never read a book or went to automotive school. He simply had a feel for working on cars."

Goober tells Andy he will "go right down" to the courthouse, and Andy returns home to finish packing for his trip. While Andy is packing, the telephone rings. Andy learns that there is still no one at the courthouse. Andy goes to investigate and finds Goober outside the courthouse working on Gilly Walker's car.

Frustrated, Andy tells Goober to go back to the filling station. Andy returns home and decides to ask Aunt Bee to take Goober's place. Goober shows up soon afterward and tells Andy he has fixed Gilly's car and is now free. Goober promises to stay in the office, but Andy refuses the offer. Aunt Bee points out that it might be better if there were a man at the courthouse, so Andy reluctantly agrees. He tells Goober, "When you get down there, you stay inside the courthouse. Don't you go outside the courthouse."

Gilly drives by and sees Goober walking to the courthouse. He stops to complain about a new problem with his engine. Gilly drives Goober down to the courthouse so he can listen to the engine on the way.

Remembering his promise to Andy, Goober takes Gilly's engine apart and brings it inside "to get it right." Goober begins with the engine but continues until the entire car is disassembled. Gilly and Floyd watch Goober while he works.

"We had three different cars in various stages of being torn apart," says George. "I also know that they actually ran because I would start the engines up."

Andy returns from the conference and is stunned when he enters the office and finds Gilly's car. The telephone rings. Goober starts the engine while Andy is on the telephone. When Andy hangs up the telephone, he tells Goober that he has to go to Mrs. Corey's house. Andy warns Goober that he'd "better have a good start getting this car out of here" by the time he returns.

When Andy returns, he is angered by Goober's slow progress. Andy announces, "Now, Goober, I'm going to get out of here because if I don't I'm liable to start hollering. When I get done hollering, I'm liable to take one of these guns out of this rack here and shoot you. Now, I'm going home, and when I come back here in the morning I want all traces of that car to be gone."

"It never concerned us that Andy was coming across angrier than usual," says Sam. "We thought Andy's anger was justified. After all, most people would get upset if they found a car in their workplace or living room."

When Andy arrives home, Aunt Bee tells him that Sheriff Jackson, the president of the Sheriffs' Association called, and Aunt Bee told him Andy was at the courthouse. Sheriff Jackson is planning to pay Andy a visit.

Andy fears that he will become the "laughingstock of the whole state" if Sheriff Jackson sees the car inside the courthouse. He rushes to the office and finds the "car back together." Gilly has decided to sell the car, and Floyd is considering buying it. Floyd, however, couldn't make up his mind with the body off, so Goober "put it together for a few minutes, so Floyd could try it out." Andy frantically tries removing a car door.

Sheriff Jackson and his assistant enter the office. When the sheriff inquires about the car's presence, Goober explains, "I took the car apart piece by piece and got it right in here. It belongs to Gilly Walker. You wouldn't believe how he abuses that car. Speed, speed, speed, that's all he ever thinks about." After thinking the situation over, Sheriff Jackson decides the car is part of a safety display. Andy's reputation is saved.

"Bill and I had decided on this solution to Andy's problem before writing the script," says Sam. "The fact that the visiting officer thinks the car is part of a safety display may be too much of a coincidence to be entirely believable. But sometimes you have to make drastic cuts for time, and sometimes they're not always the right cuts."

In the epilogue, Andy and Goober bid Sheriff Jackson and his assistant goodbye. After their departure, Andy invites Goober inside the office. He walks straight to the gun rack, removes a gun, points it at Goober, and says, "Get it out. I said, get it out, right now." Goober immediately goes to work.

"The Case of the Punch in the Nose"

Episode 152

First Broadcast on
March 15, 1965

Written by
**Bill Idelson and
Sam Bobrick**

Directed by
Coby Ruskin

"The case was never properly disposed of."
—BARNEY FIFE

"I once had an uncle who punched several people in the nose for stupid reasons," says writer Sam Bobrick. "I thought an episode inspired by my uncle's behavior would work well on *TAGS*. We presented the idea to producer Aaron Ruben. He liked it, and we began working on the script."

The opening scene in Bill and Sam's script finds Andy and Barney sorting through some old files. Barney comes across an assault case dated August 9, 1946, that involved Floyd Lawson and Charlie Foley. The case file doesn't say who assaulted whom. Barney reads the file and discovers that the case never came to trial, "nothing resolved, no verdict, no nothing."

"The date of the assault case was picked randomly," says Sam. "We wanted a date far enough in the past to emphasize the fact that Barney had to go a long way to stir up trouble."

Barney feels they ought to do something because "an assault was committed, an arrest was made, and nothing ever happened." Barney decides to reopen the case and begins his investigation by talking to Floyd. Floyd is reading a newspaper when Andy and Barney enter the barbershop. He has just read about the engagement of Bobby Gribble and Emma Larch and shares this news. Andy is interested, but Barney is focused solely on the investigation. He asks Floyd about the assault but gets nowhere.

"Howard McNear was the funniest man in acting I ever worked with," says George Lindsey. "He did something with his role of Floyd Lawson that couldn't be duplicated. He put his own stamp on it. I loved watching him act. I would often go down to the studio and watch him when I wasn't even working."

After leaving the barbershop, Barney goes next door to talk to Charlie Foley. Mr. Foley remembers the case and tells Barney he fell asleep in the barber chair. While he was sleeping, Floyd cut his hair and gave him a shave. He hadn't asked for the shave. When he refused to pay for it, an argument followed, and Floyd punched him in the nose. Foley had an eyewitness to back up his statement. He identifies the witness as "Goober in the garage. He was a little boy then. He saw the whole thing."

While Barney is talking to Mr. Foley, Andy and Floyd are back in the barbershop discussing Barney's interest in the case. Floyd observes that he thinks Barney's trouble is that he's not married. He says, "Now if he was married, these little things wouldn't bother him."

"Bill and I felt that Mayberry's slow pace left Barney with too much time on his hands," says Sam. "We expressed this through Floyd's comment about Barney not being married. Floyd felt Barney needed something like marriage to occupy his time. If he were married he would have been busy trying to make the marriage work and would not have been concerned with petty stuff."

Barney returns to the barbershop and tells Foley's version of what happened. He has asked Mr. Foley and Goober to come by so the assault can be reenacted. While waiting, Floyd gives his version. According to Floyd, Foley "asked for that shave." Floyd denies punching Foley.

When Foley and Goober arrive, Foley and Floyd start arguing about what actually happened. Barney insists that the case be reenacted. Andy takes Barney aside and asks him to stop his investigation. While the two are talking, Floyd and Mr. Foley resume arguing, and Floyd hits Foley in the nose.

Mr. Foley follows Andy into the courthouse and demands that Floyd be arrested. Foley says, "I have three witnesses. You all saw the whole thing." Andy replies that he didn't see anything because he was talking to Barney. Foley insists that Barney and Goober must have seen it. When they enter the office, Foley says to Barney, "All right, tell the truth. You saw him haul off and hit me in cold blood."

"Mr. Foley's dialogue was inspired by the title of Truman Capote's book *In Cold Blood*," says Sam. "The book was very popular at the time, and we thought the phrase would be a comical way to describe a punch in the nose."

Barney tells Foley he didn't see the assault because he was talking to Andy. Goober didn't see anything either because he was reading a comic book. Foley insists Goober saw Floyd "hit me on the nose" and calls Goober a "liar." The two argue, and Foley punches Goober in the nose.

The animosity Barney rekindles between Floyd and Mr. Foley stirs up the whole town, and numerous nose punches follow. Otis, "a distant kin of Foley's," punches Floyd in the nose. Goober punches Gilly Walker in the nose. Opie gets into a fight with his best friend, Johnny Paul. Lamar Tuttle, "a cousin of Floyd's," punches Otis in the nose.

The rash of assaults angers Andy. He tells Barney that things have gone far enough, and he wants them stopped. When Barney responds that the assaults are not their fault, Andy yells, "No, it's not our fault. It's your fault! You started the whole blame thing!" When Barney attempts to justify his actions, Andy tells him to "shut up."

"We felt that Andy's angry outburst was justified," says Sam. "Andy begged Barney to back off earlier, and Barney refused. Andy knew Barney was the troublemaker, so he had reason to be mad."

Eventually, Andy decides to have Floyd and Mr. Foley sit down and talk about the situation. He sends Barney to get Floyd and Foley and bring them to the courthouse. After the two principals are gathered, Andy begins "a hearing so we can settle this thing between you two fellows once and for all." Barney insists that Goober "really ought to be here," so Andy sends Barney to get him.

After Barney leaves, Andy attempts to have Floyd and Foley "settle this thing like friends." He reminds the two that they are old friends and tells them that being ready to forgive is the first law of friendship. Andy believes that what happened can be made right with "a warm, forgiving handshake "The two realize that Andy is right, shake hands, and forgive each other.

"This is another incidence of an important lesson developing as the script was written," says Sam. "We resolved the problem by having Andy tell the two principals to 'let sleeping dogs lie.'"

Barney and Goober enter the courthouse soon after the case is resolved. Dissatisfied with how Andy has handled the situation, Barney wants to continue his investigation. As he rushes out of the office, Goober says, "You know, Andy, Barney's a wonderful fellow, but sometimes I just don't understand him, do you?" Andy answers, "Yeah, he's a nut."

"Barney's actions were justified by the fact that 'justice is blind,'" explains Sam. "Barney is leaving no stone unturned to clear up a best-forgotten episode, no matter what the outcome."

When Goober asks where Barney has gone, Andy suddenly realizes that he's gone to the barbershop. Andy and Goober hurry outside and see Barney walking toward them, holding his nose. He has been punched.

In the epilogue, Barney has gotten a haircut. He refuses to pay Floyd an extra twenty-five cents for tonic he says he did not request. This repeats the situation between Floyd and Mr. Foley that led to the first punch in the nose. Hoping to prevent a possible punch in the nose, Andy insists that Barney pay the twenty-five cents.

"Sometimes repetition is important in comedy writing, sometimes it isn't," says Sam. "On the other hand, sometimes it isn't, and sometimes it is. On the other hand . . ."

"Opie's Newspaper"

"This is a nonpolice story. Such episodes lent diversity to story areas."
—HARVEY BULLOCK

"When I was a ten-year-old kid, my pal and I built a lean-to on the side of our garage. Inside was the office of *The Keyhole Journal*," says writer Harvey Bullock. "We 'printed' (we actually duplicated pages by using carbon paper and a gummy roller) about twenty copies of the one-page first edition. All items in the paper were gossip tidbits—whose girl was seen riding in whose car, who really craves whom although she pretends she doesn't. These tidbits would be followed by reports about mysterious doings, such as reports of garments missing from clotheslines, followed by more romantic revelations.

"The other kids didn't react much. Some of the girls named in the paper got oafish. The grown-ups giggled, if they bothered to read it at all. But we did attract one advertiser. A neighbor gave us fifteen cents to run a notice that he was selling Airway vacuum cleaners. We shut down after three issues. Boredom set in, and there were other fields to conquer. But the memory of the experience stayed with me and inspired 'Opie's Newspaper.'"

The episode begins with Opie selling Andy a copy of his newspaper, *The Mayberry Sun*. Opie and his friend Howie "put the paper out on the print machine Howie got for his birthday." After discussing the paper's poor sales, Opie leaves the courthouse, and Barney enters.

Barney has just come from the barbershop and shares with Andy his distaste for gossip. Barney says his haircut took a long time because Floyd was gossiping with another customer about the widow Saunders. Barney claims he was reading an article in the "*Geographic*" and "turned a deaf ear to the whole thing." He then proceeds to repeat in great detail the story about the widow Saunders and a dishtowel salesman from Raleigh.

"For some mysterious reason there is comedy in ultra-specifics, notably in small-town gossip where every minute happenstance is fodder for conversation," says Harvey. "The opening scene is heightened by Barney's transparent,

Episode 153

First Broadcast on March 22, 1965

Written by **Harvey Bullock**

Directed by **Coby Ruskin**

473

disdainful dismissal of gossip, which in reality he avidly cherishes—like everyone else."

After Barney repeats the gossip, Andy reads aloud from Opie's newspaper. In response, Barney comments that the paper is "darn cute."

"The items Andy reads to Barney were about kids and resembled news in *The Keyhole Journal*," says Harvey. "Barney's initial appraisal of the newspaper was all momentary approval to set up the contrast with his upcoming apoplexy when he later realizes how he's been misquoted in the second edition."

Opie returns while Andy and Barney are discussing his paper and tells them the paper's sales have not increased. Barney tells Opie, "If the papers aren't moving, there must be a reason why. Maybe you're not getting the right kind of copy. Copy, that's newspaper talk for stories." Barney goes on to tell how he had his own sports column in high school called "Pick-ups and Splashes From Floor and Pool." He acknowledges that the column only appeared once, because it was "too controversial and ahead of its time." Barney says, "I always had printer's ink in my veins. Guess I always had a nose for news." Barney advises Opie to increase the paper's scope and illustrates the point by pointing out that although Karen Folker, who is mentioned in Opie's paper, may be "hot copy for the fifth grade, uptown she don't mean a thing."

"Barney's exposition on 'hot copy' is another of his great and cherished assumptions as an authority," says Harvey. "He uses newspaper slang to mark himself as a veteran.

"In junior high school, I wrote a sports column with that exact awful name 'Pick-ups and Splashes From Floor and Pool.' I remembered it while writing the script and knew such a cornball title would fit Barney nicely."

Opie shares Barney's advice with Howie, and the two decide to model their paper after *Mayberry Gazette*'s "Mayberry After Midnight" column. The boys begin gathering material.

The two make note of Aunt Bee's comment that "Mrs. Foster's chicken à la king tasted like wallpaper paste," Andy's remark that "sometimes the preacher can be as dry as dust," and Barney's observation that Harold Grigsby's wife is "a blonde right out of a bottle." All three items are reported in *The Mayberry Sun*'s second edition.

"Most of the items in the second edition were tailored to Mayberry folk, with a hidden bomb in each," says Harvey. "I custom-fabricated the gossip items by figuring in advance which ones would lead to Andy, Barney, and Aunt Bee paying penance."

Opie hands papers to Andy, Barney, and Aunt Bee while the three are sitting in the Taylor kitchen. The hot weather is of more importance than the paper, and Barney comments, "Well, the weather's been changed so much lately, it must be the bomb."

Clifford Is a Raindrop

I tem in *The Mayberry Sun*: "Myra Lambert got a part in the school play, and she will be a raindrop."

In the navy, right after World War II, I was assigned as a welfare/recreation officer in Hawaii to work with Joe Delaney, a Red Cross representative. Sailors would often come begging for news of their family back in the States. They had received no mail for some time and were worried and distraught. Kindly Joe would immediately send requests back to the Red Cross field worker in the sailor's hometown. The field worker would then visit the family and report back to Joe.

One concerned sailor pleaded for help in finding out about his family. So Joe sent off a request to the stateside field worker. The worker visited the family and found out all was going well. In fact, Clifford, a younger brother, had been given the role of a raindrop in the school play. In an effort to make her report more colorful, the field worker began with "Clifford is a raindrop."

Joe Delaney got word the report was received, hastily called the sailor into our office, grabbed the report, and read aloud, "Clifford is a raindrop."

Both men were stunned speechless. The poor sailor, staring beseechingly, asked, "What's going on?"

They finally sorted out things, but the ridiculous incident always stuck in my mind. Even now, fifty years later, if someone asks me, "What's new?" I almost automatically reply, "Well, Clifford is a raindrop."—HARVEY BULLOCK

"Barney's line about 'it must be the bomb' was an oft-stated casual throwaway line in the aftermath of World War II," says Harvey. "When I see it now in the script, I wince. It was ill-advised because I labored to keep topical items out of Mayberry. The writers were able to present Mayberry as a small Eden, which time had passed. I tried not to make references that would date stories. Also, any reference to the bomb was negative and unnecessary."

Barney casually glances at Opie's paper and sees its contents. Andy, Barney, and Aunt Bee all realize that "this town will be too hot to live in" if the paper is read.

The three find Opie in Howie's garage. Andy asks where he delivered all the papers. When Opie answers, "Just on Willow Avenue, Elm, and Maple," the adults rush out in hopes of collecting the papers before they are noticed.

Andy, Aunt Bee, and Barney learn the consequences of gossip while they collect the papers. Mrs. Foster sees her moments after Aunt Bee has removed Opie's paper from her mailbox. Aunt Bee explains she was just passing by and wanted Mrs. Foster's recipe for chicken à la king. Mrs. Foster invites Aunt Bee and Andy over for a leftover chicken à la king supper. Barney almost gets "a load of buckshot" from Harold Grigsby. Unaware that Barney is retrieving a paper, Grigsby thinks Barney came by to see his wife. After reading Andy's remark in Opie's paper, the preacher has Andy "hog-tied into teaching Sunday School for a full month of Sundays."

"Obviously the gossip was designed so that our characters who swap stories have to eventually pay the price," says Harvey. "It was also fun to write a story where the most upright of citizens are found to have human foibles."

Andy, Barney, and Aunt Bee successfully collect the papers before any great harm is done. Three hours later, there have been no telephone calls complaining about the paper. Andy says, "I guess we got away with it. At least it's over. Maybe the boys learned a lesson out of this." Aunt Bee responds, "Maybe all of us could learn something from this. We're responsible for all this loose talk going around town. If we want the boys to behave better, we better set them a better example."

Opie comes in to say good night and apologizes for the trouble the paper caused. He says, "I guess it was kind of dumb of us to print up two whole pages of that stuff." When Andy, Aunt Bee, and Barney begin to panic about another page, Opie explains that they "bundled it up and threw it in the trash. I even saw the truck come pick it up. So nobody will ever get to read it."

Curiosity gets the best of the three adults. Later in the evening, Andy, Barney, and Aunt Bee meet unexpectedly at the city dump. Each supposedly has come to make sure the other page "was burned proper." When the bundled pages are found, Andy says, "We can go ahead and get rid of these. Yes, sir, and the quicker the better." Andy removes three pages from the bundle, hands copies to Aunt Bee and Barney, keeps one for himself, and throws the rest into a smoking barrel. The three begin reading.

"The earlier admittance of blame and the steely determination by Aunt Bee (which they all accept) that none of them will ever again indulge in mindless gossip set up the concluding laugh," says Harvey. "All of this noble intent, however, is quickly put aside when they find out more 'hot stuff' is available.

"As I reread the script, I noticed one major flaw. How did Aunt Bee get to the city dump that night? I keep hoping I will remember some correction or addition I made to cover up this gaping hole, but I cannot."

In the epilogue, Opie delivers "a new, revised edition" of *The Mayberry Sun* to the courthouse. Opie assures Andy and Barney that "there's nothing about grown-ups at all" in the paper. After Opie leaves, Andy and Barney read the paper's schoolyard gossip. Barney comments, "Opie told the truth. He's not writing about grown-ups." Andy replies, "No, but they sure caught our style good though, didn't they?"

"The Luck of Newton Monroe"

Episode 156

First Broadcast on
April 12, 1965

Written by
**Bill Idelson and
Sam Bobrick**

Directed by
Coby Ruskin

Don Rickles
Guest Stars as
Newton Monroe

"I think the 'fly' gag is one of the great pieces of television history."
—GEORGE LINDSEY

"I knew Don Rickles very well," says Andy Griffith's manager Richard O. Linke. "I suggested to Andy that Don would be great in the part of Newton Monroe. I made the suggestion only because Andy allowed me to. Andy said, 'Yeah, you're right. He'd be good in the part.' Andy then passed the suggestion on to producer Aaron Ruben, and Don was hired."

In the opening scene of "The Luck of Newton Monroe," Andy and Barney are relaxing on the Taylor front porch on a Sunday afternoon. A fly catches their attention. The fly lands on Barney's knee. Barney quickly swipes at the fly, catches it, holds his hand up to Andy's ear so he can confirm the catch, and then lets the fly go. "Well, it's Sunday," Barney says in explanation.

After releasing the fly, Barney tells Andy that the next day is Thelma Lou's birthday, and he needs to buy her a present. He then shares his plans for the rest of the afternoon. He plans to "go down to the filling station, get me a bottle of pop, go home, take a nap, then go over to Thelma Lou's and watch a little TV." Barney repeats the plan three times.

"I don't remember writing the 'fly' gag," says writer Sam Bobrick. "Most likely it was an addition written by either Aaron Ruben, Andy Griffith, or Don Knotts. Barney's recitation of his plan for Sunday afternoon was scripted. The afternoon's dull activities were the result of Barney's minimal expectations, especially in his social life."

After leaving Andy, Barney walks to Wally's filling station. Barney is greeted by Goober, who is excited about a transistor radio he has just purchased from a traveling salesman named Newton Monroe. Floyd Lawson is also at Wally's and has purchased a wristwatch.

Newton compliments Floyd on his purchase and tells him the watch goes well with his "green pants and black-and-white sports shoes." Floyd concurs and replies, "Sort of a symphony, isn't it?"

478

"Floyd was a wonderful character to write for," says Sam. "His lines were shaped primarily by his personality, and they often seemed to write themselves. Floyd's 'symphony' comment just seemed right for the character."

Barney asks Newton if he has anything in the trunk of his car for a girl. Newton suggests a ring, but Barney says he prefers something "a little less personal. "When Newton suggests a pencil sharpener, Barney likes the idea. Newton, however, remembers "just the thing"—a fur piece. Barney examines the fur and hands it back to Newton, saying he doesn't want to spend that much because "she has a birthday every year." Newton informs Barney the fur piece sells for "thirteen-and-a-quarter" because he got it at "a fantastic buy at a warehouse." Barney makes the purchase.

The next day, Barney tells Andy how pleased Thelma Lou was with her birthday present. Andy asks Barney how much he paid for the fur. After learning how inexpensive the fur was, Andy voices his suspicion that Newton is "selling stolen goods."

Floyd and Goober are inside the courthouse when Andy and Barney arrive. The two feel they have been "gypped by that fellow selling stuff over at the filling station." Goober's radio "don't play no more," and the second hand on Floyd's watch is "spinning around like a pinwheel."

The telephone rings. It is Thelma Lou, who is upset because the fur on her fur piece is starting to fall out "in bunches."

Andy and Barney learn that Newton is "just up the block" and decide to confront him about the defective merchandise.

The master shot for the confrontation shows Andy, Barney, and Newton standing in front of Dave's Coffee Shop. Apparently, there was an oversight in the editing process because the medium shots and close-ups place the three in front of a jewelry store.

This error was the result of filming the scene with one camera. After the master shot was completed, the camera was moved, perhaps for better lighting, to a different location where the additional shots were photographed.

Newton shows Andy the bill of sale for his merchandise. Although Newton is not selling stolen goods, Andy discovers that he doesn't have a peddler's license to operate in Mayberry. Andy asks Newton to leave town. Newton, however, cannot resist the inquiries of an eager customer and makes another sale after Andy's warning. Barney sees the infraction and "nails" him.

Andy tells Newton, "I'm not going to stand still while you sell that junk on the streets. Now, you were peddling without a license. You're still peddling without a license. I don't know what else to tell you. I'm going to have to book you."

Seeking revenge, Barney doesn't allow Newton to "do much sitting" in jail. He puts Newton to work planting a tree. In the process, Newton breaks a water pipe.

Later in the afternoon, Barney telephones Thelma Lou. He has purchased another birthday present. Barney tells Thelma Lou that it's a surprise, but he promises her that she's "never had anything like it." Andy overhears the conversation. After Barney hangs up, he asks Barney what he got Thelma Lou. Barney answers, "A pineapple skinner from Newton. I looked all over, and I couldn't find anything. It was only two bucks."

"There was no romance in Barney's soul," says Sam. "This is reflected in his idea of an appropriate birthday gift and his satisfaction with his purchase of a pineapple skinner. We selected a pineapple skinner because it seemed funny and very Barney Fife-ish."

Barney has Newton "down in the basement cleaning the furnace." Andy suggests that Barney "let up on" Newton. When Barney responds that he is teaching Newton a lesson, Andy suggests that he's really "getting a little revenge."

"Through Barney's behavior, Bill and I were trying to show that good people can get angry, and it's okay," says Sam. "I always hated shows that were devoid of all human emotions. People get mad, and it's better for them—and Barney—to let it out on occasion."

Andy calls to Newton through the heating vent and asks how's he doing. Newton replies that he's just starting the fire. Andy reminds him to open the flue, but minutes later black smoke pours out of the vent.

After the fire is out, Barney has Newton mop the office floor. Newton "spills the bucket" and breaks the bookcase glass while mopping. Barney yells, "Can't you do anything in this world right? He's inept," and storms out. In response to Barney's reprimand, Newton feels he is "a born loser."

Andy sympathizes with Newton and decides to help him restore his self-confidence. He gives Newton the job of painting the Taylor front porch. Andy tells Newton he can paint the porch when nobody's watching. After Newton finishes, Andy and Barney check his work. The front porch is a mess, so Andy and Barney repaint it.

The next morning, Andy takes Newton to look at the porch. Andy gives Newton the credit for the beautiful paint job. Newton comments that the porch does look great. Andy tells him, "It just shows you what a little confidence will do. And I got a surprise for you. I'm going to suspend your sentence."

Later in the day, Andy and Barney return to the office. Newton is at the front door, paintbrush in hand. With his confidence restored, he joyfully says, "I'm not inept. I'm ept. I don't have to be a salesman if I don't want to be. I'm a painter. Sheriff, I'm going to paint the courthouse for free."

In the epilogue, Barney questions Andy about the wisdom of getting Newton a sales job at a Mt. Pilot hardware store. Andy responds, "If Newton doesn't do well, they'll get rid of him. Besides he's out of our hair. Let's just forget about it." Andy and Barney find two packages. The packages are "tokens of Newton's gratitude." Barney gets "that pencil sharpener," and Andy gets a "battery-operated razor." When Barney tries out the razor, it grabs the skin on his face and will not let go.

1965–1966

"Aunt Bee the Swinger"

"Is he married?"—Aunt Bee's question after learning Congressman John Canfield is retiring to Mayberry

"As I mentioned earlier, I worked on *Gomer Pyle, U.S.M.C.* after the first two seasons of *The Griffith Show*," says Jack. "In 1965, I found time to do five more Griffith scripts. Before *The Griffith Show* ever happened, Charles Stewart and I wrote for *The Real McCoys* for two seasons. All the while, we were writing scripts for *The Danny Thomas Show*. After writing twenty-nine Griffith scripts, thirty scripts for *The Real McCoys*, and a hundred scripts for Danny Thomas, Charles and I decided to go our separate ways. We had worked together for ten years, and they were great. Writing with a partner is like a marriage, and sometimes there are divorces. Writing alone was, well, lonesome, but I wanted to try it. After a few years, I worked with a partner again, Norman Paul. We wrote a lot of shows for the Norman Lear Company."

"Aunt Bee the Swinger" begins with Andy, Opie, and Aunt Bee eating breakfast. Andy is reading the newspaper column, "Little Known Facts Known by Few." He mutters aloud, "That's something." The comment attracts Opie's attention. He asks what Andy is reading.

The script direction has *Andy reading a column from the paper about vitamins _____, _____, and _____ the body can store; however, the body will not tolerate an excess of vitamins _____ and _____. One theory states that if you eat too much polar bear liver, it will kill you.*

The vitamins the body can store are A, D, E, and K. The vitamins the body cannot retain are B complex and C. The body cannot tolerate an excess of vitamins A and D. (The vitamins named in the filmed episode were filled into the blanks in Jack's script.)

"I researched the information on the vitamins, but I left it up to producer Aaron Ruben to fill in the blanks," says Jack. "I made up 'Polar bear liver will kill you.' I guess at that point, I got a little silly."

Episode 160

First Broadcast on October 4, 1965

Written by
Jack Elinson

Directed by
Larry Dobkin

Charlie Ruggles
Guest Stars as
Congressman
John Canfield

"Aunt Bee the Swinger" is the first *The Andy Griffith Show* episode filmed in color. "Opie's Job," Episode #161, was the first color episode broadcast. (Episodes were not always broadcast in the order of production.)

Aunt Bee is also reading the newspaper and comments on an article about Congressman John Canfield. The article reports that Canfield has decided to not "run" again and will be returning to Mayberry to live.

Aunt Bee is pleased with the news. She admires the picture of Canfield that accompanies the article.

Aunt Bee describes Canfield as "a nice-looking man" and asks Andy if he (Canfield) is married. Aunt Bee learns he is not.

"The Aunt Bee character always seemed to get the short end of the stick when it came to being the center of a story," says Jack. "I zeroed in on getting a story for her and came up with this one. Since she was unmarried, I thought a romantic story would be nice."

Later in the day, Canfield returns to Mayberry. He is talking with Floyd and two townsmen. He explains that he could have "stayed in politics and gone on to become president of the United States or he could retire." (The dialogue is deleted in the filmed episode.)

Andy joins the group and warmly welcomes Canfield back home. The men begin sharing the latest gossip. Andy shares the news that he recently saw Wayne Fremont and Harriet Pope together in Mt. Pilot. Floyd, aware that Canfield has been away from Mayberry for a while, informs the congressman that he had new linoleum put down in the barbershop four years ago. (The gossip is deleted from the filmed episode.)

Aunt Bee and Helen Crump emerge from the food market across the street and notice the men talking with John Canfield. Aunt Bee agrees with Helen's comment that Canfield is "good-looking" and shares with Helen that "he is a bachelor."

Helen is pleased with the news and sees a possibility for Aunt Bee in what she has learned.

"I watched most of the Griffith episodes over the years even though I was not writing for the series, so I was up to speed on the Andy/Helen relationship," says Jack. "I thought Aneta Corsaut was wonderful as Andy's girlfriend."

Andy sees Helen approaching and stops Canfield from walking away. He introduces the two, puts his arm around Helen, and invites Canfield to come over for "supper at the house."

Canfield gets the impression that Andy and Helen are married. Andy straightens out the misunderstanding. Helen is "wistful" about her marital status.

Canfield accepts the invitation. After his departure, Andy, sensing that Helen is interested in pairing Canfield with Aunt Bee, reminds her of how mad she gets when people try to match the two of them together. Helen defends herself. She is "just trying to get two nice people, Aunt Bee and Canfield, together."

Andy describes Helen's desire to play matchmaker as "the same thing that makes women stick out a left-hand signal to make a right-hand turn." (Andy's illogical comment was wisely deleted from the script.)

Andy comes home for lunch and breaks the news that Canfield is coming over for supper that night. Aunt Bee is flustered and begins thinking about the preparations for the meal. She is distracted and accidentally pours coffee over the sandwich she made for Andy's lunch.

"In my script, Aunt Bee picks up a glass and pours milk from a bottle into it until the glass overflows," says Jack. "This provided the proof that Aunt Bee was excited about Canfield coming for supper. I don't know why this was changed to pouring coffee over Andy's sandwich. Maybe the prop man was out of milk."

That night, Canfield knocks on the front door. Opie is sitting in the living room reading a comic book. As Andy passes by on his way to the door, he takes the comic away and hands Opie a book.

"The comic book 'hunk' was not in my script," says Jack. "That must have been Aaron Ruben's idea, and I'm sure that was the Bible that Andy handed Opie."

Andy welcomes Canfield and introduces Opie to him. The men take a seat. Canfield looks around and says that the house hasn't changed.

Andy points out that the only new thing is one of the slogans framed on the wall. The family got tired of "A Stitch in Time" and changed it to "Haste Makes Waste."

Andy changes the subject. He asks Canfield if he attends Washington Senators' baseball games. Canfield replies, "Well, we in the House don't have too much to do with the Senate." (The presupper chat is deleted from the filmed episode.)

The women are upstairs making last-minute preparations. Helen assures Aunt Bee that she looks "beautiful." Helen suggests a "booster shot" of perfume before Aunt Bee meets Canfield.

Andy introduces Aunt Bee to their guest. Canfield wastes no time in turning on the charm. He looks at Aunt Bee and acknowledges that "good looks certainly run" in the Taylor family.

After supper, pie is served in the living room. Canfield compliments the supper as one of the best meals he has ever had.

Opie has heard enough and asks for permission to go outside and play under the streetlight.

"Opie's line 'Can I go outside?' also wasn't in my script," says Jack. "That was another touch by Aaron."

After Opie's departure, Canfield talks about Washington. The big city, according to him, is packed with excitement. He feels he may have some difficulty adjusting to Mayberry's slow-paced lifestyle.

Aunt Bee defends Mayberry. She informs Canfield that Mayberry has its social functions like any big city.

In response, Canfield boldly asks Aunt Bee to show him around and asks her for a date the following night. Aunt Bee turns down the invitation. She has a previous appointment.

The women return to the kitchen to "clear things away." Helen quizzes Aunt Bee about her conflicting "appointment." Aunt Bee confesses that she made up the excuse. She turned down Canfield's invitation because a woman shouldn't appear too anxious.

"A woman or a man playing hard to get goes back to Adam and Eve," says Jack. "Aunt Bee was just being the proper lady that a woman that age would be."

Later, Canfield is ready to call it a night. He is almost out the door when Aunt Bee says she will be able to get out of her previous engagement. Canfield is delighted. The date is confirmed.

"Aunt Bee suddenly going in reverse and accepting Canfield's invitation is definitely a standard comedy device," says Jack. "A perfect example was done on *The Jack Benny Show*. In a restaurant, Jack is having lunch with another guy. When the check comes, Jack, who's famous for his cheapness, surprisingly grabs the check, saying, 'I'll take it.' The other guy says, 'I'll take it,' and without missing a beat, Jack says, 'Okay' and hands the check to the other guy. That was great comedy and it inspired how Aunt Bee accepted the date."

The morning after Aunt Bee's date, Andy is in the kitchen preparing breakfast. Opie enters and asks where Aunt Bee is. Andy answers that she is still sleeping. She didn't get back from her date until after one o'clock.

Aunt Bee enters the kitchen full of energy. She takes over the breakfast preparations and gives a date report. She and Canfield ate at a restaurant, danced for two hours at the Shrine Club, and took a long walk afterward. She had a wonderful time. Three future dates have already been planned.

"The dates were shown in montage," says Jack. "There was a quick scene of Aunt Bee and Canfield going into a movie house. That was followed by the shooting of arrows. After that was a scene at a carnival hot dog stand and then a scene showing Aunt Bee and Canfield riding a tandem bicycle. The whole idea of this montage was to show all the fun and very active things they were doing."

A few days later, Andy and Helen are sitting on the front porch. They discuss Aunt Bee "running around with Canfield until all hours." Andy doesn't see how Aunt Bee can keep up the pace.

Helen sees a neighbor, Mr. Branch, staring at them from across the street. Helen suggests that Andy speak to him. Andy is reluctant and explains that Branch never speaks back; he just nods.

Mr. Branch continues to stare. Andy speaks, and Mr. Branch then nods, turns, and goes inside his house.

"I have no memory of why the silent man was in the scene," says Jack. "It had nothing to do with the story. He could have been put in this script by Aaron

Ruben. I don't know if that was the only time Mr. Branch was seen in the series or if he became a running character during the later years after I left. (Mr. Branch decided to remain inside his house. He never appeared in the series again.)

The *Mayberry Jet set returns*. Aunt Bee and Canfield spent the day in Mt. Pilot shopping. The two have plans to go square dancing that night. Aunt Bee, full of excitement, skips across the porch.

That night at the square dance, Andy and Helen step outside to get some fresh air. Aunt Bee and Canfield follow. Canfield expresses his desire that the band pick up the beat a little bit. Helen refers to Aunt Bee as a ~~"ball of fire~~" that can't be stopped.

The next morning, Andy hears Aunt Bee moaning. *The ~~belle of the~~ ball is a very pooped lady.*

He investigates and finds Aunt Bee soaking her feet in a pan of water. Aunt Bee explains that she didn't want to take a bath. She decided to wash her feet instead. Andy finds a bottle of liniment. It confirms his suspicion that Aunt Bee's dating activities have begun taking their toll.

"In my mind, Aunt Bee was in her sixties and not as spry as she used to be," says Jack. "This explains how pooped she is from all the action. Her line about not wanting to take a whole bath is just a lame excuse of a very tired elderly lady."

A stuffed toy is placed on a chair in a corner of Aunt Bee's bedroom. The toy is a recreation of the cartoon character Baba Looey, the sidekick of ~~Quick Draw McGraw~~. The toy is a prize won at the carnival. Aunt Bee can be seen holding it in the "dating" montage.

That afternoon Aunt Bee receives a ~~telephone call from Canf~~ield. He called to cancel an afternoon picnic outing and a date planned for that night.

~~Aunt Bee, reflecting~~ on the ~~cancellat~~ion, believes it is the result of her pressing too hard. In her mind, Canfield has discovered that she couldn't keep up with his lady friends in Washington and is leaving her behind.

Andy decides to investigate the reason for the date's cancelation. He confronts Canfield and is surprised when Canfield admits he can't keep up with Aunt Bee. He canceled the date so he could get some rest.

"I now realize It is out of Andy's character to march over to Canfield and ask him why his date with Aunt Bee was canceled," says Jack. "That doesn't sound like Andy. If I had to do it over, I would have had Andy coming over to talk about something else and then casually mention that it was too bad he and Aunt Bee couldn't get together that night. Andy would be subtle about it."

In the epilogue, Aunt Bee and Canfield are relaxing on the Taylor front porch. Andy plays his guitar. Helen is seated beside him. Andy finishes the song and comments on the pleasures of a nice quiet evening. Canfield agrees.

Andy resumes playing and whistles the melody. The music reflects the peaceful mood of the evening.

Andy finishes and suggests to Helen that they walk down to the drugstore for a Cherry Smash. The two get to their feet and discover that "Ginger Rogers and Fred Astaire" are asleep.

"Since Aunt Bee and Canfield did so much dancing earlier in the episode, the team of Astaire and Rogers came to mind," says Jack. "I was a big fan of those two."

"When I did the story outline for this script, I actually started with the end and then went backward to the beginning," says Jack. "The story was simple. Two people along in their years, meet and have a ball dating like a couple of teenagers, and then both collapse. The whole script was heading for that ending."

"Malcolm at the Crossroads"

Episode 164

First Broadcast on
September 27, 1965

Written by
Harvey Bullock

Directed by
Gary Nelson

**Bernard Fox and
Howard Morris**
Guest Star as
Malcolm Merri-
weather and
Ernest T. Bass

"This is a bit of a mystery script because of massive changes, including the substitution of Ernest T., which made it more interesting."
—HARVEY BULLOCK

"I can't recall the events that led to the massive revisions this script underwent," says writer Harvey Bullock. "It must have been producer Bob Ross's idea. The bully character was originally named Spike Jenson. He never appeared and was replaced (quite wisely) by Ernest T. Bass.

"Bob Ross replaced Aaron Ruben as producer at the beginning of *TAGS*'s sixth season. Aaron Ruben left to produce *Gomer Pyle, U.S.M.C.* Bob was a good friend and very talented. He had written on the old *Amos 'n' Andy* shows, and when I first met him, we shared offices while he was the editor/producer of *I'm Dickens, He's Fenster.*"

The revised script begins with Andy walking down a Mayberry street. He stops and watches Ernest T. Bass., who is working as a school-crossing guard to earn money so he and his girlfriend Romeena can get married. Ernest T. needs twelve dollars for the honeymoon. "Tents cost money," according to Ernest T. He also plans to "get a lantern too."

At this point, Ernest T. throws a rock at a passing car. Andy warns him that if he throws any more rocks he will be fired. Ernest T. promises he "won't throw one more rock." After Andy walks away, Ernest T. pulls a brick out of his sack and says, "Didn't say nothing about no brick."

On his way back to the courthouse, Andy hears a commotion down the street. Malcolm Merriweather has returned and has recklessly ridden his bicycle into a car. Luckily, Malcolm is unhurt. Andy welcomes him back to Mayberry. Malcolm tells Andy he would like to "stay a bit this time and try my hand at being an American." Malcolm plans to make his "own way" while in Mayberry and is looking for "a solid position." Andy suggests he check out the barbershop bulletin board.

Andy and Malcolm walk to the barbershop where Floyd helps them check the bulletin board. Malcolm says he has experience as a valet and a falcon keeper. Floyd carefully scans the job listings but finds openings for neither. He promises Malcolm, "The first thing that comes in for falcon keeping, I won't give it to no one else."

"I really enjoyed working with Howard McNear, who portrayed Floyd Lawson," says Bernard Fox. "We didn't get to talk much, but the wonderful way he came out with 'falcon keeper, falcon keeper' as he scanned the bulletin board rings in my ears to this day."

Later in the day, Andy returns to the school crossing and sees Ernest T. throwing a brick at a car. He fires Ernest T. and offers the position to Malcolm. Malcolm accepts and performs his new duties in a militaristic style influenced from his experience as a Coldstream Guard. The militaristic style impresses the boys who use the school crossing.

"Bernard Fox was of great help suggesting English phrases," says Harvey. "Although, I think the Coldstream Guard, which was an actual and very historic regiment, was my idea."

"I suggested many of Malcolm's English phrases," says Bernard. "The collarless shirt Malcolm wears was also my idea. Most working-class men in England wore collarless shirts. The idea was that you bought a shirt with two collars so that you could put a fresh collar on without having to wash the whole shirt. Presumably, because of the general coolness of the weather in England, the shirt itself didn't become too offensive."

Ernest T. becomes angry when he discovers that Malcolm has taken his job. To make matters worse, Malcolm is an "Englishter." Ernest T.'s parents were Irish and, according to Ernest T.'s mother, "Englishters" and the Irish are enemies. Ernest T. thus challenges Malcolm to a fight.

"I also enjoyed working with Howie Morris," says Bernard. "I thought Howie was a very funny man. It was a pleasure to appear with him and act as his straight man."

Malcolm decides to leave town quietly. On his way out of Mayberry, he sees a group of boys imitating his military style at the school crossing and changes his mind. Malcolm seeks out Goober, who used to be a bully when he was younger, and requests fighting lessons. Goober agrees, and Malcolm begins training.

"There was some difference between writing for Goober and writing for Gomer," says Harvey. "Gomer was soft, gullible, and affable. Goober was more slangy, energized, but self-effacing. Their voices also affected the kind of lines that could be written for each. Gomer had a smooth, if sometimes high-pitched voice. Goober's speech was raspy and punchy. But, all in all, there were more similarities between the two than differences."

Malcolm's training reveals his inadequacies as a fighter. He is "decked" by

Goober, gets tangled up as he is jumping rope, and hits himself in the face with a punching bag.

"I do believe the punching bag hitting me in the face was my own little bit of masochism," says Bernard. "It took about three takes to get it right. The continued bopping of the nose caused some concern, but it was worth it to get it right."

On the day of the fight, Andy, who is aware that Malcolm will likely "get killed," tells Ernest T. that if he goes through with the fight he is going to jail. Ernest T. doesn't care.

Andy decides to try a different approach. As the fighters are making their final preparations, Andy tells Ernest T. that it will be fun to watch two Irishmen fight. Andy explains that Malcolm's mother is from County Cork. Ernest T. immediately has a change of heart, "Well, never let it be said that Ernest. T. Bass ever spilt a drop of Irish blood." Ernest T. runs toward Malcolm, jumps in his arms, and kisses him on the forehead.

"I recall most clearly the incident of Howie jumping into my arms," says Bernard. "We were rehearsing on the patio of Howie's home. I suggested that Howie leap up and wrap his legs around my neck. The producer and director felt that it couldn't be done. I said I thought it could. I put my fists up, and as Howie took a flying leap, I bent my knees, caught Howie in my arms, and slid him up to my shoulders!

"Incidentally, I had often wondered why we were rehearsing at Howie's home. Only recently, he explained that his wife had just arrived home after giving birth. The producer, director, and Andy had agreed that we would rehearse at his house so that he would be immediately available if needed."

In the epilogue, Andy, Malcolm, and Ernest T. are in the courthouse. Ernest T. invites Malcolm "up to his cave to eat." Ernest T. asks Malcolm what part of County Cork his "mommy" is from. Malcolm answers that she's not from County Cork. He adds that she was born in the heart of London. Ernest T. realizes that Malcolm is a "full-blooded Englishter" after all. Andy jumps up from his desk and positions himself between Ernest T. and Malcolm as Ernest T. lunges for Malcolm. Ernest T. jumps into Andy's arms, and Malcolm crawls through Andy's legs to escape.

"I remember that prior to this episode there was some talk about fitting me in as a series regular," says Bernard. "Ray Saffian Allen, who was a good friend, called me to tell me that the agent who was negotiating for me at the time was screwing things up by telling them that I was practically signed to several other series, none of which was true. Ray said the agent was going to blow the deal. Ray suggested that I get my tail over there and attempt to patch things up with Aaron Ruben.

"Instead of meeting with Aaron, I was ushered into the presence of Bob Ross, whom I didn't know from Adam. Mr. Ross chomped on a mouthful of food as I explained that the agent was exaggerating, I had no intention of signing with another series, and that I was, in fact, looking forward to joining *TAGS*. It wasn't easy to make out his speech through a mouthful of mush, but I do believe I heard him say, 'In other words, we have first refusal?' I agreed and left without so much as a 'Bon appétit,' and that was that. Ray Allen did tell me that several scripts were written, but the recurring role never occurred. Inasmuch as the series didn't last that much longer, it really didn't matter very much. But who knows what adventures Malcolm might have cycled into and around Mayberry?"

"Off to Hollywood"

"Buy something absolutely unnecessary and then it's a blast."—AUNT BEE

"After five seasons with *The Griffith Show*, Aaron Ruben created *Gomer Pyle, U.S.M.C.*, which was a spin-off from *TAGS*," says Andy Griffith's manager Richard O. Linke. "Aaron had to leave because he was the producer of the new series. Luckily, fate showed its strong hand. I knew Bob Ross, and so did Andy. He was a writer and took over as producer of *TAGS*. I want to tell you, it was unreal. It was like we never dropped a beat, and that was unusual. Normally, you might find another producer/writer who is talented but doesn't fit in or who doesn't come up with the goods. But that wasn't the case with Bob. And Bob was such a genteel man, such a nice and talented fellow, that it just flowed."

"Off to Hollywood" begins with Goober and new Mayberry deputy Warren Ferguson discussing an unopened letter addressed to Andy from Belmont Studios, Hollywood, California. The two are curious about the letter's contents. Warren rhetorically asks Goober, "Do you know what your sharpies do when they want to see what's inside a letter?" Warren then follows with his trademark, "huh, huh, huh?" and holds the envelope up to the light.

"Warren's 'huh, huh, huh?' was not scripted," says writer Sam Bobrick. "That was one of Jack Burns's own devices. Writing for Jack was quite different from writing for Don Knotts. No one was ever easier for us to write for than Barney Fife. He was every writer's dream."

Andy enters the office as Warren and Goober are examining the envelope. Andy opens the letter and finds it contains a check for one thousand dollars. Belmont Studios has purchased the rights to make a movie about Andy. The movie is based on the magazine article, "Sheriff Without a Gun." Andy decides to go home and tell the family.

"The idea to have the Taylors travel to Hollywood was Bob Ross's idea," says Sam. "Bob also pointed out to us that a magazine article about Andy had been mentioned in a previous episode ["TV or Not TV," Episode 150] and suggested the story idea that a studio buy the rights to make a movie based on Andy's life."

Episode 166

First Broadcast on October 25, 1965

Written by
Bill Idelson and Sam Bobrick

Directed by
Alan Rafkin

Aunt Bee and Opie excitedly inspect the check. Aunt Bee wants to call Clara Edwards, but Andy would like to "kind of keep it to ourselves." Opie questions Andy about how he plans to spend the money. Andy "figured we'd put this right in the bank." This disappoints Aunt Bee and Opie. Aunt Bee suggests Andy "spend some of it" on something unnecessary. Andy does feel they "ought to celebrate." He suggests they invite Helen over for supper. Aunt Bee suggests starting the meal "with a crabmeat cocktail. At least, let's do something crazy."

Andy returns to the courthouse and finds it overflowing with people who want to see the check. Goober has spread the word. He takes the check from Andy and proudly shows it off.

Floyd remains behind after everyone else leaves. He says to Andy, "You know those two acres that I've got over on the north side. Well, it's a beautiful spot. Fill in that swamp, and it would be a paradise." Floyd is willing to sell the land "at two hundred an acre. Of course, if it happened to be a personal friend of mine, I'd shave it to one fifty." Although Andy isn't interested, Floyd tells him he doesn't have to make up his mind right away. "Just one of these days, put your wading boots on and go over and have a look at it."

"After learning about Andy's money, Floyd offers to sell him some swampland," says Sam. "By this time Bill and I understood the characters very well and knew the swampland sales pitch was perfect for Floyd. We always enjoyed writing for Floyd and imagining how Howard McNear would perform the material."

That evening at supper, Helen suggests Andy use the money "to live it up a little." She asks, "When was the last time you people took a trip?" Andy mentions the possibility of taking a trip to Asheville, North Carolina, to see cousin Evin Moore.

"The name of Andy Griffith's cousin was not in our script," says Sam. "I imagine Andy used the name to recognize his own cousin. Minor changes like this were usually made during the script read-through and approved by the producer."

Aunt Bee suggests visiting Hollywood, California. Andy protests, "Well, that's three thousand miles away—and the money! We'll have to think about this a lot."

Eventually, Andy is persuaded to spend the money on a trip to Hollywood. After the decision is made, Andy and Aunt Bee concern themselves with preparations for their departure. The two discuss taking Opie out of school, and Andy shares with Aunt Bee his concern about leaving an inexperienced man like Warren in charge of the office. The discussion takes place in the kitchen. Aunt Bee is seated at the table, snapping green beans as she talks.

"I don't think the bean snapping was included in our script," says Sam. "It was a nice realistic southern touch that was likely the input of either Bob Ross or Andy Griffith."

When Andy arrives at the courthouse, he finds a large number of "the boys." The men have gathered to look at Andy's Hollywood travel folders. The group has picked out a motel for Andy to stay in while in Hollywood. Floyd is excited about a folder from "Senior Citizen's Lodge on Route 66."

Aunt Bee purchases a new outfit for Opie to wear on the trip. The red shorts and a shirt with a white-flower print, along with a pair of sandals are "just what little boys wear in Hollywood." Opie doesn't like the outfit. Hoping to encourage Opie, Andy compliments his appearance. Aunt Bee tells Opie, "I told you your father would like it, and I'm so happy because that comes in men's sizes too. Father-and-son sets, and I got you the same outfit. Andy, why don't you go up and try on your outfit?" Andy protests, "It's so late and everything." Opie asks, "If Pa doesn't have to wear his, do I have to wear mine?" Aunt Bee responds, "Andy!"

This sets up a wonderful visual gag. Andy is shown in close-up, reacting to the news that he has to put on his "Hollywood" outfit. The close-up immediately cuts to another shot of Andy in the same pose. The camera pans backward and reveals Andy and Opie dressed identically.

"The matching father-and-son outfits were what we thought Aunt Bee's image of Hollywood would be," says Sam. "It was the first of several visual gags we used in the script."

Much of the humor in the episode comes from the small town's reaction to the Taylors' trip. Andy receives numerous requests to get an autograph or take a "Hollywood" picture for someone. He is asked to call someone's West-Coast relative, and even gets a request to "stand on the corner of Hollywood and Vine and say 'hello' from Floyd."

On the day of their departure, a large group, dressed in their Sunday best, gathers at the bus stop to bid the Taylors farewell. The town band plays.

At the bus stop, Warren volunteers to load Andy's luggage. He throws the bags over the top of the bus. When Andy lifts a suitcase, the handle comes off in his hand.

"Bill and I were somewhat reluctant to use visual gags on *The Griffith Show* because Andy preferred that the humor come from the personalities of the characters," says Sam. "We did, however, occasionally use visual humor if we felt it worked well in a scene."

In the epilogue, the Taylors are shown aboard the airplane on their way to Hollywood. Andy is finally able to relax after the frantic activity of preparing for the trip. Aunt Bee says, "Suddenly Mayberry seems far away, doesn't it? Main Street, and the people, and our house." She looks perplexed and asks, "Andy, did you turn off the gas?" Andy shouts, "Stewardess, stewardess, when's the first stop?"

"There was never any reluctance in ending the episode with the old 'did I turn off the gas' routine," says Sam. "I still have those doubts when I leave the house. The routine is tried but true."

"Taylors in Hollywood"

Episode 167

First Broadcast on
November 1, 1965

Written by
**Bill Idelson and
Sam Bobrick**

Directed by
Alan Rafkin

"~~This is Andy Taylor~~. I'm ~~the Taylor~~ they're making that movie about, *~~Sheriff Without a Gun~~*."—A~~NDY~~, on the phone with Belmont Studios

"The Hollywood-trip idea was conceived as a multiepisode series," says writer Sam Bobrick. "Bill and I got the assignment to write the first two Hollywood episodes. As I recall, this episode seemed tougher than usual to write because much of what happened was an overexaggeration of reality. Exaggerated situations always seemed to work better in Mayberry than in the outside world."

Bill and Sam begin their script with the Taylors' plane landing in Hollywood. The family is taken by bus to the Piedmont Hotel, where they will be staying during their two-week vacation.

On the way to the hotel, Andy discovers that the man sitting behind him is a relief bus driver originally from Ruby Creek, North Carolina. Andy strikes up a conversation with the man. The fellow points out several famous sites as the bus travels down Sunset Boulevard.

The Taylors' hotel is the last stop on the route. After all the other passengers have gotten off, the relief driver arranges to have the bus go up Beverly Drive so the Taylors can see a movie star's home. The bus stops in front of Cesar Romero's house.

"The famous sites (Dino's restaurant, Schwab's Drugstore, Whisky a Go Go, and the Blair House) were a combination of places we suggested in the script and those selected by the film crew," says Sam. "I don't know if the house the bus stopped in front of was actually the home of Cesar Romero. We included the stop at a movie star's home because we thought it would be typical small-town behavior to have the Taylors greatly admire anyone connected with film whether they were hot or not. Cesar Romero, by the way, was not."

After the Taylors arrive at their hotel, they are escorted to their room by a bellboy. The bellboy tells Andy that the suite overlooks the pool. When Andy walks to the window, the bellboy says, "If you look over there, you can see the diving board." Andy stands on his tiptoes. After the bellboy gives further instructions about exactly where to look, Andy finally sees the diving board. The bellboy explains how to adjust the air conditioner, holds out his hand for a tip, and says, "If there's anything else, just call room service." Andy doesn't get the hint. The bellboy points to the air-conditioner thermostat and holds out his hand again. Andy finally gets the message and tips him.

"Bellboys have traditionally been comic targets," says Sam. "The view of the pool and the bellboy's desire for a tip were inspired by actual experiences that happened to us. We exaggerated them, of course, for the script."

Once the Taylors are settled in, Aunt Bee insists that Andy call "those movie people" and tell them he is in town. Before making the call, Andy adjusts his tie. Andy identifies himself to the Belmont Pictures' operator, "This is Andy Taylor," and is transferred to the tailor shop. The call is then transferred back to the operator, to the tailor shop again, and back to the operator.

"The adjustment of the tie before placing the phone call was not scripted," says Sam. "It was a nice touch and likely resulted from Andy Griffith's acting instincts. Being transferred to the tailor shop was a routine play on words and a lot of fun to write."

The director of *Sheriff Without a Gun* returns Andy's call and invites the family to come over to the studio to watch the shooting of a scene. The Taylors rush over to the studio and meet the director, A. J. Considine. Mr. Considine introduces the Taylors to the actor who will be portraying Andy in the movie, Bryan Bender. When Andy notices that Bender is bald, he is speechless.

The Taylors watch the shooting of a scene that depicts a cigar-smoking Andy beating up and capturing the Calhoun boys single-handedly. Andy and Opie are thrilled, but Aunt Bee doesn't like the scene "one little bit."

Later that evening after the Taylors have returned to their hotel, Aunt Bee is still quite upset. She tells Andy, "I never saw anything so outlandish in my whole life. It's an exaggeration. It's nothing but a lot of humbug." Aunt Bee feels they are making a "roughneck" out of Andy's character. She insists that Andy "march right up to Mr. Considine and tell him to make things more the way they really are." Andy promises to do so when they return to the studio the following day.

The next day, Andy approaches the director but is asked to wait until the next scene has been shot. The scene is set in the Taylor home. A young and thin Aunt Bee gets a rifle and bravely defends Andy when the Calhoun boys attack the house.

"I was a little uncomfortable with the movie scenes," says Sam. "They were melodramatic, which was acceptable, but we may have exaggerated them a little too much. Even a B film wouldn't have been that bad."

At the scene's conclusion, Andy is going to tell Considine that the scene was "stupid." Aunt Bee stops Andy and says, "Just a minute. I'm not absolutely sure I've been quite right about this." Andy reminds her, "Yesterday you were crying about it." Aunt Bee replies, "I know, but somehow today it seems a little better. It's a movie, Andy. They have to take liberties in order to make it interesting."

When A. J. Considine comes over and asks Andy what he wanted to talk about, Aunt Bee responds, "We were just going to say how happy we are about the way you're making the picture. And that actress who plays me—she's marvelous."

In the epilogue, the Taylors have returned to their hotel room and are discussing what they are going to do that night. Andy suggests they go down to Grauman's Chinese Theater and take a walk down to Hollywood and Vine. Opie says, "If we were back in Mayberry, do you know what I would be doing right now? Watching the *Jerome Sanger Show* on TV." Aunt Bee responds, "And I would be watching it with you. You know, I'm very fond of that program myself." Andy says, "Yeah, that's a good show, but we're in Hollywood now. What's it going to be?" When Opie and Aunt Bee do not answer, Andy telephones room service and asks them to "send up a television set."

"I was relieved when this script was finished. In the next script, we returned to Mayberry, which was a more familiar and comfortable setting," says Sam.

"Aunt Bee Takes a Job"

"With that little lady, Miss Taylor, out front, this whole thing will take on a complete air of respectability."—RALPH KINGSLEY, counterfeiter

"I don't remember where the idea for this story came from," says writer Sam Bobrick. "I do, however, remember Frances Bavier, who portrayed Aunt Bee. She was a sweet and talented lady. I enjoyed writing for Aunt Bee. She was an easy character to work with."

Bill and Sam's script begins in the Taylor home. Andy is looking at the evening paper when Aunt Bee asks him to turn to the want ads. She points out a job listing for a receptionist's job, which reads: "Wanted: Female. Easy part-time work, afternoons. Apply in person, 177 Main Street." Aunt Bee shares her intention to apply for the position.

The next day, Aunt Bee goes to the address listed in the paper and finds the job is with a print shop. Aunt Bee enters and waits in the outer office with another applicant, Violet Rose Shumaker. Violet Rose is a shapely young woman, who is surprised when she learns Aunt Bee is also answering the ad.

"Violet Rose Shumaker was inspired by a personal memory," says Sam. "The prettiest girl in my high school was a girl named Violet Rose Daisy. We felt Aunt Bee's competition for the job should be a younger woman, so we made note of that in the script. I don't remember what the actress cast in the role looked like, but I hope she did Violet Rose justice."

Aunt Bee is interviewed by the print shop's owners, Ralph Kingsley and Arnold Finch. She tells the two that she hasn't worked for several years, that she doesn't type or take dictation, and that she isn't very good with figures. She says, "The only reason I'm here is I have too much time on my hands."

Despite these revelations, Aunt Bee is hired. She stops by the courthouse to share the news with Andy. Aunt Bee tells Andy and Warren Ferguson that Mr. Kingsley had said she was just the person they were looking for. Aunt Bee hurries home to get ready for her new job.

After Aunt Bee's departure, Andy tells Warren he wishes the new owners luck

Episode 171

First Broadcast on December 6, 1965

Written by
Bill Idelson and Sam Bobrick

Directed by
Alan Rafkin

because the previous owners did not do well financially. Warren replies, "Oh, that was probably mismanagement, Andy. You know there's nothing wrong with the printing business. A good printing shop can be a moneymaking thing."

In the next scene, a printing press is shown in close-up. As the camera pulls back, Mr. Kingsley and Mr. Finch are revealed. The two are printing ten-dollar bills.

When Andy stops by the print shop, Mr. Kingsley comes out of the back room to greet him. Andy welcomes Mr. Kingsley to town and thanks him for hiring his aunt. Kingsley is pleased to know "the nice lady that works for us is the aunt of a sheriff." He calls Mr. Finch out of the back room and introduces him to Andy.

After Andy leaves, Mr. Finch says, "Ralph, I think we should have hired Violet Rose Shumaker." Mr. Kingsley replies, "No, we couldn't be in better hands."

Aunt Bee begins her first day at work "right on time." A short time after her arrival, she knocks on the door of the back room to give Mr. Kingsley an order from a friend of hers. Mr. Kingsley opens the door and says, "Miss Taylor, about coming in the back. Mr. Finch is something of an artist, you see, and he gets very nervous when he's disturbed." Aunt Bee agrees not to disturb Mr. Finch. She gives Mr. Finch her friend's order and another order for "one hundred business cards for my nephew."

A customer named Mr. Clark enters the print shop. He has come by to pick up a package of wedding announcements, which are actually counterfeit bills. Aunt Bee notifies Mr. Kingsley. While Mr. Kingsley is getting the announcements, Aunt Bee asks Mr. Clark if the announcements are for himself. Mr. Clark is caught off guard and tells her the wedding will be on Thursday.

Later that afternoon, Andy receives a telegram stating that counterfeit bills have turned up in Raleigh. Andy believes the bills might start showing up in Mayberry soon. He decides to warn Mayberry's merchants.

Warren has the responsibility of notifying the owners of the print shop. He enters the shop and walks into the back room unannounced. Warren tells Kingsley and Finch to be on the lookout for counterfeit bills. He then says, "If you do see a bill that looks the least bit phony, bring it right to me. You see, my eyes are 'specially trained for that type of thing." Warren picks up a newly printed counterfeit bill and points out the differences between it and a phony.

In this scene, Warren is presented as a one-dimensional, know-it-all character. Bill and Sam use his self-professed "expertise" to set up the humor that results from his total ignorance. This was an approach that was previously used with Barney Fife. Barney, however, was a more fully developed and likeable character. His know-it-all behavior was countered by qualities of caring and, at times, humility.

A few days later, Mr. Clark returns to pick up some birth announcements, again actually counterfeit bills. This surprises Aunt Bee. When she inquires about the matter, Mr. Clark explains, "We're adopting a kid."

"Having the customer pick up wedding and birth announcements within a few days of each other seemed like a funny idea," says Sam. "It worked well, and Frances Bavier's reactions to the situation were wonderful."

Because the bank is closed after Aunt Bee gets off work, she asks Mr. Clark to cash her paycheck for her. Mr. Clark cashes the check with three ten-dollar bills.

Aunt Bee celebrates her first paycheck by purchasing a dress, a football for Opie, groceries, and Andy's business cards. The cards are printed in green ink.

Soon after, Andy gets a telephone call. It is Weaver's Department Store. A counterfeit bill has shown up in Mayberry!

Aunt Bee rushes to the print shop to warn Mr. Kingsley about the counterfeit bills. Mr. Kingsley and Mr. Finch decide "to get out of here." The two tell Aunt Bee they are closing up because they've "hit a slump."

Mr. Kingsley and Mr. Finch carry the printing press outside, load it in their car, and prepare to drive away. Warren, who is "out spreading the word," rushes up in the squad car, accidentally rams the back of the counterfeiters' car, and locks bumpers.

Meanwhile, Andy is at the courthouse considering the facts. He discovers the identity of the counterfeiters by putting together a series of clues. The owners of the grocery, sporting-goods store, and department store have reported counterfeit bills. Aunt Bee made purchases in all three places. Andy's business cards are printed in green ink.

"Bill and I had worked out the details that identify the counterfeiters while constructing the story outline," says Sam. "We knew where we were going before we began writing the script."

Andy rushes to the print shop. Moments before his arrival, Warren and the two counterfeiters unlock the car bumpers. Mr. Kingsley and Mr. Finch jump in their car and make a hasty departure.

Andy runs up, pulls Warren's revolver out of its holster, aims, and shoots out the rear tire of the counterfeiters' car. Aunt Bee says, "I can't believe it. Just because they're going out of business is no reason to shoot at them." Andy runs to the car and arrests the counterfeiters.

In the epilogue, Warren gives the jailed counterfeiters a sandwich. He says to them, "I still get a kick out of you fellows thinking you could pull that counterfeiting deal here in Mayberry. You must think we're real idiots. You think we wear these uniforms for our looks? That's sixty cents for the sandwiches." Mr. Kingsley gives Warren a counterfeit bill and says, "Keep the change." Warren is overjoyed until Andy points out the bill is counterfeit.

"We concluded the script by repeating the comic idea presented earlier," says Sam. "Repetition is an important comic tool. Sometimes it works, sometimes it doesn't. As a writer, you get a sense of these things."

"The Cannon"

First Broadcast on
November 22, 1965

Written by
Jack Elinson

Directed by
Alan Rafkin

"My memory is even worse than I thought. Would you believe that I forgot that Don Knotts left the show?"—JACK ELINSON

"The first season episode 'The Horse Trader' kicked me into 'The Cannon,'" says Jack. "I don't know why I should be so smitten with cannons. During World War II, the German cannons made my soldier life miserable. I should hate them."

"The Cannon" begins in the barbershop. Andy and Floyd are seated in chairs. Goober is in the barber chair. All three are reading magazines.

Goober reads aloud an advertisement for an imitation alligator wallet. (In the script the wallet is made of *genuine pin seal leather*.) It sells for $1.95. All three agree the wallet is a great value but decline the offer.

Deputy Warren Ferguson rushes in almost breathless. Warren has "big news, big news. It could be the biggest thing that ever happened in Mayberry." When asked by Andy to identify the news, Warren responds, "It is big."

Warren's "big news" dialogue is almost identical to Barney Fife's "big news" about the escaped convict in the series' second episode, "Manhunt."

"I forgot why Don Knotts left the show," says Jack. "Here I am reading a script with Barney, replaced by Warren Ferguson! It's not fair to compare Jack Burns to Don. Don's shoes are much too large for anyone to fill. Without Don, the laugh meter really plunged."

Warren announces that the governor has accepted the invitation to participate in Mayberry's upcoming Founders' Day celebration. The State Mobile Museum, displaying "all kinds of historical things," will accompany the governor's visit.

The museum contains old coins, paintings, swords used by famous generals, jewelry, and a lavaliere worn by Martha Washington.

"I had to create some valuable things for the theft I had planned for later in the episode, so I came up with the mobile museum," says Jack.

Goober, Floyd, and Warren suggest that the governor's attendance calls for a real "bang-up" celebration. The festivities should include a parade, street decorations, and music by the Mayberry Band. Andy schedules a meeting of the Founders' Day committee to make further plans.

Later in the day, Andy presides over the meeting. The committee consists of Goober, Floyd, Warren, Aunt Bee, and two Mayberry citizens, Frank Chase and John.

Aunt Bee has already planned out the governor's luncheon menu. The first course will be shrimp cocktails if "enough little forks" can be found in Mayberry. The main course will be chicken à la king. Ladyfingers and coffee will be served for dessert.

"Whenever my wife and I have friends over for dinner, she always gets shrimp cocktails as one of the appetizers," says Jack. "It's a lot classier than a cheese spread or cocktail hot dogs."

Frank has the parade planned. The procession will be led into town by the Mayberry Marching Band. The squad car and the governor's car will follow. A convertible with the top down will be next. A motorcycle ridden by one of Mayberry's citizens will bring up the rear.

Frank has something different planned for the convertible. The number-one industry in North Carolina is tobacco. Frank would like for the current Miss Tobacco, dressed in a bathing suit, to ride in the convertible.

Andy asks who the current Miss Tobacco is and is told "old man Dobbin's daughter." Andy recalls, "It was her turn."

Aunt Bee protests what she considers, a risqué idea. Frank assures her the bathing suit will be covered. Miss Tobacco will wear a garland of tobacco leaves as a crown and additional leaves will be draped over her shoulders. (The Miss Tobacco title was changed to Miss Potato, as potatoes are the "most important thing" grown around Mayberry.)

"In my script, it was the 'Tobacco Queen,' not the 'Potato Queen,'" says Jack. "Andy's great line, 'Oh, that's right, it is her turn' came from Andy Griffith or perhaps Bob Ross, the producer and story consultant who replaced Aaron Ruben. It was fun writing what a small town thinks a big parade should be."

All Founders' Day preparations are assigned. Floyd oversees the decorations. He promises the town will be a "mass of red, white, and blue." John will work with the marching band. The band, according to Andy, "didn't deserve any prizes for their Labor Day performance." The mobile museum will be guarded by Warren and Goober.

"The detailed planning for the celebration emphasized just how important the parade and the governor's visit were," says Jack. "To the folks in Mayberry, this equals the Macy's Thanksgiving Day parade and a visit from the president."

After the meeting's adjournment, Aunt Bee asks Frank if his wife, Martha, has any cocktail forks. Frank hasn't seen any. (Jack Elinson intended "the cocktail forks" to become a "runner" in the episode. This dialogue and another "fork" reference were deleted from the script.)

A few days later, Andy and Warren are *walking the street next to city hall*. The buildings are decorated with colorful bunting. Andy acknowledges that Floyd did a good job.

Warren agrees and says his Uncle Floyd has a "knack" for decorating. Warren remembers his mother telling him, when Floyd was deciding on a career, that it was a toss-up between art school or barber college. (This interesting fact about a possible art-related vocation for Floyd is deleted from the filmed episode.)

The script direction narrates, *Andy and Warren approach an area just beyond the city hall where there's a little clearing and the Civil War cannon is set in front. Andy points out the place where the mobile museum will be placed. Warren looks at the cannon and suddenly gets an idea.*

Warren reminds Andy that the governor's visit is the most important event Mayberry has had in years. He asks Andy to affirm this, "Am I right, huh, huh, huh?"

"The 'huh' repetitions were definitely a Jack Burns trademark," says Jack. "I put some of them in the script to indicate where Burns might use them."

Warren would like to fire the cannon in the governor's honor. Andy turns down the idea. The cannon will not be fired!

The mobile museum arrives. Warren and Goober are ordered to keep a constant guard on the museum. Warren takes the first watch. Goober leaves to put on the deputy uniform he has been issued.

Goober returns. The waist of his uniform's pants is pulled high, giving him an uncomfortable and comical appearance.

"I had seen Goober at work in a lot of episodes, so I was familiar with the character," says Jack. "In my mind, he wasn't that different from Gomer Pyle. Both characters were good-natured happy guys. After Jim Nabors moved on to his own series, George Lindsey took over nicely."

Goober discovers that Warren is not guarding the museum. Instead, he is bending over, peering into the barrel of the canon. Warren has discovered that there is something stuck in the barrel. Goober investigates. The museum is no longer either deputy's top priority.

A man and a woman, Jack and Stella Butler, approach the unattended museum, look over at the occupied deputies, and start checking the lock on the museum's door. Andy walks up and surprises them. He informs the couple that the museum will not be open until the next day.

Andy sees Warren and Goober by the cannon. He informs them that they are to quit fooling with the cannon and get back to guarding the museum.

Nearby, Jack and Stella are watching. The Mayberry Police force looks to them like the "Keystone Cops." The two exchange confident smiles and assure one another that what they have planned should be a "pushover."

The second act begins early on Founders' Day. Harry Boswell, *a bookkeeper-type little man*, is practicing his welcoming speech. Harry, the head of the Department of Water and Power, will officially greet the governor. Harry is filling in for the mayor, who is vacationing in Hawaii.

"I was just setting up the scene with Harry Bosworth practicing his speech," says Jack. "I thought I might get a chuckle or two out of how dull Harry was."

Andy, Frank, and John gather around the speaker's stand. Andy asks John how the band is coming along. John reports that the band's playing has "a lot of rough spots" when they are standing still. Marching may make their musical performance even worse. John shares one positive note. Jesse Earle Hagen is coming over from Mt. Pilot to play bass.

"Jesse Earle Hagen was not mentioned in the script," says Jack. "The name was inspired by the real Earle Hagen. Earle was the musical director. I imagine it was Andy Griffith's idea to mention him by name."

Andy, on his way to the parade, stops by the mobile museum. Warren reports that he knows what is stuck in the cannon . . . a cannonball! Andy is not interested. He reminds Warren to keep the museum locked until after the speeches are given and leaves.

Jack and Stella are watching. The two plan to make their move "when everybody is around the stand listening to the speeches."

Jack tells Warren he is a state policeman and asks for the museum's keys. Warren is puzzled. No official authorization to hand over the keys was ever received.

Jack blames the lack of communication on "the folks in Raleigh." Warren is sympathetic to Jack's situation and hands over the museum keys. Warren looks at *Jack's blouse which has no insignias.* Jack explains that the plain uniform makes the museum security look less like a police operation.

"As for the thief's uniform, it wouldn't have hurt to have given him a badge and some official papers," says Jack. "In my script, I just wrote he is wearing a nondescript uniform. I should have added more details."

The script direction narrates. *As Jack makes a pretense of taking over his post at the museum, Warren is about to walk away when his eyes light on the cannon again. He steps over to it and starts peering into the breech.*

Meanwhile, Floyd, Aunt Bee, Harry Bosworth, and Frank are seated at the back of the speaker's stand. They anxiously await the governor's arrival. Frank predicts that the parade will take about three minutes. Floyd does some quick figuring and says to Frank, "You figure they'll do a block a minute."

"It was fun showing a small-town parade where minutia is taken very seriously," says Jack. "Floyd's calculation of the parade speed was especially enjoyable."

Warren and Goober are still occupied with the cannon. Warren asks if Goober knows what is stuck inside the barrel. (Jack Burns answers with his irritating unscripted trademark "huh. huh.")

Warren feels it is possible that the cannon could still be fired.

The governor arrives. His parade escort stops in front of the speaker's stand. The governor, George C. Handley, mounts the stage.

Andy introduces the governor to each member of the Founders' Day committee. Floyd greets the governor as "your honorable, his excellency, his George C." This joke was set up earlier when the committee is awaiting the governor's arrival. Floyd asks Aunt Bee how he should address the governor. (The setup was deleted.)

After her introduction, the Potato Queen, wearing a crown adorned with potatoes, hands the governor a potato. The governor doesn't know what to do with it. He fiddles with the vegetable for fifteen seconds before setting it down. (The presentation of the potato and the governor's baffled response were not scripted. The queen's first name in the script was Sharman. This was changed to Sharon.)

Meanwhile, Jack and Stella are putting their "plan" into action. The script direction narrates: *Jack is poised for action as he looks at Goober and Warren. Their backs are to him. He then turns in the direction of a station wagon and throws a signal. Stella seated in the vehicle notes and signals back. Jack takes another look at Goober and Warren who are preoccupied with the cannon, then takes the keys out of his pocket and enters the museum.*

Back at the stand, the governor steps up to the podium and addresses the "good people of Mayberry."

Goober and Warren are busy looking into a hole in the breech of the cannon. Warren describes it as "the black hole of Calcutta" and asks Goober for a match.

"I don't know where it came from, but 'the black hole of Calcutta' is a phrase I've always known," says Jack. "If you want to describe complete blackness, you'd always say it's like 'the black hole of Calcutta.' I know there are a lot of black holes all over the world, but for some reason, Calcutta seems to have the very best black holes."

Stella pulls the station wagon up to the museum. She gets out and goes to an open window. Jack starts handing out valuables. Stella places them in the vehicle's back seat.

Warren is lighting a match and is about to hold it down to the hole in the cannon's breech.

The robbery is finished. Jack and Stella get into the station wagon and prepare to make their getaway.

Back at the podium, the governor proclaims that "Mayberry is one of the few towns left in America where one can enjoy true peace and tranquility."

Suddenly a loud boom from the cannon accompanied by an "impact against metal" is heard.

"It's always funny when people are saying something while the opposite is happening," says Jack. "The governor's comments are like someone boasting about what a quiet neighborhood they're living in just as another thundering airplane flies by overhead."

Andy instructs the governor to go on with his speech. Andy leaves the podium and rushes to the museum. He arrives and discovers that Goober and Warren have shot the front wheel off a station wagon.

Andy is concerned about the dazed passengers' welfare. Warren helps them out of the damaged station wagon. Meanwhile, Goober has noticed the historical treasures loaded into the vehicle's back seat.

Andy looks at Jack and Stella and identifies them as "the two tourists from yesterday." Warren suddenly realizes he has captured a couple of crooks. Andy instructs Warren to arrest them and rushes back to the speaker's stand.

Andy returns and informs the governor "the noise was a one-gun salute in his honor."

"I won't deny that the ending is far-fetched, but I thought about the ending long before doing another cannon story," says Jack. "I remembered an old joke I always loved. There's an old cannon in the town square. Each day, at noon, the cannon fired a ceremonial shot. This went on for years and years. Then one day, at noon, there was no shot. It was deadly quiet, whereupon everybody looked at each other and said, 'What was that?!' That kicked me in reverse . . . having a cannon that is silent for years and suddenly fires a shot. Then I went back to figure out how to get there. Again, I know it's a wild idea, but if anybody was disturbed by it, please forgive me. I was only having fun."

"Girl-Shy"

Episode 173

First Broadcast on
December 20, 1965

Written by
**Bill Idelson and
Sam Bobrick**

Directed by
Lee Philips

"I never chased a woman in my life. I'm a gentleman! I'm from Boston!"
—WARREN FERGUSON

"When Don Knotts announced that he didn't want to go on with the show after the fifth year, we were really disappointed because he and Andy were a great team," says Andy Griffith's manager Richard O. Linke. "It worried Andy and me. We could see going into the sixth year and having the ratings plummet. As soon as that happened, your fate was determined. You knew the show would be canceled.

"After Don left, the producers were scurrying around, saying, 'We're going to try this person, we're going to try that person.' There was a comedy team that was starting to do well, Burns and Schreiber. Somebody told us about the two guys, especially Jack Burns.

"Burns and Schreiber were appearing in a nightclub in San Diego. Andy flew down with producer Bob Ross and executive producer Sheldon Leonard with the idea of trying Jack Burns out on TAGS. The three liked what they saw, and Jack was hired."

"I don't remember what inspired the idea to center a story on sleepwalking," says writer Sam Bobrick. "Sometimes ideas came easy, sometimes they didn't. It would take us anywhere from three hours to three days to develop a story idea."

"Girl-Shy" begins with Warren Ferguson bringing his television into the courthouse. Warren explains to Andy that his landlady's brother is visiting, the hotel is full, and he is going to spend the night in the back room so the out-of-town visitor can have his room. The television leads Andy to inquire, "Hey, Warren, how's your social life? You been going out much?" Warren answers, "No, not too much. Actually, I've been pretty busy." Andy tells Warren that he and Helen are "thinking about going to a Chinese restaurant up in Mt. Pilot tonight, and we were wondering if you would like to come along." Warren agrees to come. Andy adds that Helen's "got a little girl she can get for you." Warren is stunned and says,

508

"Girl? You mean a date? I just remembered something, Andy. My blue suit is in the cleaners'. If I'm not dressed properly, I just wouldn't enjoy the evening."

Later that evening, Andy stops by the courthouse on his way to Mt. Pilot to pick up a tie clip.

"The courthouse desk may seem an odd place for Andy to keep a tie clip since he normally doesn't wear a tie with his uniform, but we didn't concern ourselves much with it," says Sam.

The telephone rings. There has been a wreck out on the highway, and Andy is needed to help clear the traffic. Helen, who is out in the car, at first decides to wait in the courthouse. She asks Warren if he would like to join her for something to eat, but he declines the invitation. Helen decides to go ahead and get something to eat. She wonders out loud whether she should "come back here and brush up on my typing or go to a movie." Warren replies, "Our typewriter's in pretty bad shape. The s keeps sticking." After hearing this, Helen decides to go to a movie.

After Helen leaves, Goober comes by the courthouse to watch an episode of *International Secret Agent F45* with Warren. Agent F45 is "suave," and the episode includes a "steamy" love scene.

"The *International Secret Agent F45* title was inspired by the popularity of the James Bond movies at the time," says Sam.

After the program, Warren falls asleep in the back room. Helen returns to the courthouse. Influenced by the television love scene, Warren sleepwalks out of the back room. He talks to Helen romantically, just like Secret Agent F45, and chases her into a cell.

Andy eventually returns, and Helen angrily tells him that his "shy little deputy, Warren, chased me." Andy wakes Warren, but Warren remembers nothing and is shocked by Helen's accusation. Warren claims he was asleep until Andy woke him. He says, "I never chased a woman in my life, I swear. I'm a gentleman! I'm from Boston!"

"Warren's comment that 'he's never chased a woman . . . he's from Boston' seemed to fit," says Sam. "After all, Warren was a bit of a know-it-all, and I'm sure he thought coming from Boston gave him an edge up on Mayberry residents."

The next day Warren tells Goober that he is a sleepwalker, and last night in his sleep he chased Helen Crump all around the courthouse. Something usually triggers Warren's sleepwalking. He thinks the fact that Andy tried to fix him up with a date and he then saw Secret Agent F45 set things in motion. Goober advises Warren to explain this to Andy, but Warren refuses. He feels Andy would not want a sleepwalking deputy. Instead he decides to "stay awake, so it can't happen again."

Meanwhile, Andy visits Helen at school and promises to "straighten this thing out." Andy asks Helen to stop by the office on her way home to see if he has found out anything.

Andy summons Warren to the courthouse. The telephone rings soon after Warren arrives. It is Mrs. Purvis. Andy says, "Oh, yes, Mrs. Purvis. Up in the tree again, is he? Did you try poking him? Look, Mrs. Purvis, I can't come over there every time you and Mr. Purvis have a fight and get him down out of a tree."

"The joke about Mr. Purvis was the result of great comic ingenuity and a touch of immaturity," says Sam. "We presented the joke through a telephone conversation, so the audience would initially think Andy and Mrs. Purvis were talking about a cat up a tree."

Warren falls asleep while Andy is on the telephone. After Andy leaves to get Mr. Purvis out of the tree, Helen stops by on her way home from school. Warren sleepwalks and the "romantic" chase is repeated.

Andy returns, learns about the incident, and fires Warren. Warren goes home and begins packing his belongings. He has decided to leave town.

Goober stops by Warren's room, and Warren asks him if he would like to buy his television set. Warren turns on the television to demonstrate that the set works fine just as a Fred Astaire movie begins.

Goober advises Warren to confess to Andy. He points out that Warren has nothing to lose, so Warren agrees.

Warren goes over to the Taylor home. Andy telephones Helen and asks her to come over. Helen arrives, sees Warren, and becomes angry. While she and Andy argue in the kitchen, Warren falls asleep on the couch. Hoping to drown out Andy and Helen's loud voices, Aunt Bee turns on the radio. Moments later, Andy and Helen are summoned from the kitchen. Warren is dancing in his sleep with Aunt Bee, just like Fred Astaire.

After his sleepwalking is revealed, Andy and Helen take Warren home. Referring to his sleepwalking, Warren says, "I got a feeling it may never happen again. These things, once they're out, that's it—thing of the past." As Andy and Helen leave, the episode concludes with Warren handcuffing himself to his bed before falling asleep.

"We never concerned ourselves with why Warren didn't confess the sleepwalking when it first happened," says Sam. "Perhaps he wasn't aware until later that revealing it would make it disappear. We were simply looking for a quick solution and hoping the audience wouldn't question its logic."

"Jack Burns was a very funny guy," says Richard O. Linke. "Unfortunately, he didn't work out. The ironic thing was, with Don Knotts leaving and Jack not working out, the ratings kept getting better and better. I remember saying to Andy at the time, 'In my mind, you are the star. You set the tempo of the show. You're the focal point, everything revolves around you. The flow of the show depends on the star, not the second or third banana.'"

"The Return of Barney Fife"

"She was the only girl I ever loved. She's the only girl I ever will love."
—**BARNEY**, mourning the loss of Thelma Lou

Episode 176

First Broadcast on
January 10, 1966

Written by
**Bill Idelson and
Sam Bobrick**

Directed by
Alan Rafkin

"The class-reunion storyline was the idea of producer Bob Ross," says writer Sam Bobrick. "It seemed like a good idea since most people have been to class reunions. We knew Don Knotts was available, and a reunion provided an excuse to bring Barney back to Mayberry."

Bill and Sam begin their reunion script with Andy, Helen, Aunt Bee, and Floss, a former classmate of Andy's, preparing for the 1948 Mayberry Union High School class reunion. Andy hangs a "Welcome Back" banner, while the "girls" work on the name badges. Andy and Aunt Bee look through the letters of the people that are coming. Aunt Bee looks at a letter from Sharon DeSpain, one of Andy's former girlfriends. Andy then opens another letter and says, "Guess who's coming back? Barney!"

Many of the details about Andy's graduating class are consistent with the "Class Reunion" episode written by Jim Fritzell and Everett Greenbaum. However, the year Andy graduated is different. In the first "reunion" episode, it is 1945.

"Bill and I tried to be consistent with the first reunion episode, but obviously we slipped up on the year," says Sam. "I don't know why it wasn't corrected. I imagine it was simply overlooked."

Barney returns to Mayberry and is welcomed back by Andy. The two talk about Barney's life in Raleigh. The high-school reunion is also discussed, and Barney asks if Thelma Lou is coming. Andy replies, "Gee, we haven't heard from her yet. She moved out of town about a month after you left. She might show up, though."

It is agreed that Barney will stay at the Taylors' house while in Mayberry. Barney "brought along a few little things." He gives Opie "an official ink pad we use at the print department." Aunt Bee receives a box of imported handkerchiefs from Tijuana. Barney gives Andy a tie clip and says, "A lot of people clip them right on the front of their shirt, even when they don't wear a tie. It's smart."

That evening after supper, Andy and Barney relax on the front porch. Barney asks, "Thelma Lou's not coming, huh?" Andy answers, "I don't guess so." Barney replies, "That's too bad. She'd get a kick out of seeing how I've come up in the world." Andy asks if Barney is still sweet on her. Barney answers, "No, no, once it's gone, it's gone, Ange. You can't go back. Course, sometimes a man wonders."

Andy and Barney reminisce about their high-school days and sing the Mayberry Union High School song. Helen steps onto the porch soon after the singing is finished and tells them that she's just heard that Thelma Lou is coming to the reunion after all. Barney is overjoyed.

On the night of the reunion, Andy impatiently waits for Barney to get ready. Andy says to Aunt Bee, "He hasn't changed much. He's still the slowest man in the world." This remark seems out of place. There was no previous reference in the series to Barney being slow.

"We weren't concerned that Barney had not previously been referred to as slow," says Sam. "Andy's comment fit the scene, so we used it."

Barney eventually comes downstairs. He proudly shows off his shirt "with initials on it." As Andy and Barney depart, Aunt Bee says, "Now, you boys drive carefully and have a good time. Don't stay out too late." Andy replies, "We won't, 'Mama.'"

"Having Aunt Bee remind Andy and Barney to drive carefully, as if they were two teenage boys, and Andy's 'mama' reply were ways of showing that time stands still for some people," says Sam.

At the reunion, Andy and Helen enjoy the music of Carl Benson's Wildcats, and Barney talks with two of his former teachers. When Thelma Lou arrives, Barney walks over and asks her to dance. As the two dance, Barney apologizes "for not writing to you for all that time" and says "a lot of things have been happening to me career wise. The future looks pretty rosy." Barney shows off the initials on his shirt.

"When Barney points out the initials on his shirt pocket, it is his way of showing growth and sophistication," says Sam.

Floss interrupts Barney and Thelma Lou and asks Thelma Lou to come with her "so she can be registered and get her name badge." While Thelma Lou is away, Barney tells Andy, "She looks just great." Andy asks if "it" is still there, and Barney answers, "Well, I'm not saying it is, and I'm not saying it ain't. I'm not going to rush into anything. I'll tell you one thing though—she's still crazy about me."

Thelma Lou returns with a male companion and introduces her new husband to Andy and Barney. The two have been married six weeks.

"Barney, of course, was shattered by the news that Thelma Lou was married," says Sam. "The fact that she married just six weeks earlier made it even sadder."

"In my mind, and no one else agreed with me, I decided that Thelma Lou didn't actually get married," says Betty Lynn, who portrayed Thelma Lou. "She knew this fellow at work and when they had the reunion and everyone would be coming back, she said to this fellow, 'Listen, I don't want to go back to Mayberry like I was. I'm going to tell them I got married. Would you do me a favor and come with me?' This was all in my head, and that's what I believed because I knew in my heart that Thelma Lou would never marry anybody but Barney Fife. They all said, 'No, no, you really got married.' But I knew better. Barney was the love of Thelma Lou's life."

Barney consoles himself by attempting to get drunk on the fruit punch. Andy says, "I'm sorry, Barn. I know it must have been a shock." Barney responds in a slurred voice, "Sure, it was a shock. So what? It wasn't the first one in my life. It won't be the last. That's life. Don't worry about it, Ange. I'll get over it. If I can't do it one way, I'll do it another." Barney takes another drink of punch. Andy replies, "Well, if you're trying to get drunk, you won't do it that way. There's nothing in the punch but fruit juice." Barney immediately sobers up.

"Having Barney get drunk on nonalcoholic fruit punch seemed funny, and Don Knotts was wonderful in the scene," says Sam.

Floss joins Andy and Barney. She introduces the two to a former classmate, Nettie Albright. Nettie ignores Andy and tells Barney, "You know, I've been wanting to talk to you. I hear that wonderful things have been happening to you." Nettie is not surprised by Barney's success. She always knew he would do well. Nettie admits that in school Barney was always her "idol." Barney takes an immediate interest in Nettie and invites her to dance.

"Barney's sudden interest in Nettie was his attempt to bounce back from the devastating news of Thelma Lou's marriage," says Sam.

Thelma Lou's marriage comes close to shattering the series' premise that all problems have a solution. In previous episodes, Andy could solve Barney's problems with a wise word or a face-saving action. But Thelma Lou's marriage is different. There is nothing Andy can say or do that will undo the marriage and make things right. The substitution of Nettie Albright's attention for the loss of Thelma Lou is not believable. This is not the solution to "losing the only girl I'll ever love."

The epilogue captures Barney's sadness over losing Thelma Lou. The school song is played very slowly in the background as Andy and Barney drive home from the reunion. Barney turns off the engine, and the two classmates remain seated in the car. Andy says, "That was something about Thelma Lou being married, wasn't it?" Barney answers, "Yeah," and begins talking enthusiastically about Nettie. Barney falls silent. Andy eventually asks, "You want to go in?" Barney answers, "Yeah."

"It was our intention to end on a melancholy note," says Sam. "The reunion has had an impact on Andy and Barney. In that brief moment of silence in the car, they both realized you can't really 'go home again.'"

"The Legend of Barney Fife"

Episode 177

First Broadcast on
January 17, 1966

Written by
Harvey Bullock

Directed by
Alan Rafkin

"A true living legend, that Barney Fife. I mean he's something, isn't he?"
—WARREN FERGUSON

"Don Knotts's picture will always be on every *TAGS* writer's piano."
—HARVEY BULLOCK

"The *TAGS* writers' seminars had stopped by this time," says writer Harvey Bullock. "There were some writers who found they didn't like the seminar pooling. They would rather cherish and develop their own ideas to fruition. Perhaps some of them thought they were giving away more good ideas than they received. Whatever, I enjoyed the seminars. After the seminars stopped, the producer's door remained open to the writers whose work he knew.

"The big mystery to me is that I don't recall working with producer Bob Ross. I knew him, of course. He was a very affable, talented friend and neighbor at the studio, but I can't bring up any remembrance of working a Griffith show with him.

"To the best of my recollection, the 'legend' story was devised by Aaron Ruben and myself. Aaron must have known that Don Knotts was available and mentioned it in one of our meetings. I jumped at the chance to write the episode."

Harvey's script begins in the Taylor kitchen. It is the morning after the class reunion, and Barney is still in bed. Andy says he'd better get down to the courthouse. Aunt Bee asks if Andy is going to wait for Barney. Andy answers, "The way he was carrying on at the reunion last night, he's liable to sleep the clock around."

"I had heard the phrase, 'sleep the clock around,' from my parents," says Harvey. "It popped into my head as I was writing the opening scene, and I gave it to Andy."

Barney comes down a short time later. Andy invites Barney to accompany him to the courthouse. Andy wants to introduce Barney to the new deputy, Warren Ferguson. Aunt Bee says that Warren is doing "a wonderful job." Barney is somewhat hesitant to meet his replacement and tells Andy he plans to return to Raleigh as soon as Goober finishes repairing the fuel pump on his car.

While Andy goes to get the keys to the squad car, Barney and Aunt Bee remain in the kitchen. Barney remarks that he is glad the new deputy is working out so well. Aunt Bee responds, "Oh yes, he's a graduate of the sheriff's academy. Finished fourth in his class. Andy was even able to take off two weeks last fall— something he was never able to do before." Barney is hurt by the implication.

Uncomfortable with the praise given to Warren, Barney decides he'd "better head on back to Raleigh." He calls to check on the car and learns it will be an hour before the repairs will be finished. Reluctantly, Barney goes with Andy to the courthouse and is introduced to Warren.

"Jack Burns had just started the show when this script was written," says Harvey. "He had done successful comedy with Avery Schreiber, but anybody who replaced Don Knotts was sticking his head into a guillotine. Viewers were attuned to the incomparable Don Knotts, and they like familiarity. No one else could be the deputy. It was also more difficult for the writers to make Jack's character function. Don had spoiled us. Moreover, I'm sure this was apparent—and depressing to Jack. He couldn't win."

Barney is surprised to learn that Warren admires his work as a former deputy and sees him as "a living legend." Enjoying the adulation, Barney decides there is no real rush to get back to Raleigh.

Warren steps into the back room to fix Barney a cup of coffee. While he is out of the room, Barney tells Andy that Warren's admiration is understandable. He says, "Lots of persons have an idol." Barney's childhood idol was "Skeets Gallagher, sidekick to Tailspin Tommy."

"I always liked the name 'Skeets Gallagher,'" says Harvey. "It was borrowed from a 1930s comic-book series. The name was sort of wacky and sounded funny."

Later in the day, the newspaper sends over a reporter to ask some questions for a story about the high-school reunion. Andy and Warren convince the reporter to include a story on Barney's return to Mayberry. Barney just happens to have packed his deputy's uniform, so Warren drives him over to Andy's house so he can put it on for a picture to accompany the newspaper's story.

Barney and Warren return to the courthouse. The photographer wants to take the picture outside. When Andy, Warren, and the photographer step outside, they are joined by Floyd.

"Floyd has no comedic lines in the street scene," says Harvey. "This can happen when a script is hurriedly trimmed for length. The vital-to-the-storylines are sometimes kept at the expense of cutting optional comedy lines. There's no telling what comic gems Floyd would have spoken if he had been given the time."

Barney remains inside the courthouse to adjust his tie. The telephone rings. When Barney answers, he is told a convict, Avery Noonan, has escaped and may be heading toward Mayberry. Barney was responsible for Noonan's initial arrest and is warned that Noonan may be seeking revenge.

A Quick Answer

I had no idea that "The Legend of Barney Fife" would be my final *TAGS* script, but that's the way it turned out. At the time, my partner Ray Allen and I were venturing into the beguiling world of feature pictures, which took most of our time and energy. I wrote most of *TAGS* by myself, and I wanted to get back to a full-time partnership with Ray. We continued the occasional TV script but concentrated primarily on films. In addition, *TAGS* without Barney wasn't as appealing.

I cherish having written for *TAGS* and am enormously grateful to the many fans who keep the show alive. *TAGS* was the central achievement of my writing career, and my relationship to it is my most important and pleasing identity.

When new friends hear I was a TV/film writer, inevitably they ask, "What shows did you write?" Well, after forty years and hundreds of scripts, I have quite a choice. But I never even skip a beat. I simply answer, *The Andy Griffith Show*.—HARVEY BULLOCK

Barney immediately decides to "pass up the newspaper story" and get out of town. Goober telephones to tell Barney he'll be getting a new fuel pump from Mt. Pilot in the morning. Barney instructs Goober to put the old fuel pump back on his car.

Barney decides to go to Andy's house and pack. He exits the courthouse dressed in Andy's raincoat with his hat pulled down over his eyes. While waiting in the Taylor home for Goober to return his car, Barney places a dresser in front of his bedroom door.

"I might have been pushing Barney's reaction a little," admits Harvey. "Farce is the most difficult of all comedy to make work, but Don gave the writers such latitude. Putting the dresser up against the door was such a cliché, I hoped it wouldn't be too wild. For a touch of normalcy, I had Andy notice it and then had Barney offer the almost credible reason that he was looking for a collar button."

Goober returns Barney's car and follows Andy inside the house.

"Goober's main story function is to compound Barney's problem of getting out of town," says Harvey. "He has mostly straight lines that progress the story but are not comedic in themselves."

As Barney is preparing to depart, the warden from the county work farm telephones Andy's house with the news that Noonan "was seen hopping a southbound train" and may be headed toward Mayberry. The warden is surprised that Barney didn't tell Andy about Noonan. Aware that Noonan is out to get Barney, Andy now understands why Barney is in such a hurry to leave Mayberry.

Moments later Warren arrives and tells Andy that he just got a call from the station master. It seems "some fellow by the name of Avery Noonan is sneaking around down at the depot." Warren has brought Barney's old gun and tells him, "I knew you'd want to get in on this one."

Barney rushes outside and quickly gets into his car, but the old fuel pump falls off when he starts the engine. Barney is thus temporarily stranded in Mayberry and has no reason not to accompany Warren and Andy to the depot.

At the depot, Andy and Warren stalk Noonan while Barney waits by the squad car. In the script, Harvey describes Barney, waiting by the car, as *nervous and unhappy with himself. A battle is going on within him. He finally comes to a decision, swallows, braces himself, and opens the depot door quietly.*

Andy has already spotted Noonan inside the depot and is preparing to apprehend him. He changes his plans, however, when he sees Barney enter. Andy gives Noonan time to confront Barney, before he drops a heavy sack on the convict. Andy then unselfishly gives all the credit for the capture to Barney.

As the epilogue begins, Barney is shown closing the cell door on Noonan, signifying that the arrest was his. The newspaper is sending a reporter over, and Barney asks Andy to "swing" the credit for the capture to Warren. Barney says, "Sometimes it don't hurt to shade things a little when you want to help someone. After all, Ange, I've had my place in the sun here for a lot of years. Now a nice fellow like that comes along, a little pat on the back will make him feel good. It's his town out there now, Ange. It's not mine."

"Barney's suggestion that Andy give the credit to Warren is a very satisfying twist," say Harvey. "It shows a touch of maturity coming to Barney. Barney is taking Andy's usual role when he gives up credit to Warren."

Barney exits to look for the newspaper reporter. Warren enters the courthouse and says, "A true living legend that Barney Fife. I mean he's something, isn't he, Andy?" Andy answers, "Yes, he is. He really is."

"Wyatt Earp Rides Again"

Episode 179

First Broadcast on
January 31, 1966

Written by
Jack Elinson

Directed by
Alan Rafkin

Pat Hingle
Guest Stars as
Fred Gibson

"Are you besmirchin' the name of Earp?"—FRED GIBSON

"All stories start with a nugget," says Jack. "The nugget here was the movie *High Noon*, the best Western ever made. How could I update it to the present? Mayberry is a small town, and they have a sheriff. How could I have someone challenge Andy to a fight? That question led to the Wild West show, which led to Fred Gibson and Clarence Earp, which led to the story."

Jack begins the story with *An old jalopy comes rumbling down the street. The driver is Fred Gibson, a grizzly old character, wearing a cowboy hat, a cowboy suit made of buckskin, and boots. He looks like a road company Buffalo Bill. He hops out of the car and marches into the sheriff's office.*

Andy and Opie are inside. Both are a bit surprised by the sudden appearance of a Western-type character.

Gibson hands Andy his card. Andy reads aloud, "Gibson's Wild West Show . . . East or West Gibson's the Best."

Gibson announces that he's bringing "our great spectacular to the entertainment-starved" community of Mayberry.

Opie is overjoyed with the prospect. Andy starts to protest, but Gibson is not a fan of two-sided conversations. He verbally rolls over Andy and assigns him the task of arranging the necessary permits. Gibson has selected the fairgrounds he passed on the way in for the site of the show.

Before leaving, Gibson announces that the star of the show is Clarence Earp, great-nephew and a direct blood relative of the famous lawman Wyatt Earp. Clarence is a "two-fisted, hard-riding, and fast-shooting" cowboy.

Later in the day, Floyd, Warren, and Andy are in the barbershop. The three are discussing the Wild West show and its star, Clarence Earp.

The discussion prompts Floyd to recall the last time someone connected to a famous person was in Mayberry. That person was Harvey Kester. Harvey used to repair Gloria Swanson's radio.

Floyd also recalls the last show that passed through Mayberry. The show featured the Great Mandrake. Mandrake ate matches, candles, and torches like most people eat carrots and peas. The show didn't last long. The fire department had to keep putting Mandrake out.

"Floyd was the perfect character to talk about trivia with such great passion," says Jack. "Only he would remember who used to repair Gloria Swanson's radio and Mandrake the Fire Eater."

The conversation returns to Clarence Earp. Floyd imagines Clarence "with broad shoulders, a narrow waist, rippling muscles . . . and a steely eye looking straight ahead as he rides tall in the saddle."

The next scene *opens close* on Clarence Earp *as he rides along on horseback. He is the opposite of what Floyd has envisioned. Clarence is a diminutive milquetoasty-looking character wearing glasses.*

"The script described Clarence in great detail," says Jack. "Instead of a big tough guy, I went the other way and made him a little guy with glasses. This made it ~~funnier.~~"

~~Clarence and Gibson~~ ride up and dismount. *Now that Clarence is down on his feet, he is more incongruous than ever. He is dressed in a black broad-brimmed hat, a ~~black frock~~ coat, ~~black~~ trousers tucked into fancy boots, white shirt, and ~~black string~~ tie. These clothes look out of place on the little fellow. He wears two ~~gun belts crisscrossing~~ his waist; the belts are laden with bullets and a holster on each hip.*

Gibson has brought Clarence into town so people "could get a look at him." A crowd gathers 'round. Gibson hawks the "rootinest-tootinest Wild West Show of them all."

Sometime later, Warren is at the barbershop talking with his Uncle Floyd. Warren looks into a mirror, notices his hair has a "nice luster," and acknowledges that the scalp treatments he has been receiving from Floyd are working.

Floyd agrees and shares words of barber wisdom, "Be kind to your scalp, and it will be kind to you."

Floyd scans a newspaper and reads aloud a printed advertisement for the Wild West Show. In response, Warren questions Clarence's blood relationship with Wyatt Earp. He points out that Wyatt was over six feet tall. Clarence is scrawny.

Floyd responds with a family antidote, "That happens sometimes. Take Aunt Sophie. Her two boys never did develop the kind of muscles she had." (Floyd's words of barber wisdom and family history were sadly deleted from the script.)

Gibson and Clarence enter the barbershop. Gibson asks permission to put one of his posters in the front window. Floyd is reluctant.

Gibson places the poster in the front window and flatters Floyd with the hope of getting his approval. In his opinion, Floyd is the kind of man who would like to see some fine entertainment come into Mayberry. Floyd concedes he is "a patron of the theater."

Warren is doubtful that Clarence can perform the lassoing, the fast draw, and the knife throwing that the poster advertises.

Gibson confirms Clarence's toughness and challenges Warren to a "little arm-wrestling" contest.

Warren excels in arm wrestling. Floyd recalls that at the last Founders' Day picnic, Warren was the arm-wrestling champ and was awarded a "month's supply of mint jelly."

"I loved writing for Floyd," says Jack. "Another example of Floyd's off-the-wall comments was the comparing interest in a Wild West Show to being 'a patron of the arts.' As for the 'mint jelly award,' lines like that were common in the series to keep the small-town flavor."

The script direction narrates the contest. *Almost bored by it all, Clarence locks hands with Warren. Warren begins the intense battle, struggling, straining, and pushing, but it's like moving the Rock of Gibraltar. Warren is even more frustrated by Clarence's calmness, as he just sits there letting Warren knock himself out. Clarence decides to put an end to the farce and with one swift motion, he pins Warren's arm to the table. Clarence gets up and struts out.*

Later at the fairgrounds, Clarence demonstrates some fancy pistol twirling for Opie, his friends, and Goober. Gibson hawks Clarence's talent and toughness. He challenges Goober to a wrestling match with Clarence.

Goober hesitantly agrees. Before going into battle, he hands his tire gauge to Opie for safekeeping.

"The 'tire gauge' bit is another example of small-town behavior," says Jack. "To Goober, his tire gauge is a very precious tool like a surgeon's scalpel."

Once his tire gauge is safe, Goober lunges at Clarence, who gracefully steps aside. Clarence tosses Goober over his shoulder. After a second fall, Gibson helps Goober up and ends the match. Gibson tells the boys, "Clarence lives by the code of the West. . . . The man who can fight is the man who's right."

An excited Opie rushes to the sheriff's office and reports on the demonstration of Clarence's talents. Andy is surprised to learn that Clarence "beat up Goober."

Opie longs for the Old West days of riding, shooting, and fighting. Hearing this, Andy wishes Gibson and Clarence would stop "stirring things up" and admits he is sorry he issued the permit to set up the Wild West show.

"Andy's concern about possible trouble by Gibson and Clarence was definitely the key element of the story," says Jack. "The whole second act headed toward how Andy would solve the problem."

Act two of the episode begins with Andy joining Floyd for a chat. Floyd has been to see the Wild West show. Floyd, reflecting on the old days, tells Andy he is too gentle to have been an Old West sheriff. Floyd feels Andy would have probably been a barber. Floyd sees himself in the role of a high-stakes gambler, a bartender, or an outlaw. (Floyd's bartending and outlaw aspirations were deleted from the chat.)

The conversation is interrupted by the sound of distant yelling. Andy goes to investigate and finds Opie and Johnny Paul on the ground wrestling. Andy pulls the two apart.

Goober joins Andy. It would seem more appropriate if Floyd would have joined Andy since the two had been together when the yelling was heard. Howard McNear, who portrayed Floyd Lawson, was unable to walk or stand unassisted at this point in his career due to a stroke. It was easier to have Goober walk into the scene and restrain Opie.

Andy asks the boys why they were fighting. Opie explains there was a disagreement, and he and Johnny Paul decided to settle it according to the code of the Old West: "The man who can fight is the man who is right."

Andy has heard enough. He sends Goober to the fairgrounds to deliver a message. He wants to see Fred Gibson and Clarence Earp in his office "right now."

Goober arrives at the fairgrounds and finds Gibson regaling some spectators with stories about Wyatt Earp. According to Gibson, Earp could "shoot a fly at a hundred yards and hit whichever you wanted . . . the left wing or the right wing." Clarence can do the same.

Gibson doesn't appreciate being interrupted by Goober. Clarence gives Goober a *withering* look. An intimidated Goober delivers Andy's message in a *soft, meek* voice. (Goober's delivery of the message was deleted from the filmed episode.)

Later at the sheriff's office, Andy requests that Gibson take it a little easier "on all this talk about fighting." Gibson, Andy believes, is negatively influencing Mayberry's children.

Andy says that Gibson shouldn't "get folks all worked up just because Clarence's name is Earp. The name of Earp was important in the old days, but the name doesn't mean that much anymore."

Andy has "besmirched the name of Earp." Clarence, defending the honor of the Earp family, demands satisfaction. He challenges Andy to a fight. Andy may pick his "weapon of choice." The showdown will take place on Main Street at high noon!

"As I mentioned, *High Noon* was what got me started on this story," says Jack. "I knew I wanted to do the showdown scene. Gary Cooper did it in the Old West, and Andy would do it in Mayberry."

Later that morning, Andy is *lying on a cot gazing into space. Warren is standing alongside the cot.* (Andy lying on a cot, either in a cell or the back room, is an unfamiliar sight. In the filmed episode, Andy is seated in one of the chairs placed by the front window.)

Warren warns Andy that if he comes face to face with Clarence, he may get hurt. Andy thinks the situation over, gets an idea, and leaves to prepare for the showdown.

The script direction narrates, *A little later, the wall clock in the office now reads two minutes to twelve. The door opens and Opie comes in, wide-eyed and alarmed.*

Opie has heard about the showdown and, remembering what he has been taught by Andy, doesn't feel fighting is the way to settle things.

Andy reminds Opie that in any good Western, the ending is never given away. Following that tradition, Opie will have to wait until high noon to find out what "weapon" Andy will use. Opie assures Andy that "whatever happens," he knows his "paw" is going to win.

"Tension was definitely part of anticipating the showdown," says Jack. "Opie's faith in his dad was very important. This scene was good father and son stuff."

Jack's vision of the showdown is described in detail. *WE HEAR THE CHURCH BELL STRIKE TWELVE TIMES. The door of the office opens, and Andy steps out. Andy strolls calmly to the middle of the street and looks in the direction Clarence will be coming from. There's a moment of stark SILENCE and then WE HEAR walking HOOFBEATS. The hoofbeats STOP, and a moment later WE SEE Clarence come around the corner. Clarence walks to the center of the street and looks in Andy's direction. They walk toward each other, stop about ten feet apart, and just look at each other.*

The filmed showdown is less dramatic. There is no tolling of church bells or sound of approaching hoofbeats. Andy never walks far from the sidewalk in front of the sheriff's office. Gibson, seeing that Andy is not "armed," reasons that he wants to "fistfight." Clarence raises his fists and begins sparring with Andy. Andy directs the showdown inside the sheriff's office.

"Since I patterned the showdown after the great movie, I wanted it to be exactly the same in the staging of it," says Jack. "It may have been a little wild, but that was the point in doing this story in the first place. Sadly, the on-screen showdown was not as dramatic as what was scripted."

Inside the sheriff's office, Andy announces that he is not going to fight Clarence with his fists. His choice of weapon is a book about Wyatt Earp and his descendants. Andy has looked through the book and discovered that Clarence's name is not mentioned.

Gibson advises Clarence to pay no attention to what Andy has said. He guides Clarence toward the door but is stopped by Andy.

In Andy's opinion, if Clarence is not told the truth and continues "playing cowboy," he will "wind up in all kinds of trouble."

Gibson reflects on Andy's prediction and decides to tell Clarence the truth.

Gibson confesses that he never knew Clarence's parents or the place where he came from. When Gibson first met Clarence, he was a sickly, unsure child who was "never able to find his place" with others. Gibson gave Clarence the Earp name so he would "have a heritage to live up to."

Clarence is stunned and unsure about his future without the Earp identity.

Andy tells Clarence a "person has to be who they really are."

Gibson agrees and decides to tell Clarence his real name: Dempsey. A boxing ring bell chimes on the soundtrack to connect the name with the former heavyweight boxing champion Jack Dempsey.

"This scene does a couple of things," says Jack. "Clarence finds out he's not an Earp, and Fred Gibson explains his reasons for deceiving him. That's why I made Clarence such a wimpy little guy. Fred did a good thing by lifting Clarence's ego from zero to macho. The 'Dempsey' finish was a funny way to cut through the treacly scene. The 'here we go again' ending was the perfect comedy formula when all else fails."

"Wyatt Earp Rides Again" was the final episode Jack Burns appeared in. The writers were giving Burns "Barney" material, and it didn't work. Andy was uncomfortable with the Warren Ferguson character. This made him "hell" to be around.

"Wyatt Earp Rides Again" concluded filming on December 8, 1965. Burns was released from his *Griffith Show* contract prior to Christmas. He received his full salary for the rest of the season.

Don Knotts's departure and the absence of a deputy did not hurt the series. By the sixth season, the show had developed an atmosphere, the community, and the character relationships that the audience wanted to see, whether a deputy was in it or not.

"Aunt Bee Learns to Drive"

Episode 180

First Broadcast on
February 7, 1966

Written by
Jack Elinson

Directed by
Lee Philips

"I enjoyed writing this script because it featured Aunt Bee. I knew Frances Bavier well, as I did all the members of the cast. She was the same in real life as she was on the screen—a wonderful, lovely lady. I was happy to write a story that gave her the spotlight."—JACK ELINSON

"This was a logical story," says Jack. "Deep into the series, we never saw Aunt Bee behind the wheel. I'm surprised a story about teaching her to drive wasn't done a lot earlier."

"Aunt Bee Learns to Drive" begins with Andy seated at the breakfast table. The script direction is detailed. *He finishes, gets up with his coffee cup and an empty plate, hurries over to the sink, gives them a quick rinsing off, and then rushes toward the living room.*

In the filmed episode, Andy wears an apron that he takes off and casts aside in the living room. Andy takes the empty cup and plate to the sink, as directed in the script, but doesn't rinse off either.

"Andy wearing an apron and momentarily forgetting to remove it was not in the script," says Jack. "I imagine that was added during filming."

Aunt Bee comes down the stairs, dressed to go out. She would like Andy to drive her over to Clara's. Aunt Bee has promised to pin up Clara's blueprint. Clara would like to wear the dress to the "social tomorrow."

Andy is in a rush. He is late for a meeting in Mt. Pilot, and driving to Clara's would be out of the way. Andy promises to take Aunt Bee tomorrow. Aunt Bee assures Andy she will work out her own transportation. After he steps out, she says aloud, "I always do."

Minor changes were made in the scene's dialogue. The color of Clara's dress is dropped. She would like to wear the dress "to church on Sunday" instead of the "social tomorrow."

Aunt Bee's words of frustration were not in the script.

Later in the day, Aunt Bee comes out of the market and sees Goober putting a

"4 Sale $295" sign on the windshield of a car. Goober bought the car and has fixed it up for resale. The sign was scripted to read "For Sale $345."

Goober greets Aunt Bee and asks if she knows anyone who is looking to buy a car.

Aunt Bee was scripted to answer, "You see, this woman I know always depends on her nephew to take her everywhere, and it would be nice if she has transportation of her own."

This dialogue is crossed out on George Lindsey's script. He writes the rewording in the margin of his script. "Well, I know a woman that always has to depend on her nephew to take her places, and it would be nice if she had a car of her own."

Goober, sensing Aunt Bee might be the "woman," points out the car's features. The seats are soft, having been broken in by an overweight previous owner. The motor "purrs like a kitten."

Goober starts to tell the car's mileage but is stopped by Aunt Bee. She feels what the previous driver did with the car is none of her business.

"Aunt Bee not wanting to know the car's mileage points out the difference between men and women," says Jack. "For women, the color of a car is the main consideration, not all that stuff under the hood. The horn should sound nice, and there must be a mirror on the visor."

Aunt Bee admits she might be interested in the car. Goober offers to bring the car over after supper and show it to Andy. Aunt Bee likes the idea and plans to break the news to Andy before Goober arrives.

That evening Aunt Bee and Helen Crump are in the kitchen making the final preparations for supper. Helen is excited that Aunt Bee has decided to buy a car.

The script directions about the serving of the supper are very detailed. *The women exit to the dining room, Aunt Bee carrying the pork chops, and Helen, the bowls of vegetables. Pork chops are set in front of Andy. Beans in front of Opie.* (In the filmed episode, the ladies simply place the dishes in an empty spot on the table.)

Andy, seeing all his favorite foods, digs in. Aunt Bee, hoping the meal has put Andy in a good mood, announces that she has something she would like to say.

Aunt Bee reminds Andy of what happened that morning. She felt like a pest asking him to drive her over to Clara's. Aunt Bee would like to become more self-sufficient and has decided to . . . there is a knock on the door. Goober is early!

Andy answers the door. Goober is standing on the porch. He announces the big surprise.

Andy says Aunt Bee is not going to buy a car. Aunt Bee replies that she can afford a car and can learn to drive like everyone else.

Andy feels that Aunt Bee is not the type to drive a car. He is concerned about her age and lack of concentration. Aunt Bee protests. She feels her age and lack of concentration are not valid points.

"Andy's concern makes sense," says Jack. "Aunt Bee is on in years, and he would worry about her ability to drive. Aunt Bee has a point also. You're only as old as you feel, and she feels great. In fact, she works harder taking care of the house than most men."

Andy sees that Aunt Bee is determined and reluctantly consents to the purchase.

The next day, Floyd is seated in front of the barbershop reading a newspaper. Andy walks up and takes a seat. Floyd tells Andy he has just read an interesting article. Floyd fumbles through the paper searching for the article but is unsuccessful.

Andy shares the news that Aunt Bee has decided to take up driving. Goober will be her teacher.

Andy gets up to leave. Floyd says if he finds the interesting article in the paper, he will give Andy a yell.

In the filmed episode, Floyd finds the article before Andy's departure. He reads aloud, "The dingo dog is indigenous to Australia."

"This is typical Floyd talk," says Jack. "He's the expert of trivia. The less important something is, the more he'll talk about it. I imagine the 'dingo dog' comment came from story consultant, Bob Ross. It was a good example of the type of trivia that interested Floyd."

Later, Aunt Bee is ready for her first driving lesson. On the way to the car, Andy reminds her that her learner's permit only allows her to drive if there's another licensed driver in the car.

Aunt Bee and Goober get in the car. Goober begins the lesson by explaining the fundamentals of driving. Aunt Bee listens carefully and then asks, "Shall we drive?"

Aunt Bee starts the motor, gives the car some gas, takes her foot off the clutch, and the car leaps forward.

The car lurches down the street and runs over the curb. The lesson ends with Aunt Bee parking the car in the middle of the street.

During the lesson, Aunt Bee wears a straw hat. The hat is held in place by a black cloth that covers the ears and the back of the head. The covering helped to conceal the facial features of the stunt driver who drove the car during the street scenes.

A few days later, Goober reports to Andy that Aunt Bee is doing fine. Andy reminds Goober to teach Aunt Bee all the rules of driving. Goober responds with his trademark, "Yo." The response was changed during filming to "Don't worry about Aunt Bee. She's in good hands."

Meanwhile, Aunt Bee is in the front yard watering a plant. The car is parked on the street next to a large tree. A tree maintenance truck comes to a stop behind it.

Lowell, the driver, has come to trim the trees along the street. He asks Aunt

Bee to move her car. Lowell cannot, due to a work restriction. The car needs to be moved about eight feet.

The script direction narrates what happens next. *Aunt Bee stands there pondering the problem. Then she shrugs and making up her mind that it can do no harm, she heads for the car.*

Aunt Bee gets in the car, accidently puts the car in reverse, and backs into the tree!

Afterward, Aunt is hysterical and worried about Andy's reaction to the accident. She and Helen discuss what to do next. The two decide that the best approach would be to tell Andy the truth about the dented fender.

Later for lunch, Aunt Bee delivers a picnic basket containing all of Andy's "favorites." The food pleases Andy and puts him in a good mood.

Aunt Bee feels the time is right. She tells Andy she would like to talk about the car.

Andy, however, takes over the conversation. He says that ~~Goob~~er has given him some great reports on Au~~nt Bee's d~~riving. ~~Andy apolog~~izes for being too hard on Aunt Bee when she first talked about learning to drive. He explains that his initial concern was based on the number of accidents he has seen happen due to a driver's momentary l~~ae~~k of c~~oncentrati~~on.

Andy eventually asks A~~unt B~~ee what she wanted to tell him earlier. She replies that "Weaver's has got a sale ~~o~~n some beautiful black socks if he needs any." (This dialogue is p~~araphras~~ed in the fil~~med epi~~sode.)

Later, Aunt Bee covers the car's damaged fender with Opie's Boy Scout tent. Helen has stopped by and watches. Aunt Bee explains the covering will give her more time to think of what to do next. She plans to tell Andy the tent is protecting the car from tree sap.

The script direction narrates what happens a short time later. *Andy is driving up in the squad car. When he gets to about ten yards from Aunt Bee's car, he suddenly jams on the breaks as he spots a boy riding his bike in the middle of the street.* Andy instructs the boy to ride closer to the curb.

Andy continues to drive up to where Aunt Bee's car is parked, and he turns back to double-check on the boy. He looks back a split second too long because he bumps right into the rear of Aunt Bee's car. It's not a bad bump, but enough to alarm him. He hops out and goes to survey the front of the squad car. Seeing no damage, he looks at the back of Aunt Bee's car.

Meanwhile, Opie rides up on his bicycle. He tells Andy he heard a "bang." Andy explains that he bumped Aunt Bee's car but there doesn't seem to be any damage. Andy asks why Opie's tent is covering the back of the car.

Andy readjusts the tent to better protect the trunk from falling tree sap and discovers the damaged fender underneath. Andy believes he caused the damage.

"Aunt Bee bumping her car was the key point in the second act, and that's where I was heading," says Jack. "Andy thinking he caused the damaged fender was the funny plot twist. All these things were in the original storyline before a word of the script is written."

Inside the house, Aunt Bee looks out a front window and sees Andy staring incredulously at the damage he's caused.

Aunt Bee meets Andy at the front door. She is ready to confess. Andy speaks first and admits that he accidentally bumped into Aunt Bee's car.

The scene's script direction gives an insight into what Aunt Bee is thinking. *Aunt Bee's mind starts working, and she gradually gets the look of a prisoner who has just received a pardon.*

Andy assures Aunt Bee that he will pay to have the fender repaired. He regrets what happened. The fact that he has never had a car accident his whole life makes the situation even worse.

"When Andy tells Aunt Bee he hit her car, I was tempted to milk the moment and have her sigh with relief," says Jack. "Aunt Bee's off the hook. I considered having her not tell Andy the truth, but I couldn't do that to such a nice lady. So, I wrote, *Aunt Bee is conscience-stricken now. She can't stand to see Andy suffering. She tells the truth.*

After telling the truth, Aunt Bee asks if Andy is still going to allow her to take the driver's license test. Andy answers that if he can run into a bumper, then Aunt Bee is allowed to run into a tree. Aunt Bee can take the test.

A few days later, Aunt Bee rushes into the sheriff's office with the news that she passed the test. She has received her driver's license! She asks for Andy's permission to buy the car. Andy gives his permission. Aunt Bee is pleased. Now the car's dent can be "really" hers.

Later, Aunt Bee takes Andy, Helen, Opie, Goober, and Floyd for a ride. Floyd bestows well wishes for happy travel: "Aunt Bee, may this be the start of many miles of smooth driving. May you glide over the highways like a swan skimming across a lake."

"Besides being the master of trivia, Floyd is the biggest cornball that ever was," says Jack. "He's on a different wavelength than the rest of humanity."

The episode ends with the following script direction, *The car starts off. But it's not like a swan skimming smoothly across a lake. It lurches like a bull charging into the ring.*

"A Baby in the House"

"The baby hates me. She just hates me. Every time I pick her up she cries."
—AUNT BEE

"I don't remember this one."—SAM BOBRICK

"I have no idea where the idea for this story came from," says writer Sam Bobrick. "I enjoyed writing all our *TAGS* scripts. Other than that general recollection, I have no memories of this episode."

Bill and Sam's "forgotten" script begins in the Taylor home. Andy, Helen, Aunt Bee, and Opie are working on a crossword puzzle. The pastime is interrupted by a telephone call from Aunt Bee's niece Martha. Martha would like to leave her six-month-old baby, Evie Joy, with the Taylors for a few days, while she and her husband attend a wedding in New Jersey. Aunt Bee is excited about the opportunity, but Andy is reluctant to have a baby in the house. He eventually consents, but he tells Aunt Bee that she's going to have to "handle the whole thing."

Goober brings some of his old toys for Evie Joy before her arrival. Goober selects the toys he thinks a baby might like—checkers and a checkerboard, an old cigar box, and Goober's favorite toy, a teddy bear named Buster. Goober points out that a baby would get a "big kick" out of knocking the checkerboard over. He also points out he spent hours opening and closing the cigar box.

"Jack Burns, who portrayed deputy Warren Ferguson, was a good actor and a pleasure to work with," says George Lindsey, who portrayed Goober Pyle. "Unfortunately, who's going to take Don Knotts's place? After Jack left the show, I filled in as the comic relief."

When the baby arrives, Martha tells Aunt Bee that the baby "almost never cries."

"Whenever a script required a baby, we would notify casting director Ruth Burch, and she would make the necessary arrangements," says former *TAGS* producer Aaron Ruben. "There were strict regulations that had to be followed whenever a baby was used. Because you could only use a baby for a limited time,

First Broadcast on
March 7, 1966

Written by
**Bill Idelson and
Sam Bobrick**

Directed by
Alan Rafkin

it was standard practice to replace the baby with a doll if the baby's face was not required in a scene."

Martha asks Opie if he would like to hold the baby. Evie Joy is content in Opie's arms. When Aunt Bee takes the baby from Opie, Evie Joy begins to cry. When Andy suggests that she might be hungry, Aunt Bee hands Evie Joy to Andy while she warms a bottle. Evie Joy stops crying as soon as Andy takes her.

Soon after the parents leave, Aunt Bee discovers that Evie Joy cries whenever she holds her. This upsets Aunt Bee. Helen comes by to see how everything is going and notices that Aunt Bee has been crying. Aunt Bee confesses to Helen that "the baby hates me. She just hates me. Every time I pick her up she cries. What am I going to do for the next six days?"

That night Andy is called out to break up a fight between Jed and Carl Darling. The fight began when Jed told Carl there was no Santa Claus. The next morning Andy is "too tired to eat" breakfast. He decides to go upstairs and "get a little sleep." Andy asks Aunt Bee not to "let the baby start crying."

After Andy leaves the table, Aunt Bee asks Opie if he has to go to school right away. She asks if he would like to give Evie Joy her bottle. When Opie says he'll be late for school, she offers to write him a note. Opie, however, doesn't want to miss first-period gym. At this point, the baby starts whining.

Aunt Bee telephones Goober at the filling station to order a quart of oil and asks if he can bring it over right away. When Goober makes the delivery, Aunt Bee gets him to feed the baby.

Around noon, Evie Joy gets hungry and starts crying again. Andy wakes up and tells Aunt Bee to feed the baby, so he can get some sleep.

A kitchenware salesman rings the doorbell soon after Andy goes back to bed. Aunt Bee invites him in and looks at his merchandise while the salesman feeds Evie Joy.

Later in afternoon, the baby starts crying again. When Andy gets up, Aunt Bee asks him to give the baby her four o'clock feeding. Andy agrees but says he doesn't understand. Aunt Bee begins to cry and tells Andy she doesn't know what to do. She says, "Evie Joy hates me. Every time I pick her up, she cries."

That evening Aunt Bee goes shopping and leaves the baby with Opie and one of his friends. The boys feed Evie Joy filling from a blueberry pie. Some of the filling gets on the baby's face.

Aunt Bee goes to check on the baby when she returns. While she is upstairs, Opie tells Andy he gave the baby some blueberry pie filling. Aunt Bee sees the blue filling around Evie Joy's mouth and thinks the baby is sick. She picks the baby up, rushes downstairs, and tells Andy to call the doctor. Andy explains to Aunt Bee that the boys gave Evie Joy some pie filling.

Once the "crisis" is past, Andy realizes that Aunt Bee is "holding the baby, and she isn't crying. She's happy as a lark." He guesses that Evie Joy cried before because she sensed that Aunt Bee was nervous. She is no longer crying because she senses that Aunt Bee picked her up to protect her. The baby now feels safe in Aunt Bee's arms.

In the epilogue, Andy, Helen, Aunt Bee, and Evie Joy (resting in her crib) relax on the front porch. Helen asks if Aunt Bee would like for her to take the baby upstairs. Aunt Bee answers, "Oh, I'll take her. She's so used to me, if anyone else picked her up it might disturb her."

"Frances Bavier was a wonderful actress," says George Lindsey. "When you can work with an actress of her caliber, you're living in the lap of luxury as far as acting is concerned, because she was so good that you didn't have to worry about her. She allowed you the freedom to focus all your attention on what you were doing.

"We had the best cast on television. Every one of them was great! The years with *The Griffith Show* were my 'golden years' of television because those people were so good."

"*The Griffith Show* had a brilliant cast," says Richard O. Linke, Andy Griffith's manager. "When you put a show together and it jells, things work right. You add, subtract, and it grows into something wonderful. With *TAGS* we had something extra, not only a brilliant cast, but a happy set—and Andy Griffith set that up."

"The County Clerk"

Episode 185

First Broadcast on
March 14, 1966

Written by
**Bill Idelson and
Sam Bobrick**

Directed by
Alan Rafkin

Jack Dodson
Guest Stars as
Howard Sprague;
Mabel Albertson
Portays Howard's
Mother

"That Mr. Sprague is kind of a funny fellow, isn't he, Pa? All the kids think so. You know, he can't throw a baseball."—OPIE TAYLOR

"Producer Bob Ross was a masterful writer," said Jack Dodson. "He was largely responsible for Howard Sprague's basic character, yet he gave me the freedom to develop and enlarge the character. Bob was a fine writer and overseer and certainly ranks high among those who have influenced me. I cannot remember specifically his special suggestions for this episode, but I know he had them. They were, as usual, followed closely. To have known and worked with Bob was a great privilege."

"Jack Dodson was a consummate professional," says George Lindsey, who portrayed Goober Pyle. "He came to *The Griffith Show* from Broadway and was a very talented actor. Jack was perfect for the Howard Sprague role."

"Bob Ross wanted to use Jack Dodson and gave us suggestions about the character he had in mind for Jack to portray," says writer Sam Bobrick. "The character, Howard Sprague, was a grown man still tied to his mother's apron strings. Bill and I took this general description and wrote 'The County Clerk.'"

Bill and Sam's script begins in the courthouse. Opie is sweeping up. As Andy searches for an accident report, he says, "That beats me." "When Opie asks what's wrong, Andy says he can't find the 1953 accident reports. He says the county clerk, Howard Sprague, wants the reports for the last twenty years.

Andy decides to take over the files he has. He walks into Howard's office and meets the new county health officer, Irene Fairchild. Miss Fairchild has taken over Howard's office. Howard has moved next door into a larger office.

Andy steps next door. He delivers the accident reports and discusses "facts and figures" with Howard. While the two are talking, Miss Fairchild returns an undershirt she has found while "cleaning out her files." Howard explains that he took it off one day "when it was rather warm."

After Miss Fairchild leaves, Andy suggests that an "old bachelor" like Howard "might like to try and make a little time there." Howard responds, "Andy, with all the work I've got to do, who's got the time?"

At this point, Howard's mother stops by and greets Andy formally by saying, "Hello, Andrew."

"Mrs. Sprague was a snob," says Sam. "We had her call Andy 'Andrew' to give the audience an idea of the stuffy climate her son was raised in. Mabel Albertson, who portrayed Mrs. Sprague, was wonderful in the role."

Mrs. Sprague reminds Howard "not to be too late coming home tonight. We're playing bridge with the Albrights at seven-thirty." Mrs. Sprague asks Howard whether he had a hot meal for lunch and if he is wearing his undershirt.

That evening Andy tells Helen he was at Howard Sprague's office and noticed that "he's quite a character." Andy goes on to say he went through high school with Howard, and "he always was strange." When Helen asks in what way, Andy answers, "He kind of always kept to himself. He never went out much. Most of the time he just went straight home." When Helen wonders why, Andy says, "His mother. I was in the office today, and she came in. Boy, she's got him tied to her apron strings, and there's very little slack."

Andy tells Helen that there's a pretty girl in the office next to Howard, and he doesn't pay much attention to her. After hearing this, Helen decides it would be good for Howard to get out more often. She suggests Andy invite Howard and Irene Fairchild to join them on a dinner date to Morelli's. At first Andy refuses, but when Helen doesn't want to "go to the show" or "take a walk," he is "persuaded" to go along with her idea.

Howard is interested in Andy's invitation, but before he can accept, he has to "call mother and make sure there are no plans for tonight."

That evening Andy drops by the Spragues' house to pick up Howard. As the two are leaving, Mrs. Sprague says, "Now, don't you worry. I know I'm going to feel much better. It's nothing. Just a little headache." Howard is concerned that his mother may be having "one of her spells" and promises to "check with her later."

Howard and Irene have a wonderful time on their date until Howard calls home and gets no answer. He is concerned that his mother is sick and ends the evening early.

The next day, Andy tells Helen that it's "no good getting involved in other people's lives." Helen replies, "They were having a perfectly wonderful time. It's that mother." Helen asks Andy to talk to Mrs. Sprague about giving Howard some freedom. Andy refuses, but when Helen doesn't want to "go get a cup of coffee" or "go to the show," he is "persuaded" again to do as Helen asks.

Andy decides to handle the situation by flattering Mrs. Sprague. He tells her he's always admired the way she's devoted her life to Howard. He says, "I wouldn't recommend this to everybody, but a charming, attractive woman like yourself—you ought to go out. Go to parties. Go to dances. Have a real life for yourself." Mrs. Sprague replies, "Andrew, you've certainly given me something to think about."

The problem seems to be resolved as the episode comes to an end. Helen, Howard, and Irene are shown seated at a table at Morelli's. The three discuss the possibility of going out the next night, and Howard comments that he hasn't been out this late in years. He notes that it is almost two o'clock. The camera then cuts to the dance floor where Andy and Mrs. Sprague are dancing together.

In the epilogue, Andy expresses his anger at Helen for playing matchmaker. Helen apologizes for asking him to talk to Mrs. Sprague. Helen thinks Mrs. Sprague just needs someone her own age and immediately returns to her matchmaking ways by suggesting that she and Andy introduce Mrs. Sprague to an elderly gentleman named Mr. Judson.

"The Foster Lady"

"Of the three Aunt Bee scripts I did in this bunch, I like this one the best."
—JACK ELINSON

Episode 187

First Broadcast on
March 21, 1966

Written by
**Jack Elinson
and Iz Elinson**

Directed by
Alan Rafkin

Guest Star
Robert Emhardt
as Willard Foster

"Oddly enough, my brother Iz and I never worked together," says Jack. "Through the years, we each had different writing partners. When I started this script, he happened to be available, so I asked him to work with me on it. We both enjoyed it immensely."

"I didn't remember that of the five scripts I did in the later years, three of them were Aunt Bee stories," says Jack. "It was never planned that way. It just happened. With Don Knotts gone, there was one lead player less to work with, so maybe that's why I thought more about the Aunt Bee character."

The script direction narrates the episode's beginning. *Andy, in a squad car, is driving along on a routine patrol. Suddenly, he sees a vehicle in trouble up ahead. It's off the highway and its right front end is in a ditch. It's a spanking new Lincoln Continental, and the unhappy driver surveying the damage is a well-dressed, distinguished-looking gentleman in his fifties. He is Willard Foster. The squad car pulls off the road and stops. Andy climbs out and walks up to the man.*

Foster explains that he was taking a shortcut. He swerved to miss a cow crossing the road but unfortunately didn't miss the ditch. (The road in the filmed episode is dirt rather than a highway.)

Foster's car is leaking oil and cannot be moved. Andy volunteers to drive back to town and have "our" garageman come out and tow Foster's car into Mayberry.

Foster informs Andy there is a telephone in his car. Andy slides into the front seat and is connected by the mobile operator with Goober at the filling station.

Goober answers. "Hello . . . Oh hi, Andy." During the read-through of the script, "hi" was changed to "hey." This is an example of how carefully each word of the script was analyzed and, if need be, changed to sound "right" for the setting and the character.

Goober tows the car into town. He asks Foster's name and address for making out the repair bill. Goober asks Foster what he does for a living and learns that Foster manufactures furniture polish. He is "the Foster of Foster Furniture Polish."

Goober comments on the company's television advertisements. He likes the pretty girl in the commercials. Foster asks if the commercial motivates Goober to go out and purchase the product. Goober admits that he would prefer "going out with the girl."

Goober's comment confirms Foster's concern that people are too busy looking at the girl to pay much attention to the product.

The repair will take the better part of the day, so Andy invites Foster home for lunch. He is sure Aunt Bee, a faithful user of his polish, would love to meet Mr. Foster.

"This is the setup scene for the story," says Jack. "When Andy said that Aunt Bee would love to meet Foster, I'm sure the audience knew exactly where we were going."

During lunch, Aunt Bee affirms that Foster's Furniture Polish gives a hard glossy shine and is long-lasting. Foster is impressed by Aunt Bee's sincerity and choice of words. He suddenly has an idea. A real person, who uses his product, may be a more effective spokesperson than the actress who currently appears in his commercials.

Foster turns his attention to the delicious meal. Aunt Bee has other ideas. She returns to the subject of the furniture polish commercials. She feels an average woman in a small town who uses the product would be an effective spokesperson.

Foster gets a "wild thought." Would Aunt Bee be willing to go on television and promote his polish? The commercials could be filmed in the Taylor home for a natural effect. If everything works out, Aunt Bee would be the new "Foster Lady."

"Foster stealing the idea from Aunt Bee's hints is definitely an old writer's formula," says Jack. "It's a tried-and-true comic tool that worked well in this story."

Sometime later, Andy joins Floyd and Goober who are seated on the bench outside the sheriff's office. He shares Aunt Bee's big news. Floyd sees "Mayberry's lady of the hour" approaching in the distance. He and Goober applaud Aunt Bee's good fortune.

Aunt Bee is excited and nervous about the opportunity. Reflecting on the surprises of life, she says she never dreamed when she used to watch Clara Kimball Young from the second balcony of the theater that she too would someday become an actress.

"Somewhere in Aunt Bee's past life, she remembers a two-balcony theater and a play starring Clara Kimball Young," says Jack. "We made the name up along with the theater."

Later at home, the excitement continues. Aunt Bee stands in front of a mirror and rehearses her sales pitch.

Andy and Opie enter. They praise Aunt Bee's performance. Andy jokingly compares Aunt Bee with Elizabeth Taylor and says both actresses are having quite a year.

"Elizabeth Taylor had a big year in 1965, as she had in the years before and after," says Jack. "When you think of glamour, you think of Elizabeth Taylor and Aunt Bee."

A few days later, "the television invaders from Raleigh" arrive. In the group is Jim Martin, the director; Bob Saunders, his assistant; Sid Hickox, the cameraman; and Eva ~~Kryger~~, the make-up woman.

"All the names of the crew, with the exception of the director, were our crew's real names," says Jack. "The names were written in the script. The assistant director role was performed by an actor. The cameraman and make-up woman were members of *The Griffith Show* crew. Eva Kryger was *The Griffith Show*'s hair stylist rather than the makeup woman."

Aunt Bee and Opie welcome the group. The crew is eager to "get the show on the road" and quickly transform the living room into "a movie set."

The director reminds Aunt Bee that there will be no script. She will deliver the sales pitch in her own words. He instructs Aunt Bee to "relax and be herself."

Andy and Goober enter. They join Opie on the sidelines and watch the commercial's first take.

The script direction narrates, *Aunt Bee knows the camera is rolling and freezes. She just stands there, staring straight ahead, petrified.*

The director encourages Aunt Bee to relax and sets up another take. *When Aunt Bee feels it, she holds the can of furniture polish up to the camera and begins to speak. Her voice is wooden, and she speaks in an artificial stilted fashion. The director blinks his eyes, not believing how bad Aunt Bee is.*

~~Goober and O~~pie see the performance differently. They feel Aunt Bee is doing great and has real talent. Andy is not so sure.

Sometime later, Mr. Foster arrives. He has come to see how the production is going. Floyd has joined the audience and is enthralled with the proceedings. Aunt Bee finishes another stilted performance and signs off with a thrown kiss à la *Dinah Shore.*

Director Martin reports to Foster that things are "going a little slow." Foster joins the audience and is introduced to Floyd. Floyd mentions that he has been using Foster's Furniture Polish for years and volunteers to fill the role of "the Foster Man" if the need arises.

"Floyd isn't bashful, that's for sure," says Jack. "He has his eye on the role of the Foster Man. You have to admire him for his sweet innocence."

Another attempt to film the commercial begins. *Now that Mr. Foster is watching, Aunt Bee really gives it her all. She breaks into a big artificial toothy smile. Foster can't believe what he's seeing. Aunt Bee isn't measuring up.*

Floyd again responds to the performance with applause. He says aloud, "I've taken it to my heart. Oh, that's lovely" and wipes the beginning of a tear away with his finger. (Floyd's response was deleted from the script.)

Aunt Bee does another take. *She's rolling now, bubbling and full of confidence.*

Floyd's appreciation of Aunt Bee's performance grows. Her acting, in his opinion, is "just like poetry."

Aunt Bee has come up with a jingle to go along with the commercial. She sings it. In response, Director Martin calls a break for lunch.

The script direction narrates, *Aunt Bee breezes into the kitchen. Martin, a beaten man, comes over to Foster and Andy. Words are not necessary. All three know that Aunt Bee is not making it.*

Martin has not gotten one good take. He believes the audience would laugh at Aunt Bee if a commercial was broadcast.

Foster reflects on this and says that some of the most successful commercials are funny. Martin agrees and believes Aunt Bee's overacting would be hilarious.

Andy listens quietly. He is concerned with how Aunt Bee will feel when she finds out people are laughing at her. Foster turns a deaf ear to the concern.

"Andy's concern about Aunt Bee's feelings is exactly the same as the audience's concern," says Jack. "Andy is simply speaking for them. The lesson to not make fun of someone doesn't have to be learned. It's already there in the audience's mind."

Andy is trying to decide what to do. *Finally, he gets a look of determination and heads for the kitchen.*

He finds Aunt Bee ecstatic with how things are going. Andy agrees and then directs the conversation toward how Aunt Bee's future success will result in "a few changes around here."

Andy believes he will eventually have to hire someone to come in to look after the house and do the cooking. Aunt Bee asks why.

Andy explains that Aunt Bee is going to be a big celebrity. She will likely have her hands full with answering fan mail, looking over contracts, and being interviewed. Her role as the Foster Lady will also require a great deal of travel.

Aunt Bee doesn't want somebody else in her kitchen. She likewise doesn't want her club and social activities in Mayberry to be interrupted by travel.

Aunt Bee hurries out of the kitchen and into the living room. She tells Mr. Foster that she has decided not to become the Foster Lady. The life of a celebrity is not for her. *This show is off the road.*

The solution to the problem is very similar to the resolution in the season-five episode "The Pageant." In the episode, Aunt Bee gives up the lead role of "Lady Mayberry" in the Centennial Pageant because it is interfering with her duties at home. Her poor acting is never mentioned.

"I never saw 'The Pageant' and was not aware of it," says Jack. "When I pitched the story, nobody mentioned a similarity to a previous episode."

The episode concludes with the Taylors watching "The Rex Benson Show . . . featuring Rex Benson and the Sing Songers." The program is presented by Foster Furniture Polish and will air the new commercial.

"'Rex Benson and the Sing Songers' was just a corny name we made up," says Jack. "The 'Andrews Sisters' was already taken."

The commercial features the "Foster Lady" speaking in a flat overdramatic voice. The "Lady" sings Aunt Bee's jingle. The commercial ends with the sound of kisses being thrown. Andy, Aunt Bee, and Opie laugh heartily.

Aunt Bee says the "Foster Lady's" performance was very good. She admits that she could have played the commercial for comedy as well, if "they'd wanted her to."

The script ends with . . . *Andy nods amused, as we: FADE OUT.*

"It was a happy finish," says Jack. "Aunt Bee's feelings weren't hurt and her confidence that she could have made it funny if that's what they wanted was funny in itself."

"I have no recollection of why this was my last *Andy Griffith Show* script," says Jack. "Sometime later, I realized that my *Griffith Show* days were over. As I reread our scripts, I'm impressed with how good they are. Charles and I were consistently good writers. The scripts were made even better by the leadership of Andy Griffith. He always knew what was right for the show. Don Knotts was a comedy writer's dream. He made what was funny on paper even funnier on screen. The other cast members and production crew were great. Aaron Ruben was a wonderful producer and story consultant. His contributions were immense. "*The Andy Griffith Show* is a true classic, and I thank Andy Griffith, Sheldon Leonard, and fate for allowing me to be a part of it."

Season Wrap-Up

The Andy Griffith Show ended its sixth season ranked sixth in the A. C. Nielsen ratings. The show was broadcast on Monday nights at 9:00 p.m. The sort of people who regularly viewed *The Griffith Show* was examined by pollsters for a six-week period during the latter months of 1967. The results showed that the show was primarily watched by southern and rural audiences earning less than five thousand dollars annually, the majority of whom were blue-collar workers.

1966–1967

"Big Fish in a Small Town"

"I like to approach fishing like everything else—from a scientific standpoint."—HOWARD SPRAGUE

"I don't have any particular memories of writing this script, except it was hard, backbreaking work, as all of them were."—BILL IDELSON

Episode 198

First Broadcast on November 28, 1966

Written by
Bill Idelson and Sam Bobrick

Directed by
Lee Philips

"The story idea for 'Big Fish in a Small Town' must have been mine," says writer Bill Idelson. "I was always a rabid fisherman, while Sam Bobrick probably never fished a day in his life, so the notion probably originated with me. I was always struck by the fact that in many places I fished there was a monster, legendary fish. Everyone knew about it, many had claimed to have seen it, a few claimed to have hooked it, but no one had landed it."

Bill and Sam's script begins in the barbershop. Fishing season starts the next day. Floyd and Goober are getting ready and "have a million things to do." Howard Sprague drops by for a haircut, learns about the opening of the new season, and hints that he would like to join Floyd and Goober the next day. The two attempt to discourage Howard because he is a "beginner" fisherman. They don't invite him to join them. Howard decides to get his haircut "later in the week."

After leaving the barbershop, Howard steps next door to the courthouse and finds Andy and Opie also getting ready for the new fishing season. Howard asks if he could "tag along" the following day. Andy reluctantly agrees.

The next morning, Howard arrives at the Taylors' house loaded down with fishing gear. Howard has an umbrella, a portable radio, a flashlight, a thermometer, and a depth finder. Howard has packed "two roast chickens, a quart of potato salad, and a lemon pie."

After arriving at Tucker's Lake, Andy, Opie, and Howard begin a day of fishing. Andy and Opie bait their hooks and discuss the possibility of catching "Old Sam," a legendary silver carp.

"The selection of 'Old Sam' for the fish's name was in part a little inside joke,"

says Bill. "He was named after Sam Bobrick, but mostly, I think the name was chosen because Old Sam was a homey, sort of appropriate name for the fish.

"We never consulted a fishing manual about anything in the script. There was a lot of bull in these scripts at times. The decision to make Old Sam a silver carp draws a blank. I never fished for such a fish and don't recall hearing about them. I wouldn't be surprised if it wasn't a suggestion from Andy."

"My personal memories of this episode are fairly clear, mostly because it was such an interesting show to shoot and because we had such comradeship on it," said Jack Dodson, who portrayed Howard Sprague. "We normally rehearsed for one day and shot for three days. Rehearsal laid out the scenes for the crew as well as the cast. Changes were made as we shot, but they were rarely major. For this episode, which was almost all on location, we had little blocking rehearsal at the studio. This episode required more location shooting than normal, and working on water posed more than the usual problems for the crew, but nothing major.

"The series' regular cast members traveled to the location in their own cars. The crew was transported by bus from the studio. All the fishing sequences and most of the exteriors were shot at the lake in Franklin Canyon, which was about a ten-mile trip from the studio. All the interiors were shot at the Desilu Studios in the heart of Hollywood. Mayberry's street scenes were filmed at Forty Acres near MGM in Culver City, about a half hour from Desilu."

Determined to catch fish, Howard wanders down to the lakeshore. He repeat-

"Hey, That's Sheldon's Chair."

At the weekly script read-through, I usually sat across the table from Sheldon Leonard, beside Andy. Bob Ross always sat at the head of the table, the director at the opposite end, and Andy in the middle, to Bob's right. We actors did not always have the same seat at the table, but there was no competition for the seats. No particular emphasis was placed on where you sat—just that the seats for Sheldon, Bob, Andy, and the director were always reserved.—JACK DODSON

edly interrupts the other fishermen with his amateur casting. Howard calls on Andy to help him untangle his line from a tree branch. After Andy untangles the line, he says, "If you just wouldn't try casting, Howard. Why don't you bottom-fish like Opie and me?" Influenced by a book he has read, Howard insists on casting. Howard calls Andy a second time to remove his hook from the seat of his pants. Howard requests Andy's assistance a third time, but this time he is not in trouble. Howard has caught a fish, and to everyone's surprise, it is Old Sam!

After catching the fish, Howard returns to town and displays Old Sam in a tank on Main Street. A newspaper reporter interviews Howard for a "front-page" story. Howard tells the reporter, "I had been using a variety of complicated lures, but after lunch I had some potato salad left, and that's what got him."

"The fish was provided by a wildlife facility," said Jack. "The scenes with the fish in the lake were easily set up because the fish was rather passive. The street scene back in Mayberry was shot inside the studio instead of at Forty Acres because of tight schedule demands."

After the interview Howard runs home to change clothes. While Howard is away Goober, Floyd, and Opie wonder aloud what Howard plans to do with the fish and ask Andy to find out.

Andy learns that Howard has decided to donate Old Sam to an aquarium in Raleigh. Goober and Floyd are disappointed with Howard's decision. Floyd says, "That fish doesn't belong in an aquarium. Old Sam was born and bred right in Tucker's Lake, and that is where he ought to be." Reflecting on the thought of Old Sam no longer being in Tucker's Lake, Goober says, "It's like the end of something, ain't it?"

Howard invites Opie to join him on a trip to Raleigh to visit the aquarium. Opie agrees but is unenthusiastic when he sees Old Sam. Howard notices Opie's disappointment and points out that he put Old Sam in the aquarium because he thought it would be nice for "a lot of other people to see Old Sam. He's kind of unusual. That's what an aquarium is for." Opie admits that the aquarium is good, but he points out that Old Sam had been in Tucker's Lake so long, "and everybody talked about him so much—tried to catch him all the time."

"Howard was intrinsic to the story, as a villain in a way, since he had recently come to town. For him to land Old Sam was an ironic, even bitter pill to swallow," says Bill. "Another ironic twist was that Howard used potato salad as bait to catch the fish. It was ironic for Old Sam, who had every kind of exotic lure thrown his way, to succumb to an outrageous offering by an alien. If Old Sam were to be landed, it should have been by one of the old residents, who probably would have released him into the lake."

After talking with Opie, Howard realizes Old Sam belongs in Tucker's Lake. Howard and Opie return to Mayberry.

Andy, Goober, and Floyd are fishing at Tucker's Lake when Floyd says, "Hey, did you see that? There was a big one went by. He went right past my line. He was as big as Old Sam. Every bit as big." Andy and Goober think Floyd is "imagining things."

Howard and Opie walk up soon afterward and are told about the big fish. Howard tells the three that what they saw might have been Old Sam. He goes on to say that a "couple of minutes ago, Opie and I let Old Sam go about fifty yards down there." Floyd asks why he decided to put the fish back in the lake. Howard answers, "You know, Opie and I went up to the aquarium in Raleigh. Well, we were standing by the tank there, and Old Sam came right over to the glass of the tank . . . and started moving his mouth. Well, we stood there and watched him for a while, and we finally figured out what he was trying to say. He was trying to tell us, 'Gosh, would I like to see Goober, and Floyd, and Andy, and everybody again.' Well, after that, I just had to put him back."

"I think the script also served to further develop Howard as a character, and that was why it was necessary to find a decent, sympathetic resolution to what was going to happen to Old Sam," says Bill. "I remember this came in for a lot of discussion. Putting the fish back in the lake immediately after it was caught was discussed but rejected for some reason, and the final conclusion came about by committee, as many of these things did."

The decision to return Old Sam to the lake was necessary. The town of Mayberry is a small, familiar, and secure place. Traditions and legends are tightly protected. The premise of Mayberry required that Old Sam would swim in Tucker's Lake forever, thus keeping the possibility of catching the legendary fish just one cast away.

"A Visit to Barney Fife"

"Bill and I were told by producer Bob Ross that Don Knotts was available for a *TAGS* guest appearance," says writer Sam Bobrick. "We were eager to write for Don again and came up with the idea to have Andy visit Barney in Raleigh. Bob liked the idea, and we were given the assignment."

"A Visit to Barney Fife" begins with Andy stopping by the Raleigh Police Department. Andy arrives earlier than expected and finds Barney painting the captain's office. After the two exchange greetings, Andy learns that Barney has been transferred from "fingerprints to the detective bureau." Barney has invited Andy to come by because he "heard that there's going to be an opening in our department, and I immediately thought of you."

Barney introduces Andy to his coworkers, and it quickly becomes evident to Andy that Barney is not respected by the other detectives.

Barney shows Andy his small corner desk and shares with him a newspaper story about a series of supermarket robberies. The master shot for this scene shows Andy in the foreground and Barney seated at his desk with his back against the wall. After the master shot was photographed, the actors performed the scene a second time with the wall behind Barney removed and the camera positioned in its place. The master shot and the secondary shot were then edited together for the finished film.

Barney leaves the office early and takes Andy, who plans to stay a few days, to the boardinghouse where he has recently moved. Andy meets the Parker family, who owns the house. The family consists of Ma, Ma's boys Leroy and Henny, and daughter, Agnes Jean, who "is a real charmer." Afterward, Andy and Barney go up to Barney's room to get settled in.

Barney proudly points out his accommodations and the decorative touches he has made. The room has a private sink with a faucet that "says cold, but it's hot," a double bed, a real leather chair, and a view "between two telephone poles" of

Episode 211

First Broadcast on
January 16, 1967

Written by
**Bill Idelson and
Sam Bobrick**

Directed by
Lee Philips

Why They Watch

When *The Andy Griffith Show* first came out, Andy was really discouraged because the reviews in New York and Los Angeles were not too good. One columnist called the show "corn-pone humor." The critics thought it was a cartoon kind of show with cartoon characters—Andy being the exception.

Andy was really upset. I said to him, "Forget those guys. Give me Ohio, Kansas. Give me the whole South. Give me Texas, Oklahoma, Indiana, Illinois."

The show found an audience in Middle America and became popular because people identified with it. They had the same problems the people of Mayberry had. Most towns have a goofball like Gomer or Goober Pyle. The audience would see Gomer and Goober, or one of the other wonderful characters we had, and think, "They remind me of someone I know."

In the mind of the audience *The Andy Griffith Show* was about real people who lived in a real town—a town where people cared about one another.
—RICHARD O. LINKE

I guess *The Andy Griffith Show* will go down as the best show that's ever been on and ever will be on television.—GEORGE LINDSEY

city hall. Barney has decorated the room with his Mayberry High School pennant and prints of *The Laughing Cavalier* and *Blue Boy.*

"Bill and I included some suggestions for decorating Barney's room in the script," says Sam. "The prop department added to this, and the end result fit Barney perfectly."

Later at dinner, the Parkers question Barney about the rash of supermarket robberies. Andy reminds Barney that the investigation is confidential. Barney, however, ignores Andy's warning. Flattered by the Parkers' interest in what he has to say, Barney explains in great detail the bureau's "zone detection system."

The next day, Andy meets with Captain Dewhurst about the job opening in the department. Andy is not interested in the job but meets with the captain in order to please Barney. During the meeting, Andy learns that the opening is for Barney's job.

That evening, Andy asks Barney if he's ever thought about coming back to Mayberry and tells him his job is still open. Barney answers, "Well, that's awful nice of you, Ange, but I got everything going for me here—a big job. I got a terrific future."

The Parkers return from shopping and interrupt the conversation. Barney tells Andy that none of the family members go shopping without the others. After the Parkers go into the house, Andy notes that they didn't purchase much. He adds, "I mean, for a whole big family, they just came back with two little sacks."

At this point, a news flash is broadcast over the radio. Another supermarket robbery has occurred, this time on the city's south side. Barney tells Andy that there has to be a leak some place. He notes, "That's the eighth time in a row we've staked out two zones and they've hit the third."

Andy and Barney rush over to the scene of the robbery. Captain Dewhurst and two detectives have been at the store for an hour and are looking around in back when the two arrive. The store manager is standing alone at the cash register. Unaware of the man's identity, Barney arrests the manager.

Captain Dewhurst releases the manager and sends Barney across the street to "get five coffees." While Barney is away, Dewhurst tells Andy that it's a rough case. He notes, "We're up against a gang that knows every move we make. Now, if we could only figure out a way to learn their moves." Andy thinks the situation over carefully.

The next day, Andy decides to "set up" the Parkers by sharing with them some "inside" information. He tells them that according to Captain Dewhurst, it was a good thing the robbers hit the night before because Saturday is a big shopping day. There will be more money involved, and the money will have to stay in the supermarket the whole weekend because the banks will be closed. Andy adds that the police have noticed that "the gang" never hits twice in the same area, so Captain Dewhurst does not plan to stake out the supermarket that was just robbed.

That evening, Andy suggests that he and Barney "go over to that supermarket that was knocked off last night and just kind of look around." Barney feels it would be a waste of time but agrees to stake out the store.

The Parkers decide to follow Andy's lead and are caught robbing the supermarket by Andy and Barney.

In the epilogue, Barney receives credit for "cracking the case." Thanks to Andy, Barney's status in the bureau is restored, and his job, at least for a while, is secure.

"I had received an offer to write for *The Smothers Brothers Show* around the time this script was written," says Sam. "Bill also had received various offers. I went on to do *The Smothers Brothers Show*, and 'A Visit to Barney Fife' became my final *TAGS* script.

"I enjoyed writing for the Smothers Brothers, but I missed writing for Andy and Don. They were a fabulous team. I always enjoyed writing for them. After Don left, however, some of the magic disappeared. It did not seem to be as much fun without him. So, maybe it was the right time for me to move on to something else."

Mayberry Days Lecture with Jack Elinson

Saturday, September 30, 2000

N. Brower: Jack, it's a real honor and a pleasure to have you here. Let's start at the very beginning. Where were you born?

J. Elinson: New York City.

N. Brower: When were you born?

J. Elinson: 1922, April 21.

N. Brower: Where did you grow up?

J. Elinson: In the Bronx. I stayed at home until World War II. I was drafted, and I was away for three years. I came back and stayed in New York for another year or so. I ended up going to California in 1948.

N. Brower: What type of work did your parents do?

J. Elinson: My dad was a house painter. My mother and father both came from Russia in the great immigration from East Europe. My mother was what all mothers were back then, a housekeeper taking care of the family.

N. Brower: How many brothers and sisters did you have?

J. Elinson: Three brothers and one sister.

N. Brower: One of your brothers was Iz Elinson. Was that a nickname?

J. Elinson: His official name was Irving, but everybody called him Iz.

N. Brower: How did Iz influence your life?

J. Elinson: Well, he made my life actually. In 1938, Iz was already a professional and very successful comedy writer. So, he opened doors for me that were very hard to get in.

I have Iz to thank for even thinking of becoming a comedy writer. In those days that wasn't an occupation that anybody really knew about. People listened to the radio and thought that comedians made it up as they went along. I never would have thought of that particular kind of work unless my brother had done it first. I realized that maybe I could do it, and with his help I did.

N. Brower: What were some of your early writing jobs?

J. Elinson: My brother Iz was working as a clerk for the Borden's Milk Company. He had a hobby of writing topical jokes, and he sent them in to the columnist

Walter Winchell. Winchell started using them, and Iz became Winchell's biggest contributor of topical jokes.

When I was sixteen years old, I went to Iz and said I'd like to try it. Iz said I'll call Winchell and tell him I've got a kid brother, and he can expect you to send him jokes in longhand. I started to do it, and low and behold, I became a contributor to Winchell's column. My first joke in the column was when I was sixteen years old.

I remember in high school, I was so cocky, I walked around saying I bet I'm the only one in this entire school that had his name in Winchell's column.

N. Brower: When did you first meet your writing partner, Charles Stewart?

J. Elinson: It was shortly before the Danny Thomas work. We met very simply. We both ended up at the same agent—oddly enough, a man with the last name Stewart, Jack Stewart. Chuck was working alone, and I was working alone. The agent came to us one day and said why don't you two guys team up. It seemed like a very good idea because we weren't doing all that great by ourselves, so we became partners.

N. Brower: How did you start writing for producer Sheldon Leonard?

J. Elinson: What happened was Sheldon Leonard was the director of the *Danny Thomas Show* in the early years, and in the fourth season they upped him to being the producer of the show. So, Sheldon was now in charge of hiring writers. In 1957, he called around and asked about me and Chuck. We went over there to try out, and it turned out to be the best thing that ever happened to us. We ended up being on the *Thomas Show* for eight years and wrote over one hundred episodes.

N. Brower: What do you consider to be your writing strengths and Charles Stewart's writing strengths?

J. Elinson: Charles Stewart did the typing, and I did the pacing and worrying. We were pretty well balanced. I might have been stronger in the comedy department. Chuck was stronger in the structure and the language in the script, but it was fifty-fifty. We just sat down, started on page one, and went line by line until we reached page forty or whatever finished it.

N. Brower: Where did you go each day to write?

J. Elinson: We rented an apartment, and that became our office. We bounced around from apartment to apartment as the years went by. We were known as freelance writers even though we were regulars on the *Danny Thomas Show*. That's why we had to find our own space.

N. Brower: How did you come to write for *The Andy Griffith Show*?

J. Elinson: When it all started and was set to go on, Sheldon Leonard, the boss of the whole operation, asked us if we would write some scripts for *The Andy Griffith Show* and get it rolling.

That emerged into a pattern where for the first two seasons of *The Griffith Show*, we wrote fifteen *The Andy Griffith Show* scripts a year for two years. At the same time, we wrote half of the Danny Thomas scripts for the two years. We were going back and forth between one show and the other.

N. Brower: What guidelines were you given for the storylines of the first few scripts?

J. Elinson: We sat down with Sheldon. This was all before Aaron Ruben was hired. They were still in the process of finding a producer. Chuck and I had a session with Sheldon and some other writers, and we bounced stories around. We settled on six storylines and started to write.

N. Brower: How much input did you have in developing the main characters?

J. Elinson: Andy, of course, was Andy Griffith. That's the whole reason it became a project. He was so strong and so different. Andy came ready-made. We didn't have to make up too much on Andy.

Opie was a little five-year-old boy. ~~Chuck~~ and I both had our own children, so we knew about ~~five-year-old boys.~~ Opie came from real-life experience.

Ronny Howard was absolutely the ~~best child~~ actor ever. No one has come along to beat him. He was just unbelievable.

Aunt Bee was just a very sweet woman, a ~~family woman~~. She herself was not married, so it was kind of nice for her to move in with the boys. At the time, my sister-in-law had an ~~Aunt Bea~~. She was a nurse. It sounded pretty good for someone coming from a small town. We decided to spell the name ~~B-E-E~~, which is ~~uncommon~~. To us, it sounded a little more country, small town. ~~It was that simple.~~

N. Brower: *The Andy Griffith Show* was shot with one camera. It was not shot before a live audience and thus was able to go on location. How did that affect your writing as opposed to writing for *The Danny Thomas Show*, which was shot with three cameras before a live audience?

J. Elinson: We had fun with the two systems because *The Danny Thomas Show* was like a little play in front of a live audience. We were limited by the sets. There was the permanent set of the apartment and a few other interiors.

That's why we got a kick when it was our time to write an *Andy Griffith* script because it was a little movie, and we could go anywhere we wanted. If we needed a scene on location like the fishing thing or the squad car going down a country road, it was possible.

We felt with *The Griffith Show* we had a lot more freedom. We could do a lot of little, short scenes outdoors.

On *The Danny Thomas Show* we had to make our scenes as long as possible so there were not too many stops. We wanted to make it like a little play.

N. Brower: How was the premier episode chosen?

J. Elinson: We had six shows made. We zeroed in on "The New Housekeeper" or "Manhunt" to be the opening show. We on the staff, Sheldon Leonard and the writers, felt that "Manhunt" would be a better show to start the series because that show was the first time you saw Don Knotts at work with the Barney Fife character. He just blew everybody away. He was just so funny, so great.

We felt that if we were going to start off, let's start off strong with big laughs and a character like Barney. In "The New Housekeeper," Barney didn't have that much to do. That show basically involved Andy, Aunt Bee, and Opie. It was a softer show and gentler. So we voted for "Manhunt."

CBS, which had the final say, voted for "The New Housekeeper" because they liked the wholesomeness of it and its softness. They liked what we thought might be the weakness.

CBS won the toss, and we started with "The New Housekeeper." We were keeping our fingers crossed. We got great ratings with that first night, but in this business, it's the second week that really counts. Did the audience like it enough to come back, or did they dislike it and turn the channel? To our relief, they came back. The ratings were just as good if not higher on the second show. As it turned out, CBS's hunch was right.

I feel whatever show, whether it was "The New Housekeeper" or "Manhunt," would have scored anyway. It's very easy to have hindsight when you look back, but there was a little argument about what should be first.

N. Brower: "The New Housekeeper" has a wonderful "running away from home" scene between Andy and Opie. The scene powerfully communicates the love between father and son. What does it feel like to see a scene on paper come alive on screen?

J. Elinson: I've forgotten what I was feeling when I first saw the episode broadcast forty years ago. I was just nervous about the show being on the air. Watching it now, and I know the script, of course, I was beginning, if you can believe it, to get a little tear in my eye.

Andy uses the technique you see in the scene all through the series. If there was a problem, without shouting, without saying you can't do that, he solved it. He never once raised his voice to anybody. He slyly got to where he wanted it to go, and he was always kind.

N. Brower: When you watch the Andy and Opie scene, does it make you think back to your own relationship with your sons when they were little boys?

J. Elinson: I had three little sons and none of them wanted to run away from home. Sometimes I wished they would run away, but I couldn't move them.

N. Brower: What award did you and Charles Stewart win for your second *The Andy Griffith Show* script, "Manhunt"?

J. Elinson: The Writer's Guild of America gave us the award for Best Script for that season for "Manhunt." I guess maybe that's why, when people ask me what my favorite show might be, I always answer "Manhunt." Probably the award has a lot to do with that.

N. Brower: Three things happen in "Manhunt" for the first time. First, Barney only has one bullet. This will become a Barney Fife trademark throughout the series. Second, if Barney has a bullet in his gun, he is going to accidentally fire it. That will happen repeatedly. Thirdly, Otis Campbell, one of our beloved characters, is introduced. Otis reaches through the bars, gets the keys, and releases himself from jail. This is another trademark behavior.

J. Elinson: We just came up with Barney having one bullet and accidentally shooting his gun. We knew that what we had here was a very incompetent person, but Barney wanted to be Clint Eastwood. We knew an incompetent guy like this was going to do everything wrong. Andy would gently trust Barney with one bullet. Barney could only put the bullet in the gun on special occasions. It normally stayed in his pocket. Shooting off the gun just came naturally. It came out of a fact that was very simple. Barney was a crazy guy who couldn't be a competent deputy. Accidently firing the gun was just a thought we came across. We didn't write it as a runner. It just became one. That was one of the funniest things we created, and it was so simple. It was just there.

Every town has a town drunk. So, we created Otis. He comes in at the end of every week after he has been drinking. He knows that nobody has to take him in. He opens the cell door and locks himself inside. When it's time to leave he reaches out and takes the key.

That whole thing was a funny way of having a man go to jail. We all know that's not the way it happens, but that's part of a small town. Otis can be trusted even though he is drunk. He was always a sweet guy whether he was drunk or sober. Otis was harmless.

N. Brower: "The Guitar Player" was the third episode of "The Andy Griffith Show." Whose idea was it to write an episode that featured music?

J. Elinson: Music was one thing we knew that we were going to be doing. Andy Griffith could strum a guitar and sing. So, we created a story that would bring in music. That was how we got to "The Guitar Player."

N. Brower: Elvis Presley was discharged from the army on March 5, 1960. Did that give you an idea to create the Jim Lindsey character?

J. Elinson: I think so. As I remember, Jim Lindsey became a big-shot musician. He was almost like a small-town Elvis Presley. In "The Return of the Guitar Player" episode, he wasn't doing too good. He was an Elvis Presley that lost his stuff.

N. Brower: Your fourth *Griffith Show* episode was "Ellie Comes to Town." What guidelines were you given for Elinor Donahue's character, Ellie Walker?

J. Elinson: The reason we had a woman come in at that point was since Andy was single, the obvious thing was maybe we could get a romance going. That would allow us to write future stories along that line.

We created a woman who came to Mayberry. A very bright woman. The fact that she was a pharmacist meant she went to college. She wasn't just an ordinary gal. This, oddly enough, when we look back, was the start of feminism on television. We were among the first writers to take a crack at feminism. Ellie was sweet and pretty and all that, but she could take care of herself.

N. Brower: You continued the feminist idea with another episode, "Ellie Runs for Council."

J. Elinson: We had Ellie run for council to show her strength. In a little town like Mayberry, people didn't even think of women in politics. This was a little touch of feminism. Wouldn't it be interesting if a woman runs and then have Andy and Ellie, who like each other very much, suddenly oppose one another? This was one of the few times when Andy got a little annoyed. Ellie running for council! What the hell is this? The story was a battle of the sexes, which is a very good formula for comedy.

N. Brower: Don Knotts really stands out in "The New Doctor." Barney schedules an appointment so he can go undercover and find out if the new doctor is romantically interested in Ellie Walker. Barney forgets his mission when he learns he has an iron deficiency. What was it like writing for Don Knotts?

J. Elinson: Chuck and I fell in love with Don Knotts. This man could do anything. He performed the material better than it was written. His face was so funny and the physical examination in "The New Doctor" was the perfect Don Knotts scene.

N. Brower: "The New Doctor also has a wonderful front porch scene that captures the spirit of Mayberry. Andy, Aunt Bee, and Opie have gathered on the front porch. Andy strums his guitar, Aunt Bee reads the newspaper, and Opie plays with his blocks.

J. Elinson: Andy playing the guitar was scripted. We didn't tell Andy Griffith what to play. He knew music and picked out the songs. The scene was originally set inside the house. I imagine the director, or the producer, Aaron Ruben, moved it to the front porch because it was a quieter place. What you see on-screen is a collaboration with a lot of script revisions along the way.

N. Brower: Which of your second-season episodes stands out in your mind?

J. Elinson: I loved "Barney and the Choir." I always fall on the floor when I see it. I have to admit that was about as broad as we got in the series. It was totally unbelievable. It was sketch comedy, which was not the way the series was running. The whole idea was so funny we couldn't afford not to do it. It was hilarious.

I remember "Guest of Honor" because we introduced Barney's "Nip It in the Bud" in that episode. It was something that came out naturally as we were writing. We never dreamed the phrase would become such a big thing. When Barney said, "Nip it, nip it, nip it," it was very funny. Whenever we had a chance to use that phrase, we did. We would sometimes milk the laugh and have Barney go crazy, repeating it over and over.

During the second season, we used Floyd the barber more often. I didn't know the actor, Howard McNear, that well. Chuck and I were busy holed up in a room writing the next script. Once in a while, we'd take a break and get down to the set just to see what was going on. I didn't get to know Howard personally, but we were all like a family at the studio. I thought Howard's performance as the barber was wonderful. We knew he was always good for a laugh.

Another episode that stands out was the last script we wrote that season, "Andy on Trial." Barney taking the stand to defend Andy was the most dramatic scene we ever did in the series. There was no attempt at laughs. This was straight. Straight as an arrow. It was a beautiful scene. You saw how Barney was so pained that he had to say what he said about Andy's misconduct. Barney then defends Andy. That was one of the best pieces of work we ever did.

Acknowledgments

My thanks go out to everyone who helped make this book possible: Jim Clark, Presiding Goober of *The Andy Griffith Show Rerun Watchers Club*, for providing pictures, writing the foreword, and being a decades-long Mayberry friend; Dennis Beal, for providing a video copy of my 2000 Mayberry Days lecture with Jack Elinson; and Paul Mulik, who allowed access to his online Mayberry scripts.

Thanks to Blair, my publisher, for taking an interest in this project. A special thank you is due to Lynn York for her insights and guidance.

I thank the late Jack Dodson, Hoke Howell, Jack Prince, Hal Smith, Jean Carson, Bernard Fox, Jeffery Hayden, Rance and Jean Howard, Mitch Jaynes, George Lindsey, Richard O. Linke, Betty Lynn, Howard Morris, Aaron Ruben, Jay Sandrich, and Amzie Strickland. Their kindness and cooperation are not forgotten.

Thanks to writers Sam Bobrick and Bill Idelson for sharing their memories.

A special word of thanks to Everett Greenbaum and Harvey Bullock. Everett felt "it was important to keep the memories alive" and faithfully answered my questions. Harvey's answers were unparalleled in detail and length. He touched my heart and became my friend.

A big thank you to Jack Elinson, who sadly never got to see the result of his faithful correspondence. His participation, however, gave him a reason to revisit his scripts. The time that had passed since their creation allowed him to view the scripts with an unbiased critical eye. Jack was rewarded by discovering just how good his Mayberry writing was.

Thanks to Andy Griffith for generously donating his Mayberry scripts to the UNC Chapel Hill library. His voice speaks loudly in their pages.

Printed in the USA
CPSIA information can be obtained
at www.ICGtesting.com
JSHW060145060923
47814JS00004B/3